Sublinear Computation Paradigm

T0237559

Naoki Katoh · Yuya Higashikawa ·
Hiro Ito · Atsuki Nagao ·
Tetsuo Shibuya · Adnan Sljoka ·
Kazuyuki Tanaka · Yushi Uno
Editors

Sublinear Computation Paradigm

Algorithmic Revolution in the Big Data Era

Springer

Editors
Naoki Katoh
Graduate School of Information Science
University of Hyogo
Kobe, Hyogo, Japan

Hiro Ito
School of Informatics and Engineering
University of Electro-Communications
Chofu, Tokyo, Japan

Tetsuo Shibuya
Human Genome Center
University of Tokyo
Minato, Tokyo, Japan

Kazuyuki Tanaka
Graduate School of Information Science
Tohoku University
Sendai, Miyagi, Japan

Yuya Higashikawa
Graduate School of Information Science
University of Hyogo
Kobe, Hyogo, Japan

Atsuki Nagao
Department of Information Science
Ochanomizu University
Bunkyo, Tokyo, Japan

Adnan Sljoka
Center for Advanced Intelligence Project
RIKEN
Chuo, Tokyo, Japan

Yushi Uno
Graduate School of Engineering
Osaka Prefecture University
Sakai, Osaka, Japan

ISBN 978-981-16-4097-1 ISBN 978-981-16-4095-7 (eBook)
https://doi.org/10.1007/978-981-16-4095-7

© The Editor(s) (if applicable) and The Author(s) 2022. This book is an open access publication.
Open Access This book is licensed under the terms of the Creative Commons Attribution 4.0 International License (http://creativecommons.org/licenses/by/4.0/), which permits use, sharing, adaptation, distribution and reproduction in any medium or format, as long as you give appropriate credit to the original author(s) and the source, provide a link to the Creative Commons license and indicate if changes were made.
The images or other third party material in this book are included in the book's Creative Commons license, unless indicated otherwise in a credit line to the material. If material is not included in the book's Creative Commons license and your intended use is not permitted by statutory regulation or exceeds the permitted use, you will need to obtain permission directly from the copyright holder.
The use of general descriptive names, registered names, trademarks, service marks, etc. in this publication does not imply, even in the absence of a specific statement, that such names are exempt from the relevant protective laws and regulations and therefore free for general use.
The publisher, the authors and the editors are safe to assume that the advice and information in this book are believed to be true and accurate at the date of publication. Neither the publisher nor the authors or the editors give a warranty, expressed or implied, with respect to the material contained herein or for any errors or omissions that may have been made. The publisher remains neutral with regard to jurisdictional claims in published maps and institutional affiliations.

This Springer imprint is published by the registered company Springer Nature Singapore Pte Ltd.
The registered company address is: 152 Beach Road, #21-01/04 Gateway East, Singapore 189721, Singapore

Preface

This book gives an overview of cutting-edge work on a new paradigm called the "sublinear computation paradigm," which was proposed in the large multiyear academic research project "Foundations of Innovative Algorithms for Big Data" in Japan. In today's rapidly evolving age of big data, massive increases in big data have led to many new opportunities and uncharted areas of exploration, but have also brought new challenges. To handle the unprecedented explosion of big data sets in research, industry, and other areas of society, there is an urgent need to develop novel methods and approaches for big data analysis. To meet this need, we are pursuing innovative changes in algorithm theory for big data. For example, polynomial-time algorithms have thus far been regarded as "fast," but if we apply an $O(n^2)$-time algorithm to a petabyte-scale or larger big data set, we will encounter problems in terms of computational resources or running time. To deal with this critical computational and algorithmic bottleneck, we require linear, sublinear, and constant-time algorithms. In this project, which ran from October 2014 to September 2021, we have proposed the sublinear computation paradigm in order to support innovation in the big data era. We have created a foundation of innovative algorithms by developing computational procedures, data structures, and modeling techniques for big data. The project is organized into three teams that focus on sublinear algorithms, sublinear data structures, and sublinear modeling. Our work has provided high-level academic research results of strong computational and algorithmic interest, which are presented in this book.

This book consists of five parts: Part I, which consists of a single chapter introducing the concept of the sublinear computation paradigm; Parts II, III, and IV review results on sublinear algorithms, sublinear data structures, and sublinear modeling, respectively; and Part V presents some application results.

We deeply appreciate the members of this project and everyone else who was involved. This project was conducted as a subproject of the research project "Advanced Core Technologies for Big Data Integration," which was supervised by Prof. Masaru Kitsuregawa. We would like to express our gratitude to him and everyone involved in that project. We also thank the editorial office of Springer for the opportunity to publish this book.

Kobe, Japan
Tokyo, Japan
Kobe, Japan

Naoki Katoh
Hiro Ito
Yuya Higashikawa

Contents

Part IV Sublinear Modelling

Part V Applications

Part I
Introduction

Chapter 1
What Is the Sublinear Computation Paradigm?

Naoki Katoh and Hiro Ito

Abstract This chapter introduces the "sublinear computation paradigm." A sublinear-time algorithm is an algorithm that runs in time sublinear in the size of the instance (input data). In other words, the running time is $o(n)$, where n is the size of the instance. This century marks the start of the era of big data. In order to manage big data, polynomial-time algorithms, which are considered to be efficient, may sometimes be inadequate because they may require too much time or computational resources. In such cases, sublinear-time algorithms are expected to work well. We call this idea the "sublinear computation paradigm." A research project named "Foundations on Innovative Algorithms for Big Data (ABD)," in which this paradigm is the central concept, was started under the CREST program of the Japan Science and Technology Agency (JST) in October 2014 and concluded in September 2021. This book mainly introduces the results of this project.

1.1 We Are in the Era of Big Data

The twenty-first century can be called the era of Big Data. The number of webpages on the Internet was estimated to be more than 1 trillion (=10^{12}) in 2008 [22], and the number of websites grows ten times in these 10 years [21]. Thus the number of webpages is estimated to be more than 10 trillion (=10^{13}) now. If we assume that 10^6 bytes($\approx 10^7$ bits) of data is contained in a single webpage on average,[1] then the total amount of the data stored on the Internet would be more than 100 exabits (=10^{20} bits)! The various actions that everyone performs are collected by our smartphones and are stored in the memory of storage devices around the world. The remarkable development of computer memory has made it possible to store this information.

[1]Note that one 1080×1920 pixel digital photo consists of more than 2×10^6 pixels.

N. Katoh
University of Hyogo, 8-2-1 Gakuennishi-machi, Nishi-ku, Kobe, Hyogo 651-2197, Japan
e-mail: naoki.katoh@gsis.u-hyogo.ac.jp

H. Ito (✉)
The University of Electro-Communications, 1-5-1 Chofugaoka, Chofu, Tokyo 182-8585, Japan
e-mail: itohiro@uec.ac.jp

© The Author(s) 2022

N. Katoh et al. (eds.), *Sublinear Computation Paradigm*,
https://doi.org/10.1007/978-981-16-4095-7_1

However, the ability to store data and the ability to make good use of the data are different problems. The speed of the data transfer using IEEE 802.11ac is 6.9 Gbps. Using this, it would take 1.7 days to read 1 petabit (10^{15} bit) of data. To read 1 exabit (10^{18} bit) of data, we would need over 4 years! Although the speed of data transfer is expected to continue to increase, the amount of available data is also expected to grow even faster.

This situation can create new problems that did not arise in past centuries, such as requiring a huge amount of time just to read an entire dataset. We are thus faced with new problems in terms of computation.

1.2 Theory of Computational Complexity and Polynomial-Time Algorithms

In the area of the theory of computational complexity, the term "polynomial-time algorithms" is often as a synonym for "efficient algorithms." A *polynomial-time algorithm* is an algorithm that runs in time expressed by a function polynomial of the size of the instance (i.e., the input). For example, consider the sorting problem that takes a set of positive integers $a_1, \ldots, a_n$ as input and outputs a permutation $\pi : \{1, \ldots, n\} \to \{1, \ldots, n\}$ such that $a_{\pi(i)} \leq a_{\pi(i+1)}$ for every $i \in \{1, \ldots, n-1\}$. In this problem, the input is expressed by n integers and thus the input size is n.[2]

We now briefly introduce the theory of computational complexity. Theoretically, the computation time of an algorithms is expressed in terms of the number of basic units of calculations (i.e., the basic arithmetic operations, reading or writing a value in a cell in memory, and comparison of two values[3]). The complexity is then expressed as a function of n, say $T(n)$, where n is the (data) size of the input. If there exists a fixed integer k such that $T(n) = O(n^k)$, then we say that the algorithm runs in polynomial time.

For example, the sorting problem can be solved in $O(n \log n)$ time, which is polynomial, and it has been proven that this is the minimum in the big-O sense, meaning that no algorithm exists that runs in $o(n \log n)$-time. In contrast, for the *partitioning problem*, which is the problem of finding a subset B of a given set A consisting of n integers $a_1, \ldots, a_n$ such that $\sum_{a_i \in B} a_i = \frac{1}{2} \sum_{a_i \in A} a_i$, no polynomial-time algorithms have been found and the majority of researchers believe that no such algorithm exists.[4]

---

[2] More rigorously, representing an integer a requires around $\log_2 a$ bits. However, in the area of the theory of computational complexity, we usually use the assumption that one integer is stored in one cell (byte) of the memory. Since this assumption may cause some strange results if pathologically huge integers are used, these integers are prohibited.

[3] In order to avoid excessive calculations, we assume that each integer consists of at most $\log_2 n$ bits, where n is the number of integers treated in the instance.

[4] This is equivalent to the well-known "P vs. NP problem," which is one of the seven Millennium Prize open problems in mathematics.

For many problems, constructing an exponential-time algorithm is easy. For the partitioning problem, for example, an algorithm that tests all subsets of A clearly solves the problem, and this requires $2^n \cdot O(n)$ time, which is exponential. Therefore, the existence of an exponential-time algorithm is considered to be trivial for many cases. Constructing polynomial-time algorithms, however, requires additional ideas in many cases.

1.3 Polynomial-Time Algorithms and Sublinear-Time Algorithms

1.3.1 A Brief History of Polynomial-Time Algorithms

The idea that "polynomial-time algorithms are efficient" is sometimes called Cobham's Thesis or Cobham–Edmonds' Thesis, which is named after Alan Cobham and Jack Edmonds [4]. Cobham [3] identified tractable problems with the complexity class P, which is the class of problems solvable in polynomial-time with respect to the input size. Edmonds also stated the same thing in [7].

Although these papers were published in 1965, the idea behind this thesis seems to have been a commonly held belief among researchers in the late in 1950s. For example, Kruskal's algorithm and Prim's algorithms, which are both almost linear-time algorithms for the minimum spanning tree problem, were presented in 1956 [16] and 1957 [17], respectively. Dijkstra's algorithm, which is an almost linear-time algorithm for the shortest path problem with positive edge lengths, was presented in 1959 [6]. Ford and Fulkerson presented the augmenting path algorithm for the maximum flow problem in 1956 [8]. The blossom algorithm was proposed by Jack Edmonds in 1961 for the maximum matching problem on general (i.e., not necessarily bipartite) graphs [7].

In 1971, Cook proposed the idea of NP-completeness and proved that the satisfiability problem (SAT) is NP-complete [5]. NP-complete problems are intuitively the most difficult problems among the class NP. NP is the set of problems that can be solved in polynomial-time by nondeterministic Turing machines. Although we do not have a proof yet, many researchers believe that no polynomial-time algorithms exist for any NP-complete problems.[5] Cook's study created a new field of research through which countlessly many combinatorial problems have been found to be NP-complete [10].

By definition, it is trivial that every problem in NP can be solved in exponential time (by a Turing machine). The theory of NP-completeness explicitly and firmly fixed the idea that "polynomial-time algorithms are efficient" in the minds of researchers. We would like to call this idea the *polynomial computation paradigm*.

[5] This is the "P vs. NP problem," which is one of the seven Millennium Prize open problems in mathematics at the end of the twntieth century.

Many important polynomial-time algorithms are now known, including the two basic polynomial-time algorithms for the linear programming problem (LP), namely the ellipsoid method proposed by Khachiyan in 1979 [15] and the interior-point method proposed by Karmarkar in 1984 [13], the strongly polynomial-time algorithm for the minimum cost flow problem proposed by Éva Tardos in 1985 [19], the linear-time shortest path algorithm with positive integer edge lengths proposed by Mikkel Thorup in 1997 [20], and the deterministic polynomial-time algorithm for primality test proposed by Agrawal, Kayal, and Saxena in 2002 [1]. These algorithms pioneered new perspectives in the field of algorithm research. They are gems that were found under the polynomial computation paradigm.

1.3.2 Emergence of Sublinear-Time Algorithms

Although linear-time algorithms have naturally considered the fastest, since intuitively we basically have to read all the data when solving a problem, the new idea of "sublinear-time algorithms" emerged at the end of the twentieth century. Sublinear-time algorithms run by reading only a sublinear (i.e., $o(n)$) amount of data from the input.

The most popular framework for sublinear-time algorithms is "property testing." This idea was first presented by Rubinfeld and Sudan [18] in 1996 (although it appeared even earlier at a conference version in 1992) in the context of program checking. In this paper, they introduced the ideas of "distance" between an instance (e.g., a function) and a property (e.g., linearity), and "ϵ-farness." They also gave constant-time testers for some properties of functions. The first study giving the notion of constant-time testability of combinatorial (mainly graph) structures was given by Goldreich, Goldwasser, and Ron [11], which was present a conference in 1995 (STOC'95). After the turn of the century, many studies that follow this idea of testability have appeared and the importance of this field is growing [2, 9].

1.3.3 Property Testing and Parameter Testing

We say that a *testing algorithm* (or *tester* for short) for a property $\mathcal{P}$ accepts a given instance I with probability at least $2/3$ if I has $\mathcal{P}$ and rejects it with probability at least $2/3$ if I is far from having $\mathcal{P}$. $\mathcal{P}$ is defined as a (generally infinitely large) subset of instances. The distance between I and $\mathcal{P}$ is defined as the minimum Hamming distance between I and $I' \in \mathcal{P}$. The distance is normalized to be in $[0, 1]$ (i.e., $\text{dist}(I, \mathcal{P}) \in [0, 1]$). If an instance has the property, the distance is zero (i.e., $\text{dist}(I, \mathcal{P}) = 0$ if $I \in \mathcal{P}$). If $\text{dist}(I, \mathcal{P}) \geq \epsilon$ for an $\epsilon \in [0, 1]$, then we say that I is ϵ-far from $\mathcal{P}$ and otherwise ϵ-close. A tester rejects I with probability at least $2/3$ if I is ϵ-far from $\mathcal{P}$.

For a property, if a tester exists whose running time[6] is bounded by a constant independent of the size of the input, then we call the property is *testable*.[7] This framework is called *property testing*.

Property testing is a relaxation of the framework of decision problems. In contrast, a relaxation of the framework of optimization problems is *parameter testing*. In parameter testing, we try to find an approximation to the value of the objective function with an additive error of at most ϵN from the optimum value, where N is the maximum value of the objective function.

This idea appeared at the end of the twentieth century, and was further developed in this century. See Chaps. 2 and 3 for these themes.

1.4 Ways to Decrease Computational Resources

In addition to property and parameter testing, there are various methods for decreasing the amount of computational resources needed for handling big data. Although some methods may require linear computation, each of them has strong merits. We briefly introduce these methods in this section.

1.4.1 Streaming Algorithms

Property testing generally uses the assumption that an algorithm can read any position (cell) of the input. However, this may be difficult in some situations, such as if the data arrives as a stream (sequence) and the algorithm is required to read the values one by one in the order of arrival. The key assumption of this framework is that an algorithm does not have enough memory to store the entire input. For example, to find the maximum value in a sequence of integers $a_1, \ldots, a_n$, it is enough to use $O(1)$ cells of memories.[8]

Although this method requires linear computation time, since it must read all of the data, the amount of memory is constant in many cases. If we assume that the order of data arrival in the stream is random, then it becomes close to the setting of (nonadaptive[9]) property testing. In this book, streaming algorithms are covered in Chap. 16.

---

[6] Normally we also use the "query complexity" besides the running time. See Chap. 2 for details.

[7] Sometimes "testable" means that the problem has an algorithm with a sublinear query complexity, and *strongly testable* may be used for distinguishing constant query complexity from mere sublinear query complexity.

[8] We assume that each memory cell can store any one integer among $\{a_1, \ldots, a_n\}$.

[9] *Nonadaptive* means that the query (of an algorithm) cannot depend on any answer of the queries; in other words, the queries are fixed before the algorithm starts.

1.4.2 Compression

Compression is a traditional and typical method for treating digital data. Basically, there are two types of compression: one type is compression of data without losing any information. In this type of compression, there is an information-theoretical lower bound on the data size. This method is used when the original data needs be reconstructed perfectly from the compressed data, and it thus called *lossless compression* or *reversible compression*. The other type of compression allows discarding of some of the data such that the compressed data is an inexact approximation. Although some of these algorithms can compress data drastically, it is not possible to reconstruct the original data perfectly from the compressed data, and these algorithms are thus called *lossy compression* or *irreversible compression*. This method works remarkably well in the field of music and image compression. See Chaps. 6, 7, 10, and 16 in this book for results from this area.

1.4.3 Succinct Data Structures

When compressed data is used, it essentially needs to be decompressed. However, decompression requires extra computation. It is therefore useful to be able to use compressed data as-is without decompression. Succinct data structures are a framework that realizes this idea. Specifically, succinct data structures use an amount of space that is close to the information-theoretical lower bound while still allowing efficient (fast) query operations. These structures involve a tradeoff between space and time. See Chaps. 8 and 9 for details.

1.5 Need for the Sublinear Computation Paradigm

1.5.1 Sublinear and Polynomial Computation Are Both Important

Even though the sublinear computation paradigm has become necessary, it does *not* mean that the polynomial computation paradigm is obsolete. Polynomial computation is still important in normal computations. The typical cases where the sublinear computations are needed are when we need to treat big data. In such cases, traditional polynomial computation is sometimes too slow.

This relationship between the polynomial computation paradigm and the sublinear computation paradigm is analogous to the relationship between *Newtonian mechanics* and *the theory of relativity* in physics. While Newton mechanics is used for normal physical calculations, the theory of relativity is needed if we try to calculate the motion of very fast objects such as rockets, satellites, or electrons. We entered the era of the theory of relativity in the twentieth century and the era of sublinear computation era in the twenty-first century.

1.5.2 *Research Project ABD*

A research project named "Foundations on Innovative Algorithms for Big Data (ABD),"[10] in which the sublinear computation paradigm is the central concept was started by JST, CREST, Japan in October 2014 and concluded in September 2021. The total budget was more than 300 million yen. Although the project had 24 members at its inception, many more researchers later joined and the final number of regular members exceeded 40 in total. The leader of the project was Prof. Naoki Katoh of University of Hyogo.[11] The project consisted of three groups: the Sublinear Algorithm Group (Team A) led by Prof. Katoh; the Sublinear Data Structure Group (Team D) led by Prof. Tetsuo Shibuya of the University of Tokyo; and the Sublinear Modeling Group (Team M) led by Prof. Kazuyuki Tanaka of Tohoku University. In this project, we worked on problems in big data computation. The main purpose of this book is to introduce the results of this project. A special issue of The Review of Socionetwork Strategies [14] is also available for this project. While some of the methods adopted in this project are not sublinear, we are confident that every piece of research concluded under the project is useful and will form the foundations of innovative algorithms for big data!

1.5.3 *The Organization of This Book*

This part of the book, Part I, has provided an introduction. Parts II, III, and IV present the theoretical results of Teams A, D, and M, respectively. Application results leading to scientific and technological innovation are compiled in Part V.

References

1. M. Agrawal, N. Kayal, N. Saxena, PRIMES P. Ann. Math. **160** (2004)
2. A. Bhattacharyya, Y. Yoshida, Property Testing—Problems and Techniques (Springer, 2021) (to be published in 2021)
3. A. Cobham, The intrinsic computational difficulty of functions, Logic, methodology and philosophy of science, in *Proceedings of the 1964 International Congress*, ed. by Y. Bar-Hillel,

[10] http://crest-sublinear.jp/en/.

[11] Although he was at Kyoto University when the project started, he later moved to Kwansei Gakuin University because of his retirement before finally moving again to his present position.

Studies in Logic and the Foundations of Mathematics (North-Holland Publishing Company, Amsterdam, 1965), pp. 24–30
4. Cobham's thesis, Wikipedia, https://en.wikipedia.org/wiki/Cobham%27s_thesis#cite_note-7
5. S. A. Cook,The complexity of theorem proving procedures, in *Proceedings of the STOC'71* (1971), pp. 151–158
6. E.W. Dijkstra, A note on two problems in connexion with graphs. Numerische Mathematik **1**, 269–271 (1959)
7. J. Edmonds, Jack, Paths, trees, and flowers. Can. J. Math. **17**, 449–467 (1965)
8. L.R. Ford, D.R. Fulkerson, Maximal flow through a network. Can. J. Math. **8**, 399–404 (1956)
9. O. Goldreich, *Introduction to Property Testing* (Cambridge University Press, 2017)
10. M.R. Garey, D.S. Johnson, *Computers and Intractability—A Guide to the Theory of NP-Completeness* (W. H, Freeman and Company, 1979)
11. O. Goldreich, S. Goldwasser, D. Ron, Property testing and its connection to learning and approximation. J. ACM **45**(4), 653–750 (1998)
12. O. Goldreich, D. Ron, Property testing in bounded degree graphs. Proc. STOC **1997**, 406–415 (1997)
13. N. Karmarkar, A new polynomial time algorithm for linear programming. Combinatorica **4**, 373–395 (1984)
14. N. Katoh et. al. (eds.), Special issue on foundations of innovative algorithms for big data—sublinear computational paradigm and its expansions. Rev. Socionetwork Strategies **13**(2), (2019)
15. L.G. Khachiyan, A polynomial algorithm in linear programming. Doklady Akademii Nauk SSSR **244**, 1093–1096 (1979)
16. J.B. Kruskal, On the shortest spanning subtree of a graph and the traveling salesman problem. Proc. AMS **7**(1), 48–50 (1956)
17. R.C. Prim, Shortest connection networks and some generalizations. Bell Syst. Tech. J. **36**, 1389–1401 (1957)
18. R. Rubinfeld, M. Sudan, Robust characterizations of polynomials with applications to program testing. SIAM J. Comput. Vo. **25**(2), 252–271 (1996)
19. É. Tardos, A strongly polynomial minimum cost circulation algorithm. Combinatorica **3**, 247–255 (1985)
20. M. Thorup, Undirected single source shortest paths with positive integer weights in linear time. J. ACM **46**, 362–394 (1999) (Conference version was in FOCS'97)
21. "Total number of Websites," internet lives starts. https://www.internetlivestats.com/total-number-of-websites/
22. "We knew the web was big...," Google Official Blog. https://googleblog.blogspot.com/2008/07/we-knew-web-was-big.html

Open Access This chapter is licensed under the terms of the Creative Commons Attribution 4.0 International License (http://creativecommons.org/licenses/by/4.0/), which permits use, sharing, adaptation, distribution and reproduction in any medium or format, as long as you give appropriate credit to the original author(s) and the source, provide a link to the Creative Commons license and indicate if changes were made.

The images or other third party material in this chapter are included in the chapter's Creative Commons license, unless indicated otherwise in a credit line to the material. If material is not included in the chapter's Creative Commons license and your intended use is not permitted by statutory regulation or exceeds the permitted use, you will need to obtain permission directly from the copyright holder.

Part II
Sublinear Algorithms

Chapter 2
Property Testing on Graphs and Games

Hiro Ito

Abstract Constant-time algorithms are powerful tools, since they run by reading only a constant-sized part of each input. Property testing is the most popular research framework for constant-time algorithms. In property testing, an algorithm determines whether a given instance satisfies some predetermined property or is far from satisfying the property with high probability by reading a constant-sized part of the input. A property is said to be testable if there is a constant-time testing algorithm for the property. This chapter covers property testing on graphs and games. The fields of graph algorithms and property testing are two of the main streams of research on discrete algorithms and computational complexity. In the section on graphs in this chapter, we present some important results, particularly on the characterization of testable graph properties. At the end of the section, we show results that we published in 2020 on a complete characterization (necessary and sufficient condition) of testable monotone or hereditary properties in the bounded-degree digraphs. In the section on games, we present results that we published in 2019 showing that the generalized chess, Shogi (Japanese chess), and Xiangqi (Chinese chess) are all testable. We believe that this is the first results for testable EXPTIME-complete problems.

2.1 Introduction

The development of efficient algorithms for problems on big data problems is an urgent task. Constant-time algorithms are a powerful tool for this since they run by reading only a constant-sized part of each input. In other words, the running time is invariant regardless of the size of the input. Property testing is the most popular research framework for constant-time algorithms. In property testing, an algorithm determines whether a given instance satisfies some predetermined property or is far from satisfying that property with high probability by reading a constant-sized part of the input. This section presents some results mainly concerning property testing that have recently been obtained in the ABD Project.

H. Ito (✉)
The University of Electro-Communications, 1-5-1 Chofugaoka, Chofu, Tokyo 182-8585, Japan
e-mail: itohiro@uec.ac.jp

© The Author(s) 2022
N. Katoh et al. (eds.), *Sublinear Computation Paradigm*,
https://doi.org/10.1007/978-981-16-4095-7_2

2.2 Basic Terms and Definitions for Property Testing

This section gives some of the basic terms that are needed in order to explain our results. Property testing works on many different types of models, including graphs, functions, strings, grammars, and images. Although the details of the definitions differ slightly between the different models, since the basic ideas are the same for all of models, we present only the definitions for digraphs.

Let $\mathbb{N} = \{0, 1, 2, \ldots\}$ be the set of natural numbers. In this chapter, we sometimes omit floor or ceiling functions. For example, if we write $s = \sqrt{n}$ in a context where s must be an integer and n is not necessarily a square number, then $\sqrt{n}$ should be taken to mean $\lfloor \sqrt{n} \rfloor$ or $\lceil \sqrt{n} \rceil$. This allows us to disregard integrality issues that make no real difference to any of our proofs.

2.2.1 *Graphs and the Three Models for Property Testing*

A directed graph or *digraph* G is defined as a pair of finite sets (V, E), where V is a finite set of *vertices* and $E \subseteq V \times V$ is a set of directed edges, or *edges* for short. The vertex set V and the edge set E of a graph G are sometimes written as V_G and E_G, respectively. If the direction of each edge is ignored (i.e., $(u, v) = (v, u)$ for any $u, v \in V$), then the digraph is called a *graph* (or an *undirected graph* if we want to indicate undirectedness explicitly). Every graph can be represented as a digraph by using reflectivity on edges; in other words if $(u, v) \in E$, then $(v, u) \in E$ for every $u, v \in V$. Thus, graphs can be regarded as special cases of digraphs. This section mainly treats (undirected) graphs. Digraphs are considered in Sect. 2.4. Many of the terms and symbols we define for graphs are also used for digraphs.

The *order* of a graph G is given by $|V_G|$ and the *size* of a graph G is given by $|E_G|$. A graph (resp., digraph) of order n is also called an *n-graph* (resp., *n-digraph*). The number of vertices adjacent to a vertex v in a graph G is denoted by $\deg_G(v)$. If G is clear from the context, the subscript G may be omitted. In property testing, since an algorithm reads only a part of an instance (input), it gets information about the instances through oracles, which depend on how to the graphs are represented. There are three known models for treating graphs in property testing: the dense-graph model; the bounded-degree (graph) model; and the general-graph model.

In *the dense-graph model*, the *edge oracle* is used: If an algorithm queries whether $(u, v) \in E$ or not, the oracle answers correctly: the answer is 1 if $(u, v) \in E$ and 0 otherwise. This model basically treats dense (i.e., $|E| = \Omega(n^2)$) graphs. This is because if $|E| = o(n^2)$, then the edge oracle answers "0" almost every time when n is large, making the queries useless.[1]

In the *bounded-degree model*, there is a restriction such that the degree of every vertex is bounded by a predetermined integer $d \geq 1$, that is, $\deg(v) \leq d$ ($\forall v \in V$). From this restriction, it follows that the number of edges in a graph is at most $dn/2$ (or

[1] It works only for determining whether a given graph is sparse.

dn for a digraph); in other words, the graph is sparse (note that d is a constant). This model assumes that for every vertex v, the vertices adjacent to v are ordered. This model uses the *adjacent-vertex oracle*: If an algorithm queries for the ith ($1 \le i \le d$) adjacent vertex of v by giving a pair (v, i), the oracle answers the name (ID) of the vertex if exists and returns a predetermined special symbol such as $\perp$ otherwise. A graph where the degree is bounded by d is also called a *d-bounded-degree graph*.

The *general-graph model* is a mixed model of the dense-graph model and the bounded-degree model. Although this model does not have any maximum degree-bound, there is a fixed upper bound d on the *average* degree. In many cases d is a constant and the graphs in this model are sparse. However, if $d = \Theta(n)$, graphs in the model may be dense. This model allows all oracles that are allowed in the other two models in addition to the *degree oracle*: If an algorithm queries the degree of a vertex v, it replies with the correct answer $\deg(v)$.

2.2.2 Properties, Distances, and Testers

The set of graphs considered in each model—that is, the dense-graph model, the bounded-degree model, or the general-graph model—is denoted by Γ. The subset of Γ such that the order of the graph is n is denoted by Γ_n. Hence $\Gamma = \bigcup_{n \in \mathbb{N}} \Gamma_n$.

A *property* is defined as a (generally infinitely large) subset of graphs closed under isomorphism.[2] For example "planarity" is defined as the set of all planar graphs. For a property $\mathcal{P}$, we define $\mathcal{P}_n$ as $\mathcal{P} \cap \Gamma_n$. Thus, clearly $\mathcal{P} = \bigcup_{n \in \mathbb{N}} \mathcal{P}_n$.

Property testing is a relaxation of a decision problem. The object of a property testing is to distinguish with high probability whether a given instance satisfies some predetermined property or the instance is "far" from satisfying the property. This requires a mathematical definition of "far."

Let G and G' both be n-graphs; $G, G' \in \Gamma_n$. The distance between the two graphs is defined as the Hamming distance between them divided by the largest Hamming distance in the model (for normalization). Thus, the distance depends on the models (i.e., how the graphs are represented). We explain this by using the dense-graph model. Let $\delta_{E_G} : V \times V \to \{0, 1\}$ be the characteristic function on E_G, that is, $\delta_{E_G}(u, v) = 1$ if $(u, v) \in E_G$ and 0 otherwise. The distance between G and G' is defined as follows: We denote by $m(G, G')$ the number of edges that need to be deleted from and/or inserted into G in order to make $G = G'$, i.e.

$$m(G, G') := |\{(u, v) \in V \times V \mid \delta_{E_G}(u, v) \neq \delta_{E_{G'}}(u, v)\}|$$

Using this, we define the distance between G and G' as follows[3]:

[2] Intuitively this means to ignore the labels on vertices and edges.

[3] Although the maximum number of edges in any (undirected) graph of order n is $n(n-1)/2$, we use n^2 for the denominator for simplicity.

$$\mathrm{dist}(G, G') := \frac{m(G, G')}{n^2}. \tag{2.1}$$

Note that $0 \le \mathrm{dist}(G, G') \le 1$ for every G and G'. In the bounded-degree model and the general-graph model, the distance is defined as follows[4]:

$$\mathrm{dist}(G, G') := \frac{m(G, G')}{dn}, \tag{2.2}$$

where d is the upper bound on the maximum (resp., the average) vertex-degrees for the bounded-degree model (resp., the general-graph model).

By using the distance between graphs, the distance beetween a graph $G \in \Gamma_n$ and a property $\mathcal{P}$ is defined as follows:

$$\mathrm{dist}(G, \mathcal{P}) := \begin{cases} \min_{G' \in \mathcal{P}_n} \mathrm{dist}(G, G') & \text{if } \mathcal{P}_n \neq \emptyset, \\ \infty & \text{otherwise.} \end{cases}$$

This applies to all the models. For a real value $0 \le \epsilon \le 1$, we say that G is ϵ-*far* from G' (resp., $\mathcal{P}$) if $\mathrm{dist}(G, G') > \epsilon$ (resp., $\mathrm{dist}(G, \mathcal{P}) > \epsilon$) and ϵ-*close* otherwise.

A *testing algorithm* for a property $\mathcal{P}$ is an algorithm that, given query access (by the oracles) to an instance G and given $0 < \epsilon \le 1$, accepts every $G \in \mathcal{P}$ with probability at least $2/3$, and rejects every G that is ϵ-far from $\mathcal{P}$ with probability at least $2/3$. If a testing algorithm accepts every $G \in \mathcal{P}$ with probability 1, then the algorithm is called a *one-sided-error*. The number of queries made by an algorithm to the given oracle is called the *query complexity* of the algorithm. If the query complexity of a testing algorithm is bounded by a constant that is independent of n (but that may depend on ϵ and d), then the algorithm is called a *tester*. A property is *testable*[5] if there is a tester for the property.

2.3 Important Known Results in Property Testing on Graphs

This section gives a very brief overview of important known results in property testing on graphs, particularly on the characterization and general properties of testability. See a recent review [11] or books [4, 8] for details.

---

4 Although the maximum number of edges of any d-bounded-degree (undirected) graph of order n is $dn/2$, we use dn for the denominator for simplicity.

5 Sometimes "testable" means that the problem has an algorithm with sublinear query complexity, and *strongly testable* may be used to distinguish constant query complexity from mere sublinear query complexity.

2.3.1 Results for the Dense-Graph Model

Alon et al. [2] found a combinatorial characterization (necessary and sufficient condition) of testable properties for the dense-graph model. We first present the theorem without defining the terms used in it.

Theorem 2.1 *For the dense-graph model, a graph property is testable if and only if it is regular-reducible.*

This theorem utilize the extremely powerful monumental Szemérédi's regularity lemma, which we now introduce briefly. For a pair of subsets of vertices $A, B \subseteq V$ of a graph $G = (V, E)$, $\text{den}(A, B) := \frac{|E(A,B)|}{|A||B|}$ is called the *density* of the pair. A family of subsets $\mathcal{V} = \{V_1, \ldots, V_k\}$ $(V_i \subseteq V, \forall i \in \{1, \ldots, k\})$ is called a *partition* of V if $V_i \cap V_j = \emptyset$ for all $1 \leq i < j \leq k$ and $V = V_1 \cup \cdots \cup V_k$. A partition $\mathcal{V} = \{V_1, \ldots, V_k\}$ of the vertex set of a graph is called an *equipartition* if $|V_i|$ and $|V_j|$ differ by no more than 1 for all $1 \leq i < j \leq k$.

Definition 2.1 (ϵ-*regular*) Let $0 < \epsilon \leq 1$ be a real number and $A, B \subseteq V$. A pair (A, B) is called ϵ-*regular* if $|\text{den}(A, B) - \text{den}(X, Y)| \leq \epsilon$ for any two subsets $X \subseteq A$ and $Y \subseteq B$ satisfying $|X| \geq \epsilon|A|$ and $|Y| \geq \epsilon|B|$. An equipartition $\mathcal{V} = \{V_1, \ldots, V_k\}$ of the vertex set of a graph is called ϵ-*regular* if all but at most ϵk^2 of the pairs (V_i, V_j) $(i, j \in \{1, \ldots, k\})$ are ϵ-regular.

Definition 2.2 (*regularity-instance*) A *regularity-instance* R is given by an error-parameter $0 < \epsilon \leq 1$, an integer k, a set of $\binom{k}{2}$ real numbers $0 \leq \eta_{i,j} \leq 1$ indexed by $1 \leq i < j \leq k$, and a set $\overline{R}$ of pairs (i, j) of size at most ϵk^2. A graph is said to satisfy the *regularity-instance* if it has an equipartition $\mathcal{V} = \{V_1, \ldots, V_k\}$ such that for all $(i, j) \notin \overline{R}$ the pair (V_i, V_j) is ϵ-regular and satisfies $|E(V_i, V_j)| = \eta_{i,j}|V_i||V_j|$. The *complexity* of the regularity instance is $\max(k, 1/\epsilon)$.

Definition 2.3 (*regular-reducible*) A graph property $\mathcal{P}$ is *regular-reducible* if for any $\delta > 0$ there exists $r = r_{\mathcal{P}}(\delta)$ such that for any n there is a family $\mathcal{R}$ of at most r regularity-instances each of complexity at most r, such that the following holds for every $\epsilon > 0$ and every n-graph G:

1. If $G \in \mathcal{P}$, then for some $R \in \mathcal{R}$, G is δ-close to R.
2. If G is ϵ-far from $\mathcal{P}$, then for any $R \in \mathcal{R}$, G is $(\epsilon - \delta)$-far from R.

Theorem 2.2 (Szemérédi's regularity lemma [2, 17]) *For every pair of an integer t and a real number $\epsilon > 0$ there exists an integer $T = T_2(t, \epsilon)$ such that any graph with $n \geq T$ vertices has an ϵ-regular equipartition of order k, where $t \leq k \leq T$.*

An intuitive explanation of the regularity lemma is that, for any $\epsilon > 0$, every graph $G = (V, E)$ has an ϵ-approximation of a constant-sized edge-weighted graph, where the edge weight approximates the density of the corresponding vertex pair. Intuitively, a property being regular-reducible means that it can be represented by a constant number of equipartitions based on the regularity lemma; in other words, the regularity lemma holds for testing the property. See [11] also for details.

Representative regular-reducible properties are monotone or hereditary properties, which are defined as follows.

Definition 2.4 A graph property $\mathcal{P}$ is *monotone* if for every $G \in \mathcal{P}$ and $e \in E_G$, $G - \{e\} \in \mathcal{P}$. A graph property $\mathcal{P}$ is *hereditary* if for every $G \in \mathcal{P}$ and $v \in V_G$, $G - \{v\} \in \mathcal{P}$.

Planarity, bipartiteness, k-colorability (for any $k \in \mathbb{N}$), H-freeness (for any graph H),[6] and disconnectedness are all monotone. The former four properties are also hereditary, but the last one, disconnectedness, is not.[7] A well-known non-monotone and hereditary property is perfectness: A graph is said to be *perfect* if for every induced subgraph, the chromatic number of the subgraph equals the clique number (= the order of the largest clique) of the subgraph. Every monotone or hereditary property is regular-reducible (see [2] for details).

We can say that Theorem 2.1 solves the problem of characterizing testable properties in the dense-graph model in a sense. However, the constants that appear in the algorithms obtained by Theorem 2.1 are incredibly (maybe more than astronomically) huge! Thus, developing faster (i.e., smaller constant complexity) algorithms remains an issue for each problem.

2.3.2 *Results for the Bounded-Degree Model*

Whereas the combinatorial characterization of testable properties as shown in Theorem 2.1 was obtained for the dense-graph model, no perfect results have been obtained for the bounded-degree model despite many attempts to achieve this goal. However, progress is being made in steps. We now have an important characterization of testable properties in the bounded-degree model called "hyperfiniteness." We also found another characterization called "forbidden configurations," for one-sided error testability, which is explained in Sect. 2.4.

Definition 2.5 Let $\epsilon > 0, t > 0$, and $d > 0$. Let $G = (V, E)$ be a d-bounded-degree n-graph. If one can remove at most ϵdn edges from G such that each connected component of the resulting graph has at most t vertices, then G is called (ϵ, t)-*hyperfinite* (with respect to degree bound d). For a function $\rho : \mathbb{R}^+ \to \mathbb{R}^+$, if G is $(\epsilon, \rho(\epsilon))$-hyperfinite for every $\epsilon > 0$, then G is called ρ-*hyperfinite*. A set $\mathcal{G}$ of d-degree-bounded graphs is called ρ-*hyperfinite* if $\forall G \in \mathcal{G}$ is ρ-hyperfinite. $\mathcal{G}$ is called *hyperfinite* if there is a function ρ such that $\mathcal{G}$ is ρ-hyperfinite.

Newman and Sohler [15] presented the following theorem.

[6] If a graph includes no H as a subgraph, then it is called H-*free*.

[7] If a graph consisting of one connected component of order $n - 1$ and one isolated vertex is disconnected, removing the isolated vertex from the graph makes it connected.

Theorem 2.3 *In the bounded-degree model, every graph property is testable for any hyperfinite family of graphs.*

While this is a sufficient condition, the following necessary condition related to hyperfiniteness was obtained by Fichtenberger et al. [5].

Definition 2.6 A *subproperty* of a property $\mathcal{P}$ is a property that is a subset of $\mathcal{P}$. A property is *non-trivially testable* if it is testable and there exists $\epsilon > 0$ such that there is an infinite number of graphs that are ϵ-far from the property.

Theorem 2.4 *Every testable property of bounded-degree graphs is either finite or contains an infinite hyperfinite subproperty. Furthermore, the complement of every non-trivially testable graph property contains an infinite hyperfinite subproperty.*

These theorems show that there is a deep relation between hyperfiniteness and testability on bounded-degree graphs. We have found, however, no necessary and sufficient condition of graph testability even for a one-sided error. Recently we found necessary and sufficient conditions for one-sided-error testability on subclasses of properties of digraphs[8] [12]. This was obtained through the ABD Project, and is explained in Sect. 2.4.

2.3.3 Results for the General-Graph Model

There were previously no general classes of testable properties for the general-graph model. Through the ABD Project, a class that models complex networks called Hierarchical Scale Free ($\mathcal{HSF}$) was founded that is testable. We present an outline of the result below, and the details are available in [10, 11].

Definition 2.7 *For positive real numbers* $c > 0$ and $\gamma > 1$, *a class of scale-free (multi)graphs* $\mathcal{SF}(c, \gamma)$ *consists of (multi)graphs* $G = (V, E)$ *for which the following condition holds: Let* v_i *be the number of vertices* v *of degree* i*. Then:*

$$\nu_i \leq cni^{-\gamma}, \quad \forall i \in \{2, 3, \ldots, \}. \tag{2.3}$$

A *clique* is a subgraph in which there exists an edge between every pair of vertices. For a nonnegative integer $c \geq 0$, a *c-isolated clique* is a clique such that the number of outgoing edges (edges between the clique and the other vertices) is less than ck, where k is the number of vertices of the clique. A 1-isolated clique is sometimes simply called an *isolated clique* (see [9] for details). Let $\mathcal{E}(G)$ be the graph obtained from G by contracting all isolated cliques.[9]

---

[8] Note that any undirected graph can be represented by a digraph, i.e., the set of digraphs can be regarded as including the set of undirected graphs.

[9] Two distinct isolated cliques never overlap, except in the special case of *double-isolated-cliques*, which consists of two isolated cliques of size k that share $k - 1$ vertices. A double-isolated-clique

Definition 2.8 For positive real numbers $c > 0, \gamma > 1$ and a positive integer $n_0 \geq 1$, a class of *hierarchical scale-free (multi)graphs* $\mathcal{HSF} = \mathcal{HSF}(c, \gamma, n_0)$ consists of (multi)graphs $G = (V, E)$ for which the following conditions hold:

(i) $G \in \mathcal{SF}(c, \gamma)$,
(ii) Consider the infinite sequence of graphs $G_0 = G, G_1 = \mathcal{E}(G_0), G_2 = \mathcal{E}(G_1), \ldots$. If $|V_{G_i}| \geq n_0$, then G_i includes at least one isolated clique $Q \subseteq V$ with $|Q| \geq 2$. (Note that if G_k has no such isolated clique, then $G_k = G_{k+1} = G_{k+2} = \cdots$.)

For a graph G and a nonnegative integer $d \geq 0$, $G|d$ is the graph obtained by deleting all edges incident to each vertex v of degree more than d. Note that $G|d$ is a d-bounded-degree graph. The following properties were obtained by [10].

Lemma 2.1 *For every $\mathcal{SF} = \mathcal{SF}(c, \gamma)$ with $\gamma > 2$, and every positive real number $\epsilon > 0$, there exists a constant $\delta = \delta(\epsilon, c, \gamma)$ such that for every graph $G \in \mathcal{SF}$, $G|\delta$ is ϵ-close to G.*

This lemma looks useful since it means that for any $\epsilon > 0$, any scale-free graph is ϵ-close to a bounded-degree graph. This lemma is applied in the proof of the following theorem, which is the main theorem of [10].

Theorem 2.5 *Every property is testable for $\mathcal{HSF}(c, \gamma, n_0)$ with $\gamma > 2$.*

In the general-graph model, no other universal (constant-time) tester is known, but universal testing algorithms with polylog(n)-time query complexity have been found for forests [14] and outerplanar graphs [3].

2.4 Characterization of Testability on Bounded-Degree Digraphs

2.4.1 Bounded-Degree Model of Digraphs

As mentioned previously, there is no complete characterization of testable graph properties in bounded-degree graphs even for one-sided-errors. Through the ABD project, however, we have obtained a characterization for one-sided-error testable properties of monotone and hereditary properties of bounded-degree digraphs [12], which we briefly explain in this section. The set of digraphs can be regarded to include the set of undirected graphs by introducing reflexivity, i.e., $\forall u, v \in V$, if $(u, v) \in E$, then $(v, u) \in E$.

In this section, we consider the bounded-degree model on digraphs. For a digraph $G = (V, E)$ and a vertex $v \in V$ we denote by $N_G^+(v)$ the set of outgoing neighbours

---

Q has no edge between Q and the other part of the graph (i.e., $\deg_G(Q) = 0$), and thus we specially define that a double-isolated-clique in G is contracted into a vertex in $\mathcal{E}(G)$. Under this assumption, $\mathcal{E}(G)$ is uniquely defined.

of v, i.e., $N_G^+(v) := \{u \in V \mid (v, u) \in E\}$. Similarly, $N_G^-(v) := \{u \in V \mid (u, v) \in E\}$ and $N_G(v) := N_G^+(v) \cup N_G^-(v)$. The *out-degree* of v is $\deg_G^+(v) := |N_G^+(v)|$, and the *in-degree* of v is $\deg_G^-(v) := |N_G^-(v)|$. The subscript G can be omitted if it is clear.

For a (di)graph $G = (V, E)$ and $F \subseteq E$, we denote by $G - F$ the graph $(V, E - F)$. For a (di)graph $G = (V, E)$ and $W \subseteq V$, we denote by $G[W]$ the subgraph of G induced by W (i.e., $G[W]$ contains all edges in E_G whose both endpoints are in W). $G[V - W]$ can be denoted by $G - W$.

In the bounded-degree model for digraphs, there are two submodels: In one, only the out-degree is bounded; in the other, both the in-degree and out-degree are bounded.[10] The former case is represented by $F(d)$ model and the latter one by $FB(d)$ model.[11] The $F(d)$ model is clealy wider than the $FB(d)$ model. Moreover, every undirected d-bounded graph can be formulated by the $FB(d)$ model by replacing each undirected edge by a pair of anti-parallel directed edges. That is, the $FB(d)$ model (and thus the $F(d)$ model as well) is regarded as including the undirected d-bounded degree model.

2.4.2 Monotone Properties and Hereditary Properties

This section extends the monotone and hereditary properties that were defined in Definition 2.4 to digraphs.

We first introduce the following notation for characterizing the testability of these properties. Let $\mathcal{H}$ be a set of digraphs. We call $\mathcal{H}$ an *r-set* if every member $H \in \mathcal{H}$ has at most r vertices (i.e., H is an r'-digraph for some $r' \leq r$). A digraph G is *$\mathcal{H}$-free* if for every $H \in \mathcal{H}$, G contains no subgraph that is isomorphic to H. A digraph G is *induced $\mathcal{H}$-free* if for every $H \in \mathcal{H}$, G contains no induced subgraph that is isomorphic to H. We denote by $\mathcal{P}_{\mathcal{H}}$ (resp., $\mathcal{P}^*_{\mathcal{H}}$) the property that contains all digraphs that are $\mathcal{H}$-free (resp., induced $\mathcal{H}$-free). $\mathcal{P}_{\mathcal{H},n}$ (resp., $\mathcal{P}^*_{\mathcal{H},n}$) is the subproperty of $\mathcal{P}_{\mathcal{H}}$ that consists of all n-digraphs in $\mathcal{P}_{\mathcal{H}}$ (resp., $\mathcal{P}^*_{\mathcal{H}}$). We can easily confirm that $\mathcal{P}_{\mathcal{H}}$ is monotone and $\mathcal{P}^*_{\mathcal{H}}$ is hereditary for any $\mathcal{H}$.

Let $H = (V, E)$ be a digraph. For a subset $W \subseteq V$, if by disregarding the directions of the edges of H, W induces a connected component in the resulting undirected graph, then we say that $H[W]$, which is the directed subgraph of H induced by W, is a *component* of H. A digraph H is *rooted* if every component H' of H has a vertex v such that for every $u \in V_{H'}$ there exists a dipath (= directed path) from v to u.

---

[10] Clearly the case in which only the *in*-degree is bounded can be formulated by the model in which only the *out*-degree is bounded by changing the edge direction.

[11] F and B mean forward and backward, respectively.

2.4.3 Characterizations

By using these terms, the characterizations of testable monotone or hereditary properties for the $F(d)$ model were given in [12].

Theorem 2.6 *Let $P = \bigcup_{n\in\mathbb{N}} \mathcal{P}_n$ be a monotone property in the $F(d)$-model. Then $\mathcal{P}$ is testable if and only if there is a function $r : (0, 1) \to \mathbb{N}$ such that for any $0 < \epsilon < 1$ and $n \in \mathbb{N}$, there is an $r(\epsilon)$-set of rooted digraphs $\mathcal{H}_n$ such that the property $\mathcal{P}_{\mathcal{H}_n,n}$ satisfies the following two conditions:*
(a) $\mathcal{P}_n \subseteq \mathcal{P}_{\mathcal{H}_n,n}$
(b) $\mathcal{P}_{\mathcal{H}_n,n}$ is $\epsilon/2$-close to $\mathcal{P}_n$.

Theorem 2.7 *Let $\mathcal{P}$ be a hereditary property in the $F(d)$-model. Then $\mathcal{P}$ is testable if and only if there are functions $r : (0, 1) \to \mathbb{N}$ and $N : (0, 1) \to \mathbb{N}$ such that for any $0 < \epsilon < 1$, there is an $r(\epsilon)$-set of rooted digraphs $\mathcal{H}$ such that for every $n \geq N(\epsilon)$, $\mathcal{P}^*_{\mathcal{H},n}$ satisfies the following two conditions:*
(a) $\mathcal{P}_n \subseteq \mathcal{P}^*_{\mathcal{H},n}$
(b) $\mathcal{P}^*_{\mathcal{H},n}$ is $\epsilon/2$-close to $\mathcal{P}_n$.

Condition (b) in both Theorems 2.6 and 2.7 is necessary, since there exists a monotone and hereditary property that is testable with a one-sided-error and has no $\mathcal{H}_n$ such that $|\mathcal{H}_n|$ is bounded by a constant $(r(\epsilon))$ and "$\mathcal{P}_n = \mathcal{P}_{\mathcal{H}_n,n}$ or $\mathcal{P}_n = \mathcal{P}^*_{\mathcal{H}_n,n}$": One of these properties is $\mathcal{P}_{C_{\sqrt{n}}} (= \mathcal{P}^*_{C_{\sqrt{n}}})$ on the $F(1)$-model,[12] where C_k is the set of directed cycles (or *dicycles*, for short) of length in $[3, k]$, i.e., $\mathcal{P}_{C_{\sqrt{n}}}$ is the property of having no dicycle of length in $[3, \sqrt{n}]$. This property is clearly monotone and hereditary. To express $\mathcal{P}_{C_{\sqrt{n}}}$ by using a set $\mathcal{H}$ of forbidden subgraphs (or forbidden induced subgraphs), $\mathcal{H}$ must includes $C_{\sqrt{n}}$, and thus $|\mathcal{H}|$ cannot be bounded by any constant. However, this property is testable with a one-sided-error as shown below.

Lemma 2.2 *$\mathcal{P}_{C_{\sqrt{n}}}$ on the $F(1)$-model is one-sided-error testable with query complexity $O(\epsilon^{-2})$.*

To prove this lemma, we will use the following lemma, which is often effective for estimating the query complexity of testers.

Lemma 2.3 *For any real number x, the following inequality holds:*

$$e^x \geq x + 1. \tag{2.4}$$

The proof of this lemma is trivial from the differentiation of $e^x - (x + 1)$, and is omitted here.

Proof of Lemma 2.2: If $n \leq 2/\epsilon$, then we can get the complete data of the graph in time $2/\epsilon$. Thus it is enough to consider the case of $n > 2/\epsilon$. We use the following algorithm for the tester:

---

[12] $\mathcal{P}_{C_{\sqrt{n}}} \neq \mathcal{P}^*_{C_{\sqrt{n}}}$ on the $F(d)$-model for $d \geq 2$.

Choose $s = 2/\epsilon$ vertices $v_1, \ldots, v_s$ from V uniformly at random, and denote them by S. For each $v_i \in S$, check whether there is a dicycle of length at most s that includes v_i by following each outgoing edge successively whenever it exists. (Note that in the $F(1)$-model, the outgoing edge of each vertex exists uniquely if it exists.) If a dicycle of length in $[3, s]$ is found, then it is rejected; otherwise, it is accepted.

We show that the above algorithm is the desired one-sided-error tester. It is clearly a one-sided-error, since it never rejects without finding a short (i.e., length of at most s) dicycle. Thus, it is enough to show that the algorithm rejects with probability at least $2/3$ if the input is ϵ-far from $\mathcal{P}_{C_{\sqrt{n}}}$.

Assume that the input $G = (V, E)$ is ϵ-far from $\mathcal{P}_{C_{\sqrt{n}}}$, i.e., that G contains more than ϵn dicycles of length in $[3, \sqrt{n}]$. Let $\mathcal{C}$ be the set of such dicycles. We divide $\mathcal{C}$ into the following two sets:

$\mathcal{C}_{\text{short}} = \{C \in \mathcal{C} \mid$ the length of C is at most s.$\}$

$\mathcal{C}_{\text{long}} = \{C \in \mathcal{C} \mid$ the length of C is more than s (and at most $\sqrt{n}$).$\}$

From $|\mathcal{C}| > \epsilon n$, $|\mathcal{C}_{\text{short}}| > \epsilon n/2$ or $|\mathcal{C}_{\text{long}}| > \epsilon n/2$ holds.

First, we assume that $|\mathcal{C}_{\text{long}}| > \epsilon n/2$. Clearly no pair of dicycles in $\mathcal{C}$ shares a common vertex, and thus more than $\epsilon s n/2 = n$ vertices are included in the graph contradiction. Thus, $|\mathcal{C}_{\text{long}}| \leq \epsilon n/2$.

From this, it follows that $|\mathcal{C}_{\text{short}}| > \epsilon n/2$. Since no pair of dicycles in $\mathcal{C}$ shares a common vertex and each dicycle has at least three vertices, then the dicycles in $\mathcal{C}_{\text{short}}$ contain more than $3\epsilon n/2$ vertices. Let W be the set of such vertices. If the algorithm finds at least one vertex from W, then it will find a short dicycle that includes the vertex and rejects the input. From $|W| > 3\epsilon n/2$, it follows that the probability that a chosen vertex is not in W is less than $1 - 3\epsilon/2$. Thus, the probability that all of s vertices chosen by the algorithm are not in W is less than

$$(1 - 3\epsilon/2)^s \leq e^{-3\epsilon s/2} = e^{-3} < \frac{1}{3}.$$

Note that the first inequality above uses the inequality (2.4). The probability that the algorithm finds at least one vertex from W is, therefore, more than $2/3$. The query complexity of this tester is clearly $O(\epsilon^{-2})$. □

Since $\mathcal{P}_{C_{\sqrt{n}}}$ is both monotone and hereditary, Theorems 2.6 and 2.7 hold. If we apply Theorem 2.6, then $\mathcal{H}_n = C_{\min\{2/\epsilon, \sqrt{n}\}}$ for each n. If we apply Theorem 2.7, then $N(\epsilon) = 4/\epsilon^2$ and $\mathcal{H} = C_{2/\epsilon}$. From this discussion, we observe that $N(\epsilon)$ is essential in Theorem 2.7.

2.4.4 An Idea to Extend the Characterizations Beyond Monotone and Hereditary

We would like to extend Theorems 2.6 and 2.7 to general properties. We denote by $\mathcal{P}_{\deg^+(d-1)}$ the property consisting of digraphs having no vertex with out-degree $d - 1$ on the $F(d)$-model. $\mathcal{P}_{\deg(d-1)}$ is one-sided-error testable as shown below.

Let $G = (V, E)$ be an input. The algorithm for $\mathcal{P}_{\deg^+(d-1)}$ chooses $2/\epsilon$ vertices from V uniformly at random and checks their out-degrees. If it finds a vertex of degree $d - 1$, then it is rejected; otherwise, it is accepted. This algorithm is a one-sided-error, since it never rejects if there is no vertex of out-degree $d - 1$. If G is ϵ-far from $\mathcal{P}_{\deg^+(d-1)}$, then there are more than ϵn vertices of out-degrees $d - 1$. Thus, the probability that there is no vertex of out-degree $d - 1$ in the selected $2/\epsilon$ vertices by the algorithm is less than

$$(1-\epsilon)^{\frac{2}{\epsilon}} \le \left(e^{-\epsilon}\right)^{\frac{2}{\epsilon}} = e^{-2} < \frac{1}{3}.$$

Note that this also uses the inequality (2.4).

Hence, the above algorithm is a one-sided-error tester for $\mathcal{P}_{\deg^+(d-1)}$. However, expressing this property by using forbidden subgraphs or forbidden induced subgraphs like Theorems 2.6 or 2.7 is impossible.[13]

To extend the idea of "forbidden something" to non-monotone and non-hereditary properties, we [12] introduced the idea of "configurations," by generalizing subgraphs and induced subgraphs. A similar idea has also appeared in [16].

Definition 2.9 A *configuration* is a pair $O = (H, L)$, where $H = (W, F)$ is a digraph in the $F(d)$-model, $L : W \to \{\text{developed}, \text{frontier}\}$ is a function, and the out-degree of every frontier vertex is 0. The configuration is *rooted* if H is rooted.

Definition 2.10 Let $O = (H = (W, F), L)$ and $G = (V, E)$ be a configuration and a graph respectively in the $F(d)$-model. We say that G has an *O-appearance* if there is an injective mapping $\phi : W \to V$ satisfying the condition that $\forall v \in W$ with $L(v) =$ developed, the following two conditions hold:

(i) $\forall u \in W$, $(v, u) \in F$ if and only if $(\phi(v), \phi(u)) \in E$.
(ii) If $(\phi(v), x) \in E$, then $\exists u \in W$, $\phi(u) = x$.

We say that G is *O-free* if G has no O-appearance. For a set $\mathcal{O}$ of configurations, we say that G is *$\mathcal{O}$-free* if $\forall O \in \mathcal{O}$, G is O-free. □

As we have already stated, $\mathcal{P}_{\deg^+(d-1)}$ cannot be defined by any set of forbidden subgraphs or induced subgraphs. However, it can be defined by using $\mathcal{O}$-freeness. That is, let $O_{\deg^+(d-1)} = (H = (W, F), L)$ be a configuration such that $W = \{v_0, v_1, \dots, v_{d-1}\}$, $E = \{(v_0, v_1), (v_0, v_2), \dots, (v_0, v_{d-1})\}$, $L(v_0) =$ developed, and $L(v_1) = L(v_2) = \dots = L(v_{d-1}) =$ frontier. Then $\mathcal{P}_{\deg(d-1)}$ is defined by the set of $O_{\deg(d-1)}$-free graphs.

The idea of configuration-free (or forbidden configurations) may work for characterizing general one-sided-error testable properties on the $F(d)$-model. See [12] for details.

[13] This follows from the fact that $\mathcal{P}_{\deg^+(d-1)}$ is neither monotone nor hereditary, and from Theorems 2.6, and 2.7.

2.5 Testable EXPTIME-Complete Games

This section presents results on the testability of combinatorial games, particularly the generalized chess, Shogi (Japanese chess), and Xiangqi (Chinese chess). Given any position on a $\sqrt{n} \times \sqrt{n}$ board with $O(n)$ pieces, the generalized chess, Shogi, and Xiangqi problems are the problems of determining the property that "the player who moves first has a winning strategy." These problems are known or believed to be EXPTIME-complete [1, 6, 7]. In [13], we proposed that this property is testable for chess, Shogi, and Xiangqi. The Shogi tester and Xiangqi tester are one-sided-error testers, and surprisingly, the chess tester is a no-error tester. Many problems have been revealed to be testable, but most of such problems belong to class NP. We think that this is the first result on the constant-time testability of EXPTIME-complete problems. This section presents these results. We mainly focus on chess, followed by Shogi, but omit the explanation for Xiangqi since the method is similar to the one for Shogi. See [13] for details.

2.5.1 *Definitions*

We begin by focusing mainly on generalized chess. Generalized chess is played on a $\sqrt{n} \times \sqrt{n}$ board with $O(n)$ pieces, including two kings. White moves first and black plays after white. A position is defined by fixing each piece to a particular cell on the board. At any given position S, the problem is to determine whether white wins if both players play optimally. The basic rules are the same as those in the original chess and are omitted here.

In chess, there are six different types of pieces: king (K), queen (Q), bishop (B), knight (N), rook (R), and pawn (P). There are only two pieces of kings; one white and one black. For each of the other piece-types (i.e., bishop, knight, rook, and pawn), there exist at most cn pieces for both white and black, respectively, where c is a constant. Piece-numbers from 1 to cn are given to each white or black piece of each piece-type; in other words, each piece has its own *piece ID* (k, o, ℓ) comprising a piece-type $k \in \{K, Q, B, N, R, P\}$, an owner-color $o \in \{\text{white}, \text{black}\}$, and a piece-number $\ell \in \{1, \ldots, cn\}$.

An algorithm can find the given position through the following oracles.

- *Piece oracle*: Given a piece ID (k, o, ℓ), the piece oracle answers an ordered pair (i, j) that provides the cell (i, j), $i, j \in \{0, 1, \ldots, \sqrt{n}\}$ where it lies. (i and j represent the column number and row number, respectively, and if $i = j = 0$, it denotes that the piece is not in the game (such a piece is called an *unused* piece). This oracle is expressed as $q_1(k, o, \ell) = (i, j)$.
- *Coordinate oracle*: Given a coordinate $(i, j), i, j \in \{0, 1, \ldots, \sqrt{n}\}$, the coordinate oracle answers the piece ID (k, o, ℓ) of the piece that lies on the cell if one exists. If no piece lies on the cell, the oracle answers $k = o = \ell = 0$. This oracle is expressed as $q_2(i, j) = (k, o, \ell)$.

When we explicitly identify position S, we express the oracles as $q_1(k, o, \ell; S)$ and $q_2(i, j; S)$, respectively. We introduce the assumption that all pieces can be arranged on the board simultaneously, and it thus follows that $2 \times (5cn + 1) \leq n$. For simplicity, we assume that

$$c \leq 1/11. \tag{2.5}$$

A position S is called a *winner* if white has a winning strategy (i.e., white will win if the players start from S and play optimally) and a *loser* otherwise. Note that a loser not only includes cases where white loses but also where the game ends in a draw.

A position is fixed by querying the piece oracle for every piece. The number of different queries for the piece oracle is at most n, and thus a position is fixed by the maximum of n data. From this, we define the *distance* between positions S and S' as

$$\mathrm{dist}(S, S') := \frac{|\{(i, j) \mid q_2(i, j; S) \neq q_2(i, j; S')\}|}{n}. \tag{2.6}$$

Clearly $0 \leq \mathrm{dist}(S, S') \leq 1$.

Positions S and S' are called *isomorphic* if we can make S identical to S' by only changing their piece-numbers (neither changing the piece-type nor owner-color is allowed). A set of positions that is closed under isomorphism is called a *property*. The distance between a position S and a property $\mathcal{P}$ is defined as follows:

$$\mathrm{dist}(S, \mathcal{P}) := \min_{S' \in \mathcal{P}} \mathrm{dist}(S, S'). \tag{2.7}$$

For a positive $\epsilon > 0$, S is ϵ-*far* from $\mathcal{P}$ if $\mathrm{dist}(S, \mathcal{P}) > \epsilon$; otherwise, it is ϵ-*close*. Let $\mathcal{W}$ be the set of winners. $\mathcal{W}$ is clearly closed under isomorphism and thus $\mathcal{W}$ is a property.

For generalized Shogi and Xiangqi, similar definitions are used. They can be easily deduced and are omitted here. See [13] for details.

2.5.2 Testers for Generalized Chess, Shogi, and Xiangqi

The following theorem was presented in [13]. Note that a *no-error* tester is a one-sided-error tester that always rejects every input that is ϵ-far from the property; that is, it always accepts or rejects with no-error if the input is in the property or ϵ-far from the property.

Theorem 2.8 *There exists a no-error tester with query complexity $O(\epsilon^{-1})$ for the generalized chess problem, there exists a one-sided-error tester with query complexity $O(\epsilon^{-2})$ for the generalized Shogi problem, and there exists a one-sided-error tester with query complexity $O(\epsilon^{-1})$ for the generalized Xiangqi problem.*

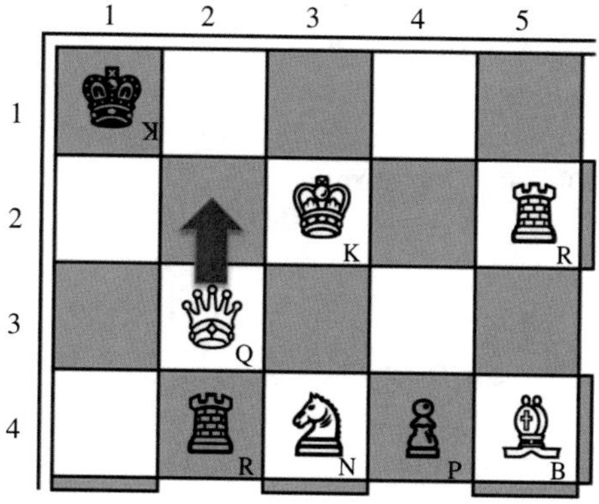

Fig. 2.1 The black king will be checkmated by white's next move, as indicated by the arrow

Proof of the chess part of Theorem 2.8 Let S be a given position. Let S' be the position made from S by changing the pieces in cells (i, j), $i \in \{1, 2, 3, 4\}$ and $j \in \{1, 2, 3, 4, 5\}$, as shown in Fig. 2.1.

The pieces that were in these cells in S are changed to be unused pieces, and the pieces that appear in these cells in S' are moved from other cells or unused pieces. In S', the white king is safe and the black king will be checkmated by white's next move (moving the queen from (3, 2) to (2, 2)), meaning that S' is a winner. The distance between S and S' is at most $20 + 8 = 28$. Thus, if $n \geq 28/\epsilon$, then $\text{dist}(S, S') \leq 28/n \leq \epsilon$. Hence, S is ϵ-close to $\mathcal{W}$, and it is sufficient to accept it. If $n < 28/\epsilon$, it is sufficient to read all of the information by calling the piece oracle for all pieces, which requires $O(\epsilon^{-1})$ queries.

This algorithm always accepts a winner. Moreover, if a given position S is ϵ-far from $\mathcal{W}$, then $n < 28/\epsilon$ and the algorithm knows the complete information for S. Therefore, this algorithm is no-error. □

The algorithms for the generalized Shogi and Xiangqi problems are a little more complicated. The reason is that in Shogi and Xiangqi there are fouls based on positions. A player who plays the fouls loses. In Shogi, the following fouls need to be considered in the generalized Shogi problem.

- *Nifu (double pawn)*: two or more unpromoted[14] pawns that belong to the same player must not be in the same column simultaneously.
- *Dead end*: pawns, lances, and knights[15] can never be moved or dropped onto cells from which a subsequent move cannot be made. Therefore, white (resp., black) unpromoted pawns and lances can never be in the first (resp., $\sqrt{n}$th) row, and white (resp., black) knights can never be in the first or second (resp., $\sqrt{n}$th or $(\sqrt{n} - 1)$th) rows.

[14] If a piece of some piece-type can be promoted (to a stronger piece) when it enters the opponent's camp.

[15] These three pieces can move only forward.

In a given position S, if there is a white piece that plays a fault, then white cannot win,[16] and thus the position is not a winner. However, if the number of pieces related to fouls is small (e.g., smaller than $\epsilon n/2$), we can remove the fouls and make white win, i.e., the position is ϵ-close to $\mathcal{W}$. To detect this, we need to perform preprocessing and the tester may have error when the input is ϵ-far from $\mathcal{W}$. For Xiangqi, a similar discussion applies. See [13] for details.

2.6 Summary

In this chapter, we introduced basic terminology and important results for property testing, which is the most examined framework for constant- or sublinear-time algorithms. In particular we presented two of our resent esults: The first is the complete characterization of one-sided-error testable monotone or hereditary properties on bounded-out-degree digraphs, and the other one is the testers for the generalized chess, Shogi, and Xiangqi problems, which are all EXPTIME-complete.

The 21st century can be called the era of big data, and the larger big data becomes, the more we need sublinear- and constant-time algorithms. The importance of this area will continue to grow. The number of fields in which constant-algorithms are efficiently applied will increase, and new techniques will be found accordingly. We eagerly await these developments.

References

1. H. Adachi, H. Kamekawa, S. Iwata, Shogi on $n \times n$ board is complete in exponential time. IEICE J. **J70-D**(10), 1843–1852 (1987). (In Japanese)
2. N. Alon, E. Fischer, I. Newman, A. Shapira, A combinatorial characterization of the testable graph properties: it's all about regularity. SIAM J. Comput. **39**(1), 143–167 (2009)
3. J. Babu, A. Khoury, I. Newma, Every property of outerplanar graphs is testable, in *Proceedings of the RANDOM 2016*, LIPICS, pp. 21:1–21:19 (2016)
4. A. Bhattacharyya, Y. Yoshida, *Property Testing: Problems and Techniques* (Springer, Berlin, 2021) (scheduled to be published in 2021)
5. H. Fichtenberger, P. Peng, C. Sohler, Every Testable (Infinite) Property of Bounded-Degree Graphs Contains an Infinite Hyperfinite Subproperty (2018). arXiv: 1811.02937 (also appeared in SODA2019)
6. R.H. Fleischer, S.U. Khan, Xiangqi and combinatorial game (2002)
7. A.S. Fraenkel, D. Lichtenstein, Computing a perfect strategy of $n \times n$ chess requires time exponential in n. J. Comb. Theory Ser. A **31**, 199–214 (1981)
8. O. Goldreich, *Introduction to Property Testing* (Cambridge University Press, Cambridge, 2017)
9. H. Ito, K. Iwama, Enumeration of isolated cliques and pseudo-cliques. ACM Trans. Algorithms **5**(4), Article 40, 1–13 (2009)
10. H. Ito, Every property is testable on a natural class of scale-free multigraphs, in *Proceedings of ESA 2016*, LIPICS, Vol. 49 (ISBN 978-3-95977-005-7) (2016), pp. 21:2–21:15

[16] If both players play fouls, the game is a draw.

11. H. Ito, What graph properties are constant-time testable?—dense graphs, sparse graphs, and complex networks. The Rev Socionetw Strat, Springer **13**(2), 101–121 (2019)
12. H. Ito, A. Khoury, I. Newman, On the characterization of 1-sided error strongly-testable graph properties for bounded-degree graphs. J. Comput. Compl. Springer **29**, Article Number 1, 1–45 (2020)
13. H. Ito, A. Nagao, T. Park, Generalized shogi, chess, and xiangqui are constant-time testable. IEICE Trans. **E102-A**(9), 1126–1133 (2019)
14. M. Kusumoto, Y. Yoshida, Testing forest-isomorphizm in the adjacency list model, in *Proceedings of ICALP2014* (1), LNSC 8572 (2014), pp. 763–774
15. I. Newman, C. Sohler, Every property of hyperfinite graphs is testable, in *Proceedings STOC 2011* (ACM, 2011), pp. 675–784. (Journal version: SIAM J. Comput. vol. 42, No. 3, pp. 1095–1112 (2013).)
16. Oded Goldreich, Dana Ron, Property testing in bounded degree graphs. Algorithmica **32**(2), 302–343 (2002)
17. E. Szemerédi, Regular partitions of graphs, in Proceedings of the Colloquim International CNRS, eds. by J.C. Bermond, J.C. Fournier, M. Las Vergnas, D. Sotteau (CNRS, Paris, 1978), pp. 399–401

Open Access This chapter is licensed under the terms of the Creative Commons Attribution 4.0 International License (http://creativecommons.org/licenses/by/4.0/), which permits use, sharing, adaptation, distribution and reproduction in any medium or format, as long as you give appropriate credit to the original author(s) and the source, provide a link to the Creative Commons license and indicate if changes were made.

The images or other third party material in this chapter are included in the chapter's Creative Commons license, unless indicated otherwise in a credit line to the material. If material is not included in the chapter's Creative Commons license and your intended use is not permitted by statutory regulation or exceeds the permitted use, you will need to obtain permission directly from the copyright holder.

Chapter 3
Constant-Time Algorithms for Continuous Optimization Problems

Yuichi Yoshida

Abstract In this chapter, we consider constant-time algorithms for continuous optimization problems. Specifically, we consider quadratic function minimization and tensor decomposition, both of which have numerous applications in machine learning and data mining. The key component in our analysis is *graph limit theory*, which was originally developed to study graphs analytically.

3.1 Introduction

In this chapter, we turn our attention to constant-time algorithms for continuous optimization problems. Specifically, we consider quadratic function minimization and tensor decomposition, both of which have numerous applications in machine learning and data mining. The key component in our analysis is *graph limit theory*, which was originally developed to study graphs analytically.

We introduce graph limit theory in Sect. 3.2, and then discuss quadratic function minimization and tensor decomposition in Sects. 3.3 and 3.4, respectively. Throughout this chapter, we assume the real RAM model, in which we can perform basic algebraic operations on real numbers in one step. For a positive integer n, let $[n]$ denote the set $\{1, 2, \ldots, n\}$. For real values $a, b, c \in \mathbb{R}$, $a = b \pm c$ is used as shorthand for $b - c \le a \le b + c$. The algorithms and analysis presented in this chapter are based on [5, 6].

3.2 Graph Limit Theory

This section reviews the basic concepts of graph limit theory. For further details, refer to the book by Lovász [7].

Y. Yoshida (✉)
National Institute of Informatics 2-1-2 Hitotsubashi, Chiyoda-ku, Tokyo, Japan
e-mail: yyoshida@nii.ac.jp

© The Author(s) 2022
N. Katoh et al. (eds.), *Sublinear Computation Paradigm*,
https://doi.org/10.1007/978-981-16-4095-7_3

We call a (measurable) function $\mathcal{W} : [0,1]^K \to \mathbb{R}$ a *dikernel of order* K. We define

$$|\mathcal{W}|_F = \sqrt{\int_{[0,1]^K} \mathcal{W}(\boldsymbol{x})^2 \mathrm{d}\boldsymbol{x}}, \qquad \text{(Frobenius norm)}$$

$$|\mathcal{W}|_{\max} = \max_{\boldsymbol{x}\in[0,1]^K} |\mathcal{W}(\boldsymbol{x})|, \qquad \text{(Max norm)}$$

$$|\mathcal{W}|_{\square} = \sup_{S_1,\ldots,S_K \subseteq [0,1]} \left| \int_{S_1\times\cdots\times S_K} \mathcal{W}(\boldsymbol{x})\mathrm{d}\boldsymbol{x}. \right| \qquad \text{(Cut norm)}$$

We note that these norms satisfy the triangle inequality. For two dikernels $\mathcal{W}$ and $\mathcal{W}'$, we define their *inner product* as $\langle \mathcal{W}, \mathcal{W}' \rangle = \int_{[0,1]^K} \mathcal{W}(\boldsymbol{x})\mathcal{W}'(\boldsymbol{x})\mathrm{d}\boldsymbol{x}$. For a dikernel $\mathcal{W} : [0,1]^2 \to \mathbb{R}$ and a function $f : [0,1] \to \mathbb{R}$, we define a function $\mathcal{W}f : [0,1] \to \mathbb{R}$ as $(\mathcal{W}f)(x) = \langle \mathcal{W}(x,\cdot), f \rangle$.

Let λ be a Lebesgue measure. A map $\pi : [0,1] \to [0,1]$ is said to be *measure-preserving* if the pre-image $\pi^{-1}(X)$ is measurable for every measurable set X, and $\lambda(\pi^{-1}(X)) = \lambda(X)$. A *measure-preserving bijection* is a measure-preserving map whose inverse map exists and is also measurable (and, in turn, also measure-preserving). For a measure-preserving bijection $\pi : [0,1] \to [0,1]$ and a dikernel $\mathcal{W} : [0,1]^K \to \mathbb{R}$, we define a dikernel $\pi(\mathcal{W}) : [0,1]^K \to \mathbb{R}$ as $\pi(\mathcal{W})(x_1,\ldots,x_K) = \mathcal{W}(\pi(x_1),\ldots,\pi(x_K))$.

A partition $\mathcal{P} = (V_1,\ldots,V_p)$ of the interval $[0,1]$ is called an *equipartition* if $\lambda(V_i) = 1/p$ for every $i \in [p]$. For a dikernel $\mathcal{W} : [0,1]^K \to \mathbb{R}$ and an equipartition $\mathcal{P} = (V_1,\ldots,V_p)$ of $[0,1]$, we define $\mathcal{W}_{\mathcal{P}} : [0,1]^K \to \mathbb{R}$ as the dikernel obtained by averaging each $V_{i_1} \times \cdots \times V_{i_K}$ for $i_1,\ldots,i_K \in [p]$. More formally, we define

$$\mathcal{W}_{\mathcal{P}}(\boldsymbol{x}) = \frac{1}{\prod_{k\in[K]} \lambda(V_{i_k})} \int_{V_{i_1}\times\cdots\times V_{i_K}} \mathcal{W}(\boldsymbol{x}')\mathrm{d}\boldsymbol{x}' = p^K \int_{V_{i_1}\times\cdots\times V_{i_K}} \mathcal{W}(\boldsymbol{x}')\mathrm{d}\boldsymbol{x}',$$

where i_k is the unique index such that $x_k \in V_{i_k}$ for each $k \in [K]$. The following lemma states that any dikernel $\mathcal{W} : [0,1]^K \to \mathbb{R}$ can be well approximated by $\mathcal{W}_{\mathcal{P}}$ for some equipartition $\mathcal{P}$ into a small number of parts.

Lemma 3.1 (Weak regularity lemma for dikernels *[4]*) *Let* $\mathcal{W}^1,\ldots,\mathcal{W}^T : [0,1]^K \to \mathbb{R}$ *be dikernels. Then, for any* $\epsilon > 0$, *there exists an equipartition* $\mathcal{P}$ *into* $|\mathcal{P}| \leq 2^{O(T/\epsilon^{2K})}$ *parts, such that for every* $t \in [T]$,

$$|\mathcal{W}^t - \mathcal{W}^t_{\mathcal{P}}|_{\square} \leq \epsilon |\mathcal{W}^t|_F.$$

We can construct the dikernel $\mathcal{X} : [0,1]^K \to \mathbb{R}$ from a tensor $X \in \mathbb{R}^{N_1\times\cdots\times N_K}$ as follows. For an integer $n \in \mathbb{N}$, let $I_1^n = [0, \frac{1}{n}]$, $I_2^n = (\frac{1}{n}, \frac{2}{n}], \ldots, I_n^n = (\frac{n-1}{n}, \ldots, 1]$. For $x \in [0,1]$, we define $i_n(x) \in [n]$ as the unique integer such that $x \in I_i^n$. We then define $\mathcal{X}(x_1,\ldots,x_K) = X_{i_{N_1}(x_1)\cdots i_{N_K}(x_K)}$. The main motivation of creating a dikernel from a tensor is that, in doing so, we can define the distance between two tensors

X and Y of different sizes via the cut norm—that is, $|\mathcal{X} - \mathcal{Y}|_\square$, where $\mathcal{X}$ and $\mathcal{Y}$ are dikernels corresponding to X and Y, respectively.

Let $\mathcal{W} : [0, 1]^K \to \mathbb{R}$ be a dikernel and $S_k = (x_1^k, \ldots, x_s^k)$ for $k \in [K]$ be sequences of elements in $[0, 1]$. Then, we define a dikernel $\mathcal{W}|_{S_1,\ldots,S_K} : [0, 1]^K \to \mathbb{R}$ as follows: We first extract a tensor $W \in \mathbb{R}^{s\times\cdots\times s}$ by setting $W_{i_1\cdots i_K} = \mathcal{W}(x_{i_1}^1, \ldots, x_{i_K}^K)$. Next, we define $\mathcal{W}|_{S_1,\ldots,S_K}$ as the dikernel corresponding to $W|_{S_1,\ldots,S_K}$. The following is the key technical lemma in the analysis of the algorithms given in the subsequent sections.

Lemma 3.2 *Let $\mathcal{W}^1, \ldots, \mathcal{W}^T : [0, 1]^K \to [-L, L]$ be dikernels. Let $S_1, \ldots, S_K$ be sequences of s elements uniformly and independently sampled from $[0, 1]$. Then, with probability at least $1 - \exp(-\Omega_K(s^2(T/\log s)^{1/K}))$, there exists a measure-preserving bijection $\pi : [0, 1] \to [0, 1]$ such that, for every $t \in [T]$, we have*

$$|\mathcal{W}^t - \pi(\mathcal{W}^t|_{S_1,\ldots,S_K})|_\square = L \cdot O_K\left(\frac{T}{\log s}\right)^{1/2K},$$

where $O_K(\cdot)$ and $\Omega_K(\cdot)$ hide factors depending on K.

3.3 Quadratic Function Minimization

Background

Quadratic functions are one of the most important function classes in machine learning, statistics, and data mining. Many fundamental problems such as linear regression, k-means clustering, principal component analysis, support vector machines, and kernel methods can be formulated as a minimization problem of a quadratic function. See, e.g., [8] for more details.

In some applications, it is sufficient to compute the minimum value of a quadratic function rather than its solution. For example, Yamada et al. [13] proposed an efficient method for estimating the Pearson divergence, which provides useful information about data, such as the density ratio [10]. They formulated the estimation problem as the minimization of a squared loss and showed that the Pearson divergence can be estimated from the minimum value. Least-squares mutual information [9] is another example that can be computed in a similar manner.

Despite its importance, minimization of quadratic functions suffers from the issue of scalability. Let $n \in \mathbb{N}$ be the number of variables. In general, this kind of minimization problem can be solved by quadratic programming (QP), which requires poly(n) time. If the problem is convex and there are no constraints, then the problem is reduced to solving a system of linear equations, which requires $O(n^3)$ time. Both methods easily become infeasible, even for medium-scale problems of, say, $n > 10000$.

Although several techniques have been proposed to accelerate quadratic function minimization, they require at least linear time in n. This is problematic when handling

Algorithm 1

Input: $n \in \mathbb{N}$, query access to a matrix $A \in \mathbb{R}^{n\times n}$ and to vectors $\boldsymbol{d}, \boldsymbol{b} \in \mathbb{R}^n$, and $\epsilon, \delta \in (0, 1)$.
1: $S \leftarrow$ a sequence of $s = s(\epsilon, \delta)$ indices independently and uniformly sampled from $[n]$.
2: **return** $\frac{n^2}{s^2} \min_{\boldsymbol{v}\in\mathbb{R}^n} p_{s,A|_S,\boldsymbol{d}|_S,\boldsymbol{b}|_S}(\boldsymbol{v})$.

large-scale problems, where even linear time is slow or prohibitive. For example, stochastic gradient descent (SGD) is an optimization method that is widely used for large-scale problems. A nice property of this method is that, if the objective function is strongly convex, it outputs a point that is sufficiently close to an optimal solution after a constant number of iterations [1]. Nevertheless, each iteration needs at least $\Omega(n)$ time to access the variables. Another popular technique is low-rank approximation such as Nyström's method [12]. The underlying idea is to approximate the input matrix by a low-rank matrix, which drastically reduces the time complexity. However, we still need to compute the matrix vector product of size n, which requires $\Omega(n)$ time. Clarkson et al. [2] proposed sublinear-time algorithms for special cases of quadratic function minimization. However, these are "sublinear" with respect to the number of pairwise interactions of the variables, which is $\Theta(n^2)$, and the algorithms require $O(n \log^c n)$ time for some $c \geq 1$.

Constant-time algorithm for quadratic function minimization
Let $A \in \mathbb{R}^{n\times n}$ be a matrix and $\boldsymbol{d}, \boldsymbol{b} \in \mathbb{R}^n$ be vectors. Then, we consider the following quadratic problem:

$$\underset{\boldsymbol{v}\in\mathbb{R}^n}{\text{minimize}}\ p_{n,A,\boldsymbol{d},\boldsymbol{b}}(\boldsymbol{v}),\ \text{where } p_{n,A,\boldsymbol{d},\boldsymbol{b}}(\boldsymbol{v}) = \langle \boldsymbol{v}, A\boldsymbol{v}\rangle + n\langle \boldsymbol{v}, \text{diag}(\boldsymbol{d})\boldsymbol{v}\rangle + n\langle \boldsymbol{b}, \boldsymbol{v}\rangle, \tag{3.1}$$

where $\langle\cdot,\cdot\rangle$ denotes the inner product and $\text{diag}(\boldsymbol{d})$ denotes a diagonal matrix in which the diagonal entries are specified by $\boldsymbol{d}$. Note that although a constant term can be included in (3.1), it is omitted here because it is irrelevant when optimizing (3.1), and hence we omit it.

Let $z^* \in \mathbb{R}$ be the optimal value of (3.1) and let $\epsilon, \delta \in (0, 1)$ be parameters. Then, our goal is then to compute z with $|z - z^*| = O(\epsilon n^2)$ with probability at least $1 - \delta$ in constant time. We further assume that we have query access to A, $\boldsymbol{b}$, and $\boldsymbol{d}$, with which we can obtain their entry by specifying an index. We note that z^* is typically $\Theta(n^2)$ because $\langle \boldsymbol{v}, A\boldsymbol{v}\rangle$ consists of $\Theta(n^2)$ terms, and $\langle \boldsymbol{v}, \text{diag}(\boldsymbol{d})\boldsymbol{v}\rangle$ and $\langle \boldsymbol{b}, \boldsymbol{v}\rangle$ consist of $\Theta(n)$ terms. Hence, we can regard the error of $\Theta(\epsilon n^2)$ as an error of $\Theta(\epsilon)$ for each term, which is reasonably small in typical situations.

Let $\cdot|_S$ be an operator that extracts a submatrix (or subvector) specified by an index set $S \subset \mathbb{N}$. Our algorithm is then given by Algorithm 1, where the parameter $s := s(\epsilon, \delta)$ is determined later. In other words, we sample a constant number of indices from the set $[n]$, and then solve the problem (3.1) restricted to these indices.

Note that the number of queries and the time complexity are $O(s^2)$ and $\text{poly}(s)$, respectively.

The goal of the rest of this section is to show the following approximation guarantee of Algorithm 1.

Theorem 3.1 *Let $\boldsymbol{v}^*$ and z^* be an optimal solution and the optimal value, respectively, of problem (3.1). By choosing $s(\epsilon, \delta) = 2^{\Theta(1/\epsilon^2)} + \Theta(\log \frac{1}{\delta} \log\log \frac{1}{\delta})$, with probability at least $1 - \delta$, a sequence S of s indices independently and uniformly sampled from $[n]$ satisfies the following: Let $\tilde{\boldsymbol{v}}^*$ and $\tilde{z}^*$ be an optimal solution and the optimal value, respectively, of the problem $\min_{\boldsymbol{v}\in\mathbb{R}^s} p_{s,A|_S,\boldsymbol{d}|_S,\boldsymbol{b}|_S}(\boldsymbol{v})$. Then, we have*

$$\left|\frac{n^2}{s^2}\tilde{z}^* - z^*\right| \leq \epsilon L M^2 n^2,$$

where

$$L = \max\left\{\max_{i,j} |A_{ij}|, \max_{i} |d_i|, \max_{i} |b_i|\right\} \text{ and } M = \max\left\{\max_{i\in[n]} |v_i^*|, \max_{i\in[n]} |\tilde{v}_i^*|\right\}.$$

We can show that M is bounded when A is symmetric and full rank. To see this, we first note that we can assume $A + n\text{diag}(\boldsymbol{d})$ is positive-definite, as otherwise $p_{n,A,\boldsymbol{d},\boldsymbol{b}}$ is not bounded and the problem is uninteresting. Then, for any set $S \subseteq [n]$ of s indices, $(A + n\text{diag}(\boldsymbol{d}))|_S$ is again positive-definite because it is a principal submatrix. Hence, we have $\boldsymbol{v}^* = (A + n\text{diag}(\boldsymbol{d}))^{-1} n\boldsymbol{b}/2$ and $\tilde{\boldsymbol{v}}^* = (A|_S + n\text{diag}(\boldsymbol{d}|_S))^{-1} n\boldsymbol{b}|_S/2$, which means that M is bounded.

3.3.1 Proof of Theorem 3.1

To use dikernels in our analysis, we first introduce a continuous version of $p_{n,A,\boldsymbol{d},\boldsymbol{b}}$. The real-valued function $P_{n,A,\boldsymbol{d},\boldsymbol{b}}$ on the functions $f : [0, 1] \to \mathbb{R}$ is defined as

$$P_{n,A,\boldsymbol{d},\boldsymbol{b}}(f) = \langle f, \mathcal{A} f\rangle + \langle f^2, \mathcal{D}1\rangle + \langle f, \mathcal{B}1\rangle,$$

where $\mathcal{D}$ and $\mathcal{B}$ are the dikernels corresponding to $\boldsymbol{d}\boldsymbol{1}^\top$ and $\boldsymbol{b}\boldsymbol{1}^\top$, respectively, $f^2 : [0, 1] \to \mathbb{R}$ is a function such that $f^2(x) = f(x)^2$ for every $x \in [0, 1]$ and $1 : [0, 1] \to \mathbb{R}$ is a constant function that has a value of 1 everywhere. The following lemma states that the minimizations of $p_{n,A,\boldsymbol{d},\boldsymbol{b}}$ and $P_{n,A,\boldsymbol{d},\boldsymbol{b}}$ are equivalent:

Lemma 3.3 *Let $A \in \mathbb{R}^{n\times n}$ be a matrix and $\boldsymbol{d}, \boldsymbol{b} \in \mathbb{R}^{n\times n}$ be vectors. Then, we have*

$$\min_{\boldsymbol{v}\in[-M,M]^n} p_{n,A,\boldsymbol{d},\boldsymbol{b}}(\boldsymbol{v}) = n^2 \cdot \inf_{f:[0,1]\to[-M,M]} P_{n,A,\boldsymbol{d},\boldsymbol{b}}(f).$$

for any $M > 0$.

Proof First, we show that $n^2 \cdot \inf_{f:[0,1]\to[-M,M]} P_{n,A,\boldsymbol{d},\boldsymbol{b}}(f) \le \min_{\boldsymbol{v}\in[-M,M]^n} p_{n,A,\boldsymbol{d},\boldsymbol{b}}(\boldsymbol{v})$. Given a vector $\boldsymbol{v} \in [-M, M]^n$, we define $f : [0, 1] \to [-M, M]$ as $f(x) = v_{i_n(x)}$. Then,

$$\langle f, \mathcal{A}f\rangle = \sum_{i,j\in[n]} \int_{I_i^n}\int_{I_j^n} A_{ij} f(x) f(y) \mathrm{d}x\mathrm{d}y = \frac{1}{n^2}\sum_{i,j\in[n]} A_{ij} v_i v_j = \frac{1}{n^2}\langle \boldsymbol{v}, A\boldsymbol{v}\rangle,$$

$$\begin{aligned}\langle f^2, \mathcal{D}1\rangle &= \sum_{i,j\in[n]} \int_{I_i^n}\int_{I_j^n} d_i f(x)^2 \mathrm{d}x\mathrm{d}y = \sum_{i\in[n]} \int_{I_i^n} d_i f(x)^2 \mathrm{d}x \\ &= \frac{1}{n}\sum_{i\in[n]} d_i v_i^2 = \frac{1}{n}\langle \boldsymbol{v}, \mathrm{diag}(\boldsymbol{d})\boldsymbol{v}\rangle,\end{aligned}$$

$$\langle f, \mathcal{B}1\rangle = \sum_{i,j\in[n]} \int_{I_i^n}\int_{I_j^n} b_i f(x) \mathrm{d}x\mathrm{d}y = \sum_{i\in[n]} \int_{I_i^n} b_i f(x) \mathrm{d}x = \frac{1}{n}\sum_{i\in[n]} b_i v_i = \frac{1}{n}\langle \boldsymbol{v}, \boldsymbol{b}\rangle.$$

Hence, we have $n^2 P_{n,A,\boldsymbol{d},\boldsymbol{b}}(f) \le p_{n,A,\boldsymbol{d},\boldsymbol{b}}(\boldsymbol{v})$.

Next, we show that $\min_{\boldsymbol{v}\in[-M,M]^n} p_{n,A,\boldsymbol{d},\boldsymbol{b}}(\boldsymbol{v}) \le n^2 \cdot \inf_{f:[0,1]\to[-M,M]} P_{n,A,\boldsymbol{d},\boldsymbol{b}}(f)$. Let $f : [0, 1] \to [-M, M]$ be a measurable function. For $x \in [0, 1]$, we then have

$$\begin{aligned}&\frac{\partial P_{n,A,\boldsymbol{d},\boldsymbol{b}}(f(x))}{\partial f(x)} \\ &= \sum_{i\in[n]} \int_{I_i^n} A_{i i_n(x)} f(y)\mathrm{d}y + \sum_{j\in[n]} \int_{I_j^n} A_{i_n(x) j} f(y)\mathrm{d}y + 2d_{i_n(x)} f(x) + b_{i_n(x)}.\end{aligned}$$

Note that the form of this partial derivative depends on only $i_n(x)$. Hence, in the optimal solution $f^* : [0, 1] \to [-M, M]$, we can assume $f^*(x) = f^*(y)$ if $i_n(x) = i_n(y)$. In other words, f^* is constant on each of the intervals $I_1^n, \ldots, I_n^n$. For such f^*, we define the vector $\boldsymbol{v} \in \mathbb{R}^n$ as $v_i = f^*(x)$, where $x \in [0, 1]$ is any element in I_i^n. Then, we have

$$\begin{aligned}\langle \boldsymbol{v}, A\boldsymbol{v}\rangle &= \sum_{i,j\in[n]} A_{ij} v_i v_j = n^2 \sum_{i,j\in[n]} \int_{I_i^n}\int_{I_j^n} A_{ij} f^*(x) f^*(y)\mathrm{d}x\mathrm{d}y = n^2\langle f^*, \mathcal{A}f^*\rangle, \\ \langle \boldsymbol{v}, \mathrm{diag}(\boldsymbol{d})\boldsymbol{v}\rangle &= \sum_{i\in[n]} d_i v_i^2 = n\sum_{i\in[n]} \int_{I_i^n} d_i f^*(x)^2\mathrm{d}x = n\langle (f^*)^2, \mathcal{D}1\rangle, \\ \langle \boldsymbol{v}, \boldsymbol{b}\rangle &= \sum_{i\in[n]} b_i v_i = n\sum_{i\in[n]} \int_{I_i^n} b_i f^*(x)\mathrm{d}x = n\langle f^*, \mathcal{B}1\rangle.\end{aligned}$$

Hence, we have $p_{n,A,\boldsymbol{d},\boldsymbol{b}}(\boldsymbol{v}) \le n^2 P_{n,A,\boldsymbol{d},\boldsymbol{b}}(f^*)$.

Proof (*of Theorem* 3.1) We instantiate Lemma 3.2 with $s = 2^{\Theta(1/\epsilon^2)} + \Theta(\log\frac{1}{\delta}\log\log\frac{1}{\delta})$ and the dikernels $\mathcal{A}$, $\mathcal{D}$, and $\mathcal{B}$. Then, with probability at least $1-\delta$, there exists a measure-preserving bijection $\pi : [0, 1] \to [0, 1]$ such that

$$\max\Big\{|\langle f, (\mathcal{A} - \pi(\mathcal{A}|_S))f\rangle|, |\langle f^2, (\mathcal{D} - \pi(\mathcal{D}|_S))1\rangle|, |\langle f, (\mathcal{B} - \pi(\mathcal{B}|_S))1\rangle|\Big\} \le \frac{\epsilon L M^2}{3}$$

for any function $f : [0, 1] \to [-M, M]$. Conditioned on this event, we have

$$\begin{aligned}
\tilde{z}^* &= \min_{v \in \mathbb{R}^s} p_{s,A|_S,d|_S,b|_S}(v) = \min_{v \in [-M,M]^s} p_{s,A|_S,d|_S,b|_S}(v) \\
&= s^2 \cdot \inf_{f:[0,1]\to[-M,M]} P_{s,A|_S,d|_S,b|_S}(f) \qquad \text{(By Lemma 3)} \\
&= s^2 \cdot \inf_{f:[0,1]\to[-M,M]} \Big(\langle f, (\pi(\mathcal{A}|_S) - \mathcal{A}) f \rangle + \langle f, \mathcal{A} f \rangle + \langle f^2, (\pi(\mathcal{D}|_S) - \mathcal{D}) 1 \rangle + \\
&\qquad \langle f^2, \mathcal{D} 1 \rangle + \langle f, (\pi(\mathcal{B}|_S) - \mathcal{B}) 1 \rangle + \langle f, \mathcal{B} 1 \rangle \Big) \\
&\le s^2 \cdot \inf_{f:[0,1]\to[-M,M]} \Big(\langle f, \mathcal{A} f \rangle + \langle f^2, \mathcal{D} 1 \rangle + \langle f, \mathcal{B} 1 \rangle \pm \epsilon L M^2 \Big) \\
&= \frac{s^2}{n^2} \cdot \min_{v \in [-M,M]^n} p_{n,A,d,b}(v) \pm \epsilon L M^2 s^2. \qquad \text{(By Lemma 3)} \\
&= \frac{s^2}{n^2} \cdot \min_{v \in \mathbb{R}^n} p_{n,A,d,b}(v) \pm \epsilon L M^2 s^2 = \frac{s^2}{n^2} z^* \pm \epsilon L M^2 s^2.
\end{aligned}$$

Rearranging the inequality, we obtain the desired result.

3.4 Tensor Decomposition

Background

We say that a tensor (or a multidimensional array) is of *order* K if it is a K-dimensional array. Each dimension is called a *mode* in tensor terminology. Tensor decomposition, which approximates the input tensor by a number of smaller tensors, is a fundamental tool for dealing with large tensors because it drastically reduces memory usage.

Among the many existing tensor decomposition methods, *Tucker decomposition* [11] is a popular choice. To some extent, Tucker decomposition is analogous to singular-value decomposition (SVD). Whereas SVD decomposes a matrix into left and right singular vectors that interact via singular values, Tucker decomposition of an order-K tensor consists of K factor matrices that interact via the so-called core tensor. The key difference between SVD and Tucker decomposition is that, in the latter, the core tensor does not need to be diagonal and its "rank" can differ for each mode. We refer to the size of the core tensor, which is a K-tuple, as the *Tucker rank* of a Tucker decomposition.

We are usually interested in obtaining factor matrices and a core tensor to minimize the *residual error*—the error between the input and low-rank approximated tensors. Sometimes, however, knowing the residual error itself is a task of interest. The residual error tells us how suitable a low-rank approximation is to approximate the input tensor in the first place, and is also useful to predetermine the Tucker rank. In real applications, Tucker ranks are not explicitly given, and we must select them by considering the tradeoff between space usage and approximation accuracy. For example, if the selected Tucker rank is too small, we risk losing essential information in the input tensor, whereas if the selected Tucker rank is too large, the computational cost of computing the Tucker decomposition (even if we allow for approximation methods) increases considerably along with space usage. As with the case of the matrix rank, one might think that a reasonably good Tucker rank can be found using a grid search. Unfortunately, grid search for an appropriate Tucker rank is challenging because, for an order-K tensor, the Tucker rank consists of K free parameters and the search space grows exponentially in K. Hence, we want to evaluate each grid point as quickly as possible.

Although several practical algorithms have been proposed, such as the higher order orthogonal iteration (HOOI) [3], they are not sufficiently scalable. For each mode, HOOI iteratively applies SVD to an unfolded tensor—a matrix that is reshaped from the input tensor. Given an $N_1 \times \cdots \times N_K$ tensor, the computational cost is hence $O(K \max_k N_k \cdot \prod_k N_k)$, which crucially depends on the input size $N_1, \ldots, N_K$. Although there are several approximation algorithms, their computational costs are still intensive.

Constant-time algorithm for the Tucker fitting problem
The problem of computing the residual error is formalized as the following *Tucker fitting* problem: Given an order-K tensor $X \in \mathbb{R}^{N_1 \times \cdots \times N_K}$ and integers $R_k \leq N_k$ ($k = 1, \ldots, K$), we want to compute the following normalized residual error:

$$\ell_{R_1,\ldots,R_K}(X) := \min_{G \in \mathbb{R}^{R_1 \times \cdots \times R_K}, \{U^{(k)} \in \mathbb{R}^{N_k \times R_k}\}_{k \in [K]}} \frac{\left| X - [\![G; U^{(1)}, \ldots, U^{(K)}]\!] \right|_F^2}{\prod_{k \in [K]} N_k}, \quad (3.2)$$

where $[\![G; U^{(1)}, \ldots, U^{(K)}]\!] \in \mathbb{R}^{N_1 \times \cdots \times N_K}$ is an order-K tensor, defined as

$$[\![G; U^{(1)}, \ldots, U^{(K)}]\!]_{i_1 \cdots i_K} = \sum_{r_1 \in [R_1], \ldots, r_K \in [R_K]} G_{r_1 \cdots r_K} \prod_{k \in [K]} U^{(k)}_{i_k r_k}$$

for every $i_1 \in [N_1], \ldots, i_K \in [N_K]$. Here, G is the core tensor, and $U^{(1)}, \ldots, U^{(K)}$ are the factor matrices. Note that we are not concerned with computing the minimizer, but only want to compute the minimum value. In addition, we do not need the exact minimum. Indeed, a rough estimate still helps to narrow down promising rank candidates. The question here is how quickly we can compute the normalized residual error $\ell_{R_1,\ldots,R_K}(X)$ with moderate accuracy.

In this section, we consider the following simple sampling algorithm, and show that it can be used to approximately solve the Tucker fitting problem. First, given an order-K tensor $X \in \mathbb{R}^{N_1 \times \cdots \times N_K}$, Tucker rank $(R_1, \ldots, R_K)$, and sample size $s \in \mathbb{N}$, we sample a sequence of indices $S_k = (x_1^k, \ldots, x_s^k)$ uniformly and independently from $[N_k]$ for each mode $k \in [K]$. We then construct a mini-tensor $X|_{S_1,\ldots,S_K} \in \mathbb{R}^{s \times \cdots \times s}$, where $(X|_{S_1,\ldots,S_K})_{i_1,\ldots,i_K} = X_{x^1_{i_1},\ldots,x^K_{i_K}}$. Finally, we compute $\ell_{R_1,\ldots,R_K}(X|_{S_1,\ldots,S_K})$ using an arbitrary solver, such as HOOI, and output the obtained value. The details are provided in Algorithm 2. Note that the time complex-

Algorithm 2 Sampling algorithm for the Tucker fitting problem

Input: $N_1, \ldots, N_K \in \mathbb{N}$, query access to a tensor $X \in \mathbb{R}^{N_1 \times \cdots \times N_K}$, Tucker rank $(R_1, \ldots, R_k)$, and $\epsilon, \delta \in (0, 1)$.
1: **for** $k = 1$ to K **do**
2: $\quad S_k \leftarrow$ a sequence of $s = s(\epsilon, \delta)$ indices uniformly and independently sampled from $[N_k]$.
3: Construct a mini-tensor $X|_{S_1,\ldots,S_K}$.
4: **return** $\ell_{R_1,\ldots,R_K}(X|_{S_1,\ldots,S_K})$.

ity for computing $\ell_{R_1,\ldots,R_K}(X|_{S_1,\ldots,S_K})$ does not depend on the input size $N_1, \ldots, N_K$ but rather on the sample size s, meaning that the algorithm runs in *constant time*, regardless of the input size.

The goal of the rest of this section is to show the following approximation guarantee of Algorithm 2.

Theorem 3.2 *Let $X \in \mathbb{R}^{N_1 \times \cdots \times N_K}$ be a tensor, $R_1, \ldots, R_K$ be integers, and $\epsilon, \delta \in (0, 1)$. For $s(\epsilon, \delta) = 2^{\Theta(1/\epsilon^{2K-2})} + \Theta(\log \frac{1}{\delta} \log \log \frac{1}{\delta})$, we have the following. Let $S_1, \ldots, S_K$ be sequences of indices as defined in Algorithm 2. Let $(G^*, U_1^*, \ldots, U_K^*)$ and $(\tilde{G}^*, \tilde{U}_1^*, \ldots, \tilde{U}_K^*)$ be minimizers of problem (3.2) on X and $X|_{S_1,\ldots,S_K}$ for which the factor matrices are orthonormal, respectively. Then we have*

$$\ell_{R_1,\ldots,R_K}(X|_{S_1,\ldots,S_K}) = \ell_{R_1,\ldots,R_K}(X) \pm O(\epsilon L^2(1 + 2MR)),$$

with probability at least $1 - \delta$, where $L = |X|_{\max}$, $M = \max\{|G^*|_{\max}, |\tilde{G}^*|_{\max}\}$, and $R = \prod_{k \in [K]} R_k$.

We remark that, for the matrix case (i.e., $K = 2$), $|G^*|_{\max}$ and $|\tilde{G}^*|_{\max}$ are equal to the maximum singular values of the original and sampled matrices, respectively.

3.4.1 Preliminaries

Let $X \in \mathbb{R}^{N_1 \times \cdots N_K}$ be a tensor. We define

$$|X|_F = \sqrt{\sum_{i_1,\ldots,i_K} X_{i_1 \cdots i_K}^2}, \qquad \text{(Frobenius norm)}$$

$$|X|_{\max} = \max_{i_1 \in [N_1],\ldots,i_K \in [N_K]} |X_{i_1 \cdots i_K}|, \qquad \text{(Max norm)}$$

$$|X|_\Box = \max_{S_1 \subseteq [N_1],\ldots,S_K \subseteq [N_K]} \left| \sum_{i_1 \in S_1,\ldots,i_K \in S_K} X_{i_1 \cdots i_K} \right|. \qquad \text{(Cut norm)}$$

We note that these norms satisfy the triangle inequality.

For a vector $\boldsymbol{v} \in \mathbb{R}^n$ and a sequence $S = (x_1, \ldots, x_s)$ of indices in $[n]$, we define the *restriction* $\boldsymbol{v}|_S \in \mathbb{R}^s$ of $\boldsymbol{v}$ as $(\boldsymbol{v}|_S)_i = v_{x_i}$ for $i \in [s]$. Let $X \in \mathbb{R}^{N_1 \times \cdots \times N_K}$ be a tensor, and $S_k = (x_1^k, \ldots, x_s^k)$ be a sequence of indices in $[N_k]$ for each mode $k \in [K]$. Then, we define the *restriction* $X|_{S_1,\ldots,S_K} \in \mathbb{R}^{s\times\cdots\times s}$ of X to $S_1 \times \cdots \times S_K$ as $(X|_{S_1,\ldots,S_K})_{i_1\cdots i_K} = X_{x_{i_1}^1,\ldots,x_{i_K}^K}$ for each $i_1 \in [N_1], \ldots, i_K \in [N_k]$.

For a tensor $G\in\mathbb{R}^{R_1\times\cdots\times R_K}$ and vector-valued functions $\{F^{(k)} : [0,1]\to\mathbb{R}^{R_k}\}_{k\in[K]}$, we define an order-$K$ dikernel $[\![G; F^{(1)}, \ldots, F^{(K)}]\!] : [0,1]^K \to \mathbb{R}$ as

$$[\![G; F^{(1)}, \ldots, F^{(K)}]\!](x_1, \ldots, x_K) = \sum_{r_1\in[R_1],\ldots,r_K\in[R_K]} G_{r_1,\ldots,r_K} \prod_{k\in[K]} F^{(k)}(x_k)_{r_k}$$

We note that $[\![G; F^{(1)}, \ldots, F^{(K)}]\!]$ is a continuous analogue of Tucker decomposition.

3.4.2 Proof of Theorem 3.2

To prove Theorem 3.2, we first consider the dikernel counterpart to the Tucker fitting problem, in which we want to minimize the following:

$$\ell_{R_1,\ldots,R_K}(\mathcal{X}) := \inf_{G\in\mathbb{R}^{R_1\times\cdots\times R_K},\{f^{(k)}:[0,1]\to\mathbb{R}^{R_k}\}_{k\in[K]}} \left|\mathcal{X} - [\![G; f^{(1)}, \ldots, f^{(K)}]\!]\right|_F^2, \tag{3.3}$$

The following lemma, which is proved in Sect. 3.4.3, states that the Tucker fitting problem and its dikernel counterpart have the same optimum values.

Lemma 3.4 *Let $X \in \mathbb{R}^{N_1\times\cdots\times N_K}$ be a tensor, and let $R_1, \ldots, R_K \in \mathbb{N}$ be integers. Then, we have*

$$\ell_{R_1,\ldots,R_K}(X) = \ell_{R_1,\ldots,R_K}(\mathcal{X}).$$

For a set of vector-valued functions $F = \{f^{(k)} : [0,1] \to \mathbb{R}^{R_k}\}_{k\in[K]}$, we define $|F|_{\max} = \max_{k\in[K],r\in[R_k],x\in[0,1]} f_r^{(k)}(x)$. For a dikernel $\mathcal{X} : [0,1]^K \to \mathbb{R}$, we define a dikernel $\mathcal{X}^2 : [0,1]^K \to \mathbb{R}$ as $\mathcal{X}^2(\boldsymbol{x}) = \mathcal{X}(\boldsymbol{x})^2$ for every $\boldsymbol{x} \in [0,1]^K$. The following lemma, which is proved in Sect. 3.4.4, states that if $\mathcal{X}$ and $\mathcal{Y}$ are close in the cut norm, then the optimum values when the Tucker fitting problem is applied to them are also close.

Lemma 3.5 *Let $\mathcal{X}, \mathcal{Y} : [0,1]^K \to \mathbb{R}$ be dikernels with $|\mathcal{X} - \mathcal{Y}|_\square \le \epsilon$ and $|\mathcal{X}^2 - \mathcal{Y}^2|_\square \le \epsilon$. For $R_1, \ldots, R_K \in \mathbb{N}$, we have*

$$\ell_{R_1,\ldots,R_K}(\mathcal{X}) = \ell_{R_1,\ldots,R_K}(\mathcal{Y}) \pm 2\epsilon\Big(1 + R\big(|G_{\mathcal{X}}|_{\max}|F_{\mathcal{X}}|_{\max}^K + |G_{\mathcal{Y}}|_{\max}|F_{\mathcal{Y}}|_{\max}^K\big)\Big),$$

where $(G_{\mathcal{X}}, F_{\mathcal{X}} = \{f_{\mathcal{X}}^{(k)}\}_{k\in[K]})$ and $(G_{\mathcal{Y}}, F_{\mathcal{Y}} = \{f_{\mathcal{Y}}^{(k)}\}_{k\in[K]})$ are solutions to problem (3.3) on $\mathcal{X}$ and $\mathcal{Y}$, respectively, which have objective values exceeding the infima by at most ϵ, and $R = \prod_{k\in[K]} R_k$.

Proof (*of Theorem* 3.2) We apply Lemma 3.2 to $\mathcal{X}$ and $\mathcal{X}^2$. Thus, with probability at least $1-\delta$, there exists a measure-preserving bijection $\pi : [0,1] \to [0,1]$ such that

$$|\mathcal{X} - \pi(\mathcal{X}|_{S_1,\dots,S_K})|_\square \le \epsilon L \quad \text{and} \quad |\mathcal{X}^2 - \pi(\mathcal{X}^2|_{S_1,\dots,S_K})|_\square \le \epsilon L^2.$$

In the following, we assume that this has happened. By Lemma 3.5 and the fact that $\ell_{R_1,\dots,R_K}(\mathcal{X}|_{S_1,\dots,S_K}) = \ell_{R_1,\dots,R_K}(\pi(\mathcal{X}|_{S_1,\dots,S_K}))$, we have

$$\ell_{R_1,\dots,R_K}(\mathcal{X}|_{S_1,\dots,S_K}) = \ell_{R_1,\dots,R_K}(\mathcal{X}) \pm \epsilon L^2\Big(1 + 2R(|G|_{\max}|F|_{\max}^K + |\tilde{G}|_{\max}|\tilde{F}|_{\max}^K)\Big),$$

where $(G, F = \{f^{(k)}\}_{k\in[K]})$ and $(\tilde{G}, \tilde{F} = \{\tilde{f}^{(k)}\}_{k\in[K]})$ are as in the statement of Lemma 3.5. From the proof of Lemma 3.4, we can assume that $|G|_{\max} = |G^*|_{\max}$, $|\tilde{G}|_{\max} = |\tilde{G}^*|_{\max}$, $|F|_{\max} \le 1$, and $|\tilde{F}|_{\max} \le 1$ (owing to the orthonormality of $U_1^*, \dots, U_K^*$ and $\tilde{U}_1^*, \dots, \tilde{U}_K^*$). It follows that

$$\ell_{R_1,\dots,R_K}(\mathcal{X}|_{S_1,\dots,S_K}) = \ell_{R_1,\dots,R_K}(\mathcal{X}) \pm \epsilon L^2\Big(1 + 2R(|G^*|_{\max} + |\tilde{G}^*|_{\max})\Big). \quad (3.4)$$

Then, we have

$$\begin{aligned}
\ell_{R_1,\dots,R_K}(X|_{S_1,\dots,S_K}) &= \ell_{R_1,\dots,R_K}(\mathcal{X}|_{S_1,\dots,S_K}) && \text{(By Lemma 4)}\\
&= \ell_{R_1,\dots,R_K}(\mathcal{X}) \pm \epsilon L^2\Big(1 + 2R(|G^*|_{\max} + |\tilde{G}^*|_{\max})\Big) && \text{(By 4)}\\
&= \ell_{R_1,\dots,R_K}(X) \pm \epsilon L^2\Big(1 + 2R(|G^*|_{\max} + |\tilde{G}^*|_{\max})\Big). && \text{(By Lemma 4)}
\end{aligned}$$

Hence, the proof is complete.

3.4.3 *Proof of Lemma 3.4*

We say that a vector-valued function $f : [0,1] \to \mathbb{R}^R$ is *orthonormal* if $\langle f_r, f_r\rangle = 1$ for every $r \in [R]$ and $\langle f_r, f_{r'}\rangle = 0$ if $r \ne r'$. First, we calculate the partial derivatives of the objective function. We omit the proof because it is a straightforward (but tedious) calculation.

Lemma 3.6 *Let $\mathcal{X} \in [0,1]^K \to \mathbb{R}$ be a dikernel, $G \in \mathbb{R}^{R_1\times\cdots R_K}$ be a tensor, and $\{f^{(k)} : [0,1] \to \mathbb{R}^{R_k}\}_{k\in[K]}$ be a set of orthonormal vector-valued functions. Then, we have*

$$\frac{\partial}{\partial f_{r_0}^{(k_0)}(x_0)} \left| \mathcal{X} - [\![G; f^{(1)}, \ldots, f^{(K)}]\!] \right|_F^2$$
$$= 2 \sum_{r_1,\ldots,r_K : r_{k_0} = r_0} G_{r_1 \cdots r_K} \int_{[0,1]^K : x_{k_0} = x_0} \mathcal{X}(\boldsymbol{x}) \prod_{k \in [K] \setminus \{k_0\}} f_{r_k}^{(k)}(x_k) \mathrm{d}\boldsymbol{x}$$
$$- 2 \sum_{r_1,\ldots,r_K} G_{r_1 \cdots r_K} G_{r_1 \cdots r_{k_0 - 1} r_0 r_{k_0 + 1} \cdots r_K} f_{r_{k_0}}^{(k_0)}(x_0).$$

Proof (*of Lemma* 3.4) First, we show that (LHS) $\leq$ (RHS). Consider a sequence of solutions for the continuous problem (3.3) for which the objective values attain the infimum. For Tucker decompositions, it is well known that there exists a minimizer for which the factor matrices $U^{(1)}, \ldots, U^{(K)}$ are orthonormal. By similar reasoning, we can show that the vector-valued functions $f^{(1)}, \ldots, f^{(K)}$ in each solution of the sequence are orthonormal. As the objective function is coercive with respect to tensor G, we can take a subsequence for which G converges. Let G^* be the limit. Now, for any $\delta > 0$, we can create a matrix $\tilde{G}$ by perturbing G^* so that (i) by fixing G to $\tilde{G}$ in the continuous problem, the infimum increases only by δ, and (ii) a matrix constructed from $\tilde{G}$ is invertible and has a condition number at least $\delta' = \delta'(\delta) > 0$.

Now, consider a sequence of solutions for the continuous problem (3.3) with G fixed to $\tilde{G}$ for which the objective values attain the infimum. We can show that the partial derivatives converge to zero almost everywhere. For any $\epsilon > 0$, there then exists a solution $(\tilde{G}, f^{(1)}, \ldots, f^{(K)})$ in the sequence such that the partial derivatives are at most ϵ almost everywhere.

Then by Lemma 3.6, for any $k_0 \in [K]$, $r_0 \in [R_k]$, and almost all $x \in [0, 1]$, we have

$$\sum_{r_1,\ldots,r_K} \tilde{G}_{r_1 \cdots r_K} \tilde{G}_{r_1 \cdots r_{k_0 - 1} r_0 r_{k_0 + 1} \cdots r_K} f_{r_{k_0}}^{(k_0)}(x_0)$$
$$= \sum_{r_1,\ldots,r_K : r_{k_0} = r_0} \tilde{G}_{r_1 \cdots r_K} \int_{[0,1]^K : x_{k_0} = x_0} \mathcal{X}(\boldsymbol{x}) \prod_{k \in [K] \setminus \{k_0\}} f_{r_k}^{(k)}(x_k) \mathrm{d}\boldsymbol{x} \pm \epsilon(k_0, r_0, x), \quad (3.5)$$

where $\epsilon(k_0, r_0, x) = O(\epsilon)$. Now, we consider a system of linear equations consisting of (3.5) for $r_0 = 1, \ldots, R_{k_0}$, where the variables are $f_1^{k_0}(x_0), \ldots, f_{R_{k_0}}^{k_0}(x_0)$. We can assume that the matrix involved in this system is invertible and has a positive condition number. For any $k \in [K], r \in [R_k]$ and almost every pair $x, x' \in [0, 1]$ with $i_{N_k}(x) = i_{N_k}(x')$, we then have $f_{r_0}^{(k_0)}(x) = f_{r_0}^{(k_0)}(x') \pm O(\epsilon/\delta')$. For each $k \in [K]$, we can define a matrix $U^{(k)} \in \mathbb{R}^{N_k \times R_k}$ as $U_{ir}^{(k)} = f_r^{(k)}(x)$, where $x \in [0, 1]$ is an arbitrary value with $i_{N_k}(x) = i$. Then, we have

$$\frac{1}{N}\left|X - [\![\tilde{G}; U^{(1)}, \ldots, U^{(K)}]\!]\right|_F^2 = \frac{1}{N}\sum_{i_1,\ldots,i_K}\left(X_{i_1\cdots i_K} - [\![\tilde{G}; U^{(1)}, \ldots, U^{(K)}]\!]_{i_1\cdots i_K}\right)^2$$
$$= \sum_{i_1,\ldots,i_K}\int_{I_{i_1}^{N_1}\times\cdots\times I_{i_K}^{N_K}}\left(\mathcal{X}(\boldsymbol{x}) - [\![\tilde{G}; f^{(1)}, \ldots, f^{(K)}]\!](\boldsymbol{x}) \pm O(\epsilon/\delta')\right)^2 \mathrm{d}\boldsymbol{x}$$
$$= \left|\mathcal{X} - [\![\tilde{G}; f^{(1)}, \ldots, f^{(K)}]\!]\right|_F^2 \pm O(\epsilon^2 N/(\delta')^2)$$

for $N = \prod_{k\in[K]} N_k$. As the choice of ϵ and δ are arbitrary, we obtain (LHS) $\leq$ (RHS).

Second, we show that (RHS) $\leq$ (LHS). Let $U^{(k)} \in \mathbb{R}^{N_k\times R_k}$ $(k \in [K])$ be matrices. We define a vector-valued function $f^{(k)} : [0, 1] \to \mathbb{R}^{R_k}$ as $f_r^{(k)}(x) = U^{(k)}_{i_{N_k}(x)r}$ for each $k \in [K]$ and $r \in [R_k]$. Then, we have

$$\left|\mathcal{X} - [\![G; f^{(1)}, \ldots, f^{(K)}]\!]\right|_F^2 = \int_{[0,1]^K}\left(\mathcal{X}(\boldsymbol{x}) - [\![G; f^{(1)}, \ldots, f^{(K)}]\!](\boldsymbol{x})\right)^2 \mathrm{d}\boldsymbol{x}$$
$$= \sum_{i_1,\ldots,i_K}\int_{\prod_{k\in[K]} I_{i_k}^{N_k}}\left(\mathcal{X}(\boldsymbol{x}) - [\![G; f^{(1)}, \ldots, f^{(K)}]\!](\boldsymbol{x})\right)^2 \mathrm{d}\boldsymbol{x}$$
$$= \frac{1}{N}\sum_{i_1,\ldots,i_K}\left(X_{i_1\cdots i_K} - [\![G; U^{(1)}, \ldots, U^{(K)}]\!]_{i_1\cdots i_K}\right)^2$$
$$= \frac{1}{N}\left|X - [G; U^{(1)}, \ldots, U^{(K)}]\right|_F^2,$$

from which the claim follows.

3.4.4 Proof of Lemma 3.5

For a sequence of functions $f^{(1)}, \ldots, f^{(K)}$, we define their tensor product $\bigotimes_{k\in[K]} f^{(k)} \in [0, 1]^K \to \mathbb{R}$ as $\bigotimes_{k\in[K]} f^{(k)}(x_1, \ldots, x_K) = \prod_{k\in[K]} f^{(k)}(x_k)$, which is a dikernel of order-K.

The cut norm is useful for bounding the absolute value of the inner product between a tensor and a tensor product:

Lemma 3.7 *Let $\epsilon \geq 0$ and $\mathcal{W} : [0, 1]^K \to \mathbb{R}$ be a dikernel with $|\mathcal{W}|_\square \leq \epsilon$. Then, for any functions $f^{(1)}, \ldots, f^{(K)} : [0, 1] \to [-L, L]$, we have $|\langle \mathcal{W}, \bigotimes_{k\in[K]} f^{(k)}\rangle| \leq \epsilon L^K$.*

Proof For $\tau \in \mathbb{R}$ and the function $h : [0, 1] \to \mathbb{R}$, let $L_\tau(h) := \{x \in [0, 1] \mid h(x) = \tau\}$ be the level set of h at τ. For $f'^{(i)} = f^{(i)}/L$, we have

$$\begin{aligned}
\left|\left\langle \mathcal{W}, \bigotimes_{k\in[K]} f^{(k)}\right\rangle\right| &= L^K \left|\left\langle \mathcal{W}, \bigotimes_{k\in[K]} f'^{(k)}\right\rangle\right| \\
&= L^K \left| \int_{[-1,1]^K} \prod_{k\in[K]} \tau_k \int_{\prod_{k\in[K]} L_{\tau_k}(f'^{(k)})} \mathcal{W}(\boldsymbol{x}) \mathrm{d}\boldsymbol{x} \mathrm{d}\boldsymbol{\tau} \right| \\
&\leq L^K \int_{[-1,1]^K} \prod_{k\in[K]} |\tau_k| \left| \int_{\prod_{k\in[K]} L_{\tau_k}(f'^{(k)})} \mathcal{W}(\boldsymbol{x}) \mathrm{d}\boldsymbol{x} \mathrm{d}\boldsymbol{\tau} \right| \\
&\leq \epsilon L^K \int_{[-1,1]^K} \prod_{k\in[K]} |\tau_k| \mathrm{d}\boldsymbol{\tau} = \epsilon L^K.
\end{aligned}$$

Thus, we have the following:

Lemma 3.8 *Let $\mathcal{X}, \mathcal{Y} : [0,1]^K \to \mathbb{R}$ be dikernels with $|\mathcal{X} - \mathcal{Y}|_\square \leq \epsilon$ and $|\mathcal{X}^2 - \mathcal{Y}^2|_\square \leq \epsilon$, where $\mathcal{X}^2(\boldsymbol{x}) = \mathcal{X}(\boldsymbol{x})^2$ and $\mathcal{Y}^2(\boldsymbol{x}) = \mathcal{Y}(\boldsymbol{x})^2$ for every $\boldsymbol{x} \in [0,1]^K$. Then, for any tensor $G \in \mathbb{R}^{R_1\times\cdots\times R_K}$ and a set of vector-valued functions $F = \{f^{(k)} : [0,1] \to \mathbb{R}^{R_k}\}_{k\in[K]}$, we have*

$$\left|\mathcal{X} - [\![G; f^{(1)}, \ldots, f^{(K)}]\!]\right|_F^2 = \left|\mathcal{Y} - [\![G; f^{(1)}, \ldots, f^{(K)}]\!]\right|_F^2 \pm \epsilon\Big(1 + 2R|G|_{\max}|F|_{\max}^K\Big),$$

where $R = \prod_{k\in[K]} R_K$.

Proof We have

$$\begin{aligned}
&\left| |\mathcal{X} - [\![G; f^{(1)}, \ldots, f^{(K)}]\!]|_F^2 - |\mathcal{Y} - [\![G; f^{(1)}, \ldots, f^{(K)}]\!]|_F^2 \right| \\
&= \Big| \int_{[0,1]^K} \Big(\mathcal{X}(\boldsymbol{x}) - [\![G; f^{(1)}, \ldots, f^{(K)}]\!](\boldsymbol{x})\Big)^2 \mathrm{d}\boldsymbol{x} \\
&\quad - \int_{[0,1]^K} \Big(\mathcal{Y}(\boldsymbol{x}) - [\![G; f^{(1)}, \ldots, f^{(K)}]\!](\boldsymbol{x})\Big)^2 \mathrm{d}\boldsymbol{x} \Big| \\
&= \left| \int_{[0,1]^K} \Big(\mathcal{X}(\boldsymbol{x})^2 - \mathcal{Y}(\boldsymbol{x})^2\Big) \mathrm{d}\boldsymbol{x} - 2\int_{[0,1]^K} (\mathcal{X}(\boldsymbol{x}) - \mathcal{Y}(\boldsymbol{x}))[\![G; f^{(1)}, \ldots, f^{(K)}]\!](\boldsymbol{x}) \mathrm{d}\boldsymbol{x} \right| \\
&\leq |\mathcal{X}^2 - \mathcal{Y}^2|_\square + 2 \sum_{r_1\in[R_1],\ldots,r_k\in[R_k]} |G_{r_1\cdots r_K}| \cdot \left|\left\langle \mathcal{X} - \mathcal{Y}, \bigotimes_{k\in[K]} f_{r_k}^{(k)} \right\rangle\right| \\
&\leq \epsilon + 2\epsilon R|G|_{\max}|F|_{\max}^K
\end{aligned}$$

by Lemma 3.7.

Proof (*of Lemma* 3.5) By Lemma 3.8, we have

$$\begin{aligned}
\left|\mathcal{Y} - [\![G_\mathcal{Y}; f_\mathcal{Y}^{(1)}, \ldots, f_\mathcal{Y}^{(K)}]\!]\right|_F^2 &\leq \left|\mathcal{Y} - [\![G_\mathcal{X}; f_\mathcal{X}^{(1)}, \ldots, f_\mathcal{X}^{(K)}]\!]\right|_F^2 + \epsilon \\
&\leq \left|\mathcal{X} - [\![G_\mathcal{X}; f_\mathcal{X}^{(1)}, \ldots, f_\mathcal{X}^{(K)}]\!]\right|_F^2 + \Big(2\epsilon + 2\epsilon R|G_\mathcal{X}\|_{\max}\|F_\mathcal{X}\|_{\max}^K\Big).
\end{aligned}$$

Similarly, we have

$$\left\| \mathcal{X} - [\![G_{\mathcal{X}}; f_{\mathcal{X}}^{(1)}, \ldots, f_{\mathcal{X}}^{(K)}]\!] \right\|_F^2 \leq \left\| \mathcal{X} - [\![G_{\mathcal{Y}}; f_{\mathcal{Y}}^{(1)}, \ldots, f_{\mathcal{Y}}^{(K)}]\!] \right\|_F^2 + \epsilon$$
$$\leq \left\| \mathcal{Y} - [\![G_{\mathcal{Y}}; f_{\mathcal{Y}}^{(1)}, \ldots, f_{\mathcal{Y}}^{(K)}]\!] \right\|_F^2 + \left(2\epsilon + 2\epsilon R \|G_{\mathcal{Y}}\|_{\max} \|F_{\mathcal{Y}}\|_{\max}^K \right).$$

Hence, the claim follows.

References

1. L. Bottou, Stochastic learning, in *Advanced Lectures on Machine Learning* (2004), pp. 146–168
2. K.L. Clarkson, E. Hazan, D.P. Woodruff, Sublinear optimization for machine learning. J. ACM **59**(5), 23:1–23:49 (2012)
3. Lieven De Lathauwer, Bart De Moor, Joos Vandewalle, On the best rank-1 and rank-$(r_1, r_2, \ldots, r_n)$ approximation of higher-order tensors. SIAM J. Matrix Anal. Appl. **21**(4), 1324–1342 (2000)
4. A. Frieze, R. Kannan, The regularity lemma and approximation schemes for dense problems, in *FOCS* (1996), pp. 12–20
5. K. Hayashi, Y. Yoshida, Minimizing quadratic functions in constant time, in *NIPS* (2016), pp. 2217–2225
6. K. Hayashi, Y. Yoshida, Fitting low-rank tensors in constant time, in *NIPS* (2017), pp. 2473–2481
7. L. Lovász, *Large Networks and Graph Limits* (American Mathematical Society, 2012)
8. K.P. Murphy, *Machine Learning: A Probabilistic Perspective* (The MIT Press, 2012)
9. Taiji Suzuki, Masashi Sugiyama, Least-squares independent component analysis. Neural Comput. **23**(1), 284–301 (2011)
10. M. Sugiyama, T. Suzuki, T. Kanamori, *Density Ratio Estimation in Machine Learning* (Cambridge University Press, 2012)
11. Ledyard R. Tucker, Some mathematical notes on three-mode factor analysis. Psychometrika **31**(3), 279–311 (1966)
12. K.I. Christopher, in *Using the Nyström Method to Speed up Kernel Machines, NIPS* eds. by C. Williams, M. Seeger (2001)
13. M. Yamada, T. Suzuki, T. Kanamori, H. Hachiya, M. Sugiyama, Relative density-ratio estimation for robust distribution comparison, in *NIPS* (2011)

Open Access This chapter is licensed under the terms of the Creative Commons Attribution 4.0 International License (http://creativecommons.org/licenses/by/4.0/), which permits use, sharing, adaptation, distribution and reproduction in any medium or format, as long as you give appropriate credit to the original author(s) and the source, provide a link to the Creative Commons license and indicate if changes were made.

The images or other third party material in this chapter are included in the chapter's Creative Commons license, unless indicated otherwise in a credit line to the material. If material is not included in the chapter's Creative Commons license and your intended use is not permitted by statutory regulation or exceeds the permitted use, you will need to obtain permission directly from the copyright holder.

Chapter 4
Oracle-Based Primal-Dual Algorithms for Packing and Covering Semidefinite Programs

Khaled Elbassioni and Kazuhisa Makino

Abstract *Packing and covering* semidefinite programs (SDPs) appear in natural relaxations of many combinatorial optimization problems as well as a number of other applications. Recently, several techniques have been proposed that utilize the particular structure of this class of problems in order to obtain more efficient algorithms than those offered by general SDP solvers. For certain applications, it may be necessary to deal with SDPs with a very large number of (e.g., exponentially or even infinitely many) constraints. In this chapter, we give an overview of some of the techniques that can be used to solve this class of problems, focusing on multiplicative weight updates and logarithmic-potential methods.

4.1 Packing and Covering Semidefinite Programs

We denote by $\mathbb{S}^n$ the set of all $n \times n$ real symmetric matrices and by $\mathbb{S}^n_+ \subseteq \mathbb{S}^n$ the set of all $n \times n$ positive semidefinite (psd) matrices. We consider the following pairs of *packing-covering* semidefinite programs (SDPs):

$$\begin{aligned} z_I^* = \max\ & C \bullet X && \text{(PACKING- I)} \\ \text{s.t.}\ & A_i \bullet X \leq b_i, \forall i \in [m] \\ & X \in \mathbb{S}^n,\ X \succeq 0 \end{aligned}$$

$$\begin{aligned} z_I^* = \min\ & b^T y && \text{(COVERING- I)} \\ \text{s.t.}\ & \sum_{i=1}^{m} y_i A_i \succeq C \\ & y \in \mathbb{R}^m,\ y \geq 0, \end{aligned}$$

K. Elbassioni (✉)
Khalifa University of Science and Technology, P.O. Box 127788, Abu Dhabi, United Arab Emirates
e-mail: khaled.elbassioni@ku.ac.ae

K. Makino
Research Institute for Mathematical Sciences (RIMS), Kyoto University, Kyoto 606-8502, Japan
e-mail: makino@kurims.kyoto-u.ac.jp

© The Author(s) 2022

N. Katoh et al. (eds.), *Sublinear Computation Paradigm*,
https://doi.org/10.1007/978-981-16-4095-7_4

$$z^*_{II} = \min C \bullet X \quad \text{(Covering- II)}$$
$$\text{s.t. } A_i \bullet X \ge b_i, \forall i \in [m]$$
$$X \in \mathbb{S}^n,\ X \succeq 0$$

$$z^*_{II} = \max b^T y \quad \text{(Packing- II)}$$
$$\text{s.t.} \sum_{i=1}^{m} y_i A_i \preceq C$$
$$y \in \mathbb{R}^m,\ y \ge 0,$$

where $C, A_1, \ldots, A_m \in \mathbb{S}^n_+$ are (non-zero) psd matrices, and $b = (b_1, \ldots, b_n)^T \in \mathbb{R}^m_+$ is a non-negative vector. In the above, $C \bullet X := \mathrm{Tr}(CX) = \sum_{i=1}^n \sum_{j=1}^n c_{ij} x_{ij}$, and "$\succeq$" is the *Löwner order* on matrices: $A \succeq B$ if and only if $A - B$ is psd. This type of SDP arises in many applications. See, for example, [14, 15] and the references therein.

We assume the following throughout this chapter:

(A) $b_i > 0$ and hence $b_i = 1$ for all $i \in [m]$.

It is known that, under assumption (A), *strong duality* holds for problems (Packing- I) and (Covering- I) (resp., (Packing- II) and (Covering- II)). Let $\epsilon \in (0, 1]$ be a given constant. We say that (X, y) is an ϵ*-optimal* primal-dual solution for (Packing- I)-(Covering- I) if (X, y) is a primal-dual feasible pair such that

$$C \bullet X \ge (1 - \epsilon) b^T y \ge (1 - \epsilon) z^*_I. \tag{4.1}$$

Similarly, we say that (X, y) is an ϵ-optimal primal-dual solution for (Packing- II)-(Covering- II) if (X, y) is a primal-dual feasible pair such that

$$C \bullet X \le (1 + \epsilon) b^T y \le (1 + \epsilon) z^*_{II}. \tag{4.2}$$

In this chapter, we allow the number of constraints m in (Packing- I) (resp., (Covering- II)) to be *exponentially* (or even infinitely) large, so we assume the availability of the following *oracle*:

Max(Y)(resp., Min(Y)) : Given $Y \in \mathbb{S}^n_+$, find $i \in \mathrm{argmax}_{i \in [m]} A_i \bullet Y$ (resp., $i \in \mathrm{argmin}_{i \in [m]} A_i \bullet Y$).

Note that an *approximation* oracle computing the above maximum (resp., minimum) within a factor of $(1 - \epsilon)$ (resp., $(1 + \epsilon)$) is also sufficient for our purposes. A primal-dual solution (X, y) to (Covering- I) (resp., (Packing- II)) is said to be η*-sparse* if the size of $\mathrm{supp}(y) := \{i \in [m] : y_i > 0\}$ is at most η.

When $C = I = I_n$ (which is the identity matrix in $\mathbb{R}^{n \times n}$) and $b = \mathbf{1}_m$ (which is the vector containing all ones in $\mathbb{R}^m$), we say that the packing-covering SDPs are in *normalized* form. It can be shown (see, e.g., [7, 16]) that, to within a multiplicative factor of $(1 + \epsilon)$ in the objective, any pair of packing-covering SDPs of the form (Packing- I)-(Covering- I) can be brought to normalized form in $O(n^3)$ time while increasing the oracle time by only $O(n^\omega)$, where ω is the exponent of matrix multiplication, under the following assumption:

(B-I) There exist r matrices, say $A_1, \ldots, A_r$, such that $\hat{A} := \sum_{i=1}^{r} A_i \succ 0$. In particular, $\mathrm{Tr}(X) \le \tau := \frac{r}{\lambda_{\min}(\hat{A})}$ for any optimal solution X for (PACKING- I), and we may assume that $r = 1$ and $A_1 = \frac{1}{\tau} I$.

Similarly, it can be shown that, to within a multiplicative factor of $(1+\epsilon)$ in the objective, any pair of packing-covering SDPs of the form (PACKING- II)-(COVERING- II) can be brought to normalized form in $O(n^3)$ time, while increasing the oracle time by only $O(n^{\omega})$. Moreover, we may assume in this normalized form that

(B-II) $\lambda_{\min}(A_i) = \Omega\big(\frac{\epsilon}{n} \cdot \min_{i'} \lambda_{\max}(A_{i'})\big)$ for all $i \in [m]$,

where, for a psd matrix $B \in \mathbb{S}_+^n$, we denote by $\{\lambda_j(B) : j = 1, \ldots, n\}$ the eigenvalues of B, and by $\lambda_{\min}(B)$ and $\lambda_{\max}(B)$ the minimum and maximum eigenvalues of B, respectively. Given additional $O(mn^2)$ time, we may also assume that

(B-II') $\frac{\lambda_{\max}(A_i)}{\lambda_{\min}(A_i)} = O\big(\frac{n^2}{\epsilon^2}\big)$ for all $i \in [m]$.

Thus, the remainder of this chapter focuses on normalized problems.

Mixed packing and covering SDPs.
We also consider the following *mixed* packing-covering feasibility SDPs:

$$
\begin{aligned}
& A_i \bullet X \le b_i, \quad \forall i \in [m_p] \qquad\qquad \text{(MIX- PACK- COVER)}\\
& B_i \bullet X \ge d_i, \quad \forall i \in [m_c]\\
& X \in \mathbb{S}^n, \ X \succeq 0,
\end{aligned}
$$

where $A_1, \ldots, A_{m_p}, B_1, \ldots, B_{m_c} \in \mathbb{R}^{n \times n}$ are psd matrices, and $b = (b_1, \ldots, b_{m_p})^T$, $d = (d_1, \ldots, d_{m_c})^T$ are non-negative real vectors.

A matrix $X \in \mathbb{S}_+^n$ is an ϵ-approximate solution for (MIX- PACK- COVER) if $A_i \bullet X \le b_i$ for all $i \in [m_p]$ and $B_i \bullet X \ge (1-\epsilon)d_i$ for all $i \in [m_c]$.

4.2 Applications

4.2.1 *SDP relaxation for Robust* MAXCUT

Given a simple undirected graph $G = (V, E)$ on $n = |V|$ vertices with non-negative edge weights $w \in \mathbb{R}_+^E$, the objective in the well-known MAXCUT problem is to find a subset of the vertices $X \subset V$ that maximizes the weight of the cut: $w(X, V \setminus X) := \sum_{u \in X,\, v \in V \setminus X} w_{uv}$. The best-known approximation algorithm (with approximation ratio 0.878…) [10] for MAXCUT is based on the following SDP relaxation:

$$\max\ L(w) \bullet X \qquad \text{(MaxCut- SDP)}$$

$$\text{s.t.}\quad \mathbf{1}_i\mathbf{1}_i^T \bullet X = 1,\ \ \forall i \in [n] \qquad (4.3)$$
$$X \in \mathbb{R}^{n\times n},\ X \succeq 0.$$

By simply changing the equality in (4.3) into an inequality, this can be written in the form (PACKING- I), with $A_i := \mathbf{1}_i\mathbf{1}_i^T$ and $C := L(w) \succeq 0$ being the *Laplacian* matrix of G, defined as follows:

$$L_{ij}(w) = \begin{cases} \sum_{k=1}^n w_{ik} & \text{if } i = j, \\ -w_{ij} & \text{if } \{i, j\} \in E, \\ 0 & \text{otherwise.} \end{cases}$$

Based on this relaxation, the following result is obtained using the *scalar multiplicative weights update (MWU)* method:

Theorem 4.1 ([18]) *There is a randomized algorithm for finding an ϵ-optimal solution for (*MAXCUT- SDP*) in time $\tilde{O}(\frac{nm}{\epsilon^3})$, where n and m respectively denote the number of vertices and edges in a given graph.*

Under the *robust optimization* framework, one assumes the weights are *not known precisely*, but instead are given by a *convex uncertainty* set $\mathcal{W} \subseteq \mathbb{R}^n_+$, where it is necessary to find a (near)-optimal solution under the *worst-case* choice $w \in \mathcal{W}$ in the uncertainty set:

$$\max \min_{w\in\mathcal{W}} L(w) \bullet X \qquad \text{Robust- MaxCut- SDP}$$

$$\text{s.t.}\quad \mathbf{1}_i\mathbf{1}_i^T \bullet X \le 1,\ \ \forall i \in [n] \qquad (4.4)$$
$$X \in \mathbb{R}^{n\times n},\ X \succeq 0.$$

By "guessing" the value τ of an optimal solution (via binary search), (4.4) can be reduced to

$$\begin{aligned} & \min\ I \bullet X \\ \text{Robust- MaxCut- SDP}\quad \text{s.t.}\quad & \mathbf{1}_i\mathbf{1}_i^T \bullet X \ge 1,\ \ \forall i \in [n] \\ & \frac{1}{\tau} L(w) \bullet X \ge 1,\ \ \forall w \in \mathcal{W} \\ & X \in \mathbb{R}^{n\times n},\ X \succeq 0. \end{aligned}$$

Thus, we obtain a covering SDP (of type (COVERING- II)) with an *infinite* number of constraints, given by a minimization oracle over the convex set $\mathcal{W}$. We can use the *matrix logarithmic-potential* method to obtain the following result:

Theorem 4.2 *There is a randomized algorithm that finds an ϵ-optimal solution for (4.4) in time $\tilde{O}\big(\frac{n^{\omega+1}}{\epsilon^{2.5}} + \frac{n\mathcal{T}}{\epsilon^2}\big)$, where $\mathcal{T}$ is the time needed to optimize a linear function over $\mathcal{W}$.*

Note that for this reduction to remain valid, it is sufficient to find an ϵ-optimal solution to (4.4) for any $\epsilon = o\big(\frac{1}{n}\big)$.

4.2.2 Mahalanobis Distance Learning

Given a psd matrix $X \in \mathbb{S}^n$, the *X-Mahalanobis distance* between two points $a, b \in \mathbb{R}^n$ is defined as

$$d_X(a, b) := \sqrt{(a-b)^T X (a-b)}.$$

The distance function $d_X(\cdot, \cdot)$ is a semi-metric; that is, it is symmetric ($d_X(a, b) = d_X(a, b)$) and satisfies the triangle inequality ($d_X(a, c) \le d_X(a, b) + d_M(b, c)$), and it is also a metric if $X \succ 0$ (as in this case, $d_X(a, b) = 0$ if and only if $a = b$).

The *Mahalanobis distance learning* problem is defined as follows [28]: Given sets $\mathcal{C}_s$ and $\mathcal{C}_d$ of *similar* and *dissimilar* pairs of points in $\mathbb{R}^n$, respectively, a similarity parameter $\sigma_s \in \mathbb{R}_+$ and a dissimilarity parameter $\sigma_d \in \mathbb{R}_+$, the objective is to find a matrix X such that all the pairs in $\mathcal{C}_s$ are "close" and all the pairs in $\mathcal{C}_d$ are "far" with respect to the distance function $d_X(\cdot, \cdot)$:

$$(a-b)^T X (a-b) \le \sigma_s, \ \forall (a, b) \in \mathcal{C}_s \tag{4.5}$$

$$(a-b)^T X (a-b) \ge \sigma_d, \ \forall (a, b) \in \mathcal{C}_d \tag{4.6}$$

$$X \in \mathbb{S}^n, \ X \succeq 0. \tag{4.7}$$

Note that this can be written in the form (MIX- PACK- COVER), with $|\mathcal{C}_s|$ packing constraints of the form $A_{a,b} \bullet X \le \sigma_s$, where $A_{a,b} = (a-b)(a-b)^T$ for $(a, b) \in \mathcal{C}_s$, and $|\mathcal{C}_d|$ covering constraints of the form $B_{a,b} \bullet X \ge \sigma_d$, where $B_{a,b} = (a-b)(a-b)^T$ for $(a, b) \in \mathcal{C}_d$.

We can use the *scalar MWU* method to obtain the following result:

Theorem 4.3 *There is a deterministic algorithm that finds an ϵ-feasible solution for (4.5)-(4.2.2) in time $\tilde{O}(\frac{m(m+n^3)}{\epsilon^2})$, where n is the dimension of the point sets and $m := |\mathcal{C}_s|^2 + |\mathcal{C}_d|^2$.*

We remark that it is plausible that further improvements (possibly by another factor of $O(m)$) are possible via *rank-one tricks* and the use of *approximate eigenvalue* computations.

4.2.3 Related Work

Problems (PACKING- I)-(COVERING- I) and (PACKING- II)-(COVERING- II) can be solved using general SDP solvers, such as interior-point methods. For example, the barrier method (see, e.g., [22]) can compute a solution within an *additive* error of ϵ from the optimal in time $O(\sqrt{n}m(n^3 + mn^2 + m^2)\log\frac{1}{\epsilon})$ (see also [1, 27]). However, due to the special nature of (PACKING- I)-(COVERING- I) and (PACKING- II)-(COVERING- II), better algorithms can be obtained. Most of the improvements are obtained by using *first-order methods* [2, 3, 5, 6, 8, 15–18, 21, 23, 24], or second-order methods [13, 14]. In general, we can classify these algorithms according to whether they are *(semi) width-independent*, are *parallel*, *output sparse solutions*, or are *oracle-based*, as follows.

(I) *(Semi) width-independent*: The running time of the algorithm depends *polynomially* on the bit length of the input. For example, in the of case of (PACKING- I)-(COVERING- I), the running time is poly$(n, m, \mathcal{L}, \log\tau, \frac{1}{\epsilon})$, where $\mathcal{L}$ is the maximum bit length needed to represent any number in the input. In contrast, the running time of a width-dependent algorithm depends polynomially on a "width parameter" ρ, which is polynomial in $\mathcal{L}$ and τ.

(II) *Parallel*: The algorithm takes polylog$(n, m, \mathcal{L}, \log\tau)\cdot$ poly$(\frac{1}{\epsilon})$ time on a poly $(n, m, \mathcal{L}, \log\tau, \frac{1}{\epsilon})$ number of processors.

(III) *Sparse*: The algorithm outputs an η-sparse solution to (COVERING- I) (resp., (PACKING- II)) for $\eta =$ poly$(n, \log m, \mathcal{L}, \log\tau, \frac{1}{\epsilon})$ (resp., $\eta =$ poly$(n, \log m, \mathcal{L}, \frac{1}{\epsilon})$), where τ is a parameter that bounds the trace of any optimal solution X;

(IV) *Oracle-based*: The only access the algorithm has to the matrices $A_1, \ldots, A_m$ is via the maximization/minimization oracle, and hence the running time is independent of m.

Table 4.1 below gives a summary[1] of the most relevant results together with their classifications according to the four criteria above. We note that almost all of these algorithms for packing/covering SDPs are generalizations of similar algorithms for packing/covering linear programs (LPs), and most of them are essentially based on an *exponential potential function* in the form of *scalar exponentials*, such as [3, 18], or *matrix exponential* [2, 5, 6, 15, 17]. For instance, several of these results use the scalar or matrix versions of the MWU method (see, e.g., [4]), which are extensions of similar methods for packing/covering LPs [9, 11, 25, 29].

In [12], a different type of algorithm was given for covering LPs (indeed, more generally, for a class of concave covering inequalities) based on a *logarithmic* potential function. In [7], it was shown that this approach could be extended to provide sparse solutions for both versions of packing and covering SDPs.

As we can see from the table, among all the algorithms, only the matrix (MWU and logarithmic-potential) algorithms are oracle-based (and hence produce sparse

[1] We provide rough estimates of the bounds, as some of them are not stated explicitly in the corresponding paper in terms of the parameters we consider here.

Table 4.1 Different algorithms for packing/covering SDPs

Paper	Problem	Technique	Most expensive operation	# Iterations	Width-indep.	Parallel	Sparse	Oracle-based
[3, 18]	(PACKING- I) (COVERING- II)	MWU	Max/min eigenvalue of a psd matrix $\tilde{O}(\frac{n^2}{\epsilon})$	$O(\frac{\rho \log m}{\epsilon^2})$	No	No	No*	No
[6]	(PACKING- I) (COVERING- II)	Matrix MWU	Matrix exponential $O(n^3)$	$O(\frac{\rho^2 \tau^2 \log n}{\epsilon^2 (z_I^*)^2})$	No	No	No*	Yes
[13, 15]	(PACKING- I)	Nesterov's smoothing technique [20, 21]	Matrix exponential $O(n^3)$	$O(\frac{\tau \log m}{\epsilon})$	No	No	No	No
[14]	(COVERING- II)	Nesterov's smoothing technique [20, 21]	Min eigenvalue of a non-psdmatrix $O(n^3)$	$O(\frac{\rho^2 \log(nm)}{\epsilon})$	No	No	No	No
[16]	(PACKING- I) & (COVERING- II)	MWU technique [20, 21]	Eigenvalue decomposition $O(n^3)$	$O(\frac{\log^{13} n \log m}{\epsilon^{13}})$	Yes	Yes	No	No
[23, 24]	(PACKING- II)& (COVERING- II)	Matrix MWU	Matrix exponential $O(n^3)$	$O(\frac{\log^3 m}{\epsilon^3})$	Yes	Yes	No	No
[2]	(PACKING- I)& (COVERING- II)	Gradient Descent + Mirror Descent	Matrix exponential $O(n^3)$	$O(\frac{\log^2(mn) \log \frac{1}{\epsilon}}{\epsilon^2})$	Yes	Yes	No	No
This chapter (Sect. 4.5)	(PACKING- II)& (COVERING- II)	Matrix MWU	Matrix exponential $O(n^3)$	$O(\frac{n \log n}{\epsilon^2})$	Yes	No	Yes	Yes
[7]	(PACKING- II) & (COVERING- II) (PACKING- II) & (COVERING- II)	Matrix Logarithmic potential [12]	Matrix inversion $O(n^{\omega})$	$O(n \log(n\mathcal{L}\tau) + \frac{n}{\epsilon^2})$ $O(n \log(n/\epsilon) + \frac{n}{\epsilon^2})$	Yes	No	Yes	Yes

*In fact, these algorithms find sparse solutions in the sense that the dependence of the size of the support of the dual solution on m is at most logarithmic. However, the dependence of the size of the support on the bit length $\mathcal{L}$ is not polynomial

solutions) in the sense described above. However, the overall running time of the matrix MWU algorithm is larger by a factor of (roughly) $\Omega(n^{3-\omega})$ than that of the logarithmic-potential algorithm, where ω is the exponent of matrix multiplication. Moreover, we cannot extend the matrix MWU algorithm to solve (PACKING- I)-(COVERING- I) (in particular, it seems tricky to bound the number of iterations).

4.3 General Framework for Packing-Covering SDPs

Given a pair of packing-covering SDPs (PACKING- I)-(COVERING- I) or (COVERING- II)-(PACKING- II), we consider the following general framework in which each constraint is assigned a weight reflecting how satisfied the constraint is given the current solution:

1 Initialize constraint weights
2 **while** *the stopping criterion is not satisfied* **do**
3 | Form a "*weighted average*" of all the inequalities into a single inequality
4 | /* If we maintain weights for primal $\longrightarrow$ *scalar* version */
5 | /* If we maintain weights for dual $\longrightarrow$ *matrix* version */
6 | Solve a *fractional knapsack problem* to determine the *direction* of the next update
7 | Update the *primal* (or sometimes *dual*) variables in the chosen direction
8 | Update the *weights* to reflect which constraints become more satisfied
9 | /* Weights (*essentially*) $\longleftrightarrow$ *dual* (or sometimes *primal*) variables */
10 **end**

Algorithm 1: A general framework for solving packing-covering SDPs

We obtain different algorithms depending on how the weights are defined. We write $a_i := A_i \bullet X \geq 0$. Since $a_{\max} := \max\{a_1, \ldots, a_m\}$ (resp., $a_{\min} := \min\{a_1, \ldots, a_m\}$) is *not a smooth* function (in X), it is more convenient to work with a *smooth approximation* of it, which is provided by the weighted average formed in step 3 in the framework. There are several ways to do this, for example:

- *Exponential averaging*: The weights are $\overline{p}_i := \frac{(1+\epsilon)^{a_i}}{\sum_{i'=1}^{m}(1+\epsilon)^{a_{i'}}}$ (resp., $\overline{p}_i := \frac{(1-\epsilon)^{a_i}}{\sum_{i'=1}^{m}(1-\epsilon)^{a_{i'}}}$).
  The following claim justifies the use of these sets of weights.

Lemma 4.1 *If* $a_{\max} \geq \frac{1+\epsilon}{\epsilon}\log_{1+\epsilon}\frac{m}{\epsilon}$ $\left(\textit{resp., } a_{\min} \geq \frac{1}{\epsilon}\log_{\frac{1}{1-\epsilon}}\left(\frac{m \cdot a_{\max}}{\epsilon \cdot a_{\min}}\right)\right)$, *then*

$$\frac{a_{\max}}{1+\epsilon} \leq \sum_{i=1}^{m}\overline{p}_i a_i \leq a_{\max} \quad \left(\textit{resp., } a_{\min} \leq \sum_{i=1}^{m}\overline{p}_i a_i \leq (1+\epsilon)a_{\min}\right).$$

- *Logarithmic potential averaging*: The weights are $\overline{p}_i = \frac{\epsilon}{m}\frac{\theta^*}{\theta^*-a_i}$ (resp., $\overline{p}_i = \frac{\epsilon}{m}\frac{\theta^*}{a_i-\theta^*}$), where θ^* is the minimizer (resp., maximizer) of the potential function

$$\Phi(\theta) = \ln\left(\theta \cdot \sqrt[\epsilon/m]{\prod_{i=1}^{m} \frac{1}{\theta - a_i}}\right) \quad \left(\text{resp.}, \Phi(\theta) = \ln\left(\theta \cdot \sqrt[\epsilon/m]{\prod_{i=1}^{m} (a_i - \theta)}\right)\right).$$

(It can be easily verified that $\sum_i \overline{p}_i = 1$.) The following claim justifies the use of these sets of weights.

Lemma 4.2

$$\frac{(1-\epsilon)a_{\max}}{1-\epsilon/m} \le \sum_{i=1}^{m} \overline{p}_i a_i \le a_{\max} \quad \left(\textit{resp.}, a_{\min} \le \sum_{i=1}^{m} \overline{p}_i a_i \le \frac{a_{\min}(1+\epsilon)}{1+\epsilon/m}\right).$$

4.4 Scalar Algorithms

4.4.1 Scalar MWU Algorithm for (Packing-I)-(Covering-I)

Given a normalized pair of packing-covering SDPs of type I (Packing- I)-(Covering- I), and a feasible primal solution X, we use the exponential weight $p_i := (1+\epsilon)^{A_i \bullet X}$, for $i \in [m]$. Averaging the inequalities with respect to the weights $\overline{p}_i := \frac{p_i}{\sum_i p_i}$, we arrive at the following problem:

$$\begin{aligned} &\max\ I \bullet X \\ \text{s.t.}\ &\sum_i \overline{p}_i A_i \bullet X \le 1, \quad \forall i \in [m] \\ &X \in \mathbb{R}^{n\times n},\ X \succeq 0. \end{aligned} \tag{4.8}$$

Letting $\overline{A} := \sum_i \overline{p}_i A_i$ and writing $X = \sum_{v \in B_n} \lambda_v v v^T$, where $B_n := \{v \in \mathbb{R}^n : \|v\| = 1\}$ and $\lambda_v \ge 0$ for all $v \in B_n$, we obtain the following *(infinite-dimensional) knapsack* problem

$$\begin{aligned} &\max \sum_{v \in B_n} \lambda_v \\ \text{s.t.}\ &\sum_{v \in B_n} \lambda_v \overline{A} \bullet v v^T \le 1, \quad \forall i \in [m] \\ &\lambda_v \ge 0, \quad \forall v \in B_n. \end{aligned} \tag{4.9}$$

An optimal solution is attained at a vector $v \in B_n$ which *minimizes* $v^T \overline{A} v$. This is the basis vector corresponding to $\lambda_{\min}(\overline{A})$.

Thus, using this set of weights in our general framework (Algorithm 1) yields the following procedure (for a vector $p \in \mathbb{R}^m$, we write $\overline{p}_i := \frac{p_i}{\sum_i p_i}$):

1 $t \leftarrow 0$; $X(0) \leftarrow 0$; $y(0) \leftarrow 0$; $M(0) \leftarrow 0$; $T \leftarrow \epsilon^{-2} \ln m$
2 **while** $M(t) < T$ **do**
3 $\quad p_i(t) = (1+\epsilon)^{A_i \bullet X(t)}$ /* Update the weights */
4 $\quad v(t) = \operatorname{argmin}_{v:\|v\|=1} \sum_i \overline{p}_i(t) A_i \bullet vv^T$ /* Find an eigenvector corresponding to the smallest eigenvalue of the average inequality matrix */
5 $\quad \delta(t) = 1/\max_i A_i \bullet v(t)v(t)^T$ /* Define the update step size */
6 $\quad X(t+1) = X(t) + \delta(t)v(t)v(t)^T$; $y(t+1) \leftarrow y(t) + \delta(t)\overline{p}_i(t)$ /* Update the primal-dual solutions */
7 $\quad M(t+1) = \max_i A_i \bullet X(t+1)$ /* Compute the largest LHS */
8 $\quad t \leftarrow t+1$
9 **end**
10 **output** $(\hat{X}, \hat{y}) = \left(\frac{X(t)}{M(t)}, \frac{y(t)}{(1-1.5\epsilon)M(t)}\right)$

Algorithm 2: Scalar MWU algorithm for (PACKING- I)-(COVERING- I)

The stopping criterion is that the left-hand side (LHS) of at least one inequality in (PACKING- I) reaches some threshold $T := \epsilon^{-2} \ln m$, with respect to the current solution $X(t)$. The step size (step 5) is chosen such that in each iteration of the while-loop, this right-hand size increases by at least 1, thus guaranteeing termination in mT iterations.

Theorem 4.4 *Given a real $\epsilon \in (0, 1]$, Algorithm 2 outputs an ϵ-optimal solution for (PACKING- I)-(COVERING- I) in $O(m \log m/\epsilon^2)$ iterations, where each iteration requires an oracle call that computes an eigenvector corresponding to the minimum eigenvalue of a psd matrix.*

For a given matrix $M \in \mathbb{R}^{n \times n}$, computing $\lambda_{\min}(M)$ (almost) exactly requires $O(n^3)$ time via a full eigenvalue decomposition of the matrix. If M is psd, a faster approximation of $\lambda_{\min}(M)$ can be obtained (using Lanczos' algorithm with a random start) via the following result.

Theorem 4.5 ([19]) *Let $M \in \mathbb{S}_+^n$ be a psd matrix with N non-zeros and $\gamma \in (0, 1)$ be a given constant. Then, there is a randomized algorithm that computes, with high (i.e., $1 - o(1)$) probability a unit vector $v \in \mathbb{R}^n$ such that $v^T M v \geq (1-\gamma)\lambda_{\max}(M)$. The algorithm takes $O\left(\frac{\log n}{\sqrt{\gamma}}\right)$ iterations, each requiring $O(N)$ arithmetic operations.*

By applying the lemma to $(\overline{A})^{-1}$, we can approximate $\lambda_{\min}(\overline{A})$ in $\tilde{O}(n^{\omega})$ time.

4.4.2 *Scalar Logarithmic Potential Algorithm For (PACKING-I)–(COVERING-I)*

Given a normalized pair of packing-covering SDPs of type I (PACKING- I)-(COVERING- I) and a feasible primal solution X, we use the logarithmic-potential weights $\overline{p}_i = \frac{\epsilon}{m} \frac{\theta^*}{\theta^* - A_i \bullet X}$ for $i \in [m]$. Averaging the inequalities with respect to this set of weights, we arrive at the knapsack problem (4.9). This gives rise to the following procedure:

$s \leftarrow 0$; $\varepsilon_0 \leftarrow \frac{1}{4}$; $t \leftarrow 0$; $\nu(0) \leftarrow 1$; $X(0) \leftarrow \mathbf{1}_i\mathbf{1}_i^T$ (for an arbitrary $i \in [n]$)
while $\varepsilon_s > \epsilon$ **do**
  $\delta_s \leftarrow \frac{\varepsilon_s^3}{32m}$ **while** $\nu(t) > \varepsilon_s$ **do**
    $\theta(t) \leftarrow \theta^*(t)^{\delta_s}$, where $\theta^*(t)$ is the smallest positive root of the equation

$$\frac{\varepsilon_s\theta}{m}\sum_i \frac{1}{\theta - A_i \bullet X(t)} = 1$$

$$y(t) \leftarrow \overline{p}(t), \text{ where } \overline{p}_i(t) := \frac{\varepsilon_s\theta(t)}{m}\frac{1}{\theta(t) - A_i \bullet X(t)}, \text{ for } i \in [n]$$

/* Set the dual solution */ $v(t) = \text{argmin}_{v:||v||=1} \overline{A}(t) \bullet vv^T$, where $\overline{A}(t) := \sum_i \overline{p}_i(t)A_i$ /* Find the eigenvector corresponding to the smallest eigenvalue of the average inequality matrix */

$$\nu(t+1) \leftarrow \frac{\overline{A}(t) \bullet X(t) - \overline{A}(t) \bullet v(t)v(t)^T}{\overline{A}(t) \bullet X(t) + \overline{A}(t) \bullet v(t)v(t)^T}$$ /* Compute the error */

$$\tau(t+1) \leftarrow \frac{\varepsilon_s\theta(t)\nu(t+1)}{4m(\overline{A}(t) \bullet X(t) + \overline{A}(t) \bullet v(t)v(t)^T)}$$ /* Compute the step size */

$X(t+1) \leftarrow (1 - \tau(t+1))X(t) + \tau(t+1)v(t)v(t)^T$ /* Update the primal solution */ $t \leftarrow t+1$

  end
  $\varepsilon_{s+1} \leftarrow \frac{\varepsilon_s}{2}$
  $s \leftarrow s+1$
end
output $(\hat{X}, \hat{y}) = \left(\frac{X(t-1)}{(1-\varepsilon_{s-1}/m)\theta(t-1)}, \frac{(1+\varepsilon_{s-1})y(t-1)}{(1-\varepsilon_{s-1})(1-2\varepsilon_{s-1})\theta(t-1)}\right)$

Algorithm 3: Scalar logarithmic-potential algorithm for (PACKING- I)-(COVERING- I)

In the above, for given numbers $x \in \mathbb{R}_+$ and $\delta \in (0, 1)$, we define the δ-(upper) approximation x^δ of x to be a number satisfying: $x \le x^\delta < (1+\delta)x$.

Theorem 4.6 *Given $\epsilon \in (0, 1]$, Algorithm 3 outputs an ϵ-optimal solution for* (COVERING- I)*-*(PACKING- I) *in $O(m \log \psi + m/\epsilon^2)$ iterations, where $\psi := \frac{\lambda_{\max}(\overline{A}(0))}{\lambda_{\min}(\overline{A}(0))}$ and each iteration requires an oracle call that computes an eigenvector corresponding to the minimum eigenvalue of a psd matrix.*

4.5 Matrix Algorithms

4.5.1 *Matrix MWU Algorithm For (COVERING-II)-(PACKING-II)*

Let $F(y) := \sum_{i=1}^{m} y_i A_i$. Then, we can rewrite the normalized version of (PACKING-II) as follows:

$$\begin{aligned} z_I^* &= \max \mathbf{1}^T y \qquad \text{(PACKING- II)} \\ \text{s.t. } & \lambda_j(F(y)) \le 1, \quad \forall j \in [n] \\ & y \in \mathbb{R}^m, \ y \ge 0. \end{aligned}$$

Averaging the inequalities with respect to the weights $\overline{p}_j := \frac{p_j}{\sum_j p_j}$, where $p_j := (1+\epsilon)^{\lambda_j(F(y))}$, we get

$$\begin{aligned} & \max \mathbf{1}^T y \\ \text{s.t. } & \sum_j \overline{p}_j \lambda_j(F(y)) \le 1, \quad \forall j \in [n] \\ & y \in \mathbb{R}^m, \ y \ge 0. \end{aligned}$$

Using the *eigenvalue decomposition*: $F(y) = U \Lambda U^T$, where Λ is the diagonal matrix containing the eigenvalues of $F(y)$ and $UU^T = I$, and letting

$$\overline{P} := U \begin{bmatrix} \overline{p}_1 & 0 & \cdots & 0 \\ 0 & \overline{p}_2 & \cdots & 0 \\ \cdots & \cdots & \cdots & \cdots \\ 0 & 0 & \cdots & \overline{p}_n \end{bmatrix} U^T = \frac{(1+\epsilon)^{F(y)}}{\text{Tr}((1+\epsilon)^{F(y)})},$$

we obtain the following knapsack problem:

$$\begin{aligned} & \max \mathbf{1}^T y \\ \text{s.t. } & \sum_i (\overline{P} \bullet A_i) y_i \le 1, \quad \forall j \in [n] \\ & y \in \mathbb{R}^m, \ y \ge 0. \end{aligned}$$

An optimal solution is attained at the basis vector $y = \mathbf{1}_i \in \mathbb{R}_+^m$ that minimizes $\overline{P} \bullet A_i$. This gives rise to the following matrix MWU algorithm:

Theorem 4.7 *Given an real $\epsilon \in (0, 1]$, Algorithm 2 outputs an ϵ-optimal solution for (COVERING- II)-(PACKING- II) in $O(n \log n/\epsilon^2)$ iterations, where each iteration requires matrix exponential computation, two oracle calls that computes the max-*

1 $t \leftarrow 0$; $y(0) \leftarrow 0$; $X(0) \leftarrow 0$; $M(0) \leftarrow 0$; $T \leftarrow \epsilon^{-2} \ln n$
2 **while** $M(t) < T$ **do**
3 $\quad P(t) = (1+\epsilon)^{\sum_{i=1}^{m} y_i(t) A_i}$ /* Update the weight matrix by exponentiation */
4 $\quad i(t) \leftarrow \text{argmin}_i\, A_i \bullet P(t)$ $\delta(t) \leftarrow 1/\lambda_{\max}(A_{i(t)})$ /* Define the update step size */
$\quad X(t+1) \leftarrow X(t) + \frac{\delta(t) P(t)}{I \bullet P(t)}$; $y(t+1) \leftarrow y(t) + \delta(t) \mathbf{1}_{i(t)}$ /* Update the primal-dual solution */
5 $\quad M(t+1) \leftarrow \lambda_{\max}(\sum_i y_i(t) A_i)$ /* Compute the largest eigenvalue of LHS of dual */
6 $\quad t \leftarrow t+1$
7 **end**
8 $L(t) \leftarrow \min_i A_i \bullet X(t)$
9 **output** $(\hat{X}, \hat{y}) = \left(\frac{X(t)}{L(t)}, \frac{y(t)}{M(t)}\right)$

Algorithm 4: Matrix MWU algorithm for (PACKING- II)-(COVERING- II)

imum eigenvalue of a psd matrix, and a single oracle call to the minimization in step 4.

The most demanding step in the above algorithm is the matrix exponential computation, which can be done in $O(n^3)$ time via a complete eigenvalue decomposition. A more efficient approximation, particularly when the matrices A_i are sparse, can be obtained via the following result.

Theorem 4.8 ([26]) *There is an algorithm for approximating the matrix exponential e^F in time $O(n^2 r \log^3 \frac{1}{\epsilon})$, where r denotes the number of non-zeros in $F \in \mathbb{S}^n$, and ϵ is the approximation accuracy.*

We remark that a matrix MWU algorithm and a theorem similar to Algorithm 4 and Theorem 4.7 for (PACKING- I)-(COVERING- I) have not yet been discovered and are left as open problems.

4.5.2 *Matrix Logarithmic Potential Algorithm For (PACKING-I)-(COVERING-I)*

Let $F(y) := \sum_{i=1}^{m} y_i A_i$. Then, we can rewrite the normalized version of (COVERING-I) as

$$\begin{aligned} z_I^* &= \min \mathbf{1}^T y && \text{(PACKING- II)} \\ \text{s.t. } & \lambda_j(F(y)) \geq 1, \quad \forall j \in [n] \\ & y \in \mathbb{R}^m, \; y \geq 0. \end{aligned}$$

Averaging the inequalities with respect to the weights $\overline{p}_j := \frac{\epsilon}{n} \frac{\theta^*}{\lambda_j(F(y)) - \theta^*}$, we get

$$\begin{aligned} \min\ & \mathbf{1}^T y \\ \text{s.t.}\ & \sum_j \overline{p}_j \lambda_j(F(y)) \geq 1, \ \ \forall j \in [n] \\ & y \in \mathbb{R}^m, \ y \geq 0. \end{aligned}$$

Using the *eigenvalue decomposition*: $F(y) = U \Lambda U^T$, where Λ is the diagonal matrix containing the eigenvalues of $F(y)$ and $UU^T = I$, and letting

$$\overline{P} := U \begin{bmatrix} \overline{p}_1 & 0 & \cdots 0 \\ 0 & \overline{p}_2 & \cdots 0 \\ \cdots & \cdots & \cdots \\ 0 & 0 & \cdots \overline{p}_n \end{bmatrix} U^T = \frac{\epsilon\theta^*}{n}(F(y) - \theta^* I)^{-1},$$

we obtain the following knapsack problem:

$$\begin{aligned} \min\ & \mathbf{1}^T y \\ \text{s.t.}\ & \sum_i (\overline{P} \bullet A_i) y_i \geq 1, \forall j \in [n] \\ & y \in \mathbb{R}^m, \ y \geq 0. \end{aligned}$$

An optimal solution is attained at the basis vector $y = \mathbf{1}_i \in \mathbb{R}^m_+$ that maximizes $\overline{P} \bullet A_i$. This gives rise to the following matrix logarithmic-potential algorithm:

1 $s \leftarrow 0; \varepsilon_0 \leftarrow \frac{1}{2}; t \leftarrow 0; \nu(0) \leftarrow 1; y(0) \leftarrow \frac{1}{r}\sum_{i=1}^r \mathbf{1}_i$
2 **while** $\varepsilon_s > \epsilon$ **do**
3 $\quad \delta_s \leftarrow \frac{\varepsilon_s^3}{32n}$
4 $\quad$ **while** $\nu(t) > \varepsilon_s$ **do**
5 $\quad\quad \theta(t) \leftarrow \theta^*(t)_{\delta_s}$, where $\theta^*(t)$ is the smallest positive root of the equation $\frac{\varepsilon_s \theta}{n}\mathrm{Tr}(F(y(t)) - \theta I)^{-1} = 1$
$\quad\quad X(t) \leftarrow \frac{\varepsilon_s \theta(t)}{n}(F(y(t)) - \theta(t) I)^{-1}$ /* Set the primal solution */ $i(t) \leftarrow \mathrm{argmax}_i\, A_i \bullet X(t)$ /* Call the maximization oracle */
6 $\quad\quad \nu(t+1) \leftarrow \frac{X(t) \bullet A_{i(t)} - X(t) \bullet F(y(t))}{X(t) \bullet A_{i(t)} + X(t) \bullet F(y(t))}$ /* Compute the error */
7 $\quad\quad \tau(t+1) \leftarrow \frac{\varepsilon_s \theta(t) \nu(t+1)}{4n(X(t) \bullet A_{i(t)} + X(t) \bullet F(y(t)))}$ /* Compute the step size */
$\quad\quad y(t+1) \leftarrow (1 - \tau(t+1))y(t) + \tau(t+1)\mathbf{1}_{i(t)}$ /* Update the dual solution */ $t \leftarrow t+1$
8 $\quad$ **end**
9 $\quad \varepsilon_{s+1} \leftarrow \frac{\varepsilon_s}{2}$
10 $\quad s \leftarrow s+1$
11 **end**
12 **output** $(\hat{X}, \hat{y}) = \left(\frac{(1-\varepsilon_{s-1})X(t-1)}{(1+\varepsilon_{s-1})^2\theta(t-1))}, \frac{y(t-1)}{\theta(t-1)}\right)$

Algorithm 5: Matrix logarithmic-potential algorithm for (PACKING- I)-(COVERING- I)

The most demanding steps are the computation of $\theta(t)$ and $X(t)$ in steps 5 and 5, respectively. Computing $\theta(t)$ can be done via binary search over a region determined by repeated matrix multiplications and approximate minimum eigenvalue computation (cf. Theorem 4.5). Once $\theta(t)$ is determined, computing $X(t)$ requires a single matrix inversion. The overall running time per iteration is $\tilde{O}(n^{\omega})$ plus the time needed by the maximization oracle in step 5.

Theorem 4.9 *Given $\epsilon \in (0, 1]$, Algorithm 5 outputs an ϵ-optimal solution for* (COVERING- I)*-*(PACKING- I) *in $O(n \log \psi + \frac{n}{\epsilon^2})$ iterations, where $\psi := \frac{r \cdot \max_i \lambda_{\max}(A_i)}{\lambda_{\min}(\hat{A})}$ and each iteration requires $O(\log \frac{n}{\epsilon})$ matrix multiplications and a single oracle call to the maximization in step 5.*

4.5.3 *Matrix Logarithmic Potential Algorithm For* (PACKING-II)*-*(COVERING-II)

A symmetric version of Algorithm 5 for (PACKING- II)-(COVERING- II) can be given as follows:

1 $s \leftarrow 0$; $\varepsilon_0 \leftarrow \frac{1}{4}$; $t \leftarrow 0$; $\nu(0) \leftarrow 1$; $y(0) \leftarrow \mathbf{1}_i$ (for an arbitrary $i \in [m]$)
2 while $\varepsilon_s > \epsilon$ **do**
3 $\quad \delta_s \leftarrow \frac{\varepsilon_s^3}{32n}$ **while** $\nu(t) > \varepsilon_s$ **do**
4 $\quad\quad \theta(t) \leftarrow \theta^*(t)^{\delta_s}$, where $\theta^*(t)$ is the smallest positive root of the equation
$\quad\quad \frac{\varepsilon_s \theta}{n} \mathrm{Tr}(\theta I - F(y(t)))^{-1} = 1$ $\;X(t) \leftarrow \frac{\varepsilon_s \theta(t)}{n}(\theta(t) I - F(y(t)))^{-1}$ /* Set the primal solution */ $i(t) \leftarrow \mathrm{argmin}_i\, A_i \bullet X(t)$ /* Call the minimization oracle */
$\quad\quad \nu(t+1) \leftarrow \frac{X(t) \bullet F(y(t)) - X(t) \bullet A_{i(t)}}{X(t) \bullet A_{i(t)} + X(t) \bullet F(y(t))}$ /* Compute the error */
$\quad\quad \tau(t+1) \leftarrow \frac{\varepsilon_s \theta(t) \nu(t+1)}{4n(X(t) \bullet A_{i(t)} + X(t) \bullet F(y(t)))}$ /* Compute the step size */
$\quad\quad y(t+1) \leftarrow (1 - \tau(t+1)) y(t) + \tau(t+1) \mathbf{1}_{i(t)}$ /* Update the dual solution */
$\quad\quad t \leftarrow t + 1$
5 $\quad$ **end**
6 $\quad \varepsilon_{s+1} \leftarrow \frac{\varepsilon_s}{2}$
7 $\quad s \leftarrow s + 1$
8 end
9 output $(\hat{X}, \hat{y}) = \left(\frac{(1+\varepsilon_{s-1}) X(t-1)}{(1-2\varepsilon_{s-1})^2 \theta(t-1)}, \frac{y(t-1)}{\theta(t-1)} \right)$

Algorithm 6: Materix logarithmic-potential algorithm for (PACKING- II)-(COVERING- II)

Theorem 4.10 *Given $\epsilon \in (0, 1]$, Algorithm 6 outputs an ϵ-optimal solution for* (PACKING- II)*-*(COVERING- II) *in $O(n \log \psi + \frac{n}{\epsilon^2})$ iterations, where $\psi := O(\log \frac{n}{\epsilon})$ and each iteration requires $O(\log \frac{n}{\epsilon})$ matrix inversions and a single oracle call to the minimization in step 4.*

Acknowledgements We thank Waleed Najy for many helpful discussions on this topic. This work was partially supported by JST CREST JPMJCR1402 and Grants-in-Aid for Scientific Research. The research of the first author was partially supported by Abu Dhabi Education & Knowledge – Abu Dhabi Award for Research Excellence (AARE18-152).

References

1. F. Alizadeh, Interior point methods in semidefinite programming with applications to combinatorial optimization. SIAM J. Optim. **5**(1), 13–51 (1995)
2. Z. Allen-Zhu, Y.T. Lee, L. Orecchia, Using optimization to obtain a width-independent, parallel, simpler, and faster positive sdp solver, in *Proceedings of the Twenty-seventh Annual ACM-SIAM Symposium on Discrete Algorithms*, SODA '16 (Society for Industrial and Applied Mathematics, Philadelphia, PA, USA, 2016), pp. 1824–1831
3. S. Arora, E. Hazan, S. Kale, Fast algorithms for approximate semidefinite programming using the multiplicative weights update method (2005), pp. 339–348
4. S. Arora, E. Hazan, S. Kale, The multiplicative weights update method: a meta-algorithm and applications. Theory Comput. **8**(1), 121–164 (2012)
5. S. Arora, S. Kale, A combinatorial, primal-dual approach to semidefinite programs (2007), pp. 227–236
6. S. Arora, S. Kale. A combinatorial, primal-dual approach to semidefinite programs. J. ACM **63**(2), 12:1–12:35 (2016)
7. K. Elbassioni, K. Makino, Oracle-based primal-dual algorithms for packing and covering semidefinite programs, in *27th Annual European Symposium on Algorithms, ESA 2019, September 9–11, 2019, Munich/Garching, Germany* (2019), pp. 43:1–43:15
8. D. Garber, E. Hazan, Sublinear time algorithms for approximate semidefinite programming. Math. Program. **158**(1–2), 329–361 (2016)
9. N. Garg, J. Könemann, Faster and simpler algorithms for multicommodity flow and other fractional packing problems. SIAM J. Comput. **37**(2), 630–652 (2007)
10. M.X. Goemans, D.P. Williamson, Improved approximation algorithms for maximum cut and satisfiability problems using semidefinite programming. J. ACM **42**(6), 1115–1145 (1995)
11. M.D. Grigoriadis, L.G. Khachiyan, A sublinear-time randomized approximation algorithm for matrix games. Operat. Res. Lett. **18**(2), 53–58 (1995)
12. M.D. Grigoriadis, L.G. Khachiyan, L. Porkolab, J. Villavicencio, Approximate max-min resource sharing for structured concave optimization. SIAM J. Optim. **41**, 1081–1091 (2001)
13. G. Iyengar, D. J. Phillips, C. Stein, Approximation algorithms for semidefinite packing problems with applications to maxcut and graph coloring, in *Integer Programming and Combinatorial Optimization (IPCO)*, eds. by M. Jünger, V. Kaibel (Berlin, Heidelberg, 2005), pp. 152–166
14. G. Iyengar, D.J. Phillips, C. Stein, Feasible and accurate algorithms for covering semidefinite programs, in *Algorithm Theory—SWAT 2010*, ed. by H. Kaplan (Berlin, Heidelberg, 2010), pp. 150–162.
15. G. Iyengar, D.J. Phillips, C. Stein, Approximating semidefinite packing programs. SIAM J. Optim. **21**(1), 231–268 (2011)
16. R. Jain, P. Yao, A parallel approximation algorithm for positive semidefinite programming. In *IEEE 52nd Annual Symposium on Foundations of Computer Science, FOCS 2011, Palm Springs, CA, USA, October 22-25, 2011* (2011), pp. 463–471
17. R. Jain, P. Yao, A parallel approximation algorithm for mixed packing and covering semidefinite programs. CoRR (2012). arXiv:abs/1201.6090
18. P. Klein, H.-I. Lu, Efficient approximation algorithms for semidefinite programs arising from max cut and coloring, in *Proceedings of the Twenty-eighth Annual ACM Symposium on Theory of Computing*, STOC '96 (ACM, New York, NY, USA, 1996), pp. 338–347

19. Z. Leyk, H. Woźniakowski, Estimating a largest eigenvector by lanczos and polynomial algorithms with a random start. Numer. Linear Algebra Appl. **5**(3), 147–164 (1999)
20. Y. Nesterov, Smooth minimization of non-smooth functions. Math. Program. **103**(1), 127–152 (2005)
21. Y. Nesterov, Smoothing technique and its applications in semidefinite optimization. Math. Program. **110**(2), 245–259 (2007)
22. Y. Nesterov, A. Nemirovskii, Interior-Point Polynomial Algorithms in Convex Programming. Society for Industrial and Applied Mathematics (1994)
23. R. Peng, K. Tangwongsan, Faster and simpler width-independent parallel algorithms for positive semidefinite programming, in *Proceedings of the Twenty-fourth Annual ACM Symposium on Parallelism in Algorithms and Architectures*, SPAA '12 (ACM, New York, NY, USA, 2012), pp. 101–108
24. R. Peng, K. Tangwongsan, P. Zhang, Faster and simpler width-independent parallel algorithms for positive semidefinite programming. CoRR (2016). arXiv:abs/1201.5135
25. S.A. Plotkin, D.B. Shmoys, É. Tardos, Fast approximation algorithms for fractional packing and covering problems (1991), pp. 495–504
26. J. van den Eshof, M. Hochbruck, Preconditioning lanczos approximations to the matrix exponential. SIAM J. Sci. Comput. **27**(4), 1438–1457 (2006)
27. L. Vandenberghe, S. Boyd, Semidefinite programming. SIAM Rev. **38**(1), 49–95 (1996)
28. E.P. Xing, M.I. Jordan, S.J. Russell, A.Y. Ng, Distance metric learning with application to clustering with side-information, in *Advances in Neural Information Processing Systems 15*, ed. by S. Becker, S. Thrun, K. Obermayer (MIT Press, Cambridge, 2003), pp. 521–528
29. N.E. Young, Sequential and parallel algorithms for mixed packing and covering (2001), pp. 38–546

Open Access This chapter is licensed under the terms of the Creative Commons Attribution 4.0 International License (http://creativecommons.org/licenses/by/4.0/), which permits use, sharing, adaptation, distribution and reproduction in any medium or format, as long as you give appropriate credit to the original author(s) and the source, provide a link to the Creative Commons license and indicate if changes were made.

The images or other third party material in this chapter are included in the chapter's Creative Commons license, unless indicated otherwise in a credit line to the material. If material is not included in the chapter's Creative Commons license and your intended use is not permitted by statutory regulation or exceeds the permitted use, you will need to obtain permission directly from the copyright holder.

Chapter 5
Almost Linear Time Algorithms for Some Problems on Dynamic Flow Networks

Yuya Higashikawa, Naoki Katoh, and Junichi Teruyama

Abstract Motivated by evacuation planning, several problems regarding *dynamic flow networks* have been studied in recent years. A dynamic flow network consists of an undirected graph with positive edge lengths, positive edge capacities, and positive vertex weights. The road network in an area can be treated as a graph where the edge lengths are the distances along the roads and the vertex weights are the number of people at each site. An edge capacity limits the number of people that can enter the edge per unit time. In a dynamic flow network, when particular points on edges or vertices called *sinks* are given, all of the people are required to evacuate from the vertices to the sinks as quickly as possible. This chapter gives an overview of two of our recent results on the problem of locating multiple sinks in a dynamic flow path network such that the max/sum of evacuation times for all the people to sinks is minimized, and we focus on techniques that enable the problems to be solved in almost linear time.

5.1 Introduction

Recently, many parts of the world have been affected by disasters including earthquakes, nuclear plant accidents, volcanic eruptions, and flooding, highlighting the urgent need for orderly evacuation planning. One powerful tool for evacuation planning is the *dynamic flow model* introduced by Ford and Fulkerson [10], which represents movement of commodities over time in a network. In this model, we are given a graph with *source* vertices and *sink* vertices. Each source vertex is associated with a positive weight, called a *supply*; each sink vertex is associated with a positive weight, called a *demand*; and each edge is associated with a positive length and capacity.

Y. Higashikawa (✉) · N. Katoh · J. Teruyama
University of Hyogo, Kobe, Japan
e-mail: higashikawa@gsis.u-hyogo.ac.jp

N. Katoh
e-mail: naoki.katoh@gsis.u-hyogo.ac.jp

J. Teruyama
e-mail: junichi.teruyama@gsis.u-hyogo.ac.jp

© The Author(s) 2022

N. Katoh et al. (eds.), *Sublinear Computation Paradigm*,
https://doi.org/10.1007/978-981-16-4095-7_5

Table 5.1 Summary of minmax k-sink problems

Path	General capacities: $O(n \log n + k^2 \log^4 n)$, $O(n \log^3 n)$ [7]
	Uniform capacity: $O(n + k^2 \log^2 n)$, $O(n \log n)$ [7]
Tree	General capacities: $O(\max\{k, \log n\} \cdot kn \log^4 n)$ [9]
	Uniform capacity: $O(\max\{k, \log n\} \cdot kn \log^3 n)$ [9]
General graph	General capacities: FPTAS for a fixed k [3]
	Uniform capacity: FPTAS for a fixed k [3]

An edge capacity limits the amount of supply that can enter the edge per unit time. One variant of the dynamic flow problem is the *quickest transshipment problem*, in which the objective is to send exactly the right amount of supply out of sources into sinks while satisfying demand constraints in the minimum overall time. Hoppe and Tardos [17] provided a polynomial time algorithm for this problem in the case where the transit times are integral. However, the complexity of their algorithm is very high. Finding a practical polynomial time solution to this is still an open problem. Readers are referred to a recent survey by Skutella [20] on dynamic flows.

This chapter discusses related problems called *k-sink problems* [3, 5–9, 14–16, 18], in which the objective is to find the locations of k sinks in a given dynamic flow network so that all the supply is sent to the sinks as quickly as possible. The following two criteria can be naturally considered for determining the optimality of the locations: minimization of *evacuation completion time* and *aggregate evacuation time* (i.e., *average evacuation time*). We call the k-sink problem that requires finding the locations of k sinks that minimize the evacuation completion time (resp., the aggregate evacuation time) the *minmax* (resp., *minsum*) *k-sink problem*. Although several papers have studied minmax k-sink problems in dynamic flow networks [3, 7–9, 14, 15, 18], minsum k-sink problems in dynamic flow networks have not been studied except for the case of path networks [5, 6, 15, 16].[1] Tables 5.1 and 5.2 summarize the previous results for the minmax k-sink problems and the minsum k-sink problems, respectively.

There are two models for the evacuation method. Under the *confluent flow model*, all the supply leaving a vertex must evacuate to the same sink through the same edges, and under the *non-confluent flow model*, there is no such restriction. To our knowledge, almost all of the papers that deal with the k-sink problems [3, 5–9, 15] adopt the confluent flow model, while only one paper [16] handles both of the models.

Although it may seem natural to model the evacuation behavior of people by treating each supply as a discrete quantity as in [17, 18], almost all of the previous papers on sink problems [3, 7–9, 14–16] have treated each supply as a continuous

[1] Note that the minsum 1-sink problem in general networks can be solved in polynomial time by applying the following two facts: (1) Baumann and Skutella [2] provided a polynomial time algorithm for the problem of computing a dynamic flow to a fixed sink in a general network while minimizing the aggregate evacuation time. (2) For the minsum 1-sink problem in general networks, one can prove that there exists an optimal sink located at a vertex in a similar manner to the well-known *node optimality theorem* for the 1-median problem [12].

Table 5.2 Summary of minsum k-sink problems

Path	General capacities: $O(kn \log^4 n)$ [6] $\min\{O(kn \log^3 n), n2^{O(\sqrt{\log k \log \log n})} \log^3 n\}$ [16]
	Uniform capacity: $O(kn \log^3 n)$ [5] $\min\{O(kn \log^2 n), n2^{O(\sqrt{\log k \log \log n})} \log^2 n\}$ [16]
Tree	Open
General graph	

quantity since it is easier to treat the problems mathematically and the effect is negligible when the number of people is large. Throughout this chapter, we adopt the model with continuous supplies.

We also give an overview of two of our recent results [7, 16] on the problems of locating multiple sinks on dynamic flow path networks such that the max/sum of evacuation times for all the people to sinks is minimized, and we focus on algorithmic frameworks that enable solving the problems in almost linear time.

5.2 Preliminaries

For two real values a, b with $a < b$, let $[a, b] = \{t \in \mathbb{R} \mid a \le t \le b\}$, $[a, b) = \{t \in \mathbb{R} \mid a \le t < b\}$, $(a, b] = \{t \in \mathbb{R} \mid a < t \le b\}$, and $(a, b) = \{t \in \mathbb{R} \mid a < t < b\}$, where $\mathbb{R}$ is the set of real values. For two integers i, j with $i \le j$, let $[i..j] = \{h \in \mathbb{Z} \mid i \le h \le j\}$, where $\mathbb{Z}$ is the set of integers. A dynamic flow path network $\mathcal{P}$ is given as a 5-tuple $(P, \mathbf{w}, \mathbf{c}, \mathbf{l}, \tau)$, where P is a path with vertex set $V = \{v_i \mid i \in [1..n]\}$ and edge set $E = \{e_i = (v_i, v_{i+1}) \mid i \in [1..n-1]\}$, $\mathbf{w}$ is a vector $\langle w_1, \ldots, w_n \rangle$ of which each component w_i is the *weight* of vertex v_i representing the amount of supply (e.g., the number of evacuees or cars) located at v_i, $\mathbf{c}$ is a vector $\langle c_1, \ldots, c_{n-1} \rangle$ of which each component c_i is the *capacity* of edge e_i representing the upper bound on the flow amount that can enter e_i per unit time, $\mathbf{l}$ is a vector $\langle \ell_1, \ldots, \ell_{n-1} \rangle$ of which each component ℓ_i is the *length* of edge e_i (i.e., the distance between two end vertices of e_i), and τ is the time taken for unit supply to move unit distance along any edge.

We say that a point p lies on path $P = (V, E)$, denoted by $p \in P$, if p lies on a vertex $v \in V$ or an edge $e \in E$. We assume that path P can be represented by a horizontal line segment along which the vertices $v_1, v_2, \ldots, v_n$ are arranged in order from left to right. For two points $p, q \in P$, $p \prec q$ means that p lies to the left side of q. For two points $p, q \in P$, $p \preceq q$ means that $p \prec q$ or p and q lie at the same location. For two points $p, q \in P$ such that $p \preceq q$, p divides an edge (v_i, v_{i+1}) in the ratio $r_p : 1 - r_p$, and q divides an edge (v_j, v_{j+1}) in the ratio $r_q : 1 - r_q$, let $L(p, q)$ be the distance between p and q, that is, $L(p, q) = (1 - r_p)\ell_i + r_q \ell_j + \sum_{h=i+1}^{j-1} \ell_h$ (where $\sum_{h=i+1}^{i} \ell_h = 0$ and $\sum_{h=i+1}^{i-1} \ell_h = -\ell_i$). Let us consider two integers $i, j \in [1..n]$ with $i < j$. We denote by $P_{i,j}$ a *subpath* of P from v_i to v_j, and by $\mathcal{P}_{i,j}$ a subnetwork of $\mathcal{P}$ consisting of subpaths $P_{i,j}$. Let $L_{i,j}$ be the distance between v_i and v_j, that is, $L_{i,j} = \sum_{h=i}^{j-1} \ell_h$, and let $C_{i,j}$ be the minimum capacity among all the edges between v_i and v_j, that is, $C_{i,j} = \min\{c_h \mid h \in [i..j-1]\}$. For $i \in [1..n]$, we denote the sum of weights from v_1 to v_i by $W_i = \sum_{j=1}^{i} w_j$. Note that, given a dynamic flow path network $\mathcal{P}$, if we construct two lists of W_i and $L_{1,i}$ for all $i \in [1..n]$ in $O(n)$ preprocessing time, we can obtain W_i for any $i \in [1..n]$ and $L_{i,j} = L_{1,j} - L_{1,i}$ for any $i, j \in [1..n]$ with $i < j$ in $O(1)$ time. In addition, $C_{i,j}$ for any $i, j \in [1..n]$ with $i < j$ can be obtained in $O(1)$ time with $O(n)$ preprocessing time, which is known as the *range minimum query* [1, 4].

A *k-sink* $\mathbf{x}$ is a k-tuple $(x_1, \ldots, x_k)$ of points on P such that $x_i \prec x_j$ for any $i < j$. We assume that no two sinks lie on the same edge.[2] We define the function Id for point $p \in P$ as follows: the value $\mathrm{Id}(p)$ is an integer such that $v_{\mathrm{Id}(p)} \preceq p \prec v_{\mathrm{Id}(p)+1}$ holds, that is, if p lies on edge (v_i, v_{i+1}) or at vertex v_i, $\mathrm{Id}(p) = i$. A *divider* $\mathbf{d}$ is a $(k-1)$-tuple $(d_1, \ldots, d_{k-1})$ of real values such that $0 \le d_i < d_j \le W_n$ for any $i < j$. A pair $(\mathbf{x}, \mathbf{d})$ is called *valid* if and only if $W_{\mathrm{Id}(x_i)} \le d_i \le W_{\mathrm{Id}(x_{i+1})}$ holds for any i. A valid pair $(\mathbf{x}, \mathbf{d})$ determines what amount of supply from which vertex flows to which sink so that the portion $d_i - d_{i-1}$ of supply is assigned to flow to sink x_i, where $d_0 = 0$ and $d_k = W_n$. More precisely, given a valid pair $(\mathbf{x}, \mathbf{d})$, the portion $W_{\mathrm{Id}(x_i)} - d_{i-1}$ of supply that originates from the left side of x_i flows to sink x_i, and the portion $d_i - W_{\mathrm{Id}(x_i)}$ of supply that originates from the right side of x_i also flows to sink x_i. For instance, under the non-confluent flow model, if $W_{h-1} < d_i < W_h$ where $h \in [1..n]$, the portion $d_i - W_{h-1}$ of the w_h supply at v_h flows to sink x_i and the rest of the $W_h - d_i$ supply flows to sink x_{i+1}. The difference between the confluent flow model and the non-confluent flow model is that the confluent flow model requires that each value d_i of a divider $\mathbf{d}$ must take a value in $\{W_1, \ldots, W_n\}$, whereas the non-confluent flow model does not. For a dynamic flow path network $\mathcal{P}$ and a valid pair $(\mathbf{x}, \mathbf{d})$, the *evacuation completion time* $\mathsf{CT}(\mathcal{P}, \mathbf{x}, \mathbf{d})$ is the time at which all the supply completes the evacuation. The *aggregate evacuation time* $\mathsf{AT}(\mathcal{P}, \mathbf{x}, \mathbf{d})$ is the sum of the evacuation completion time for all the supply. Explicit definitions of these are given in Sect. 5.3.

5.3 Objective Functions

Suppose that we are given a divider $\mathbf{d} = (d_1, \ldots, d_{k-1})$. This $\mathbf{d}$ implies that we have k 1-sink subproblems. The ith subproblem consists of a subnetwork $\mathcal{P}_{h,h'}$ such that the weight of v_j is w_j for $j \in [h+1..h'-1]$, while those of v_h and $v_{h'}$ are $W_h - d_{i-1}$ and $d_i - W_{h'-1}$, respectively, where $W_{h-1} < d_{i-1} \le W_h$ and $W_{h'-1} < d_i \le W_{h'}$. To explicitly define the evacuation completion time and the aggregate evacuation time,

---

[2] It turns out that this assumption does not result in a loss of generality once the cost function is introduced later. If some adjacent two sinks x_i and x_{i+1} lie on edge (v_j, v_{j+1}), that is, $v_j \prec x_i \prec x_{i+1} \prec v_{j+1}$, moving x_i to v_j or moving x_{i+1} to v_{j+1} does not increase the cost.

we first consider the case of the 1-sink problem, and then extend the argument to the general case of the k-sink problem.

5.3.1 Objective Functions for the 1-Sink Problem

Given a dynamic flow path network $\mathcal{P} = (P, \mathbf{w}, \mathbf{c}, \mathbf{l}, \tau)$ with n vertices, we assign a unique sink to a point x, that is, $\mathbf{x} = (x)$ and $\mathbf{d} = ()$, which is the 0-tuple. We consider only the case where x is on an edge e_i excluding its end vertices, that is, $v_i \prec x \prec v_{i+1}$, since the case where x is on a vertex can be treated similarly. In this case, all the supply on the left side of x (i.e., at $v_1, \ldots, v_i$) flows to the right toward sink x, and all the supply on the right side of x (i.e., at $v_{i+1}, \ldots, v_n$) flows to the left toward sink x.

To treat this case, we introduce some new notation. Let the function $\theta^{x,+}(z)$ denote the time at which the first $z - W_i$ of supply on the right side of x completes its evacuation to sink x (where $\theta^{x,+}(z) = 0$ for $z \in [0, W_i]$). Similarly, let $\theta^{x,-}(z)$ denote the time at which the first $W_i - z$ of supply on the left side of x completes its evacuation to sink x (where $\theta^{x,-}(z) = 0$ for $z \in [W_i, W_n]$). Higashikawa [13] showed that the values $\theta^{x,+}(W_n)$ and $\theta^{x,-}(0)$, which are the evacuation completion times for all the supply on the right and left sides of x, respectively, are given by the following formulae:

$$\theta^{x,+}(W_n) = \max\left\{\frac{W_n - W_{j-1}}{C_{i,j}} + \tau \cdot L(x, v_j) \mid j \in [i+1..n]\right\}, \text{ and} \tag{5.1}$$

$$\theta^{x,-}(0) = \max\left\{\frac{W_j}{C_{j,i+1}} + \tau \cdot L(v_j, x) \mid j \in [1..i]\right\}. \tag{5.2}$$

Using these, the evacuation completion time $\mathsf{CT}(\mathcal{P}, (x), ())$ is given by

$$\mathsf{CT}(\mathcal{P}, (x), ()) = \max\left\{\theta^{x,+}(W_n), \theta^{x,-}(0)\right\}. \tag{5.3}$$

We can generalize formulae (5.1) and (5.2) to the case of any $z \in [0, W_n]$ as follows:

$$\theta^{x,+}(z) = \max\{\theta^{x,+,j}(z) \mid j \in [i+1..n]\}, \tag{5.4}$$

where $\theta^{x,+,j}(z)$ for $j \in [i+1..n]$ is defined as

$$\theta^{x,+,j}(z) = \begin{cases} 0 & \text{if } z \le W_{j-1}, \\ \frac{z - W_{j-1}}{C_{i,j}} + \tau \cdot L(x, v_j) & \text{if } z > W_{j-1}, \end{cases} \tag{5.5}$$

and

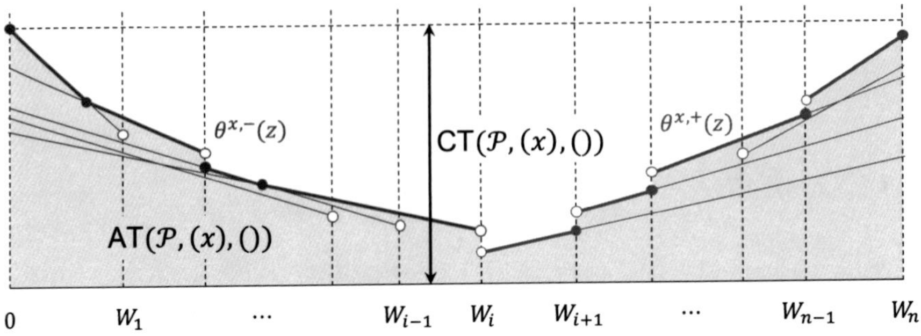

Fig. 5.1 The blue (resp., red) thick half-open segments indicate the function $\theta^{x,+}(z)$ (resp., $\theta^{x,-}(z)$). The gray area indicates $\mathsf{AT}(\mathcal{P}, (x), ())$

$$\theta^{x,-}(z) = \max\{\theta^{x,-,j}(z) \mid j \in [1..i]\}, \tag{5.6}$$

where $\theta^{x,-,j}(z)$ is defined for $j \in [1..i]$ as

$$\theta^{x,-,j}(z) = \begin{cases} \frac{W_j - z}{C_{j,i+1}} + \tau \cdot L(v_j, x) & \text{if } z < W_j, \\ 0 & \text{if } z \geq W_j. \end{cases} \tag{5.7}$$

Then, the aggregate evacuation times for the supply on the right and left sides of x are

$$\int_{W_i}^{W_n} \theta^{x,+}(z)dz \quad \text{and} \quad \int_0^{W_i} \theta^{x,-}(z)dz,$$

respectively. Thus, the aggregate evacuation time $\mathsf{AT}(\mathcal{P}, (x), ())$ is given by

$$\mathsf{AT}(\mathcal{P}, (x), ()) = \int_0^{W_i} \theta^{x,-}(z)dz + \int_{W_i}^{W_n} \theta^{x,+}(z)dz. \tag{5.8}$$

See also Fig. 5.1.

5.3.2 Objective Functions for k-Sink

Let us consider a valid pair consisting of a k-sink $\mathbf{x} = (x_1, \ldots, x_k)$ and a divider $\mathbf{d} = (d_1, \ldots, d_{k-1})$ such that each sink is on an edge excluding its end vertices, that is, $v_{\mathrm{Id}(x_i)} \prec x_i \prec v_{\mathrm{Id}(x_i)+1}$. In this situation, for each $i \in [1..k]$, the first $d_i - W_{\mathrm{Id}(x_i)}$ of supply on the right side of x_i and the first $W_{\mathrm{Id}(x_i)} - d_{i-1}$ of supply on the left side of x_i move to sink x_i. By the argument of the previous section, the evacuation completion times for the supply on the right and left sides of x_i are represented by

$$\theta^{x_i,+}(d_i) \text{ and } \theta^{x_i,-}(d_{i-1}),$$

respectively. Thus, the evacuation completion time $\mathsf{CT}(\mathcal{P}, \mathbf{x}, \mathbf{d})$ is given by

$$\mathsf{CT}(\mathcal{P}, \mathbf{x}, \mathbf{d}) = \max\left\{\theta^{x_i,+}(d_i), \theta^{x_i,-}(d_{i-1}) \mid i \in [1..k]\right\}, \tag{5.9}$$

where $d_0 = 0$ and $d_k = W_n$. The aggregate evacuation times for the supply on the right and left sides of x_i are

$$\int_{W_{\mathrm{Id}(x_i)}}^{d_i} \theta^{x_i,+}(z)dz \quad \text{and} \quad \int_{d_{i-1}}^{W_{\mathrm{Id}(x_i)}} \theta^{x_i,-}(z)dz,$$

respectively. Thus, the aggregate evacuation time $\mathsf{AT}(\mathcal{P}, \mathbf{x}, \mathbf{d})$ is given by

$$\mathsf{AT}(\mathcal{P}, \mathbf{x}, \mathbf{d}) = \sum_{i \in [1..k]} \left(\int_{d_{i-1}}^{W_{\mathrm{Id}(x_i)}} \theta^{x_i,-}(z)dz + \int_{W_{\mathrm{Id}(x_i)}}^{d_i} \theta^{x_i,+}(z)dz \right), \tag{5.10}$$

where $d_0 = 0$ and $d_k = W_n$.

5.4 Minmax k-Sink Problems on Paths

In this section, we consider the minmax k-sink problems on path networks under the confluent flow model, which is precisely defined as

(MINMAX-k-SINK-PATH-CONFLUENT-FLOW)
Input: A dynamic flow path network $\mathcal{P} = (P, \mathbf{w}, \mathbf{c}, \mathbf{l}, \tau)$.
Goal: Find a solution $(\mathbf{x}, \mathbf{d})$ to the problem

$$\begin{array}{lll} \text{min.} & \mathsf{CT}(\mathcal{P}, \mathbf{x}, \mathbf{d}) & \\ \text{s.t.} & \mathbf{x} = (x_1, \ldots, x_k) \in P^k, & x_h \prec x_l \ \forall h < l, \\ & \mathbf{d} = (d_1, \ldots, d_{k-1}) \in \{W_h \mid h \in [1..n]\}^{k-1}, & W_{\mathrm{Id}(x_h)} \le d_h \le W_{\mathrm{Id}(x_{h+1})} \ \forall h. \end{array}$$

For the MINMAX-k-SINK-PATH-CONFLUENT-FLOW problem, [7] reported the following result, which is the best so far:

Theorem 5.1 *([7]) The* MINMAX-k-SINK-PATH-CONFLUENT-FLOW *problem can be solved in $O(\min\{n \log n + k^2 \log^4 n, n \log^3 n\})$ time. Moreover, if the capacities of $\mathcal{P}$ are uniform, the* MINMAX-k-SINK-PATH-CONFLUENT-FLOW *problem can be solved in $O(\min\{n + k^2 \log^2 n, n \log n\})$ time.*

Theorem 5.1 implies that the problem is solved in almost linear time for any k. In [7], two kinds of algorithms are provided: One is an $O(n \log n + k^2 \log^4 n)$ time algorithm based on the *parametric search method*, and the other is an $O(n \log^3 n)$ time algorithm based on the *sorted matrix method*.

Both algorithms require repeatedly solving the problems of locating 1-sink for multiple choices of different subnetworks. Note that the optimal solution for the problem of locating 1-sink on $\mathcal{P}_{i,j}$ is a point x^* that minimizes the following expression over $x \in P_{i,j}$

$$\mathsf{CT}(\mathcal{P}_{i,j}, (x), ()) = \max\left\{\theta^{x,+}(W_j), \theta^{x,-}(W_{i-1})\right\}. \tag{5.11}$$

Both algorithms also require repeatedly performing *feasibility tests* for multiple choices of different subnetworks. We say that $\mathcal{P}_{i,j}$ is (t, q)*-feasible* if and only if the answer of the following decision problem is "yes":

(FEASIBILITY-TEST-FOR-SUBPATH)
Input: A dynamic flow path network $\mathcal{P} = (P, \mathbf{w}, \mathbf{c}, \mathbf{l}, \tau)$, a positive real $t \in \mathbb{R}^+$, integers q, i, j satisfying $q \in [1..k]$ and $i, j \in [1..n]$ with $i < j$.
Goal: Determine whether there exists a pair of vectors $(\mathbf{x}', \mathbf{d}')$ such that

$$\begin{aligned} &\mathsf{CT}(\mathcal{P}_{i,j}, \mathbf{x}', \mathbf{d}') \le t, && \\ &\mathbf{x}' = (x_1, \ldots, x_q) \in P_{i,j}^q, && x_h \prec x_l \ \forall h < l, \\ &\mathbf{d}' = (d_1, \ldots, d_{q-1}) \in \{W_h \mid h \in [i..j]\}^{q-1}, && W_{\mathrm{Id}(x_h)} \le d_h \le W_{\mathrm{Id}(x_{h+1})} \ \forall h. \end{aligned}$$

Note that [7] developed a data structure called the *CUE tree* to efficiently compute $\theta^{x,-}(W_{i-1})$ and $\theta^{x,+}(W_j)$ for any integers $i, j \in [1..n]$ with $i < j$ and any $x \in P_{i,j}$. For the case of general edge capacities, the CUE tree can be constructed in $O(n \log n)$ time, and $\theta^{x,-}(W_{i-1})$ and $\theta^{x,+}(W_j)$ can be computed in $O(\log^2 n)$ time by using the CUE tree. See [7] for more detail.

Lemma 5.1 *([7]) Given a dynamic flow path network $\mathcal{P} = (P, \mathbf{w}, \mathbf{c}, \mathbf{l}, \tau)$ with n vertices, the CUE tree can be constructed in $O(n \log n)$ time. Moreover, if the capacities of $\mathcal{P}$ are uniform, the CUE tree can be constructed in $O(n)$ time.*

Lemma 5.2 *([7]) Given a dynamic flow path network $\mathcal{P} = (P, \mathbf{w}, \mathbf{c}, \mathbf{l}, \tau)$ with n vertices, suppose that the CUE tree is available. Then, for any integers $i, j \in [1..n]$ with $i < j$ and any $x \in P_{i,j}$, $\theta^{x,-}(W_{i-1})$ and $\theta^{x,+}(W_j)$ can be computed in $O(\log^2 n)$ time. Moreover, if the capacities of $\mathcal{P}$ are uniform, $\theta^{x,-}(W_{i-1})$ and $\theta^{x,+}(W_j)$ can be computed in $O(\log n)$ time.*

In the rest of this section, we first describe how feasibility tests are performed in Sect. 5.4.1 and how the 1-sink problem for a subnetwork is solved in Sect. 5.4.2, and then show the frameworks of the parametric search method in Sect. 5.4.3 and the sorted matrix method in Sect. 5.4.4.

5.4.1 Feasibility Test

In [7], to solve the MINMAX-k-SINK-PATH-CONFLUENT-FLOW problem, an algorithm repeatedly tests the (t, q)-feasibility of $\mathcal{P}_{i,j}$ for multiple choices of different 4-tuples (t, q, i, j). Let $\mathsf{CT}_{\mathsf{OPT}}(q, i, j)$ denote the optimal cost for the problem of locating q-sink on $\mathcal{P}_{i,j}$. Then, for a positive real $t \in \mathbb{R}^+$, integers q, i, j satisfying $q \in [1..k]$ and $i, j \in [1..n]$ with $i < j$, $\mathcal{P}_{i,j}$ is (t, q)-feasible if and only if $\mathsf{CT}_{\mathsf{OPT}}(q, i, j) \le t$ holds.

Lemma 5.3 ([7]) *Given a dynamic flow path network $\mathcal{P} = (P, \mathbf{w}, \mathbf{c}, \mathbf{l}, \tau)$ with n vertices, suppose that the CUE tree is available. For integers q, i, j satisfying $q \in [1..k]$ and $i, j \in [1..n]$ with $i < j$, the (t, q)-feasibility of $\mathcal{P}_{i,j}$ can be tested in $O(\min\{n \log^2 n, k \log^3 n\})$ time. Moreover, if the capacities of $\mathcal{P}$ are uniform, the (t, q)-feasibility of $\mathcal{P}_{i,j}$ can be tested in $O(\min\{n, k \log n\})$ time.*

Proof We prove only the case of general capacities. For the case of uniform capacity, see [7].

To determine the (t, q)-feasibility of $\mathcal{P}_{i,j}$, we first place the sinks consecutively from left to right as far to the right as possible. We then compute the maximum integer h such that $\theta^{v_h,-}(W_{i-1}) \le t$ and $\theta^{v_{h+1},-}(W_{i-1}) > t$ holds. Next, we solve

$$\theta^{v_{h+1},-}(W_{i-1}) - \alpha \cdot \tau \ell_h = t \tag{5.12}$$

for α. If $\alpha < 1$, we move the leftmost sink x_1 to the point that divides edge $e_h = (v_h, v_{h+1})$ at a ratio of $1 - \alpha : \alpha$, otherwise we place x_1 at v_h. We then compute the maximum integer l_1 such that $\theta^{x_1,+}(W_{l_1}) \le t$ and $\theta^{x_1,+}(W_{l_1+1}) > t$ holds. We thus determine the maximal subnetwork $\mathcal{P}_{i,l_1}$ such that $\mathsf{CT}_{\mathsf{OPT}}(1, i, l_1) \le t$. In the same manner, we repeatedly isolate the maximal subnetworks $\mathcal{P}_{i,l_1}, \mathcal{P}_{l_1+1,l_2}, \mathcal{P}_{l_2+1,l_3}, \ldots,$ and if the qth subnetwork is found to have $l_q < j$, then $\mathcal{P}_{i,j}$ is not (t, q)-feasible, otherwise it is (t, q)-feasible.

Let us now look at the time complexity. Isolating $\mathcal{P}_{i,l_1}$ consists of (a) computing h, (b) solving the equation for α, and (c) computing l_1. Obviously (b) takes $O(1)$ time. For (a), applying a binary search takes $O(\log^3 n)$ time because we compute $\theta^{v_a,-}(W_{i-1})$ over $a \in [i..j]$ $O(\log n)$ times and each $\theta^{v_a,-}(W_{i-1})$ can be computed in $O(\log^2 n)$ time using the CUE tree by Lemma 5.2. Similarly (c) takes $O(\log^3 n)$ time by binary search. In this way, we can isolate at most q subnetworks in $O(q \log^3 n) = O(k \log^3 n)$ time. However, if we simply scan from left to right instead of using a binary search for (a) and (c), that is, if we compute $\theta^{v_a,-}(W_{i-1})$ for $a = i, i+1, \ldots, h, h+1$ and $\theta^{x_1,-}(W_b)$ for $b = h+1, h+2, \ldots, l_1, l_1+1$, it takes $O((l_1 - i) \log^2 n)$ time to determine P_{i,l_1}. In this way, we can isolate at most p subnetworks in $O((j - i) \log^2 n) = O(n \log^2 n)$ time. □

5.4.2 Solving the 1-Sink Problem

Lemma 5.4 *([7]) Given a dynamic flow path network $\mathcal{P} = (P, \mathbf{w}, \mathbf{c}, \mathbf{l}, \tau)$ with n vertices, suppose that the CUE tree is available. For any integers i, j satisfying $i, j \in [1..n]$ with $i < j$, $\mathsf{CT}_{\mathsf{OPT}}(1, i, j)$ can be computed in $O(\log^3 n)$ time. Moreover, if the capacities of $\mathcal{P}$ are uniform, $\mathsf{CT}_{\mathsf{OPT}}(1, i, j)$ can be computed in $O(\log n)$ time.*

Proof We prove only the case of general capacities. See [7] for the case of uniform capacity.

Recalling Eq. (5.11), we have

$$\begin{aligned} \mathsf{CT}_{\mathsf{OPT}}(1, i, j) &= \min_{x \in P_{i,j}} \mathsf{CT}(\mathcal{P}_{i,j}, (x), ()) \\ &= \min_{x \in P_{i,j}} \max\left\{\theta^{x,+}(W_j), \theta^{x,-}(W_{i-1})\right\}. \end{aligned} \tag{5.13}$$

Because $\theta^{x,+}(W_j)$ and $\theta^{x,-}(W_{i-1})$ are monotonically decreasing and monotonically increasing, respectively, in $x \in P_{i,j}$, if an integer $h \in [i..j]$ satisfies $\theta^{v_h,-}(W_{i-1}) \le \theta^{v_h,+}(W_j)$ and $\theta^{v_{h+1},-}(W_{i-1}) > \theta^{v_{h+1},+}(W_j)$, then there exists x^* that minimizes $\mathsf{CT}(\mathcal{P}_{i,j}, (x), ())$ on edge e_h including v_h and v_{h+1}. We can apply binary search to compute this h, which can be done in $O(\log^3 n)$ time using the CUE tree (see Lemma 5.2). Once h is determined, x^* can be computed as follows: We solve

$$\theta^{v_{h+1},-}(W_{i-1}) - \alpha \cdot \tau\ell_h = \theta^{v_h,+}(W_j) - (1-\alpha) \cdot \tau\ell_h \tag{5.14}$$

for α in $O(1)$ time. If $\alpha \le 0$, let $x^* = v_{h+1}$ and compute $\mathsf{CT}_{\mathsf{OPT}}(1, i, j) = \mathsf{CT}(\mathcal{P}_{i,j}, (v_{h+1}), ())$. If $\alpha \ge 1$, let $x^* = v_h$ and compute $\mathsf{CT}_{\mathsf{OPT}}(1, i, j) = \mathsf{CT}(\mathcal{P}_{i,j}, (v_h), ())$. Otherwise, let x^* be the point that divides edge $e_h = (v_h, v_{h+1})$ at a ratio of $1 - \alpha : \alpha$ and compute $\mathsf{CT}_{\mathsf{OPT}}(1, i, j) = \theta^{v_{h+1},-}(W_{i-1}) - \alpha \cdot \tau\ell_h = \theta^{v_h,+}(W_j) - (1-\alpha) \cdot \tau\ell_h$. Using the CUE tree, we can compute these values in $O(\log^2 n)$ time. Thus, $\mathsf{CT}_{\mathsf{OPT}}(1, i, j)$ can be computed in $O(\log^3 n) + O(1) + O(\log^2 n) = O(\log^3 n)$ time. □

5.4.3 Parametric Search Method

In the parametric search method, we first compute the maximum integer i_1 such that $\mathcal{P}_{i_1+1,n}$ is not $(\mathsf{CT}_{\mathsf{OPT}}(1, 1, i_1), k-1)$-feasible and store $t_1 = \mathsf{CT}_{\mathsf{OPT}}(1, 1, i_1 + 1)$ as a feasible value. Note that $t^* = \mathsf{CT}_{\mathsf{OPT}}(k, 1, n)$ satisfies $\mathsf{CT}_{\mathsf{OPT}}(1, 1, i_1) < t^* \le t_1$. To compute i_1, we apply binary search by executing $O(\log n)$ tests for $(\mathsf{CT}_{\mathsf{OPT}}(1, 1, a), k-1)$-feasibility of $\mathcal{P}_{a+1,n}$ over $1 \le a \le n$. For an integer a, we can compute $\mathsf{CT}_{\mathsf{OPT}}(1, 1, a)$ in $O(\log^3 n)$ time by Lemma 5.4. Also, by Lemma 5.3, we can test whether $\mathcal{P}_{a+1,n}$ is $(\mathsf{CT}_{\mathsf{OPT}}(1, 1, a), k-1)$-feasible in $O(k \log^3 n)$ time. Summarizing these arguments, we can compute i_1 and t_1 in $\{O(\log^3 n) + O(k \log^3 n)\}$

$\times\ O(\log n) = O(k \log^4 n)$ time. Next, we compute the maximum integer i_2 such that $\mathcal{P}_{i_2+1,n}$ is not $(\mathsf{CT}_{\mathsf{OPT}}(1, i_1+1, i_2), k-2)$-feasible and store $t_2 = \mathsf{CT}_{\mathsf{OPT}}(1, i_1 + 1, i_2 + 1)$ as a feasible value, which can be done in $O(k \log^4 n)$ time in the same manner as in the computation of (i_1, t_1). Sequentially, we determine $(i_3, t_3), \ldots, (i_{k-1}, t_{k-1})$ in $(k-3) \times O(k \log^4 n)$ time and eventually compute $t_k = \mathsf{CT}_{\mathsf{OPT}}(1, i_{k-1} + 1, n)$ in $O(\log^3 n)$ time. Note that $t^* = \min\{t_i \mid i = 1, 2, \ldots, k\}$ holds, which can be computed in $O(k)$ time. We then execute a (t^*, k)-feasibility test for $\mathcal{P}$ in $O(k \log^3 n)$ time, so that the optimal k-sink is obtained. We thus see that the problem can be solved in $(k-1) \times O(k \log^4 n) + O(\log^3 n) + O(k) + O(k \log^3 n) = O(k^2 \log^4 n)$ time once the CUE tree is constructed. Since it takes $O(n \log n)$ time to construct the CUE tree by Lemma 5.1, the total time complexity is $O(n \log n + k^2 \log^4 n)$.

For the case of uniform capacity, the same argument holds. Applying Lemmas 5.1, 5.3, and 5.4, we have a total time complexity of $O(n + k^2 \log^2 n)$.

5.4.4 Sorted Matrix Method

A matrix A is *sorted* if and only if each row and column of A is sorted in non-decreasing order. The sorted matrix method is based on the following lemma shown in [11]:

Lemma 5.5 *([11]) Consider a minimization problem Q with an instance $\mathcal{I}$ of size n. Suppose that the feasibility of any value for $\mathcal{I}$ can be tested in $g(n)$ time. Let A be an $n \times n$ sorted matrix such that each element can be computed in $f(n)$ time. Then, the minimum element of A that is feasible for Q can be found in $O(nf(n) + g(n) \log n)$ time.*

In [7], an $n \times n$ matrix A is defined such that the (i, j)th entry of A is given by

$$A[i, j] = \begin{cases} \mathsf{CT}_{\mathsf{OPT}}(1, n-i+1, j) & \text{if } n-i+1 \le j \\ 0 & \text{otherwise.} \end{cases} \tag{5.15}$$

Note that we do not actually compute all the elements of A, but compute the element $A[i, j]$ on demand as needed.

Let us confirm that matrix A is sorted. It is also clear that matrix A includes $\mathsf{CT}_{\mathsf{OPT}}(1, l, r)$ for every pair of integers (l, r) such that $l, r \in [1..n]$ with $l < r$. In addition, there exists a pair (l, r) such that $\mathsf{CT}_{\mathsf{OPT}}(1, l, r) = \mathsf{CT}_{\mathsf{OPT}}(k, 1, n)$. These facts imply that the minimum element $A[i, j]$ such that $\mathcal{P}$ is $(A[i, j], k)$-feasible is $\mathsf{CT}_{\mathsf{OPT}}(k, 1, n)$, and hence we can apply Lemma 5.5 to solve the MINMAX- k- SINK-PATH- CONFLUENT- FLOW problem as follows: Once the CUE tree is constructed, we have $f(n) = O(\log^3 n)$ by Lemma 5.4 and $g(n) = O(n \log^2 n)$ by Lemma 5.3, so the problem can be solved in $O(n \log^3 n)$ time. Because it takes $O(n \log n)$ time to construct the CUE tree by Lemma 5.1, the total time complexity is $O(n \log n) + O(n \log^3 n) = O(n \log^3 n)$.

For the case of uniform capacity, the same argument holds. Applying Lemmas 5.1, 5.3, and 5.4, we have a total time complexity of $O(n \log n)$.

5.5 Minsum k-Sink Problems on Paths

In this section, our task is to find a valid pair $(\mathbf{x}, \mathbf{d})$ that minimizes the aggregate evacuation time $\mathsf{AT}(\mathcal{P}, \mathbf{x}, \mathbf{d})$. This task can be precisely represented as follows:

(MINSUM-k-SINK-PATH)
Input: A dynamic flow path network $\mathcal{P} = (P, \mathbf{w}, \mathbf{c}, \mathbf{l}, \tau)$.
Goal: Find a solution $(\mathbf{x}, \mathbf{d})$ to the problem

$$\begin{array}{lll} \text{min.} & \mathsf{AT}(\mathcal{P}, \mathbf{x}, \mathbf{d}) & \\ \text{s.t.} & \mathbf{x} = (x_1, \ldots, x_k) \in P^k, & x_h \prec x_l \ \forall h < l, \\ & \mathbf{d} = (d_1, \ldots, d_{k-1}) \in \mathbb{R}^{k-1}, & W_{\mathrm{Id}(x_h)} \leq d_h \leq W_{\mathrm{Id}(x_{h+1})} \ \forall h. \end{array}$$

(MINSUM-k-SINK-PATH-CONFLUENT-FLOW)
Input: A dynamic flow path network $\mathcal{P} = (P, \mathbf{w}, \mathbf{c}, \mathbf{l}, \tau)$.
Goal: Find a solution $(\mathbf{x}, \mathbf{d})$ to the problem

$$\begin{array}{lll} \text{min.} & \mathsf{AT}(\mathcal{P}, \mathbf{x}, \mathbf{d}) & \\ \text{s.t.} & \mathbf{x} = (x_1, \ldots, x_k) \in P^k, & x_h \prec x_l \ \forall h < l, \\ & \mathbf{d} = (d_1, \ldots, d_{k-1}) \in \{W_h \mid h \in [1..n]\}^{k-1}, & W_{\mathrm{Id}(x_h)} \leq d_h \leq W_{\mathrm{Id}(x_{h+1})} \ \forall h. \end{array}$$

For the MINSUM-k-SINK-PATH problem, [16] reported the following result, which is the best so far:

Theorem 5.2 *([16]) The MINSUM-k-SINK-PATH/MINSUM-k-SINK-PATH-CONFLUENT-FLOW problems can be solved in* $\min\{O(kn \log^3 n), n2^{O(\sqrt{\log k \log \log n})} \log^3 n\}$ *time. Moreover, if the capacities of $\mathcal{P}$ are uniform, then both the problems can be solved in* $\min\{O(kn \log^2 n), n2^{O(\sqrt{\log k \log \log n})} \log^2 n\}$ *time.*

For the confluent flow model, it was shown in [6, 15] that for the minsum k-sink problems, there exists an optimal k-sink such that all of the k sinks are at vertices. [16] extended this fact to the non-confluent flow model.

Lemma 5.6 *([6, 15, 16]) For the minsum k-sink problem in a dynamic flow path network, there exists an optimal k-sink such that all of the k sinks are at vertices under the confluent/non-confluent flow model.*

Lemma 5.6 implies that it is sufficient to consider only the case where every sink is at a vertex. Thus, we suppose $\mathbf{x} = (x_1, \ldots, x_k) \in V^k$, where $x_i \prec x_j$ for $i < j$.

The fundamental idea of [16] for solving the MINSUM-k-SINK-PATH problem is to reduce it to the *minimum k-link path problem*. In the minimum k-link path problem, we are given a weighted complete directed acyclic graph (DAG) $G = (V', E', w')$ with $V' = \{v'_i \mid i \in [1..n]\}$ and $E' = \{(v'_i, v'_j) \mid i, j \in [1..n], i < j\}$. Each edge (v'_i, v'_j) is associated with a weight $w'(i, j)$. A *k-link* path is a path that contains exactly k edges. The task is to find a k-link path from v'_1 to v'_n that minimizes the sum of weights of k edges. The minimum k-link path problem is represented as follows:

(MINIMUM-k-LINK-PATH)
Input: A weighted complete DAG $G = (V', E', w')$.
Goal: Find a k-link path $(v'_{a_0} = v'_1, v'_{a_1}, v'_{a_2}, \ldots, v'_{a_{k-1}}, v'_{a_k} = v'_n)$ from v'_1 to v'_n.

$$\begin{array}{lll} \text{min.} & \displaystyle\sum_{i=1}^{k} w'(a_{i-1}, a_i) & \\ \text{s.t.} & a_i \in [0..n], & a_0 = 1, a_k = n, a_h < a_l \ \forall h < \ell. \end{array}$$

Schieber [19] showed that the MINIMUM-k-LINK-PATH can be solved in almost linear time[3] regardless of k if the weight function w' satisfies the *concave Monge property*.

Definition 5.1 *(Concave Monge property)* We say that a function $f : \mathbb{Z} \times \mathbb{Z} \to \mathbb{R}$ satisfies the concave Monge property if for any integers i, j with $i + 1 < j$, $f(i, j) + f(i + 1, j + 1) \leq f(i + 1, j) + f(i, j + 1)$ holds.

Lemma 5.7 *([19]) Given a weighted complete DAG with n vertices, if the weight function satisfies the concave Monge property, the* MINIMUM-k-LINK-PATH *can be solved in* $\min\{O(kn), n2^{O(\sqrt{\log k \log \log n})}\}$ *time.*

Higashikawa et al. [16] presented a reduction from MINSUM-k-SINK-PATH to MINIMUM-$(k + 1)$-LINK-PATH such that the weight function w' satisfies the concave Monge property. Let a dynamic flow path network $\mathcal{P} = (P = (V, E), \mathbf{w}, \mathbf{c}, \mathbf{l}, \tau)$ with n vertices be an instance of MINSUM-k-SINK-PATH. We prepare a weighted complete DAG $G = (V', E', w')$ with $n + 2$ vertices, where $V' = \{v'_i \mid i \in [0..n + 1]\}$ and $E' = \{(v'_i, v'_j) \mid i, j \in [0..n + 1], i < j\}$. We set the weight function w' as

$$w'(i, j) = \begin{cases} \mathsf{AT}_{\mathsf{OPT}}(i, j) & i, j \in [1..n], i < j, \\ \mathsf{AT}(\mathcal{P}_{i,n}, (v_i), ()) & i \in [1..n] \text{ and } j = n + 1, \\ \mathsf{AT}(\mathcal{P}_{1,j}, (v_j), ()) & i = 0 \text{ and } j \in [1..n], \\ \infty & i = 0 \text{ and } j = n + 1, \end{cases} \tag{5.16}$$

where $\mathsf{AT}_{\mathsf{OPT}}(i, j)$ is the optimal aggregate evacuation time required to move all the supply between v_i and v_j to one of two sinks v_i or v_j. On the weighted complete DAG G constructed as above, let us consider a $(k + 1)$-link path $(v'_{a_0} =$

[3] Note that we assume that the weight function w' is not given explicitly, but that a value $w'(i, j)$ can be obtained in constant time whenever required.

$v'_0, v'_{a_1}, \ldots, v'_{a_k}, v'_{a_{k+1}} = v'_{n+1})$ from v'_0 to v'_{n+1}, where $a_1, \ldots, a_k$ are integers satisfying $0 < a_1 < a_2 < \cdots < a_k < n+1$. The sum of weights of this $(k+1)$-link path is

$$\sum_{i=0}^{k} w'(a_i, a_{i+1}) = \mathsf{AT}(\mathcal{P}_{1,a_1}, (v_{a_1}), ()) + \sum_{i=1}^{k-1} \mathsf{AT}_{\mathsf{OPT}}(a_i, a_{i+1}) + \mathsf{AT}(\mathcal{P}_{a_k,n}, (v_{a_k}), ()).$$

This value is equivalent to $\min_{\mathbf{d}} \mathsf{AT}(\mathcal{P}, \mathbf{x}, \mathbf{d})$ for a k-sink $\mathbf{x} = (v_{a_1}, v_{a_2}, \ldots, v_{a_k})$, which implies that a minimum $(k+1)$-link path on G corresponds to an optimal k-sink location for a dynamic flow path network $\mathcal{P}$.

Let us consider the following subtasks:

(MINSUM-FLOW-FOR-SUBPATH)
Input: A dynamic flow path network $\mathcal{P} = (P, \mathbf{w}, \mathbf{c}, \mathbf{l}, \tau)$, integers $i, j \in [1..n]$ with $i < j$.
Goal: Find a value d such that

$$\begin{array}{ll} \text{min.} & \mathsf{AT}(\mathcal{P}_{i,j}, \mathbf{x} = (v_i, v_j), \mathbf{d} = (d)) \\ \text{s.t.} & W_i \le d \le W_{j-1}. \end{array}$$

(MINSUM-FLOW-FOR-SUBPATH-CONFLUENT-FLOW)
Input: A dynamic flow path network $\mathcal{P} = (P, \mathbf{w}, \mathbf{c}, \mathbf{l}, \tau)$, integers $i, j \in [1..n]$ with $i < j$.
Goal: Find a value d such that

$$\begin{array}{ll} \text{min.} & \mathsf{AT}(\mathcal{P}_{i,j}, \mathbf{x} = (v_i, v_j), \mathbf{d} = (d)) \\ \text{s.t.} & d \in \{W_h \mid h \in [i..j-1]\}. \end{array}$$

Note that [16] developed a data structure to efficiently solve both of these problems. This data structure can be constructed in $O(n \log^2 n)$ time and can be used to solve MINSUM-FLOW-FOR-SUBPATH/MINSUM-FLOW-FOR-SUBPATH-CONFLUENT-FLOW in $O(\log^3 n)$ time. See [16] for details.

Lemma 5.8 ([16]) *For a given dynamic flow path network $\mathcal{P}$ with n vertices, there exists a segment tree $\mathcal{T}$ that satisfies the following conditions:*

1. $\mathcal{T}$ can be constructed in $O(n \log^2 n)$ time.
2. MINSUM-FLOW-FOR-SUBPATH/MINSUM-FLOW-FOR-SUBPATH-CONFLUENT-FLOW can be solved in $O(\log^3 n)$ time by using $\mathcal{T}$.
3. If the capacities of $\mathcal{P}$ are uniform, then MINSUM-FLOW-FOR-SUBPATH/MINSUM-FLOW-FOR-SUBPATH-CONFLUENT-FLOW can be solved in $O(\log^2 n)$ time by using $\mathcal{T}$.

Because w' satisfies the concave Monge property (see Sect. 5.5.2), Lemmas 5.7 and 5.8 lead to Theorem 5.2.

In the rest of this section, we first observe the properties of the aggregate evacuation time in Sect. 5.5.1 and then show that the weighted function w' obtained by the reduction satisfies the concave Monge property in Sect. 5.5.2.

5.5.1 Property of Aggregate Evacuation Time

Recalling that we consider only the case where every sink is at a vertex, we simply use $\theta^{i,+}(z)$ and $\theta^{i,-}(z)$ instead of $\theta^{v_i,+}(z)$ and $\theta^{v_i,+}(z)$, respectively.

We next give the general form of the aggregate evacuation time. Let $\phi^{i,+}(z)$ denote the aggregate evacuation time when the first $z - W_i$ of supply on the right side of v_i flows to sink v_i. Similarly, we denote by $\phi^{i,-}(z)$ the aggregate evacuation time when the first $W_{i-1} - z$ of supply on the left side of v_i flows to sink v_i. Therefore, we have

$$\phi^{i,+}(z) = \int_{W_i}^{z} \theta^{i,+}(t)dt = \int_{0}^{z} \theta^{i,+}(t)dt \quad \text{and}$$
$$\phi^{i,-}(z) = \int_{z}^{W_{i-1}} \theta^{i,-}(t)dt = \int_{z}^{W_n} \theta^{i,-}(t)dt = -\int_{W_n}^{z} \theta^{i,-}(t)dt \qquad (5.17)$$

(see Fig. 5.2). For $i, j \in [1..n]$ with $i < j$, we define

$$\phi^{i,j}(z) = \phi^{i,+}(z) + \phi^{j,-}(z) = \int_{0}^{z} \theta^{i,+}(t)dt + \int_{z}^{W_n} \theta^{j,-}(t)dt \qquad (5.18)$$

for $z \in [W_i, W_{j-1}]$.

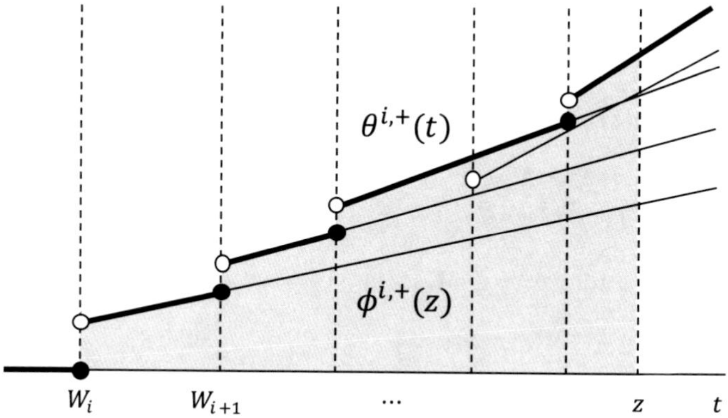

Fig. 5.2 Thick half-open segments represent the function $\theta^{i,+}(t)$ and the gray area represents $\phi^{i,+}(z)$ for some $z > W_i$

Suppose that we are given a k-sink $\mathbf{x} = (x_1, \ldots, x_k) \in V^k$ and a divider $\mathbf{d} = (d_1, \ldots, d_{k-1})$. Recalling the definition of $\mathrm{Id}(p)$ for $p \in P$, we have $x_i = v_{\mathrm{Id}(x_i)}$ for all $i \in [1..k]$. Because each sink is at a vertex, by simply modifying the integration intervals in Eq. (5.10), the aggregate evacuation time $\mathsf{AT}(\mathcal{P}, \mathbf{x}, \mathbf{d})$ is given by

$$\begin{aligned}\mathsf{AT}(\mathcal{P}, \mathbf{x}, \mathbf{d}) &= \sum_{i\in[1..k]} \left(\int_{d_{i-1}}^{W_{\mathrm{Id}(x_i)-1}} \theta^{x_i,-}(z)dz + \int_{W_{\mathrm{Id}(x_i)}}^{d_i} \theta^{x_i,+}(z)dz \right) \\ &= \sum_{i\in[1..k]} \left(\int_{d_{i-1}}^{W_{\mathrm{Id}(x_i)-1}} \theta^{\mathrm{Id}(x_i),-}(z)dz + \int_{W_{\mathrm{Id}(x_i)}}^{d_i} \theta^{\mathrm{Id}(x_i),+}(z)dz \right). \end{aligned} \quad (5.19)$$

By Eqs. (5.17), (5.18) and (5.19), we have

$$\begin{aligned}\mathsf{AT}(\mathcal{P}, \mathbf{x}, \mathbf{d}) &= \sum_{i\in[1..k]} \left(\int_{d_{i-1}}^{W_{\mathrm{Id}(x_i)-1}} \theta^{\mathrm{Id}(x_i),-}(z)dz + \int_{W_{\mathrm{Id}(x_i)}}^{d_i} \theta^{\mathrm{Id}(x_i),+}(z)dz \right) \\ &= \sum_{i\in[1..k]} \left(\phi^{\mathrm{Id}(x_i),-}(d_{i-1}) + \phi^{\mathrm{Id}(x_i),+}(d_i) \right) \\ &= \phi^{\mathrm{Id}(x_1),-}(0) + \sum_{i\in[1..k-1]} \phi^{\mathrm{Id}(x_i),\mathrm{Id}(x_{i+1})}(d_i) + \phi^{\mathrm{Id}(x_k),+}(W_n). \end{aligned} \quad (5.20)$$

In the rest of this section, we show the important properties of $\phi^{i,j}(z)$. Let us first confirm that by Eq. (5.17), both $\phi^{i,+}(z)$ and $\phi^{j,-}(z)$ are convex in z since $\theta^{i,+}(z)$ and $-\theta^{j,-}(z)$ are non-decreasing in z, and therefore $\phi^{i,j}(z)$ is convex in z. We have a more useful lemma that gives the conditions for the minimizer of $\phi^{i,j}(z)$.

Lemma 5.9 ([16]) *For any $i, j \in [1..n]$ with $i < j$, there uniquely exists*

$$z^* \in \operatorname*{arg\,min}_{z\in[W_i, W_{j-1}]} \max\{\theta^{i,+}(z), \theta^{j,-}(z)\}.$$

Furthermore, $\phi^{i,j}(z)$ is minimized on $[W_i, W_{j-1}]$ when $z = z^*$.

Proof By Eqs. (5.4) and (5.5), $\theta^{i,+}(z)$ is strictly increasing in $z \in [W_i, W_n]$. Similarly, by Eqs. (5.6) and (5.7), $\theta^{j,-}(z)$ is strictly decreasing in $z \in [0, W_{j-1}]$. Thus, there uniquely exists $z^* \in [W_i, W_{j-1}]$.

We then see that for any $z' \in [W_i, z^*]$,

$$\begin{aligned}\phi^{i,j}(z^*) - \phi^{i,j}(z') &= \phi^{i,+}(z^*) + \phi^{j,-}(z^*) - (\phi^{i,+}(z') + \phi^{j,-}(z')) \\ &= \int_{z'}^{z^*} \theta^{i,+}(t)dt - \int_{z'}^{z^*} \theta^{j,-}(t)dt \\ &= \int_{z'}^{z^*} \left\{\theta^{i,+}(t) - \theta^{j,-}(t)\right\} dt \le 0,\end{aligned}$$

and for any $z'' \in [z^*, W_{j-1}]$,

$$\begin{aligned}\phi^{i,j}(z^*) - \phi^{i,j}(z'') &= \phi^{i,+}(z^*) + \phi^{j,-}(z^*) - (\phi^{i,+}(z'') + \phi^{j,-}(z')) \\ &= \int_{z''}^{z^*} \theta^{i,+}(t)dt - \int_{z''}^{z^*} \theta^{j,-}(t)dt \\ &= -\int_{z^*}^{z''} \left\{\theta^{i,+}(t) - \theta^{j,-}(t)\right\} dt \le 0,\end{aligned}$$

which imply that z^* minimizes $\phi^{i,j}(z)$ on $[W_i, W_{j-1}]$. □

In the following sections, this z^* is called the *pseudo-intersection point*[4] of $\theta^{i,+}(z)$ and $\theta^{j,-}(z)$.

5.5.2 Concave Monge Property

We now show that the function w' defined in Eq. (5.16) satisfies the concave Monge property under the non-confluent flow model. We omit the proof for the confluent flow model, since the proof can be constructed similarly to the one for the confluent flow model. See [16] for details.

Let us give some observations of $\mathsf{AT}_{\mathsf{OPT}}(i, j)$. Under the non-confluent flow model, for any $i, j \in [1..n]$ with $i < j$, $\mathsf{AT}_{\mathsf{OPT}}(i, j) = \min_{z \in [W_i, W_{j-1}]} \phi^{i,j}(z)$. Lemma 5.9 implies that $\phi^{i,j}(z)$ on $[W_i, W_{j-1}]$ is minimized when z is the pseudo-intersection point of $\theta^{i,+}(z)$ and $\theta^{j,-}(z)$. For any $i, j \in [1..n]$ with $i < j$, let $\alpha^{i,j}$ denote the pseudo-intersection point of $\theta^{i,+}(z)$ and $\theta^{j,-}(z)$.

Thus, we have

$$\mathsf{AT}_{\mathsf{OPT}}(i, j) = \phi^{i,j}(\alpha^{i,j}) = \int_0^{\alpha^{i,j}} \theta^{i,+}(z)dz + \int_{\alpha^{i,j}}^{W_n} \theta^{j,-}(z)dz. \qquad (5.21)$$

We give the following two lemmas.

Lemma 5.10 *([16]) For any integer* $i \in [1..n-1]$ *and any* $z \in [0, W_n]$,

$$\theta^{i,+}(z) \ge \theta^{i+1,+}(z) \text{ and } \theta^{i,-}(z) \le \theta^{i+1,-}(z)$$

hold.

Proof We give the proof of only $\theta^{i,+}(z) \ge \theta^{i+1,+}(z)$ because the other case can be proved in a similar way. By Eq. (5.5), for any $j \in [i+2..n]$, we have

[4] The reason why we use the term "pseudo-intersection" is that the two functions $\theta^{i,+}(z)$ and $\theta^{j,-}(z)$ are not continuous, in general, whereas the "intersection" is usually defined for continuous functions.

$$\theta^{i,+,j}(z) - \theta^{i+1,+,j}(z) = \begin{cases} 0 & \text{if } z \le W_{j-1}, \\ \frac{z-W_{j-1}}{C_{i,j}} + \tau \cdot L_{i,j} & \text{if } W_{j-1} < z \le W_j, \\ \frac{(z-W_{j-1})(C_{i+1,j}-C_{i,j})}{C_{i,j}C_{i+1,j}} + \tau \cdot \ell_i & \text{if } z > W_j. \end{cases}$$

Because $C_{i+1,j} - C_{i,j} = \min\{c_h \mid h \in [i+1..j-1]\} - \min\{c_h \mid h \in [i..j-1]\} \ge 0$, $\theta^{i,+,j}(z) - \theta^{i+1,+,j}(z) \ge 0$ holds. Therefore, we have $\theta^{i,+}(z) \ge \theta^{i+1,+}(z)$ since $\theta^{i,+}(z) = \max\{\theta^{i,+,j}(z) \mid j \in [i+1..n]\}$ by Eq. (5.4). □

Lemma 5.11 *([16]) For any $i, j \in [1..n]$ with $i < j$,*

$$\alpha^{i,j} \le \alpha^{i+1,j} \le \alpha^{i+1,j+1} \text{ and } \alpha^{i,j} \le \alpha^{i,j+1} \le \alpha^{i+1,j+1}$$

hold.

Proof We give the proof of only $\alpha^{i,j} \le \alpha^{i+1,j}$ because the other cases can be proved in a similar way. For any $i, j \in [1..n]$ with $i < j$ and positive constant ϵ, we have

$$\theta^{i+1,+}(\alpha^{i,j} - \epsilon) \le \theta^{i,+}(\alpha^{i,j} - \epsilon) < \theta^{j,-}(\alpha^{i,j} - \epsilon)$$

because $\theta^{i,+}(z) \ge \theta^{i+1,+}(z)$ holds by Lemma 5.10 and $\theta^{j,-}(z)$ is a non-increasing function. This implies that $\alpha^{i,j} \le \alpha^{i+1,j}$ holds, which completes the proof. □

Let us show that the function w' defined in Eq. (5.16) satisfies the concave Monge property under the non-confluent flow model.

Lemma 5.12 *([16]) The weight function w' defined in Eq. (5.16) satisfies the concave Monge property under the non-confluent flow model.*

Proof If we show that, for any $i, j \in [0..n]$ with $i < j$,

$$w'(i, j) + w'(i+1, j+1) \le w'(i, j+1) + w'(i+1, j) \tag{5.22}$$

holds, thus completing the proof. Note that condition (5.22) holds for $i = 0$ and $j = n$, because the right-hand side of (5.22) contains $w'(0, n+1) = \infty$ and other terms are finite. Let us consider the following three cases: (1) $0 < i < j < n$, (2) $i = 0$ and $0 < j < n$, (3) $0 < i < n$ and $j = n$.

Case 1. Consider the case of $0 < i < j < n$. By Eq. (5.16), for any $(i', j') \in \{(i, j), (i, j+1), (i+1, j), (i+1, j+1)\}$, we have $w'(i', j') = \mathsf{AT}_{\mathsf{OPT}}(i', j')$. Recall that $\alpha^{i,j}$ is the pseudo-intersection point of $\theta^{i,+}(z)$ and $\theta^{j,-}(z)$, and we have

$$w'(i, j) = \mathsf{AT}_{\mathsf{OPT}}(i, j) = \phi^{i,j}(\alpha^{i,j}) = \int_0^{\alpha^{i,j}} \theta^{i,+}(z)dz + \int_{\alpha^{i,j}}^{W_n} \theta^{j,-}(z)dz. \tag{5.23}$$

For any $i, j \in [1..n-1]$ with $i < j$, Eq. (5.23) and Lemma 5.11 state that

$$
\begin{aligned}
& w'(i, j+1) + w'(i+1, j) - w'(i, j) - w'(i+1, j+1) \\
&= \phi^{i,j+1}(\alpha^{i,j+1}) + \phi^{i+1,j}(\alpha^{i+1,j}) - \phi^{i,j}(\alpha^{i,j}) - \phi^{i+1,j+1}(\alpha^{i+1,j+1}) \\
&= \int_{\alpha^{i,j}}^{\alpha^{i,j+1}} \theta^{i,+}(z)dz + \int_{\alpha^{i,j+1}}^{\alpha^{i+1,j+1}} \theta^{j+1,-}(z)dz \\
&\quad - \int_{\alpha^{i,j}}^{\alpha^{i+1,j}} \theta^{j,-}(z)dz - \int_{\alpha^{i+1,j}}^{\alpha^{i+1,j+1}} \theta^{i+1,+}(z)dz. \qquad (5.24)
\end{aligned}
$$

Now, we show that for any $z \in [\alpha^{i,j}, \alpha^{i+1,j+1})$,

$$\min\{\theta^{i,+}(z), \theta^{j+1,-}(z)\} \geq \max\{\theta^{j,-}(z), \theta^{i+1,+}(z)\}$$

holds. First, for any $z \in [0, W_n]$, $\theta^{i,+}(z) \geq \theta^{i+1,+}(z)$ and $\theta^{j,-}(z) \leq \theta^{j+1,-}(z)$ hold by Lemma 5.10. For any $z \geq \alpha^{i,j}$, $\theta^{i,+}(z) \geq \theta^{j,-}(z)$ holds because $\alpha^{i,j}$ is the pseudo-intersection point of $\theta^{i,+}(z)$ and $\theta^{j,-}(z)$. Similarly, for any $z < \alpha^{i+1,j+1}$, we have $\theta^{i+1,+}(z) \leq \theta^{j+1,-}(z)$. Therefore, for any $z \in [\alpha^{i,j}, \alpha^{i+1,j+1})$, $\min\{\theta^{i,+}(z), \theta^{j+1,-}(z)\} \geq \max\{\theta^{j,-}(z), \theta^{i+1,+}(z)\}$ holds.

Thus, Eq. (5.24) continues as

$$
\begin{aligned}
& w'(i, j+1) + w'(i+1, j) - w'(i, j) - w'(i+1, j+1) \\
\geq & \int_{\alpha^{i,j}}^{\alpha^{i+1,j+1}} \min\{\theta^{i,+}(z), \theta^{j+1,-}(z)\} - \int_{\alpha^{i,j}}^{\alpha^{i+1,j+1}} \max\{\theta^{j,-}(z), \theta^{i+1,+}(z)\}dz \\
\geq & \ 0,
\end{aligned}
$$

and then condition (5.22) holds for any i, j with $0 < i < j < n$.

Case 2. Consider the case of $i = 0$ and $j \in [1..n-1]$. Recall that $w'(0, j) = \phi^{j,-}(0)$ and $w'(0, j+1) = \phi^{j+1,-}(0)$ by Eq. (5.16). In this case, we have

$$
\begin{aligned}
& w'(0, j+1) + w'(1, j) - w'(0, j) - w'(1, j+1) \\
&= \phi^{j+1,-}(0) + \phi^{1,j}(\alpha^{1,j}) - \phi^{j,-}(0) - \phi^{1,j+1}(\alpha^{1,j+1}) \\
&= \int_0^{W_n} \theta^{j+1,-}(z)dz + \int_0^{\alpha^{1,j}} \theta^{1,+}(z)dz + \int_{\alpha^{1,j}}^{W_n} \theta^{j,-}(z)dz \\
&\quad - \int_0^{W_n} \theta^{j,-}(z)dz - \int_0^{\alpha^{1,j+1}} \theta^{1,+}(z)dz - \int_{\alpha^{1,j+1}}^{W_n} \theta^{j+1,-}(z)dz \\
&= \int_0^{\alpha^{1,j+1}} \theta^{j+1,-}(z)dz - \int_0^{\alpha^{1,j}} \theta^{j,-}(z)dz - \int_{\alpha^{1,j}}^{\alpha^{1,j+1}} \theta^{1,+}(z)dz,
\end{aligned}
$$

where the last equality uses $\alpha^{1,j} \leq \alpha^{1,j+1}$ by Lemma 5.11. By Lemma 5.10, we have $\theta^{j+1,-}(z) \geq \theta^{j,-}(z)$ for any $z \in [0, W_n]$. Using the same argument as in the previous case, for any $z < \alpha^{1,j+1}$, we have $\theta^{1,+}(z) < \theta^{j+1,-}(z)$. Thus, we have

$$
\begin{aligned}
& w'(0, j+1) + w'(1, j) - w'(0, j) - w'(1, j+1) \\
&= \int_0^{\alpha^{1,j+1}} \theta^{j+1,-}(z)dz - \int_0^{\alpha^{1,j}} \theta^{j,-}(z)dz - \int_{\alpha^{1,j}}^{\alpha^{1,j+1}} \theta^{1,+}(z)dz \\
&= \int_0^{\alpha^{1,j}} \left\{\theta^{j+1,-}(z) - \theta^{j,-}(z)\right\} dz + \int_{\alpha^{1,j}}^{\alpha^{1,j+1}} \left\{\theta^{j+1,-}(z) - \theta^{1,+}(z)\right\} dz \geq 0.
\end{aligned}
$$

Case 3. Consider the case of $j = n$ and $i \in [1..n-1]$. Recall that $w'(i, n+1) = \phi^{i,+}(W_n)$ and $w'(i+1, n+1) = \phi^{i+1,+}(W_n)$ by Eq. (5.16). Similar to the second case, we use the facts that $\alpha^{i,n} \leq \alpha^{i+1,n}$ by Lemma 5.11, $\theta^{i,+}(z) \geq \theta^{i+1,+}(z)$ for any $z \in [0, W_n]$ by Lemma 5.10, and $\theta^{i,+}(z) \geq \theta^{n,-}(z)$ for any $z \geq \alpha^{i,n}$. Then, we have

$$
\begin{aligned}
& w'(i, n+1) + w'(i+1, n) - w'(i, n) - w'(i, n+1) \\
&= \phi^{i,+}(W_n) + \phi^{i+1,n}(\alpha^{i+1,n}) - \phi^{i,n}(\alpha^{i,n}) - \phi^{i+1,+}(W_n) \\
&= \int_0^{W_n} \theta^{i,+}(z)dz + \int_0^{\alpha^{i+1,n}} \theta^{i+1,+}(z)dz + \int_{\alpha^{i+1,n}}^{W_n} \theta^{n,-}(z)dz \\
&\qquad - \int_0^{\alpha^{i,n}} \theta^{i,+}(z)dz - \int_{\alpha^{i,n}}^{W_n} \theta^{n,-}(z)dz - \int_0^{W_n} \theta^{i+1,+}(z)dz \\
&= \int_{\alpha^{i,n}}^{W_n} \theta^{i,+}(z)dz - \int_{\alpha^{i,n}}^{\alpha^{i+1,n}} \theta^{n,-}(z)dz - \int_{\alpha^{i+1,n}}^{W_n} \theta^{i+1,+}(z)dz \\
&= \int_{\alpha^{i,n}}^{\alpha^{i+1,n}} \left\{\theta^{i,+}(z) - \theta^{n,-}(z)\right\} dz + \int_{\alpha^{i+1,n}}^{W_n} \left\{\theta^{i,+}(z) - \theta^{i+1,+}(z)\right\} dz \geq 0.
\end{aligned}
$$

Thus, for any $i, j \in [0..n]$ with $i < j$, condition (5.22) holds. This implies that the function w' satisfies the concave Monge condition. □

Acknowledgements We thank Robert Benkoczi, Binay Bhattacharya, Mordecai J. Golin, and Tsunehiko Kameda for many helpful discussions on this topic. This work was supported by JST CREST Grant Number JPMJCR1402, JSPS KAKENHI Grant Number 19H04068, and JSPS KAKENHI Grant Number 20K19746.

References

1. S. Alstrup, C. Gavoille, H. Kaplan, T. Rauhe, Nearest common ancestors: a survey and a new distributed algorithm, in *Proceedings of the fourteenth annual ACM symposium on Parallel algorithms and architectures* (2002), pp. 258–264
2. Nadine Baumann, Martin Skutella, Earliest arrival flows with multiple sources. Math. Operat. Res. **34**(2), 499–512 (2009)
3. R. Belmonte, Y. Higashikawa, N. Katoh, Y. Okamoto, Polynomial-time approximability of the k-sink location problem. *CoRR* (2015). arXiv:abs/1503.02835
4. M.A. Bender, M. Farach-Colton, The lca problem revisited, in *Latin American Symposium on Theoretical Informatics* (Springer, Berlin, 2000), pp. 88–94

5. R. Benkoczi, B. Bhattacharya, Y. Higashikawa, T. Kameda, N. Katoh, Minsum k-sink problem on dynamic flow path networks, in *International Workshop on Combinatorial Algorithms*, (Springer, Berlin, 2018), pp. 78–89
6. Robert Benkoczi, Binay Bhattacharya, Yuya Higashikawa, Tsunehiko Kameda, Naoki Katoh, Minsum k-sink problem on path networks. Theor. Comput. Sci. **806**, 388–401 (2020)
7. B. Bhattacharya, M.J. Golin, Y. Higashikawa, T. Kameda, N. Katoh, Improved algorithms for computing k-sink on dynamic flow path networks, in *Workshop on Algorithms and Data Structures* (Springer, Berlin, 2017), pp. 133–144
8. D. Chen, M. Golin, Sink evacuation on trees with dynamic confluent flows, in *27th International Symposium on Algorithms and Computation (ISAAC 2016)*. Schloss Dagstuhl-Leibniz-Zentrum fuer Informatik (2016)
9. D. Chen, M.J. Golin, Minmax centered k-partitioning of trees and applications to sink evacuation with dynamic confluent flows. *CoRR* (2018). arXiv:abs/1803.09289
10. L.R. Jr Ford, D.R. Fulkerson, Constructing maximal dynamic flows from static flows. *Operations research*, **6**(3), 419–433 (1958)
11. G.N. Frederickson, D.B. Johnson, Finding kth paths and p-centers by generating and searching good data structures. J. Algorithms 4(1):61–80 (1983)
12. S.L. Hakimi, Optimum locations of switching centers and the absolute centers and medians of a graph. Operat. Res. **12**(3), 450–459 (1964)
13. Y. Higashikawa, Studies on the space exploration and the sink location under incomplete information towards applications to evacuation planning (2014)
14. Y. Higashikawa, M.J. Golin, N. Katoh, Minimax regret sink location problem in dynamic tree networks with uniform capacity. J. Graph Algorithms Appl. **18.4**, 539–555 (2014)
15. Y. Higashikawa, M.J. Golin, N. Katoh, Multiple sink location problems in dynamic path networks. Theor. Comput. Sci. **607**, 2–15D (2015)
16. Y. Higashikawa, N. Katoh, J. Teruyama, K. Watase, Almost linear time algorithms for minsum k-sink problems on dynamic flow path networks, in *International Conference on Combinatorial Optimization and Applications* (Springer, Berlin, 2020), pp. 198–213
17. Bruce Hoppe, Éva. Tardos, The quickest transshipment problem. Math. Operat. Res. **25**(1), 36–62 (2000)
18. Satoko Mamada, Takeaki Uno, Kazuhisa Makino, Satoru Fujishige, An $o(n \log^2 n)$ algorithm for the optimal sink location problem in dynamic tree networks. Discrete Appl. Math. **154**(16), 2387–2401 (2006)
19. Baruch Schieber, Computing a minimum weight k-link path in graphs with the concave monge property. J. Algorithms **29**(2), 204–222 (1998)
20. M. Skutella, An introduction to network flows over time, in *Research Trends in Combinatorial Optimization* (Springer, Berlin, 2009), pp. 451–482

Open Access This chapter is licensed under the terms of the Creative Commons Attribution 4.0 International License (http://creativecommons.org/licenses/by/4.0/), which permits use, sharing, adaptation, distribution and reproduction in any medium or format, as long as you give appropriate credit to the original author(s) and the source, provide a link to the Creative Commons license and indicate if changes were made.

The images or other third party material in this chapter are included in the chapter's Creative Commons license, unless indicated otherwise in a credit line to the material. If material is not included in the chapter's Creative Commons license and your intended use is not permitted by statutory regulation or exceeds the permitted use, you will need to obtain permission directly from the copyright holder.

Part III
Sublinear Data Structures

Chapter 6
Information Processing on Compressed Data

Yoshimasa Takabatake, Tomohiro I, and Hiroshi Sakamoto

Abstract We survey our recent work related to information processing on compressed strings. Note that a "string" here contains any fixed-length sequence of symbols and therefore includes not only ordinary text but also a wide range of data, such as pixel sequences and time-series data. Over the past two decades, a variety of algorithms and their applications have been proposed for compressed information processing. In this survey, we mainly focus on two problems: recompression and privacy-preserving computation over compressed strings. Recompression is a framework in which algorithms transform a given compressed data into another compressed format without decompression. Recent studies have shown that a higher compression ratio can be achieved at lower cost by using an appropriate recompression algorithm such as preprocessing. Furthermore, various privacy-preserving computation models have been proposed for information retrieval, similarity computation, and pattern mining.

6.1 Restructuring Compressed Data

Data compression plays a central role in the efficient transmission and storage of data. Recent developments have also shown that data compression is a useful tool for processing highly repetitive data which contains long common substrings. Typical examples of highly repetitive data include collections of genomes taken from similar species and versioned documents. Popular compressors for highly repetitive data include Lempel-Ziv 77 (LZ77) [40], run-length encoded Burrows-Wheeler transform (RLBWT) [8], and grammar-based compression [34]. For each of these compression methods, researchers have developed techniques for operating on compressed data. For example, there are indexes based on LZ77 [37], RLBWT [17], and grammar-based compression [11]. Although recent studies [33, 36, 45] have investigated the fundamentals of these techniques and obtained a unified view of the compressibility of highly repetitive data, each compressed format still has pros and cons that cannot

Y. Takabatake · T. I · H. Sakamoto (✉)
Kyushu Institute of Technology, Kitakyushu, Japan
e-mail: hiroshi@ai.kyutech.ac.jp

© The Author(s) 2022

N. Katoh et al. (eds.), *Sublinear Computation Paradigm*,
https://doi.org/10.1007/978-981-16-4095-7_6

be ignored in practice. LZ77 usually achieves better compression than other compression methods, the index based on RLBWT (called r-index) supports very fast pattern search, and grammar-based compression is easy to handle in both theory and practice. Thus, in order to take advantage of the virtues of the different compressed formats, it is useful to have algorithms that can efficiently convert one compressed format to another. In this section, we present some examples of these algorithms.

6.1.1 Preliminaries

Let Σ be an ordered alphabet, that is, a set of characters that has a total order. A string over Σ is a sequence of characters chosen from Σ. The length of a string w is denoted by $|w|$. For any $1 \leq i \leq |w|$, the ith character of w is denoted by $w[i]$. The substring of w starting at i and ending at j is denoted by $w[i...j]$. The substring $w[i...j]$ is called a *prefix* (resp., *suffix*) if $i = 1$ (resp., $j = |w|$). The reversed string of w is denoted by w^R, namely, $w^R = w[|w|]w[|w| - 1] \cdots w[2]w[1]$.

Let T be a string of length n over Σ. We consider the following three compression schemes for T.

LZ77: LZ77 is characterized by greedy factorization $T = f_1 f_2 \cdots f_z$ of T. The ith factor f_i is a single character if the character does not appear in $f_1 f_2 \cdots f_{i-1}$, and otherwise, the longest substring such that there is another occurrence s_i of f_i with $s_i \leq |f_1 f_2 \cdots f_{i-1}|$. The position s_i is called the reference position of the ith LZ77 factor f_i. We can store T in $O(z)$-space because each factor f_i (in the second case) can be replaced with a pair $(s_i, |f_i|)$.

BWT, RLBWT: For simplicity, we assume that T is extended by the end marker \$, which is a special character not in Σ and lexicographically smaller than any character in Σ, that is, $T[n + 1] = \$$. The Burrows-Wheeler transform [8] is a permutation L of characters in $T[1 \ldots n + 1]$ obtained as follows: $L[i]$ is the character preceding the lexicographically ith smallest suffix among all non-empty suffixes of T with the exception that $L[i] = \$$ when the ith smallest suffix is T itself (and therefore has no preceding character). The resulting string L can be interpreted as a sequence obtained by sorting characters in T according to their context (succeeding suffixes). Since characters sharing similar context tend to be identical, L is well compressible by run-length encoding. The run-length encoded BWT is called RLBWT.

Let $\mathsf{SA}[1 \ldots n + 1]$ denote the suffix array of $T[1 \ldots n + 1]$, where $\mathsf{SA}[i]$ is the starting position of the lexicographically ith smallest suffix. We consider SA as a mapping from BWT position to text position and say that the BWT position i corresponds to the text position $\mathsf{SA}[i]$. One crucial operation on the BWT string L is the so-called LF mapping that maps a BWT position i to the BWT position corresponding to text position $\mathsf{SA}[i] - 1$. LF mapping can be implemented by a rank data structure on L that returns the number of occurrences of a character c in $L[1 \ldots i]$ for any character c and BWT position i.

By using LF mapping, we can also support backward search. For any string w that appears in T, there is a unique maximal interval $[b \ldots e]$ such that the lexicographically ith suffix is prefixed by w iff $i \in [b \ldots e]$. Note that $e - b + 1$ is the number of occurrences of w in T and the text positions corresponding to these positions represent the occurrences of w. A single step of the backward search computes the cw-interval from the w-interval by using the same mechanism as LF mapping, where c is a character. The index based on backward search on BWT is known as the FM-index [14]. Although it was previously known that the occurrences of a pattern can be counted by a backward search implemented in RLBWT space [41], it was recently reported that RLBWT can be augmented with an $O(r)$-space data structure to report all the occurrences of the pattern efficiently. The index based on RLBWT is called the r-index [17].

Grammar compression: Grammar compression is a general framework of data compression in which a context-free grammar (CFG) $\mathcal{S} = (\Sigma, \mathcal{V}, \mathcal{D})$ that derives a single string T is considered to be a compressed representation of T, where Σ is the set of characters (terminals), $\mathcal{V}$ is the set of variables (non-terminals), $\mathcal{D}$ is the set of deterministic production rules whose right-hand sides are strings over $(\mathcal{V} \cup \Sigma)$, and the last variable derives T.[1] The compressed size of $\mathcal{S}$ is expressed by the sum of the lengths of right-hand sides of the production rules in $\mathcal{S}$. We consider run-length encoding right-hand sides of CFGs, and call such CFGs *run-length encoded CFGs (RLCFGs)*. The compressed size of an RLCFG is expressed by the sum of run-length encoded sizes of right-hand sides of the production rules.

Algorithm 1: Supposing that we have parsed suffix $T[p + 1 \ldots]$, compute the length of the next LZ77 factor ending at p.

$p' \leftarrow p$;
$w \leftarrow \varepsilon$;
$c \leftarrow T[p']$;
while *cw-interval contains a text position larger than p'* **do**
    $p' \leftarrow p' - 1$;
    $w \leftarrow cw$;
    $c \leftarrow T[p']$;
return $\min(1, p' - p)$;

6.1.2 RLBWT to LZ77

Algorithms to compute LZ77 from RLBWT are considered in [3, 32, 46, 47, 49]. An essential task when computing LZ77 is to search for the longest prefix of $T[|f_1 f_2 \cdots f_{i-1}| + 1 \cdots]$ that occurs before and compute an occurrence $s_i \leq |f_1 f_2 \cdots f_{i-1}|$ of f_i. The basic idea is to use the backward search on RLBWT of T^R to perform this task. One difficulty is ignoring the BWT positions that correspond

[1] We treat the last variable as the starting variable.

to the suffixes starting after $|f_1 f_2 \cdots f_{i-1}|$ during the backward search. In [49], it is shown that keeping at most $2r$ BWT positions is sufficient to compute the longest prefix and a reference position for the LZ77 factor. This subsection gives a brief review of this idea.

For the sake of this explanation, consider the case of LZ77 parsing from right to left (i.e., we conceptually compute the LZ77 factorization for T^R) so that backward search on T (instead of the reversed one) can be used. Supposing that we have parsed suffix $T[p+1\ldots]$, Algorithm 1 shows how to compute the length of the next factor ending at p. To check whether the cw-interval contains a text position larger than p', we partition SA into r subintervals and maintain at most two positions for each subinterval, which is the LF-mapped interval of a run of L. Suppose that the cw-interval $[b\ldots e]$ is non-empty and $[b\ldots e]$ is covered by consecutive subintervals $[b_1\ldots e_1], [b_2\ldots e_2], \ldots, [b_k\ldots e_k]$ with minimal integer k, that is, $b_1 \leq b < e_1 + 1 = b_2 < e_2 + 1 = b_3 < \cdots < e_{k-1} + 1 = b_k \leq e \leq e_k$. If $k = 1$, the characters of L in w-interval consist of a single character c and all positions in w-interval are LF-mapped to cw-interval. Therefore, cw-interval contains a text position larger than p' iff w-interval satisfies the condition in the previous step. For the case of $k > 1$, we mark the closest positions from the boundaries of subintervals that correspond to text positions larger than p'. Using this information, we can check whether $\mathsf{SA}[b_1\ldots e_1]$ and/or $\mathsf{SA}[b_k\ldots e_k]$ contain a text position larger than p'. We also maintain the data structure to check whether a subinterval in $[b_2\ldots e_2], \ldots, [b_{k-1}\ldots e_{k-1}]$ contains a text position larger than p', and if so we compute which interval contains that position.

In this way, we can compute the lengths of LZ77 factors. The reference position for each LZ77 factor can also be computed by maintaining text positions corresponding to the marked positions in each subinterval. The data structures use only $O(r)$ words of space.

In [46], the data structures are tuned to improve the time complexity. In [47], a fast implementation for the backward search in RLBWT space was proposed and applied to the above-mentioned algorithm. In [3], an online construction of r-index was proposed and the technique was extended to an online LZ77 factorization algorithm in RLBWT space. In [32], a different approach to converting RLBWT to LZ77 was proposed.

6.1.3 Recompression on Grammar Compression

Given that there are a number of CFGs with different properties for representing strings, we may want to transform one CFG to another without explicitly decompressing the text. In this subsection, we introduce a technique called recompression which has proven to be a powerful tool in problems related to grammar compression [26–28, 31] and word equations [29, 30].

In [27], Jeż proposed an algorithm TtoG for computing an RLCFG of T in $O(N)$ time. Let TtoG(T) denote the RLCFG of T produced by TtoG. We use the term *letters* for characters and variables introduced by TtoG. A run is called a *block* in this subsection. TtoG consists of two different types of compression, namely, block compression (BComp) and pair compression (PComp).

- BComp: Given a string w over $\Sigma = [1 \ldots |w|]$, BComp compresses w by replacing all blocks of length ≥ 2 with fresh letters. Note that BComp eliminates all blocks of length ≥ 2 in w.
- PComp: Given a string w over $\Sigma = [1 \ldots |w|]$ that contains no block of length ≥ 2, PComp compresses w by replacing all pairs from $\acute{\Sigma}\grave{\Sigma}$ with fresh letters, where $(\acute{\Sigma}, \grave{\Sigma})$ is a partition of Σ, that is, $\Sigma = \acute{\Sigma} \cup \grave{\Sigma}$ and $\acute{\Sigma} \cap \grave{\Sigma} = \emptyset$. Given the frequency table of pairs, we can deterministically compute a partition of Σ by which at least $(|w| - 1)/4$ occurrences of pairs are replaced.

TtoG compresses $T_0 = T$ by applying BComp and PComp in turns until the string is shrunk down to a single letter. Because PComp compresses a given string by a constant factor of $3/4$, the height of TtoG(T) is $O(\lg N)$.

TtoG performs level-by-level transformation of T_0 into strings $T_1, T_2, \ldots, T_{\hat{h}}$, where $|T_{\hat{h}}| = 1$. If h is even, the transformation from T_h to T_{h+1} is performed by BComp, and production rules of the form $c \rightarrow \ddot{c}^d$ are introduced. If h is odd, the transformation from T_h to T_{h+1} is performed by PComp, and production rules of the form $c \rightarrow \acute{c}\grave{c}$ are introduced. Let Σ_h be the set of letters appearing in T_h.

The advantage of TtoG is that it can be simulated on $\mathcal{S} = \mathcal{S}_0 = (\Sigma_0, \mathcal{V}, \mathcal{D}_0)$ without decompression. We consider the level-by-level transformation of $\mathcal{S}_0$ into CFGs $\mathcal{S}_1 = (\Sigma_1, \mathcal{V}, \mathcal{D}_1), \mathcal{S}_2 = (\Sigma_2, \mathcal{V}, \mathcal{D}_2), \ldots, \mathcal{S}_{\hat{h}} = (\Sigma_{\hat{h}}, \mathcal{V}, \mathcal{D}_{\hat{h}})$, where each $\mathcal{S}_h$ generates T_h. More specifically, the compression from T_h to T_{h+1} is simulated on $\mathcal{S}_h$. We can correctly compute the letters introduced in each level $h + 1$ while modifying $\mathcal{S}_h$ into $\mathcal{S}_{h+1}$; hence, we get all the letters of TtoG(T) in the end. We note that new "variables" are never introduced and modifications are made by rewriting the right-hand sides of the original variables.

We now show how PComp is performed on $\mathcal{S}_h$ for odd h. That is, we compute $\mathcal{S}_{h+1}$ from $\mathcal{S}_h$. Note that any occurrence i of a pair $\acute{c}\grave{c}$ in T_h can be uniquely associated with a variable X that is the label of the lowest node covering the interval $[i \ldots i + 1]$ in the derivation tree of $\mathcal{S}_h$ (recall that $\mathcal{S}_h$ generates T_h). We can compute the frequency table of pairs by counting pairs associated with X in $\mathcal{D}_h(X)$ and multiplying it by the number of occurrences of X in the derivation tree of $\mathcal{S}_h$. The frequency table is used to compute a partition of Σ_h, which determines the pairs to be replaced. A pair appears *explicitly* in right-hand sides or *crosses* the boundaries of variables. We can modify $\mathcal{S}_h$ so that all the crossing occurrences to be replaced appear explicitly in some right-hand side, then replace the explicit occurrences to get $\mathcal{S}_{h+1}$. In a similar way, BComp can also be performed on $\mathcal{S}_h$ for odd h.

In [23], it is shown that TtoG(T) can be used to answer the longest common extension (LCE) queries and the transformation from arbitrary CFG $\mathcal{S}$ to TtoG(T) is a key for efficient construction algorithms of LCE data structures in grammar compressed space. In [53], the recompression technique is modified to transform arbitrary CFG $\mathcal{S}$ into the CFG obtained by the RePair algorithm [38]. RePair is known to achieve the best compression performance in practice and there are many studies on computing RePair in small space. Using *online* grammar compression algorithms, such as [43, 57], the algorithm in [53] leads to the first RePair algorithm working in compressed space.

6.2 Privacy-Preserving Similarity Computation

6.2.1 Related Work

This section reviews recent results in privacy-preserving information retrieval over strings recently presented in [59]. As the number of strings containing personal information has increased, privacy-preserving computation has become increasingly important. Secure computation based on public-key encryption is one of the great accomplishments of modern cryptography because it allows untrusted parties to compute a function based on their private inputs, while revealing nothing but the result.

Rapid progress in gene sequencing technology has expanded the range of applications of edit distance to include personalized genomic medicine, diagnosis of diseases, and preventive treatment (e.g., see [1]). However, because the genome of a person is ultimately personal information that uniquely identifies the owner, the parties involved should not share personal genomic data in plaintext. We therefore consider a secure two-party model for edit distance computation: Two untrusted parties generating their own public and private keys have strings x and y, respectively, and they want to jointly compute $f(x, y)$ for a given metric f without revealing anything about their individual strings.

Homomorphic encryption (HE) is an emerging technique for such secure multi-party computation. HE is a kind of public-key encryption between two parties Alice and Bob where Bob wants to send a secret message to Alice. In this model, Bob generates his secret key and public key prior to communication, say sk and pk, where pk is known to everyone. Alice then sends the encrypted message $E(m, pk)$ to Bob and he decrypts m by using his secret key sk using the property $E(E(m, pk), sk) = m$. If it is not necessary to specify the owner of pk and sk, we simply write $E(m)$ for simplicity.

A public-key encryption $E()$ has the additive homomorphic property if we can obtain $E(m + n)$ from $E(m)$ and $E(n)$ without decryption, and the multiplicative property is similarly defined. If $E()$ is additive, Alice can obtain the summation of many people's secret numbers without revealing their private numbers.

The first public-key encryption algorithm RSA [51] is multiplicative because it has the following property: Let (e, n) be a public key and (d, n) be a secret key, respectively, where e, d, n are integers. For a message m, its encryption is computed by $c = (m^e \mod n)$ and is decrypted by $c^d = m^{ed} \equiv m \mod n$. We can easily check the multiplicative property $(m_1^e \mod n) \cdot (m_2^e \mod n) = (m_1 m_2)^e \mod n$. The Paillier encryption system [48] was the first system to have the additive property. This means that parties can jointly compute the encrypted value $E(x+y)$ directly based on only two encrypted integers $E(x)$ and $E(y)$.

By taking advantage of the homomorphic property, researchers have proposed HE-based privacy-preserving protocols for computing the Levenshtein distance $d(x, y)$. For example, Inan et al. [25] designed a three-party protocol where two parties securely compute $d(x, y)$ by enlisting the help of a reliable third party. Rane and Sun [50] then improved this three-party protocol to develop the first two-party protocol.

In this review, we focus on an extended Levenshtein distance called the *edit distance with moves* (EDM) which allows any substring to be moved with unit cost in addition to the standard operations of inserting, deleting, and replacing a character. Based on the EDM, we can find a set of approximately maximal common substrings appearing in two strings, which can be used to detect plagiarism in documents or long repeated segments in DNA sequences. As an example, consider two unambiguously similar strings $x = a^N b^N$ and $y = b^N a^N$, which can be transformed into each other by a single move. While the exact EDM is simply $\mathrm{EDM}(x, y) = 1$, the Levenshtein distance has the undesirable value $d(x, y) = 2N$. The n-gram distance is preferable to the Levenshtein distance in this case, but it requires huge time/space complexity depending on N.

Although computation of $\mathrm{EDM}(x, y)$ is NP-hard [55], Cormode and Muthukrishnan [12] were able to find an almost linear-time approximation algorithm. Many techniques have been proposed for computing the EDM. For example, Ganczorz et al. [18] proposed a lightweight probabilistic algorithm. In these algorithms, each string x is transformed into a characteristic vector v_x consisting of nonnegative integers representing the frequencies of particular substrings of x. For two strings x and y, we then have the approximate distance guaranteeing $L_1(v_x, v_y) = O(\lg^* N \lg N)\mathrm{EDM}(x, y)$ for $N = |x| + |y|$.

In Appendix A of [15], there is a subtle flaw in the ESP algorithm [12] that achieves this $O(\lg^* N \lg N)$ bound. However, this flaw can be remedied by an alternative algorithm called HSP [15]. Because $\lg^* N$ increases extremely slowly,[2] we employ $L_1(v_x, v_y)$ as a reasonable approximation to $\mathrm{EDM}(x, y)$.

Basically, the ESP tree is a special type of grammar compression referred to in the previous section where the length of the right-hand side of any production rule is just two or three. Therefore, $\mathrm{EDM}(x, y)$ is approximated by the compressed expressions for the strings x and y. The relationship between grammar compression (including ESP) and its applications has been widely investigated in the past two decades (see, e.g., [10, 21, 24, 39, 42, 52, 54, 56–58]).

[2] $\lg^* N$ is the number of times the logarithm function lg can be iteratively applied to N until $\lg^* N \leq 1$.

Recently, Nakagawa et al. proposed the first secure two-party protocol for EDM (sEDM) [44] based on HE. However, their algorithm suffers from a bottleneck during the step where the parties construct a shared labeling scheme. Yoshimoto improved the previous algorithm to make it easier to use in practice [59]. We review the practical algorithm here.

6.2.2 Edit Distance with Moves

Based on the notation for strings in the previous section, $\mathrm{EDM}(S, S')$ is the length of the shortest sequence of edit operations that transforms S into S', where the permitted operations (each having unit cost) are inserting, deleting, or renaming one symbol at any position, or moving an arbitrary substring. Unfortunately, as Theorem 6.1 states, computing $\mathrm{EDM}(S, S')$ is NP-hard even if the renaming operations are not allowed [55], so we focus on an approximation algorithm for EDM, called Edit-Sensitive Parsing (ESP) [12].

Theorem 6.1 (Shapira and Storer [55]) *Determining* $\mathrm{EDM}(x, y)$ *is NP-hard even if only three unit-cost operations are allowed, namely, inserting a character, deleting a character, and moving a substring.*

ESP constructs a parsing tree, called an ESP tree, for a given string S, where internal nodes are labeled *consistently*, that is, internal nodes have a common name if and only if they derive the same string. After two ESP trees T_S and $T_{S'}$ are constructed for given strings S and S' for comparison in EDM, the characteristic vectors v_S and $v_{S'}$ are defined such that $v_S[i]$ is the frequency of the ith label in T_S. $EDM(S, S')$ is then approximated by $L_1(v_S, v_{S'})$ with the following lower/upper bounds.

Theorem 6.2 (Cormode and Muthukrishnan [12]) *Let T_S and $T_{S'}$ be consistently labeled ESP trees for $S, S' \in \Sigma^*$, and let v_S be the characteristic vector for S, where $v_S[k]$ is the frequency of label k in T_S. Then,*

$$\frac{1}{2}\mathrm{EDM}(S, S') \leq L_1(v_S, v_{S'}) = O(\lg^* N \lg N)\mathrm{EDM}(S, S')$$

for $L_1(v_S, v_{S'}) = \sum_{i=1}^{k} |v_S[i] - v_{S'}[i]|$.

In Fig. 6.1, we illustrate an example of consistent labeling of the trees T_S and $T_{S'}$ together with the resulting characteristic vectors. Since the strings S and S' are parsed offline, the problem of preserving privacy is reduced to designing a secure protocol for creating consistent labels and computing the L_1-distance between the trees.

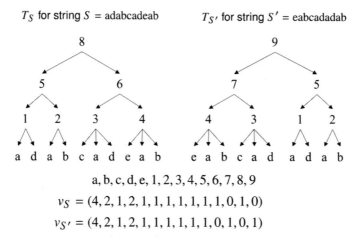

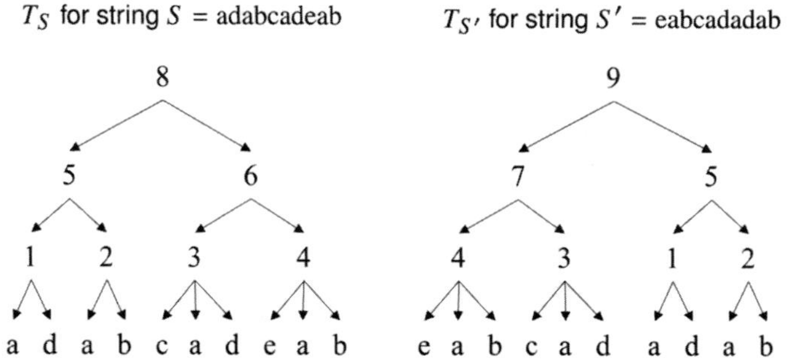

$$\text{a, b, c, d, e}, 1, 2, 3, 4, 5, 6, 7, 8, 9$$
$$v_S = (4, 2, 1, 2, 1, 1, 1, 1, 1, 1, 1, 0, 1, 0)$$
$$v_{S'} = (4, 2, 1, 2, 1, 1, 1, 1, 1, 1, 0, 1, 0, 1)$$

Fig. 6.1 Example of approximate EDM. For strings $S = adabcadeab$ and $S' = eabcadadab$, S is transformed into S' by two moves of substrings, that is, $\text{EDM}(S, S') = 2$. After constructing ESP trees T_S and $T_{S'}$ with consistent labeling, the corresponding characteristic vectors v_S and $v_{S'}$ are computed offline. The exact $\text{EDM}(S, S')$ is approximated by $L_1(v_S, v_{S'}) = 4$

6.2.3 Homomorphic Encryption

We now briefly review the framework of homomorphic encryption. Let (pk, sk) be a key pair for a public-key encryption scheme, and let $E_{pk}(x)$ be the encrypted value of a message x and $D_{sk}(C)$ be the decrypted value of a ciphertext C, respectively. We say that the encryption scheme is *additively homomorphic* if we have the following properties: (1) There is an operation $h_+(\cdot, \cdot)$ for $E_{pk}(x)$ and $E_{pk}(y)$ such that $D_{sk}(h_+(E_{pk}(x), E_{pk}(y))) = x + y$. (2) For any r, we can compute the scalar multiplication such that $D_{sk}(r \cdot E_{pk}(x)) = r \cdot x$.

An additive homomorphic encryption scheme that allows a sufficient number of these operations is called an additive HE.[3] Paillier's encryption scheme [48] is the first secure additive HE. However, there are not many functions that can be evaluated by using only additive homomorphism and scalar multiplication.

The multiplication $D_{sk}(h_\times(E_{pk}(x), E_{pk}(y))) = x \cdot y$ is another important homomorphism. If we allow both additive and multiplicative homomorphism as well as scalar multiplication (called a fully homomorphic encryption, FHE [19] for short), it follows that we can perform any arithmetic operation on ciphertexts. For example, if we can use sufficiently large number of additive operations and a single multiplicative operation over ciphertexts, we obtain the inner-product of two encrypted vectors.

However, there is a trade-off between the available homomorphic operations and their computational cost. To avoid this difficulty, we focus on leveled HE (LHE) where the number of homomorphic multiplications is restricted beforehand. In particular,

[3] In general, the number of applicable operations over ciphertexts is bounded by the size of (pk, sk).

L2HE (Additive HE that allows a single homomorphic multiplication) has attracted a great deal of attention. The BGN encryption system is the first L2HE and was invented by Boneh et al. [6] by assuming a single multiplication and sufficient numbers of additions. Using BGN, we can securely evaluate formulas in disjunctive normal form. Following this pioneering study, many practical L2HE protocols have been proposed [2, 9, 16, 22].

In terms of EDM computation, although Nakagawa et al. [44] introduced an algorithm for computing the EDM based on L2HE, their algorithm is very slow for large strings. Following on from this work, Yoshimoto et al. proposed another novel secure computation of EDM for large strings based on the faster L2HE proposed by Attrapadung et al. [2]. To our knowledge, there is no secure two-party protocol for EDM computation that uses only the additive homomorphic property. Whether we can compute EDM using a two-party protocol based on additive HE alone is an interesting question.

For the benefit of the reader, we give a simple review of the mechanism used by BGN, the first L2HE. For plaintexts $m_1, m_2 \in \{1, \ldots, M\}$ and their corresponding ciphertexts C_1 and C_2, the ciphertexts of $m_1 + m_2$ and $m_1 m_2$ can be computed directly from C_1 and C_2 without decrypting m_1 and m_2, provided $m_1 + m_2, m_1 m_2 \leq M$.

For large primes q_1 and q_2, the BGN encryption scheme is based on two multiplicative cyclic groups $\mathbb{G}$ and $\mathbb{G}'$ of order $q_1 q_2$, two generators g_1 and g_2 of $\mathbb{G}$, an inverse function $(\cdot)^{-1} : \mathbb{G} \to \mathbb{G}$, and a bihomomorphism $e : \mathbb{G} \times \mathbb{G} \to \mathbb{G}'$. By definition, $e(\cdot, x)$ and $e(x, \cdot)$ are group homomorphisms for all $x \in \mathbb{G}$. In addition, we assume that both the inverse function $(\cdot)^{-1}$ and the bihomomorphism e can be computed in polynomial time in terms of the security parameter $\log_2 q_1 q_2$. Such a system $(\mathbb{G}, \mathbb{G}', g_1, g_2, (\cdot)^{-1}, e)$ can be generated by, for example, letting $\mathbb{G}$ be a subgroup of a supersingular elliptic curve and e be a Tate pairing [6]. The BGN encryption scheme proceeds as follows.

Key generation: Randomly generate two sufficiently large primes q_1 and q_2, then use these to define $(\mathbb{G}, \mathbb{G}', g_1, g_2, (\cdot)^{-1}, e)$ as described above. Choose two random generators g and u of $\mathbb{G}$, set $h = u^{q_2}$, and let M be a positive integer bounded above by a polynomial function of the security parameter $\log_2 p_1 p_2$. The public key is then $pk = (p_1 p_2, \mathbb{G}, \mathbb{G}', e, g, h, M)$ and the private key is $sk = q_1$.

Encryption: Encrypt the message $m \in \{0, \ldots, M\}$ using pk and a random $r \in \mathbb{Z}_n$ to $C = g^m h^r \in \mathbb{G}$ yielding the ciphertext C.

Decryption: Find the integer m such that $C^{q_1} = (g^m h^r)^{q_1} = (g^{q_1})^m$ using a polynomial time algorithm. There is a known algorithm for this with time complexity of $O(\sqrt{M})$.

Homomorphic properties: For the ciphertexts $C_1 = g^{m_1} h^{r_1}$ and $C_2 = g^{m_2} h^{r_2}$ in $\mathbb{G}$ corresponding to the messages m_1 and m_2, anyone can calculate the encrypted value of $m_1 + m_2$ and $m_1 m_2$ directly from C_1 and C_2 without knowing m_1 and m_2, as follows.

– **Additive homomorphism**:

$$C_a = C_1 C_2 h^r = (g^{m_1} h^{r_1})(g^{m_2} h^{r_2}) h^r = g^{m_1+m_2} h^{r_1+r_2+r}$$

gives the encrypted value of $m_1 + m_2$.

– Multiplicative homomorphism: $C_m = e(C_1, C_2)h^r \in \mathbb{G}'$ gives the encrypted value of $m_1 m_2$, because

$$\begin{aligned} C_m^{q_1} &= e(C_1, C_2) \\ &= \left[e(g_1, g_2)^{m_1 m_2} e(g_1, g_2)^{q_2 m_1 r_1} e(g_2, g_1)^{q_2 m_2 r_1} e(g_1, g_2)^{q_2 r}\right]^{q_1} \\ &= \left(e(g_1, g_2)^{q_1}\right)^{m_1 m_2}, \end{aligned}$$

where we decrypt C_m, by computing $m_1 m_2$ from $(g(g_1, g_2)^{q_1})^{m_1 m_2}$ and $e(g_1, g_2)^{q_1}$.

Note that $C_1, C_2 \in \mathbb{G}'$ also have additive homomorphic properties, so BGN allows a single multiplication and unlimited additions over ciphertexts.

6.2.4 L2HE-Based Algorithm for Secure EDM

We now explain the algorithm for computing approximate EDM based on L2HE [59]. Two parties $\mathcal{A}, \mathcal{B}$ have strings $S_\mathcal{A}, S_\mathcal{B}$, respectively. First, they compute the corresponding ESP trees $T_\mathcal{A}$ and $T_\mathcal{B}$ offline and they assign tentative labels to internal nodes of $T_\mathcal{A}$ and $T_\mathcal{B}$ using a hash function $h : X \to \{1, 2, \dots, n\}$ for $X \subseteq \{0, 1, \dots, m\}$ of n different labels in $T_\mathcal{A}$ and $T_\mathcal{B}$ with a fixed m. The goal is to securely relabel X using a bijection: $X \to \{1, 2, \dots, n\}$, as described in Algorithm 2. We suppose that $\mathcal{A}$ and $\mathcal{B}$ generate their own public and private keys prior to the computation.

In Algorithm 2, we assume an L2HE scheme allowing a single multiplicative operation and a sufficient number of additive operations over encrypted integers. Because these operations are usually implemented by AND ($\cdot$) and XOR ($\oplus$) logic gates (e.g., [7]), we introduce the following notation for these gates. First, $E_\mathcal{A}(x)$ denotes the ciphertext generated by encrypting plaintext x with $\mathcal{A}$'s public key, and $E_\mathcal{A}(x, y, z)$ is an abbreviation for the vector $(E_\mathcal{A}(x), E_\mathcal{A}(y), E_\mathcal{A}(z)$. Here, $E_\mathcal{A}(x, y, z) \cdot E_\mathcal{A}(a, b, c)$ denotes $(E_\mathcal{A}(x \cdot a), E_\mathcal{A}(y \cdot b), E_\mathcal{A}(z \cdot c))$ and $E_\mathcal{A}(x, y, z) \oplus E_\mathcal{A}(a, b, c)$ denotes $(E_\mathcal{A}(x \oplus a), E_\mathcal{A}(y \oplus b), E_\mathcal{A}(z \oplus c))$ for each bit $x, y, z, a, b, c \in \{0, 1\}$. Using this notation, we describe the proposed protocol in Algorithm 2.

Next, we define the protocol security based on a model where both parties are assumed to be *semi-honest*, that is, corrupt parties merely cooperate to gather information out of the protocol, but do not deviate from the protocol specification. The security is defined as follows.

Definition 6.1 (Semi-honest security [20]) A protocol is secure against semi-honest adversaries if each party's observation of the protocol can be simulated using only the input they hold and the output that they receive from the protocol.

Intuitively, this definition tells us that a corrupt party is unable to learn any extra information that cannot be derived from the input and output explicitly (for details, see [20]). Under this assumption, since the algorithm is symmetric with respect

Algorithm 2 for consistently labeling $T_{\mathcal{A}}$ and $T_{\mathcal{B}}$ [59]

Preprocessing (tentative labeling): Parties $\mathcal{A}$ and $\mathcal{B}$ agree to use a hash function H with a range $\{0, \ldots, m\}$ for sufficiently large m. Both parties compute $T_{\mathcal{A}}$ and $T_{\mathcal{B}}$ corresponding to their respective strings offline. The label of internal node u is assigned $H(s(u))$ where $s(u)$ is the string of all leaves of u. Now, parties $\mathcal{A}$ and $\mathcal{B}$ have tentative label sets $[T_{\mathcal{A}}], [T_{\mathcal{B}}] \subseteq \{0, \ldots, m\}$, respectively.

Goal: Change all the labels using a bijection: $[T_{\mathcal{A}}] \cup [T_{\mathcal{B}}] \to \{1, \ldots, n\}$ without either party having to reveal anything about their private strings.

Notation: $E_{\mathcal{A}}(x)$ denotes the ciphertext of a message x encrypted by an L2HE with $\mathcal{A}$'s public key.

Sharing a dictionary:
Step 1: Party $\mathcal{A}$ computes the bit vector $\mathbf{X}[1 \ldots m]$ such that $\mathbf{X}[\ell] = 1$ iff $\ell \in [T_{\mathcal{A}}]$. Similarly, party $\mathcal{B}$ computes $\mathbf{Y}[1 \ldots m]$ such that $\mathbf{Y}[\ell] = 1$ iff $\ell \in [T_{\mathcal{B}}]$.
Step 2: $\mathcal{A}$ sends $E_{\mathcal{A}}(\mathbf{X})$ to $\mathcal{B}$ and $\mathcal{B}$ sends $E_{\mathcal{B}}(\mathbf{Y})$ to $\mathcal{A}$.
Step 3: $\mathcal{B}$ computes $(E_{\mathcal{A}}(\mathbf{X}) \oplus E_{\mathcal{A}}(\mathbf{Y})) \oplus (E_{\mathcal{A}}(\mathbf{X}) \cdot E_{\mathcal{A}}(\mathbf{Y})) = E_{\mathcal{A}}(\mathbf{X} \cup \mathbf{Y})$ and $\mathcal{A}$ computes $(E_{\mathcal{B}}(\mathbf{X}) \oplus E_{\mathcal{B}}(\mathbf{Y})) \oplus (E_{\mathcal{B}}(\mathbf{X}) \cdot E_{\mathcal{B}}(\mathbf{Y})) = E_{\mathcal{B}}(\mathbf{X} \cup \mathbf{Y})$.

Relabeling $[T_{\mathcal{A}}]$ **using** $E_{\mathcal{A}}(\mathbf{X} \cup \mathbf{Y})$ ($[T_{\mathcal{B}}]$ is relabeled in a symmetrical fashion)
Step 4: $\mathcal{A}$ computes $E_{\mathcal{B}}(L_\ell) = E_{\mathcal{B}}\left(\sum_{i=1}^{\ell}(\mathbf{X} \cup \mathbf{Y})[i]\right)$ for all $\ell \in [T_{\mathcal{A}}]$.
Step 5: $\mathcal{A}$ sends all $E_{\mathcal{B}}(L_\ell + r_\ell)$ to $\mathcal{B}$ choosing r_ℓ uniformly at random from $\mathbb{N}$.
Step 6: $\mathcal{B}$ decrypts all $L_\ell + r_\ell$ and sends them back to $\mathcal{A}$.
Step 7: $\mathcal{A}$ recreates $L_\ell \in \{1, \ldots, n\}$ for all $\ell \in [T_{\mathcal{A}}]$ by subtracting r_ℓ.

to $\mathcal{A}$ and $\mathcal{B}$, the following theorem proves the security of our algorithm's against semi-honest adversaries.

Theorem 6.3 (Yoshimoto et al. [59]) *Let* $[T_{\mathcal{A}}]$ *be the set of labels appearing in* $T_{\mathcal{A}}$. *The only knowledge that a semi-honest* $\mathcal{A}$ *can gain by executing Algorithm 2 is the distribution of the labels* $\{L_\ell \mid \ell \in [T_{\mathcal{A}}]\}$ *over* $[1, \ldots, n]$.

Theorem 6.4 (Yoshimoto et al. [59]) *Algorithm 2 assigns consistent labels using the injection:* $[T_{\mathcal{A}}] \cup [T_{\mathcal{B}}] \to \{1, 2, \ldots, n\}$ *without revealing the parties' private information. It has round and communication complexities of* $O(1)$ *and* $O(\alpha(n \lg n + m + rn))$, *respectively, where* $n = |[T_{\mathcal{A}}] \cup [T_{\mathcal{B}}]|$, m *is the modulus of the rolling hash used for preprocessing,* $r = \max\{r_1, \ldots, r_n\}$ *is the security parameter, and* α *is the cost of executing a single encryption, decryption, or homomorphic operation.*

Table 6.1 Comparison of the communication and round complexities of secure EDM computation models [44, 59] as well as a naive algorithm. Here, N is the total length of both parties' input strings, n is the number of characteristic substrings determining the approximate EDM, and m is the range of the rolling hash $H(\cdot)$ for the substrings satisfying $m > n$. "Naive" is the baseline method that uses $H(\cdot)$ as the labeling function for the characteristic substrings

Method	#Communication	#Round
Naive	$O(m \lg m)$	$O(1)$
Nakagawa et al. [44]	$O(n \lg n)$	$O(\lg N)$
Yoshimoto et al. [59]	$O(n \lg n + m)$	$O(1)$

6.2.5 Result and Open Question

The complexities of related algorithms are summarized in Table 6.1. Computing the approximate EDM involves two phases: the shared labeling of characteristic substrings (Phase 1) and the L_1-distance computation of characteristic vectors (Phase 2).

Let the parties have strings x and y, respectively. In the offline case (i.e., there is no need for privacy-preserving communication), they construct the respective parsing trees T_x and T_y by the bottom-up parsing called ESP [12], where the node labels must be *consistent*, meaning that two labels are equal if they correspond to the same substring. In such an ESP tree, a substring derived by an internal node is called a characteristic substring. In a privacy-preserving model, the two parties need to jointly compute these consistent labels without revealing whether a characteristic substring is common to both of them (Phase 1). After computing all the labels in T_x and T_y, they jointly compute the L_1-distance of two characteristic vectors containing the frequencies of all labels in T_x and T_y (Phase 2).

As reported in [44], a bottleneck exists in Phase 1. The task is to design a bijection $f : X \cup Y \to \{1, 2, \ldots, n\}$ where X and Y ($|X \cup Y| = n$) are the sets of characteristic substrings for the parties, respectively. Since X and Y are computable without communication, the goal is to jointly compute $f(w)$ for any $w \in X$ without revealing whether $w \in Y$. This problem is closely related to the private set operation (PSO) where parties possessing their private sets want to obtain the results for several set operations, such as intersection or union. Applying the Bloom filter [5] and HE techniques, various protocols for PSO have been proposed [4, 13, 35]. However, these protocols are not directly applicable to our problem because they require at least three parties for the security constraints. In contrast, the algorithm reviewed here introduced a novel secure two-party protocol for Phase 1.

As shown in Table 6.1, the recent result eliminates the $O(\lg N)$ round complexity using the proposed method that can achieve $O(1)$ round complexity while maintaining the efficiency of communication complexity. Furthermore, the practical performance of the algorithms for real DNA sequences was reported in [44].

Acknowledgements The authors were supported by JST CREST (JPMJCR1402) and JSPS KAKENHI (16K16009, 17H01791, 17H00762, and 18K18111).

References

1. M. Akgün, A.O. Bayrak, B. Ozer, M.S. Sağiroğlu, Privacy preserving processing of genomic data: A survey. Journal of Biomedical Informatics **56**, 103–111 (2015)
2. N. Attrapadung, G. Hanaoka, S. Mitsunari, Y. Sakai, K. Shimizu, T. Teruya, Efficient two-level homomorphic encryption in prime-order bilinear groups and a fast implementation in webassembly. In *ASIACCS* (2018), pp. 685–697
3. H. Bannai, T. Gagie, T. I, Refining the r-index. Theor. Comput. Sci. **812**, 96–108 (2020)
4. M. Blanton, E. Aguiar, Private and oblivious set and multiset operations. In *ASIACCS* (2012), pp. 40–41
5. B.H. Bloom, Space/time trade-offs in hash coding with allowable errors. Commun. ACM **13**(7), 422–426 (1970)
6. D. Boneh, E.J. Goh, K. Nissim, Evaluating 2-DNF formulas on ciphertexts. In *TCC* (2005), pp. 325–341
7. Z. Brakerski, C. Gentry, V. Vaikuntanathan, (Leveled) Fully homomorphic encryption without bootstrapping. In *ITCS* (2012), pp. 309–325
8. M. Burrows, D.J. Wheeler, *A Block-Sorting Lossless Data Compression Algorithm* (Technical report, HP Labs, 1994)
9. D. Catalano, D. Fiore, Using linearly-homomorphic encryption to evaluate degree-2 functions on encrypted data. In *CCS* (2015), pp. 1518–1529
10. M. Charikar, E. Lehman, D. Liu, R. Panigrahy, M. Prabhakaran, A. Sahai, and A. Shelat. The smallest grammar problem. IEEE Trans. Inform. Theory, 51(7), 2554–2576, 2005
11. F. Claude, G. Navarro, Improved grammar-based compressed indexes. In *SPIRE* (2012), pp. 180–192
12. G. Cormode, S. Muthukrishnan, The string edit distance matching problem with moves. ACM Trans. Algor. **3**(1), 2 (2007)
13. A. Davidson, C. Cid, An efficient toolkit for computing private set operations. In *ACISP* (2017), pp. 261–278
14. P. Ferragina, G. Manzini, Opportunistic data structures with applications. In *FOCS* (2000), pp. 390–398
15. J. Fischer, T. I, D. Köppl, Deterministic sparse suffix sorting on rewritable texts (2015)
16. D.M. Freeman, Converting pairing-based cryptosystems from composite-order groups to prime-order groups. In *EUROCRYPT* (2010), pp. 44–61
17. T. Gagie, G. Navarro, N. Prezza, Fully functional suffix trees and optimal text searching in bwt-runs bounded space. J. ACM **67**(1), 2:1–2:54 (2020)
18. M. Ganczorz, P. Gawrychowski, A. Jez, T. Kociumaka, Edit distance with block operations. In *ESA* (2018), pp. 33:1–33:14
19. C. Gentry, Fully homomorphic encryption using ideal lattices. In *STOC* (2009)
20. O. Goldreich, *Foundations of Cryptography*, vol. Volume (Cambridge University Press, II, 2004)
21. K. Goto, H. Bannai, S. Inenaga, M. Takeda, LZD factorization: Simple and practical online grammar compression with variable-to-fixed encoding. In *CPM* (2015), pp. 219–230
22. G. Herold, J. Hesse, D. Hofheinz, C. Ràfols, A. Rupp, Polynomial spaces: a new framework for composite-to-prime-order transformations. In *CRYPTO* (2014), pp. 261–279
23. T. I, Longest common extensions with recompression. In *CPM* 2017, pp. 18:1–18:15
24. T. I, W. Matsubara, K. Shimohira, S. Inenaga, H. Bannai, M. Takeda, K. Narisawa, A. Shinohara, Detecting regularities on grammar-compressed strings. Inf. Comput. **240**, 74–89 (2015)

25. A. Inan, S. Kaya, Y. Saygin, E. Savas, A. Hintoglu, A. Levi, Privacy preserving clustering on horizontally partitioned data. Data and Knowledge Engineering **63**(3), 646–666 (2007)
26. A. Jeż, Compressed membership for NFA (DFA) with compressed labels is in NP (P). In *STACS* (2012), pp. 136–147
27. A. Jeż. Approximation of grammar-based compression via recompression. Theor. Comput. Sci., 592:115–134, 2015
28. A. Jeż, Faster fully compressed pattern matching by recompression. ACM Trans. Algor. **11**(3), 20:1–20:43 (2015)
29. A. Jeż. One-variable word equations in linear time. Algorithmica, 74(1), 1–48, 2016
30. A. Jeż, Recompression: A simple and powerful technique for word equations. J. ACM **63**(1), 4 (2016)
31. A. Jeż, M. Lohrey, Approximation of smallest linear tree grammar. In *STACS* (2014), pp. 445–457
32. D. Kempa, Optimal construction of compressed indexes for highly repetitive texts. In *SODA* (2019), pp. 1344–1357
33. D. Kempa, N. Prezza, At the roots of dictionary compression: string attractors. In *STOC* (2018), pp. 827–840
34. J.C. Kieffer, E.H. Yang, Grammar-based codes: A new class of universal lossless source codes. IEEE Trans. Information Theory **46**(3), 737–754 (2000)
35. L. Kissner, D.X. Song, Privacy-preserving set operations. In *CRYPTO* (2005), pp. 241–257
36. T. Kociumaka, G. Navarro, N. Prezza, Towards a definitive measure of repetitiveness (2019)
37. S. Kreft and G. Navarro. On compressing and indexing repetitive sequences. Theor. Comput. Sci., 483:115–133, 2013
38. N.J. Larsson, A. Moffat, Offline dictionary-based compression. In *DCC* (1999), pp. 296–305
39. E. Lehman, *Approximation Algorithms for Grammar-Based Compression* (MIT, 2002). (PhD thesis)
40. A. Lempel, J. Ziv, On the complexity of finite sequences. IEEE Trans. Information Theory **22**(1), 75–81 (1976)
41. V. Mäkinen, G. Navarro, J. Sirén, N. Välimäki, Storage and retrieval of highly repetitive sequence collections. Journal of Computational Biology **17**(3), 281–308 (2010)
42. S. Maruyama, H. Sakamoto, and M. Takeda. An online algorithm for lightweight grammar-based compression. Algorithms, 5:213–235, 2012
43. T. Masaki, T. Kida, Online grammar transformation based on Re-Pair algorithm. In *DCC* (2016), pp. 349–358
44. S. Nakagawa, T. Sakamoto, Y. Takabatake, T. I, K. Shin, H. Sakamoto, Privacy-preserving string edit distance with moves. In *SISAP* (2018), pp. 226–240
45. G. Navarro, N. Prezza, Universal compressed text indexing. Theor. Comput. Sci. **762**, 41–50 (2019)
46. T. Nishimoto, Y. Tabei, Conversion from RLBWT to LZ77. In *CPM* (2019), pp. 9:1–9:12
47. T. Ohno, K. Sakai, Y. Takabatake, T. I, H. Sakamoto, A faster implementation of online RLBWT and its application to LZ77 parsing. J. Discrete Algorithms **52–53**, 18–28 (2018)
48. P. Paillier, Public-key cryptosystems based on composite degree residuosity classes. In *EUROCRYPT* (1999), pp. 223–238
49. A. Policriti, N. Prezza, Computing LZ77 in run-compressed space. In *DCC* (2016), pp. 23–32
50. S. Rane, W. Sun, Privacy preserving string comparisons based on levenshtein distance. In *WIFS* (2010), pp. 1–6
51. R. Rivest, A. Shamir, and L. Adleman. A method for obtaining digital signatures and public-key cryptosystems. Commun. ACM, 21(2), 120–126, 1978
52. W. Rytter. Application of Lempel-Ziv factorization to the approximation of grammar-based compression. Theor. Comp. Sci., 302(1–3):211–222, 2003
53. K. Sakai, T. Ohno, K. Goto, Y. Takabatake, T. I, H. Sakamoto, Repair in compressed space and time. In *DCC* (2019), pp. 518–527
54. H. Sakamoto. A fully linear-time approximation algorithm for grammar-based compression. J. Discrete Algorithms, 3(2–4), 416–430, 2005

55. D. Shapira and J.A. Storer. Edit distance with move operations. J. Discrete Algorithms, 5(2), 380–392, 2007
56. Y. Tabei, H. Saigo, Y. Yamanishi, S.J. Puglisi, Scalable partial least squares regression on grammar-compressed data matrices. In *KDD* (2016), pp. 1875–1884
57. Y. Takabatake, T. I, H. Sakamoto, A space-optimal grammar compression. In *ESA* (2017), pp. 67:1–67:15
58. E.-H. Yang, D.-K. He, Efficient universal lossless data compression algorithms based on a greedy sequential grammar transform - part two: with context models. IEEE Trans. Inform. Theory **49**(11), 2874–2894 (2003)
59. Y. Yoshimoto, M. Kataoka, Y. Takabatake, T. I, K. Shin, H. Sakamoto, Faster privacy-preserving computation of edit distance with moves. In *WALCOM* (2020), pp. 308–320

Open Access This chapter is licensed under the terms of the Creative Commons Attribution 4.0 International License (http://creativecommons.org/licenses/by/4.0/), which permits use, sharing, adaptation, distribution and reproduction in any medium or format, as long as you give appropriate credit to the original author(s) and the source, provide a link to the Creative Commons license and indicate if changes were made.

The images or other third party material in this chapter are included in the chapter's Creative Commons license, unless indicated otherwise in a credit line to the material. If material is not included in the chapter's Creative Commons license and your intended use is not permitted by statutory regulation or exceeds the permitted use, you will need to obtain permission directly from the copyright holder.

Chapter 7
Compression and Pattern Matching

Takuya Kida and Isamu Furuya

Abstract We introduce our research on compressed pattern matching technology that combines data compression and pattern matching. To show the results of this work, we explain the collage system proposed by Kida et al. in 2003 that is a unifying framework for compressed pattern matching, and we explain the Repair-VF method proposed by Yoshida and Kida in 2013 and the MR-Repair method proposed by Furuya et al. in 2019 as grammar compressions suitable for compressed pattern matching.

7.1 Introduction

Data compression is a technology that reduces the space used to store data by compactly expressing the redundancy contained in the data. It is mainly used for efficiently storing large amounts of data and reducing communication costs. If we consider the conversion of information to digital data as a kind of data compression, it has a long history that can be traced back to the Morse code developed in the 1830s. Many compression methods have been proposed depending on the type and application of data [43–46].

Information retrieval has also long been studied as a technique for efficiently finding a target part from a large-scale dataset or data group [3, 11, 13, 14, 30, 39, 55], and there are various methods depending on the required specifications. In particular, the approaches differ between searching for images and audio data and searching for documents (*text*). In this chapter, we focus on the latter task of text searching.

T. Kida (✉)
Faculty of Engineering, Hokkai-Gakuen University, 1-1, S26-W11, Chuo-ku, Sapporo 064-0926, Japan
e-mail: kida@lst.hokkai-s-u.ac.jp

I. Furuya
Graduate School of IST, Hokkaido University, N14-W9, Kitaku, Sapporo 060-0814, Japan
e-mail: furuya@ist.hokudai.ac.jp

© The Author(s) 2022

N. Katoh et al. (eds.), *Sublinear Computation Paradigm*,
https://doi.org/10.1007/978-981-16-4095-7_7

One of the basic problems in text searching is the *pattern matching problem*, which is also called the string matching problem. This is the problem of finding the occurrences of keywords (*patterns*) in a target text. Broadly speaking, there are two approaches to solving this problem. One is to build an index for the input text in advance, which is called *text indexing*. A text index allows for efficient searching when the target text is static and is not subsequently updated. The other is to access the input text sequentially from the beginning to the end while checking if the given pattern matches at the current reference position in the text. This is called *text scanning*. Text scanning is applicable even if the text is updated from time to time and it does not require index structures. In general, text indexing is superior in terms of search speed, while text scanning is superior in terms of search flexibility. By convention, "pattern matching" often refers to the latter, text scanning, in a narrow sense.

In this chapter, we outline a fusion technology of data compression and pattern matching called *compressed pattern matching*. First, in Sect. 7.2, we look back on the history of this field of study. Then, in Sect. 7.3, we provide some notation and definitions that are used in the following sections. In addition, we recall grammar compression, which is the key compression scheme for compressed pattern matching. Next, in Sect. 7.4, we introduce the general framework of compressed pattern matching proposed by Kida et al. [21]. In Sects. 7.5 and 7.6, we present outlines of Repair-VF and MR-Repair, respectively, which are the results of our work in this study. Finally, we conclude in Sect. 7.7.

7.2 History of Compressed Pattern Matching Research

The technology of combining data compression and pattern matching emerged in the early 1990s. This has come to be known as the *compressed pattern matching problem* [1], which is the problem of performing pattern matching without first decompressing the compressed input text. Formally, when a text $T = t_1 t_2 \dots t_u$ (t_i is a symbol) is given in compressed form $Z = z_1 z_2 \dots z_n$ (z_i is an element of the compressed text), and pattern P is given, the problem is to find all occurrences of P in T using only Z and P. A simple method is to first decompress Z to T and then use some commonly used pattern matching algorithm. However, this approach requires $O(m + u)$ time for pattern matching in addition to the decompression time.

The optimal algorithm for the compressed pattern matching problem is one that performs pattern matching in $O(m + n)$ time in the worst case. However, it is not easy to achieve both efficient compression of text data and fast pattern matching on it. In the initial research in this field, individual pattern matching algorithms were developed for each compression method. For example, Eilam-Tzoreff and Vishkin et al. [15] proposed an algorithm for run-length compression, Gąsieniec et al. [18] and Farach Thorup et al. [16] proposed algorithms for LZ77, and Amir et al. [2] proposed an algorithm for LZW [54]. However, these algorithms tend to be complicated, and as Manber [29] pointed out, it is questionable as to whether they are more practical than the simple method.

From the late 1990s to the early 2000s, several efficient methods for compressed pattern matching emerged [22, 38, 41]. For the first time, it was shown experimentally that these methods can perform pattern matching faster than the simple method. Furthermore, methods have appeared that can perform pattern matching faster by about the compression ratio than matching on the original text. The key is to select a compression method suitable for pattern matching even at the expense of compression ratio. In fact, Byte Pair Encoding (BPE), which was used by Shibata et al. [48] for this purpose, has a compression ratio of at most about 50% for natural language texts, while the LZ-family methods can compress the same texts to about 30% or less. However, text compression by BPE offers an advantage for pattern patching because all the codewords are fixed at 8 bits and the correspondence between each codeword and a portion of the text is relatively clear.

This caused a paradigm shift. Whereas individual pattern matching algorithms were previously developed for each data compression method, we realized that in order to increase the matching speed it would be better to develop a new data compression method suitable for pattern matching. In fact, in the 2000s, several data compression methods were proposed for this purpose.

One of the main groups of compression methods based on this idea are the compression methods proposed by Brisaboa et al. [7–9] and by Klein and Ben-Nissan [24]. These are based on a technique called *dense coding* [8]. Dense coding divides an input (natural language) text into words, and then encodes them so that the codewords become shorter in descending order of the frequency of the words. In addition, each codeword is assigned a bit pattern that has an explicit end to facilitate codeword extraction. Although dense coding offers good performance in terms of both compression ratio and pattern matching speed, some ingenuity is required to apply it to data such as DNA sequences that cannot be divided into words.

The other system is *grammar-based compression* (or *grammar compression*) [23] with fixed-length coding. This idea is an extension of BPE and can be applied even if an input text cannot be separated into words. One direct improvement of BPE is a method using a context-sensitive grammar by Maruyama et al. [34], while for compression methods based on context-free grammar we have the methods by Klein and Shapira [25] and Uemura et al. [51]. In both methods, a modified version of suffix tree [53] is used as a dictionary tree for constructing grammar.

In this chapter, for convenience, we refer to the former system as the dense coding system and the latter as the VF coding system.

In the 2010s, new data compression algorithms began to appear that achieved compression performance comparable to well-known compression tools such as Gzip and Bzip while maintaining properties suitable for pattern matching. Among the two systems described above, the VF coding system has difficulties in terms of compression rate and compression speed. Therefore, research looked into searching for and improving grammar compression, which is the basis of the VF coding system. Among this work, the algorithm RePair [26], which was proposed before the name "grammar compression" was used, has attracted attention because of its excellent compression ratio. Yoshida and Kida et al. [56] proposes a variant of RePair, called Repair-VF, which reduces the decrease in compression ratio by suppressing unnecessary grammar rules while encoding the output using fixed length codewords. The time and space complexities required for Repair-VF are both $O(n)$ for text of length n, which is the same as the original RePair. Repair-VF realizes high-speed pattern matching on compressed text while having a good compression ratio comparable to Gzip.

Very recently, we proposed a novel variant of RePair, called MR-RePair [17], which constructs more compact grammars than RePair, particularly for highly repetitive texts. This achievement comes from an analysis of RePair. We show in [17] that the main process of RePair, that is, the step by step substitution of the most frequent symbol pairs, works within the corresponding most frequent *maximal repeats*. We then reveal in [17] the relationship between maximal repeats and grammars constructed by RePair.

7.3 Preliminaries

7.3.1 Definitions of Notation and Terms

Let Σ be an *alphabet*, that is, an ordered finite set of symbols. An element $T = t_1 \dots t_n$ of Σ^* is called a *string* or a *text*, where $|T| = n$ denotes its length. Let ε be an empty string of length 0, that is, $|\varepsilon| = 0$. We denote a concatenation of two strings $x, y \in \Sigma$ by $x \cdot y$, or xy for simplicity if no confusion occurs.

If $T = xyz$ with $x, y, z \in \Sigma^*$, then x, y, z are called a *prefix*, *substring*, and *suffix* of T, respectively. Let $T[i : j] = t_i \cdots t_j$ for any $1 \le i \le j \le n$ denote a substring of T beginning at i and ending at j in T, and let $T[i] = t_i$ denote the i th symbol of T. Let $w[i : j] = \varepsilon$ if $j < i$ for simplicity.

7.3.2 Grammar Compression

A *context-free grammar* (*CFG* or simply *grammar*) G is defined as a four-tuple $G = \{V, \Sigma, S, R\}$, where V denotes an ordered finite set of variables, Σ denotes an ordered finite alphabet, R denotes a finite set of binary relations called *production rules* (or *rules*) between V and $(V \cup \Sigma)^*$, and $S \in V$ denotes a special variable called *start variable*. A production rule refers to the situation where a variable is substituted and written in the form $v \to w$, with $v \in V$ and $w \in (V \cup \Sigma)^*$. Let $X, Y \in (V \cup \Sigma)^*$. If there are $x_l, x, x_r, y \in (V \cup \Sigma)^*$ such that $X = x_l x x_r$, $Y = x_l y x_r$, and $x \to y \in R$, we write $X \to Y$, and denote the reflexive transitive closure of $\to$ as $\stackrel{*}{\Rightarrow}$. Let $val(v)$ be a string derived from v, that is, $v \stackrel{*}{\Rightarrow} val(v)$. We define grammar $\hat{G} = \{\hat{V}, \hat{\Sigma}, \hat{S}, \hat{R}\}$ as a *subgrammar* of G if $\hat{V} \subseteq V$, $\hat{\Sigma} \subseteq (V \cup \Sigma)$, and $\hat{R} \subseteq R$.

Given a text T, *grammar compression* is a method for lossless text data compression that constructs a restricted CFG uniquely deriving the text T. For G to be deterministic, the production rule for each variable $v \in V$ must be unique. In what follows, we assume that every grammar is deterministic and each production rule is $v_i \to expr_i$, where $expr_i$ is an expression either $expr_i = a$ $(a \in \Sigma)$ or $expr_i = v_{j_1} v_{j_2} \dots v_{j_n}$ $(i > j_k$ for all $1 \leq k \leq j_n)$. To estimate the effectiveness for compression, we use the size of the constructed grammar, which is defined as the total length of the right-hand side of all production rules of the grammar.

While the problem of constructing the smallest such grammar for a given text is known to be NP-hard [10], several approximation algorithms have been proposed. One of them is RePair [26], which is an off-line grammar compression algorithm. Despite its simple scheme, RePair is known for its high compression in practice [12, 19, 52], and hence, it has been comprehensively studied. Some examples of studies on the RePair algorithm include its extension to an online algorithm [35], practical working time/space improvements [6, 47], applications to various fields [12, 27, 49], and theoretical analysis of generated grammar sizes [10, 40, 42].

7.4 Framework for Compressed Pattern Matching

A grammar compressed text can be expressed in a framework called collage systems [21]. A pattern matching algorithm on the compressed text can then be obtained as an instance of the general algorithm on the collage system. Algorithm on collage systems can be understood as an extension of the Knuth-Morris-Pratt method (KMP method) [14].

7.4.1 KMP Method

The KMP method a well-known linear-time algorithm for pattern matching on an ordinary (uncompressed) text. Its movement can be modeled as a linear automaton (KMP automaton) for a given pattern P.

For a given pattern P, a KMP automaton consists of two functions:

$$\begin{aligned} \text{goto function} g &: Q \times \Sigma \to Q \cup \{\mathit{fail}\}, \\ \text{failure function} f &: Q \setminus \{0\} \to Q, \end{aligned}$$

where $Q = \{0, 1, \dots, |P|\}$ is the set of states, and *fail* is a special symbol that is not included in Q. For $j \in Q$ and $a \in \Sigma$, the goto function g returns $j + 1$ if $P[j + 1] = a$ holds, otherwise it returns *fail*. For $j = 0$, let $g(0, a) = 0$ for all $a \in \Sigma$ where $P[1] \neq a$ holds. For $j \in Q \setminus \{0\}$, the failure function f returns the maximum integer k such that $P[1 : k] = P[j - k + 1 : j]$ holds.

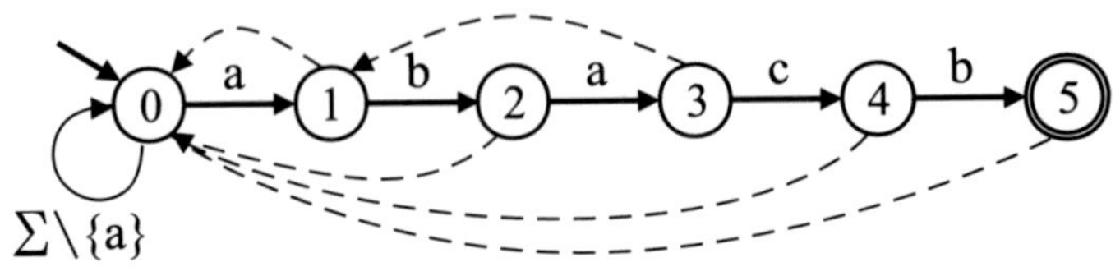

Fig. 7.1 KMP automaton for P = abacb. In this figure, each circle indicates a state, and the double circle indicates the final state. Solid arrows and dashed arrows indicate the goto function and failure function, respectively

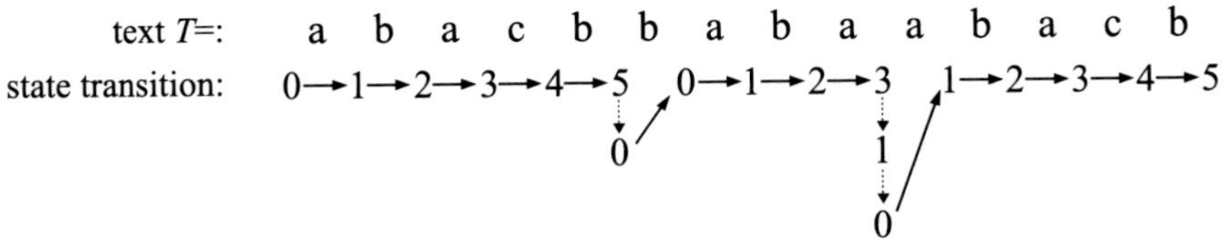

Fig. 7.2 Movement of KMP automaton. Solid arrows and dashed arrows indicate state transitions caused by the goto function and the failure function, respectively

The automaton repeats state transitions by tracing g corresponding to the characters read one by one from the input text. If g returns *fail*, then f is repeatedly called with the current state number to go back until a transition by g succeeds with the same character. When the automaton finally reaches the rightmost state, it can be judged that P has occurred.

Figure 7.1 shows the KMP automaton for pattern P = abacb. The movement of the KMP automaton in Fig. 7.1 for the text T = abacbbabaabacb is shown in Fig. 7.2. In this example, it can be judged that P has occurred when the automaton reaches the state number 5.

To eliminate the failure function, we define the state transition function $\delta : Q \times \Sigma \to Q$ as follows:

$$\delta(j, a) = \begin{cases} g(j, a) & \text{if } g(j, a) \neq \textit{fail}, \\ \delta(f(j), a) & \text{otherwise} \end{cases}$$

Moreover, we extend it to $Q \times \Sigma^*$ as follows:

$$\delta^*(j, \varepsilon) = j, \quad \delta^*(j, ua) = \delta(\delta^*(j, u), a),$$

where $j \in Q$, $u \in \Sigma^*$, and $a \in \Sigma$.

7.4.2 Collage System

A *collage system* is a pair $\langle \mathcal{D}, \mathcal{S} \rangle$ defined as follows: $\mathcal{D}$ is a sequence of assignments $X_1 = expr_1; X_2 = expr_2; \cdots; X_n = expr_n$, where each X_k is a token and $expr_k$ is any of the form:

a	for $a \in \Sigma \cup \{\varepsilon\}$,	*(primitive assignment)*
$X_i X_j$	for $i, j < k$,	*(concatenation)*
$^{[j]}X_i$	for $i < k$ and an integer j,	*(prefix truncation)*
$X_i^{[j]}$	for $i < k$ and an integer j,	*(suffix truncation)*
$(X_i)^j$	for $i < k$ and an integer j.	*(j times repetition)*

Let the set of all tokens in $\mathcal{D}$ be denoted by $F(\mathcal{D})$. Each token represents a string obtained by evaluating the expression as it implies. Let the string represented by token $X \in F(\mathcal{D})$ be denoted by $X.u$. For example, for $X_1 = \mathtt{a}$; $X_2 = \mathtt{b}$; $X_3 = X_1 \cdot X_2$; $X_4 = (X_3)^3$; $X_5 = X_4^{[1]}$, $X_4.u = \mathtt{ababab}$ and $X_5.u = \mathtt{ababa}$. However, in this section we identify token X with the string it represents, and simply denote both by X unless confusion occurs.

Let the number of assignments in $\mathcal{D}$ be the *size* of $\mathcal{D}$, and denote it by $||\mathcal{D}||$, that is, $||\mathcal{D}|| = |F(\mathcal{D})| = n$. For a sequence $\mathcal{S} = X_{i_1}, X_{i_2}, \ldots, X_{i_k}$ of tokens defined in $\mathcal{D}$, we denote by $|\mathcal{S}|$ the number k of tokens in $\mathcal{S}$.

The collage system $\langle \mathcal{D}, \mathcal{S} \rangle$ represents the string obtained by concatenating $X_{i_1}, \ldots, X_{i_k}$. That is, $\mathcal{D}$ and $\mathcal{S}$ correspond to the dictionary and compressed text in a compression method, respectively. Both $\mathcal{D}$ and $\mathcal{S}$ can be encoded in various ways. The compression ratios therefore depend on their encoding sizes rather than $||\mathcal{D}||$ and $|\mathcal{S}|$.

A collage system is said to be *truncation-free* if $\mathcal{D}$ contains no truncation operation. A collage system is said to be *regular* if $\mathcal{D}$ contains neither truncation nor repetition operations. A regular collage system is said to be *simple* if for every assignment $X = YZ$, $|Y.u| = 1$ or $|Z.u| = 1$.

7.4.3 Pattern Matching on Collage Systems

The basic idea of pattern matching on a collage system is to simulate the movement of the KMP automaton on uncompressed text. Using the state transition function δ^* of the KMP automaton defined in Sec. 7.4.1, we define the function $Jump : Q \times F(\mathcal{D}) \to Q$ as follows:

$$Jump(j, X) = \delta^*(j, X.u).$$

The intent of *Jump* is to simulate the state transition of the original KMP automaton by jumping when it receives token X. Moreover, for any $j \in Q$ and $X \in F(\mathcal{D})$, we define the set $Output(j, X) = Occ_P(P[1:j] \cdot X.u)$, where $Occ_P(x)$ indicates the set of all indices of occurrences of P within x.

Fig. 7.3 A matching algorithm on a collage system

Input. Collage system $\langle \mathcal{D}, \mathcal{S} \rangle$ and pattern $P = P[1:m]$.
Output. All positions of occurrences of P in T:

```
  /* Preprocessing */
  Collect the information required to calculate Jump and Output;
  /* Scanning compressed text */
  let S = X_{i_1} X_{i_2} ... X_{i_n}.
  ℓ := 0; state := 0;
  for k := 1 to n do begin
    for each p ∈ Output(state, X_{i_k}) do
      pattern P occurs at ℓ + p − m + 1;
    state = Jump(state, X_{i_k});
    ℓ := ℓ + |X_{i_k}|
  end
```

For a given collage system $\langle \mathcal{D}, \mathcal{S} \rangle$ representing text T and for a given pattern P, the pattern matching algorithm preprocesses the information required to calculate *Jump* and *Output* from $\mathcal{D}$, and then performs matching while scanning a sequence of tokens in $\mathcal{S}$ one by one from the head (Fig. 7.3).

From the results of [21], the following theorem is obtained.

Theorem 1 (Theorem 3 of [21]) *For a collage system $\langle \mathcal{D}, \mathcal{S} \rangle$, the compressed pattern matching problem can be solved in $O(||\mathcal{D}|| + |\mathcal{S}| + m^2 + R)$ time using $O(||\mathcal{D}|| + m^2)$ space if $\langle \mathcal{D}, \mathcal{S} \rangle$ is regular, where R is the number of occurrences of pattern P in the text represented by $\langle \mathcal{D}, \mathcal{S} \rangle$.*

This theorem applies to both RePair and Repair-VF because texts compressed by these can be described by regular collage systems.

7.5 Repair-VF

This section first introduces RePair and then gives an outline of Repair-VF. Repair-VF has a structure that combines RePair with a fixed-length coding. Please refer to the literature [56] for the details of Repair-VF and experimental results for its performance.

7.5.1 RePair

RePair is a grammar compression algorithm that was proposed by Larsson and Moffat [26]. For input text T, let $G = \{V, \Sigma, S, R\}$ be the grammar constructed by RePair. The RePair procedure can then be described by the following steps:

Step 1. Replace each symbol $a \in \Sigma$ with a new variable v_a and add $v_a \to a$ to R.
Step 2. Find the most frequent pair p in T.

	a	b	r	a	c	a	d	a	b	r	a
$v_\alpha \to \alpha$ (α = a,b,r,c,d)	v_a	v_b	v_r	v_a	v_c	v_a	v_d	v_a	v_b	v_r	v_a
$v_1 \to v_a v_b$	v_1		v_r	v_a	v_c	v_a	v_d	v_1		v_r	v_a
$v_2 \to v_1 v_r$	v_2			v_a	v_c	v_a	v_d	v_2			v_a
$v_3 \to v_2 v_a$	v_3				v_c	v_a	v_d	v_3			
$S \to v_3 v_c v_a v_d v_3$	S										

Fig. 7.4 Example of the grammar generation process of RePair for T = abracadabra. The generated grammar is $\{\{v_a, v_b, v_r, v_c, v_1, v_2, v_3, S\}$, {a,b,r,c,d}, S, $\{v_a \to$ a, $v_b \to$ b, $v_r \to$ r, $v_c \to$ c, $v_d \to$ d, $v_1 \to v_a v_b$, $v_2 \to v_1 v_c$, $v_3 \to v_2 v_d$, $S \to v_3 v_c v_a v_d v_3\}\}$ with a size of 16

Step 3. Replace every occurrence (or as many occurrences as possible if p is a pair consisting of the same symbol) of p with a new variable v, and then, add $v \to p$ to R.

Step 4. Re-evaluate the frequencies of pairs for the updated text generated in Step 3. If the maximum frequency is 1, add $S \to$ (current text$T$) to R, and terminate. Otherwise, return to Step 2.

Figure 7.4 illustrates an example of the grammar generation process of RePair.

The following theorem relates to the performance of RePair shown by Larsson and Moffat [26].

Theorem 2 ([26]) *RePair works in $O(n)$ expected time and $5n + 4k^2 + 4k' + \lceil\sqrt{n+1}\rceil - 1$ words of space, where n is the length of the source text, k denotes the cardinality of the source alphabet, and k' denotes the cardinality of the final dictionary.*

7.5.2 *Outline of Repair-VF*

The original RePair encodes the rules in R excluding S using Elias gamma coding, that is, each codeword has a variable length, whereas Repair-VF uses a fixed-length code. The right side of S corresponds to the compressed text, and is converted to a sequence of fixed-length codewords of the rules in S.

Consider the number of fixed-length coded rules. In the process of Step 1 of RePair, $|\Sigma|$ rules are created. In addition, the process of Step 3 of RePair replaces the most frequent pair and at the same time adds one rule to R. Let s be the number of rules which are added to R in Step 3. The total number of rules is then $|\Sigma| + s$, and thus each symbol can be fixed-length encoded with $\lceil\log(|\Sigma| + s)\rceil$ bits. The information about Σ can be restored from the rules added in Step 3, so there is no need to explicitly save it. Therefore, only the rules added in Step 3 and the right side of S added last in Step 4 need to be saved. In the former, the right side of each rule consists of two symbols, so the total number of symbols to be saved is $2s$. Since the latter depends on the input text T, let n be the length of T. The number of bits of the output compressed data is then

$$(2s + n)\lceil \log(|\Sigma| + s)\rceil \tag{7.1}$$

bits in total.

We want to find the best s that minimizes the total number of output bits. Note that the final output tends to be smaller as s increases up to some point. In RePair, Step 3 is repeated until the frequency of the most frequent pair becomes 1. In the case of using a fixed-length code as above, this increases useless rules. Increasing the number of rules can increase the bit length per symbol, resulting in a longer final bit length. We can eliminate the waste by terminating the process in the middle. However, it is difficult to determine on the fly the s at which the output becomes minimal. Even after the first time the output size increases, the length of S may become shorter by continuing Step 3, and the output size may decrease again.

Therefore, during the processing of RePair, we record the minimum value of the output size and the corresponding s by calculating Equation (7.1) every time a rule is added in Step 3. Note that the calculation of Equation (7.1) does not require actual coding or outputting since a fixed-length code is used. Finally, when S is output in Step 4, we can obtain the smallest output by outputting while expanding the rules added after the best s.

This is *Repair-VF* (called Repair-VF-best in the original paper). The suffix "VF" comes from an abbreviation for variable-to-fixed length coding (VF coding). For the input text T, each rule of the output grammar G corresponds to a substring of T, and the right-hand side of S can be regarded as the variable length factorization of T. Thus, Repair-VF can be viewed as a VF coding from the viewpoint of information source coding.

7.6 MR-Repair

In this section we outline MR-Repair, which is a method to reduce the output grammar size by focusing on the relationship between RePair and maximal repeats. Please refer to the literature [17] for the details of MR-Repair and experimental results for its performance.

7.6.1 Maximal Repeats

Let s be a substring of text T. If the frequency of s is greater than 1, s is called a *repeat*. A *left* (or *right*) *extension* of s is any substring of T in the form ws (or sw), where $w \in \Sigma^*$. We define s as a *left* (or *right*) *maximal* if left (or right) extensions of s occur a strictly lower number of times in T than s. Accordingly, s is a maximal repeat of T if s is both left and right maximal. In this paper, we only consider strings with a length of more than 1 as maximal repeats. For example, the substring `abra` of $T =$ `abracadabra` is a maximal repeat, whereas `br` is not.

The following theorem describes an essential property of RePair, that is, RePair recursively replaces the most frequent maximal repeats.

Theorem 3 (Theorem 1 of [17]) *Let T be a given text, under the condition that every most frequent maximal repeat of T does not appear overlapping itself. Let f be the frequency of the most frequent pairs of T, and t be a text obtained after all pairs with frequency f in T are replaced by variables. There is then a text s such that s is obtained after all maximal repeats with frequency f in T are replaced by variables, and s and t are isomorphic to each other.*

7.6.2 MR Order

According to Theorem 1 of [17], if there is just one most frequent maximal repeat in the current text, then RePair replaces all occurrences of it step by step. However, a problem arises if there are two or more most frequent maximal repeats, with some of them overlapping. In this case, the selection order of pairs (of course, they are most frequent) affects the priority of maximal repeats. We call this order of selecting (summarizing) maximal repeats the *maximal repeat selection order* (or simply *MR-order*). Note that the selection order of pairs actually depends on the implementation of RePair. If there are several distinct most frequent pairs with overlaps, RePair constructs grammars with different sizes according to the selection order of the pairs.

However, the following theorem states that the MR-order rather than the replacement order of pairs determines the size of the grammar generated by RePair.

Theorem 4 (Theorem 2 of [17]) *The sizes of grammars generated by RePair are the same if they are generated in the same MR-order.*

7.6.3 Algorithm

The main strategy of the proposed method is to recursively replace the most frequent maximal repeats instead of the most frequent pairs.

Definition 1 (*Definition 3 of* [17]) For an input text T, let $G = \{V, \Sigma, S, R\}$ be the grammar generated by MR-Repair. MR-Repair constructs G through the following steps:

Step 1. Replace each symbol $a \in \Sigma$ with a new variable v a and add $v_a \rightarrow a$ to R.

Step 2. Find the most frequent maximal repeat r in T.

Step 3. Check if $|r| > 2$ and $r[1] = r[|r|]$, and if so, use $r[1 : |r| - 1]$ instead of r in Step 4.

	a	b	r	a	c	a	d	a	b	r	a
$v_\alpha \rightarrow \alpha$ (α = a,b,r,c,d)	v_a	v_b	v_r	v_a	v_c	v_a	v_d	v_a	v_b	v_r	v_a
$v_1 \rightarrow v_a v_b v_r$	v_1			v_a	v_c	v_a	v_d	v_1			v_a
$v_2 \rightarrow v_1 v_a$	v_2				v_c	v_a	v_d	v_2			
$S \rightarrow v_2 v_c v_a v_d v_2$	S										

Fig. 7.5 Example of the grammar generation process of MR-Repair for T = abracadabra. The generated grammar is $\{\{v_a, v_b, v_r, v_c, v_d, v_1, S\}, \{a, b, r, c, d\}, S, \{v_a \rightarrow a, v_b \rightarrow b, v_r \rightarrow r, v_c \rightarrow c, v_d \rightarrow d, v_1 \rightarrow v_a v_b v_r, v_2 \rightarrow v_1 v_a, S \rightarrow v_2 v_c v_a v_d v_2\}\}$ with a size of 15

Step 4. Replace every occurrence of r with a new variable v and then add $v \rightarrow r$ to R.

Step 5. Re-evaluate the frequencies of maximal repeats for the updated text generated in Step 4. If the maximum frequency is 1, add $S \rightarrow$ (current text) to R and terminate. Otherwise, return to Step 2.

Figure 7.5 shows an example of the grammar generation process of MR-Repair. As shown in this figure, the size of the grammar generated by MR-Repair is smaller than that generated by RePair shown in Figure reffig:repair.

Theorem 5 (Theorem 5 of [17]) *Assume that RePair and MR-Repair work based on the same MR-order for a given text. Let* g_{rp} *and* g_{mr} *be the sizes of the grammars generated by RePair and MR-Repair, respectively. Then,* $\frac{1}{2} g_{rp} < g_{mr} \leq g_{rp}$ *holds.*

7.7 Conclusion

In this chapter, we outlined research on compressed pattern matching and showed that we can speed up pattern matching by selecting a suitable compression method. This has led to the development of compression methods that are useful for pattern matching. Whereas the initially developed compression methods had low compression performance, Repair-VF [56] achieves both a good compression rate and good matching speed by combining advanced grammar compression with fixed-length code. Collage systems [21] provide a unified algorithm for compressed pattern matching, allowing us to obtain an efficient pattern matching algorithm for grammar compression as an instance of the unified algorithm.

Since proposing Repair-VF, we have proposed several improvements for it. LT-Repair [35] improves RePair processing semi-online by adding the constraint called the *left-tall condition* to its grammar. This makes it possible to efficiently compress large-scale text data with small memory.

MR-Repair [17], which we have recently proposed, is a method that reduces the output grammar size by focusing on the relationship between RePair and maximal repeats. Although heuristic improvements [4, 20, 28, 36] focusing on non-maximal repetitive substrings have previously been proposed, MR-Repair is superior because it has been proven to generate theoretically smaller grammar than the original RePair. A topic for future work is to see whether compressed pattern matching using these methods can be performed efficiently.

In the present work, we mainly explained the compressed pattern matching problem based on text scanning. However, the *succinct index* technology which combines text index and data compression was also established in 2000. This is an indexing technology that utilizes a succinct data structure that can solve query processing with a small space of almost the information-theoretic lower bound. Succinct index has an excellent property that allows full-text searching while compressing a target text smaller than the original text. For details of this technology, refer to the excellent book by Navarro [37].

In terms of online grammar compression methods, there exists FOLCA proposed by Maruyama et al. [33] and its improvement SOLCA proposed by Takabatake et al. [50]. FOLCA is based on a string factorization called edit-sensitive parsing. It performs factorization and grammar generation in parallel while reading an input text sequentially from the beginning. It is known that *straight line programs* (restricted CFGs) generated by FOLCA can be used as index structures [5].

In recent years, Martinez et al. [31] proposed a novel compression method called Marlin and an improvement of it [32]. These methods achieve both decompression at ultrahigh-speed and good performance in terms of compression ratio. If we can decompress compressed data at sufficiently high speed, we can perform pattern matching efficiently even if it is performed after decompressing the data. Comparative studies on these approaches are also left for future work.

References

1. A. Amir, G. Benson, Efficient two-dimensional compressed matching, in *Proc. Data Compression Conference*, p. 279 (1992)
2. A. Amir, G. Benson, M. Farach, Let sleeping files lie: pattern matching in Z-compressed files. J. Comput. Syst. Sci. **52**, 299–307 (1996)
3. A. Apostolico, Z. Galil, *Pattern Matching Algorithms* (Oxford University Press, 1997)
4. A. Apostolico, S. Lonardi, Off-line compression by greedy textual substitution. Proc. IEEE **88**(11), 1733–1744 (2000)
5. D. Belazzougui, P. Cording, S. Puglisi, Y. Tabei, Access, rank, and select in grammar-compressed strings, in *Algorithms—ESA 2015, LNCS*, vol. 9294 (Springer, 2015), pp. 142–154
6. P. Bille, I.L. Gørtz, N. Prezza, *Space-Efficient Re-pair Compression* (2017), pp. 171–180
7. N. Brisaboa, A. Fariña, J. López Rodríguez, G. Navarro, E. Lopez, A new searchable variable-to-variable compressor. Data Compression Conf. **DCC2010**, 199–208 (2010)
8. N. Brisaboa, E. Iglesias, G. Navarro, J. Paramá, An efficient compression code for text databases. Eur. Conf. Inform. Retrieval (ECIR'03) **2633**, 468–481 (2003)
9. N. Brisaboa, G. Navarro, M. Esteller, (S,C)-dense coding: An optimized compression code for natural language text databases, in *String Processing and Information Retrieval (SPIRE2003), LNCS*, vol. 2857 (2003), pp. 122–136
10. M. Charikar, E. Lehman, D. Liu, R. Panigrahy, M. Prabhakaran, A. Sahai, A. Shelat, The smallest grammar problem. Inform. Theory, IEEE Trans. **51**, 2554–2576 (2005)
11. C. Charras, T. Lecroq, *Handbook of Exact String Matching Algorithms* (College Publications, 2004)

12. F. Claude, G. Navarro, Fast and compact web graph representations. ACM Trans. Web **4**(4) (2010). https://doi.org/10.1145/1841909.1841913
13. M. Crochemore, C. Hancart, T. Lecroq, *Algorithms on Strings* (Cambridge University Press, 2007)
14. M. Crochemore, W. Rytter, *Jewels of Stringology* (World Scientific, 2002). https://doi.org/10.1142/4838
15. T. Eilam-Tzoreff, U. Vishkin, Matching patterns in strings subject to multi-linear transformations. Theor. Comput. Sci. **60**(3), 231–254 (1988)
16. M. Farach, M. Thorup, String-matching in Lempel-Ziv compressed strings. Algorithmica **20**(4), 388–404 (1998). ((previous version in STOC'95))
17. I. Furuya, T. Takagi, Y. Nakashima, S. Inenaga, H. Bannai, T. Kida, MR-RePair: grammar compression based on maximal repeats, in *Data Compression Conference (DCC2019)* (IEEE Computer Society, 2019), pp. 508–517
18. L. Gąsieniec, M. Karpinski, W. Plandowski, W. Rytter, Efficient algorithms for Lempel-Ziv encoding, in *Proceedings of the 4th Scandinavian Workshop on Algorithm Theory, LNCS*, vol. 1097, (Springer, 1996), pp. 392–403
19. R. González, G. Navarro, Compressed text indexes with fast locate, in *Combinatorial Pattern Matching*. ed. by B. Ma, K. Zhang (Springer, Berlin Heidelberg, Berlin, Heidelberg, 2007), pp. 216–227
20. S. Inenaga, T. Funamoto, M. Takeda, A. Shinohara, Linear-time off-line text compression by longest-first substitution, in *String Processing and Information Retrieval. SPIRE 2003, LNCS*, vol. 2857 (Springer, 2003), pp. 137–152
21. T. Kida, T. Matsumoto, Y. Shibata, M. Takeda, A. Shinohara, S. Arikawa, Collage system: a unifying framework for compressed pattern matching. Theor. Comput. Sci. **298**(1), 253–272 (2003). https://doi.org/10.1016/S0304-3975(02)00426-7
22. T. Kida, M. Takeda, A. Shinohara, M. Miyazaki, S. Arikawa, Multiple pattern matching in LZW compressed text. J. Discrete Algor. **1**(1), 133–158 (2000). (previous version in DCC'98 and CPM'99)
23. J.C. Kieffer, E. Yang, Grammar-based codes: a new class of universal lossless source codes. IEEE Trans. Inform. Theory **46**(3), 737–754 (2000)
24. S. Klein, M. Ben-Nissan, Using fibonacci compression codes as alternatives to dense codes. Data Compression Conf. **DCC2008**, 472–481 (2008)
25. S. Klein, D. Shapira, Improved variable-to-fixed length codes, in *String Processing and Information Retrieval (SPIRE 2008), LNCS*, vol. 5280, (Springer, 2008), pp. 39–50
26. N.J. Larsson, A. Moffat, Offline dictionary-based compression, in *Data Compression Conference (DCC'99)*, (IEEE Computer Society, 1999), pp. 296–305
27. M. Lohrey, S. Maneth, R. Mennicke, Xml tree structure compression using re-pair. Inform. Syst. **38**(8), 1150–1167 (2013)
28. M. Gańczorz, A. Jeż, Improvements on repair grammar compressor. Data Compression Conf. **DCC2017**, 181–190 (2017)
29. U. Manber, A text compression scheme that allows fast searching directly in the compressed file. ACM Trans. Inform. Syst. **15**(2), 124–136 (1997). (previous version in CPM'94)
30. C.D. Manning, P. Raghavan, H. Schuetze, *Introduction to Information Retrieval* (Cambridge University Press, 2008)
31. M. Martinez, M. Haurilet, R. Stiefelhagen, J. Serra-Sagristà, Marlin: a high throughput variable-to-fixed codec using plurally parsable dictionaries, in *Data Compression Conference (DCC2017)*, (IEEE Computer Society, 2017), pp. 161–170
32. M. Martinez, K. Sandfort, D. Dubé, J. Serra-Sagristà, Improving marlin's compression ratio with partially overlapping codewords, in *Data Compression Conference (DCC2018)* (IEEE Computer Society, 2018), pp. 325–334
33. S. Maruyama, Y. Tabei, Fully online grammar compression in constant space, in *Data Compression Conference (DCC2014)*, (IEEE Computer Society, 2014), pp. 173–182
34. S. Maruyama, Y. Tanaka, H. Sakamoto, M. Takeda, Context-sensitive grammar transform: compression and pattern matching. IEICE. Trans. **93-D**, 219–226 (2010). https://doi.org/10.1587/transinf.E93.D.219

35. T. Masaki, T. Kida, Online grammar transformation based on re-pair algorithm, in *Data Compression Conference (DCC2016)*, (IEEE Computer Society, 2016), pp. 349–358
36. R. Nakamura, H. Bannai, S. Inenaga, M. Takeda, Simple linear-time off-line text compression by longest-first substitution, in *Data Compression Conference (DCC'07)*, (IEEE Computer Society, 2007), pp. 123–132
37. G. Navarro, *Compact Data Structures: A Practical Approach*, 1st edn. (Cambridge University Press, USA, 2016)
38. G. Navarro, M. Raffinot, A general practical approach to pattern matching over Ziv-Lempel compressed text. Combinat. Pattern Matching (CPM'99), LNCS **1645**, 14–36 (1999)
39. G. Navarro, M. Raffinot, *Flexible Pattern Matching in Strings: Practical On-Line Search Algorithms for Texts and Biological Sequences* (Cambridge University Press, 2002)
40. G. Navarro, L. Russo, *Repair Achieves High-Order Entropy* (2008), pp. 537–537
41. G. Navarro, J. Tarhio, Boyer-moore string matching over Ziv-Lempel compressed text, in *Proceedings of the CPM'2000, LNCS*, vol. 1848, (Springer, 2000), pp. 166–180
42. C. Ochoa, G. Navarro, Re-pair and all irreducible grammars are upper bounded by high-order empirical entropy. IEEE Trans. Inform. Theory **65**(5), 3160–3164 (2019)
43. D. Salomon, *Data Compression: The Complete Reference*, 4th edn. (Springer, 2006)
44. D. Salomon, G. Motta, *Handbook of Data Compression*, 5th edn. (Springer, 2009)
45. K. Sayood, *Lossless Compression Handbook* (Academic Press, 2002)
46. K. Sayood, *Introduction to Data Compression*, 4th edn. (Morgan Kaufmann, 2012)
47. K. Sekine, H. Sasakawa, S. Yoshida, T. Kida, *Adaptive Dictionary Sharing Method for Repair Algorithm*, (2014), p. 425
48. Y. Shibata, T. Kida, S. Fukamachi, M. Takeda, A. Shinohara, T. Shinohara, S. Arikawa, Speeding up pattern matching by text compression, in *Proceedings of the 4th Italian Conference on Algorithms and Complexity, LNCS*, vol. 1767, (Springer, 2000), pp. 306–315
49. Y. Tabei, H. Saigo, Y. Yamanishi, S.J. Puglisi, *Scalable partial least squares regression on grammar-compressed data matrices*, vol. KDD '16, (Association for Computing Machinery, New York, NY, USA, 2016), pp. 1875–1884. (https://doi.org/10.1145/2939672.2939864)
50. Y. Takabatake, I. Tomohiro, H. Sakamoto, A space-optimal grammar compression, in *25th Annual European Symposium on Algorithms (ESA2017), LIPIcs*, vol. 87, (Schloss Dagstuhl-Leibniz-Zentrum für Informatik, 2017), pp. 67:1–67:15
51. T. Uemura, S. Yoshida, T. Kida, T. Asai, S. Okamoto, Training parse trees for efficient vf coding, in *String Processing and Information Retrieval (SPIRE 2010), LNCS*, vol. 6393, (Springer, 2010), pp. 179–184
52. R. Wan, *Browsing and Searching Compressed Documents* (The University of Melbourne, Melbourne, Australia, 2003). (Ph.D. thesis)
53. P. Weiner, *Linear Pattern Matching Algorithm* (1973), pp. 1–11
54. T.A. Welch, A technique for high performance data compression. IEEE Comput. **17**, 8–19 (1984)
55. I.H. Witten, A. Moffat, T.C. Bell, *Managing Gigabytes: Compressing and Indexing Documents and Images*, 2nd edn. (Morgan Kaufmann, 1999)
56. S. Yoshida, T. Kida, A variable-length-to-fixed-length coding method using a Re-Pair algorithm. IPSJ Online Trans. **6**, 121–127 (2013)

Open Access This chapter is licensed under the terms of the Creative Commons Attribution 4.0 International License (http://creativecommons.org/licenses/by/4.0/), which permits use, sharing, adaptation, distribution and reproduction in any medium or format, as long as you give appropriate credit to the original author(s) and the source, provide a link to the Creative Commons license and indicate if changes were made.

The images or other third party material in this chapter are included in the chapter's Creative Commons license, unless indicated otherwise in a credit line to the material. If material is not included in the chapter's Creative Commons license and your intended use is not permitted by statutory regulation or exceeds the permitted use, you will need to obtain permission directly from the copyright holder.

Chapter 8
Orthogonal Range Search Data Structures

Kazuki Ishiyama and Kunihiko Sadakane

Abstract We first review existing space-efficient data structures for the orthogonal range search problem. Then, we propose two improved data structures, the first of which has better query time complexity than the existing structures and the second of which has better space complexity that matches the information-theoretic lower bound.

8.1 Introduction

Consider a set P of n points in the d-dimensional space $\mathbb{R}^d$. Given an orthogonal range $Q = \left[l_0^{(Q)}, u_0^{(Q)}\right] \times \left[l_1^{(Q)}, u_1^{(Q)}\right] \times \cdots \times \left[l_{d-1}^{(Q)}, u_{d-1}^{(Q)}\right]$, the problem of answering queries for information on $P \cap Q$, the subset of P contained in the range Q, is called the *orthogonal range search* problem, and is one of the fundamental problems in computational geometry.

The information obtained about $P \cap Q$ differs depending on the query. The most basic queries are the *reporting* query, which enumerates all the points in $P \cap Q$, and the *counting* query, which returns the number of points $|P \cap Q|$. There are other queries such as the *emptiness* query, which checks whether $P \cap Q$ is empty or not, and aggregate queries, which compute the summation, average, or variance of weights of points in the query range.

Applications of the orthogonal range search problem include database searches [21]. For example, assuming there is a database of employees of a company, then a query to count the number of employees whose duration of service is at least x_1 years and at most x_2 years, age is at least y_1 and at most y_2, and annual income is at least z_1 and at most z_2, can be formalized as an orthogonal range search problem. Other applications include geographical information systems, CAD, and computer graphics.

K. Ishiyama · K. Sadakane (✉)
Graduate School of Information Science and Technology, The University of Tokyo, 7-3-1 Hongo, Bunkyo-ku, Tokyo 113-8656, Japan
e-mail: sada@mist.i.u-tokyo.ac.jp

© The Author(s) 2022

N. Katoh et al. (eds.), *Sublinear Computation Paradigm*,
https://doi.org/10.1007/978-981-16-4095-7_8

In such applications, it is common to perform multiple queries on the same point set P. We therefore consider constructing the problem as an indexing problem: Given a point set P a priori, we first construct some data structure D from P. Then, when a query range Q is given, we answer the query using the data structure D.

8.1.1 Existing Work

In many existing works, the number n of points is regarded as a variable for evaluating time complexity and the number d of dimensions is regarded as a constant. However, in this chapter, we regard d as a variable too. For the computation model, we use w-bit word RAM where $w = \Theta(\lg n)$ bits. That is, a constant number of coordinate values can be treated in constant time. Then, it takes $O(d)$ time to check whether a point is inside a query range.

If more space than $\Theta(dn)$ words is allowed to be used for the space complexity of data structures and if we assume that d is a constant, then we can perform the counting and reporting queries in time polynomial to $\log n$. *Range trees* [2, 14, 15, 23] are such data structures. Range trees support counting queries in $O\left(d \log^{d-1} n\right)$ time and reporting queries in $O\left(d \log^{d-1} n + dk\right)$ time using $O\left(dn \log^{d-1} n\right)$ word space, where $k = |P \cap Q|$, that is, the number of points enumerated by a reporting query using the fractional cascading technique [15, 23]. Although these data structures are time-efficient, it is desirable to develop more space-efficient data structures.

Some data structures having linear space complexity have been proposed. For example, quad trees [6] were the first data structures used for orthogonal range search. Unfortunately, quad trees have terrible worst-case behaviors. To overcome this, kd-tree [1] is used. The query time complexity of the kd-tree is $O\left(d^2 n^{\frac{d-1}{d}}\right)$ for counting and $O\left(d^2 n^{\frac{d-1}{d}} + dk\right)$ for reporting [13].

These data structures store the coordinates of points separately in plain form, and therefore can be applied to the case of real-valued coordinates. However, if the coordinates take integer values from 0 to $n-1$, then there exist data structures with even smaller space complexity and query time complexity. For example, Chazelle [4] proposed a data structure for the two-dimensional case with linear space complexity and time complexity of $O(\lg n)$ for counting and $O(\lg n + k \lg^{\varepsilon} n)$ for reporting where $0 < \varepsilon < 1$ is any constant. Note that although the assumption that each coordinate value is an integer from 0 to $n-1$ seems too strict, as is explained in Sect. 8.2.2, any orthogonal range search problem in d-dimensional space can be reduced into one on the $[n]^d$ grid, and therefore the assumption does not create any difficulties.

There has also been research on succinct data structures for the orthogonal range search problem. The wavelet tree [9] is a data structure which was originally proposed for representing compressed suffix arrays, and it later turned out that wavelet tree can support various queries efficiently [18]. For the orthogonal range search problem, wavelet tree can support counting queries in $O(\lg n)$ time and reporting queries in $O((1+k)\lg n)$ time [8]. Bose et al. [3] proposed improved succinct data structures that support counting queries in $O(\lg n/\lg\lg n)$ time and reporting queries in $O(((1+k)\lg n/\lg\lg n)$ for two-dimensional cases.

For higher dimensions, Okajima and Maruyama [20] proposed the KDW-tree, which is a succinct data structure for any dimensionality. The query time complexity of the KDW-tree is smaller than that of the kd-tree. If we assume d is a constant, counting queries take $O\left(n^{\frac{d-2}{d}}\lg n\right)$ time and reporting queries take $O\left(\left(n^{\frac{d-2}{d}}+k\right)\lg n\right)$ time. The KDW-tree has been shown to be practical by numerical experiments.

8.1.2 *Our Results*

We show space and time complexities of data structures for the orthogonal range search problem explained in Sect. 8.1.1 and our proposed data structures in Table 8.1. Note that these are for the case where the coordinates are integers from 0 to $n-1$, and the space complexities are measured in bits. Table 8.1 shows reporting time complexities. Counting time complexities can be obtained by letting $k=0$.

Our data structures are space-efficient for high-dimensional orthogonal range search problems.

Our first data structure has the same space complexity as the KDW-tree and better query time complexities. Note that the result in Table 8.1 is for the case of $d \geq 3$. If $d=2$, we can improve the $n^{\frac{d-2}{d}}$ term to $\lg n$. This result appeared in [11].

Note that, as shown in Sect. 8.2.1, the necessary space to represent a set of n points in d-dimensional space such that each coordinate takes an integer value from 0 to $n-1$ is $(d-1)n\lg n+\Theta(n)$ bits. This means that if we assume d is a constant, the space complexity of the KDW-tree and our first data structure does not match the information-theoretic lower bound asymptotically.

Table 8.1 Comparison of complexities. The results or KDW-tree and Ours 1 are for $d \geq 3$. Note that k is the number of points enumerated by a reporting query. The time complexities for counting queries are obtained by letting $k=0$ in the time complexities for reporting queries

Data structure	Dim.	Space (bits)	Query time
kd-tree [1]	d	$O(dn\lg n)$	$O\left(d^2 n^{\frac{d-1}{d}}+dk\right)$
Wavelet tree [9]	2	$n\lg n+o(n\lg n)$	$O((1+k)\lg n)$
Bose et al. [3]	2	$n\lg n+o(n\lg n)$	$O\left((1+k)\frac{\lg n}{\lg\lg n}\right)$
KDW-tree [20]	d	$d\{n\lg n+o(n\lg n)\}$	$O\left(\left(\mathrm{poly}(d)\cdot n^{\frac{d-2}{d}}+dk\right)\lg n\right)$
Ours 1	d	$d\{n\lg n+o(n\lg n)\}$	$O\left(\left(d^3 n^{\frac{d-2}{d}}+dk\right)\frac{\lg n}{\lg\lg n}\right)$
Ours 2	d	$(d-1)\{n\lg n+o(n\lg n)\}$	$O(dn\lg n)$

Our second data structure uses $(d-1)n\lg n + (d-1)\cdot o(n\lg n)$ bits of space. This asymptotically matches the information-theoretic lower bound even if d is assumed to be a constant. Therefore, we can say this data structure is truly succinct. Unfortunately, the worst-case query time complexity is $O(dn\lg n)$, which is not fast in theory. However, this data structure is fast in practice for the case where the number d of dimensions is large but the number d' of dimensions used for a query is small. This kind of query often occurs in the database search applications shown in Sect. 8.1. This result appeared in [10].

8.2 Preliminaries

In this paper, we assume that coordinates of points are non-negative integers. As will be explained in Sect. 8.2.2, we sometimes assume that coordinates are integers from 0 to $n-1$. Therefore, we define [n] as the set $\{0, 1, \ldots, n-1\}$. For a d-dimensional space, we denote each dimension by dim. 0, dim. $1, \ldots,$ dim. $d-1$, coordinate values of a point by 0-th coordinate value, 1-th coordinate value, $\ldots$, $d-1$-th coordinate value. For a rooted tree, we assume the depth of the root node is 0. Throughout the paper, log x denotes the natural logarithm and lg x denotes the base 2 logarithm.

Next, we define two concepts used in this chapter. The first one is containment degree. This is the concept of an inclusion relationship between two orthogonal ranges introduced in [20]. For two d-dimensional orthogonal ranges $Q = \left[l_0^{(Q)}, u_0^{(Q)}\right] \times \cdots \times \left[l_{d-1}^{(Q)}, u_{d-1}^{(Q)}\right]$ and $R = \left[l_0^{(R)}, u_0^{(R)}\right] \times \cdots \times \left[l_{d-1}^{(R)}, u_{d-1}^{(R)}\right]$, we define $\mathrm{CDeg}(R, Q)$ as

$$\mathrm{CDeg}(R, Q) = \#\left\{i \in [d] \;\middle|\; \left[l_i^{(R)}, u_i^{(R)}\right] \subseteq \left[l_i^{(Q)}, u_i^{(Q)}\right]\right\}$$

and call it the containment degree of R with respect to Q. This is the number of dimensions, in each of which R is contained in Q. The containment degree is an important concept for analyzing time complexities of orthogonal range search algorithms.

Next, we explain z-value. This is a projection of multi-dimensional data onto one-dimensional data as proposed by Morton [17]. Consider a point $p = (p_0, p_1, \ldots, p_{d-1})$ in the d-dimensional space where the coordinate values are integers. If coordinate values are expressed as l-bit binary numbers $p_0 = b_0^0 b_0^1 \cdots b_0^{l-1}$, $p_1 = b_1^0 b_1^1 \cdots b_1^{l-1}, \ldots, p_{d-1} = b_{d-1}^0 b_{d-1}^1 \cdots b_{d-1}^{l-1}$, the z-value $z(p)$ of point p is defined as

$$z(p) = b_0^0 b_1^0 \cdots b_{d-1}^0 b_0^1 b_1^1 \cdots b_{d-1}^1 \cdots b_0^{l-1} b_1^{l-1} \cdots b_{d-1}^{l-1}.$$

In the case of a two-dimensional space, if we arrange grid points in increasing order of z-value, we see a z-shape curve as shown in Fig. 8.1. We therefore call the value z-value.

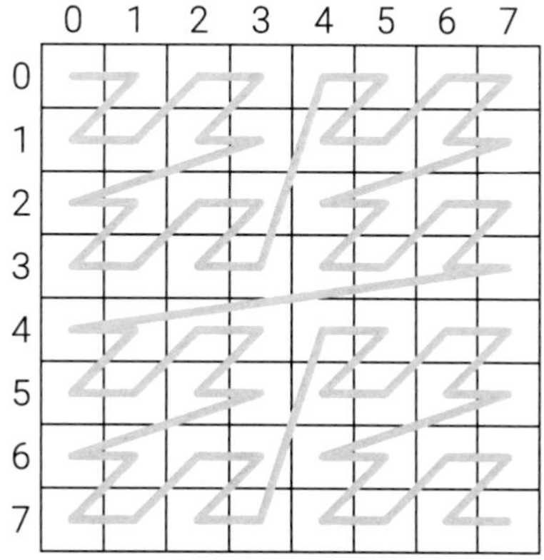

Fig. 8.1 Curve obtained by joining grid points in z-valueorder in two-dimensional space

8.2.1 Succinct Data Structures and Information-Theoretic Lower Bound

Succinctness of data structures was proposed by Jacobson [12] and is one of the criteria for measuring space complexities of data structures. It is defined as follows.

Let n be the number of different values that an object can take. Then, we need at least $\lceil \lg n \rceil$ bits of space to represent the object. If the space complexity $S(n)$ of a data structure representing the object satisfies $S(n) = \lg n + o(\lg n)$ bits, we say the data structure is *succinct* and $\lceil \lg n \rceil$ bits is the *information-theoretic lower bound* of the size of representations of the object. Note that succinct data structures not only offer data compression, but also support some efficient queries. For orthogonal range search, a naive algorithm supports linear time queries by scanning an array containing coordinate values of points. Succinct data structures are therefore expected to answer queries in sublinear time.

The space complexity of $\lg n + o(\lg n)$ bits in the definition of succinct data structures indicates that the size of auxiliary indexing data structures added to the data is negligibly small compared with the size of the data itself ($\lg n$ bits). In other words, the space complexity of succinct data structures asymptotically matches the information-theoretic lower bound when $n \to \infty$.

We compute the information-theoretic lower bound for representing a set of points with integer coordinates. Assume that i-th coordinate value takes integer values from 0 to $U_i - 1$. Because the number of grid points is $\prod_{i=0}^{d-1} U_i$, the number of different sets of n points is

$$\binom{\prod_{i=0}^{d-1} U_i}{n}.$$

By using Stirling's approximation formula

$$\log n! = n \log n - n + O(\log n),$$

we obtain

$$\begin{aligned}
\log \binom{U}{n} &= \log U! - \log(U-n)! - \log n! \\
&= U \log U - U - (U-n)\log(U-n) + (U-n) - n\log n + n + O(\log U) \\
&= U \log \frac{U}{U-n} + n \log \frac{U-n}{n} + O(\log U) \\
&= U \log \left(1 + \frac{n}{U-n}\right) + n \log \frac{U}{n}\left(1 - \frac{n}{U}\right) + O(\log U) \\
&= U \left(\frac{n}{U-n} - \Theta\left(\left(\frac{n}{U-n}\right)^2\right)\right) + n \log \frac{U}{n} - \Theta\left(\frac{n^2}{U}\right) + O(\log U) \\
&= n \log U - n \log n + \Theta(n).
\end{aligned}$$

Therefore, the information-theoretic lower bound of the size for representing the point set is

$$\lg \binom{\prod_{i=0}^{d-1} U_i}{n} = \sum_{i=0}^{d-1} n \lg U_i - n \lg n + \Theta(n).$$

Note that storing coordinate values of the points explicitly using $\sum_{i=0}^{d-1} \lceil \lg U_i \rceil$ use $n \lg n$ bit more space than the information-theoretic lower bound.

8.2.2 Assumptions on Point Sets

Because data structures such as kd-tree or range trees that have linear or larger space complexities usually store the coordinates of points in a plain format, we do not care whether they are integers or real values. However, if we consider succinct data structures, we usually assume that coordinates values are integers from 0 to $n-1$. We also assume that for any points $p, q \in P$ and any $i \in [d]$, the i-th coordinate value p_i of p and the i-th coordinate value q_i of q are different. Although this assumption may appear to be unrealistic and too strong, for the orthogonal range search problem, it is known that an arbitrary point set on $\mathbb{R}^d$ can be transformed into a point set on $[n]^d$ [7].

Consider a set P of n points on $\mathbb{R}^d$. We create another point set P' on $[n]^d$ as follows. The set P' also contains n points and there is a one-to-one correspondence between points in P and points in P'. Assume that $p \in P$ corresponds to $p' \in P'$. Then, the i-th coordinate value p'_i of p' is then defined from the i-th coordinate value p_i of p as

$$p'_i = \#\{q \in P \mid q_i < p_i\}. \tag{8.1}$$

That is, the i-th coordinate value of p' is the number of points in P such that the i-th coordinate value is smaller than p_i. This is called the rank value of p with respect to the i-th coordinate value, and the transformation is called the transformation into rank space. We use arrays $C_0, C_1, \ldots, C_{d-1}$ each of length n. The array C_i stores the i-th coordinate values of points in P in increasing order.

By using the point set P' on the rank space and the arrays C_i ($i = 0, \ldots, d-1$) that contain the original coordinate values of the points in P, we can reduce the problem of orthogonal range search on the original point set P into that on P'. Assume that a query range $Q = \left[l_0^{(Q)}, u_0^{(Q)}\right] \times \cdots \times \left[l_{d-1}^{(Q)}, u_{d-1}^{(Q)}\right] \subset \mathbb{R}^d$ is given for a point set P. From the construction of P', there exists a range $Q' = \left[l_0^{(Q')}, u_0^{(Q')}\right] \times \cdots \times \left[l_{d-1}^{(Q')}, u_{d-1}^{(Q')}\right] \subset [n]^d$ such that

$$p \in Q \iff p' \in Q'.$$

The boundaries of this Q' are computed by

$$l_i^{(Q')} = \#\left\{p \in P \;\middle|\; p_i < l_i^{(Q)}\right\}$$
$$u_i^{(Q')} = \#\left\{p \in P \;\middle|\; p_i \le u_i^{(Q)}\right\} - 1.$$

These are computed in $\mathrm{O}(d \lg n)$ time by binary searches on the arrays C_i. Then, the counting query is performed by using Q'. For the reporting query, after finding a point $p' \in P'$ which is included in the query range Q' in the rank space, we need to recover the original coordinates of the point $p \in P$. This is done in $\mathrm{O}(d)$ time using the arrays C_i containing the coordinates of the original points by

$$p_i = C_i[p'_i].$$

Thus, an orthogonal range search problem on $\mathbb{R}^d$ can be transformed into that on $[n]^d$. Note that if coordinates are transformed as in Eq. (8.1), the identical coordinate values in $\mathbb{R}^d$ are transformed into identical coordinate values in $[n]^d$. By shifting values by one for the identical coordinate values, we can transform the coordinate values so that for any two distinct points $p', q' \in P'$ and any $i \in [d]$, the i-th coordinate value p'_i of p' is different from the i-th coordinate value q'_i of q'.

If the original points have integer coordinate values, we can reduce the space [19]. Consider the case where P is a point set on $[U]^d$, that is, each coordinate value takes an integer value from 0 to $U - 1$. In this case, the point set P' in the rank space does not change. However, we store the coordinates of the original point set P in a different way. We store them using multi-sets $M_0, M_1, \ldots, M_{d-1}$, each of which corresponds to one of the d dimensions. The multi-set M_i stores the i-th coordinate value of the points in P. We use the data structure of [22] to store multi-sets.

Lemma 8.1 *There exists a data structure using* $n \lg(U/n) + O(n)$ *which supports a selectm query on a multi-set* M_i *in constant time.*

A selectm query on a multi-set M finds the j-th smallest element in M. That is, $C_i[j]$ is obtained by finding the j-th smallest element in array C_i. Therefore, if a query range Q on $[U]^d$ is given, it can be transformed into a query range Q' on the rank space by binary searches using selectm queries, and the original coordinate values are obtained by d many selectm queries.

Assume that there exists a succinct data structure D' for a point set P' on $[n]^d$. Then, the space complexity of D' is $(d-1)n \lg n + (d-1) \cdot o(n \lg n)$ bits, as shown in Sect. 8.2.1. If we add d data structures of Lemma 8.1, the total space complexity becomes $dn \lg U - n \lg n + (d-1) \cdot o(n \lg n)$ bits. This is succinct for the point set P on $[U]^d$. Therefore, if there exists a succinct data structure for a point set on $[n]^d$, we can construct a succinct data structure for a point set on $[U]^d$. From here onward, we consider only point sets on $[n]^d$.

8.3 kd-Tree

kd-tree [1] is a well-known data structure that partitions the space recursively. It is used not only for the orthogonal range search problem, but also for the nearest neighbor search problem.

8.3.1 Construction of kd-Trees

We explain the algorithm for constructing a kd-tree of a point set P for the two-dimensional case. First, we find the point p for which the x-coordinate is the median of the point set P, and store p at the root of the kd-tree. Next, we divide the set $P \setminus \{p\}$ into two: the set P_{left} that stores points with x-coordinates smaller than that of p, and the set P_{right} that stores points with x coordinates larger than that of p. We add two children $v_{\text{left}}, v_{\text{right}}$ to the root of the kd-tree. Next, from P_{left} (P_{right}), we find p_{left} (p_{right}) for which the y-coordinate is the median of the set, and we store p_{left} (p_{right}) in v_{left} (v_{right}). Similarly, we divide the set $P_{\text{left}} \setminus \{p_{\text{left}}\}$ ($P_{\text{right}} \setminus \{p_{\text{right}}\}$) into two subsets according to y-coordinates, find medians with respect to x-coordinates, and store them in children of v_{left} (v_{right}), and repeat this recursively. Figure 8.2 shows an example of partitioning a point set.

For a d-dimensional space, we partition the space based on the first dimension, the second dimension, and so on. After partitioning the space based on the d-th dimension, we use the first dimension again.

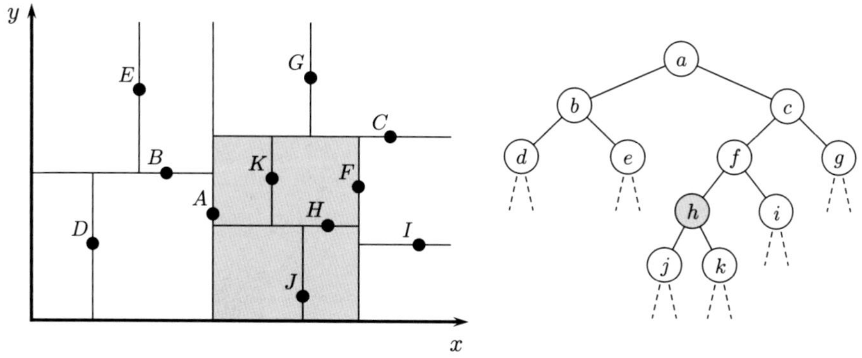

Fig. 8.2 Partitioning of a space based on the point set (left) and the corresponding kd-tree (right). Points $A, B, C, \ldots$ correspond to nodes $a, b, c, \ldots$. The range corresponding to node h is shown in gray in the left figure

8.3.2 *Range Search Algorithm*

An important concept for understanding range searches using a kd-tree is the correspondence between nodes of the kd-tree and ranges. In Sect. 8.3.1, we explained that each node of the kd-tree stores a point. We can also consider that each node corresponds to an orthogonal range. Let $V(v)$ denote the point in P stored in node v and $R(v)$ denote the corresponding range. Then $R(v)$ is defined as follows:

- For the root node r of the kd-tree, the range $R(r)$ is the whole space.
- For a node v at depth l, the range $R(v_{\mathrm{left}})$ for the left child v_{left} of v is obtained as follows. We partition $R(v)$ into two by the hyperplane that is perpendicular to the $(l \bmod d)$-th axis and contains $V(v)$. Then, $R(v_{\mathrm{left}})$ is the range with the smaller $(l \bmod d)$-th coordinate value and $R(v_{\mathrm{right}})$ is the range with the larger $(l \bmod d)$-th coordinate value.

For example, in Fig. 8.2, the range $R(h)$ corresponding to node h is the gray area.

The algorithm for reporting queries using a kd-tree is as follows. The algorithm searches the space by traversing tree nodes from the root. Each time a node v is visited, the algorithm checks whether the corresponding point $V(v)$ $(\in P)$ is contained in the query range Q or not. If the range $R(v)$ is fully contained in the query range Q, the algorithm outputs all the points stored in the sub-tree rooted at v. If $R(v)$ and Q has no intersection, the algorithm terminates the search of the sub-tree. For a counting query, instead of outputting all the points when $R(v)$ is contained in Q, the algorithm finds and accumulates the size of the sub-tree rooted at v. Although it may seem impossible to execute the algorithm since the range $R(v)$ for node v is not explicitly stored in the kd-tree, if the range $R(v)$ for node v is known, then we know the coordinate values of the hyperplane partitioning the range from the coordinate values of point $V(v)$, and we can compute $R(v_{\mathrm{left}})$ and $R(v_{\mathrm{right}})$. Therefore, we can execute the algorithm by keeping the range $R(v)$ during the search.

8.3.3 Complexity Analyses

The time complexity of kd-trees is analyzed in [13]. A counting query takes $O\left(d \cdot n^{\frac{d-1}{d}} + 2^d\right)$ time. In general, we assume d is a constant and write the complexity as $O\left(n^{\frac{d-1}{d}}\right)$. For a reporting query, we output all coordinates of points in Q. Because a point can be output in constant time, the query time complexity is $O\left(n^{\frac{d-1}{d}} + k\right)$.

If $d \geq \lg n$, the height of the kd-tree is at most d, and therefore the space is partitioned at most d times. Then, it is necessary to traverse all the nodes and a query takes $O(n)$ time.

8.4 Wavelet Tree

Wavelet tree is a succinct data structure supporting various queries on strings and integer sequences efficiently. It was originally proposed for representing compressed suffix arrays [9], but it later became known that wavelet tree can support more operations [18]. Orthogonal range search in two-dimensional space is one of these operations [16].

8.4.1 Construction

The two-dimensional point sets P that can be represented directly using wavelet tree are those where the coordinates take integer values from 1 to n and the x-coordinate values are all distinct. As explained in Sect. 8.2.2, without loss of generality, we can transform any point set into a point set in $[n]^d$ space. For such a two-dimensional point set P, consider an integer sequence C that contains the y-coordinates of the points in increasing order of x-coordinates. For example, for the point set in Fig. 8.3, the corresponding integer sequence C is $4, 2, 7, 5, 0, 3, 1, 6$. For this sequence C, we construct a wavelet tree as follows.

First, we consider that the root of the wavelet tree corresponds to C. Note that we do not store C directly in the wavelet tree. We then focus on the most significant (highest) bit of the $\lceil \lg n \rceil$-bit binary representation of each integer in C. If it is 0 (1), the integer is moved into the left (right) child of the root. We consider that each child node of the root corresponds to an integer sequence containing the numbers in the original array C in the same order. For example, in the example in Fig. 8.3, integers from 0 to 3 go to the left child, and integers from 4 to 7 go to the right child. Therefore, the left child corresponds to an integer sequence $2, 0, 3, 1$, and the right child $4, 7, 5, 6$.

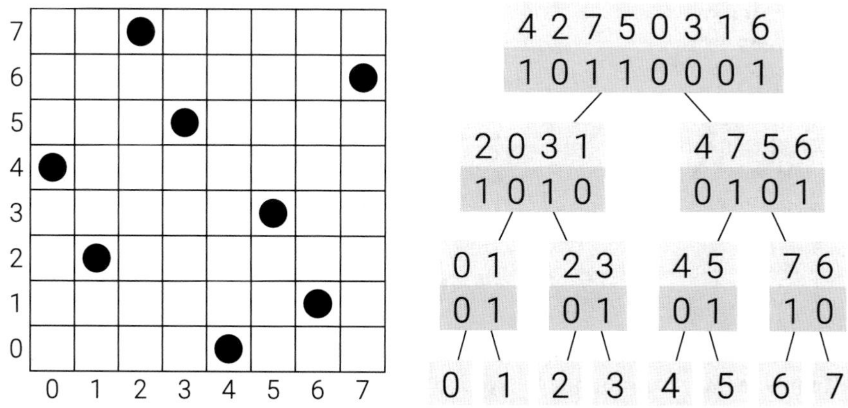

Fig. 8.3 A two-dimensional point set P (left) and the corresponding wavelet tree (right)

Next, for each integer sequence of child nodes, we focus on the second most significant bit of the binary representation of each number. We move a number with 0 bit to the left, and a number with 1 bit to the right. Similarly, we repeat this until the integer sequence of a node consists of the identical integer.

Note that we do not store integer sequences in nodes of the wavelet tree. In each node, we store a bit string of the same length as the corresponding integer sequence. The i-th bit of the bit string is 0 (1) if the i-th integer in the integer sequence goes to the left (right) child. In other words, a bit string stored in a node of depth l is the concatenation of the $(l + 1)$-th highest bit of each integer in the integer sequence corresponding to the node. In the example in Fig. 8.3, the integer sequence corresponding to the root node is $4, 2, 7, 5, 0, 3, 1, 6$, and because integers from 0 to 3 go to the left child and integers from 4 to 7 go to the right child, the bit string stored in the root node is $1, 0, 1, 1, 0, 0, 0, 1$. Note that we do not store bit strings at leaf nodes. We show the information stored in the wavelet tree in the right tree in Fig. 8.3. Only bit strings drawn above the dark gray rectangles, that is, those in the lower row of each node, are stored.

Note that although it may seem impossible to recover the original information (the integer sequence) from these bit strings, it is possible. Consider the recovery of the fourth integer of the wavelet tree in Fig. 8.3 (right). From the bit string stored in the root node, we know that the first bit of the integer is 1. Because this 1 bit corresponding to the fourth integer is the third 1 in the bit string, we know that the integer to be recovered corresponds to the third bit of the bit string in the right child of the root node. If we look at the third bit of the right child, we know that the second bit of the integer is 0. Further, this 0 bit is the second 0 in the bit string, the integer to be recovered corresponds to the second bit of the left child of the current node. Finally, from the second bit of the left child, we know the last bit of the integer to be recovered is 1. Therefore, the fourth integer is 101 in binary, that is, 5. This is shown in Fig. 8.4.

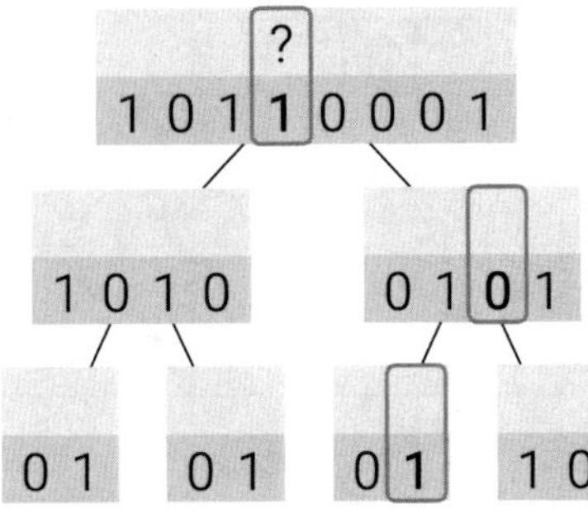

Fig. 8.4 In the wavelet tree in Fig. 8.3, we recover the fourth integer. By looking at the bits enclosed in boxes, we know that the fourth integer is 101 in binary, that is, 5

In this recovery operation, we need to compute the number of zeros/ones in the first i bits of a bit string. This operation is also used in the range search algorithm in the next section. If we look at bits one by one from the beginning of a bit string, it takes $\mathrm{O}(n)$ time, which is too slow. We therefore represent the bit string of each node by the following data structure [5, 12].

Lemma 8.2 *For a bit string of length n, there exists a data structure using* $n + o(n)$ *bits which answers a rank/select query in constant time, where the rank query* $\mathrm{rank}_b(B, i)$ *is to count the number of b bits* ($b = 0, 1$) *in the bits from* $B[0]$ *to* $B[i]$ ($i \geq 0$) *of a bit string B, and the select query* $\mathrm{select}_b(B, i)$ *is to return the position of the i-th b* ($i \geq 1$, $b = 0, 1$) *in a bit string B.*

The select query is also necessary for range searches using a wavelet tree.

8.4.2 Range Search Algorithm

We explain how to solve the two-dimensional range search problem using a wavelet tree. First, we explain the counting query, which is performed by a recursive function as in Algorithm 1. For a query range $Q = [l, r] \times [b, t]$, the argument of the function is $\textsc{WTCounting}(l, r, b, t, v_{\mathrm{root}}, 0, 2^{\lceil \lg n \rceil} - 1)$, where v_{root} is the root node of the wavelet tree. The left (right) child of node v is represented by v_{left} (v_{right}). The bit string stored in node v is represented by $v.B$.

We explain the algorithm in Fig. 8.5 using the example of searching a range $Q = [1, 6] \times [1, 4]$ for the point set P in Fig. 8.3.

The search algorithm traverses the tree from the root. During the search, the algorithm keeps the interval I of an integer sequence (or bit string) corresponding to an interval of the x-coordinate of the query range. In the example in Fig. 8.5, we focus on the interval $I = [1, 6]$ at the root node. To move to the left child, we need to compute the interval corresponding to the query range. This is done by a rank query that counts the number of zeros from the beginning of the bit string to a specified position. In the bit string stored in the root node, the number of zeros from the beginning to the 0-th position (in general, if the interval is $I = [l, r]$, to $(l - 1)$-th

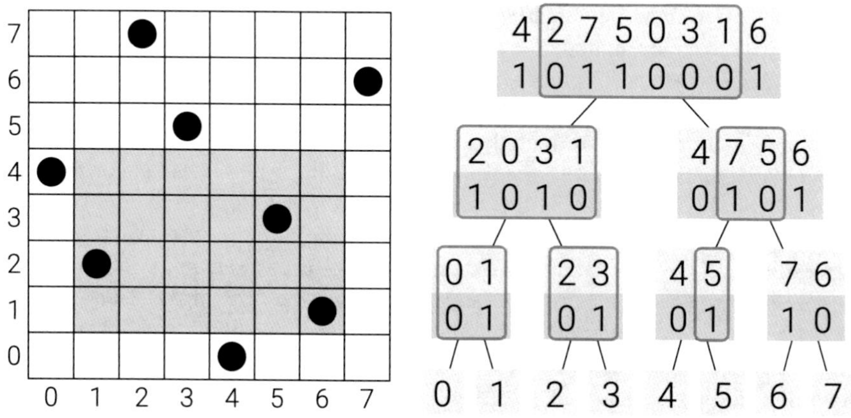

Fig. 8.5 Behavior of the algorithm when searching a range of [1, 6] × [1, 4] for the two-dimensional point set in Fig. 8.3

Algorithm 1 WTCOUNTING($x_1, x_2, y_1, y_2, v, a, b$)

Input: A node v of the wavelet tree and an interval $[x_1, x_2]$ in the corresponding bit string, the interval $[a, b]$ of y coordinate corresponding to node v, and the interval $[y_1, y_2]$ of y coordinate for the query range.

Output: The number of points stored in the sub-tree rooted at v and contained in Q.

if $x_1 > x_2$ **then**
    return 0
else if $[a, b] \cap [y_1, y_2] = \varnothing$ **then**
    return 0
else if $[a, b] \subseteq [y_1, y_2]$ **then**
    return $x_2 - x_1 + 1$
end if
$x_1^l \leftarrow \text{rank}_0\,(v.B, x_1 - 1)$
$x_2^l \leftarrow \text{rank}_0\,(v.B, x_2) - 1$
$x_1^r \leftarrow x_1 - x_1^l$
$x_2^r \leftarrow x_2 - x_2^l - 1$
$m \leftarrow \lfloor (a + b)/2 \rfloor$
return WTCOUNTING($x_1^l, x_2^l, y_1, y_2, v_{\text{left}}, a, m$)
    +WTCOUNTING($x_1^r, x_2^r, y_1, y_2, v_{\text{right}}, m + 1, b$)

---

position) is 0, so we know the interval corresponding to the query starts at position 0. Because the number of zeros from the beginning to the 6-th position (in general, if the interval is $I = [l, r]$, to r-th position) is four, we know the interval ends at position 3. Thus, we obtain the interval $I = [0, 3]$ for the left child. Similarly, for the right child, by using rank queries counting the number of ones, we can obtain the interval $I = [1, 2]$.

We repeat this process by going down the tree maintaining an interval. When we reach a leaf, we can determine if the y-coordinate of the point is included in the query range. However, we can sometimes determine this at an earlier stage. For example, in Fig. 8.5, after obtaining the interval $I = [1, 2]$ at the left child of the root, for the right child of the current node the interval of the y-coordinate corresponding to the node is $[2, 3]$, which is completely included in the interval $[1, 4]$ of the y-coordinate of the query range. Therefore, for the two points we focus on at this node, both the x- and y-coordinates are included in the query range, and we found two points in the query range. However, after computing the interval $I = [1, 2]$ for the right child of the root, the interval of the y-coordinate corresponding to the right child of the current node is $[6, 7]$, which has no intersection with the interval $[1, 4]$ of the y-coordinate of the query range. We do not need to further search the sub-tree.

As observed above, in a range search using a wavelet tree, if the query range is $Q = [l, r] \times [b, t]$, we first focus on points for which the x-coordinates are contained in Q, that is, contained in the range $[l, r] \times [0, n - 1]$. Next, the process of traversing down the tree corresponds to partitioning the range into two according to the y-coordinate. If an obtained range is completely contained in the query range, or does not intersect with the query range, we terminate searching the sub-tree.

For counting queries, it is sufficient to sum the number of points. For reporting queries, the extra work of computing the coordinates of the points is also required. This is shown in Algorithm 2.

The outline of the reporting query is the same as the counting query. In Algorithm 1, we obtain the number of points in Line 2. We change it one by one to output coordinates of points corresponding to the interval $[x_1, x_2]$ of the bit string $v.B$. The x- and y-coordinates of each point are obtained by WTREPORTX

Algorithm 2 WTREPORTING($x_1, x_2, y_1, y_2, v, a, b$)

Input: A node v of the wavelet tree, the interval $[x_1, x_2]$ of the bit string stored in it, the interval $[a, b]$ of y coordinates corresponding to the range for v, and the interval $[y_1, y_2]$ of y coordinates for the query range.

Output: Coordinates of point stored in the sub-tree rooted at v and contained in Q.

1: **if** $x_1 > x_2$ **then**
2:     terminate
3: **else if** $[a, b] \cap [y_1, y_2] = \varnothing$ **then**
4:     terminate
5: **else if** $[a, b] \subseteq [y_1, y_2]$ **then**
6:     **for** $i = x_1$ to x_2 **do**
7:         $x \leftarrow$ WTREPORTX(v, i)
8:         $y \leftarrow$ WTREPORTY(v, i, a, b)
9:         Output (x, y)
10:     **end for**
11: **end if**
12: $x_1^l \leftarrow$ rank$_0$($v.B, x_1 - 1$)
13: $x_2^l \leftarrow$ rank$_0$($v.B, x_2$) $- 1$
14: $x_1^r \leftarrow x_1 - x_1^l$
15: $x_2^r \leftarrow x_2 - x_2^l - 1$
16: $m \leftarrow \lfloor (a + b)/2 \rfloor$
17: WTREPORTING($x_1^l, x_2^l, y_1, y_2, v_{\text{left}}, a, m$)
18: WTREPORTING($x_1^r, x_2^r, y_1, y_2, v_{\text{right}}, m + 1, b$)

Algorithm 3 WTREPORTX(v, i)

Input: A node v of the wavelet tree and an integer i.
Output: The x coordinate value of the point corresponding to the i-th bit of the bit string stored in v.

1: **if** v is the root **then**
2:     **return** i
3: **else if** v is the left child of v_{parent} **then**
4:     $i \leftarrow \text{select}_0 \left(v_{\text{parent}}.B, i + 1 \right)$
5:     **return** WTREPORTX(v_{parent}, i)
6: **else**
7:     $i \leftarrow \text{select}_1 \left(v_{\text{parent}}.B, i + 1 \right)$
8:     **return** WTREPORTX(v_{parent}, i)
9: **end if**

Algorithm 4 WTREPORTY(v, i, a, b)

Input: A node v of the wavelet tree, the interval $[a, b]$ of y coordinate corresponding to the range for v, and an integer i.
Output: The y coordinate value of the point corresponding to the i-th bit of the bit string stored in v.

1: **if** $a = b$ **then**
2:     **return** a
3: **else if** $v.B[i] = 0$ **then**
4:     $i \leftarrow \text{rank}_0 (v.B, i) - 1$
5:     **return** WTREPORTY$(v_{\text{left}}, i, a, \lfloor (a + b)/2 \rfloor)$
6: **else**
7:     $i \leftarrow \text{rank}_1 (v.B, i) - 1$
8:     **return** WTREPORTY$(v_{\text{right}}, i, \lfloor (a + b)/2 \rfloor + 1, b)$
9: **end if**

---

and WTREPORTY, respectively. The algorithm WTREPORTY for computing the y-coordinate (Algorithm 4) is similar to the algorithm for recovering a value of the original integer array explained in Sect. 8.4.1. We compute the y-coordinates by traversing down the tree using rank queries.

In contrast, the algorithm WTREPORTX for computing the x-coordinate (Algorithm 3) traverses up the tree using select queries. We explain this by example. In Fig. 8.5, assume that at node v, which is the right child of the left child of the root, we find that points corresponding to the interval $I = [0, 1]$ are contained in the query range. Consider the computation of the x-coordinate of the point corresponding to the bit $v.B[1]$. First, the node v we focus on is the right child of its parent. We find the position of the second 1 in the parent by a select query. Then we know that the point corresponds to the bit $v'.B[2]$ in the parent node v'. Next, because the current node is the left child of the parent (the root), we find the position of the third 0 in the bit string of the parent by a select query. Now we know that the point corresponds to the bit $r.B[5]$ at the root node r. That is, the x-coordinate of the point is 5.

As shown above, we can traverse the nodes of the wavelet tree using rank and select queries on bit strings. For range searches, we traverse down the tree from the root computing the intervals of the x-coordinate corresponding to the query range.

If we find a node where the corresponding interval of the y-coordinate is contained in the query range, we answer the query by computing the length of the interval or coordinate values by traversing the tree.

8.4.3 Complexity Analyses

We now analyze the space complexity of the wavelet tree and query time complexities for the orthogonal range search problem.

First, we analyze the space complexity. The height of the wavelet tree is $\lceil \lg n \rceil$. The total length of bit strings stored in the nodes with the same depth is always n. Therefore, the total length of all the bit strings in the wavelet tree is $n \lg n$. We can concatenate all the bit strings and store only a long bit string. Then it is not necessary to store the tree structure of the wavelet tree. By using the data structure of Lemma 8.2 for this long bit string, the space complexity is $n \lg n + o(n \lg n)$ bits in total.

Next, we consider query time complexities. For a counting query, we consider the number of visited nodes. In the wavelet tree, each time we traverse an edge toward a leaf, points with small y-coordinates go to the left child, and points with large y-coordinates go to the right child. At leaves we can consider that all points are sorted in increasing order of y-coordinates. This means that leaf nodes corresponding to the interval of y-coordinates of the query range exist in a consecutive place in the wavelet tree. Now, consider the set M of nodes of the wavelet tree defined as follows. The set M contains a maximal node v such that the y-coordinates corresponding to the leaf nodes in the sub-tree rooted at v are contained in the query range, that is, the y-coordinates of the leaves in the sub-tree of v are contained in the query range but the sub-tree of the parent of v contains some node for which the corresponding y-coordinate is not contained in the query range. This is the set of nodes from which we do not further search the sub-tree for a counting query using the wavelet tree, and in Fig. 8.6, it is shown as dark gray nodes.

Let A be the set of nodes that are ancestors of nodes of M. This is the set of nodes visited before reaching nodes of M which are shown as light gray nodes in Fig. 8.6. The number of nodes visited in a counting query is then $|A| + |M|$. We now consider the size of M and A.

For the size of the set M, the following lemma holds.

Lemma 8.3 *It holds* $|M| = O(\lg n)$.

Proof (Lemma 8.3) The set M is constructed as follows. Let M' be the set of leaf nodes of the wavelet tree corresponding to the interval of y-coordinates in the query range. For the nodes of M', if two nodes v_1 and v_2 have a common parent node v, we remove v_1 and v_2 from M' and add v to M'. By repeating this process until there are no such pairs of nodes, the set M' coincides with M.

For each depth of the wavelet tree, the number of nodes of depth belonging to M is then at most two, because if there exist more than two nodes, two of them must have the same parent. This completes the proof that $|M| = O(\lg n)$.

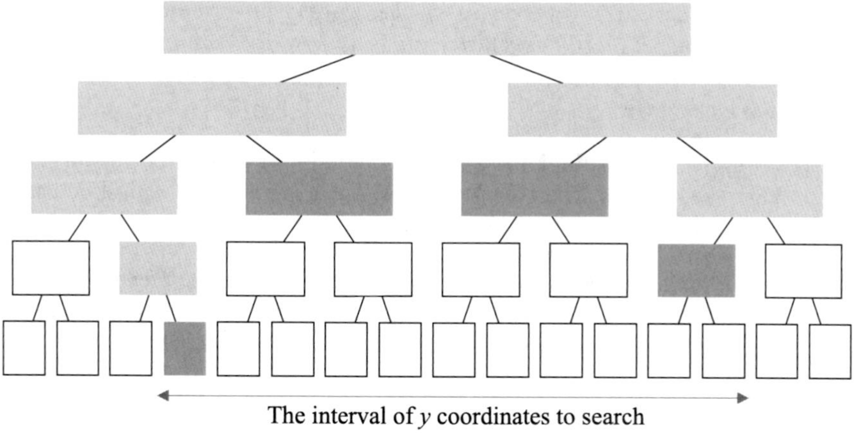

Fig. 8.6 Nodes visited by a counting query. We traverse light gray nodes, and when we reach a dark gray node, we do not further search the nodes below it

For the size of the set A, the following lemma holds.

Lemma 8.4 *It holds* $|A| = \mathrm{O}(\lg n)$.

Proof (Lemma 8.4) Consider a node v in the set A. In the set of leaf nodes in the sub-tree rooted at v, there must exist a leaf node where the corresponding y-coordinate is included in the query range and a leaf node where the corresponding y-coordinate is not included in the query range. Therefore, for each depth of the wavelet tree, there are at most two such nodes in A, because if there exists more than two such nodes, for a node in the middle, the corresponding y-coordinates of the leaves in the sub-tree rooted at that node are contained in the query range. This completes the proof that $|A| = \mathrm{O}(\lg n)$.

From the above discussion, the number of nodes visited in a counting query is $|A| + |M| = \mathrm{O}(\lg n)$. When we visit a new node, we use a constant number of rank queries. Because a rank query takes constant time (Lemma 8.2), the time complexity of a counting query using the wavelet tree is $\mathrm{O}(\lg n)$.

For a reporting query, it is necessary to compute coordinates of points in the query range. As explained in Sect. 8.4.2, x-coordinates are computed by traversing up the tree and y-coordinates are computed by traversing down the tree, with the coordinates of each point computed by visiting $\mathrm{O}(\lg n)$ nodes. Moving to an adjacent node in the wavelet tree is done by a constant number of rank/select queries, and each rank/select query takes constant time (Lemma 8.2). Therefore, the coordinates of a point are obtained in $\mathrm{O}(\lg n)$ time, and the time complexity for a reporting query using the wavelet tree is $\mathrm{O}((1 + k) \lg n)$, where k is the number of output points.

We obtain the following theorem.

Theorem 8.1 *The space complexity of the wavelet tree representing a two-dimensional point set on* $[n]^2$ *is* $n \lg n + o(n \lg n)$ *bits, and a counting query takes* $O(\lg n)$ *time, and a reporting query takes* $O((k+1)\lg n)$ *time, where k is the number of points to enumerate.*

As shown in Sect. 8.2.1, the information-theoretic lower bound for a point set on $[n]^2$ is $n \lg n + O(n)$ bits. Therefore, the wavelet tree is a succinct data structure.

Theorem 8.2 *Let P be a set of points on* $M = [1..n] \times [1..n]$ *in which all points have distinct x-coordinates. Then, there exists a data structure using* $n \lg n + o(n \lg n)$ *bits that answers a counting query in* $O(\lg \lg n)$ *time and a reporting query in* $O((1+k)\lg n / \lg \lg n)$ *time, where k is the number of points to output.*

8.5 Proposed Data Structure 1: Improved Query Time Complexity

This data structure uses the idea of adding data structures to the kd-tree to improve the query time complexity [20]. First, we explain the idea of [20] in Sect. 8.5.1. Next, we explain the algorithm of range search in Sect. 8.5.3, and analyze the time complexity in Sect. 8.5.4.

8.5.1 Idea for Improving the Time Complexity of the kd-Tree

The method proposed in [20] improves the query time complexity of the kd-tree by adding d many wavelet trees to the kd-tree such that the term $n^{(d-1)/d}$ is replaced by $n^{(d-2)/d}$ ($\lg n$ if $d = 2$), at the cost of increasing the total complexity by a factor of $O(\lg n)$. Note that we assume point sets are on $[n]^d$.

First, we construct the kd-tree for a given set P of points in the d-dimensional space. Next, we label the nodes of the kd-tree with numbers based on the inorder traversal of a binary tree defined as follows:

- If the root node has a left child, we traverse the sub-tree rooted at the node.
- Examine the root node.
- If the root node has a right child, we traverse the sub-tree rooted at the node.

Figure 8.7 shows an example of a point set (left) and numbers assigned based on the inorder traversal of the kd-tree of the set (right).

Next, we make point sets P_i $(i = 0, \ldots, d-1)$ with n points on $[n]^2$. The two-dimensional point set P_i is created as follows. If a point p in the original d-dimensional point set P has the i-th coordinate value p_i and the inorder position of the node of the kd-tree containing p is j, we add point (j, p_i) to P_i. Figure 8.8 shows the point sets P_0, P_1 created from the point set in Fig. 8.7.

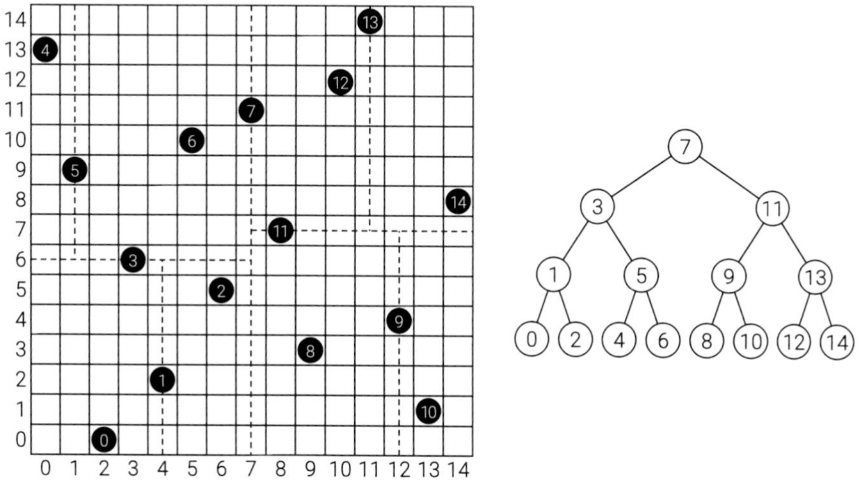

Fig. 8.7 A two-dimensional point set (left) and the corresponding kd-tree (right). The numbers of nodes are assigned by an inorder traversal of the kd-tree. The dashed lines in the left figure show the partition of the space by the kd-tree

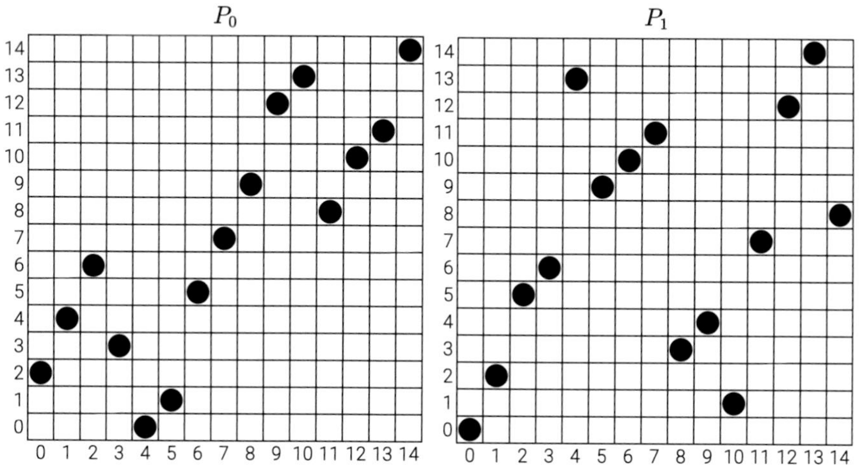

Fig. 8.8 Two-dimensional point sets obtained from the point set in Fig. 8.7

From these two-dimensional point sets $P_0, \ldots, P_{d-1}$, we construct wavelet trees $W_0, \ldots, W_{d-1}$. The wavelet trees W_i can be thought of as constructed from an integer sequence A_i containing the i-th coordinate value of points in P in the order of the kd-tree.

These data structures can be used for range searches as follows. Given a query range Q, we perform the original search using the kd-tree. In the original algorithm, as explained in Sect. 8.3, we traverse the kd-tree and shrink the range $R(v)$, and when

CDeg$(R(v), Q) = d$ (i.e., $R(v) \subseteq Q$), we know that all the points in the sub-tree rooted at v are contained in Q. By using the d wavelet tree, we can terminate the search when CDeg$(R(v), Q) = d - 1$. Assume that when a node v is visited, $R(v)$ is contained in Q for all dimensions except for i. The inorder numbers of nodes in the sub-tree rooted at node v have consecutive values. Let $[a, b]$ be the interval for the numbers. Then, the points in this interval are contained in Q except for dim. i. This implies that points in P_i that are contained in the range $[a, b] \times [l_i^{(Q)}, u_i^{(Q)}]$ are contained in Q even for dim. i. Therefore, after finding the node v, it is sufficient to search the range $[a, b] \times [l_i^{(Q)}, u_i^{(Q)}]$ of P_i using wavelet trees W_i.

The number of nodes of the kd-tree visited by this method is $O(n^{(d-2)/d})$ ($O(\lg n)$ for the case $d = 2$). The search of the last dimension using the wavelet tree takes $O(\lg n)$ time for a counting query. Therefore, the time complexity for a counting query using the kd-tree is improved to $O(n^{(d-2)/d} \lg n)$ ($O(\lg^2 n)$ for the case $d = 2$).

8.5.2 *Index Construction*

We now explain the proposed data structure. First, we construct the kd-tree for a given point set P. Note that this kd-tree is temporarily built in order to construct our data structure, and is not included in the final structure. Next, as in Sect. 8.5.1, we number the nodes of the kd-tree by an inorder traversal, and create d many two-dimensional point sets $P_0, \ldots, P_{d-1}$. For each P_i, we create the data structure of [3]. Let B_i be this data structure. Finally, we discard the kd-tree. The final data structure consists of $B_0, \ldots, B_{d-1}$.

8.5.3 *Range Search Algorithm*

We explain the algorithm for a reporting query using the data structure explained in the previous section. The pseudocode is shown in Algorithm 5. This algorithm simulates a search of the kd-tree using $B_0, \ldots, B_{d-1}$. We explain it in comparison with the search algorithm of the kd-tree. Note that we explain the algorithm assuming the inorder number of each node v of the kd-tree is also assigned to the point $V(v)$ stored in v. That is, if we say a point with number j, it is the point stored in the node with inorder position j. We also assume that for an interval $[a, b]$ of point numbers, $R([a, b])$ denotes the range containing points that have numbers in $[a, b]$. In Algorithm 5, the interval $[a, b]$ of point numbers always corresponds to the interval of inorder numbers of nodes in the sub-tree rooted at a node v of the kd-tree. Therefore, $R([a, b])$ coincides with $R(v)$.

If we use the kd-tree, we shrink the focused range $R(v)$ by going down the tree. In the proposed method, by shrinking the interval $[a, b]$ of point numbers, we reduce the corresponding range $R([a, b])$. Because the kd-tree stores the point $V(v)$ corresponding to a node v, we can obtain the information of the point used for

Algorithm 5 REPORTING($[a, b], Q$)

Input: An interval of point numbers $[a, b]$ and a query range Q.
Output: Points with numbers in $[a, b]$ and which are contained in range Q.

```
if Deg(R([a, b]), Q) = d − 1 then
    For the last dimension i such that R([a, b]) is not yet contained in Q, search [a, b] ×
    [l_i^(Q), u_i^(Q)] of P_i using B_i and enumerate points contained in Q. For each point, compute
    coordinates using B_0, ..., B_{d−1}.
else if R([a, b]) has no intersection with Q then
    terminate
else if a = b then
    Examine the point with number a. If it is in Q, output it.
else
    c ← ⌈(a + b)/2⌉
    Output the point with number c if it is in Q.
    REPORTING([a, c − 1], Q)
    REPORTING([c + 1, b], Q)
end if
```

partitioning the space. In contrast, in the proposed method, points are not explicitly stored. However, if the focused interval $[a, b]$ coincides with the interval of inorder numbers for the sub-tree rooted at a node v, we find $c = \lceil (a + b)/2 \rceil$ is the number of the points used for partitioning.[1] Furthermore, the intervals $[a, c - 1]$ and $[c + 1, b]$ correspond to the intervals of the numbers for sub-trees rooted at the left and right child of v, respectively. Therefore, by a recursive search of Algorithm 5, we can obtain the correct partitioning points.

For the range $R([a, b])$, we can compute the ranges after a partition from the range before partition and the coordinates of the point used for partitioning similarly to the case of the kd-tree.

8.5.4 *Complexity Analyses*

We now analyze the complexities of the algorithm. First, we consider its space complexity. We use d data structures of Bose et al. [3] each of which uses $n \lg n + o(n \lg n)$ bits as in Theorem 8.2. The total space complexity is then $dn \lg n + o(dn \lg n)$ bits.

Next, we consider the query time complexity. If we use the same analysis as in [20], assuming d is a constant, we can show the number of nodes corresponding to cells with containment degree of at most $d - 1$ is $O\left(n^{\frac{d-2}{d}}\right)$. Here, we derive the query time complexity using a novel analysis for non-constant d.

---

[1] In the kd-tree, at each depth, we partition the space by the median of the point set with respect to a dimension, and therefore $c = \lceil (a + b)/2 \rceil$ is the number of the point used for partitioning. If the point set contains an even number of points, we can obtain the correct partitioning point using a predetermined rule.

The proposed method partitions the space for each dimension in order, in the same fashion as for the kd-tree. As in [20], we define a series of partitions with respect to dim. 0 to dim. d-1 as a cycle. We then calculate the number $T_m(n, d)$ of nodes at which the containment degree with respect to Q is at most $d-2$ in the m-th cycle. When the $(m-1)$-th cycle has finished, the space is partitioned into $2^{d(m-1)}$ many cells. Among them, we count the number of cells for which the containment degree with respect to Q is at most $d-2$. These cells contain a $(d-2)$-dimensional face of Q (an edge of a cuboid if $d=3$). A $(d-2)$-dimensional face of a d-dimensional orthogonal range Q is obtained by choosing two dimensions from the d-dimensions and choosing the upper side or the lower side of the range for each of the two dimensions. Therefore, Q has $\binom{d}{2}2^2$ many $(d-2)$-dimensional faces. When the $(m-1)$-th cycle has finished, because each dimension is partitioned into 2^{m-1} cells, the number of cells containing a $(d-2)$-dimensional face is at most $2^{(m-1)(d-2)}$. Then after the $(m-1)$-th cycle, the number of cells to be searched is at most

$$\binom{d}{2}2^2 \cdot 2^{(m-1)(d-2)}.$$

In the sub-trees rooted at these nodes, the number of nodes in the m-th cycle is $2^d - 1$. Therefore, it holds that

$$\begin{aligned} T_m(n, d) &\le \left(2^d - 1\right)\binom{d}{2}2^2 \cdot 2^{(m-1)(d-2)} \\ &< 2^3 d(d-1)2^{(d-2)m}. \end{aligned}$$

Let $N(n, d)$ be the number of nodes for which the containment degree with respect to Q is at most $d-2$. It then holds that

$$\begin{aligned} N(n, d) &= \sum_{m=1}^{\frac{1}{d}\lg n} T_m(n, d) \\ &< 2^3 d(d-1) \sum_{m=1}^{\frac{1}{d}\lg n} 2^{(d-2)m} \\ &= 2^3 d(d-1) \frac{2^{d-2}\left(2^{\frac{d-2}{d}\lg n} - 1\right)}{2^{d-2} - 1} \\ &= \mathrm{O}\left(d^2 \cdot n^{\frac{d-2}{d}}\right). \end{aligned}$$

We use the fact that the containment degree is weakly increasing as we traverse down the tree. In the proposed method, we terminate the search when the containment degree reaches $d-1$. The visited nodes are then those with containment degree of at most $d-2$ and their child nodes. There are at most $2N(n, d)$ such nodes. The proposed method virtually traverses the kd-tree. It takes $\mathrm{O}\left(d \frac{\lg n}{\lg\lg n}\right)$ time to compute the coordinates of a point stored in a node. When a node for which the containment degree with respect to Q is $d-1$, we search the last one dimension in $\mathrm{O}\left(\frac{\lg n}{\lg\lg n}\right)$ time. The time complexity of a counting query is then $\mathrm{O}\left(d^3 n^{\frac{d-2}{d}} \frac{\lg n}{\lg\lg n}\right)$. For a reporting query, it takes $\mathrm{O}\left(d \frac{\lg n}{\lg\lg n}\right)$ time to compute the coordinates of a point. The total time complexity is then $\mathrm{O}\left(\left(d^3 n^{\frac{d-2}{d}} + dk\right) \frac{\lg n}{\lg\lg n}\right)$, where k is the number of points in Q. In summary, we obtain the following:

Theorem 8.3 *For an orthogonal range search problem on the $[n]^d$ space, there exists a data structure that has space complexity of $dn \lg n + \mathrm{o}(dn \lg n)$ bits and which answers a counting query in $\mathrm{O}\left(d^3 n^{\frac{d-2}{d}} \frac{\lg n}{\lg\lg n}\right)$ time and a reporting query in $\mathrm{O}\left(\left(d^3 n^{\frac{d-2}{d}} + dk\right) \frac{\lg n}{\lg\lg n}\right)$, where k is the number of points in the query range.*

8.6 Proposed Data Structure 2: Succinct and Practically Fast

The second proposed method is a data structure that is succinct and practically fast. In this method, we use $d-1$ many wavelet trees to represent a point set on $[n]^d$. In Sect. 8.6.1, we explain how to construct the data structure. In Sect. 8.6.2, we explain the algorithm for the orthogonal range search problem. In Sect. 8.6.3, we analyze the space and time complexities.

8.6.1 Index Construction

In this method, we assume that the points of P have distinct values in the 0-th coordinate value.

First, we create length-n integer arrays $A_1, \ldots, A_{d-1}$. The array A_i corresponds to dim. i, and stores the i-th coordinate value of the points in increasing order of the 0-th coordinate value. Next, for those arrays we create wavelet trees $W_1, \ldots, W_{d-1}$. The wavelet trees W_i can be considered to represent the two-dimensional point set P_i generated from the d-dimensional point set P by projecting the points onto the plane spanned by the 0-th axis and the i-th axis. Figure 8.9 shows an example.

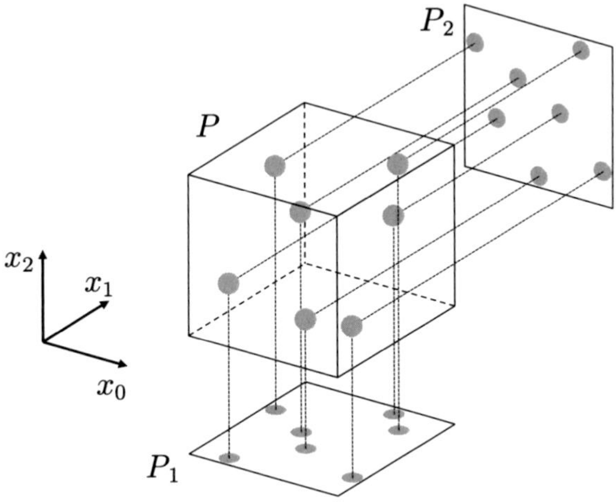

Fig. 8.9 A three-dimensional point set P and two-dimensional point sets P_1, P_2 generated by projecting P onto each plane

---

Algorithm 6 REPORT(Q)

Input: A query range $Q = \left[l_0^{(Q)}, u_0^{(Q)}\right] \times \cdots \times \left[l_{d-1}^{(Q)}, u_{d-1}^{(Q)}\right]$.

Output: The coordinates of points of P contained in Q.

1: $D := \varnothing$
2: **for** $i = 1$ to $d - 1$ **do**
3:   **if** $\left[l_i^{(Q)}, u_i^{(Q)}\right] \subsetneq [0, n - 1]$ **then**
4:     $D = D \cup \{i\}$
5:     $c_i := \text{COUNT}\left(P_i, \left[l_0^{(Q)}, u_0^{(Q)}\right] \times \left[l_i^{(Q)}, u_i^{(Q)}\right]\right)$
6:   **end if**
7: **end for**
8: Sort elements $i_1, \ldots, i_{|D|}$ of D in increasing order of c_i.
9: $A := \text{REPORTX}\left(P_{i_1}, \left[l_0^{(Q)}, u_0^{(Q)}\right] \times \left[l_{i_1}^{(Q)}, u_{i_1}^{(Q)}\right]\right)$
10: **for** $i = i_2$ to $i_{|D|}$ **do**
11:   **for all** $a \in A$ **do**
12:     **if** The i-th coordinate of a point for which the 0-th coordinate is a and is not contained in $\left[l_i^{(Q)}, u_i^{(Q)}\right]$ **then**
13:       $A = A \setminus \{a\}$
14:     **end if**
15:   **end for**
16: **end for**
17: **for all** $a \in A$ **do**
18:   Obtain the coordinates of a point for which the 0-th coordinate is a and output them.
19: **end for**

8.6.2 Range Search Algorithm

Next, we explain how to solve the orthogonal range search problem using the data structure (Algorithm 6).

Assume that a query range $Q = \left[l_0^{(Q)}, u_0^{(Q)}\right] \times \cdots \times \left[l_{d-1}^{(Q)}, u_{d-1}^{(Q)}\right]$ is given. For each $i = 1, \ldots, d-1$ such that $\left[l_i^{(Q)}, u_i^{(Q)}\right] \neq [0, n-1]$, that is, the dimension i used for the search, we count the number of points of P_i that are contained in range $\left[l_0^{(Q)}, u_0^{(Q)}\right] \times \left[l_i^{(Q)}, u_i^{(Q)}\right]$ using wavelet trees W_i (counting query). Let m $(= |D|)$ be the number of i $(= 1, \ldots, d-1)$ such that $\left[l_i^{(Q)}, u_i^{(Q)}\right] \neq [0, n-1]$, and let $i_1, \ldots, i_m$ be the sorted ones in increasing order of the number of answers of counting queries.

Using wavelet trees W_{i_1}, we then enumerate only the x-coordinates of points of P_{i_1} contained in $\left[l_0^{(Q)}, u_0^{(Q)}\right] \times \left[l_{i_1}^{(Q)}, u_{i_1}^{(Q)}\right]$ and store them in a set A. For each element a of A and for each $i = i_2, \ldots, i_m$, we check whether the i-th coordinate of a point for which the 0-th coordinate is a is contained in the query range. The elements remaining in A correspond to points in the query range. The answer to a counting query is the cardinality of A. For a reporting query, we compute coordinates of the points and output them.

The reason we compute the number of points contained in each dimension by a counting query is twofold. Firstly, the x-coordinate (the 0-th coordinate) of points contained in the query range with respect to the i_1-th (and the 0-th) dimension can be output quickly at line 9 of the algorithm if the number of points to enumerate is small. Secondly, in the double loops from line 10 to line 16, we want to reduce the size of A as soon as possible.

8.6.3 Complexity Analyses

Consider the space and time complexities of the proposed method.

For the space complexity, we use $d-1$ many wavelet trees. Therefore, the space complexity is $(d-1)\lg n + (d-1) \cdot o(\lg n)$ bits.

For the query time complexity, let m be the number of wavelet trees used in a search. The time to perform m counting queries on wavelet tree is $O(m \lg n)$. We then sort m integers in $O(m \lg m)$ time. Next, we enumerate the x-coordinates of points contained in the query range for the dimension with the minimum number of points. Let $c_{i_1} = c_{\min}$ be the number of points to enumerate. This takes $O((1 + c_{\min}) \lg n)$ time. The time to check whether these points are contained in the query range for other dimensions is $O((m-1)c_{\min} \lg n)$. Let d' be the number of dimensions used in the query, then it holds that $m \leq d'$. Therefore, the query time complexity can be written as $O\big(d' c_{\min} \lg n + d' \lg d'\big)$.

8.7 Conclusion

In this chapter, we first reviewed data structures for high-dimensional orthogonal range search. We then proposed two data structures for the problem.

The first one simulates the search of the kd-tree using d succinct data structures for two-dimensional orthogonal range search data structures [3]. We improved the query time complexity of KDW-tree while keeping the same space complexity.

The second one is succinct and practically fast. The space complexity is $(d-1)n \lg n + (d-1) \cdot \mathrm{o}(n \lg n)$, which is succinct. The worst-case query time complexity is $\mathrm{O}(dn \lg n)$, which is not good. However, if the number d of dimensions is large but the number d' of dimensions used in a search is small, it runs fast in practice.

References

1. J.L. Bentley, Multidimensional binary search trees used for associative searching. Commun. ACM **18**(9), 509–517 (1975)
2. J.L. Bentley, Decomposable searching problems. Inf. Process. Lett. **8**(5), 244–251 (1979)
3. P. Bose, M. He, A. Maheshwari, P. Morin, Succinct orthogonal range search structures on a grid with applications to text indexing, in *Proceedings of the 11th Workshop on Algorithms and Data Structures (WADS 2009)* (Springer, 2009), pp. 98–109
4. B. Chazelle, A functional approach to data structures and its use in multidimensional searching. SIAM J. Comput. **17**(3), 427–462 (1988)
5. D. Clark, *Compact Pat Trees*. Ph.D. thesis (University of Waterloo, 1997)
6. R.A. Finkel, J.L. Bentley, Quad trees a data structure for retrieval on composite keys. Acta Inform. **4**(1), 1–9 (1974)
7. H.N. Gabow, J.L. Bentley, R.E. Tarjan, Scaling and related techniques for geometry problems, in *Proceedings of the 16th Annual ACM Symposium on Theory of Computing (STOC 1984)* (ACM, 1984), pp. 135–143
8. T. Gagie, G. Navarro, S.J. Puglisi, New algorithms on wavelet trees and applications to information retrieval. Theor. Comput. Sci. **426–427**, 25–41 (2012)
9. R. Grossi, A. Gupta, J.S. Vitter, High-order entropy-compressed text indexes, in *Proceedings of the 14th Annual ACM-SIAM Symposium on Discrete Algorithms (SODA 2003)* (SIAM, 2003), pp. 841–850
10. K. Ishiyama, K. Sadakane, Practical space-efficient data structures for high-dimensional orthogonal range searching, in *Proceedings of the 10th International Conference on Similarity Search and Applications (SISAP 2017)* (Springer, 2017), pp. 234–246
11. K. Ishiyama, K. Sadakane, A succinct data structure for multidimensional orthogonal range searching, in *Proceedings of Data Compression Conference 2017 (DCC 2017)* (2017), pp. 270–279
12. G.J. Jacobson, *Succinct Static Data Structures*. Ph.D. thesis (Pittsburgh, PA, USA, 1988)
13. D.T. Lee, C.K. Wong, Worst-case analysis for region and partial region searches in multidimensional binary search trees and balanced quad trees. Acta Inform. **9**(1), 23–29 (1977)
14. D.T. Lee, C.K. Wong, Quintary trees: a file structure for multidimensional datbase sytems. ACM Trans. Database Syst. **5**(3), 339–353 (1980)
15. G.S. Lueker, A data structure for orthogonal range queries, in *Proceedings of the 9th Annual Symposium on Foundations of Computer Science (SFCS 1978)* (IEEE, 1978), pp. 28–34
16. V. Mäkinen, G. Navarro, Position-restricted substring searching, in *Proceedings of the 7th Latin American Symposium on Theoretical Informatics (LATIN 2006)* (Springer, 2006), pp. 703–714

17. G.M. Morton, *A Computer Oriented Geodetic Data Base and a New Technique in File Sequencing* (International Business Machines Company, New York, 1966)
18. G. Navarro, Wavelet trees for all. J. Discrete Algorithms **25**, 2–20 (2014)
19. G. Navarro, *Compact Data Structures: A Practical Approach* (Cambridge University Press, 2016)
20. Y. Okajima, K. Maruyama, Faster linear-space orthogonal range searching in arbitrary dimensions, in *Proceedings of the 17th Workshop on Algorithm Engineering and Experiments (ALENEX 2015)* (SIAM, 2015), pp. 82–93
21. J. O'Rourke, J.E. Goodman, *Handbook of Discrete and Computational Geometry* (CRC Press, 2004)
22. R. Raman, V. Raman, S.R. Satti, Succinct indexable dictionaries with applications to encoding k-ary trees, prefix sums and multisets. ACM Trans. Algorithms **3**(4), Article 43 (2007)
23. D.E. Willard, *Predicate-Oriented Database Search Algorithms*. Technical report (Harvard Univ Cambridge MA Aiken Computation Lab, 1978)

Open Access This chapter is licensed under the terms of the Creative Commons Attribution 4.0 International License (http://creativecommons.org/licenses/by/4.0/), which permits use, sharing, adaptation, distribution and reproduction in any medium or format, as long as you give appropriate credit to the original author(s) and the source, provide a link to the Creative Commons license and indicate if changes were made.

The images or other third party material in this chapter are included in the chapter's Creative Commons license, unless indicated otherwise in a credit line to the material. If material is not included in the chapter's Creative Commons license and your intended use is not permitted by statutory regulation or exceeds the permitted use, you will need to obtain permission directly from the copyright holder.

Chapter 9
Enhanced RAM Simulation in Succinct Space

Taku Onodera

Abstract We describe two recent results on space-efficient functional random access memory (RAM), which is RAM with non-standard functionalities. The first is about oblivious RAM, which enables a remote database to be accessed without revealing to the database owner which part of the database is being accessed. The other is about wear leveling, which enables the number of updates to be balanced among all the memory cells regardless of the content of the computation being performed on the memory.

9.1 Introduction

Random access memory (RAM) underlies most modern computers, and improvements to the RAM itself can have a positive impact on a wide range of applications. For example, faster RAM access makes all RAM-based computations correspondingly faster. Some types of RAM improvements are not just about efficiency but also about *functionality*. An example is virtual memory in operating systems, which enables, among other things, application programs to utilize the memory without concern about cumbersome management issues such as allocation. Generally speaking, this type of RAM improvement functions by using conventional RAM to simulate "enhanced" RAM while introducing some performance overhead.

In this chapter, we describe two such enhanced RAM simulations—*oblivious RAM* (ORAM) and *wear leveling*—with the emphasis on how to minimize the space overhead. These topics were chosen mainly because the authors' knowledge of them, although there are also some conceptual similarities between ORAM and wear

T. Onodera (✉)
The University of Tokyo, Tokyo, Japan
e-mail: tk-ono@is.s.u-tokyo.ac.jp

© The Author(s) 2022

N. Katoh et al. (eds.), *Sublinear Computation Paradigm*,
https://doi.org/10.1007/978-981-16-4095-7_9

leveling. Other functionality-enhanced RAM simulations include initializable array [2], memory checking [3], locally decodable code [11], and huge random object [8].[1]

9.2 Oblivious RAM

9.2.1 Problem

Suppose you want to outsource a database, stored in RAM, to a server and want to access it in a privacy-preserving way. Although you can hide the data content by encryption, the server can still see which part of the RAM you are accessing. This is a serious issue in the current era of cloud computing. The same problem also appears when one wants to hide the details of software implemented in a physically secure processor that accesses insecure main memory.

Oblivious RAM (ORAM) is the formalization and corresponding solution of this problem. Typically, it works by storing the RAM into some data structure on the server and moves the RAM cells dynamically in the data structure as the user accesses the RAM.

As an example, consider a scheme where the server stores the RAM as-is except that each cell is encrypted by the user's key. To access the ith cell, the user performs the following procedure for $j = 1$ to N where N is the number of cells:

1. Retrieve the ith cell from the server.
2. Decrypt the retrieved cell.
3. If $i = j$:
   - For read access, copy the decrypted value to local memory.
   - For write access, change the decrypted value to the new value.
4. Re-encrypt the possibly changed decrypted value.
5. Store the re-encrypted value back in the ith cell on the server.

We assume semantically secure encryption when encryption is used in this chapter. In particular, there is an overwhelmingly high probability that the re-encrypted ciphertext looks totally different to the server from the ciphertext before re-encryption regardless of whether the plaintext is updated or not. Thus, no matter what actual access is performed, all that the server can see is that random-looking encrypted cells are updated to still random-looking re-encrypted cells in a fixed scan order. Of course, the access overhead of this method is very large since each cell access takes

[1] A huge random object, in this context, is a succinct representation of a pseudorandom object that supports certain queries. For example, a pseudorandom function can be thought of as a huge pseudorandom bitstring that is implicitly represented by a tiny seed and supports efficient random access. This is not a data structure in the conventional sense because the represented object is a pseudorandom bitstring instead of "data."

time linear to the entire RAM size. The purpose of this example is merely to illustrate the kind of security we want to achieve.

We now give a more formal problem description. We have three parties: the user, the server, and the simulator. The simulator models a program that runs in the local environment of the user. The simulator provides the user with an access interface to RAM that we call the virtual RAM while the server provides the simulator with an access interface to RAM that we call the physical RAM. That is, the user gives the simulator a series of queries of the form (type, i, v) where type $\in$ {read, write}, $i \in [N]$, and $v \in \{0, 1\}^B$. We call these virtual queries. The parameter N specifies the number of virtual cells—cells in the virtual RAM—while B specifies the size of each virtual cell. Given a virtual query, the simulator gives the server another series of queries of the form (type, i, v), where type $\in$ {read, write}, $i \in [N']$, and $v \in \{0, 1\}^{B'}$. We call these physical queries. The simulator, and thus the physical queries, is probabilistic in general.[2] The server responds to physical queries in the obvious way. That is, for (read, i, $*$) where "$*$" means that the third component is arbitrary, the server returns the value of the ith physical cell, and for (write, i, v), the server updates the value of the ith physical cell to v. If the virtual query from the user is of the form (read, i, $*$), the simulator derives the value of the ith virtual cell through the interaction with the server and returns it to the user. If the virtual query is of the form (write, i, v), the simulator updates the value of the ith virtual cell to v. The simulator must respond to the virtual queries online. We call the sequence of second components of the virtual queries (resp. physical queries) a virtual access pattern (resp. physical access pattern). For a virtual query sequence q, let $a(q)$ denote the physical access pattern induced by q. Recall that $a(q)$ is a random variable in general. The ORAM scheme is secure if $a(q_1)$ and $a(q_2)$ are indistinguishable for any virtual query sequences q_1 and q_2 of the same length. There are some variations in the exact meaning "indistinguishable". Typically used meanings of indistinguishability in descending order of security are a) equally distributed, b) statistically closely distributed, and c) computationally indistinguishable. The main performance metric of ORAM includes access overhead, which is the number of physical queries processed for each virtual query, the simulator local space size, and the server space size, which is $B'N'$ bits.

As mentioned above, the simulator models a program running in the local environment of the user. Thus, in practice, we do not distinguish the user and the simulator. For example, we refer to the simulator local space as user space.

The ORAM problem is non-trivial only if the user space is smaller than BN bits since otherwise, the simulator can store the entire RAM locally and ignore the server.

[2] The simulator of the scan-based method is deterministic, and it is not hard to see that its linear access overhead is optimal if we restrict the simulator to be deterministic. Thus, all simulators of interest are indeed probabilistic.

Table 9.1 Summary of existing results. † means amortized bound. $\approx \log N$ means $O(f(N))$ for any $f \in \omega(\log N)$. The constant factor of the user space of [26] is $\ll 1$

	Access overhead	Sever space (N')	User space	Technique	Security
[7]	$O(\sqrt{N}\log N)^{\dagger}$	$N(1+2\sqrt{N})$	$O(1)$	Square root	Computational
[9]	$O(\log^3 N)^{\dagger}$	$\Theta(N\log N)$	$O(1)$	Hierarchical	Computational
[19]	$O(\sqrt{N}\log N)$	$(1+\Theta(1))N$	$O(1)$		
[19]	$O(\log^3 N)$	$\Theta(N\log N)$	$O(1)$		
[10]	$O(\log^2 N)^{\dagger}$	$(1+\Theta(1))N$	$O(1)$		
[13]	$O(\frac{\log^2 N}{\log\log N})$	$(1+\Theta(1))N$	$O(1)$		
[20]	$O(\log N\log\log N)^{\dagger}$	$(1+\Theta(1))N$	$O(1)$		
[12]	$O(\log N)^{\dagger}$	$(1+\Theta(1))N$	$O(1)$		
[25]	$O(\log^3 N)$	$\Theta(N\log N)$	$O(1)$	Tree	Statistical
[27]	$O(\log^2 N)$	$(1+\Theta(1))N$	$\approx \log N$		
[17]	$O(\log^2 N)$	$(1+o(1))N$	$\approx \log N$		

9.2.2 *Existing Results*

Table 9.1 gives a summary of some of the existing results. Every method has physical cell size $B' = B + \Theta(\log N)$. There is an $\Omega(\log N)$ lower bound for the access overhead if the user space is at most $N^{1-\epsilon}$ for constant $\epsilon > 0$ [14].

There are mainly two types of techniques that are actively studied: hierarchical approaches and tree-based approaches.[3] Asymptotically, the state-of-the-art hierarchical method [12] has access overhead matching the lower bound mentioned above while the state-of-the-art tree-based methods have about $\log N$ times larger asymptotic access overhead. Yet, tree-based methods are still of practical interest because they tend to have much smaller access overhead constant factors than the hierarchical methods. The access overheads of tree-based methods also constrain the worst case while those of the hierarchical methods are often amortized. Although there are techniques to achieve competitive worst-case access overhead via the hierarchical methods [13, 19], they tend to be complex and add further constant factors to the performance bounds.

In the past, the ORAM research community has focused mainly on reducing the access overhead because it was the biggest obstacle to applying ORAM in practice. However, some recent studies have achieved practical access performances [16, 22] by combining tree-based ORAM with special hardware. For example, the PHANTOM secure processor system [16] supports access pattern-hiding SQL queries with a time overhead of 1.2–6 $\times$ compared to the standard insecure version. Thus, at least for tree-based ORAM, exploration of aspects other than access overhead is beginning to make sense.

---

[3] The square root method [7] was the first non-trivial ORAM and is the origin of some of the ideas underlying the hierarchical methods.

We describe the recent development of techniques for reducing the number of physical cells N' of the tree-based ORAM to $(1 + o(1))N$ [17]. Note that there also is a space overhead originating from the cell size: typically, $B' = B + c \lg N$ where c is a small constant such as 2. We ignore the cell size overhead and focus on the cell number because the typical value of B is 128 bytes in the secure processor setting and the overhead with respect to the cell size is just a few percent.

9.2.3 Tree-Based Methods

The tree-based method of Stefanov et al. [27] works as follows. The server organizes the physical cells into a complete binary tree with N leaves where each node is a bucket—a container that can accommodate a constant number of virtual cells. Each virtual cell has a position label—an integer in $[N]$—and a virtual cell with position label i is stored either in some bucket on the path from the root to the ith leaf or in a stash, which is a container in the user's local memory that can accommodate a small number of virtual cells. Let v_i be the ith virtual cell and let p_i be the position label of v_i. Suppose the user maintains p_i for all $i \in [N]$ in local memory. This requires $\Omega(N)$ user space but simplifies the exposition. We will reduce the user space later. To access v_i, the user retrieves all of the blocks on the path from the root to the p_ith leaf. Let this path be P. At this point, v_i must be in the stash. The user copies the value of v_i to somewhere in its local memory for a read query or changes it to some other value for a write query. Then, the user updates p_i to a fresh random value in $[N]$. After that, the user scans the buckets on P from the leaf to the root, and for each bucket, moves cells in the stash to the bucket greedily while respecting the position labels and the bucket capacity. See Fig. 9.1 for an example.

Sometimes, some virtual cells in the stash cannot be moved back to the tree. For example, if all cells are assigned the same position label, only $\Theta(\log N)$ physical cells can be used to store the virtual cells and thus, most virtual cells must end up in the stash. (Of course, if N is large, such an event happens only extremely rarely.) Stefanov et al. proved that if the bucket size is at least 5, the number of cells left in the stash after processing a query is exponentially small. Thus, if the stash size is $\omega(\log N)$, the stash overflows during processing a polynomial number of queries with only negligible probability.

To reduce the user space for position labels, the user outsources the position labels using the same method recursively. That is, each position label is a $\lceil \lg N \rceil$ bit integer and the table for position labels of all virtual cells can be thought of as a RAM storing the $N\lceil \lg N \rceil$-bit concatenation of the integers. Thus, the original problem of hiding the access pattern to RAM consisting of N cells, each of B bits, is reduced to hiding the access pattern to RAM consisting of $N\lceil \lg N \rceil / B$ cells, each of B bits. If, say, $B \geq 2 \lg N$, which is a completely reasonable assumption for all reasonable N,[4] the problem size (cell number) decreases exponentially and reaches $O(1)$ after

[4] Recall that the typical value of B is 128 bytes in secure processor applications.

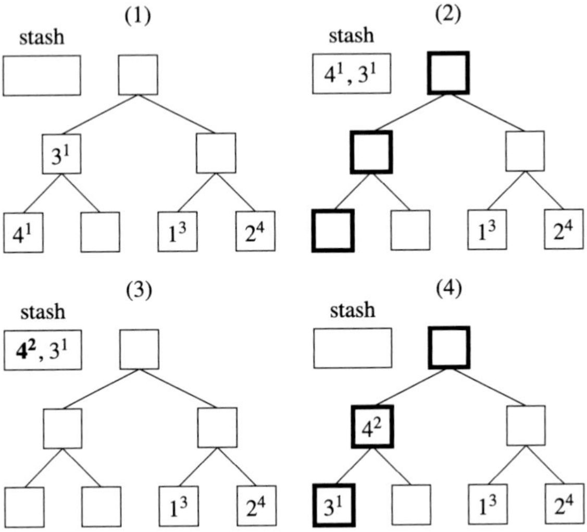

Fig. 9.1 Example access process for reading the 4th virtual cell. $N = 4$. Bucket size is 1. The expression i^j means the ith virtual cell with position label j. The path from the root to the first leaf is scanned from top to bottom in step (2) and from bottom to top in step (4)

$O(\lg N)$ levels of recursion. At that point, the user can store the $O(1)$ size RAM locally terminating the recursion.

The tree at the top level of recursion has size $\Theta(N)$ and the tree at higher recursion levels decreases exponentially. The access overhead is proportional to the sum of the heights of the trees at all recursion levels, which is $O(\log^2 N)$. The server space is proportional to the sum of the sizes of the trees at all recursion levels, which is $\Theta(N)$.

Although each recursion level requires a stash, the numbers of cells left in those stashes are independent and it turns out that the total number of cells left in all stashes is still exponentially small. Thus, $f(N)$ user space is enough for any $f(N) \in \omega(\log N)$.

9.2.4 *Succinct Construction*

The constant factor hidden in the $\Theta(N)$ server space bound of the method described above is about 10: the top-level tree has $2N$ nodes each of capacity 5 while the size of the recursive trees is negligible because typically, B is much larger than $\lg N$. (Theoretically, we assume $B = \omega(\lg N)$.) Though one can reduce this constant factor to some extent by decreasing the tree height while tuning the bucket size, it is not possible to achieve a factor ≤ 2 while maintaining a meaningful stash overflow probability, at least using the currently known analysis techniques. This method also leads to prohibitively large access overhead as the server space becomes close to $2N$. We now describe a method for achieving $(1 + o(1))N$ server space with a modest sacrifice in access overhead [17].

Fig. 9.2 Large leaf layout

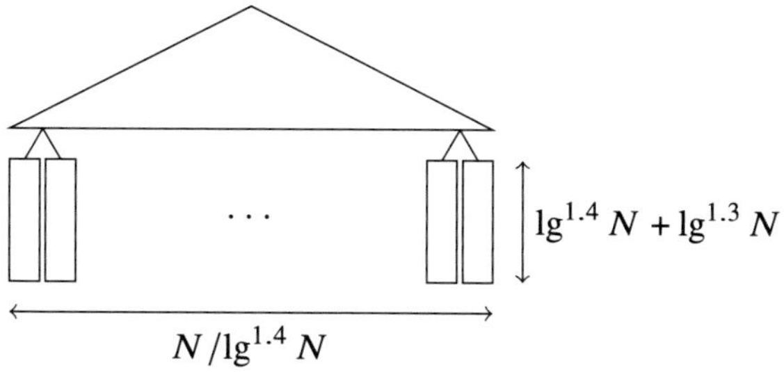

The idea is to modify the layout of the tree at the top recursion level so that the leaf number is $N/\lg^{1.4} N$ and the leaf size is $\lg^{1.4} N + \lg^{1.3} N$ (see Fig. 9.2). It is obvious that the tree size is $(1 + 1/\lg^{0.1} N)N$ while access overhead remains $O(\log^2 N)$. We now explain why the stash overflow probability remains small.

Let N_i be the number of cells with position label i for $i \in [N/\lg^{1.4} N]$. Let the load of a bucket be the number of cells stored in the bucket. At each moment in the lifetime of the scheme, N_i follows the binomial distribution with parameters N and $N/\lg^{1.4} N$ for each i. The probability that this becomes larger than $\lg^{1.4} N + \lg^{1.3} N$ is negligible. Thus, no leaf becomes full while processing a polynomial number of queries. Under this assumption, the distribution of the internal bucket loads is dominated by the distribution of the loads of the corresponding $N/\lg^{1.4} N - 1$ internal buckets in the standard N leaf layout scheme described above. This is so because the internal buckets in the large leaf layout do not need to store the cells that overflow from the leaves. Thus, assuming no leaf becomes full, the stash overflow probability of the large leaf case is negligible. The same is true even without this assumption because there is only a negligible probability that the assumed case does not occur.

We can reduce the $N/\lg^{0.1} N$ extra term on the tree size even further by "the power of two choices". That is, we give two random position labels to each virtual cell. One is primary, which determines the path on which the cell can reside, while the other is secondary, which is a dummy needed to hide the access pattern. Now, N_i is the number of virtual cells with primary position label i. We maintain N_i for all i in a sub-ORAM in the same way we store position labels in recursive ORAM. To access a virtual cell v, we retrieve all cells on the path from the root to the p_1th leaf and the path from the root to the p_2th leaf. We choose two random labels p_1', p_2' and let p_1' (resp. p_2') be the new primary (resp. secondary) label of v if $N_{p_1'} < N_{p_2'}$. Otherwise, we exchange the role of p_1' and p_2'. We then scan the paths specified by the old labels and greedily move back the cells as in the previous method. Here, N_i is not binomial but concentrated much more tightly around the mean due to the effect of the two choices. Thus, the "head space" for each leaf can be much smaller than $\lg^{1.3} N$, leading to a smaller tree size.

By tuning the parameters, the first technique (large leaf layout) alone can achieve about $(1 + \Theta(\frac{\log N}{B} + \frac{1}{\sqrt{\log N}}))N$ server space while the second technique (two choices) decreases it to $(1 + \Theta(\frac{\log N}{B} + \frac{\log\log N}{\log^2 N}))N$.[5]

9.2.5 *Open Problem*

It is unknown whether the optimal $O(\log N)$ access overhead and $(1 + o(1))N$ server space can be achieved at the same time. There are two natural approaches for answering this question affirmatively:

- Develop a technique for making hierarchical methods, such as [9], succinct and apply it to the existing optimal method [12]. This seems particularly challenging if we further require a worst-case (instead of amortized) access overhead bound because the existing techniques for achieving a worst-case access overhead bound in the hierarchical approach [13, 19] require maintaining multiple versions of the database.
- Achieve $O(\log N)$ access overhead by a tree-based approach and apply the techniques described here. The first part is already an open problem of sufficient interest.

9.3 Wear Leveling

9.3.1 *Problem*

Consider the case where you have RAM with the limitation that each cell state can be updated at most a certain number of times. Once the number of updates has reached the limit, the cell dies and you can no longer update it. The utility of the RAM quickly degrades as the cells start to die because the total amount of information that can be stored decreases, and it becomes cumbersome to manage which cells are still alive. Thus, the number of times you can support updates before cells start to die is of primary interest. This number depends heavily on the case. In the best case where the updates are uniform among the cells, you can perform nL updates where n is the number of cells and L is the number of times each cell can be updated. In contrast, in the worst case where all updates fall onto a particular cell, you can perform updates only L times. Wear leveling is the problem of prolonging the memory lifetime as much as possible while keeping the associated overhead, if any, as small as possible.

The system community has been studying wear leveling for decades. Historically, flash memory was the main motivation for studies conducted from the late 1980s to the mid 2000s [1, 6, 15]. Today, the main motivation for wear leveling comes

[5] These bounds include the cell size overhead that we ignored in the main explanation for brevity.

from phase change memory (PCM), which is an emerging next-generation memory technology that has many features, including low latency, energy efficiency, and non-volatility [5]. Each PCM cell supports only 10^8–10^9 updates, which means that cells can start dying within minutes or even seconds if no effort is made to perform wear leveling. PCM differs from flash memory in certain important respects, such as latency, access granularity, and in-place write capability, and thus requires a different wear leveling formalization than flash memory.

Most existing studies on wear leveling are conducted mainly from a practical point of view. Often, they do not have a formal problem statement or rigorous theoretical analyses. While this might not be a serious problem if the only thing that matters is the performance, some relatively recent studies have repeatedly emphasized the security aspects of wear leveling [21, 23, 24, 28, 29]. In particular, it is important to take into account the case of malicious users who actively try to reduce the memory lifetime. (Consider, for example, a computing outsourcing service.)

Below, we describe a recent theoretical study that constructed a problem formalization to capture the wear leveling for PCM explained above, and the corresponding solutions [18].

The formal problem statement is as follows. There are two parties: the user and server. The server has three resources: physical RAM, wear-free memory, and private randomness. The physical RAM is RAM that consists of N B-bit cells while the wear-free memory is RAM that consists of a small number of B-bit cells. The user provides the server with adversarially chosen read/write queries to virtual RAM—a RAM consisting of n b-bit cells—and the server must respond to these queries "correctly." That is, each request is of the form (type, i, v) where type $\in$ {read, write}, $i \in [n]$, and $v \in \{0, 1\}^b$ and, for (read, i, $*$) where "$*$" means that the third component is arbitrary, the server must return the last value written to the ith virtual cell (the v in the last query of the form (write, i, v)). The server not only needs to return the correct responses but also needs to support as many write queries as possible with high probability without updating any physical cell more than L times where L is a parameter. We assume $L = n^\delta$ for some constant $\delta > 0$. Equivalently, we define $\delta := \log_L n$ and assume it is a constant. This assumption is reasonable even though, in reality, L and n are independent, because L is 10^8–10^9 and $\log_L n$ is at most 2 or 3 for reasonable n.

The performance metric for wear leveling includes the physical memory size, the wear-free memory size, the number of write queries supported, and the access overhead, which is the number of physical RAM accesses needed for each virtual RAM access. We say a wear-leveling scheme is "optimal" if it satisfies the following conditions (asymptotic notations are in terms of $n \to \infty$):

- $N = 1 + o(1)$[6];
- With high probability, that is, $1 - O(1/n)$, it can process $(1 - o(1))NL$ write queries without updating any physical cell more than L times;

[6] We ignore the cell size overhead for brevity. Security Refresh [23] described below does not have any cell size overhead ($B' = B$) while the method of Onodera and Shibuya [18] described after that has a cell size of $B' = B + 2\lceil \lg n \rceil + 1$.

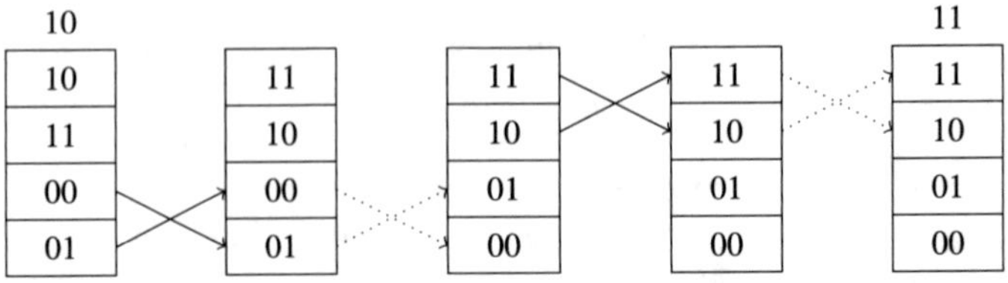

Fig. 9.3 Movement of cells in an epoch of security refresh. All the numbers are binary. $n = 4 (= N)$, $r_0 =$"10", and $r_1 =$"11". Solid arrows mean cell swaps while dotted arrows mean skipped cell swaps

- The processing time of each query is $O(1)$;
- It requires only $O(1)$ cells in the wear-free memory.

9.3.2 Security Refresh

The wear leveling scheme of Sewong et al. [23] is optimal if $L = N^\delta$ for $\delta > 1$ while it is non-optimal (in fact, "far from" optimal) for $\delta < 1$ [18].

In this method, n virtual cells are stored in the $N = n$ physical cells in permuted order. The method works in epochs. At each epoch, two random $\lg n$-bit integers r_0 and r_1 are maintained. (We assume n is a power of two for brevity.) At the start of an epoch, for each $i \in [n]$, the ith virtual cell v_i is stored in the $i \oplus r_0$th physical cell $V_{i \oplus r_0}$ where $\oplus$ means bit-wise XOR. During the epoch, each v_i is moved from $V_{i \oplus r_0}$ to $V_{i \oplus r_1}$. Note that the virtual cell stored in the destination $V_{i \oplus r_1}$ of v_i is $v_{i \oplus r_1 \oplus r_0}$ and its destination is $V_{i \oplus r_0}$; that is, v_i and $v_{i \oplus r_0 \oplus r_1}$ swap their positions. This is done as follows. For every t write queries processed where t is a parameter, we perform a remap subroutine. At the ith remap subroutine call in an epoch, we check if $i < i \oplus r_0 \oplus r_1$. If so, v_i still is in $V_{i \oplus r_0}$ and thus, we swap the contents of $V_{i \oplus r_0}$ and $V_{i \oplus r_1}$. Otherwise, v_i is already in $V_{i \oplus r_1}$ and we skip swapping. The epoch ends after the nth remap subroutine finishes. At that point, each cell v_i is stored in $V_{i \oplus r_1}$. We update r_0 to r_1, and r_1 to a fresh random $\lg n$-bit integer. Now every v_i is in $V_{i \oplus r_0}$ as required for the epoch start, and we restart another epoch at this point. See Fig. 9.3 for an example. To access v_i, we access $V_{i \oplus r_0}$ if v_i was already remapped in the epoch. (We have already seen how to check this.) Otherwise, we access $V_{i \oplus r_1}$.

The non-trivial part of the analysis is the proof of a high-probability guarantee of memory lifetime. We outline the key points. Fix a physical cell and let X_i be the number of times it is updated during the ith epoch. We need to place a bound on the probability that the sum of X_is deviates from its expected value. To do this, it suffices to bound the deviation of the sum of odd-indexed variables $X_1, X_3, \ldots$ from its expected value and do the same for the sum of even-indexed variables $X_2, X_4, \ldots$ separately. This is helpful because each X_i is a random variable that depends on r_0, r_1 in the ith epoch (and the queries) and thus, the odd-indexed variables $X_1, X_3, \ldots$ are independent of each other and so are the even-indexed variables. Regardless of the queries, X_i is bounded by the number of write queries processed in an epoch tn. Although this suggests the use of the Hoeffding inequality, it turns out that it does not work for the case $\delta < 2$, essentially because the condition $X_i \leq tn$ alone does not capture the fact that some cell being updated many, say, $\approx tn$, times in an epoch negatively affects the number of times other cells are updated in the epoch. To derive the bound for the case $1 < \delta < 2$, bound the second moment of X_i and apply the Bernstein inequality [4].

If the user tries to keep on updating v_i continuously, one of $V_{i \oplus r_0}$ and $V_{i \oplus r_1}$ is updated $tn/2 = \Omega(n)$ times during the first epoch, and this physical cell dies if $\delta < 1$. Thus, this method is not optimal for $\delta < 1$.

9.3.3 Construction for Small Write Limit Cases

We now briefly describe a method for achieving optimality for the case $\delta < 1$, that is, the memory is large [18]. The idea is to prepare spare cells and remap the frequently updated cells to free spare cells adaptively. (We maintain the write counts of cells by appending a counter to each cell.) We store pointers to the new locations in the old locations to trace the remapped cells. To keep the number of pointers to follow small, we connect pointers in a manner that is similar to the DFS of a complete d-ary tree with d^h leaves where d, h are parameters (see Fig. 9.4). As we continue to process write queries, the data structure gradually degrades: the free spare cells become scarce and the trees become saturated. To reset the degradation, we perform a Security Refresh-style mapping. That is, we treat the structure in Fig. 9.4 as residing in another RAM u and maintain a global mapping—a gradually changing one-to-one map between the cells of u and the physical cells $V_1, V_2, \ldots$. Once we have globally remapped a cell of u corresponding to a tree root, we reset the "DFS" starting from that cell. For example, if we globally remap u_i in state (5) of Fig. 9.4, we free u_{n+1}, u_{n+4}, resetting DFS for the tree from u_i to the root. Garbage such as u_{n+3} are also reclaimed sooner or later when they are globally remapped. To access v_i, the tree path traversal in u starting from i is simulated translating between addresses in u and addresses in V.

Although analysis of the bound on memory lifetime is cumbersome, the same idea as the analysis of Security Refresh applies. Indeed, the core argument is easier because the Hoeffding bound suffices.

9.3.4 Open Problem

The access overhead of the method for the small write limit case described above is about $1/\delta$. It is easy to obtain amortized $1 + o(1)$ and worst-case $\Theta(n)$ access overhead if we allow relatively large wear-free memory, for example, $O(n^\epsilon)$ for an appropriate constant $0 < \epsilon < 1$. It seems possible and practically relevant to

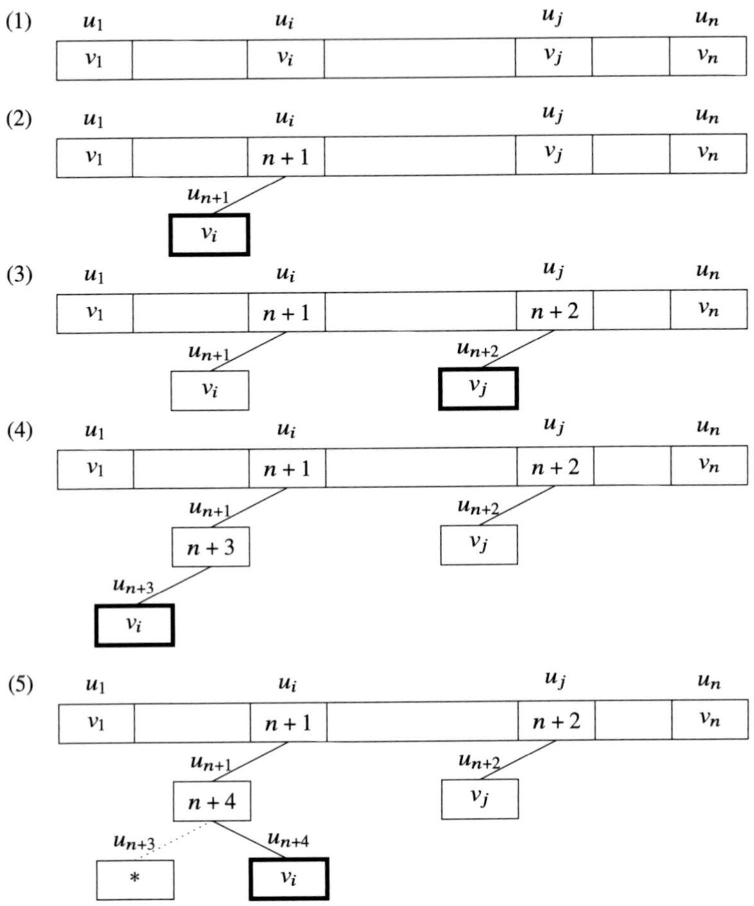

Fig. 9.4 Example evolution of u. $d = h = 2$. $u_1, \ldots, u_n$ are default locations while the rest are spare cells. Each panel shows the state just after the thick-bordered cell was allocated because the cell previously storing its content was updated and the write count reached the threshold

achieve amortized $1 + o(1)$ and worst-case $O(1)$ access overhead in this setting. A theoretically more interesting challenge is to give negative results that justify the use of such large wear-free memory.

9.4 Conclusion

We reviewed two recent studies on ORAM and wear leveling that achieve succinct space usage. Though these objects have totally different motivations and are studied in different communities, there are some similarities between them. As we mentioned in the introduction, several other concepts with similar flavors are known, including initializable RAM, memory checking, locally decodable code, and huge random objects. There are probably many more such enhanced RAM instances yet to be found, and trying to find them can be an avenue for making progress in studies of data structures.

References

1. A. Ban, Wear leveling of static areas in flash memory. US Patent 6,732,221, May 2004
2. J. Bentley, *Programming Pearls* (Addison-Wesley, Column 1, 1989)
3. Manuel Blum, Will Evans, Peter Gemmell, Sampath Kannan, Moni Naor, Checking the Correctness of Memories. Algorithmica **12**(2-3), 225–244 (1994)
4. S. Boucheron, G. Lugosi, P. Massart, *Concentration Inequalities: A Nonasymptotic Theory of Independence* (Oxford University Press, 2013). Equation (2.10)
5. J. Boukhobza, S. Rubini, R. Chen, Z. Shao, Emerging NVM: a survey on architectural integration and research challenges. ACM Trans. Des. Autom. Electron. Syst. **23**(2), 14:1–14:32 (2017)
6. Eran Gal, Sivan Toledo, Algorithms and Data Structures for Flash Memories. ACM Comput. Surv. **37**(2), 138–163 (2005)
7. O. Goldreich, Towards a theory of software protection and simulation by oblivious RAMs, in *Proceedings of the 19th Annual ACM Symposium on Theory of Computing (STOC)* (1987), pp. 182–194
8. Oded Goldreich, Shafi Goldwasser and Asaf Nussboim. On the implementation of huge random objects. In SIAM J. Comput. 39.7, 2010, pp. 2761–2822
9. Oded Goldreich, Rafail Ostrovsky, Software Protection and Simulation on Oblivious RAMs. J. ACM **43**(3), 431–473 (1996)
10. M.T. Goodrich, M. Mitzenmacher, Privacy-preserving access of outsourced data via oblivious RAM simulation, in *Proceedings of the 38th International Conference on Automata, Languages and Programming (ICALP)*, vol. II (2011), pp. 576–587
11. J. Katz, L. Trevisan, On the efficiency of local decoding procedures for error-correcting codes, in *Proceedings of the 32nd Annual ACM Symposium on Theory of Computing (STOC)* (2000), pp. 80–86
12. I. Komargodski, W.-K. Lin, K. Nayak, E. Peserico, E. Shi, OptORAMa: optimal oblivious RAM, in *Proceedings of the 39th Annual International Conference on the Theory and Applications of Cryptographic Techniques (Eurocrypt)* (2020), pp. 403–432
13. E. Kushilevitz, S. Lu, R. Ostrovsky, On the (in)security of hash-based oblivious RAM and a new balancing scheme, in *Proceedings of the 23rd Annual ACM-SIAM Symposium on Discrete Algorithms (SODA)* (2012), pp. 143–156
14. K.G. Larsen, J.B. Nielsen, Yes, there is an oblivious RAM lower bound!, in *Proceedings of the 38th International Cryptology Conference (CRYPTO)* (2018), pp. 523–542
15. K.M.J. Lofgren, R.D. Norman, G.B. Thelin, A. Gupta, Wear leveling techniques for flash EEPROM systems. US Patent 6,230,233, May 2001
16. M. Maas, E. Love, E. Stefanov, M. Tiwari, E. Shi, K. Asanovic, J. Kubiatowicz, D. Song, PHANTOM: practical oblivious computation in a secure processor, in *Proceedings of the 20th ACM SIGSAC Conference on Computer & Communications Security (CCS)* (2013), pp. 311–324
17. T. Onodera, T. Shibuya, Succinct oblivious RAM, in *Proceedings of the 35th Symposium on Theoretical Aspects of Computer Science (STACS)* (2018), pp. 1–16
18. T. Onodera, T. Shibuya, Wear leveling revisited. To appear in *The 31st International Symposium on Algorithms and Computation (ISAAC2020)*

19. R. Ostrovsky, V. Shoup, Private information storage, in *Proceedings of the 29th Annual ACM Symposium on Theory of Computing (STOC)* (1997), pp. 294–303
20. S. Patel, G. Persiano, M. Raykova, K. Yeo, PanORAMa: oblivious RAM with logarithmic overhead, in *Proceedings of the 59th Annual Symposium on Foundations of Computer Science (FOCS)* (2018), pp. 871–882
21. M.K. Qureshi, M. Franceschini, V. Srinivasan, L. Lastras, B. Abali, J. Karidis, Enhancing lifetime and security of PCM-based main memory with start-gap wear leveling, in *Proceedings of the 42nd Annual IEEE/ACM International Symposium on Microarchitecture (MICRO)* (2009), pp. 14–23
22. Ling Ren, Christopher W. Fletcher, Albert Kwon, Marten van Dijk, Srinivas Devadas, Design and Implementation of the Ascend Secure Processor. IEEE Trans. Depend. Secure Comput. **16**(2), 204–216 (2019)
23. N.H. Seong, D.H. Woo, H.-H. Lee, Security refresh: protecting phase-change memory against malicious wear out. IEEE Micro. **31**(1), 119–127 (2011)
24. André Seznec, A Phase Change Memory as a Secure Main Memory. IEEE Computer Architecture Letters **9**(1), 5–8 (2010)
25. E. Shi, T.-H.H. Chan, E. Stefanov, M. Li, Oblivious RAM with $O((\log N)^3)$ worst-case cost, in *Proceedings of the 17th International Conference on the Theory and Application of Cryptology and Information Security (Asiacrypt)* (2011), pp. 197–214
26. E. Stefanov, E. Shi, D.X. Song, Towards practical oblivious RAM, in *19th Annual Network and Distributed System Security Symposium (NDSS)* (2012)
27. E. Stefanov, M. van Dijk, E. Shi, T.-H.H. Chan, C. Fletcher, L. Ren, X. Yu, S. Devadas, Path ORAM: an extremely simple oblivious RAM protocol J. ACM **65**(4) (2018)
28. G. Wu, H. Zhang, Y. Dong, J. Hu, CAR: securing PCM main memory system with cache address remapping, in *Proceedings of the 18th IEEE International Conference on Parallel and Distributed Systems* (2012), pp. 628–635
29. H. Yu, Y. Du, Increasing endurance and security of phase-change memory with multi-way wear-leveling. IEEE Trans. Comput. **63**(5), 1157–1168 (2014)

Open Access This chapter is licensed under the terms of the Creative Commons Attribution 4.0 International License (http://creativecommons.org/licenses/by/4.0/), which permits use, sharing, adaptation, distribution and reproduction in any medium or format, as long as you give appropriate credit to the original author(s) and the source, provide a link to the Creative Commons license and indicate if changes were made.

The images or other third party material in this chapter are included in the chapter's Creative Commons license, unless indicated otherwise in a credit line to the material. If material is not included in the chapter's Creative Commons license and your intended use is not permitted by statutory regulation or exceeds the permitted use, you will need to obtain permission directly from the copyright holder.

Part IV
Sublinear Modelling

Chapter 10
Review of Sublinear Modeling in Probabilistic Graphical Models by Statistical Mechanical Informatics and Statistical Machine Learning Theory

Kazuyuki Tanaka

Abstract We review sublinear modeling in probabilistic graphical models by statistical mechanical informatics and statistical machine learning theory. Our statistical mechanical informatics schemes are based on advanced mean-field methods including loopy belief propagations. This chapter explores how phase transitions appear in loopy belief propagations for prior probabilistic graphical models. The frameworks are mainly explained for loopy belief propagations in the Ising model which is one of the elementary versions of probabilistic graphical models. We also expand the schemes to quantum statistical machine learning theory. Our framework can provide us with sublinear modeling based on the momentum space renormalization group methods.

10.1 Introduction

Statistical machine learning frameworks using **probabilistic graphical models** are useful for many applications, including information communication technologies [1–3], compressed sensing [4, 5] and neural information processing systems [6–10] in data-driven sciences.

Most probabilistic graphical models belong to the exponential family [11] and can be regarded as classical spin systems in **statistical mechanical informatics** [12–17]. However, it is well known that many applicable formulations in data sciences as well as computational sciences can be reduced to combinatorial problems with some constraint conditions which can be regarded as an **Ising Model** in statistical mechanical informatics [18, 19]. Moreover, much interest has focused on applying **quantum annealing** as a novel high-speed optimization technology to massive optimization problems [20–24].

K. Tanaka (✉)
Graduate School of Information Sciences, Tohoku University, Sendai, Japan
e-mail: kazu@tohoku.ac.jp

© The Author(s) 2022

N. Katoh et al. (eds.), *Sublinear Computation Paradigm*,
https://doi.org/10.1007/978-981-16-4095-7_10

10.2 Statistical Machine Learning

In statistical machine learning, most of the mathematical frameworks for machine learning are based on maximum likelihood frameworks [25, 26] from statistical mathematical sciences. The important points are how to assume the prior distribution and the data generative probability distribution and how to express the joint probability between the parameters and the data vector. In this section, we explore maximum likelihood frameworks in terms of model selection and parameter selection from a given data vector.

10.2.1 *Bayesian Statistics and Maximization of Marginal Likelihood*

Let us consider a graph specified by nodes and edges, (V, E), where V is the set of all nodes i and E is the set of all edges $\{i, j\}$. State variables s_i and d_i are associated with each node i. The vectors $\boldsymbol{s} = \begin{pmatrix} s_1 \\ s_2 \\ \vdots \\ s_{|V|} \end{pmatrix}$ and $\boldsymbol{d} = \begin{pmatrix} d_1 \\ d_2 \\ \vdots \\ d_{|V|} \end{pmatrix}$ correspond to the parameters and the data vector, respectively. The state spaces of s_i and d_i are given by Ω and $(-\infty, +\infty)$, respectively. Now $\rho(\boldsymbol{d}|\boldsymbol{s}, \beta)$ and $P(\boldsymbol{s}|\alpha)$ which correspond to the data generative and prior models, respectively, are assumed to be as follows:

$$\rho(\boldsymbol{d}|\boldsymbol{s}, \beta) = \prod_{i \in V} \sqrt{\frac{\beta}{2\pi}} \exp\left(-\frac{1}{2}\beta(d_i - s_i)^2\right), \tag{10.1}$$

$$P(\boldsymbol{s}|\alpha) = \frac{\prod_{\{i,j\} \in E} \exp\left(-\frac{1}{2}\alpha\left(s_i - s_j\right)^2\right)}{\sum_{s_1 \in \Omega} \sum_{s_2 \in \Omega} \cdots \sum_{s_{|V|} \in \Omega} \prod_{\{i,j\} \in E} \exp\left(-\frac{1}{2}\alpha\left(s_i - s_j\right)^2\right)}. \tag{10.2}$$

The expressions for the posterior probability $P(\boldsymbol{s}|\boldsymbol{d}, \alpha, \beta)$, joint probability $\rho(\boldsymbol{s}, \boldsymbol{d}|\alpha, \beta)$, and marginal likelihood $\rho(\boldsymbol{d}|\alpha, \beta)$ are given by Bayes formulas as follows:

$$P(\boldsymbol{s}|\boldsymbol{d}, \alpha, \beta) = \frac{\rho(\boldsymbol{s}, \boldsymbol{d}|\alpha, \beta)}{\rho(\boldsymbol{d}|\alpha, \beta)} = \frac{\rho(\boldsymbol{d}|\boldsymbol{s}, \beta)P(\boldsymbol{s}|\alpha)}{\rho(\boldsymbol{d}|\alpha, \beta)}, \tag{10.3}$$

$$\rho(\boldsymbol{s}, \boldsymbol{d}|\alpha, \beta) = \rho(\boldsymbol{d}|\boldsymbol{s}, \beta)P(\boldsymbol{s}|\alpha), \tag{10.4}$$

$$\begin{aligned} \rho(\boldsymbol{d}|\alpha, \beta) &= \sum_{s_1\in\Omega}\sum_{s_2\in\Omega}\cdots\sum_{s_{|V|}\in\Omega} \rho(\boldsymbol{s}, \boldsymbol{d}|\alpha, \beta) \\ &= \sum_{s_1\in\Omega}\sum_{s_2\in\Omega}\cdots\sum_{s_{|V|}\in\Omega} \rho(\boldsymbol{d}|\boldsymbol{s}, \beta)P(\boldsymbol{s}|\alpha). \end{aligned} \tag{10.5}$$

Estimates of the hyperparameters and the parameter vector $\widehat{\alpha}, \widehat{\beta}, \widehat{\boldsymbol{s}} = \left(\widehat{s_1}, \widehat{s_2}, \cdots, \widehat{s_{|V|}}\right)$ are determined by

$$\left(\widehat{\alpha}(\boldsymbol{d}), \widehat{\beta}(\boldsymbol{d})\right) = \underset{(\alpha,\beta)}{\text{argmax}}\,\rho\left(\boldsymbol{d}\middle|\alpha, \beta\right), \tag{10.6}$$

$$\widehat{s_i}(\boldsymbol{d}) = \underset{s_i\in\Omega}{\text{argmax}}\, P_i\left(s_i\middle|\boldsymbol{d}, \widehat{\alpha}(\boldsymbol{d}), \widehat{\beta}(\boldsymbol{d})\right)\ (i\in V). \tag{10.7}$$

Equations (10.6) and (10.7) are referred to as the **maximization of marginal likelihood (MML)** [25, 26] and the **maximization of posterior marginal (MPM)** [27], respectively.

10.2.2 Expectation-Maximization Algorithm

The expectation-maximization (EM) algorithm is often used to maximize the marginal likelihood in Eq. (10.6) [25, 26]. The $\mathcal{Q}$-function for the EM algorithm in the present framework is defined by

$$\mathcal{Q}\left(\alpha, \beta\middle|\alpha', \beta', \boldsymbol{d}\right) \equiv \sum_{s_1\in\Omega}\sum_{s_2\in\Omega}\cdots\sum_{s_{|V|}\in\Omega} P\left(\boldsymbol{s}\middle|\boldsymbol{d}, \alpha', \beta'\right)\ln\left(\rho\left(\boldsymbol{s}, \boldsymbol{d}\middle|\alpha, \beta\right)\right). \tag{10.8}$$

The EM algorithm is a procedure that performs the following procedures of **E-** and **M-step** repeatedly for $t = 0, 1, 2, \cdots$ until $\widehat{\alpha}(\boldsymbol{d})$ and $\widehat{\beta}(\boldsymbol{d})$ converge:

E-step: Compute $\mathcal{Q}\left(\alpha, \beta\middle|\alpha(\boldsymbol{d}, t), \beta(\boldsymbol{d}, t), \boldsymbol{d}\right)$ for various values of α and β.

M-step: Determine $\left(\alpha(\boldsymbol{d}, t+1), \beta(\boldsymbol{d}, t+1)\right)$ so as to satisfy the extremum conditions of $\mathcal{Q}\left(\alpha, \beta\middle|\alpha(\boldsymbol{d}, t), \beta(\boldsymbol{d}, t), \boldsymbol{d}\right)$ with respect to α and β. Update $\widehat{\alpha}(\boldsymbol{d})\leftarrow\alpha(\boldsymbol{d}, t+1)$ and $\widehat{\beta}(\boldsymbol{d})\leftarrow\beta(\boldsymbol{d}, t+1)$.

The update rule from $(\alpha(\boldsymbol{d}, t), \beta(\boldsymbol{d}, t))$ to $(\alpha(\boldsymbol{d}, t+1), \beta(\boldsymbol{d}, t+1))$ for the extremum conditions can be written as

$$\frac{1}{|E|}\sum_{\{i,j\}\in E}\sum_{s_1\in\Omega}\sum_{s_2\in\Omega}\cdots\sum_{s_{|V|}\in\Omega}\left(s_i-s_j\right)^2 P\left(s_1,s_2,\cdots,s_{|V|}\middle|\alpha(\boldsymbol{d},t+1)\right)$$
$$=\frac{1}{|E|}\sum_{\{i,j\}\in E}\sum_{s_1\in\Omega}\sum_{s_2\in\Omega}\cdots\sum_{s_{|V|}\in\Omega}\left(s_i-s_j\right)^2 P\left(s_1,s_2,\cdots,s_{|V|}\middle|\boldsymbol{d},\alpha(\boldsymbol{d},t),\beta(\boldsymbol{d},t)\right), \tag{10.9}$$

$$\frac{1}{\beta(\boldsymbol{d},t+1)}=\frac{1}{|V|}\sum_{i\in V}\sum_{s_1\in\Omega}\sum_{s_2\in\Omega}\cdots\sum_{s_{|V|}\in\Omega}(s_i-d_i)^2 P\left(s_1,s_2,\cdots,s_{|V|}\middle|\boldsymbol{d},\alpha(\boldsymbol{d},t),\beta(\boldsymbol{d},t)\right). \tag{10.10}$$

The marginal probability distributions of $P\left(\boldsymbol{s}\middle|\boldsymbol{d},\alpha,\beta\right)$ and $P\left(\boldsymbol{s}\middle|\alpha\right)$ are introduced as

$$P_i\left(s_i\middle|\boldsymbol{d},\alpha,\beta\right)\equiv\sum_{\tau_1\in\Omega}\sum_{\tau_2\in\Omega}\cdots\sum_{\tau_{|V|}\in\Omega}\delta_{s_i,\tau_i}P\left(\tau_1,\tau_2,\cdots,\tau_{|V|}\middle|\boldsymbol{d},\alpha,\beta\right)\ (i\in V), \tag{10.11}$$

$$P_{ij}\left(s_i,s_j\middle|\boldsymbol{d},\alpha,\beta\right)=P_{ji}\left(s_j,s_i\middle|\boldsymbol{d},\alpha,\beta\right)$$
$$\equiv\sum_{\tau_1\in\Omega}\sum_{\tau_2\in\Omega}\cdots\sum_{\tau_{|V|}\in\Omega}\delta_{s_i,\tau_i}\delta_{s_j,\tau_j}P\left(\tau_1,\tau_2,\cdots,\tau_{|V|}\middle|\boldsymbol{d},\alpha,\beta\right)\ (\{i,j\}\in E), \tag{10.12}$$

$$P_{ij}\left(s_i,s_j\middle|\alpha\right)=P_{ji}\left(s_j,s_i\middle|\alpha\right)$$
$$\equiv\sum_{\tau_1\in\Omega}\sum_{\tau_2\in\Omega}\cdots\sum_{\tau_{|V|}\in\Omega}\delta_{s_i,\tau_i}\delta_{s_j,\tau_j}P\left(\tau_1,\tau_2,\cdots,\tau_{|V|}\middle|\alpha\right)\ (\{i,j\}\in E). \tag{10.13}$$

In this way, the extremum conditions can be reduced to

$$\frac{1}{|E|}\sum_{\{i,j\}\in E}\sum_{s_i\in\Omega}\sum_{s_j\in\Omega}\left(s_i-s_j\right)^2 P_{ij}\left(s_i,s_j\middle|\alpha(\boldsymbol{d},t+1)\right)$$
$$=\frac{1}{|E|}\sum_{\{i,j\}\in E}\sum_{s_i\in\Omega}\sum_{s_j\in\Omega}\left(s_i-s_j\right)^2 P_{ij}\left(s_i,s_j\middle|\boldsymbol{d},\alpha(\boldsymbol{d},t),\beta(\boldsymbol{d},t)\right), \tag{10.14}$$

$$\frac{1}{\beta(\boldsymbol{d},t+1)}=\frac{1}{|V|}\sum_{i\in V}\sum_{s_i\in\Omega}(s_i-d_i)^2 P_i\left(s_i\middle|\boldsymbol{d},\alpha(\boldsymbol{d},t),\beta(\boldsymbol{d},t)\right). \tag{10.15}$$

To realize the EM procedure as a practical algorithm, **Markov chain Monte Carlo (MCMC) Methods** are often used, which are powerful probabilistic methods [28, 29]. In some recent developments, advanced mean-field methods from statistical mechanical informatics are also used as powerful deterministic algorithms, as shown in Sect. 10.3. Consider the expectation values for both sides of Eqs. (10.9) and (10.10) with respect to the state vector $\boldsymbol{d}$ of a data point according to the following probability density function where the hyperparameters α and β are set to their true values α^* and β^*, respectively:

$$\rho(\boldsymbol{d}|\alpha^*, \beta^*) = \sum_{\boldsymbol{\tau}\in\Omega^{|V|}} \rho\big(\boldsymbol{d}|\boldsymbol{\tau}, \alpha^*, \beta^*\big) P\big(\boldsymbol{\tau}|\alpha^*\big), \tag{10.16}$$

such that

$$\begin{aligned}\rho(d_1, d_2, \cdots, d_{|V|}|\alpha^*, \beta^*) = &\sum_{\tau_1\in\Omega}\sum_{\tau_2\in\Omega}\cdots\sum_{\tau_{|V|}\in\Omega} \rho(d_1, d_2, \cdots, d_{|V|}|\tau_1, \tau_2, \cdots, \tau_{|V|}, \beta^*) \\ &\times P(\tau_1, \tau_2, \cdots, \tau_{|V|}|\alpha^*) \\ &(d_1\in(-\infty, +\infty), d_2\in(-\infty, +\infty), \cdots, d_{|V|}\in(-\infty, +\infty)).\end{aligned} \tag{10.17}$$

We can then derive simultaneous equations for the statistical trajectory $\{\overline{\alpha}(\alpha^*, \beta^*, t), \overline{\beta}(\alpha^*, \beta^*, t)|t = 1, 2, 3, \cdots\}$) in the convergence process $\{(\alpha(\boldsymbol{d}, t), \beta(\boldsymbol{d}, t))|t = 1, 2, 3, \cdots\}$ of the above EM algorithm.

Equations (10.9) and (10.10) can be rewritten as follows:

$$\frac{1}{|E|}\frac{\partial}{\partial\alpha(\boldsymbol{d}, t+1)}(\ln(Z(\alpha(\boldsymbol{d}, t+1)))) = \frac{1}{|E|}\frac{\partial}{\partial\alpha(\boldsymbol{d}, t)}(\ln(Z(\boldsymbol{d}, \alpha(\boldsymbol{d}, t), \beta(\boldsymbol{d}, t)))), \tag{10.18}$$

$$\frac{1}{\beta(\boldsymbol{d}, t+1)} = \frac{1}{|V|}\frac{\partial}{\partial\beta(\boldsymbol{d}, t)}(\ln(Z(\boldsymbol{d}, \alpha(\boldsymbol{d}, t), \beta(\boldsymbol{d}, t)))), \tag{10.19}$$

where

$$Z(\alpha) \equiv \sum_{s_1\in\Omega}\sum_{s_2\in\Omega}\cdots\sum_{s_{|V|}\in\Omega}\prod_{\{i,j\}\in E}\exp\Big(-\frac{1}{2}\alpha\big(s_i - s_j\big)^2\Big), \tag{10.20}$$

$$Z(\boldsymbol{d}, \alpha, \beta) \equiv \sum_{s_1\in\Omega}\sum_{s_2\in\Omega}\cdots\sum_{s_{|V|}\in\Omega} w\big(s_1, s_2, \cdots, s_{|V|}\big|\boldsymbol{d}, \alpha, \beta\big), \tag{10.21}$$

$$\begin{aligned} w\big(\boldsymbol{s}\big|\boldsymbol{d}, \alpha, \beta\big) &= w\big(s_1, s_2, \cdots, s_{|V|}\big|d_1, d_2, \cdots, d_{|V|}, \alpha, \beta\big) \\ &\equiv \Bigg(\prod_{i\in V}\exp\Big(-\frac{1}{2}\beta(s_i - d_i)^2\Big)\Bigg)\Bigg(\prod_{\{i,j\}\in E}\exp\Big(-\frac{1}{2}\alpha\big(s_i - s_j\big)^2\Big)\Bigg). \end{aligned} \tag{10.22}$$

By taking the expectation values of both sides of Eqs. (10.18) and (10.19) with respect to the state vector of the data point $\boldsymbol{d}$ in the probability density function $\rho(\boldsymbol{d}|\alpha^*, \beta^*)$, the simultaneous deterministic equation for the statistical trajectory

$\{\overline{\alpha}(\alpha^*, \beta^*, t), \overline{\beta}(\alpha^*, \beta^*, t)|t = 1, 2, 3, \cdots\}$ of the EM procedure can be derived as follows:

$$\frac{1}{|E|}\frac{\partial}{\partial\overline{\alpha}(\alpha^*, \beta^*, t+1)}\left(\ln\left(Z\left(\overline{\alpha}(\alpha^*, \beta^*, t+1)\right)\right)\right)$$
$$= \frac{1}{|E|}\frac{\partial}{\partial\overline{\alpha}(\alpha^*, \beta^*, t)}\left(\int_{-\infty}^{+\infty}\int_{-\infty}^{+\infty}\cdots\int_{-\infty}^{+\infty}\rho\left(\boldsymbol{d}\middle|\alpha^*, \beta^*\right)\left(\ln\left(Z\left(\boldsymbol{d}, \overline{\alpha}(\alpha^*, \beta^*, t), \overline{\beta}(\alpha^*, \beta^*, t)\right)\right)\right)dd_1dd_2\cdots dd_{|V|}\right), \tag{10.23}$$

$$\frac{1}{\overline{\beta}(\alpha^*, \beta^*, t+1)} = \frac{1}{|V|}\frac{\partial}{\partial\overline{\beta}(\alpha^*, \beta^*, t)}$$
$$\left(\int_{-\infty}^{+\infty}\int_{-\infty}^{+\infty}\cdots\int_{-\infty}^{+\infty}\rho\left(\boldsymbol{d}|\alpha^*, \beta^*\right)\left(\ln\left(Z\left(\boldsymbol{d}, \overline{\alpha}(\alpha^*, \beta^* t), \overline{\beta}(\alpha^*, \beta^*, t)\right)\right)\right)dd_1dd_2\cdots dd_{|V|}\right). \tag{10.24}$$

In the case of a continuous state space $\Omega = (-\infty, +\infty)$, the posterior and prior probabilistic models correspond to Gaussian graphical models, and the statistical trajectory in Eqs. (10.23) and (10.24) can be exactly computed by means of the multi-dimensional Gaussian integral formula [30].

For a discrete state space Ω, it is generally hard to treat Eqs. (10.23) and (10.24) analytically. To estimate Eqs. (10.23) and (10.24), the following quantity is often introduced in statistical mechanical informatics [13, 17]:

$$\int_{-\infty}^{+\infty}\int_{-\infty}^{+\infty}\cdots\int_{-\infty}^{+\infty}\rho\left(\boldsymbol{d}\middle|\alpha^*, \beta^*\right)(\ln(Z(\boldsymbol{d}, \alpha, \beta)))dd_1dd_2\cdots dd_{|V|}. \tag{10.25}$$

The quantity in Eq. (10.25) can be rewritten as follows:

$$\int_{-\infty}^{+\infty}\int_{-\infty}^{+\infty}\cdots\int_{-\infty}^{+\infty}\rho\left(\boldsymbol{d}|\alpha^*, \beta^*\right)\left(\lim_{n\to+0}\frac{1}{n}\left(Z(\boldsymbol{d}, \alpha, \beta)^n - 1\right)\right)dd_1dd_2\cdots dd_{|V|}$$
$$= \lim_{n\to+0}\frac{1}{n}\int_{-\infty}^{+\infty}\int_{-\infty}^{+\infty}\cdots\int_{-\infty}^{+\infty}\rho\left(\boldsymbol{d}|\alpha^*, \beta^*\right)\left(\left(Z(\boldsymbol{d}, \alpha, \beta)^n - 1\right)\right)dd_1dd_2\cdots dd_{|V|}$$
$$= \lim_{n\to+0}\frac{1}{n}\int_{-\infty}^{+\infty}\int_{-\infty}^{+\infty}\cdots\int_{-\infty}^{+\infty}\rho\left(\boldsymbol{d}|\alpha^*, \beta^*\right)\left(\sum_{s_1\in\Omega}\sum_{s_2\in\Omega}\cdots\sum_{s_{|V|}\in\Omega}w\left(\boldsymbol{s}|\boldsymbol{d}, \alpha, \beta\right)\right)^n dd_1dd_2\cdots dd_{|V|} - 1$$
$$= \lim_{n\to+0}\frac{1}{n}\left(\int_{-\infty}^{+\infty}\int_{-\infty}^{+\infty}\cdots\int_{-\infty}^{+\infty}\rho\left(\boldsymbol{d}|\alpha^*, \beta^*\right)\right.$$
$$\left.\times\prod_{j=1}^{n}\left(\sum_{s_{1,j}\in\Omega}\sum_{s_{2,j}\in\Omega}\cdots\sum_{s_{|V|,j}\in\Omega}w\left(s_{1,j}, s_{2,j}, \cdots s_{|V|,j}|\boldsymbol{d}, \alpha, \beta\right)\right)dd_1dd_2\cdots dd_{|V|}\right) - 1$$
$$= \frac{1}{Z(\alpha^*)}\left(\sqrt{\frac{\beta^*}{2\pi}}\right)^{|V|}$$
$$\times\left\{\lim_{n\to+0}\frac{1}{n}\left(\int_{-\infty}^{+\infty}\int_{-\infty}^{+\infty}\cdots\int_{-\infty}^{+\infty}\left(\sum_{\tau_1\in\Omega}\sum_{\tau_2\in\Omega}\cdots\sum_{\tau_{|V|}\in\Omega}w\left(\tau_1, \tau_2, \cdots\tau_{|V|}|\boldsymbol{d}, \alpha^*, \beta^*\right)\right)\right.\right.$$
$$\left.\left.\times\prod_{j=1}^{n}\left(\sum_{s_{1,j}\in\Omega}\sum_{s_{2,j}\in\Omega}\cdots\sum_{s_{|V|,j}\in\Omega}w\left(s_{1,j}, s_{2,j}, \cdots s_{|V|,j}|\boldsymbol{d}, \alpha, \beta\right)\right)\right)dd_1dd_2\cdots dd_{|V|}\right\} - 1. \tag{10.26}$$

Equation (10.26) means that computation of the statistical quantity in Eq. (10.25) can be reduced, up to some normalization constant, to computation of the statistical quantity in the probabilistic model given by the weight factor

$$w\big(\tau_1, \tau_2, \cdots \tau_{|V|}\big|\boldsymbol{d}, \alpha^*, \beta^*\big)\prod_{j=1}^{n} w\big(s_{1,j}, s_{2,j}, \cdots s_{|V|,j}\big|\boldsymbol{d}, \alpha, \beta\big). \tag{10.27}$$

We remark that the weight factor (10.27) is expressed by considering some replicas of the posterior probabilistic model $P(\boldsymbol{s}|\boldsymbol{d}, \alpha, \beta)$ and the analysis starting from the weight factor (10.27) is referred to as a **replica method** [13, 17]. One possible case for analytical treatment is the EM algorithm with the prior and posterior probabilistic models in Eqs. (10.2) and (10.3) for the compete graph (V, E). The dynamics of the EM algorithm with the MCMC method can be analyzed by using the replica method and the **master equations** for **Glauber dynamics** [31].[1]

10.2.3 Expectation-Maximization Algorithm for Probabilistic Image Segmentations

This section extends the previous section to the statistical machine learning framework for probabilistic image segmentation. In probabilistic image segmentations, we consider a square grid graph (V, E) in which a light intensity vector $\boldsymbol{d}_i = (d_{i\mathrm{R}}, d_{i\mathrm{G}}, d_{i\mathrm{B}})$ for the three components red $d_{i\mathrm{R}}$, green $d_{i\mathrm{G}}$ and blue $d_{i\mathrm{B}}$ is assigned to each node i. The state vector $\boldsymbol{s}$ for the labeled configuration and the data matrix $\boldsymbol{D}$ for the color image configuration are expressed as

$$\boldsymbol{s} = \begin{pmatrix} s_1 \\ s_2 \\ s_3 \\ \vdots \\ s_{|V|} \end{pmatrix}, \quad \boldsymbol{D} = \begin{pmatrix} \boldsymbol{d}_1 \\ \boldsymbol{d}_2 \\ \boldsymbol{d}_3 \\ \vdots \\ \boldsymbol{d}_{|V|} \end{pmatrix} = \begin{pmatrix} d_{1\mathrm{R}} & d_{1\mathrm{G}} & d_{1\mathrm{B}} \\ d_{2\mathrm{R}} & d_{2\mathrm{G}} & d_{2\mathrm{B}} \\ d_{3\mathrm{R}} & d_{3\mathrm{G}} & d_{3\mathrm{B}} \\ \vdots & \vdots & \vdots \\ d_{|V|\mathrm{R}} & d_{|V|\mathrm{G}} & d_{|V|\mathrm{B}} \end{pmatrix}. \tag{10.28}$$

Here $\rho(\boldsymbol{D}|\boldsymbol{s}, \boldsymbol{a}(+1), \boldsymbol{a}(-1), \boldsymbol{C}(+1), \boldsymbol{C}(-1))$ and $P(\boldsymbol{s}|\alpha)$ are assumed to be as follows:

$$\rho(\boldsymbol{D}|\boldsymbol{s}, \boldsymbol{a}(+1), \boldsymbol{a}(-1), \boldsymbol{C}(+1), \boldsymbol{C}(-1)) = \prod_{i\in V} g\big(\boldsymbol{d}_i\big|s_i, \boldsymbol{a}(s_i), \boldsymbol{C}(s_i)\big), \tag{10.29}$$

[1] **Glauber dynamics** was proposed in Ref. [32].

$$P(\boldsymbol{s}|\alpha) = \frac{\prod_{\{i,j\}\in E} \exp(-2\alpha(1-\delta_{s_i,s_j}))}{\sum_{s_1\in\Omega}\sum_{s_2\in\Omega}\cdots\sum_{s_{|V|}\in\Omega}\prod_{\{i,j\}\in E}\exp(-2\alpha(1-\delta_{s_i,s_j}))}, \tag{10.30}$$

where

$$g\big(\boldsymbol{d_i}|s_i, \boldsymbol{a}(s_i), \boldsymbol{C}(s_i)\big) \equiv \sqrt{\frac{1}{\det(2\pi \boldsymbol{C}(s_i))}}\exp\Big(-\frac{1}{2}(\boldsymbol{d_i}-\boldsymbol{a}(s_i))\boldsymbol{C}^{-1}(s_i)(\boldsymbol{d_i}-\boldsymbol{a}(s_i))^{\mathrm{T}}\Big), \tag{10.31}$$

$$\boldsymbol{a}(+1) = \begin{pmatrix} a_{\mathrm{R}}(+1) \\ a_{\mathrm{G}}(+1) \\ a_{\mathrm{B}}(+1) \end{pmatrix},\ \boldsymbol{a}(-1) = \begin{pmatrix} a_{\mathrm{R}}(-1) \\ a_{\mathrm{G}}(-1) \\ a_{\mathrm{B}}(-1) \end{pmatrix}, \tag{10.32}$$

$$\boldsymbol{C}(+1) = \begin{pmatrix} C_{\mathrm{RR}}(+1) & C_{\mathrm{RG}}(+1) & C_{\mathrm{RB}}(+1) \\ C_{\mathrm{GR}}(+1) & C_{\mathrm{GG}}(+1) & C_{\mathrm{GB}}(+1) \\ C_{\mathrm{BR}}(+1) & C_{\mathrm{BG}}(+1) & C_{\mathrm{BB}}(+1) \end{pmatrix},\ \boldsymbol{C}(-1) = \begin{pmatrix} C_{\mathrm{RR}}(-1) & C_{\mathrm{RG}}(-1) & C_{\mathrm{RB}}(-1) \\ C_{\mathrm{GR}}(-1) & C_{\mathrm{GG}}(-1) & C_{\mathrm{GB}}(-1) \\ C_{\mathrm{BR}}(-1) & C_{\mathrm{BG}}(-1) & C_{\mathrm{BB}}(-1) \end{pmatrix}. \tag{10.33}$$

Note that the probabilistic graphical model in Eq. (10.30) is referred to as a **Potts mode** [33].

In probabilistic segmentation and clustering, $\rho(\boldsymbol{D}|\boldsymbol{s}, \boldsymbol{a}(+1), \boldsymbol{a}(-1), \boldsymbol{C}(+1), \boldsymbol{C}(-1))$ in Eq. (10.29) and $P(\boldsymbol{s}|\alpha)$ in Eq. (10.30) correspond to the data generative and prior models, respectively. The joint probability of $\boldsymbol{s}$ and $\boldsymbol{D}$ is expressed in terms of the data generative and prior distributions, $\rho(\boldsymbol{D}|\boldsymbol{s}, \boldsymbol{a}(+1), \boldsymbol{a}(-1), \boldsymbol{C}(+1), \boldsymbol{C}(-1))$ and $P(\boldsymbol{s}|\alpha)$, as follows:

$$\rho(\boldsymbol{s}, \boldsymbol{D}|\alpha, \boldsymbol{a}(+1), \boldsymbol{a}(-1), \boldsymbol{C}(+1), \boldsymbol{C}(-1)) \equiv \rho(\boldsymbol{D}|\boldsymbol{s}, \boldsymbol{a}(+1), \boldsymbol{a}(-1), \boldsymbol{C}(+1), \boldsymbol{C}(-1))P(\boldsymbol{s}|\alpha). \tag{10.34}$$

By using the joint probability distribution, the posterior probability $P(\boldsymbol{s}|\boldsymbol{D}, \alpha, \boldsymbol{a}(+1), \boldsymbol{a}(-1), \boldsymbol{C}(+1), \boldsymbol{C}(-1))$ and the marginal likelihood $\rho(\boldsymbol{D}|\alpha, \boldsymbol{a}(+1), \boldsymbol{a}(-1), \boldsymbol{C}(+1), \boldsymbol{C}(-1))$ are defined by using Bayes formulas as follows:

$$P(\boldsymbol{s}|\boldsymbol{D}, \alpha, \boldsymbol{a}(+1), \boldsymbol{a}(-1), \boldsymbol{C}(+1), \boldsymbol{C}(-1)) \equiv \frac{\rho(\boldsymbol{s}, \boldsymbol{D}|\alpha, \boldsymbol{a}(+1), \boldsymbol{a}(-1), \boldsymbol{C}(+1), \boldsymbol{C}(-1))}{\rho(\boldsymbol{D}|\alpha, \boldsymbol{a}(+1), \boldsymbol{a}(-1), \boldsymbol{C}(+1), \boldsymbol{C}(-1))}, \tag{10.35}$$

$$\begin{aligned}&\rho(\boldsymbol{D}|\alpha, \boldsymbol{a}(+1), \boldsymbol{a}(-1), \boldsymbol{C}(+1), \boldsymbol{C}(-1)) \\ &\quad\equiv \sum_{s_1\in\Omega}\sum_{s_2\in\Omega}\cdots\sum_{s_{|V|}\in\Omega} \rho(\boldsymbol{s}, \boldsymbol{D}|\alpha, \boldsymbol{a}(+1), \boldsymbol{a}(-1), \boldsymbol{C}(+1), \boldsymbol{C}(-1)).\end{aligned} \tag{10.36}$$

Estimates of the hyperparameters and parameter vector, namely, $\widehat{\alpha}(\boldsymbol{D})$, $\widehat{\boldsymbol{a}}(+1|\boldsymbol{D})$, $\widehat{\boldsymbol{a}}(-1|\boldsymbol{D})$, $\widehat{\boldsymbol{C}}(+1|\boldsymbol{D})$, $\widehat{\boldsymbol{C}}(-1|\boldsymbol{D})$, $\widehat{\boldsymbol{s}}(\boldsymbol{D}) = \big(\widehat{s_1}(\boldsymbol{D}), \widehat{s_2}(\boldsymbol{D}), \cdots, \widehat{s_{|V|}}(\boldsymbol{D})\big)$ are determined by

$$\begin{aligned}&\Big(\widehat{\alpha}(\boldsymbol{D}), \widehat{\boldsymbol{a}}(+1|\boldsymbol{D}), \widehat{\boldsymbol{a}}(-1|\boldsymbol{D}), \widehat{\boldsymbol{C}}(+1|\boldsymbol{D}), \widehat{\boldsymbol{C}}(-1|\boldsymbol{D})\Big)\\&\qquad = \arg \max_{(\alpha, \boldsymbol{a}(+1), \boldsymbol{a}(-1), \boldsymbol{C}(+1), \boldsymbol{C}(-1))} \rho\big(\boldsymbol{D}\big|\alpha, \boldsymbol{a}(+1), \boldsymbol{a}(-1), \boldsymbol{C}(+1), \boldsymbol{C}(-1)\big),\end{aligned} \tag{10.37}$$

$$\widehat{s_i}(\boldsymbol{D}) = \underset{s_i \in \Omega}{\operatorname{argmax}}\, P_i\Big(s_i\Big|\boldsymbol{D}, \widehat{\alpha}(\boldsymbol{D}), \widehat{\boldsymbol{a}}(+1|\boldsymbol{D}), \widehat{\boldsymbol{a}}(-1|\boldsymbol{D}), \widehat{\boldsymbol{C}}(+1|\boldsymbol{D}), \widehat{\boldsymbol{C}}(-1|\boldsymbol{D})\Big)\ (i \in V). \tag{10.38}$$

The $\mathcal{Q}$-function for the EM algorithm in the present framework is defined by

$$\begin{aligned}&\mathcal{Q}\big(\alpha, \boldsymbol{s}(+1), \boldsymbol{a}(-1), \boldsymbol{C}(+1), \boldsymbol{C}(-1)|\boldsymbol{s}'(+1), \boldsymbol{s}'(-1), \boldsymbol{C}'(+1), \boldsymbol{C}'(-1), \boldsymbol{D}\big)\\&\quad \equiv \sum_{s_1 \in \Omega}\sum_{s_2 \in \Omega}\cdots\sum_{s_{|V|} \in \Omega} P\big(\boldsymbol{s}|\boldsymbol{D}, \alpha, \boldsymbol{a}'(+1), \boldsymbol{a}'(-1), \boldsymbol{C}'(+1), \boldsymbol{C}'(-1)\big)\\&\qquad\qquad \times \ln(\rho(\boldsymbol{s}, \boldsymbol{D}|\alpha, \boldsymbol{a}(+1), \boldsymbol{a}(-1), \boldsymbol{C}(+1), \boldsymbol{C}(-1))).\end{aligned} \tag{10.39}$$

The EM algorithm is a procedure that performs the following **E-step** and **M-step** repeatedly for $t = 0, 1, 2, \cdots$ until $\widehat{\alpha}(\boldsymbol{D})$, $\widehat{\boldsymbol{a}}(+1, \boldsymbol{D})$, $\widehat{\boldsymbol{a}}(-1, \boldsymbol{D})$, $\widehat{\boldsymbol{C}}(+1, \boldsymbol{D})$, $\widehat{\boldsymbol{C}}(-1, \boldsymbol{D})$ converge:

E-step: Compute $\mathcal{Q}\big(\alpha, \boldsymbol{a}(+1), \boldsymbol{a}(-1), \boldsymbol{C}(+1), \boldsymbol{C}(-1)\big|\alpha(t), \boldsymbol{a}(+1, t), \boldsymbol{a}(-1, t), \boldsymbol{C}(+1, t), \boldsymbol{C}(-1, t)\big)$ for various values of $\boldsymbol{a}(+1)$, $\boldsymbol{a}(-1)$, $\boldsymbol{C}(+1)$, and $\boldsymbol{C}(-1)$.

M-step: Determine $\alpha(t+1)$, $\boldsymbol{a}(+1, t+1)$, $\boldsymbol{a}(-1, t+1)$, $\boldsymbol{C}(+1, t+1)$, and $\boldsymbol{C}(-1, t+1)$ that satisfy the extremum conditions of $\mathcal{Q}$-function with respect to $\boldsymbol{a}(+1)$, $\boldsymbol{a}(-1)$, $\boldsymbol{C}(+1)$ and $\boldsymbol{C}(-1)$ as follows:

$$\begin{aligned}&(\alpha(t+1), \boldsymbol{a}(+1, t+1), \boldsymbol{a}(-1, t+1), \boldsymbol{C}(+1, t+1), \boldsymbol{C}(-1, t+1))\\&\leftarrow \underset{\alpha, \boldsymbol{a}(+1), \boldsymbol{a}(-1), \boldsymbol{C}(+1), \boldsymbol{C}(-1)}{\text{extremum}}\\&\mathcal{Q}\big(\alpha, \boldsymbol{a}(+1), \boldsymbol{a}(-1), \boldsymbol{C}(+1), \boldsymbol{C}(-1)\big|\alpha(t), \boldsymbol{a}(+1, t), \boldsymbol{a}(-1, t), \boldsymbol{C}(+1, t), \boldsymbol{C}(-1, t), \boldsymbol{D}\big).\end{aligned} \tag{10.40}$$

Update $\widehat{\alpha}(\boldsymbol{D}) \leftarrow \alpha(t+1)$, $\widehat{\boldsymbol{a}}(+1, \boldsymbol{D}) \leftarrow \boldsymbol{a}(+1, t+1)$, $\widehat{\boldsymbol{a}}(-1, \boldsymbol{D}) \leftarrow \boldsymbol{a}(-1, t+1)$, $\widehat{\boldsymbol{C}}(+1, \boldsymbol{D}) \leftarrow \boldsymbol{C}(+1, t+1)$ and $\widehat{\boldsymbol{C}}(-1, \boldsymbol{D}) \leftarrow \boldsymbol{C}(-1, t+1)$.

By using the equalities in Eqs. (10.29), (10.30), (10.34), and (10.35), the EM algorithm by the $\mathcal{Q}$-function can be reduced to the following simultaneous update rules:

$$\begin{aligned}&\frac{1}{|E|}\sum_{\{i,j\} \in E}\sum_{s_i \in \Omega}\sum_{s_j \in \Omega}\Big(1 - \delta_{s_i, s_j}\Big)P_{ij}\big(s_i, s_j\big|\alpha(t+1)\big)\\&= \frac{1}{|E|}\sum_{\{i,j\} \in E}\sum_{s_i \in \Omega}\sum_{s_j \in \Omega}\Big(1 - \delta_{s_i, s_j}\Big)P_{ij}\big(s_i, s_j\big|\boldsymbol{D}, \alpha(t), \boldsymbol{a}(+1, t), \boldsymbol{a}(-1, t), \boldsymbol{C}(+1, t), \boldsymbol{C}(-1, t)\big),\end{aligned} \tag{10.41}$$

$$\boldsymbol{a}(s_i, t+1) = \frac{\sum_{i \in V} \boldsymbol{d}_i P_i\big(s_i \big| \boldsymbol{D}, \alpha(t), \boldsymbol{a}(+1,t), \boldsymbol{a}(-1,t), \boldsymbol{C}(+1,t), \boldsymbol{C}(-1,t)\big)}{\sum_{i \in V} P_i\big(s_i \big| \boldsymbol{D}, \alpha(t), \boldsymbol{a}(+1,t), \boldsymbol{a}(-1,t), \boldsymbol{C}(+1,t), \boldsymbol{C}(-1,t)\big)} \quad (s_i \in \Omega), \tag{10.42}$$

$$\boldsymbol{C}(s_i, t+1) = \frac{\sum_{i \in V} (\boldsymbol{d}_i - \boldsymbol{a}(s_i,t))^{\mathrm{T}} (\boldsymbol{d}_i - \boldsymbol{a}(s_i,t)) P_i\big(s_i \big| \boldsymbol{D}, \alpha(t), \boldsymbol{a}(+1,t), \boldsymbol{a}(-1,t), \boldsymbol{C}(+1,t), \boldsymbol{C}(-1,t)\big)}{\sum_{i \in V} P_i\big(s_i \big| \boldsymbol{D}, \alpha(t), \boldsymbol{a}(+1,t), \boldsymbol{a}(-1,t), \boldsymbol{C}(+1,t), \boldsymbol{C}(-1,t)\big)} \quad (s_i \in \Omega), \tag{10.43}$$

where

$$\begin{aligned} &P_i(s_i | \boldsymbol{D}, \alpha, \boldsymbol{a}(+1), \boldsymbol{a}(-1), \boldsymbol{C}(+1), \boldsymbol{C}(-1)) \\ &\equiv \sum_{\tau_1 \in \Omega} \sum_{\tau_2 \in \Omega} \cdots \sum_{\tau_{|V|} \in \Omega} \delta_{s_i, \tau_i} P\big(\tau_1, \tau_2, \cdots, \tau_{|V|} \big| \boldsymbol{D}, \alpha, \boldsymbol{a}(+1), \boldsymbol{a}(-1), \boldsymbol{C}(+1), \boldsymbol{C}(-1)\big) \; (i \in V), \end{aligned} \tag{10.44}$$

$$\begin{aligned} &P_{ij}(s_i, s_j | \boldsymbol{D}, \alpha, \boldsymbol{a}(+1), \boldsymbol{a}(-1), \boldsymbol{C}(+1), \boldsymbol{C}(-1)) \\ &= P_{ji}(s_j, s_i | \boldsymbol{D}, \alpha, \boldsymbol{a}(+1), \boldsymbol{a}(-1), \boldsymbol{C}(+1), \boldsymbol{C}(-1)) \\ &\equiv \sum_{\tau_1 \in \Omega} \sum_{\tau_2 \in \Omega} \cdots \sum_{\tau_{|V|} \in \Omega} \delta_{s_i, \tau_i} \delta_{s_j, \tau_j} P\big(\tau_1, \tau_2, \cdots, \tau_{|V|} \big| \boldsymbol{D}, \alpha, \boldsymbol{a}(+1), \boldsymbol{a}(-1), \boldsymbol{C}(+1), \boldsymbol{C}(-1)\big) \; (\{i, j\} \in E), \end{aligned} \tag{10.45}$$

$$\begin{aligned} P_{ij}(s_i, s_j | \alpha) &= P_{ji}(s_j, s_i | \alpha) \\ &\equiv \sum_{\tau_1 \in \Omega} \sum_{\tau_2 \in \Omega} \cdots \sum_{\tau_{|V|} \in \Omega} \delta_{s_i, \tau_i} \delta_{s_j, \tau_j} P\big(\tau_1, \tau_2, \cdots, \tau_{|V|} \big| \alpha\big) \; (\{i, j\} \in E). \end{aligned} \tag{10.46}$$

10.3 Statistical Mechanical Informatics

In statistical mechanical informatics [13–17], Ising models are very familiar probabilistic models for which computations are done by statistical mechanical techniques, including advanced mean-field methods, renormalization group methods, Monte Carlo simulations, and replica methods [36, 37]. This section reviews the framework of the Ising model and associated advanced mean-field methods.[2]

[2] A review of both exact results and approximate results as well as perturbative computations for Ising models is given in Refs. [34, 35].

10.3.1 Ising Model

Let us consider an Ising model defined by the following probability distribution for the state space $\Omega = \{+1, -1\}$ for the state variable s_i at each node $i\,(\in V)$:

$$P\left(s\middle|d, \frac{J}{k_B T}, \frac{h}{k_B T}\right) = P\left(s_1, s_2, \cdots, s_{|V|}\middle|d_1, d_2, \cdots, d_{|V|}, \frac{J}{k_B T}, \frac{h}{k_B T}\right)$$
$$\equiv \frac{\exp\left(-\frac{1}{k_B T}\left(\frac{1}{2}J\sum_{\{i,j\}\in E}(s_i - s_j)^2 + \frac{1}{2}h\sum_{i\in V}(s_i - d_i)^2\right)\right)}{\sum_{s_1\in\Omega}\sum_{s_2\in\Omega}\cdots\sum_{s_{|V|}\in\Omega}\exp\left(-\frac{1}{k_B T}\left(\frac{1}{2}J\sum_{\{i,j\}\in E}(s_i - s_j)^2 + \frac{1}{2}h\sum_{i\in V}(s_i - d_i)^2\right)\right)}$$
$$(J > 0,, \ T > 0, \ d_i \in (-\infty, +\infty)\ (\forall i \in V)). \tag{10.47}$$

Because $s_i{}^2 = 1\ (i\in V)$, the probability distribution $P(s)$ can be reduced to

$$P\left(s\middle|d, \frac{J}{k_B T}, \frac{h}{k_B T}\right) = \frac{1}{Z}\exp\left(-\frac{1}{k_B T}H(s)\right)\ (T > 0), \tag{10.48}$$

$$H(s) = H(s_1, s_2, \cdots, s_{|V|})$$
$$\equiv -J\sum_{\{i,j\}\in E} s_i s_j - h\sum_{i\in V} d_i s_i \ (J > 0, \ h \geq 0, \ d_i \in (-\infty, +\infty)\ (\forall i \in V)), \tag{10.49}$$

$$Z \equiv \sum_{s_1\in\Omega}\sum_{s_2\in\Omega}\cdots\sum_{s_{|V|}\in\Omega}\exp\left(-\frac{1}{k_B T}H(s)\right), \tag{10.50}$$

where $H(s)$ and Z are referred to in statistical mechanical informatics as the **energy function** (or **Hamiltonian**) and the **partition function**, respectively, the probability distribution in Eq. (10.47) is called the **Gibbs distribution**, k_B is the **Boltzmann constant**, T is the **(absolute) temperature**, J is the **(ferromagnetic) interaction**, and h is the **external field**.

Let us suppose the **Kullback-Leibler Divergence**

$$\mathrm{KL}[P||R] \equiv \sum_{s_1\in\Omega}\sum_{s_2\in\Omega}\cdots\sum_{s_{|V|}\in\Omega} R(s)\ln\left(\frac{R(s)}{P\left(s\middle|\frac{J}{k_B T}, \frac{h}{k_B T}\right)}\right), \tag{10.51}$$

which is always non-negative for two probability distributions $P\left(s\middle|\frac{J}{k_B T}, \frac{h}{k_B T}\right)$ and $R(s)$ and is regarded as a pseudo-distance between them. By substituting the explicit expression for $P(s)$ in Eqs. (10.48), (10.49) and (10.50) into Eq. (10.51), the expression for the Kullback-Leibler divergence (10.51) in terms of the partition function Z and the free energy functional $\mathcal{F}[R]$ can be derived as follows:

$$\mathrm{KL}[P||R] = \frac{1}{k_{\mathrm{B}}T}\big(k_{\mathrm{B}}T\ln(Z) + \mathcal{F}[R]\big), \tag{10.52}$$

where

$$\mathcal{F}[R] \equiv \sum_{s_1\in\Omega}\sum_{s_2\in\Omega}\cdots\sum_{s_{|V|}\in\Omega} H(\boldsymbol{s})R(\boldsymbol{s}) + k_{\mathrm{B}}T\sum_{s_1\in\Omega}\sum_{s_2\in\Omega}\cdots\sum_{s_{|V|}\in\Omega} R(\boldsymbol{s})\ln\big(R(\boldsymbol{s})\big). \tag{10.53}$$

For the free energy functional $\mathcal{F}[R]$, it is valid that

$$\operatorname*{argmin}_{R}\left\{\mathcal{F}[R]\middle|\sum_{\tau_1\in\Omega}\sum_{\tau_2\in\Omega}\cdots\sum_{\tau_{|V|}\in\Omega} R\big(\tau_1,\tau_2,\cdots,\tau_{|V|}\big) = 1\right\} = P\left(\boldsymbol{s}\middle|\frac{J}{k_{\mathrm{B}}T},\frac{h}{k_{\mathrm{B}}T}\right), \tag{10.54}$$

$$\min_{R}\left\{\mathcal{F}[R]\middle|\sum_{\tau_1\in\Omega}\sum_{\tau_2\in\Omega}\cdots\sum_{\tau_{|V|}\in\Omega} R\big(\tau_1,\tau_2,\cdots,\tau_{|V|}\big) = 1\right\} = -k_{\mathrm{B}}T\ln(Z). \tag{10.55}$$

Note that $-k_{\mathrm{B}}T\ln(Z)$ is referred to as the **free energy** for the Gibbs distribution in Eq. (10.47).

10.3.2 Advanced Mean-Field Method

This section reviews the fundamental framework of advanced mean-field methods [12], including the **mean-field approximation** [35–37] and the **Bethe approximation** [35, 39–41]. Our framework is given for the Ising model in Eqs. (10.48), (10.49), and (10.50). It is known that a generalization of the present framework can be realized by using the **cluster variation method** in Refs. [42–45].

We introduce a trial probability distribution $R(\boldsymbol{s}) = R(s_1, s_2, \cdots, s_{|V|})$ which is restricted to the following functional form:

$$R(\boldsymbol{s}) = R\big(s_1, s_2, \cdots, s_{|V|}\big) = \prod_{i\in V} R_i(s_i), \tag{10.56}$$

$$R_i(s_i) = \sum_{\tau_1\in\Omega}\sum_{\tau_2\in\Omega}\cdots\sum_{\tau_{|V|}\in\Omega} \delta_{s_i,\tau_i} R\big(\tau_1,\tau_2,\cdots,\tau_{|V|}\big)\ (i\in V). \tag{10.57}$$

By using the definition of $R_i(s_i)$ and the normalization condition

$$\sum_{\tau_1\in\Omega}\sum_{\tau_2\in\Omega}\cdots\sum_{\tau_{|V|}\in\Omega} R(\tau_1, \tau_2, \cdots, \tau_{|V|}) = 1, \tag{10.58}$$

we confirm that

$$\sum_{\tau_i\in\Omega} R_i(\tau_i) = R_i(+1) + R_i(-1) = 1 \ (i\in V). \tag{10.59}$$

By substituting the expression $R(\boldsymbol{s})$ in terms of the marginal probability distribution $R_i(s_i)$ $(i\in V)$, such that $\boldsymbol{R}_i = \begin{pmatrix} R_i(+1) & 0 \\ 0 & R_i(-1) \end{pmatrix}$ into Eqs. (10.56)–(10.53), the free energy functional $\mathcal{F}[R]$ can be reduced to the following mean-field free energy functional:

$$\mathcal{F}[R] = \mathcal{F}_{\mathrm{MF}}[\{\boldsymbol{R}_i|i\in V\}], \tag{10.60}$$

where

$$\begin{aligned}\mathcal{F}_{\mathrm{MF}}[\{\boldsymbol{R}_i|i\in V\}] &= \mathcal{F}_{\mathrm{MF}}\left[\left\{\begin{pmatrix} R_i(+1) & 0 \\ 0 & R_i(-1) \end{pmatrix}\middle| i\in V\right\}\right] \\ &\equiv -J\sum_{\{i,j\}\in E}\left(\sum_{\tau_i\in\Omega}\tau_i R_i(\tau_i)\right)\left(\sum_{\tau_j\in\Omega}\tau_j R_j(\tau_j)\right) - h\sum_{i\in V} d_i\left(\sum_{\tau_i\in\Omega}\tau_i R_i(\tau_i)\right) \\ &\quad + k_{\mathrm{B}}T\sum_{i\in V}\sum_{\tau_i\in\Omega} R_i(\tau_i)\ln(R_i(\tau_i)).\end{aligned} \tag{10.61}$$

Let us suppose the following conditional minimization of the free energy functional:

$$\begin{aligned}\widehat{\boldsymbol{R}}_i &= \left\{\begin{pmatrix} \widehat{R}_i(+1) & 0 \\ 0 & \widehat{R}_i(-1) \end{pmatrix}\middle| i\in V, s_i\in\Omega\right\} \\ &= \arg\min_{\{\boldsymbol{R}_i|i\in V\}}\left\{\mathcal{F}_{\mathrm{MF}}[\{\boldsymbol{R}_i|i\in V\}]\middle|\sum_{\tau_i\in\Omega} R_i(\tau_i) = 1, i\in V\right\}.\end{aligned} \tag{10.62}$$

First we introduce the Lagrange multiplier λ_i $(i\in V)$ to ensure the normalization conditions $\sum_{\tau\in\Omega} R_i(\tau) = 1$ $(i\in V)$ as follows:

$$\mathcal{L}_{\mathrm{MF}}[\{\boldsymbol{R}_i|i\in V\}] \equiv \mathcal{F}_{\mathrm{MF}}[\{\boldsymbol{R}_i|i\in V\}] - \sum_{i\in V}\lambda_i\Big(\sum_{\tau_i\in\Omega} R_i(\tau_i) - 1\Big). \tag{10.63}$$

$\widehat{\boldsymbol{R}}_i$ $(i\in V)$ are determined so as to satisfy the following extremum condition:

$$\left[\frac{\partial}{\partial R_i(-1)}\mathcal{L}_{\mathrm{MF}}[\{\boldsymbol{R}_i|i\in V\}]\right]_{\{\boldsymbol{R}_i=\widehat{\boldsymbol{R}}_i|i\in V\}}=0\ (i\in V), \tag{10.64}$$

$$\left[\frac{\partial}{\partial R_i(+1)}\mathcal{L}_{\mathrm{MF}}[\{\boldsymbol{R}_i|i\in V\}]\right]_{\{\boldsymbol{R}_i=\widehat{\boldsymbol{R}}_i|i\in V\}}=0\ (i\in V), \tag{10.65}$$

such that

$$\left[\frac{\partial}{\partial \boldsymbol{R}_i}\mathcal{L}_{\mathrm{MF}}[\{\boldsymbol{R}_i|i\in V\}]\right]_{\{\boldsymbol{R}_i=\widehat{\boldsymbol{R}}_i|i\in V\}}=0\ (i\in V). \tag{10.66}$$

It needs to be shown that $\widehat{\boldsymbol{R}}_i$ $(i\in V)$ are derived as follows:

$$\widehat{R}_i(s_i) = \exp\left(-1+\frac{\lambda_i}{k_{\mathrm{B}}T}\right)\exp\left(\frac{1}{k_{\mathrm{B}}T}\left(hd_i+J\sum_{j\in\partial i}\left(\sum_{\tau_j\in\Omega}\tau_j\widehat{R}_j(\tau_j)\right)\right)s_i\right)\ (i\in V,\ s_i\in\Omega). \tag{10.67}$$

Finally, λ_i needs to be determined such that it satisfies the normalization condition of the marginal probability $\widehat{R}_i(s_i)$. The marginal probabilities $\left\{\widehat{\boldsymbol{R}}_i\middle|i\in V\right\}$ are derived as

$$\widehat{R}_i(s_i)=\frac{\exp\left(\frac{1}{k_{\mathrm{B}}T}\left(hd_i+J\sum_{j\in\partial i}\left(\sum_{\tau_j\in\Omega}\tau_j\widehat{R}_j(\tau_j)\right)\right)s_i\right)}{\sum_{\tau_i\in\Omega}\exp\left(\frac{1}{k_{\mathrm{B}}T}\left(hd_i+J\sum_{j\in\partial i}\left(\sum_{\tau_j\in\Omega}\tau_j\widehat{R}_j(\tau_j)\right)\right)\tau_i\right)}\ (i\in V,\ s_i\in\Omega). \tag{10.68}$$

We introduce the local magnetization

$$m_i\equiv\sum_{\tau_i\in\Omega}\tau_i\widehat{R}_i(\tau_i). \tag{10.69}$$

By solving the simultaneous equations

$$\sum_{\tau_i\in\Omega}\widehat{R}_i(\tau_i)=\widehat{R}_i(+1)+\widehat{R}_i(-1)=1\ (i\in V), \tag{10.70}$$

$$\sum_{\tau_i\in\Omega}\tau_i\widehat{R}_i(\tau_i)=\widehat{R}_i(+1)-\widehat{R}_i(-1)=m_i\ (i\in V), \tag{10.71}$$

with respect to $\widehat{R}_i(+1)$ and $\widehat{R}_i(-1)$, we derive the following expression for the marginal probability:

$$\widehat{R}_i(s_i) = \frac{1}{2}\big(1 + m_i s_i\big) \; (i \in V). \tag{10.72}$$

The extremum conditions in Eq. (10.68) can be reduced to the following simultaneous deterministic equation of $\{m_i | i \in V\}$:

$$m_i = \tanh\left(\frac{1}{k_B T}\left(hd_i + J\sum_{j\in\partial i} m_j\right)\right) \; (i \in V), \tag{10.73}$$

which is referred to as the **mean-field equation**.[3]

By substituting Eq. (10.72) into Eq. (10.61), the mean-field free energy functional can be reduced to

$$\mathcal{F}_{\mathrm{MF}}\big[\big\{\widehat{R}_i(-1), \widehat{R}_i(+1)\big| i \in V\big\}\big] = F_{\mathrm{MF}}\big(m_1, m_2, \cdots, m_{|V|}\big), \tag{10.74}$$

$$\begin{aligned} F_{\mathrm{MF}}\big(m_1, m_2, \cdots, m_{|V|}\big) \equiv & -J\sum_{\{i,j\}\in E} m_i m_j - h\sum_{i\in V} d_i m_i \\ & + k_B T \sum_{i\in V} \frac{1}{2}(1 + m_i)\ln\left(\frac{1}{2}(1 + m_i)\right) \\ & + k_B T \sum_{i\in V} \frac{1}{2}(1 - m_i)\ln\left(\frac{1}{2}(1 - m_i)\right). \end{aligned} \tag{10.75}$$

The extremum conditions

$$\frac{\partial}{\partial m_i} F_{\mathrm{MF}}\big(m_1, m_2, \cdots, m_{|V|}\big) = 0 \; (i \in V) \tag{10.76}$$

can be reduced to the mean-field equations in Eq. (10.73).

We now explore the framework of the Bethe approximation for the Ising model in Eqs. (10.48), (10.49), and (10.50). Our framework is based on the cluster variation method [39, 42–45].

We introduce a trial probability distribution $R(\boldsymbol{s}) = R(s_1, s_2, \cdots, s_{|V|})$ that is restricted to the following functional form:

---

[3]Equation (10.73) is often referred to as the **naive mean-field equation** in statistical machine learning theory [2, 3, 12].

$$R(\boldsymbol{s}) = R(s_1, s_2, \cdots, s_{|V|}) = \left(\prod_{i\in V} R_i(s_i)\right)\left(\prod_{\{i,j\}\in E} \frac{R_{ij}(s_i, s_j)}{R_i(s_i)R_j(s_j)}\right)$$
$$= \left(\prod_{i\in V} R_i(s_i)^{1-|\partial i|}\right)\left(\prod_{\{i,j\}\in E} R_{ij}(s_i, s_j)\right), \quad (10.77)$$

where

$$R_{ij}(s_i, s_j) = R_{ji}(s_j, s_i)$$
$$\equiv \sum_{\tau_1\in\Omega}\sum_{\tau_2\in\Omega}\cdots\sum_{\tau_{|V|}\in\Omega} \delta_{s_i,\tau_i}\delta_{s_j,\tau_j} R(\tau_1, \tau_2, \cdots, \tau_{|V|}) \ (\{i, j\}\in E). \quad (10.78)$$

By using Eqs. (10.57) and (10.78), we can derive the normalization and reducibility conditions in the marginal probabilities as follows:

$$\sum_{\tau_i\in\Omega} R_i(\tau_i) = 1 \ (i\in V), \ \sum_{\tau_i\in\Omega}\sum_{\tau_j\in\Omega} R_{ij}(\tau_i, \tau_j) = 1 \ (\{i, j\}\in E), \quad (10.79)$$

$$R_i(s_i) = \sum_{\tau_j\in\Omega} R_{ij}(s_i, \tau_j), \ R_j(s_j) = \sum_{\tau_i\in\Omega} R_{ij}(\tau_i, s_j) \ (\{i, j\}\in E). \quad (10.80)$$

By substituting the explicit expression for $P(\boldsymbol{s})$ and the expression $\ln(R(\boldsymbol{s}))$ in terms of the marginal probability distributions $\boldsymbol{R}_i = \begin{pmatrix} R_i(+1) & 0 \\ 0 & R_i(-1) \end{pmatrix}$ $(i\in V)$ and $\boldsymbol{R}_{ij} = \begin{pmatrix} R_{ij}(+1,+1) & 0 & 0 & 0 \\ 0 & R_{ij}(+1,-1) & 0 & 0 \\ 0 & 0 & R_{ij}(-1,+1) & 0 \\ 0 & 0 & 0 & R_{ij}(-1,-1) \end{pmatrix}$ $(\{i, j\}\in E)$ in Eq. (10.77) into Eq. (10.51), the Kullback-Leibler divergence can be reduced to the following expression in terms of the partition function Z and the Bethe free energy functional $\mathcal{F}_{\mathrm{Bethe}}[\{\boldsymbol{R}_i|i\in V\}, \{\boldsymbol{R}_{ij}|\{i, j\}\in E\}]$:

$$\mathrm{KL}[P||R] = \frac{1}{k_{\mathrm{B}}T}\left(k_{\mathrm{B}}T\ln Z + \mathcal{F}_{\mathrm{Bethe}}\left[\{\boldsymbol{R}_i|i\in V\}, \{\boldsymbol{R}_{ij}|\{i, j\}\in E\}\right]\right), \quad (10.81)$$

where

$$\begin{aligned}
&\mathcal{F}_{\rm Bethe}\big[\{\boldsymbol{R}_i|i\in V\},\{\boldsymbol{R}_{ij}|\{i,j\}\in E\}\big]\\
&\equiv -J\sum_{\{i,j\}\in E}\left(\sum_{\tau_i\in\Omega}\sum_{\tau_j\in\Omega}\tau_i\tau_j R_{\{i,j\}}(\tau_i,\tau_j)\right)-h\sum_{i\in V}\left(\sum_{\tau_i\in\Omega}\tau_i R_i(\tau_i)\right)\\
&+k_{\rm B}T\sum_{i\in V}(1-|\partial i|)\left(\sum_{\tau_i\in\Omega}R_i(\tau_i)\ln\big(R_i(\tau_i)\big)\right)\\
&+k_{\rm B}T\sum_{\{i,j\}\in E}\left(\sum_{\tau_i\in\Omega}\sum_{\tau_j\in\Omega}R_{ij}(\tau_i,\tau_j)\ln\big(R_{ij}(\tau_i,\tau_j)\big)\right).
\end{aligned}\tag{10.82}$$

Let us suppose the following conditional minimization of the Bethe free energy functional:

$$\begin{aligned}
&\left(\left\{\widehat{\boldsymbol{R}}_i\middle|i\in V\right\},\left\{\widehat{\boldsymbol{R}}_{\{i,j\}}\middle|\{i,j\}\in E\right\}\right)\\
&=\arg\min_{\{\boldsymbol{R}_i|i\in V\},\{\boldsymbol{R}_{\{i,j\}}|\{i,j\}\in E\}}\Bigg\{\mathcal{F}_{\rm Bethe}\big[\{\boldsymbol{R}_i|i\in V\}],\{\boldsymbol{R}_{\{i,j\}}|\{i,j\}\in E\}\big]\\
&\qquad\Bigg|\sum_{\tau_i\in\Omega}R_i(\tau_i)=1\ (i\in V),\ \sum_{\tau_i\in\Omega}\sum_{\tau_j\in\Omega}R_{ij}(\tau_i,\tau_j)=1\ (\{i,j\}\in E),\\
&\qquad R_i(-1)=\sum_{\tau_j\in\Omega}R_{ij}(-1,\tau_j)\ (j\in\partial i,\ i\in V),\\
&\qquad R_i(+1)=\sum_{\tau_j\in\Omega}R_{ij}(+1,\tau_j)\ (j\in\partial i,\ i\in V)\Bigg\}.
\end{aligned}\tag{10.83}$$

We introduce the Lagrange multiplier λ_i $(i\in V)$, $\lambda_{\{i,j\}}$, $\lambda_{i,ij}(-1)=\lambda_{i,ji}(-1)$, $\lambda_{i,ij}(+1)=\lambda_{i,ji}(+1)$ $(\{i,j\}\in E)$ to ensure the normalization and reducibility conditions as follows:

$$\begin{aligned}
\mathcal{L}_{\rm Bethe}\big[\{\boldsymbol{R}_i|i\in V\},\{\boldsymbol{R}_{ij}|\{i,j\}\in E\}\big]\equiv\ &\mathcal{F}_{\rm Bethe}\big[\{\boldsymbol{R}_i|i\in V\},\{\boldsymbol{R}_{ij}|\{i,j\}\in E\}\big]\\
&-\sum_{i\in V}\lambda_i\Big(\sum_{\tau_i\in\Omega}R_i(\tau_i)-1\Big)\\
&-\sum_{\{i,j\}\in E}\lambda_{\{i,j\}}\Big(\sum_{\tau_i\in\Omega}\sum_{\tau_j\in\Omega}R_{ij}(\tau_i,\tau_j)-1\Big)\\
&-\sum_{i\in V}\sum_{j\in\partial i}\lambda_{i,ij}(-1)\Big(R_i(-1)-\sum_{\tau_j\in\Omega}R_{ij}(-1,\tau_j)\Big)\\
&-\sum_{i\in V}\sum_{j\in\partial i}\lambda_{i,ij}(+1)\Big(R_i(+1)-\sum_{\tau_j\in\Omega}R_{ij}(+1,\tau_j)\Big).
\end{aligned}\tag{10.84}$$

The marginal probabilities $\widehat{\boldsymbol{R}}_i$ $(i\in V)$ and $\widehat{\boldsymbol{R}}_{ij}$ $(\{i,j\}\in E)$ are determined so as to satisfy the following extremum condition:

$$\left[\frac{\partial}{\partial\boldsymbol{R}_i}\mathcal{L}_{\rm Bethe}\big[\{\boldsymbol{R}_i|i\in V\},\{\boldsymbol{R}_{ij}|\{i,j\}\in E\}\big]\right]_{\{\boldsymbol{R}_i=\widehat{\boldsymbol{R}}_i|i\in V\},\{\boldsymbol{R}_{ij}=\widehat{\boldsymbol{R}}_{ij}|\{i,j\}\in E\}}=0\ (i\in V),\tag{10.85}$$

$$\left[\frac{\partial}{\partial \boldsymbol{R}_{ij}}\mathcal{L}_{\mathrm{Bethe}}\left[\{\boldsymbol{R}_i|i\in V\},\{\boldsymbol{R}_{ij}|\{i,j\}\in E\}\right]\right]_{\{\boldsymbol{R}_i=\widehat{\boldsymbol{R}}_i|i\in V\},\{\boldsymbol{R}_{ij}=\widehat{\boldsymbol{R}}_{ij}|\{i,j\}\in E\}}=0\ (\{i,j\}\in E). \tag{10.86}$$

It needs to be shown that $\widehat{R}_i(s_i)$ $(i\in V)$ and $\widehat{R}_{ij}(s_i,s_j)=\widehat{R}_{ji}(s_j,s_i)$ $(\{i,j\}\in E)$ are derived as follows:

$$\widehat{R}_i(s_i)=\exp\left(-1-\frac{\lambda_i}{k_{\mathrm{B}}T(|\partial i|-1)}\right)\times\exp\left(\frac{1}{k_{\mathrm{B}}T}\left(-\frac{1}{|\partial i|-1}hd_is_i-\frac{1}{|\partial i|-1}\sum_{j\in\partial i}\lambda_{i,ij}(s_i)\right)\right)\ (i\in V), \tag{10.87}$$

$$\widehat{R}_{ij}(s_i,s_j)=\widehat{R}_{ji}(s_j,s_i)=\exp\left(-1+\frac{\lambda_{\{i,j\}}}{k_{\mathrm{B}}T}\right)\times\exp\left(\frac{1}{k_{\mathrm{B}}T}(Js_is_j-\lambda_{i,ij}(s_i)-\lambda_{j,ij}(s_j))\right)\ (\{i,j\}\in E). \tag{10.88}$$

Finally, λ_i and $\lambda_{\{i,j\}}$ need to be determined so as to satisfy the normalization condition of the marginal probabilities $\widehat{R}_i(s_i)$ and $\widehat{R}_{ij}(s_i,s_j)$.

By introducing the messages $\mu_{k\to i}(s_i)$ and $\mu_{l\to j}(s_j)$ in the transformations

$$\exp\left(-\frac{\lambda_{i,ij}(s_i)}{k_{\mathrm{B}}T}\right)=\left(\prod_{k\in\partial i\backslash\{j\}}\mu_{k\to i}(s_i)\right)\exp\left(\frac{h}{k_{\mathrm{B}}T}d_is_i\right), \tag{10.89}$$

$$\exp\left(-\frac{\lambda_{j,ij}(s_j)}{k_{\mathrm{B}}T}\right)=\left(\prod_{l\in\partial j\backslash\{i\}}\mu_{l\to j}(s_j)\right)\exp\left(\frac{h}{k_{\mathrm{B}}T}d_js_j\right). \tag{10.90}$$

The expressions of the marginal probabilities $\widehat{\boldsymbol{R}}_i$ and $\widehat{\boldsymbol{R}}_{ij}$ in Eqs. (10.87) and (10.88) can be reduced to the following expressions:

$$\widehat{R}_i(s_i)=\frac{1}{Z_i}\left(\prod_{k\in\partial i}\mu_{k\to i}(s_i)\right)\exp\left(\frac{h}{k_{\mathrm{B}}T}d_is_i\right)\ (i\in V), \tag{10.91}$$

$$\widehat{R}_{ij}(s_i, s_j) = \widehat{R}_{ji}(s_j, s_i) = \frac{1}{Z_{\{i,j\}}}\left(\prod_{k\in\partial i\backslash\{j\}} \mu_{k\to i}(s_i)\right)\left(\prod_{l\in\partial j\backslash\{i\}} \mu_{l\to j}(s_j)\right) \times\exp\left(\frac{1}{k_{\mathrm{B}}T}(Js_is_j + hd_is_i + hd_js_j)\right) \ (\{i, j\}\in E), \tag{10.92}$$

$$Z_i \equiv \sum_{\tau_i\in\Omega}\left(\prod_{k\in\partial i}\mu_{k\to i}(\tau_i)\right)\exp\left(\frac{h}{k_{\mathrm{B}}T}d_i\tau_i\right) \ (i\in V), \tag{10.93}$$

$$Z_{\{i,j\}} \equiv \sum_{\tau_i\in\Omega}\sum_{\tau_j\in\Omega}\left(\prod_{k\in\partial i\backslash\{j\}} \mu_{k\to i}(\tau_i)\right)\left(\prod_{l\in\partial j\backslash\{i\}} \mu_{l\to j}(\tau_j)\right) \times\exp\left(\frac{1}{k_{\mathrm{B}}T}(J\tau_i\tau_j + hd_i\tau_i + hd_j\tau_j)\right) \ (\{i, j\}\in E). \tag{10.94}$$

By substituting Eqs. (10.91) and (10.92) into the reducibility conditions in Eq. (10.80), the simultaneous deterministic equations for the messages can be derived as follows:

$$\mu_{j\to i}(s_i) = \frac{Z_i}{Z_{\{i,j\}}}\sum_{\tau_j\in\Omega}\left(\prod_{l\in\partial j\backslash\{i\}} \mu_{l\to j}(\tau_j)\right)\exp\left(\frac{1}{k_{\mathrm{B}}T}(Js_i\tau_j + hd_j\tau_j)\right) \ (\{i, j\}\in E), \tag{10.95}$$

$$\mu_{i\to j}(s_j) = \frac{Z_j}{Z_{\{i,j\}}}\sum_{\tau_i\in\Omega}\left(\prod_{k\in\partial i\backslash\{j\}} \mu_{k\to i}(\tau_i)\right)\exp\left(\frac{1}{k_{\mathrm{B}}T}(J\tau_is_j + hd_i\tau_i)\right) \ (\{i, j\}\in E). \tag{10.96}$$

The Bethe free energy functional is given by

$$\mathcal{F}_{\mathrm{Bethe}}\left[\{\widehat{\boldsymbol{R}}_i|i\in V\}, \{\widehat{\boldsymbol{R}}_{ij}|\{i, j\}\in E\}\right] = -k_{\mathrm{B}}T\sum_{i\in V}(1 - |\partial i|)\ln Z_i - k_{\mathrm{B}}T\sum_{\{i,j\}\in E}\ln Z_{\{i,j\}}. \tag{10.97}$$

The framework in the Bethe approximation using Eqs. (10.91), (10.92), (10.93), and (10.94) with Eqs. (10.95) and (10.96) is referred to as a **loopy belief propagation** in statistical machine learning theory [12, 46–48]. The present derivation is based on the cluster variation method in Refs. [39, 42–44], and [45]. Recently, some novel approaches for loopy belief propagation methods have been proposed, including the **approximate message passing algorithm** [49], and **replica cluster variation method** [50, 51]. A review summarizing recent developments in loopy belief propagation methods is given in Ref. [52].

By solving

$$\sum_{\tau_i\in\Omega}\sum_{\tau_j\in\Omega}\widehat{R}_{ij}(\tau_i,\tau_j)=\widehat{R}_{ij}(+1,+1)+\widehat{R}_{ij}(-1,+1)+\widehat{R}_{ij}(+1,-1)+\widehat{R}_{ij}(-1,-1)=1, \tag{10.98}$$

$$\sum_{\tau_i\in\Omega}\sum_{\tau_j\in\Omega}\tau_i\widehat{R}_{ij}(\tau_i,\tau_j)=\widehat{R}_{ij}(+1,+1)-\widehat{R}_{ij}(-1,+1)+\widehat{R}_{ij}(+1,-1)-\widehat{R}_{ij}(-1,-1)=m_i, \tag{10.99}$$

$$\sum_{\tau_i\in\Omega}\sum_{\tau_j\in\Omega}\tau_j\widehat{R}_{ij}(\tau_i,\tau_j)=\widehat{R}_{ij}(+1,+1)+\widehat{R}_{ij}(-1,+1)-\widehat{R}_{ij}(+1,-1)-\widehat{R}_{ij}(-1,-1)=m_j, \tag{10.100}$$

$$\begin{aligned}\sum_{\tau_i\in\Omega}\sum_{\tau_j\in\Omega}\tau_i\tau_j\widehat{R}_{ij}(\tau_i,\tau_j)&=\widehat{R}_{ij}(+1,+1)-\widehat{R}_{ij}(-1,+1)\\&\quad-\widehat{R}_{ij}(+1,-1)+\widehat{R}_{ij}(-1,-1)=c_{\{i,j\}}=c_{\{j,i\}},\end{aligned} \tag{10.101}$$

as simultaneous linear equations for $\widehat{R}_{ij}(+1,+1)$, $\widehat{R}_{ij}(-1,+1)$, $\widehat{R}_{ij}(+1,-1)$, and $\widehat{R}_{ij}(-1,-1)$, we can confirm the following equality:

$$\widehat{R}_{ij}(s_i,s_j)=\frac{1}{4}\big(1+m_is_i+m_js_j+c_{\{i,j\}}s_is_j\big). \tag{10.102}$$

By substituting Eqs. (10.72) and (10.102) into Eq. (10.82), the Bethe free energy functional can be reduced to

$$\mathcal{F}_{\text{Bethe}}\Big[\big\{\widehat{\boldsymbol{R}}_i\big|i\in V\big\},\big\{\widehat{\boldsymbol{R}}_{ij}\big|\{i,j\}\in E\big\}\Big]=F_{\text{Bethe}}\big(\big\{m_i\big|i\in V\big\},\big\{c_{\{i,j\}}\big|\{i,j\}\in E\big\}\big), \tag{10.103}$$

$$F_{\mathrm{Bethe}}\left(\left\{m_i \middle| i\in V\right\}, \left\{c_{\{i,j\}} \middle| \{i,j\}\in E\right\}\right) \equiv -J\sum_{\{i,j\}\in E} c_{\{i,j\}} - h\sum_{i\in V} d_i m_i$$
$$+k_{\mathrm{B}}T\sum_{i\in V}(1-|\partial i|)\sum_{s_i=\pm 1}\widehat{R}_i(s_i)\ln\left(\widehat{R}_i(s_i)\right) + k_{\mathrm{B}}T\sum_{\{i,j\}\in E}\sum_{s_j=\pm 1}\widehat{R}_{ij}(s_i,s_j)\ln\left(\widehat{R}_{ij}(s_i,s_j)\right). \tag{10.104}$$

The extremum conditions

$$\frac{\partial}{\partial m_k}F_{\mathrm{Bethe}}\left(\left\{m_i \middle| i\in V\right\}, \left\{c_{\{i,j\}} \middle| \{i,j\}\in E\right\}\right) = 0\ (k\in V), \tag{10.105}$$

$$\frac{\partial}{\partial c_{\{k,l\}}}F_{\mathrm{Bethe}}\left(\left\{m_i \middle| i\in V\right\}, \left\{c_{\{i,j\}} \middle| \{i,j\}\in E\right\}\right) = 0\ (\{k,l\}\in E) \tag{10.106}$$

can be reduced to the following simultaneous equations:

$$\frac{h}{k_{\mathrm{B}}T}d_i = \frac{1}{2}(1-|\partial i|)\sum_{\tau_i\in\Omega}\tau_i\ln\left(\widehat{R}_i(\tau_i)\right) + \frac{1}{4}\sum_{j\in\partial i}\sum_{\tau_i\in\Omega}\sum_{\tau_j\in\Omega}\tau_i\ln\left(\widehat{R}_{ij}(\tau_i,\tau_j)\right)\ (i\in V), \tag{10.107}$$

$$\frac{J}{k_{\mathrm{B}}T} = \frac{1}{4}\sum_{\tau_i\in\Omega}\sum_{\tau_j\in\Omega}\tau_i\tau_j\ln\left(\widehat{R}_{ij}(\tau_i,\tau_j)\right)\ (\{i,j\}\in E). \tag{10.108}$$

The schemes for the derivations of Eqs. (10.107) and (10.108) from the Bethe free energy (Eqs. (10.103)–(10.104)) are given in Refs. [41, 53–55].

In the advanced mean-field method, some researchers are interested in perturbative computation of the correction terms with respect to $\frac{J}{k_{\mathrm{B}}T}$ from the mean-field free energy [56, 57], which is referred to as a **Thouless-Anderson-Palmar (TAP) free energy**. The scheme used in the derivations has been extended to a classical Heisenberg model [58]. One familiar perturbative method in statistical mechanical informatics is the Plefka expansion, in which we obtain higher-order correction terms with respect to $\frac{J}{k_{\mathrm{B}}T}$ from the mean-field free energy [12]. By substituting Eq. (10.102) into Eq. (10.108), $c_{\{i,j\}}$ can be expressed in terms of m_i, m_j, and $\frac{J}{k_{\mathrm{B}}T}$. It is known that the TAP equation can be derived by expanding the expression for $c_{\{i,j\}}$ up to the second-order term $\left(\frac{J}{k_{\mathrm{B}}T}\right)^2$ with respect to an infinitesimal $\frac{J}{k_{\mathrm{B}}T}$ and by substituting it into Eq. (10.82) with Eqs. (10.72) and (10.102) [41], The fundamental framework of the TAP free energy and its expansion using the advanced mean-field method has been clarified [59]. The Bethe free energy functional and the TAP free energy as well as loopy belief propagation have been applied to Boltzmann machine learning [53, 60–64]. Some recent developments appear in Chap. 7 of Part 3 in this book.

The EM schemes with advanced mean-field methods in the previous sections have been applied to noise reduction in probabilistic image processing [30, 51, 65–69]. The basic frameworks are based on Eqs. (10.14) and (10.15) with the two-body and

Bayesian Noise Reductions by Generalized Sparse Prior

$$P(s_1, s_2, \cdots, s_{|V|} | p, \alpha, p) \propto \prod_{\{i,j\}\in E} \prod_{c\in\{\mathrm{R,G,B}\}} \exp\left(-\frac{1}{2}\alpha_c |s_{i,c} - s_{j,c}|^p\right) (0 < p \le 2)$$

$$P(d_1, d_2, \cdots, d_{|V|} | s_1, s_2, \cdots, s_{|V|}, \beta) \propto \prod_{i\in V} \prod_{c\in\{\mathrm{R,G,B}\}} \exp\left(-\frac{1}{2}\beta (d_{i,c} - s_{i,c})^2\right)$$

$$P(s_1, s_2, \cdots, s_{|V|} | d_1, d_2, \cdots, d_{|V|}, p, \alpha, \beta) \propto P(d_1, d_2, \cdots, d_{|V|} | s_1, s_2, \cdots, s_{|V|}, \beta) P(s_1, s_2, \cdots, s_{|V|} | p, \alpha)$$

R: Red
G: Green
B: Blue

State Vector of Parameters $s = (s_1, s_2, \cdots, s_{|V|})$ $\quad s_i = (s_{i,\mathrm{R}}, s_{i,\mathrm{G}}, s_{i,\mathrm{B}})$ $\quad \alpha = (\alpha_\mathrm{R}, \alpha_\mathrm{G}, \alpha_\mathrm{B})$

State Vector of Data Point $d = (d_1, d_2, \cdots, d_{|V|})$ $\quad d_i = (d_{i,\mathrm{R}}, d_{i,\mathrm{G}}, d_{i,\mathrm{B}})$

Deterministic Equations of Hyperparameters α and β

$$\frac{1}{|E|}\sum_{\{i,j\}\in E}\sum_{s_{i,c}\in\Omega}\sum_{s_{j,c}\in\Omega} |s_{i,c} - s_{j,c}|^p P_{ij}(s_{i,c}, s_{j,c} | p, \hat{\alpha}) = \frac{1}{|E|}\sum_{\{i,j\}\in E}\sum_{s_{i,c}\in\Omega}\sum_{s_{j,c}\in\Omega} |s_{i,c} - s_{j,c}|^p P_{ij}(s_{i,c}, s_{j,c} | d, p, \hat{\alpha}, \hat{\beta})$$

$$\frac{1}{\hat{\beta}} = \frac{1}{|V|}\sum_{i\in V}\sum_{c\in\{\mathrm{R,G,B}\}}\sum_{s_i\in\Omega} (s_{i,c} - d_{i,c})^2 P_{i,c}(s_{i,c} | d, p, \hat{\alpha}, \hat{\beta})$$

EM Procedure: Repeat E step and M step until α(*t*) and σ(*t*) converge

[E step] Compute

$$u_c(t+1) \leftarrow \frac{1}{|E|}\sum_{\{i,j\}\in E}\sum_{s_{i,c}\in\Omega}\sum_{s_{j,c}\in\Omega} |s_{i,c} - s_{j,c}|^p P_{ij,c}(s_{i,c}, s_{j,c} | d, p, \alpha(t), \beta(t)) (\forall c \in \{\mathrm{R,G,B}\})$$

$$\beta(t+1) = \left(\frac{1}{|V|}\sum_{i\in V}\sum_{c\in\{\mathrm{R,G,B}\}}\sum_{s_{i,c}\in\Omega} (s_{i,c} - d_{i,c})^2 P_{i,c}(s_{i,c} | d, p, \alpha(t), \beta(t))\right)^{-1}.$$

[M step] Solve $\frac{1}{|E|}\sum_{\{i,j\}\in E}\sum_{s_{i,c}\in\Omega}\sum_{s_{j,c}\in\Omega} |s_{i,c} - s_{j,c}|^p P_{ij,c}(s_{i,c}, s_{j,c} | p, \alpha(t+1)) = u_c(t+1) (\forall c \in \{\mathrm{R,G,B}\})$

with respect to $\alpha(t+1)$.

[MPM step] Update $t \leftarrow t+1$ **and** $\hat{s}_{i,c}(d,p) = \arg\max_{s_{i,c}\in\Omega} P_{i,c}(s_{i,c} | d, p, \hat{\alpha}, \hat{\beta})$ $(\forall i \in V, \forall c \in \{\mathrm{R,G,B}\})$

$$P_{i,c}(s_{i,c} | d, p, \alpha, \beta) \equiv \sum_{\tau_{1,\mathrm{R}}\in\Omega}\sum_{\tau_{1,\mathrm{G}}\in\Omega}\sum_{\tau_{1,\mathrm{B}}\in\Omega}\cdots\sum_{\tau_{|V|,\mathrm{R}}\in\Omega}\sum_{\tau_{|V|,\mathrm{G}}\in\Omega}\sum_{\tau_{|V|,\mathrm{B}}\in\Omega} \delta_{s_{i,c},\tau_{i,c}} P(\tau_1, \tau_2, \cdots, \tau_{|V|} | d_1, d_2, \cdots, d_{|V|}, p, \alpha, \beta)$$

$$P_{ij,c}(s_{i,c}, s_{i,c} | d, p, \alpha, \beta) \equiv \sum_{\tau_{1,\mathrm{R}}\in\Omega}\sum_{\tau_{1,\mathrm{G}}\in\Omega}\sum_{\tau_{1,\mathrm{B}}\in\Omega}\cdots\sum_{\tau_{|V|,\mathrm{R}}\in\Omega}\sum_{\tau_{|V|,\mathrm{G}}\in\Omega}\sum_{\tau_{|V|,\mathrm{B}}\in\Omega} \delta_{s_{i,c},\tau_{i,c}}\delta_{s_{i,c},\tau_{i,c}} P(\tau_1, \tau_2, \cdots, \tau_{|V|} | d_1, d_2, \cdots, d_{|V|}, p, \alpha, \beta)$$

$$P_{ij,c}(s_{i,c}, s_{i,c} | p, \alpha) \equiv \sum_{\tau_{1,\mathrm{R}}\in\Omega}\sum_{\tau_{1,\mathrm{G}}\in\Omega}\sum_{\tau_{1,\mathrm{B}}\in\Omega}\cdots\sum_{\tau_{|V|,\mathrm{R}}\in\Omega}\sum_{\tau_{|V|,\mathrm{G}}\in\Omega}\sum_{\tau_{|V|,\mathrm{B}}\in\Omega} \delta_{s_{i,c},\tau_{i,c}}\delta_{s_{i,c},\tau_{i,c}} P(\tau_1, \tau_2, \cdots, \tau_{|V|} | p, \alpha)$$

Compute the marginals by loopy belief propagation in each step

Fig. 10.1 Fundamental framework of Bayesian noise reduction by generalized sparse prior and additive white Gaussian noise

one-body posterior marginal probability distributions in Eqs. (10.11) and (10.12) as well as the two-body prior marginal probability distribution in Eq. (10.13). They can be computed by means of the message passing algorithms in Eqs. (10.91) and (10.92) with Eqs. (10.93), (10.94), (10.95), and (10.96) for the Ising model in Eqs. (10.47), (10.48), and (10.50) with the prior and posterior probability distributions in Eqs. (10.2) and (10.3), respectively. The framework and some numerical experimental results are shown in Figs. 10.1 and 10.2, respectively. Moreover, the loopy belief propagation is applicable to Bayesian image segmentation in the framework of Sect. 10.2.3 [70]. They are also useful for community detection be means of the stochastic block model for modular networks [71–73].

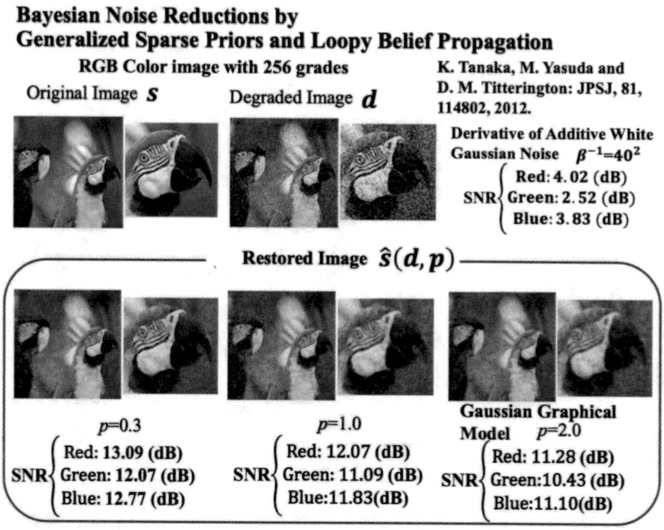

Fig. 10.2 Numerical experiments in Bayesian noise reduction by the generalized sparse prior and additive white Gaussian noise

10.3.3 Free Energy Landscapes and Phase Transitions in the Thermodynamic Limit

In this section, we consider the Ising model defined by

$$P\left(s\middle|\frac{J}{k_{\rm B}T},\frac{h}{k_{\rm B}T}\right)\equiv\frac{1}{Z\left(\frac{J}{k_{\rm B}T},\frac{h}{k_{\rm B}T}\right)}\exp\left(\frac{1}{k_{\rm B}T}H(s)\right),\tag{10.109}$$

where

$$\begin{aligned}H(s)&=H(s_1,s_2,\cdots,s_{|V|})\\&\equiv-J\sum_{\{i,j\}\in E}s_is_j-h\sum_{i\in V}s_i\ (J>0),\end{aligned}\tag{10.110}$$

$$Z\left(\frac{J}{k_{\rm B}T},\frac{h}{k_{\rm B}T}\right)\equiv\sum_{s_1\in\Omega}\sum_{s_2\in\Omega}\cdots\sum_{s_{|V|}\in\Omega}\exp\left(-\frac{1}{k_{\rm B}T}H(s)\right).\tag{10.111}$$

The energy function in Eq. (10.110) corresponds to the one in Eq. (10.49) for the case of $d_i=1$ for every node $i(\in V)$. In the present section, we consider a regular of degree 4 that includes a square grid graph with periodic boundary conditions along the x- and y-direction as shown in Fig. 10.3.

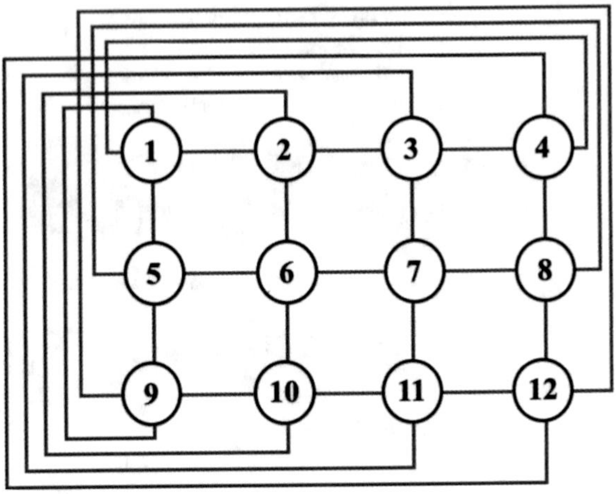

Fig. 10.3 Square grid graph (V, E) with periodic boundary conditions along the x- and y-direction in the case $V = \{1, 2, 3, 4, 5, 6, 7, 8, 9, 10, 11, 12\}$

For the Ising model in Eq. (10.110) and its partition function in Eq. (10.50), we have the free energy per node

$$f(J, h, T) = -k_{\mathrm{B}}T \times \lim_{|V|\to+\infty} \frac{1}{|V|} \ln(Z), \tag{10.112}$$

the internal energy for zero external field

$$\begin{aligned} Ju &\equiv \frac{\partial}{\partial\left(\frac{1}{k_{\mathrm{B}}T}\right)}\left(\frac{1}{k_{\mathrm{B}}T} f(J, h=0, T)\right) \\ &= \lim_{|V|\to+\infty} \frac{1}{|E|} \sum_{\{i,j\}\in E} \sum_{s} (-s_i s_j) P\left(s \left| \frac{J}{k_{\mathrm{B}}T}, \frac{h}{k_{\mathrm{B}}T} = 0\right.\right), \end{aligned} \tag{10.113}$$

and the spontaneous magnetization

$$\begin{aligned} m_{\pm} &\equiv \lim_{h\to\pm 0} \frac{\partial}{\partial\left(\frac{h}{k_{\mathrm{B}}T}\right)}\left(\frac{1}{k_{\mathrm{B}}T} f(J, h, T)\right) \\ &= \lim_{h\to\pm 0} \lim_{|V|\to+\infty} \frac{1}{|V|} \sum_{i\in V} \sum_{s} s_i P\left(s \left| \frac{J}{k_{\mathrm{B}}T}, \frac{h}{k_{\mathrm{B}}T}\right.\right), \end{aligned} \tag{10.114}$$

as important statistical quantities in the thermodynamic limit $|V| \to +\infty$. The existence of the thermodynamic limit $|V| \to +\infty$ means that the limit of the right-hand side in Eq. (10.110) converges. Sufficient conditions for the existence of the thermodynamic limit of the Ising model of Eqs. (10.109), (10.110), and (10.111) have been given by Ruelle in Ref. [38].

In the thermodynamic limit $|V| \to +\infty$ for the Ising model in Eq. (10.110) on a square grid graph with periodic boundary conditions along the x- and y-direction as shown in Fig. 10.3,

$$\frac{u}{J}=-\coth\left(\frac{2J}{k_{\mathrm{B}}T}\right)\left(1+\left(2\tanh^2\left(\frac{2J}{k_{\mathrm{B}}T}\right)-1\right)\left(\frac{2}{\pi}\right)\int_0^{\frac{\pi}{2}}\left(1-\left(\frac{2\sinh\left(\frac{2J}{k_{\mathrm{B}}T}\right)}{\cosh^2\left(\frac{2J}{k_{\mathrm{B}}T}\right)}\right)^2\sin^2(\theta)\right)^{-\frac{1}{2}}d\theta\right),\tag{10.115}$$

$$\begin{aligned}{m_{\pm}}^2 &= \lim_{|\boldsymbol{r}_i-\boldsymbol{r}_j|\to+\infty}\lim_{|V|\to+\infty}\sum_{\boldsymbol{s}} s_i s_j P\left(\boldsymbol{s}\middle|\frac{J}{k_{\mathrm{B}}T},\frac{h}{k_{\mathrm{B}}T}=0\right)\\ &=\begin{cases}0 & \left(\frac{J}{k_{\mathrm{B}}T}<\frac{1}{2}\mathrm{arcsinh}(1)\right)\\ \left(1-\sinh^{-4}\left(\frac{2J}{k_{\mathrm{B}}T}\right)\right)^{\frac{1}{4}} & \left(\frac{J}{k_{\mathrm{B}}T}>\frac{1}{2}\mathrm{arcsinh}(1)\right)\end{cases},\end{aligned}\tag{10.116}$$

where $\boldsymbol{r}_i$ is the position vector of each node $i(\in V)$ [34, 74, 75]. In Eq. (10.116), the spontaneous magnetizations m_+ and m_- correspond to each branch of $m_+\geq 0$ and $m_-\leq 0$, respectively. They are as shown in Fig. 10.4. Note that for the Ising model in Eq. (10.110) on such regular graphs,

$$m_{i,V}\left(\frac{J}{k_{\mathrm{B}}T},\frac{h}{k_{\mathrm{B}}T}\right)\equiv\sum_{\boldsymbol{s}} s_i P\left(\boldsymbol{s}\middle|\frac{J}{k_{\mathrm{B}}T},\frac{h}{k_{\mathrm{B}}T}\right),\tag{10.117}$$

for every $i(\in V)$, does not depend on i but can be expressed as $m_V\left(\frac{J}{k_{\mathrm{B}}T},\frac{h}{k_{\mathrm{B}}T}\right)$.

In the mean-field approximation of the previous subsection, the spontaneous magnetizations

$$m_{\pm}=\lim_{h\to\pm 0}\lim_{|V|\to+\infty} m_V\left(\frac{J}{k_{\mathrm{B}}T},\frac{h}{k_{\mathrm{B}}T}\right),\tag{10.118}$$

are given as solutions of the following mean-field equation:

$$m_{\pm}=\tanh\left(\frac{1}{k_{\mathrm{B}}T}(h+4Jm_{\pm})\right)\ (h\to\pm 0),\tag{10.119}$$

and the internal energy Ju in Eq. (10.113) in the mean-field approximation is given as

$$u=-{m_{\pm}}^2.\tag{10.120}$$

The solutions of Eq. (10.119) correspond to the extremum values of the following mean-field free energy:

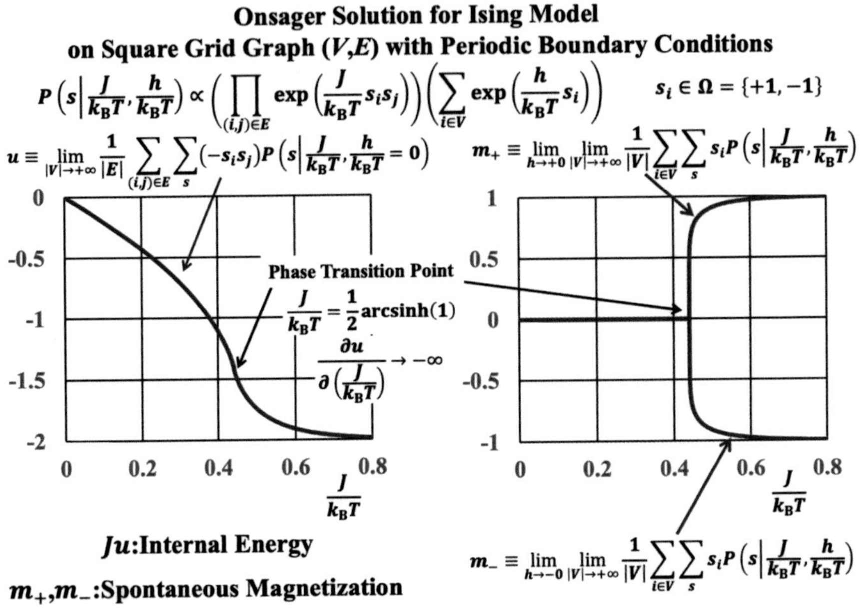

Fig. 10.4 Internal energy Ju in Eq. (10.113) and magnetization $m_\pm$ in Eq. (10.114) in the Onsager solution in the Ising model of Eqs. (10.48) and (10.50) with Eq. (10.110) on the square grid graph (V, E) with the periodic boundary conditions along the x- and y-direction

$$\begin{aligned} f_{\rm MF}(m) &\equiv \frac{1}{|V|}F_{\rm MF}\big(m_1, m_2, \cdots, m_{|V|}\big) \\ &= -2Jm^2 + k_{\rm B}T\left(\frac{1}{2}(1+m)\right)\ln\left(\frac{1}{2}(1+m)\right) \\ &\quad + k_{\rm B}T\left(\frac{1}{2}(1-m)\right)\ln\left(\frac{1}{2}(1-m)\right), \qquad (10.121) \end{aligned}$$

which corresponds to $\frac{1}{|V|}F_{\rm MF}\big(m_1, m_2, \cdots, m_{|V|}\big)$ in Eq. (10.75) for $h = 0$. The spontaneous magnetization $m_\pm$ and the internal energy u for $h = 0$ are computed by setting $0 < \left|\frac{h}{k_{\rm B}T}\right| < 10^{-5}$ and using the iteration method for Eq. (10.119) numerically. The graphs of $\left(\frac{J}{k_{\rm B}T}, u\right)$ and $\left(\frac{J}{k_{\rm B}T}, m_\pm\right)$ are shown in Fig. 10.5. Moreover, the graphs of $\left(m, \frac{1}{k_{\rm B}T}f_{\rm MF}(m)\right)$ for $\frac{J}{k_{\rm B}T} = 0.20, 0.25$, and 0.40 are shown in Fig. 10.6. It is known that the mean-field equation always has the trivial solution $m_\pm = 0$, and begins to have some non-trivial solutions for $m_+ > 0$ and $m_- < 0$. The mean-field equation (10.119) begins to have some non-trivial solutions in the region of $\frac{J}{k_{\rm B}T} > \frac{1}{4}$ by expanding the right-hand side of Eq. (10.119) around $m = 0$ and keeping the first-order term of m.

Mean Field Approximation for Ising Model
on Square Grid Graph (V,E) with Periodic Boundary Conditions

$$P\left(s\middle|\frac{J}{k_BT},\frac{h}{k_BT}\right) \propto \left(\prod_{(i,j)\in E}\exp\left(\frac{J}{k_BT}s_is_j\right)\right)\left(\sum_{i\in V}\exp\left(\frac{h}{k_BT}s_i\right)\right) \qquad s_i \in \Omega = \{+1,-1\}$$

$$m_+ \equiv \lim_{h\to+0}\lim_{|V|\to+\infty}\frac{1}{|V|}\sum_{i\in V}\sum_s s_iP\left(s\middle|\frac{J}{k_BT},\frac{h}{k_BT}\right)$$

$$u \equiv \lim_{h\to\pm0}\lim_{|V|\to+\infty}\frac{1}{|E|}\sum_{(i,j)\in E}\sum_s(-s_is_j)P\left(s\middle|\frac{J}{k_BT},\frac{h}{k_BT}\right) \qquad m_- \equiv \lim_{h\to-0}\lim_{|V|\to+\infty}\frac{1}{|V|}\sum_{i\in V}\sum_s s_iP\left(s\middle|\frac{J}{k_BT},\frac{h}{k_BT}\right)$$

——— **Global Minimum State (Stable)**

——— **Local Maximum State (Unstable)** } **for Mean Field Free Energy**

I. $h \to +0$: $\displaystyle\lim_{\frac{J}{k_BT}\to+\infty}(P_i(+1),P_i(-1))\to(1,0)$

III. $(P_i(+1),P_i(+1)) = \left(\frac{1}{2},\frac{1}{2}\right)\left(\forall\frac{J}{k_BT}>0\right)$

II. $h \to -0$: $\displaystyle\lim_{\frac{J}{k_BT}\to+\infty}(P_i(+1),P_i(-1))\to(0,1)$

$$P_i(s_i) \equiv \lim_{|V|\to+\infty}\sum_{s_1\in\Omega}\sum_{s_2\in\Omega}\cdots\sum_{s_{i-1}\in\Omega}\sum_{s_{i+1}\in\Omega}\sum_{s_{i+2}\in\Omega}\cdots\sum_{s_{|V|}\in\Omega}P\left(s\middle|\frac{J}{k_BT},\frac{h}{k_BT}\right)(\forall s_i\in\Omega)$$

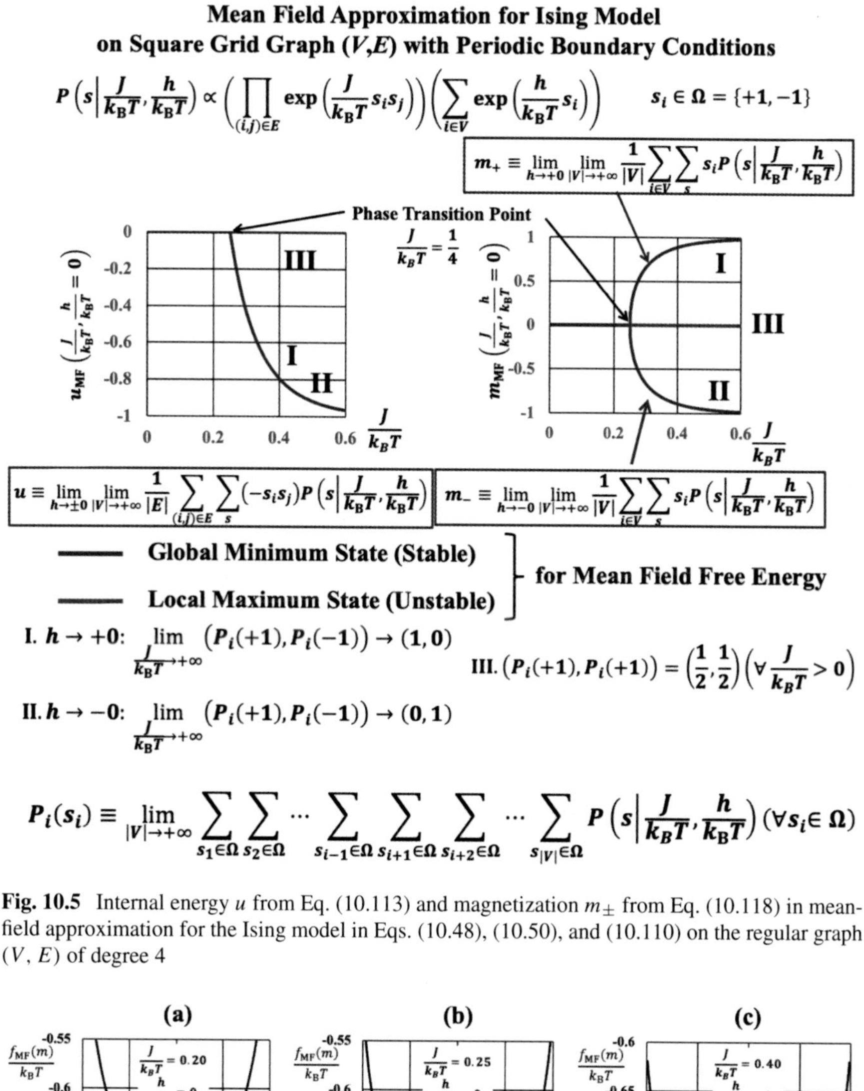

Fig. 10.5 Internal energy u from Eq. (10.113) and magnetization $m_\pm$ from Eq. (10.118) in mean-field approximation for the Ising model in Eqs. (10.48), (10.50), and (10.110) on the regular graph (V, E) of degree 4

(a)   **(b)**   **(c)**

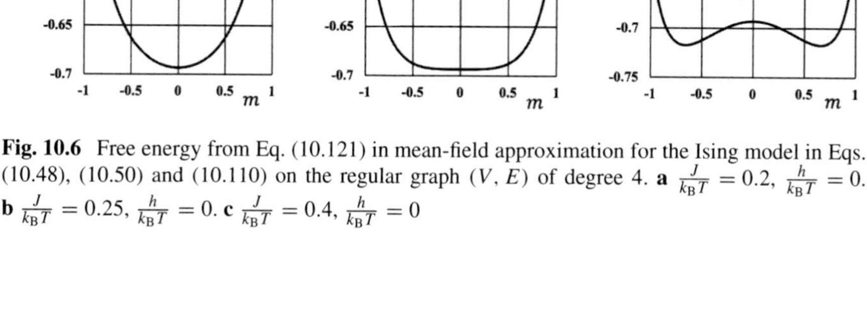

Fig. 10.6 Free energy from Eq. (10.121) in mean-field approximation for the Ising model in Eqs. (10.48), (10.50) and (10.110) on the regular graph (V, E) of degree 4. **a** $\frac{J}{k_BT} = 0.2$, $\frac{h}{k_BT} = 0$. **b** $\frac{J}{k_BT} = 0.25$, $\frac{h}{k_BT} = 0$. **c** $\frac{J}{k_BT} = 0.4$, $\frac{h}{k_BT} = 0$

Next, we consider the Bethe approximation for the Ising model in Eqs. (10.48), (10.50), and (10.110) on the regular graph (V, E) of degree 4. In this case, the average m_i, the correlation c_{ij} and the messages $\mu_{i\to j}(+1)$ and $\mu_{i\to j}(-1)$ do not depend on i and j, and can be expressed as m, c, $\mu(+1)$ and $\mu(-1)$. We now introduce

$$\Lambda \equiv \frac{1}{2}k_{\rm B}T\ln\left(\frac{\mu(+1)}{\mu(-1)}\right). \tag{10.122}$$

The message passing equations in Eqs. (10.95) and (10.96) and the magnetization are reduced to

$$\frac{\Lambda}{k_{\rm B}T} = \text{arctanh}\left(\tanh\left(\frac{J}{k_{\rm B}T}\right)\tanh\left(\frac{h+3\Lambda}{k_{\rm B}T}\right)\right). \tag{10.123}$$

Moreover, since the marginal probabilities $\widehat{R}_i(+1)$ and $\widehat{R}_i(-1)$ are also independent of i, we can derive the expression for the magnetization in terms of Λ as follows:

$$m_{\rm Bethe}\left(\frac{J}{k_{\rm B}T}, \frac{h}{k_{\rm B}T}\right) \equiv \frac{1}{|V|}\sum_{i\in V}\left(\sum_{s_i\in\Omega} s_i\widehat{R}(s_i)\right) = \tanh\left(\frac{h+4\Lambda}{k_{\rm B}T}\right). \tag{10.124}$$

For the infinitesimal small limits of h, such that $h\to +0$ and $h\to -0$, the magnetization $m_{\rm Bethe}\left(\frac{J}{k_{\rm B}T}, \frac{h}{k_{\rm B}T}\right)$ in Eq. (10.124) can be computed numerically by using the iteration method. Moreover, Eqs. (10.104) and (10.108) can be reduced to

$$\begin{aligned} f_{\rm Bethe}(m, c) &= \frac{1}{|V|}F_{\rm Bethe}\left(\{m_i|i\in V\}, \{c_{\{i,j\}}|\{i,j\}\in E\}\right) \\ &= -2Jc - hm \\ &\quad -3k_{\rm B}T\left(\frac{1}{2}(1+m)\right)\ln\left(\frac{1}{2}(1+m)\right) - 3k_{\rm B}T\left(\frac{1}{2}(1-m)\right)\ln\left(\frac{1}{2}(1-m)\right) \\ &\quad +2k_{\rm B}T\left(\frac{1}{4}(1+2m+c)\right)\ln\left(\frac{1}{4}(1+2m+c)\right) \\ &\quad +4k_{\rm B}T\left(\frac{1}{4}(1-c)\right)\ln\left(\frac{1}{4}(1-c)\right) \\ &\quad +2k_{\rm B}T\left(\frac{1}{4}(1-2m+c)\right)\ln\left(\frac{1}{4}(1-2m+c)\right), \end{aligned} \tag{10.125}$$

and

$$\frac{J}{k_{\rm B}T} = \ln\frac{(1+c)^2 - 4m^2}{(1-c)^2}, \tag{10.126}$$

such that

$$c = \frac{1}{\tanh\left(\frac{2J}{k_B T}\right)}\left(1 - \sqrt{1 - (1 - 2m^2)\tanh^2\left(\frac{2J}{k_B T}\right) - 2m^2\tanh\left(\frac{2J}{k_B T}\right)}\right). \quad (10.127)$$

The graphs of

$$\left(m, \frac{1}{k_B T} f_{\text{Bethe}}\left(m, \frac{1}{\tanh\left(\frac{2J}{k_B T}\right)}\left(1 - \sqrt{1 - (1 - 2m^2)\tanh^2\left(\frac{2J}{k_B T}\right) - 2m^2\tanh\left(\frac{2J}{k_B T}\right)}\right)\right)\right), \quad (10.128)$$

for $\frac{J}{k_B T} = 0.25$, $\frac{J}{k_B T} = \text{arctanh}\left(\frac{1}{3}\right)$, and $\frac{k_B T}{J} = 0.40$ in the case of $h = 0$ are shown in Figs. 10.7, 10.8, and 10.9, respectively. Figure 10.7 shows the internal energy u from Eq. (10.113) and the spontaneous magnetization $m_{\pm}$ in Eq. (10.118) in loopy belief propagation (Bethe approximation) for the Ising model in Eqs. (10.48), (10.50), and (10.110) on the regular graph (V, E) of degree 4. These quantities u and $m_{\pm}$ are obtained by

$$u_{\text{Bethe}}\left(\frac{J}{k_B T}, \frac{h}{k_B T} = 0\right) = \frac{\cosh\left(\frac{6\Lambda}{k_B T}\right) - \exp\left(-\frac{2J}{k_B T}\right)}{\cosh\left(\frac{6\Lambda}{k_B T}\right) + \exp\left(-\frac{2J}{k_B T}\right)}, \quad (10.129)$$

$$m_{\text{Bethe}}\left(\frac{J}{k_B T}, \frac{h}{k_B T} = 0\right) = \tanh\left(\frac{4\Lambda}{k_B T}\right), \quad (10.130)$$

where

$$\frac{\Lambda}{k_B T} = \text{arctanh}\left(\tanh\left(\frac{J}{k_B T}\right)\tanh\left(\frac{3\Lambda}{k_B T}\right)\right). \quad (10.131)$$

These always give the same results as in Eq. (10.110) on the regular graph (V, E) of degree 4. In particular, it is known that the results for Eqs. (10.48), (10.50), and (10.110) on the regular tree graph (V, E) of degree 4 are exact. It is known that Eq. (10.123) always has the trivial solution $\Lambda = 0$, but begins to have some non-trivial solutions in the region of $\frac{J}{k_B T} J > \text{arctanh}\left(\frac{1}{3}\right)$ by expanding the right-hand side of Eq. (10.123) around $\Lambda = 0$ and keeping the first-order term of Λ. In Fig. 10.7, the blue curves correspond to global minimum states that are stable states and the red lines correspond to the local maximum state that are unstable states for each value of $\frac{J}{k_B T}$ in the Bethe free energy $f_{\text{Bethe}}(m, c)$ of Eq. (10.125) for the case of $h = 0$. The Bethe free energy landscapes $f_{\text{Bethe}}(m, c)$ of Eq. (10.125) in the case of $h = 0$ for several values of $\frac{J}{k_B T}$ are shown in Figs. 10.8 and 10.9. It is known that Eq. (10.123) always has the trivial solution $\Lambda = 0$, but begins to have some non-trivial solutions in the region of $\frac{J}{k_B T} > \text{arctanh}\left(\frac{1}{3}\right)$ by expanding the right-hand side of Eq. (10.123) around $\Lambda = 0$ and keeping the first-order term of Λ. In Fig. 10.7, the blue curves correspond to global minimum states that are stable states and the red lines

Loopy Belief Propagation for Ising Model
on Regular Graph (V,E) with Degree 4

$$P\left(s\Big|\frac{J}{k_BT},\frac{h}{k_BT}\right) \propto \left(\prod_{(i,j)\in E}\exp\left(\frac{J}{k_BT}s_is_j\right)\right)\left(\sum_{i\in V}\exp\left(\frac{h}{k_BT}s_i\right)\right) \qquad s_i\in\Omega=\{+1,-1\}$$

$$m_+\equiv\lim_{h\to+0}\lim_{|V|\to+\infty}\frac{1}{|V|}\sum_{i\in V}\sum_s s_iP\left(s\Big|\frac{J}{k_BT},\frac{h}{k_BT}\right)$$

$$u\equiv\lim_{h\to\pm0}\lim_{|V|\to+\infty}\frac{1}{|E|}\sum_{(i,j)\in E}\sum_s(-s_is_j)P\left(s\Big|\frac{J}{k_BT},\frac{h}{k_BT}\right)$$

$$m_-\equiv\lim_{h\to-0}\lim_{|V|\to+\infty}\frac{1}{|V|}\sum_{i\in V}\sum_s s_iP\left(s\Big|\frac{J}{k_BT},\frac{h}{k_BT}\right)$$

—— **Global Minimum State (Stable)**

—— **Local Maximum State (Unstable)** ⎫ for Bethe Free Energy

I. $h\to+0$: $\lim_{\frac{J}{k_BT}\to+\infty}(P_i(+1),P_i(-1))\to(1,0)$

III. $(P_i(+1),P_i(+1))=\left(\frac{1}{2},\frac{1}{2}\right)\left(\forall\frac{J}{k_BT}>0\right)$

II. $h\to-0$: $\lim_{\frac{J}{k_BT}\to+\infty}(P_i(+1),P_i(-1))\to(0,1)$

$$P_i(s_i)\equiv\lim_{|V|\to+\infty}\sum_{s_1\in\Omega}\sum_{s_2\in\Omega}\cdots\sum_{s_{i-1}\in\Omega}\sum_{s_{i+1}\in\Omega}\sum_{s_{i+2}\in\Omega}\cdots\sum_{s_{|V|}\in\Omega}P\left(s\Big|\frac{J}{k_BT},\frac{h}{k_BT}\right)\ (\forall s_i\in\Omega)$$

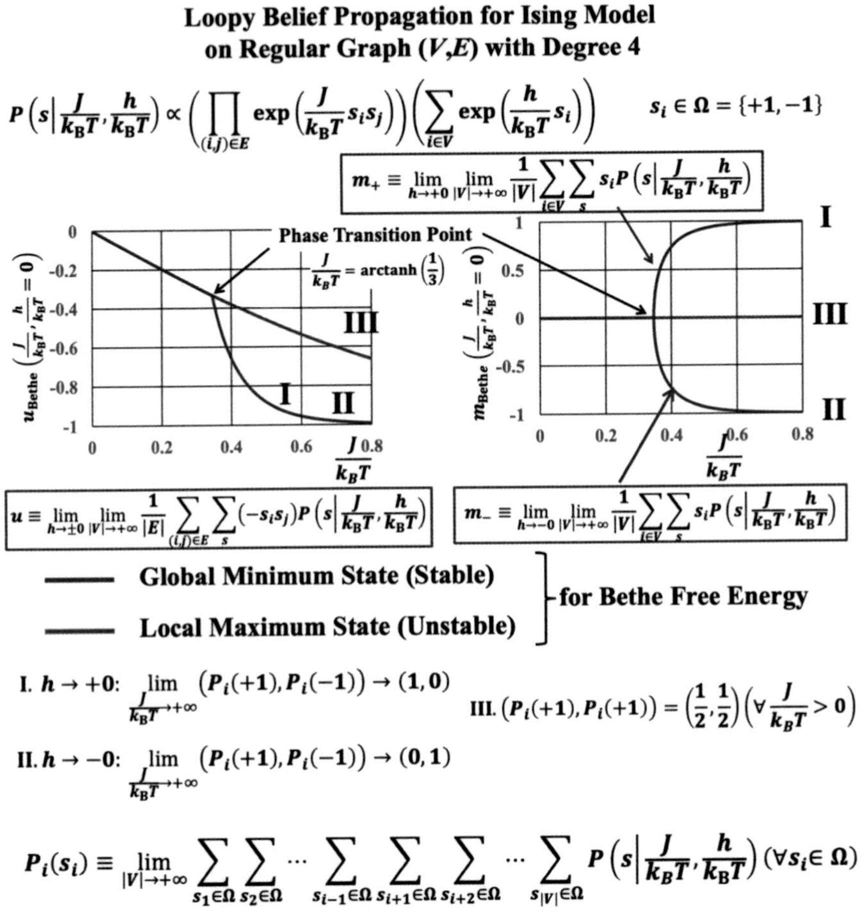

Fig. 10.7 Internal energy u from Eq. (10.113) and magnetization m from Eq. (10.118) in loopy belief propagation (Bethe approximation) for the Ising model in Eqs. (10.48), (10.50), and (10.110) on the regular graph (V,E) of degree 4

correspond to the local maximum state that are unstable states for each value of $\frac{J}{k_BT}$ in the Bethe free energy $f_{\text{Bethe}}(m,c)$ in Eq. (10.125) for the case of $h=0$. The Bethe free energy landscapes $f_{\text{Bethe}}(m,c)$ in Eq. (10.125) in the case of $h=0$ for several values of $\frac{J}{k_BT}$ are shown in Figs. 10.8 and 10.9.

Now we consider the $|\Omega|$-state Potts model [33] given by

$$P\left(s\Big|\frac{J}{k_BT},\frac{h_0}{k_BT},\frac{h_1}{k_BT},\cdots,\frac{h_{|\Omega|-1}}{k_BT}\right)$$
$$=\frac{1}{Z}\left(\prod_{\{i,j\}\in E}\exp\left(\frac{J}{k_BT}\delta_{s_is_j}\right)\right)\left(\prod_{i\in V}\prod_{n\in\Omega}\exp\left(\frac{h_n}{k_BT}\delta_{s_i,n}\right)\right), \qquad (10.132)$$

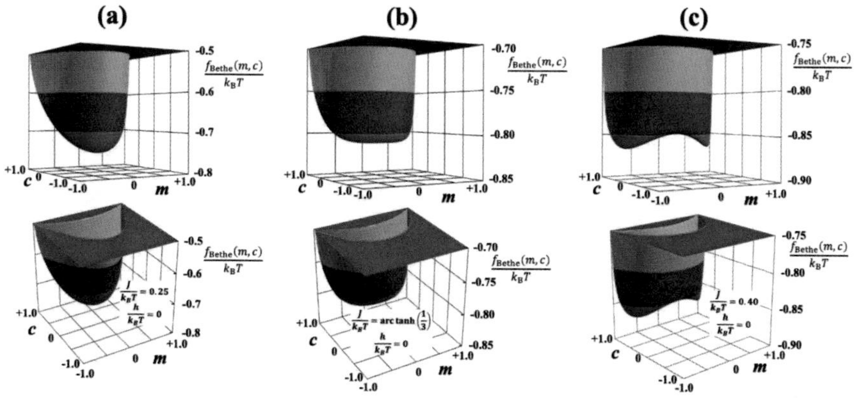

Fig. 10.8 Bethe free energy for $f_{\text{Bethe}}(m, c)$ for the Ising model in Eqs. (10.48), (10.50), and (10.110) on the regular graph (V, E) of degree 4. **a** $\frac{J}{k_B T} = 0.25$, $\frac{h}{k_B T} = 0$. **b** $\frac{J}{k_B T} = \text{arctanh}\left(\frac{1}{3}\right)$, $\frac{h}{k_B T} = 0$. **c** $\frac{J}{k_B T} = 0.4$, $\frac{h}{k_B T} = 0$

$$\hat{c}(m) \equiv \frac{1}{\tanh\left(\frac{2J}{k_B T}\right)} \left(1 - \sqrt{1 - (1 - 2m^2)\tanh^2\left(\frac{2J}{k_B T}\right) - 2m^2 \tanh\left(\frac{2J}{k_B T}\right)}\right)$$

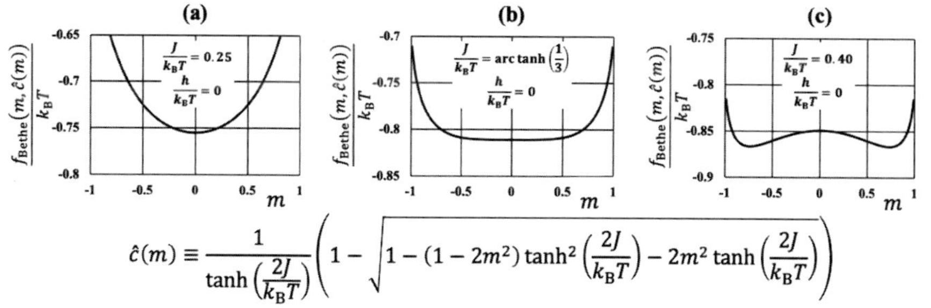

Fig. 10.9 Bethe free energy Extremum $f_{\text{Bethe}}(m, c)$ for the Ising model of Eqs. (10.48), and (10.50) with Eqs. (10.110) on the regular graph (V, E) with degree 4. **a** $\frac{J}{k_B T} = 0.25$, $\frac{h}{k_B T} = 0$. **b** $\frac{J}{k_B T} = \text{arctanh}\left(\frac{1}{3}\right)$, $\frac{h}{k_B T} = 0$. **c** $\frac{J}{k_B T} = 0.4$, $\frac{h}{k_B T} = 0$

$$Z \equiv \sum_{s_1 \in \Omega} \sum_{s_2 \in \Omega} \cdots \sum_{s_{|V|} \in \Omega} \left(\prod_{\{i,j\} \in E} \exp\left(\frac{J}{k_B T}\delta_{s_i s_j}\right)\right)\left(\prod_{i \in V}\prod_{n \in \Omega}\exp\left(\frac{h_n}{k_B T}\delta_{s_i, n}\right)\right), \quad (10.133)$$

where $\Omega = \{0, 1, 2, \cdots, |\Omega| - 1\}$. By similar arguments to those for Eqs. (10.72) and (10.102), the marginal probabilities $\widehat{R}_i(s_i)$ and $\widehat{R}_{ij}(s_i, s_j)$ can be expressed as orthonormal expansions as follows:

$$\widehat{R}_i(s_i) = \left(\frac{1}{|\Omega|}\right) + \sum_{k \in \Omega \setminus \{0\}} m_i^{(k)} \Phi_k(s_i), \quad (10.134)$$

$$\widehat{R}_{ij}(s_i, s_j) = \left(\frac{1}{|\Omega|}\right)^2 + \left(\frac{1}{|\Omega|}\right) \sum_{k\in\Omega\setminus\{0\}} m_i^{(k)} \Phi_k(s_i)$$
$$+ \left(\frac{1}{|\Omega|}\right) \sum_{l\in\Omega\setminus\{0\}} m_j^{(l)} \Phi_l(s_j) + \sum_{k\in\Omega\setminus\{0\}} \sum_{l\in\Omega\setminus\{0\}} c_{ij}^{(k,l)} \Phi_k(s_i)\Phi_l(s_j), \quad (10.135)$$

where $\{\Phi_k(s_i)|s_i\in\Omega, k\in\Omega\}$ is the set of orthonormal polynomials satisfying the following relationships:

$$\Phi_0(s_i) \equiv \left(\frac{1}{|\Omega|}\right), \quad (10.136)$$

$$\sum_{s_i\in\Omega} \Phi_k(s_i)\Phi_l(s_i) = \delta_{k,l} \ (k\in\Omega, l\in\Omega). \quad (10.137)$$

Because it is valid that

$$\sum_{s_i\in\Omega} \sum_{s_i\in\Omega} \Phi_k(s_i)\Phi_l(s_j)\delta_{s_i,s_j} = \sum_{s_i\in\Omega} \Phi_k(s_i)\Phi_l(s_i) = \delta_{k,l} \ (k\in\Omega, l\in\Omega), \quad (10.138)$$

we have the following orthonormal expansion of δ_{s_i,s_j}:

$$\delta_{s_i,s_j} = \sum_{k\in\Omega} \sum_{l\in\Omega} \left(\sum_{s_i'\in\Omega} \sum_{s_j'\in\Omega} \Phi_k(s_i')\Phi_l(s_j')\delta_{s_i',s_j'} \right) \Phi_k(s_i)\Phi_l(s_j)$$
$$= \sum_{k\in\Omega} \Phi_k(s_i)\Phi_k(s_j) \ (s_i\in\Omega, s_j\in\Omega). \quad (10.139)$$

By using Eqs. (10.134) and (10.135) and the orthonormal expansion of the two-body interaction part of the Potts model, the Bethe free energy functional for the Potts model in Eqs. (10.132) and (10.133) can be reduced to

$$\mathcal{F}_{\mathrm{Bethe}}\left[\left\{\widehat{\boldsymbol{R}}_i \middle| i\in V\right\}, \left\{\widehat{\boldsymbol{R}}_{ij} \middle| \{i, j\}\in E\right\}\right]$$
$$= F_{\mathrm{Bethe}}\left(\left\{m_i^{(k)} \middle| i\in V, k\in\Omega\setminus\{0\}\right\}, \left\{c_{\{i,j\}}^{(k,l)} \middle| \{i, j\}\in E, \ k, l\in\Omega\setminus\{0\}\right\}\right), \quad (10.140)$$

where

$$
\begin{aligned}
&F_{\text{Bethe}}\Big(\big\{m_i^{(k)}\big|i\in V,\ k\in\Omega\backslash\{0\}\big\},\ \big\{c_{\{i,j\}}^{(k,l)}\big|\{i,j\}\in E,\ k,l\in\Omega\backslash\{0\}\big\}\Big)\\
&\equiv -J\sum_{i\in V}|\partial i|\left(\frac{1}{|\Omega|}\right)^2 - J\sum_{i\in V}|\partial i|\frac{1}{|\Omega|}\sum_{k\in\Omega\backslash\{0\}} m_i^{(k)} - J\sum_{\{i,j\}\in E}\sum_{k\in\Omega\backslash\{0\}} c_{i,j}^{(k,k)}\\
&+k_{\text{B}}T\sum_{i\in V}(1-|\partial i|)\widehat{R}_i(s_i)\ln\big(\widehat{R}_i(s_i)\big)\\
&+k_{\text{B}}T\sum_{\{i,j\}\in E}\widehat{R}_{ij}(s_i,s_j)\ln\big(\widehat{R}_{ij}(s_i,s_j)\big).
\end{aligned}
\tag{10.141}
$$

For the case of spatially uniformity, $m_i^{(k)}$ and $c_{ij}^{(k,l)}$ are independent of i and $\{i, j\}$ and can be represented by $m^{(k)}$ and $c^{(k,l)}$, respectively, in the Bethe free energy in Eq. (10.141). For the three-state and four-state Potts model, the Bethe free energy in Eq. (10.141) can be represented by

$$
F_{\text{Bethe}}\left(\begin{pmatrix} m^{(1)} \\ m^{(2)} \end{pmatrix}, \begin{pmatrix} c^{(1,1)} & c^{(1,2)} \\ c^{(2,1)} & c^{(2,2)} \end{pmatrix}\right),
\tag{10.142}
$$

and

$$
F_{\text{Bethe}}\left(\begin{pmatrix} m^{(1)} \\ m^{(2)} \\ m^{(3)} \end{pmatrix}, \begin{pmatrix} c^{(1,1)} & c^{(1,2)} & c^{(1,3)} \\ c^{(2,1)} & c^{(2,2)} & c^{(2,3)} \\ c^{(3,1)} & c^{(3,2)} & c^{(3,3)} \end{pmatrix}\right),
\tag{10.143}
$$

respectively. Figures 10.10 and 10.11 show the internal energy with no external fields

$$
u = \lim_{|V|\to+\infty}\frac{1}{|E|}\sum_{\{i,j\}\in E}\sum_{s}\big(-\delta_{s_i,s_j}\big)P\left(s\middle|\frac{J}{k_{\text{B}}T},\frac{h_0}{k_{\text{B}}T}=0,\frac{h_1}{k_{\text{B}}T}=0,\cdots,\frac{h_{|\Omega|-1}}{k_{\text{B}}T}=0\right),
\tag{10.144}
$$

in loopy belief propagation (Bethe approximation) on the regular graph (V, E) of degree 4. We now consider also the moments $m^{(2)}$ and $m^{(1)}$ as **order parameters** for the three-state and four-state Potts model, respectively, for the following cases:

$$
\begin{cases}
\text{(I)} \lim_{h_0\to+0} m^{(2)},\ h_1=h_2=0,\\
\text{(II)} \lim_{h_1\to+0} m^{(2)},\ h_0=h_2=0,\\
\text{(III)} \lim_{h_2\to+0} m^{(2)},\ h_0=h_1=0,\\
\text{(IV)}\ m^{(2)} \text{ under } h_0=h_1=h_2=0 \text{ and } \mu(0)=\mu(1)=\mu(2)=\frac{1}{3},
\end{cases}
\tag{10.145}
$$

for the three-state Potts model, and

$$\begin{cases} \text{(I)} \lim_{h_0 \to +0} m^{(2)}, h_1 = h_2 = h_3 = 0, \\ \text{(II)} \lim_{h_1 \to +0} m^{(2)}, h_0 = h_2 = h_3 = 0, \\ \text{(III)} \lim_{h_2 \to +0} m^{(2)}, h_0 = h_1 = h_3 = 0, \\ \text{(IV)} \lim_{h_3 \to +0} m^{(2)}, h_0 = h_1 = h_2 = 0, \\ \text{(V)}\ m^{(2)} \text{ under } h_0 = h_1 = h_2 = 0 \text{ and } \mu(0) = \mu(1) = \mu(2) = \mu(3) = \frac{1}{4}, \end{cases} \tag{10.146}$$

for the four-state Potts model. These are also shown in Figs. 10.10 and 10.11. In Figs. 10.10 and 10.11, blue, green, and red lines show the global minimum states, local minimum states, and local maximum states, respectively, of the Bethe free energies which are given by Eq. (10.142) for the three-state Potts model and by Eq. (10.143) for the four-state Potts model. In the global minimum states, there exist discontinuous points in $m^{(2)}$ and $m^{(1)}$ as well as u. Although the first derivative Ju of the free energy with respect to $\frac{1}{k_B T}$ is always continuous, the second derivative diverges or has discontinuity in the Ising model as shown in Figs. 10.4, 10.5, and 10.7. This kind of singularity is referred to as a **second-order phase transition** in statistical mechanics. However, the first derivative Ju of the free energy with respect to $\frac{1}{k_B T}$ has a discontinuity as shown in Figs. 10.10 and 10.11. This singularity is referred to as a **first-order phase transition** in statistical mechanics. Figures 10.12 and 10.13 show the Bethe free energy landscapes

$$f_{\text{Bethe}}\left(m^{(1)}, m^{(2)}\right) \equiv \frac{1}{|V|} \underset{\begin{pmatrix} c^{(1,1)} & c^{(1,2)} \\ c^{(2,1)} & c^{(2,2)} \end{pmatrix}}{\text{extremum}} F_{\text{Bethe}}\left(\begin{pmatrix} m^{(1)} \\ m^{(2)} \end{pmatrix}, \begin{pmatrix} c^{(1,1)} & c^{(1,2)} \\ c^{(2,1)} & c^{(2,2)} \end{pmatrix}\right), \tag{10.147}$$

for the three-state Potts model and

$$f_{\text{Bethe}}\left(m^{(1)}, m^{(3)}\right) \equiv \frac{1}{|V|} \underset{m^{(2)}, \begin{pmatrix} c^{(1,1)} & c^{(1,2)} & c^{(1,3)} \\ c^{(2,1)} & c^{(2,2)} & c^{(2,3)} \\ c^{(3,1)} & c^{(3,2)} & c^{(3,3)} \end{pmatrix}}{\text{extremum}} F_{\text{Bethe}}\left(\begin{pmatrix} m^{(1)} \\ m^{(2)} \\ m^{(3)} \end{pmatrix}, \begin{pmatrix} c^{(1,1)} & c^{(1,2)} & c^{(1,3)} \\ c^{(2,1)} & c^{(2,2)} & c^{(2,3)} \\ c^{(3,1)} & c^{(3,2)} & c^{(3,3)} \end{pmatrix}\right), \tag{10.148}$$

for the four-state Potts model, respectively.

10.3.4 Ising Model on a Complete Graph

This section considers a complete graph (V, E) for which the energy function $H(s)$ is defined by

**Loopy Belief Propagation for Three State Potts Model
on Regular Graph (V,E) with Degree 4** $s_i \in \Omega = \{0, 1, 2\}$

$$P\left(s\left|\frac{J}{k_BT}, \frac{h_0}{k_BT}, \frac{h_1}{k_BT}, \frac{h_2}{k_BT}\right.\right) \propto \left(\prod_{(i,j)\in E} \exp\left(\frac{J}{k_BT}\delta_{s_i,s_j}\right)\right)\left(\prod_{i\in V} \exp\left(\sum_{n\in\Omega}\frac{h_n}{k_BT}\delta_{s_i,n}\right)\right)$$

$$m^{(k)} \equiv \lim_{|V|\to+\infty}\frac{1}{|V|}\sum_{i\in V}\sum_s \Phi_k(s_i)P\left(s\left|\frac{J}{k_BT}, \frac{h_0}{k_BT}, \frac{h_1}{k_BT}, \frac{h_2}{k_BT}\right.\right)$$

$$c^{(k,l)} \equiv \lim_{|V|\to+\infty}\frac{1}{|E|}\sum_{(i,j)\in E}\sum_s \Phi_k(s_i)\Phi_l(s_j)P\left(s\left|\frac{J}{k_BT}, \frac{h_0}{k_BT}, \frac{h_1}{k_BT}, \frac{h_2}{k_BT}\right.\right)$$

$$(\Phi_0(0), \Phi_0(1), \Phi_0(2)) \equiv \left(\frac{1}{\sqrt{3}}, \frac{1}{\sqrt{3}}, \frac{1}{\sqrt{3}}\right) \quad (\Phi_1(0), \Phi_1(1), \Phi_1(2)) \equiv \left(\frac{1}{\sqrt{2}}, 0, -\frac{1}{\sqrt{2}}\right) \quad (\Phi_2(0), \Phi_2(1), \Phi_2(2)) \equiv \left(\sqrt{\frac{1}{6}}, -\sqrt{\frac{2}{3}}, \sqrt{\frac{1}{6}}\right)$$

$$u \equiv \lim_{|V|\to+\infty}\frac{1}{|E|}\sum_{(i,j)\in E}\sum_s(-\delta_{s_i,s_j})P\left(s\left|\frac{J}{k_BT}, \frac{h_0}{k_BT}, \frac{h_1}{k_BT}, \frac{h_2}{k_BT}\right.\right) \qquad m^{(2)} \equiv \lim_{|V|\to+\infty}\frac{1}{|V|}\sum_{i\in V}\sum_s\Phi_2(s_i)P\left(s\left|\frac{J}{k_BT}, \frac{h_0}{k_BT}, \frac{h_1}{k_BT}, \frac{h_2}{k_BT}\right.\right)$$

Global Minimum State (Stable)
Local Minimum State (Metastable)   for Bethe Free Energy
Local Maximum State (Unstable)

$$F_{\text{Bethe}}\left(\begin{pmatrix} m^{(1)} \\ m^{(2)} \end{pmatrix}, \begin{pmatrix} c^{(1,1)} & c^{(1,2)} \\ c^{(2,1)} & c^{(2,2)} \end{pmatrix}\right)$$

I. $h_0 \to +0, h_1 = h_2 = 0$: $\displaystyle\lim_{\frac{J}{k_BT}\to+\infty} (P_i(0), P_i(1), P_i(2)) = (1, 0, 0)$

II. $h_1 \to +0, h_0 = h_2 = 0$: $\displaystyle\lim_{\frac{J}{k_BT}\to+\infty} (P_i(0), P_i(1), P_i(2)) = (0, 1, 0)$

III. $h_2 \to +0, h_0 = h_1 = 0$: $\displaystyle\lim_{\frac{J}{k_BT}\to+\infty} (P_i(0), P_i(1), P_i(2)) = (0, 0, 1)$

IV. $(P_i(0), P_i(1), P_i(2))$
$= \left(\frac{1}{3}, \frac{1}{3}, \frac{1}{3}\right)\left(\forall \frac{J}{k_BT} > 0\right)$

$$P_i(s_i) \equiv \lim_{|V|\to+\infty}\sum_{s_1\in\Omega}\sum_{s_2\in\Omega}\cdots\sum_{s_{i-1}\in\Omega}\sum_{s_{i+1}\in\Omega}\sum_{s_{i+2}\in\Omega}\cdots\sum_{s_{|V|}\in\Omega}P\left(s\left|\frac{J}{k_BT}, \frac{h_0}{k_BT}, \frac{h_1}{k_BT}, \frac{h_2}{k_BT}\right.\right) \quad (\forall s_i\in\Omega)$$

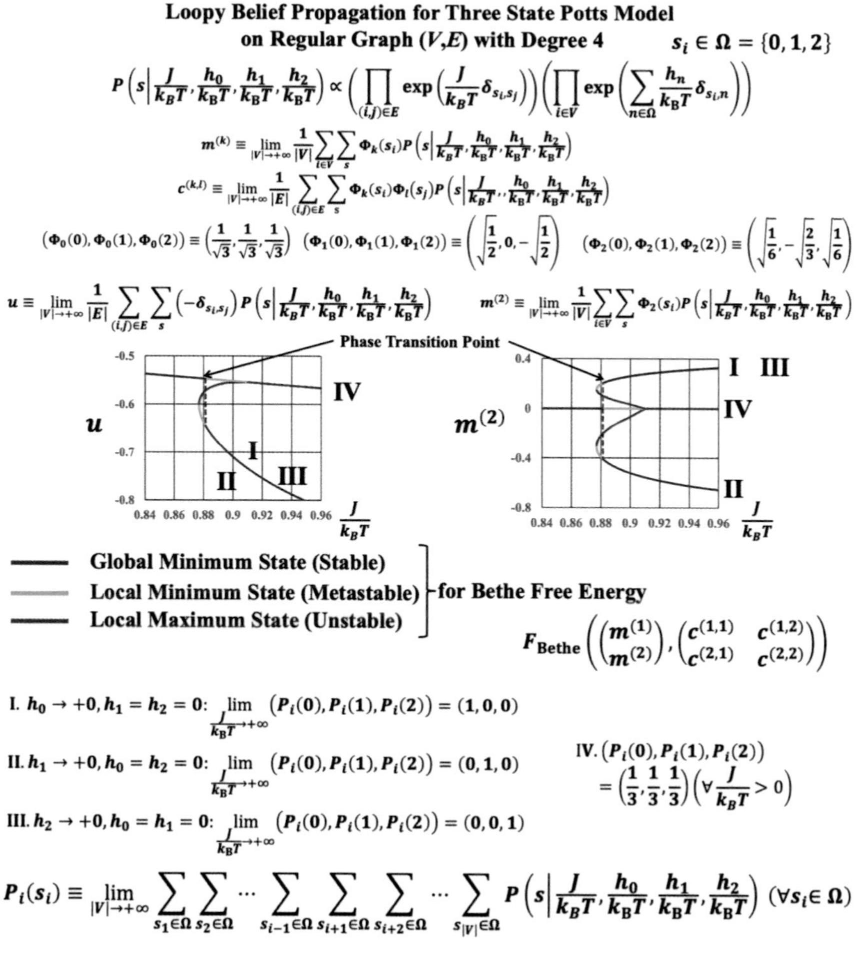

Fig. 10.10 Internal energy u in Eq. (10.144) and (I) $\displaystyle\lim_{h_0\to+0} m^{(2)}$ for $h_1 = h_2 = 0$, (II) $\displaystyle\lim_{h_1\to+0} m^{(2)}$ for $h_0 = h_2 = 0$, (III) $\displaystyle\lim_{h_2\to+0} m^{(2)}$ for $h_0 = h_1 = 0$, (IV) $m^{(2)}$ under $h_0 = h_1 = h_2 = 0$ and $\mu(0) = \mu(1) = \mu(2) = \frac{1}{3}$ such that $P_i(0) = P_i(1) = P_i(2)$ in loopy belief propagation (Bethe approximation) for the three-state Potts model in Eqs. (10.132) and (10.133) on the regular graph (V, E) of degree 4

$$H(s) = H(s_1, s_2, \cdots, s_{|V|}) \equiv -\frac{J}{|V|}\sum_{\{i,j\}\in E} s_i s_j - h\sum_{i\in V} s_i \quad (J > 0), \quad (10.149)$$

instead of Eq. (10.110) in Eqs. (10.109) and (10.111). Note that the interaction between every pair of connected nodes is set to $\frac{J}{|V|}$ to guarantee the existence of the thermodynamic limit in $|V| \to +\infty$ for the complete graph in the sense of Ruelle in Ref. [38].

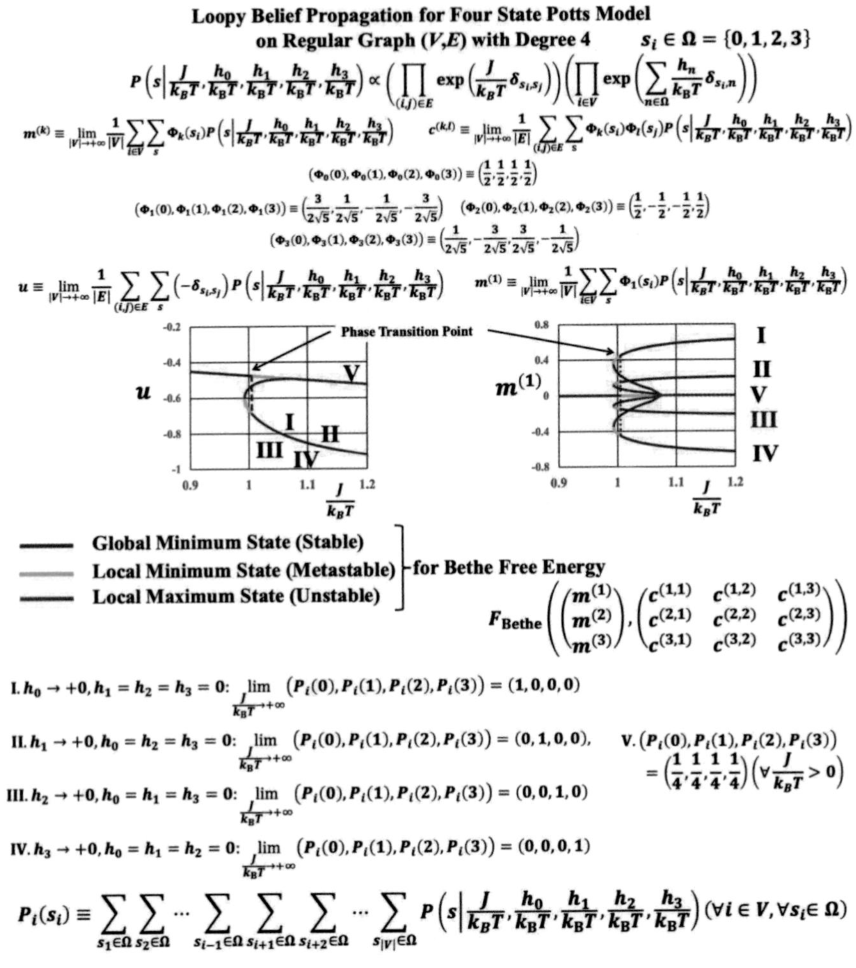

Fig. 10.11 Internal energy u in Eq. (10.144) and order parameter $m^{(1)}$ in loopy belief propagation (Bethe approximation) for the four-state Potts model in Eqs. (10.132) and (10.133) on the regular graph (V, E) of degree 4

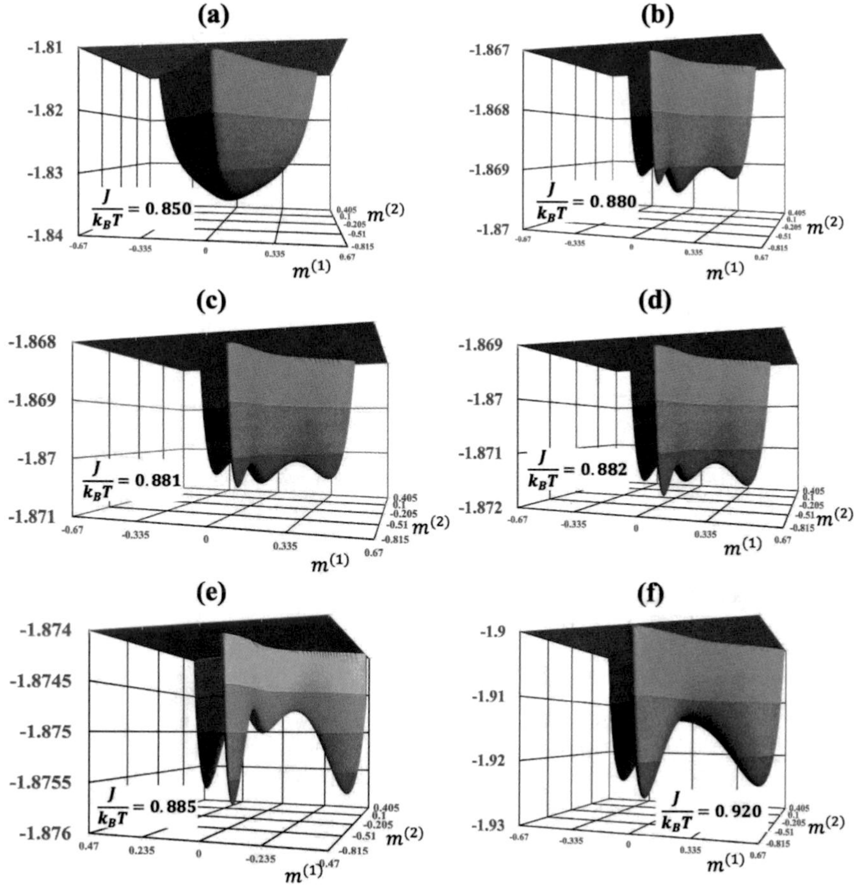

Fig. 10.12 Bethe free energy for $f_{\text{Bethe}}(m^{(1)}, m^{(2)})$ for the three-state Potts model in Eqs. (10.132) and (10.133) on the regular graph (V, E) of degree 4. **a** $\frac{J}{k_BT} = 0.850$. **b** $\frac{J}{k_BT} = 0.880$. **c** $\frac{J}{k_BT} = 0.881$. **d** $\frac{J}{k_BT} = 0.882$. **e** $\frac{J}{k_BT} = 0.885$. **f** $\frac{J}{k_BT} = 0.920$

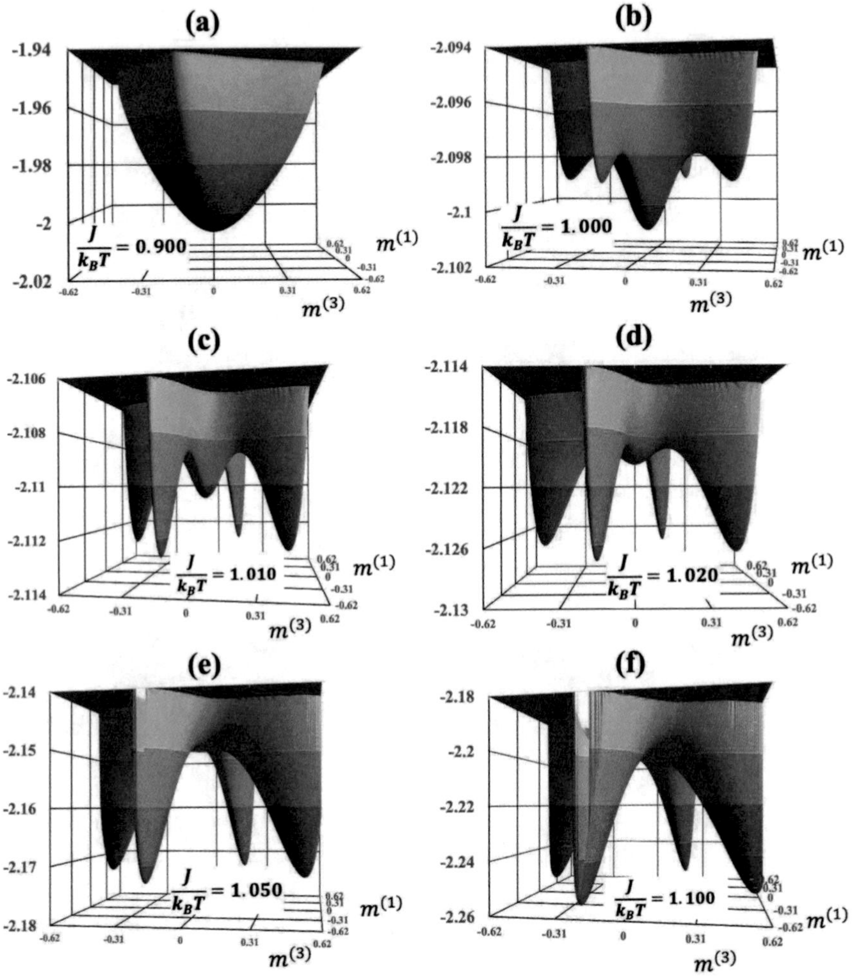

Fig. 10.13 Bethe free energy for $f_{\text{Bethe}}(m^{(1)}, m^{(2)})$ for the four-state Potts model in Eqs. (10.132) and (10.133) on the regular graph (V, E) of degree 4. **a** $\frac{J}{k_B T} = 0.900$. **b** $\frac{J}{k_B T} = 1.000$. **c** $\frac{J}{k_B T} = 1.010$. **d** $\frac{J}{k_B T} = 1.020$. **e** $\frac{J}{k_B T} = 1.050$. **f** $\frac{J}{k_B T} = 1.100$

The free energy in Eq. (10.55) is expressed as follows:

$$
\begin{aligned}
&-k_{\mathrm{B}}T\ln\left(Z\left(\frac{J}{k_{\mathrm{B}}T},\frac{h}{k_{\mathrm{B}}T}\right)\right)\\
&=-k_{\mathrm{B}}T\ln\left(\sum_{\tau_1\in\Omega}\sum_{\tau_2\in\Omega}\cdots\sum_{\tau_{|V|}\in\Omega}\exp\left(\frac{h}{k_{\mathrm{B}}T}\sum_{i\in V}\tau_i+\frac{J}{|V|k_{\mathrm{B}}T}\sum_{\{i,j\}\in E}\tau_i\tau_j\right)\right)\\
&=\frac{J}{2}-k_{\mathrm{B}}T\ln\left(\sum_{\tau_1\in\Omega}\sum_{\tau_2\in\Omega}\cdots\sum_{\tau_{|V|}\in\Omega}\exp\left(\frac{h}{k_{\mathrm{B}}T}\sum_{i\in V}\tau_i\right)\exp\left(\frac{1}{2}\left(\sqrt{\frac{J}{|V|k_{\mathrm{B}}T}}\sum_{i\in V}\tau_i\right)^2\right)\right).
\end{aligned}
\tag{10.150}
$$

By using the Gauss integral formula

$$
\frac{1}{\sqrt{2\pi}}\int_{-\infty}^{+\infty}\exp\left(-\frac{1}{2}x^2+ax\right)dx=\exp\left(\frac{1}{2}a^2\right),
\tag{10.151}
$$

the expression for the free energy is rewritten as

$$
\begin{aligned}
&-k_{\mathrm{B}}T\ln\left(Z\left(\frac{J}{k_{\mathrm{B}}T},\frac{h}{k_{\mathrm{B}}T}\right)\right)\\
&=\frac{1}{2}J-\ln\Bigg(\sum_{\tau_1\in\Omega}\sum_{\tau_2\in\Omega}\cdots\sum_{\tau_{|V|}\in\Omega}\frac{1}{\sqrt{2\pi}}\int_{-\infty}^{+\infty}e^{-\frac{1}{2}x^2}\\
&\qquad\times\exp\left(\sum_{i\in V}\left(\sqrt{\frac{J}{|V|k_{\mathrm{B}}T}}x+\frac{h}{k_{\mathrm{B}}T}\right)\tau_i\right)dx\Bigg)\\
&=\frac{1}{2}J-\ln\left(\frac{1}{\sqrt{2\pi}}\int_{-\infty}^{+\infty}e^{-\frac{1}{2}x^2}\prod_{i\in V}\left(\sum_{\tau_i\in\Omega}\exp\left(\left(\sqrt{\frac{J}{|V|k_{\mathrm{B}}T}}x+\frac{h}{k_{\mathrm{B}}T}\right)\tau_i\right)\right)dx\right)\\
&=\frac{1}{2}J-\ln\left(\frac{1}{\sqrt{2\pi}}\int_{-\infty}^{+\infty}e^{-\frac{1}{2}x^2}\prod_{i\in V}\left(2\cosh\left(\sqrt{\frac{J}{|V|k_{\mathrm{B}}T}}x+\frac{h}{k_{\mathrm{B}}T}\right)\right)dx\right).
\end{aligned}
\tag{10.152}
$$

Note that the procedure in which a new continuous variable x is introduced in Eq. (10.152) is referred to as a **Hubbard-Stratonovich transformation** [13]. Moreover, by replacing the variable x by $y=x\sqrt{|V|\left(\frac{k_{\mathrm{B}}T}{J}\right)}$, the free energy can be written as

$$
-k_{\mathrm{B}}T\ln\left(Z\left(\frac{J}{k_{\mathrm{B}}T},\frac{h}{k_{\mathrm{B}}T}\right)\right)=\frac{1}{2}J-\ln\left(\frac{1}{\sqrt{2\pi}}\int_{-\infty}^{+\infty}\exp(|V|\psi(y))dy\right),
\tag{10.153}
$$

where

$$
\psi(y)\equiv-\frac{1}{2}\left(\frac{J}{k_{\mathrm{B}}T}\right)y^2+\frac{1}{|V|}\sum_{i\in V}\ln\left(2\cosh\left(\frac{1}{k_{\mathrm{B}}T}(Jy+h)\right)\right).
\tag{10.154}
$$

We now consider the magnetization $m\left(\frac{J}{k_{\mathrm{B}}T},\frac{h}{k_{\mathrm{B}}T}\right)=\lim_{|V|\to+\infty}\frac{1}{|V|}\sum_{i\in V}\sum_{s_1\in\Omega}\sum_{s_2\in\Omega}\cdots\sum_{s_{|V|}\in\Omega}s_iP\left(s\middle|\frac{J}{k_{\mathrm{B}}T},\frac{h}{k_{\mathrm{B}}T}\right)$ for Eqs. (10.109) and (10.111) with Eq. (10.149) as follows:

$$\begin{aligned}m\left(\frac{J}{k_{\mathrm{B}}T},\frac{h}{k_{\mathrm{B}}T}\right)&=\lim_{|V|\to+\infty}\frac{1}{|V|}\frac{\partial}{\partial\left(\frac{h}{k_{\mathrm{B}}T}\right)}\left(-k_{\mathrm{B}}T\ln\left(Z\left(\frac{J}{k_{\mathrm{B}}T},\frac{h}{k_{\mathrm{B}}T}\right)\right)\right)\\&=\lim_{|V|\to+\infty}\frac{\int_{-\infty}^{+\infty}\exp\left(|V|\left(\psi(y)+\frac{1}{|V|}\ln\left(\tanh\left(\frac{1}{k_{\mathrm{B}}T}(Jy+h)\right)\right)\right)\right)dy}{\int_{-\infty}^{+\infty}\exp(|V|\psi(y))dy}.\end{aligned}\tag{10.155}$$

Because it is valid that

$$\begin{aligned}\lim_{|V|\to+\infty}\frac{\partial}{\partial y}\psi(y)&=\lim_{|V|\to+\infty}\frac{\partial}{\partial y}\left(\psi(y)+\frac{1}{|V|}\ln\left(\tanh\left(\frac{1}{k_{\mathrm{B}}T}(Jy+h)\right)\right)\right)\\&=-\frac{J}{k_{\mathrm{B}}T}\left(y-\tanh\left(\frac{1}{k_{\mathrm{B}}T}(Jy+h)\right)\right),\end{aligned}\tag{10.156}$$

we obtain the magnetization as

$$\begin{aligned}m\left(\frac{J}{k_{\mathrm{B}}T},\frac{h}{k_{\mathrm{B}}T}\right)&=\lim_{|V|\to+\infty}\frac{\exp\left(|V|\left(\psi(y_{\max})+\frac{1}{|V|}\ln\left(\tanh\left(\frac{1}{k_{\mathrm{B}}T}(Jy_{\max}+h)\right)\right)\right)\right)}{\exp\left(|V|\psi(y_{\max})\right)}\\&=\tanh\left(\frac{1}{k_{\mathrm{B}}T}(Jy_{\max}+h)\right),\end{aligned}\tag{10.157}$$

where

$$y_{\max}=\tanh\left(\frac{1}{k_{\mathrm{B}}T}(Jy_{\max}+h)\right)\tag{10.158}$$

by using a **saddle point method** [37]. Equations (10.157) and (10.158) reduce to the following mean-field equation for $m\left(\frac{J}{k_{\mathrm{B}}T},\frac{h}{k_{\mathrm{B}}T}\right)$:

$$m\left(\frac{J}{k_{\mathrm{B}}T},\frac{h}{k_{\mathrm{B}}T}\right)=\tanh\left(\frac{1}{k_{\mathrm{B}}T}\left(Jm\left(\frac{J}{k_{\mathrm{B}}T},\frac{h}{k_{\mathrm{B}}T}\right)+h\right)\right).\tag{10.159}$$

This means that it is possible to treat the Ising model on the complete graph in the thermodynamic limit analytically using the mean-field method.

By combining the replica method with the Hubbard-Stratonovich transformation and the saddle point method, it is possible to treat the random average in Eq. (10.25) for the Ising model with non-uniform external fields on the complete graph analytically [13, 76]. In statistical mechanics, this kind of approach has been developed as the **spin glass theory** [77–80]. Such computational techniques that use the replica method for Ising models with spatially non-uniform interactions and external fields on the complete graph have been used to estimate statistical performance analysis for many probabilistic information processing systems [13, 15–17].

Next, we consider the belief propagation method for the Ising model on the complete graph in Eq. (10.149) with Eqs. (10.109) and (10.111). For an infinitesimal small $|V|^{-1}$, the message passing rule in Eq. (10.95) can be expanded to

$$\begin{aligned}
\mu_{j\to i}(s_i) &= \frac{Z_i}{Z_{\{i,j\}}}\sum_{\tau_j\in\Omega}\left(\prod_{l\in\partial j\backslash\{i\}}\mu_{l\to j}(\tau_j)\right)\exp\left(\frac{1}{k_{\mathrm{B}}T}\left(\frac{J}{|V|}s_i\tau_j+h\tau_j\right)\right)\\
&= \frac{Z_i}{Z_{\{i,j\}}}\sum_{\tau_j\in\Omega}\left(\prod_{l\in\partial j\backslash\{i\}}\mu_{l\to j}(\tau_j)\right)\exp\left(\frac{h}{k_{\mathrm{B}}T}\tau_j\right)\left(1+\frac{1}{|V|}\frac{J}{k_{\mathrm{B}}T}s_i\tau_j+\mathcal{O}\left(|V|^{-2}\right)\right)\\
&= \frac{Z_iZ_j}{Z_{\{i,j\}}}\sum_{\tau_j\in\Omega}\widehat{R}_j(\tau_j)\left(1+\frac{1}{|V|}\frac{J}{k_{\mathrm{B}}T}s_i\tau_j+\mathcal{O}\left(|V|^{-2}\right)\right)\\
&= \frac{Z_iZ_j}{Z_{\{i,j\}}}\left(1+\frac{1}{k_{\mathrm{B}}T}\left(\frac{J}{|V|}\sum_{\tau_j\in\Omega}\tau_j\widehat{R}_j(\tau_j)\right)s_i+\mathcal{O}\left(|V|^{-2}\right)\right)\\
&= \frac{Z_iZ_j}{Z_{\{i,j\}}}\left(\exp\left(\frac{1}{k_{\mathrm{B}}T}\left(\frac{J}{|V|}\sum_{\tau_j\in\Omega}\tau_j\widehat{R}_j(\tau_j)\right)s_i\right)+\mathcal{O}\left(|V|^{-2}\right)\right).
\end{aligned}\tag{10.160}$$

By substituting Eq. (10.160) into Eq. (10.91), the marginal probabilities can be expressed as follows:

$$\begin{aligned}
\widehat{R}_i(s_i) &= \frac{\exp\left(\frac{1}{k_{\mathrm{B}}T}\left(\frac{J}{|V|}\sum_{j\in V\backslash\{i\}}\sum_{\tau_j\in\Omega}\tau_j\widehat{R}_j(\tau_j)+h\right)s_i\right)}{\sum_{\tau_i\in\Omega}\exp\left(\frac{1}{k_{\mathrm{B}}T}\left(\frac{J}{|V|}\sum_{j\in V\backslash\{i\}}\sum_{\tau_j\in\Omega}\tau_j\widehat{R}_j(\tau_j)+h\right)\tau_i\right)}\\
&\quad+\mathcal{O}\left(|V|^{-1}\right)\ (|V|\to+\infty,\ s_i\in\Omega, i\in V),
\end{aligned}\tag{10.161}$$

$$\widehat{R}_{ij}(s_i,s_j)=\widehat{R}_i(s_i)\widehat{R}_j(s_j)+\mathcal{O}\left(|V|^{-1}\right)\ (|V|\to+\infty,\ s_i\in\Omega, s_j\in\Omega, \{i,j\}\in E).\tag{10.162}$$

Equation (10.161) can be regarded as a system of simultaneous deterministic equations for $\left\{\widehat{R}_i(s_i)\middle|s_i\in\Omega, i\in V\right\}$ and is equivalent to the mean-field equation in Eq. (10.68) for Eq. (10.149) with Eqs. (10.109) and (10.111).

10.3.5 Probabilistic Segmentation by Potts Prior and Loopy Belief Propagation

In Sect. 10.2.3, we gave the fundamental framework of probabilistic segmentation based on the Potts prior, and reduced the framework of the EM procedure for estimating hyperparameters to the extremum conditions of the $\mathcal{Q}$-function as shown in Eqs. (10.41), (10.42), and (10.43) with Eqs. (10.44), (10.45), and (10.46). These frameworks can be realized by combining them with the loopy belief propagation in Sect. 10.3.2 to give the following practical procedures [70]:

Probabilistic segmentation algorithm (Input : $\boldsymbol{D}$**, Output :** $\widehat{\alpha}(\boldsymbol{D}), \widehat{u}(\boldsymbol{D}), \widehat{\boldsymbol{a}}(\boldsymbol{D}), \widehat{\boldsymbol{C}}(\boldsymbol{D}), \widehat{s}(\boldsymbol{D})$**)**

Step 1: Input the data vector $\boldsymbol{d}$ and set the initial values of hyperparameters $\widehat{\alpha}(\boldsymbol{D})$, $\widehat{\boldsymbol{a}}(\boldsymbol{D})$, $\widehat{\boldsymbol{C}}(\boldsymbol{D})$ and messages in the loopy belief propagation $\{\widehat{\mu}_{j\to i}(s_i, \boldsymbol{D})|i\in V, j\in\partial i, s_i\in\Omega\}$ for the posterior probability distribution. We set $t \leftarrow 0$ as the number of iterations of the EM procedure.

Step 2 (E-step) Set $t \leftarrow t+1$ and update $\widehat{u}(\boldsymbol{D}), \widehat{\boldsymbol{a}}(\boldsymbol{D}), \widehat{\boldsymbol{C}}(\boldsymbol{D}), \{\widehat{\mu}_{j\to i}(s_i, \boldsymbol{D})|s_i\in\Omega, i\in\mathcal{V}, j\in\partial i\}$ using the following procedures:

$$\mu_{j\to i}(s_i) \leftarrow \frac{\sum_{\tau_j\in\Omega}\exp\big(2\widehat{\alpha}(\boldsymbol{D})\delta_{s_i,\tau_j}\big)g\big(\boldsymbol{d}_j\big|\tau_j, \widehat{\boldsymbol{a}}(\tau_j, \boldsymbol{D}), \widehat{\boldsymbol{C}}(\tau_j, \boldsymbol{D})\big)\prod_{k\in\partial j\setminus\{i\}}\widehat{\mu}_{k\to j}(\tau_j, \boldsymbol{D})}{\sum_{\tau_i\in\Omega}\sum_{\tau_j\in\Omega}\exp\big(2\widehat{\alpha}(\boldsymbol{D})\delta_{\tau_i,\tau_j}\big)g\big(\boldsymbol{d}_j\big|\tau_j, \widehat{\boldsymbol{a}}(\tau_j, \boldsymbol{D}), \widehat{\boldsymbol{C}}(\tau_j, \boldsymbol{D})\big)\prod_{k\in\partial j\setminus\{i\}}\widehat{\mu}_{k\to j}(\tau_j, \boldsymbol{D})}$$
$$(s_i\in\Omega, i\in V, j\in\partial i), \tag{10.163}$$

$$\widehat{\mu}_{j\to i}(s_i, \boldsymbol{D}) \leftarrow \mu_{j\to i}(s_i)\ (s_i\in\Omega,\ i\in V,\ j\in\partial i), \tag{10.164}$$

$$B_i \leftarrow \sum_{\tau_i\in\Omega} g\big(\boldsymbol{d}_i\big|\tau_i, \widehat{\boldsymbol{a}}(\tau_i, \boldsymbol{D}), \widehat{\boldsymbol{\sigma}}(\tau_i, \boldsymbol{D})\big)\prod_{k\in\partial i}\widehat{\mu}_{k\to i}(\tau_i, \boldsymbol{D})\ \ (i\in V), \tag{10.165}$$

$$\begin{aligned} B_{\{i,j\}} \leftarrow \sum_{\tau_i\in\Omega}\sum_{\tau_j\in\Omega}&\Big(\prod_{k\in\partial i\setminus\{j\}}\widehat{\mu}_{k\to i}(\tau_i, \boldsymbol{D})\Big)g\big(\boldsymbol{d}_i\big|\tau_i, \widehat{\boldsymbol{a}}(\tau_i, \boldsymbol{D}), \widehat{\boldsymbol{C}}(\tau_i, \boldsymbol{D})\big)\\ &\times\exp\Big(2\widehat{\alpha}(\boldsymbol{D})\delta_{\tau_i,\tau_j}\Big)\\ &\times g\big(\boldsymbol{d}_j\big|\tau_j, \widehat{\boldsymbol{a}}(\tau_j, \boldsymbol{D}), \widehat{\boldsymbol{C}}(\tau_j, \boldsymbol{D})\big)\Big(\prod_{k\in\partial j\setminus\{i\}}\widehat{\mu}_{k\to j}(\tau_j, \boldsymbol{D})\Big)\ (\{i,j\}\in E), \end{aligned} \tag{10.166}$$

$$\boldsymbol{a}(s_i) \leftarrow \frac{\displaystyle\sum_{i\in V}\frac{1}{B_i}\boldsymbol{d}_i g\big(\boldsymbol{d}_i\big|s_i,\widehat{\boldsymbol{a}}(s_i,\boldsymbol{D}),\widehat{\boldsymbol{C}}(s_i,\boldsymbol{D})\big)\Big(\prod_{k\in\partial i}\widehat{\mu}_{k\to i}(s_i,\boldsymbol{D})\Big)}{\displaystyle\sum_{i\in V}\frac{1}{B_i}g\big(\boldsymbol{d}_i\big|s_i,\boldsymbol{a}(s_i,\boldsymbol{D}),\boldsymbol{C}(s_i,\boldsymbol{D})\big)\Big(\prod_{k\in\partial i}\widehat{\mu}_{k\to i}(s_i,\boldsymbol{D})\Big)}\ (s_i\in\Omega),\tag{10.167}$$

$$\boldsymbol{C}(s_i) \leftarrow \frac{\displaystyle\sum_{i\in V}\frac{1}{B_i}(\boldsymbol{d}_i-\widehat{a}(s_i,\boldsymbol{D}))(\boldsymbol{d}_i-\widehat{a}(s_i,\boldsymbol{D}))^{\mathrm{T}} g\big(\boldsymbol{d}_i\big|s_i,\widehat{\boldsymbol{a}}(s_i,\boldsymbol{D}),\widehat{\boldsymbol{C}}(s_i,\boldsymbol{D})\big)\Big(\prod_{k\in\partial i}\widehat{\mu}_{k\to i}(s_i,\boldsymbol{D})\Big)}{\displaystyle\sum_{i\in V}\frac{1}{B_i}g\big(\boldsymbol{d}_i\big|s_i,\widehat{\boldsymbol{a}}(s_i,\boldsymbol{D}),\widehat{\boldsymbol{C}}(s_i,\boldsymbol{D})\big)\Big(\prod_{k\in\partial i}\widehat{\mu}_{k\to i}(s_i,\boldsymbol{D})\Big)}\ (s_i\in\Omega),\tag{10.168}$$

$$\begin{aligned}\widehat{u}(\boldsymbol{D}) \leftarrow \frac{1}{|E|}\sum_{\{i,j\}\in E}\Bigg(&\frac{1}{B_{\{i,j\}}}\sum_{\tau_i\in\Omega}\sum_{\tau_j\in\Omega}(-\delta_{\tau_i,\tau_j})\exp\big(2\widehat{\alpha}(\boldsymbol{D})\delta_{\tau_i,\tau_j}\big)\\&\times\Big(\prod_{k\in\partial i\backslash\{j\}}\widehat{\mu}_{k\to i}(\tau_i,\boldsymbol{D})\Big)g\big(\boldsymbol{d}_i\big|\tau_i,\widehat{\boldsymbol{a}}(\tau_i,\boldsymbol{D}),\widehat{\boldsymbol{C}}(\tau_i,\boldsymbol{D})\big)\\&\times\Big(\prod_{k\in\partial j\backslash\{i\}}\widehat{\mu}_{k\to j}(\tau_j,\boldsymbol{D})\Big)g\big(\boldsymbol{d}_j\big|\tau_j,\widehat{\boldsymbol{a}}(\tau_j,\boldsymbol{D}),\widehat{\boldsymbol{C}}(\tau_j,\boldsymbol{D})\big)\Bigg),\end{aligned}\tag{10.169}$$

$$\widehat{\boldsymbol{a}}(s_i,\boldsymbol{D}) \leftarrow \boldsymbol{a}(s_i)\ (s_i\in\Omega),\tag{10.170}$$

$$\widehat{\boldsymbol{C}}(s_i,\boldsymbol{D}) \leftarrow \boldsymbol{C}(s_i)\ (s_i\in\Omega).\tag{10.171}$$

Here, $g\big(\boldsymbol{d}_i\big|\xi,\widehat{\boldsymbol{a}}(\xi,\boldsymbol{D}),\widehat{\boldsymbol{C}}(\xi,\boldsymbol{D})\big)$ is defined by Eq. (10.31) for each state $\xi(\in\Omega)$.

Step 3 (M-step): Set the initial values of the messages $\{\widehat{\lambda}(\xi)|\xi\in\Omega\}$ in the loopy belief propagation for the Potts prior and repeat the following procedure until $\widehat{\alpha}(\boldsymbol{d})$ and $\{\widehat{\lambda}(\xi)|\xi\in\Omega\}$ converge:

$$\lambda(s_i) \leftarrow \frac{\displaystyle\sum_{\tau_j\in\Omega}\exp\big(2\widehat{\alpha}(\boldsymbol{D})\delta_{s_i,\tau_j}\big)\widehat{\lambda}(\tau_j,\boldsymbol{D})^3}{\displaystyle\sum_{\tau_i\in\Omega}\sum_{\tau_j\in\Omega}\exp\big(2\widehat{\alpha}(\boldsymbol{D})\delta_{\tau_i,\tau_j}\big)\widehat{\lambda}(\tau_j,\boldsymbol{D})^3}\ (s_i\in\Omega),\tag{10.172}$$

$$\widehat{\lambda}(s_i, \boldsymbol{d}) \leftarrow \lambda(s_i)\ (s_i \in \Omega), \tag{10.173}$$

$$\widehat{\alpha}(\boldsymbol{D}) \leftarrow \widehat{\alpha}(\boldsymbol{D}) \times \left(\frac{1}{1+\widehat{u}(\boldsymbol{D})} \frac{\sum_{\tau_i \in \Omega} \sum_{\tau_j \in \Omega} (1-\delta_{\tau_i,\tau_j}) \widehat{\lambda}(\tau_i, \boldsymbol{D})^3 \exp\Big(2\widehat{\alpha}(\boldsymbol{D})\delta_{\tau_i,\tau_j}\Big) \widehat{\lambda}(\tau_j, \boldsymbol{D})^3}{\sum_{\tau_i \in \Omega} \sum_{\tau_j \in \Omega} \widehat{\lambda}(\tau_i, \boldsymbol{D})^3 \exp\Big(2\widehat{\alpha}(\boldsymbol{D})\delta_{\tau_i,\tau_j}\Big) \widehat{\lambda}(\tau_j, \boldsymbol{D})^3} \right)^{1/4}. \tag{10.174}$$

Step 4 Compute the output $\widehat{\boldsymbol{s}}(\boldsymbol{D}) = \big(\widehat{s_1}(\boldsymbol{D}), \widehat{s_2}(\boldsymbol{D}), \cdots, \widehat{s_{|V|}}(\boldsymbol{D})\big)$ as follows:

$$\widehat{s_i}(\boldsymbol{D}) \leftarrow \underset{s_i \in \Omega}{\operatorname{argmax}}\ g\Big(\boldsymbol{d}_i \Big| s_i, \widehat{\boldsymbol{a}}(s_i, \boldsymbol{D}), \widehat{\boldsymbol{C}}(s_i, \boldsymbol{D})\Big) \prod_{k \in \partial i} \widehat{\mu}_{k \to i}(s_i, \boldsymbol{D})\ (i \in V). \tag{10.175}$$

Stop if the hyperparameters $\widehat{\alpha}(\boldsymbol{D}), \widehat{\boldsymbol{a}}(s_i, \boldsymbol{D})\ (s_i \in \Omega)$, and $\widehat{\boldsymbol{C}}(s_i, \boldsymbol{D})\ (s_i \in \Omega)$ converge and return to **Step 2** otherwise.

Some of the numerical experimental results are shown in Fig. 10.14. The Potts prior has the first-order phase transition as shown in Sect. 10.3.6. Figure 10.14 shows how the hyperparameter $2\alpha = \frac{J}{k_B T}$ converges in the EM procedure with loopy belief propagation under the first-order phase transition.

10.3.6 Real-Space Renormalization Group Method and Sublinear Modeling of Statistical Machine Learning

First, we explore the most fundamental real-space renormalization procedure for the Ising model in Eq. (10.49) on the ring graph (V, E), where

$$E \equiv \Big\{\{1,2\}, \{2,3\}, \{3,4\}, \cdots, \{|V|-1, |V|\}, \{|V|, 1\}\Big\}, \tag{10.176}$$

in the case of $|V| = 2^L$. We have the following equality:

$$\begin{aligned}
&\sum_{s_2 \in \Omega} \sum_{s_4 \in \Omega} \sum_{s_6 \in \Omega} \cdots \sum_{s_{|V|} \in \Omega} \prod_{\{i,j\} \in E} \exp\left(\frac{1}{k_B T} J s_i s_{i+1}\right) \\
&= \left(\sum_{s_2 \in \Omega} \exp\left(\frac{1}{k_B T} J (s_1 + s_3) s_2\right)\right) \left(\sum_{s_4 \in \Omega} \exp\left(\frac{1}{k_B T} J (s_3 + s_5) s_4\right)\right) \\
&\quad \times \cdots \times \left(\sum_{s_{|V|} \in \Omega} \exp\left(\frac{1}{k_B T} J \big(s_{|V|-3} + s_{|V|-1}\big) s_{|V|-2}\right)\right)
\end{aligned}$$

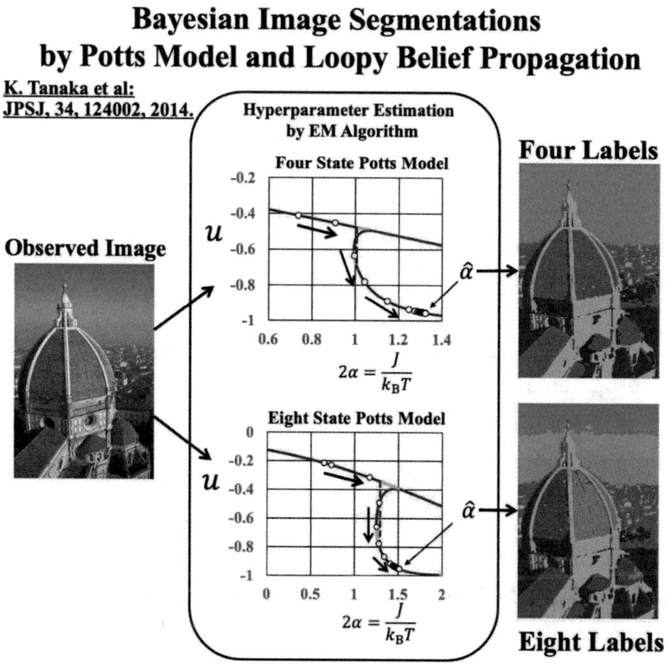

Fig. 10.14 Numerical experimental results of probabilistic segmentations by Potts prior and loopy belief propagation. The graph (V, E) is a square grid graph with periodic boundary conditions along the x- and y-directions

$$
\begin{aligned}
&\left(\sum_{s_{|V|}\in\Omega}\exp\left(\frac{1}{k_BT}J\left(s_{|V|-1}+s_1\right)s_{|V|}\right)\right)\\
&=2^{\frac{|V|}{2}}\left(\cosh\left(\frac{1}{k_BT}J\right)\right)^{\frac{1}{2}(1+s_1s_3)}\left(\cosh\left(\frac{1}{k_BT}J\right)\right)^{\frac{1}{2}(1+s_3s_5)}\\
&\quad\times\cdots\times\left(\cosh\left(\frac{1}{k_BT}J\right)\right)^{\frac{1}{2}\left(1+s_{|V|-3}s_{|V|-1}\right)}\left(\cosh\left(\frac{1}{k_BT}J\right)\right)^{\frac{1}{2}\left(1+s_{|V|-1}s_1\right)}\\
&=2^{\frac{|V|}{2}}\left(\prod_{i=0}^{\frac{|V|}{2}-2}\exp\left(\left(1+s_{2i+1}s_{2i+3}\right)\times\frac{1}{2}\ln\left(\cosh\left(\frac{2}{k_BT}J\right)\right)\right)\right)\\
&\exp\left(\left(1+s_{|V|-1}s_1\right)\times\frac{1}{2}\ln\left(\cosh\left(\frac{2}{k_BT}J\right)\right)\right).
\end{aligned}
\tag{10.177}
$$

For the $\frac{|V|}{2}$-dimensional state vector $(a_1, a_3, a_5, \cdots, a_{|V-3|}, a_{|V|-1})$, the marginal probability distribution $P_{\{1,3,5,\cdots,|V|-3,|V|-1\}}\left(a_1, a_3, a_5, \cdots, a_{|V|-3}, a_{|V|-1}\middle|\alpha\right)$ is expressed as

$$
\begin{aligned}
&P_{\{1,3,5,\cdots,|V|-3,|V|-1\}}\big(s_1, s_3, s_5, \cdots, s_{|V|-3}, s_{|V|-1}\big) \\
&\equiv \sum_{s_2\in\Omega}\sum_{s_4\in\Omega}\sum_{s_6\in\Omega}\cdots\sum_{s_{|V|-2}\in\Omega}\sum_{s_{|V|}\in\Omega} P\big(s_1, s_2, s_3, s_4, s_5, s_6, \cdots, s_{|V|-3}, s_{|V|-2}s_{|V|-1}, s_{|V|}\big) \\
&= \frac{\left(\prod_{i=0}^{\frac{|V|}{2}-2}\exp\big(\alpha^{(1)}s_{2i+1}, s_{2i+3}\big)\right)\exp\big(\alpha^{(1)}s_{|V|-1}, s_1\big)}{\sum_{a_1\in\Omega}\sum_{a_3\in\Omega}\cdots\sum_{a_{|V|-1}\in\Omega}\left(\prod_{i=0}^{\frac{|V|}{2}-2}\exp\big(\alpha^{(1)}s_{2i+1}, s_{2i+3}\big)\right)\exp\big(\alpha^{(1)}s_{|V|-1}, s_1\big)},
\end{aligned}
\tag{10.178}
$$

where

$$
\alpha^{(1)} \equiv \frac{1}{2}\ln\left(\cosh\left(\frac{2}{k_{\rm B}T}J\right)\right). \tag{10.179}
$$

The remaining nodes, which are denoted by odd numbers, are now renumbered by replacing i with $\frac{i-1}{2}$ for $i = 1, 3, 5, \cdots, |V|-3, |V|-1$ and new sets $V^{(1)}$ and $E^{(1)}$ of nodes and edges and a new state vector $\boldsymbol{s}^{(1)} = \left(s_1^{(1)}, s_2^{(1)}, s_3^{(1)}, \cdots, s_{\frac{|V|}{2}-1}^{(1)}, s_{\frac{|V|}{2}}^{(1)}\right)^{\rm T}$ are introduced as follows:

$$
V^{(1)} \equiv \left\{1, 2, , 3, 4, \cdots, \frac{|V|}{2}-1, \frac{|V|}{2}\right\}, \tag{10.180}
$$

$$
E^{(1)} \equiv \left\{\{1, 2\}, \{2, 3\}, \{3, 4\}, \cdots, \{\frac{|V|}{2}-1, \frac{|V|}{2}\}, \{\frac{|V|}{2}, 1\}\right\}, \tag{10.181}
$$

$$
s_i^{(1)} = s_{2i-1}\ (i = 1, 2, \cdots, |V|/2). \tag{10.182}
$$

For the $\frac{|V|}{2}$-dimentional state vector $\boldsymbol{s}^{(1)} = \left(s_1^{(1)}, s_2^{(1)}, s_3^{(1)}, \cdots, s_{\frac{|V|}{2}-1}^{(1)}, s_{\frac{|V|}{2}}^{(1)}\right)^{\rm T}$, we define a new renormalized probability distribution by

$$
P^{(1)}\big(\boldsymbol{s}^{(1)}\big) \equiv \frac{\prod_{\{i,j\}\in E^{(1)}}\exp\Big(\alpha^{(1)}s_i^{(1)}s_j^{(1)}\Big)}{\sum_{a_1^{(1)}\in\Omega}\sum_{a_2^{(1)}\in\Omega}\cdots\sum_{a_{|V|/2}^{(1)}\in\Omega}\prod_{\{i,j\}\in E^{(1)}}\exp\Big(\alpha^{(1)}s_i^{(1)}s_j^{(1)}\Big)}. \tag{10.183}
$$

By repeating the above renormalizing procedures,

$$\sum_{s_2^{(r-1)}\in\Omega}\sum_{s_4^{(r-1)}\in\Omega}\sum_{s_6^{(r-1)}\in\Omega}\cdots\sum_{s_{|V^{(r-1)}|}\in\Omega}\prod_{\{i,j\}\in E^{(r-1)}}\exp\left(\frac{1}{k_{\mathrm{B}}T}Js_i^{(r-1)}s_{i+1}^{(r-1)}\right)$$
$$= 2^{\frac{|V|}{2^r}}\left(\prod_{i=0}^{\frac{|V|}{2^r}-2}\exp\left((1+s_{2i+1}s_{2i+3})\times\frac{1}{2}\ln\left(\cosh\left(2\alpha^{(r-1)}\right)\right)\right)\right)$$
$$\exp\left((1+s_{|V|-1}s_1)\times\frac{1}{2}\ln\left(\cosh\left(\frac{2}{k_{\mathrm{B}}T}J\right)\right)\right), \tag{10.184}$$

$$\alpha^{(r)} \equiv \frac{1}{2}\ln\left(\cosh\left(2\alpha^{(r-1)}\right)\right), \tag{10.185}$$

$$s_i^{(r)} = s_{2i-1}^{(r-1)}\ \left(i = 1, 2, \cdots, \frac{|V|}{2^r}\right), \tag{10.186}$$

the renormalized probability of the r-th step is generated as follows:

$$P^{(r)}\left(s^{(r)}\right) \equiv \frac{\prod_{\{i,j\}\in E^{(r)}}\exp\left(\alpha^{(r)}s_i^{(r)}s_{i+1}^{(r)}\right)}{\sum_{s_1^{(r)}\in\Omega}\sum_{s_2^{(r)}\in\Omega}\cdots\sum_{s_{|V|/2^r}^{(r)}\in\Omega}\prod_{\{i,j\}\in E^{(r)}}\exp\left(\alpha^{(r)}s_i^{(r)}s_{i+1}^{(r)}\right)}, \tag{10.187}$$

where

$$V^{(r)} \equiv \left\{1, 2, \cdots, \frac{|V|}{2^r}\right\}, \tag{10.188}$$

$$E^{(r)} \equiv \left\{\{1,2\},\{2,3\},\{3,4\},\cdots,\{\frac{|V|}{2^r}-1,\frac{|V|}{2^r}\},\{\frac{|V|}{2^r},1\}\right\}. \tag{10.189}$$

Note that $V^{(0)} = V$, $E^{(0)} = E$, $\alpha^{(0)} = \frac{J}{k_{\mathrm{B}}T}$, $\boldsymbol{s}^{(0)} = \boldsymbol{s}$, and $P^{(0)}\left(\boldsymbol{s}^{(0)}\right) = P(\boldsymbol{s})$.

Equation (10.185) corresponds to the update rule from $\alpha^{(r-1)}$ $\alpha^{(r)}$. By solving Eq. (10.185) with respect to $\alpha^{(r-1)}$, we can derive the inverse transformation rule of the real-space renormalization group procedure as follows:

$$\alpha^{(r-1)} = \frac{1}{2}\text{arccosh}\big(\exp\big(2\alpha^{(r)}\big)\big). \tag{10.190}$$

If the hyperparameter $\alpha^{(r)}$ in the r-th renormalized probability distribution $P^{(r)}\big(\boldsymbol{s}^{(r)}\big)$ has been estimated from given data vectors by means of the EM algorithm for renormalized probabilistic graphical models on ring graphs $\big(V^{(r)}, E^{(r)}\big)$, we can estimate the hyperparameter $\alpha^{(0)} = \frac{J}{k_B T}$ of the probabilistic graphical models (10.49) on ring graphs (V, E) by using the inverse transformation rule of the real-space renormalization group procedure (10.190).

Now, we extend the real-space renormalization group scheme for the probabilistic graphical model on the ring graph to the square grid graph as a pair approximation in the real-space renormalization group framework as follows:

$$\exp\big(\alpha^{(r)} s_1 s_3\big) \propto \sum_{s_2\in\Omega}\sum_{s_4\in\Omega} \exp\big(\alpha^{(r-1)}(s_1s_2 + s_2s_3 + s_1s_4 + s_4s_3)\big). \tag{10.191}$$

Equation (10.191) can be reduced to

$$\alpha^{(r)} = \ln\big(\cosh\big(2\alpha^{(r-1)}\big)\big). \tag{10.192}$$

The r-th renormalized probability distribution for Eq. (10.49) is expressed as

$$P^{(r)}\big(\boldsymbol{s}^{(r)}\big) \propto \prod_{\{i,j\}\in E^{(r)}} \exp\Big(\alpha^{(r)} s_i^{(r)} s_j^{(r)}\Big). \tag{10.193}$$

The inversion formula in Eq. (10.192) can be derived as

$$\alpha^{(r-1)} = \frac{1}{2}\text{arccosh}\big(\exp\big(\alpha^{(r)}\big)\big). \tag{10.194}$$

The above framework can be extended to the $|\Omega|$-state Potts model, as shown in Fig. 10.15. The inverse renormalization group transformation can also be applied to the probabilistic segmentations in Eqs. (10.41), (10.42), and (10.43) with Eqs. (10.44), (10.45), and (10.46) in Sect. 10.2.3 [81]. One of the numerical experimental results in the inverse renormalization group transformation in probabilistic segmentations is shown in Fig. 10.16.

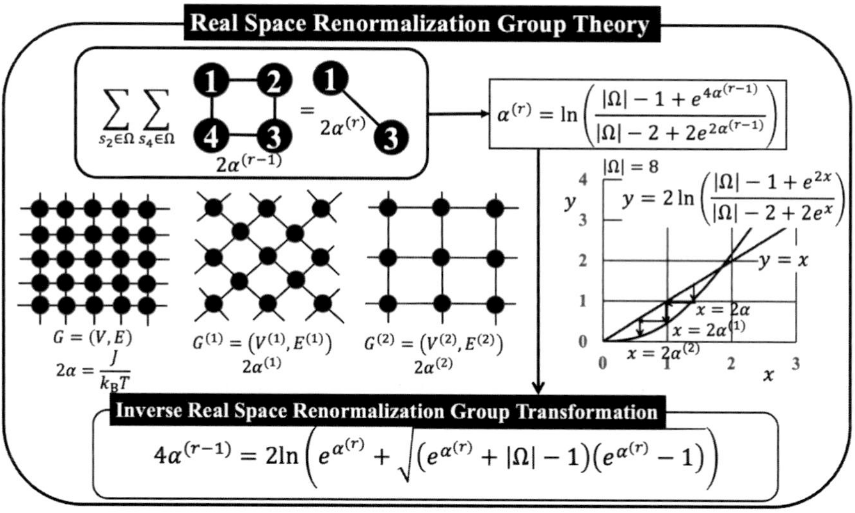

Fig. 10.15 Fundamental framework of sublinear computational modeling by the inverse renormalization group transformation in probabilistic segmentations

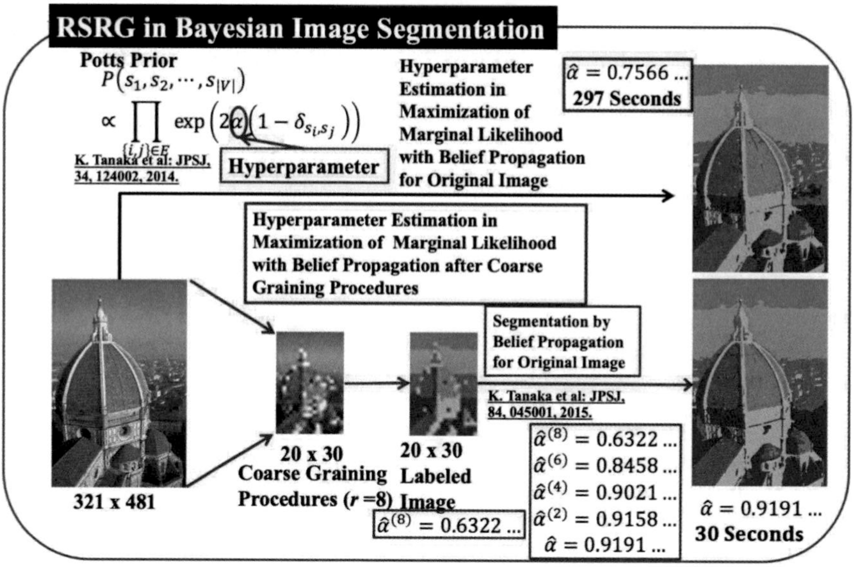

Fig. 10.16 Numerical experimental results of sublinear computational modeling in the inverse renormalization group transformation in probabilistic segmentations

10.4 Quantum Statistical Machine Learning

This section explores the fundamental frameworks of quantum probabilistic graphical models based on energy matrices and density matrices. Note that every energy matrix needs to be Hermitian and have a density matrix that is defined by all the eigenvalues and all the eigenvectors of each energy matrix. If all the off-diagonal elements of the density matrix are zero, the diagonal elements correspond to the probability distribution in the probabilistic graphical model. First, we explain general frameworks of density matrices and their differentiations and define the minimization of free energies of density matrices. Second, we give the definitions of tensor products of matrices as well as vectors. By using Pauli spin matrices as well as tensor products, we introduce quantum probabilistic graphical models. Finally, we extend the conventional EM algorithm to a quantum expectation-maximization (QEM) algorithm.

10.4.1 Elementary Function and Differentiations of Hermitian Matrices

Before proceeding with the quantum statistical mechanical extension of statistical machine learning, we need to explore some essential formulas for Hermitian matrices and their derivatives. Some fundamental properties of matrices for statistical inference have appeared in Ref. [82]. In the present section, we give some useful formulas for treating the entropy in quantum probabilistic graphical models.

We consider the $M \times M$ Hermitian matrix $\boldsymbol{A}$

$$\boldsymbol{A} = \begin{pmatrix} A_{11} & A_{12} & \cdots & A_{1M} \\ A_{21} & A_{22} & \cdots & A_{2M} \\ \vdots & \vdots & \ddots & \vdots \\ A_{M1} & A_{M2} & \cdots & A_{MM} \end{pmatrix}, \tag{10.195}$$

which satisfies $\boldsymbol{A} = \overline{\boldsymbol{A}}^{\mathrm{T}}$. Here we remark that $\boldsymbol{A}^{\mathrm{T}}$ and $\overline{\boldsymbol{A}}$ are the transpose and conjugate matrix of $\boldsymbol{A}$, respectively. We introduce vertical and horizontal basis vectors in the M-dimensional space as follows:

$$|1\rangle = \begin{pmatrix} 1 \\ 0 \\ 0 \\ 0 \\ \vdots \\ 0 \\ 0 \\ 0 \end{pmatrix}, \ |2\rangle = \begin{pmatrix} 0 \\ 1 \\ 0 \\ 0 \\ \vdots \\ 0 \\ 0 \\ 0 \end{pmatrix}, \ |3\rangle = \begin{pmatrix} 0 \\ 0 \\ 1 \\ 0 \\ \vdots \\ 0 \\ 0 \\ 0 \end{pmatrix}, \cdots, |M-1\rangle = \begin{pmatrix} 0 \\ 0 \\ 0 \\ 0 \\ \vdots \\ 0 \\ 1 \\ 0 \end{pmatrix}, |M\rangle = \begin{pmatrix} 0 \\ 0 \\ 0 \\ 0 \\ \vdots \\ 0 \\ 0 \\ 1 \end{pmatrix}, \tag{10.196}$$

and

$$\begin{cases} \langle 1| = (1, 0, 0, 0, \cdots, 0, 0, 0), \\ \langle 2| = (0, 1, 0, 0, \cdots, 0, 0, 0), \\ \langle 3| = (0, 0, 1, 0, \cdots, 0, 0, 0), \\ \vdots \\ \langle M-1| = (0, 0, 0, 0, \cdots, 0, 1, 0), \\ \langle M| = (0, 0, 0, 0, \cdots, 0, 0, 1). \end{cases} \tag{10.197}$$

We can confirm that

$$\langle i|\boldsymbol{A}|j\rangle = A_{ij} \ (i\in\{1, 2, \cdots, M\},\ j\in\{1, 2, \cdots, M\}). \tag{10.198}$$

The Hermitian matrix $\boldsymbol{A}$ is diagonalized as

$$\boldsymbol{A} = \boldsymbol{U}\boldsymbol{\Lambda}\boldsymbol{U}^{-1}, \tag{10.199}$$

$$\boldsymbol{\Lambda} \equiv \begin{pmatrix} \lambda_1 & 0 & 0 & \cdots & 0 \\ 0 & \lambda_2 & 0 & \cdots & 0 \\ 0 & 0 & \lambda_3 & \cdots & 0 \\ \vdots & \vdots & \vdots & \ddots & \vdots \\ 0 & 0 & 0 & \cdots & \lambda_M \end{pmatrix}, \tag{10.200}$$

where all the eigenvalues, $\lambda_1, \lambda_2, \cdots, \lambda_M$, are always real numbers. For the eigenvector $\boldsymbol{u}_i = \begin{pmatrix} U_{1i} \\ U_{2i} \\ \vdots \\ U_{Mi} \end{pmatrix}$ corresponding to the eigenvalue λ_i, such that $\boldsymbol{A}\boldsymbol{u}_i = \lambda_i \boldsymbol{u}_i$, for every $i\in\{1, 2, 3, \cdots, M\}$ the matrix $\boldsymbol{U}$ is defined by

$$\boldsymbol{U} \equiv (\boldsymbol{u}_1, \boldsymbol{u}_2, \boldsymbol{u}_3, \cdots, \boldsymbol{u}_M) = \begin{pmatrix} U_{11} & U_{12} & U_{13} & \cdots & U_{1M} \\ U_{21} & U_{22} & U_{23} & \cdots & U_{2M} \\ U_{31} & U_{32} & U_{33} & \cdots & U_{3M} \\ \vdots & \vdots & \vdots & \ddots & \vdots \\ U_{M1} & U_{M2} & U_{M3} & \cdots & U_{MM} \end{pmatrix}. \tag{10.201}$$

It is known that $\boldsymbol{U}$ is a unitary matrix that satisfies $\boldsymbol{U}^{-1} = \overline{\boldsymbol{U}}^{\mathrm{T}}$ for any Hermitian matrix $\boldsymbol{s}$. If λ_1 is the maximum eigenvalue, its corresponding eigenvector $\boldsymbol{u}_1$ is expressed using the following notation:

$$\boldsymbol{u}_1 = \mathrm{argmax}\boldsymbol{A}. \tag{10.202}$$

Note that argmax$\boldsymbol{A}$ is the eigenvector that corresponds to the maximum eigenvalue of $\boldsymbol{A}$.

For any Hermitian matrix $\boldsymbol{A}$, the exponential function is defined by

$$\exp(\boldsymbol{A}) \equiv \sum_{n=0}^{+\infty} \frac{1}{n!}\boldsymbol{A}^n = \boldsymbol{U}\begin{pmatrix} \exp(\lambda_1) & 0 & 0 & \cdots & 0 \\ 0 & \exp(\lambda_2) & 0 & \cdots & 0 \\ 0 & 0 & \exp(\lambda_3) & \cdots & 0 \\ \vdots & \vdots & \vdots & \ddots & \vdots \\ 0 & 0 & 0 & \cdots & \exp(\lambda_M) \end{pmatrix}\boldsymbol{U}^{-1}, \quad (10.203)$$

and $\ln(\boldsymbol{A})$ is defined by the inverse function of $\exp(\boldsymbol{A})$ such that

$$\exp(\ln(\boldsymbol{A})) = \boldsymbol{A}. \quad (10.204)$$

In the present definition, we have

$$\exp(\boldsymbol{A}\otimes\boldsymbol{I}) = (\exp(\boldsymbol{A}))\otimes\boldsymbol{I},\ \exp(\boldsymbol{I}\otimes\boldsymbol{A}) = \boldsymbol{I}\otimes(\exp(\boldsymbol{A})), \quad (10.205)$$

where $\boldsymbol{I}$ is an identity matrix.

For $|1-\lambda_1| < 1, |1-\lambda_2| < 1, \cdots, |1-\lambda_N| < 1$, $\ln(\boldsymbol{A})$ is defined by

$$\ln(\boldsymbol{A}) = \ln(\boldsymbol{I}-(\boldsymbol{I}-\boldsymbol{A})) \equiv -\sum_{n=1}^{+\infty}\frac{1}{n}(\boldsymbol{I}-\boldsymbol{A})^n = \boldsymbol{U}\begin{pmatrix} \ln(\lambda_1) & 0 & 0 & \cdots & 0 \\ 0 & \ln(\lambda_2) & 0 & \cdots & 0 \\ 0 & 0 & \ln(\lambda_3) & \cdots & 0 \\ \vdots & \vdots & \vdots & \ddots & \vdots \\ 0 & 0 & 0 & \cdots & \ln(\lambda_M) \end{pmatrix}\boldsymbol{U}^{-1}. \quad (10.206)$$

By using Eqs. (10.203) and (10.206), we can confirm that

$$\exp(\ln(\boldsymbol{A})) = \sum_{n=0}^{+\infty}\frac{1}{n!}(\ln(\boldsymbol{A}))^n = \sum_{n=0}^{+\infty}\frac{1}{n!}\boldsymbol{U}\begin{pmatrix} (\ln(\lambda_1))^n & 0 & 0 & \cdots & 0 \\ 0 & (\ln(\lambda_2))^n & 0 & \cdots & 0 \\ 0 & 0 & (\ln(\lambda_3))^n & \cdots & 0 \\ \vdots & \vdots & \vdots & \ddots & \vdots \\ 0 & 0 & 0 & \cdots & (\ln(\lambda_M))^n \end{pmatrix}\boldsymbol{U}^{-1}$$

$$= \boldsymbol{U}\begin{pmatrix} \exp(\ln(\lambda_1)) & 0 & 0 & \cdots & 0 \\ 0 & \exp(\ln(\lambda_2)) & 0 & \cdots & 0 \\ 0 & 0 & \exp(\ln(\lambda_3)) & \cdots & 0 \\ \vdots & \vdots & \vdots & \ddots & \vdots \\ 0 & 0 & 0 & \cdots & \exp(\ln(\lambda_M)) \end{pmatrix}\boldsymbol{U}^{-1}$$

$$= \boldsymbol{U}\begin{pmatrix} \lambda_1 & 0 & 0 & \cdots & 0 \\ 0 & \lambda_2 & 0 & \cdots & 0 \\ 0 & 0 & \lambda_3 & \cdots & 0 \\ \vdots & \vdots & \vdots & \ddots & \vdots \\ 0 & 0 & 0 & \cdots & \lambda_M \end{pmatrix}\boldsymbol{U}^{-1} = \boldsymbol{A}. \tag{10.207}$$

Moreover, we have

$$\begin{aligned} &\sum_{n=0}^{N}(\boldsymbol{I}-\boldsymbol{A})^n - (\boldsymbol{I}-\boldsymbol{s})\sum_{n=0}^{N}(\boldsymbol{I}-\boldsymbol{A})^n \\ &= \boldsymbol{I} + (\boldsymbol{I}-\boldsymbol{s}) + (\boldsymbol{I}-\boldsymbol{A})^2 + \cdots + (\boldsymbol{I}-\boldsymbol{A})^N \\ &\quad - (\boldsymbol{I}-\boldsymbol{s}) - (\boldsymbol{I}-\boldsymbol{A})^2 - \cdots - (\boldsymbol{I}-\boldsymbol{s})^N - (\boldsymbol{I}-\boldsymbol{A})^{N+1} \\ &= \boldsymbol{I} - (\boldsymbol{I}-\boldsymbol{A})^{N+1}, \end{aligned} \tag{10.208}$$

such that

$$\sum_{n=0}^{N}(\boldsymbol{I}-\boldsymbol{A})^n = (\boldsymbol{I}-(\boldsymbol{I}-\boldsymbol{A}))^{-1}\big(\boldsymbol{I}-(\boldsymbol{I}-\boldsymbol{A})^{N+1}\big). \tag{10.209}$$

We have

$$\boldsymbol{A}^{N+1} = \boldsymbol{U}\begin{pmatrix} (1-\lambda_1)^{N+1} & 0 & 0 & \cdots & 0 \\ 0 & (1-\lambda_2)^{N+1} & 0 & \cdots & 0 \\ 0 & 0 & (1-\lambda_3)^{N+1} & \cdots & 0 \\ \vdots & \vdots & \vdots & \ddots & \vdots \\ 0 & 0 & 0 & \cdots & (1-\lambda_M)^{N+1} \end{pmatrix}\boldsymbol{U}^{-1} \to 0 \ (N \to +\infty), \tag{10.210}$$

so it is valid that

$$\boldsymbol{A}^{-1} = (\boldsymbol{I}-(\boldsymbol{I}-\boldsymbol{A}))^{-1} = \sum_{n=0}^{+\infty}(\boldsymbol{I}-\boldsymbol{A})^n. \tag{10.211}$$

Note that exp($\boldsymbol{A}$ and $\ln(\boldsymbol{A})$ as well as $\boldsymbol{A}^{-1}$ are also Hermitian matrices in the present case. (This can be shown by using $\overline{\boldsymbol{A}^n}^{\mathrm{T}} = \big(\overline{\boldsymbol{A}}^{\mathrm{T}}\big)^n$.)

We now introduce a Hermitian matrix function $\boldsymbol{G}(x)$ for any real number x as follows:

$$\boldsymbol{G}(x) \equiv \begin{pmatrix} G_{11}(x) & G_{12}(x) & G_{13}(x) & \cdots & G_{1M}(x) \\ G_{21}(x) & G_{22}(x) & G_{23}(x) & \cdots & G_{2M}(x) \\ G_{31}(x) & G_{32}(x) & G_{33}(x) & \cdots & G_{3M}(x) \\ \vdots & \vdots & \vdots & \ddots & \vdots \\ G_{M1}(x) & G_{M2}(x) & G_{M3}(x) & \cdots & G_{MM}(x) \end{pmatrix}. \tag{10.212}$$

We have

$$G_{ij}(x) = \overline{G}_{ji}(x) \ (i \in \{1, 2, \cdots, M\},\ j \in \{1, 2, \cdots, M\}), \tag{10.213}$$

such that

$$\langle i|\boldsymbol{G}(x)|j\rangle = \langle j|\overline{\boldsymbol{G}}(x)|i\rangle \ (i \in \{1, 2, \cdots, M\},\ j \in \{1, 2, \cdots, M\}). \tag{10.214}$$

It is obvious that the derivative of the matrix $\boldsymbol{G}(x)$ with respect to x, namely,

$$\frac{d}{dx}\boldsymbol{G}(x) \equiv \begin{pmatrix} \frac{d}{dx}G_{11}(x) & \frac{d}{dx}G_{12}(x) & \frac{d}{dx}G_{13}(x) & \cdots & \frac{d}{dx}G_{1M}(x) \\ \frac{d}{dx}G_{21}(x) & \frac{d}{dx}G_{22}(x) & \frac{d}{dx}G_{23}(x) & \cdots & \frac{d}{dx}G_{2M}(x) \\ \frac{d}{dx}G_{31}(x) & \frac{d}{dx}G_{32}(x) & \frac{d}{dx}G_{33}(x) & \cdots & \frac{d}{dx}G_{3M}(x) \\ \vdots & \vdots & \vdots & \ddots & \vdots \\ \frac{d}{dx}G_{M1}(x) & \frac{d}{dx}G_{M2}(x) & \frac{d}{dx}G_{M3}(x) & \cdots & \frac{d}{dx}G_{MM}(x) \end{pmatrix} \tag{10.215}$$

is also a Hermitian matrix such that

$$\langle i|\frac{d}{dx}\boldsymbol{G}(x)|j\rangle = \langle j|\frac{d}{dx}\overline{\boldsymbol{G}}(x)|j\rangle \ (i \in \{1, 2, \cdots, M\},\ j \in \{1, 2, \cdots, M\}). \tag{10.216}$$

We have the following equalities:

$$\frac{d}{dx}(\mathrm{Tr}[\boldsymbol{G}(x)]) = \mathrm{Tr}\left[\frac{d}{dx}\boldsymbol{G}(x)\right], \tag{10.217}$$

and

$$\mathrm{Tr}\left(\left(\frac{d}{dx}\boldsymbol{G}(x)\right)\boldsymbol{G}(x)\right) = \mathrm{Tr}\left(\boldsymbol{G}(x)\left(\frac{d}{dx}\boldsymbol{G}(x)\right)\right). \tag{10.218}$$

Equation (10.218) can be confirmed as follows:

$$\begin{aligned}\mathrm{Tr}\Big(\Big(\frac{d}{dx}\boldsymbol{G}(x)\Big)\boldsymbol{G}(x)\Big) &= \sum_{i=1}^{M}\langle i|\Big(\frac{d}{dx}\boldsymbol{G}(x)\Big)\boldsymbol{G}(x)|i\rangle = \sum_{i=1}^{M}\sum_{j=1}^{M}\langle i|\Big(\frac{d}{dx}\boldsymbol{G}(x)\Big)|j\rangle\langle j|\boldsymbol{G}(x)|i\rangle \\ &= \sum_{j=1}^{M}\sum_{i=1}^{M}\langle j|\boldsymbol{G}(x)|i\rangle\langle i|\Big(\frac{d}{dx}\boldsymbol{G}(x)\Big)|j\rangle = \mathrm{Tr}\Big(\boldsymbol{G}(x)\Big(\frac{d}{dx}\boldsymbol{G}(x)\Big)\Big).\end{aligned} \tag{10.219}$$

By using Eqs. (10.217) and (10.219), we derive the following fundamental formula

$$\begin{aligned}\frac{d}{dx}\mathrm{tr}(\boldsymbol{G}(x)^n) &= \mathrm{Tr}\Big(\Big(\frac{d}{dx}\boldsymbol{G}(x)\Big)(\boldsymbol{G}(x)^{n-1})\Big) + \mathrm{Tr}\Big(\boldsymbol{G}(x)\Big(\frac{d}{dx}\boldsymbol{G}(x)^{n-1}\Big)\Big) \\ &= \mathrm{Tr}\Big(\Big(\frac{d}{dx}\boldsymbol{G}(x)\Big)(\boldsymbol{G}(x)^{n-1})\Big) \\ &\quad +\mathrm{Tr}\Big(\boldsymbol{G}(x)\Big(\Big(\frac{d}{dx}\boldsymbol{G}(x)\Big)(\boldsymbol{G}(x)^{n-2}) + \boldsymbol{G}(x)\Big(\frac{d}{dx}\boldsymbol{G}(x)^{n-2}\Big)\Big)\Big) \\ &= \mathrm{Tr}\Big(\Big(\frac{d}{dx}\boldsymbol{G}(x)\Big)(\boldsymbol{G}(x)^{n-1})\Big) \\ &\quad +\mathrm{Tr}\Big(\boldsymbol{G}(x)\Big(\frac{d}{dx}\boldsymbol{G}(x)\Big)(\boldsymbol{G}(x)^{n-2})\Big) + \mathrm{Tr}\Big(\boldsymbol{G}(x)^2\Big(\frac{d}{dx}\boldsymbol{G}(x)^{n-2}\Big)\Big) \\ &= \mathrm{Tr}\Big(\Big(\frac{d}{dx}\boldsymbol{G}(x)\Big)\boldsymbol{G}(x)^{n-1}\Big) \\ &\quad +\mathrm{Tr}\Big(\Big(\frac{d}{dx}\boldsymbol{G}(x)\Big)\boldsymbol{G}(x)\boldsymbol{G}(x)^{n-2}\Big) + \mathrm{Tr}\Big(\boldsymbol{G}(x)^2\Big(\frac{d}{dx}\boldsymbol{G}(x)^{n-2}\Big)\Big) \\ &= \mathrm{Tr}\Big(\Big(\frac{d}{dx}\boldsymbol{G}(x)\Big)2\boldsymbol{G}(x)^{n-1}\Big) + \mathrm{Tr}\Big(\boldsymbol{G}(x)^2\Big(\frac{d}{dx}\boldsymbol{G}(x)^{n-2}\Big)\Big) \\ &= \cdots \\ &= \mathrm{Tr}\Big(\Big(\frac{d}{dx}\boldsymbol{G}(x)\Big)(n-1)\boldsymbol{G}(x)^{n-1}\Big) + \mathrm{Tr}\Big(\boldsymbol{G}(x)^{n-1}\Big(\frac{d}{dx}\boldsymbol{G}(x)\Big)\Big) \\ &= \mathrm{Tr}\Big(\Big(\frac{d}{dx}\boldsymbol{G}(x)\Big)(n-1)\boldsymbol{G}(x)^{n-1}\Big) + \mathrm{Tr}\Big(\Big(\frac{d}{dx}\boldsymbol{G}(x)\Big)\boldsymbol{G}(x)^{n-1}\Big) \\ &= \mathrm{Tr}\Big(\Big(\frac{d}{dx}\boldsymbol{G}(x)\Big)n\boldsymbol{G}(x)^{n-1}\Big).\end{aligned} \tag{10.220}$$

From Eqs. (10.217) and (10.220), we can confirm the following equality:

$$\begin{aligned}
\frac{d}{dx}\mathrm{Tr}(\ln(\boldsymbol{G}(x))) &= \frac{d}{dx}\mathrm{Tr}(\ln(\boldsymbol{I}-(\boldsymbol{I}-\boldsymbol{G}(x)))) \\
&= \frac{d}{dx}\mathrm{Tr}\left(-\sum_{n=1}^{+\infty}\frac{1}{n}(\boldsymbol{I}-\boldsymbol{G}(x))^n\right) \\
&= -\sum_{n=1}^{+\infty}\frac{1}{n}\frac{d}{dx}\mathrm{Tr}\big((\boldsymbol{I}-\boldsymbol{G}(x))^n\big) \\
&= -\sum_{n=1}^{+\infty}\frac{1}{n}\mathrm{Tr}\left(\left(\frac{d}{dx}(\boldsymbol{I}-\boldsymbol{G}(x))\right)n(\boldsymbol{I}-\boldsymbol{G}(x))^{n-1}\right) \\
&= \mathrm{Tr}\left(\left(-\frac{d}{dx}(\boldsymbol{I}-\boldsymbol{G}(x))\right)\left(\sum_{n=1}^{+\infty}(\boldsymbol{I}-\boldsymbol{G}(x))^{n-1}\right)\right) \\
&= \mathrm{Tr}\left(\left(\frac{d}{dx}\boldsymbol{G}(x)\right)\left(\sum_{n=1}^{+\infty}(\boldsymbol{I}-\boldsymbol{G}(x))^{n-1}\right)\right) \\
&= \mathrm{Tr}\left(\left(\frac{d}{dx}\boldsymbol{G}(x)\right)(\boldsymbol{I}-(\boldsymbol{I}-\boldsymbol{G}(x)))^{-1}\right). \\
&= \mathrm{Tr}\left(\left(\frac{d}{dx}\boldsymbol{G}(x)\right)\big(\boldsymbol{G}(x)^{-1}\big)\right).
\end{aligned} \tag{10.221}$$

By using Eqs. (10.221), we can confirm the following equality:

$$\begin{aligned}
\frac{d}{d\boldsymbol{A}}\mathrm{Tr}[\boldsymbol{A}(\ln(\boldsymbol{A}))] &\equiv \begin{pmatrix}
\frac{d}{dA_{11}}\mathrm{Tr}[\boldsymbol{A}\ln(\boldsymbol{A})] & \frac{d}{dA_{12}}\mathrm{Tr}[\boldsymbol{A}\ln(\boldsymbol{A})] & \cdots & \frac{d}{dA_{1M}}\mathrm{Tr}[\boldsymbol{A}\ln(\boldsymbol{A})] \\
\frac{d}{dA_{21}}\mathrm{Tr}[\boldsymbol{A}\ln(\boldsymbol{A})] & \frac{d}{dA_{22}}\mathrm{Tr}[\boldsymbol{A}\ln(\boldsymbol{A})] & \cdots & \frac{d}{dA_{2M}}\mathrm{Tr}[\boldsymbol{A}\ln(\boldsymbol{A})] \\
\vdots & \vdots & \ddots & \vdots \\
\frac{d}{dA_{M1}}\mathrm{Tr}[\boldsymbol{A}\ln(\boldsymbol{A})] & \frac{d}{dA_{M2}}\mathrm{Tr}[\boldsymbol{A}\ln(\boldsymbol{A})] & \cdots & \frac{d}{dA_{MM}}\mathrm{Tr}[\boldsymbol{A}\ln(\boldsymbol{A})]
\end{pmatrix} \\
&= \ln(\boldsymbol{A}) + \boldsymbol{I}.
\end{aligned} \tag{10.222}$$

10.4.2 Minimization of Free Energy Functionals for Density Matrices

For any $M \times M$ Hermitian matrix $\boldsymbol{H}$ that satisfies $\boldsymbol{H} = \overline{\boldsymbol{H}}^{\mathrm{T}}$, the free energy functional for an $M \times M$ trial density matrix

$$\boldsymbol{R} = \begin{pmatrix}
R_{11} & R_{12} & \cdots & R_{1M} \\
R_{21} & R_{22} & \cdots & R_{2M} \\
\vdots & \vdots & \ddots & \vdots \\
R_{M1} & R_{M2} & \cdots & R_{MM}
\end{pmatrix} \tag{10.223}$$

is defined by

$$\mathcal{F}[\boldsymbol{R}] = \mathrm{Tr}[\boldsymbol{R}(\boldsymbol{H} + k_{\mathrm{B}}T\ln(\boldsymbol{R}))]. \tag{10.224}$$

The density matrix $\boldsymbol{P}$ is determined so as to satisfy the following conditional minimization with the normalization condition as follows:

$$\boldsymbol{P} = \underset{\boldsymbol{R}}{\mathrm{argmin}}\left\{\mathcal{F}[\boldsymbol{R}]\middle|\mathrm{Tr}[\boldsymbol{R}] = 1\right\}, \tag{10.225}$$

and this reduces to

$$\boldsymbol{P} = \frac{1}{Z}\exp\left(-\frac{1}{k_{\mathrm{B}}T}\boldsymbol{H}\right), \tag{10.226}$$

$$Z \equiv \mathrm{Tr}\left[\exp\left(-\frac{1}{k_{\mathrm{B}}T}\boldsymbol{H}\right)\right]. \tag{10.227}$$

First, we introduce the Lagrange multiplier λ to ensure the normalization condition as follows:

$$\mathcal{L}[\boldsymbol{R}] \equiv \mathcal{F}[\boldsymbol{R}] - \lambda\big(\mathrm{Tr}[\boldsymbol{R}] - 1\big). \tag{10.228}$$

$\widehat{\boldsymbol{R}}$ are determined so as to satisfy the following extremum condition:

$$\frac{\partial}{\partial R_{mm'}}\mathcal{L}[\boldsymbol{R}] = 0 \ (m = 1, 2, \cdots, M, \ m' = 1, 2, \cdots, M). \tag{10.229}$$

Finally, by determining λ so as to satisfy the normalization condition $\mathrm{Tr}\left[\widehat{\boldsymbol{R}}\right] = 1$, Eqs. (10.226) and (10.227) can be derived.

Because the energy matrix $\boldsymbol{H}$ is a Hermitian matrix, all the eigenvalues h_m are always real numbers and all the eigenvectors $\begin{pmatrix} \psi^{(m)}(1) \\ \psi^{(m)}(2) \\ \vdots \\ \psi^{(m)}(M) \end{pmatrix}$ can be chosen as real vectors and are defined by

$$\boldsymbol{H}\begin{pmatrix} \psi^{(m)}(1) \\ \psi^{(m)}(2) \\ \vdots \\ \psi^{(m)}(M) \end{pmatrix} = h^{(m)}\begin{pmatrix} \psi^{(m)}(1) \\ \psi^{(m)}(2) \\ \vdots \\ \psi^{(m)}(M) \end{pmatrix} \ (m = 1, 2, \cdots, M), \tag{10.230}$$

where

$$\left(\psi^{(m)}(1), \psi^{(m)}(2), \cdots, \psi^{(m)}(M)\right)\begin{pmatrix} \psi^{(m)}(1) \\ \psi^{(m)}(2) \\ \vdots \\ \psi^{(m)}(M) \end{pmatrix} = 1 \ (m = 1, 2, \cdots, M). \quad (10.231)$$

By using these eigenvalues and eigenvectors of $\boldsymbol{H}$, the density matrix can be expressed as

$$\widehat{\boldsymbol{R}} = \begin{pmatrix} \psi^{(1)}(1) & \psi^{(2)}(1) & \cdots & \psi^{(M)}(1) \\ \psi^{(1)}(2) & \psi^{(2)}(2) & \cdots & \psi^{(M)}(2) \\ \vdots & \vdots & \ddots & \vdots \\ \psi^{(1)}(M) & \psi^{(2)}(M) & \cdots & \psi^{(M)}(M) \end{pmatrix}\begin{pmatrix} p^{(1)} & 0 & \cdots & 0 \\ 0 & p^{(2)} & \cdots & 0 \\ \vdots & \vdots & \ddots & \vdots \\ 0 & 0 & \cdots & p^{(M)} \end{pmatrix}\begin{pmatrix} \psi^{(1)}(1) & \psi^{(2)}(1) & \cdots & \psi^{(M)}(1) \\ \psi^{(1)}(2) & \psi^{(2)}(2) & \cdots & \psi^{(M)}(2) \\ \vdots & \vdots & \ddots & \vdots \\ \psi^{(1)}(M) & \psi^{(2)}(M) & \cdots & \psi^{(M)}(M) \end{pmatrix}^{\mathrm{T}}, \quad (10.232)$$

where

$$p^{(m)} = \frac{\exp\left(-\frac{1}{k_{\mathrm{B}}T}h^{(m)}\right)}{\mathrm{Tr}\left[\exp\left(-\frac{1}{k_{\mathrm{B}}T}h^{(m)}\right)\right]} \ (m = 1, 2, \cdots, M). \quad (10.233)$$

This means that the probability of each state $\begin{pmatrix} \psi^{(m)}(1) \\ \psi^{(m)}(2) \\ \vdots \\ \psi^{(m)}(M) \end{pmatrix}$ is $p^{(m)}$ for $m = 1, 2, \cdots, M$.

10.4.3 Tensor Products

This section explores **tensor products (Kronecker products)** [82]. Tensor products include some fundamental mathematical concepts for achieving quantum statistical mechanical extensions of probabilistic graphical models.

We introduce tensor products for matrices and vectors by the following definitions:

$$\begin{pmatrix} A_{11} & A_{12} \\ A_{21} & A_{22} \end{pmatrix} \otimes \begin{pmatrix} B_{11} & B_{12} \\ B_{21} & B_{22} \end{pmatrix} = \begin{pmatrix} A_{11}\begin{pmatrix} B_{11} & B_{12} \\ B_{21} & B_{22} \end{pmatrix} & A_{12}\begin{pmatrix} B_{11} & B_{12} \\ B_{21} & B_{22} \end{pmatrix} \\ A_{21}\begin{pmatrix} B_{11} & B_{12} \\ B_{21} & B_{22} \end{pmatrix} & A_{22}\begin{pmatrix} B_{11} & B_{12} \\ B_{21} & B_{22} \end{pmatrix} \end{pmatrix}$$

$$= \begin{pmatrix} A_{11}B_{11} & A_{11}B_{12} & A_{12}B_{11} & A_{12}B_{12} \\ A_{11}B_{21} & A_{11}B_{22} & A_{12}B_{21} & A_{12}B_{22} \\ A_{21}B_{11} & A_{21}B_{12} & A_{22}B_{11} & A_{12}B_{12} \\ A_{21}B_{21} & A_{21}B_{22} & A_{22}B_{21} & A_{12}B_{22} \end{pmatrix}, \quad (10.234)$$

$$\begin{pmatrix} A_1 \\ A_2 \end{pmatrix} \otimes \begin{pmatrix} B_1 \\ B_2 \end{pmatrix} = \begin{pmatrix} A_1 \begin{pmatrix} B_1 \\ B_2 \end{pmatrix} \\ A_2 \begin{pmatrix} B_1 \\ B_2 \end{pmatrix} \end{pmatrix} = \begin{pmatrix} A_{11}B_{11} \\ A_{11}B_{21} \\ A_{21}B_{11} \\ A_{21}B_{21} \end{pmatrix}. \tag{10.235}$$

We remark that

$$\begin{aligned} &\left(\begin{pmatrix} A_{11} & A_{12} \\ A_{21} & A_{22} \end{pmatrix} \otimes \begin{pmatrix} B_{11} & B_{12} \\ B_{21} & B_{22} \end{pmatrix}\right)\left(\begin{pmatrix} C_{11} & C_{12} \\ C_{21} & C_{22} \end{pmatrix} \otimes \begin{pmatrix} D_{11} & D_{12} \\ D_{21} & D_{22} \end{pmatrix}\right) \\ &= \left(\begin{pmatrix} A_{11} & A_{12} \\ A_{21} & A_{22} \end{pmatrix}\begin{pmatrix} C_{11} & C_{12} \\ C_{21} & C_{22} \end{pmatrix}\right) \otimes \left(\begin{pmatrix} B_{11} & B_{12} \\ B_{21} & B_{22} \end{pmatrix}\begin{pmatrix} D_{11} & D_{12} \\ D_{21} & D_{22} \end{pmatrix}\right). \end{aligned} \tag{10.236}$$

Moreover, for the following general matrices $\boldsymbol{A}$ and $\boldsymbol{B}$,

$$\boldsymbol{A} = \begin{pmatrix} A_{11} & A_{12} & \cdots & A_{1M} \\ A_{21} & A_{22} & \cdots & A_{2M} \\ \vdots & \vdots & \ddots & \vdots \\ A_{M1} & A_{M2} & \cdots & A_{MM} \end{pmatrix}, \ \boldsymbol{B} = \begin{pmatrix} B_{11} & B_{12} & \cdots & B_{1N} \\ B_{21} & B_{22} & \cdots & B_{2N} \\ \vdots & \vdots & \ddots & \vdots \\ B_{N1} & B_{N2} & \cdots & B_{NN} \end{pmatrix}, \tag{10.237}$$

we define the tensor product $\boldsymbol{A} \otimes \boldsymbol{B}$ as

$$\begin{aligned} \boldsymbol{A} \otimes \boldsymbol{B} &= \begin{pmatrix} A_{11} & A_{12} & \cdots & A_{1M} \\ A_{21} & A_{22} & \cdots & A_{2M} \\ \vdots & \vdots & \ddots & \vdots \\ A_{M1} & A_{M2} & \cdots & A_{MM} \end{pmatrix} \otimes \begin{pmatrix} B_{11} & B_{12} & \cdots & B_{1N} \\ B_{21} & B_{22} & \cdots & B_{2N} \\ \vdots & \vdots & \ddots & \vdots \\ B_{N1} & B_{N2} & \cdots & B_{NN} \end{pmatrix} \\ &= \begin{pmatrix} A_{11}\boldsymbol{B} & A_{12}\boldsymbol{B} & \cdots & A_{1M}\boldsymbol{B} \\ A_{21}\boldsymbol{B} & A_{22}\boldsymbol{B} & \cdots & A_{2M}\boldsymbol{B} \\ \vdots & \vdots & \ddots & \vdots \\ A_{M1}\boldsymbol{B} & A_{M2}\boldsymbol{B} & \cdots & A_{MM}\boldsymbol{B} \end{pmatrix} \\ &= \begin{pmatrix} A_{11}B_{11} & A_{11}B_{12} & \cdots & A_{11}B_{1N} & A_{12}B_{11} & A_{12}B_{12} & \cdots & A_{12}B_{1N} & \cdots & A_{1M}B_{11} & A_{1M}B_{12} & \cdots & A_{1M}B_{1N} \\ A_{11}B_{21} & A_{11}B_{22} & \cdots & A_{11}B_{2N} & A_{12}B_{21} & A_{12}B_{22} & \cdots & A_{12}B_{2N} & \cdots & A_{1M}B_{21} & A_{1M}B_{22} & \cdots & A_{1M}B_{2N} \\ \vdots & \vdots & \ddots & \vdots & \vdots & \vdots & \ddots & \vdots & \ddots & \vdots & \vdots & \ddots & \vdots \\ A_{11}B_{N1} & A_{11}B_{N2} & \cdots & A_{11}B_{NN} & A_{12}B_{N1} & A_{12}B_{N2} & \cdots & A_{12}B_{NN} & \cdots & A_{1M}B_{N1} & A_{1M}B_{N2} & \cdots & A_{1M}B_{NN} \\ A_{21}B_{11} & A_{21}B_{12} & \cdots & A_{21}B_{1N} & A_{22}B_{11} & A_{22}B_{12} & \cdots & A_{22}B_{1N} & \cdots & A_{2M}B_{11} & A_{2M}B_{12} & \cdots & A_{2M}B_{1N} \\ A_{21}B_{21} & A_{21}B_{22} & \cdots & A_{21}B_{2N} & A_{22}B_{21} & A_{22}B_{22} & \cdots & A_{22}B_{2N} & \cdots & A_{2M}B_{21} & A_{2M}B_{22} & \cdots & A_{2M}B_{2N} \\ \vdots & \vdots & \ddots & \vdots & \vdots & \vdots & \ddots & \vdots & \ddots & \vdots & \vdots & \ddots & \vdots \\ A_{21}B_{N1} & A_{21}B_{N2} & \cdots & A_{21}B_{NN} & A_{22}B_{N1} & A_{22}B_{N2} & \cdots & A_{22}B_{NN} & \cdots & A_{2M}B_{N1} & A_{2M}B_{N2} & \cdots & A_{2M}B_{NN} \\ \vdots & \vdots & \ddots & \vdots & \vdots & \vdots & \ddots & \vdots & \ddots & \vdots & \vdots & \ddots & \vdots \\ A_{M1}B_{11} & A_{M1}B_{12} & \cdots & A_{M1}B_{1N} & A_{M2}B_{11} & A_{M2}B_{12} & \cdots & A_{M2}B_{1N} & \cdots & A_{MM}B_{11} & A_{MM}B_{12} & \cdots & A_{MM}B_{1N} \\ A_{M1}B_{21} & A_{M1}B_{22} & \cdots & A_{M1}B_{2N} & A_{M2}B_{21} & A_{M2}B_{22} & \cdots & A_{M2}B_{2N} & \cdots & A_{MM}B_{21} & A_{MM}B_{22} & \cdots & A_{MM}B_{2N} \\ \vdots & \vdots & \ddots & \vdots & \vdots & \vdots & \ddots & \vdots & \ddots & \vdots & \vdots & \ddots & \vdots \\ A_{M1}B_{N1} & A_{M1}B_{N2} & \cdots & A_{M1}B_{NN} & A_{M2}B_{N1} & A_{M2}B_{N2} & \cdots & A_{M2}B_{NN} & \cdots & A_{MM}B_{N1} & A_{MM}B_{N2} & \cdots & A_{MM}B_{NN} \end{pmatrix}, \end{aligned} \tag{10.238}$$

Similarly, for vectors

$$\boldsymbol{a} = \begin{pmatrix} a_1 \\ a_2 \\ \vdots \\ a_M \end{pmatrix}, \ \boldsymbol{b} = \begin{pmatrix} b_1 \\ b_2 \\ \vdots \\ b_N \end{pmatrix}, \tag{10.239}$$

the tensor product $\boldsymbol{a} \otimes \boldsymbol{b}$ is defined as

$$\boldsymbol{a} \otimes \boldsymbol{b} = \begin{pmatrix} a_1 \\ a_2 \\ \vdots \\ a_M \end{pmatrix} \otimes \begin{pmatrix} b_1 \\ b_2 \\ \vdots \\ b_N \end{pmatrix} = \begin{pmatrix} a_1 \boldsymbol{b} \\ a_2 \boldsymbol{b} \\ \vdots \\ a_M \boldsymbol{b} \end{pmatrix} = \begin{pmatrix} a_1 \begin{pmatrix} b_1 \\ b_2 \\ \vdots \\ b_N \end{pmatrix} \\ a_2 \begin{pmatrix} b_1 \\ b_2 \\ \vdots \\ b_N \end{pmatrix} \\ \vdots \\ a_M \begin{pmatrix} b_1 \\ b_2 \\ \vdots \\ b_N \end{pmatrix} \end{pmatrix} = \begin{pmatrix} a_1 b_1 \\ a_1 b_2 \\ \vdots \\ a_1 b_N \\ a_2 b_1 \\ a_2 b_2 \\ \vdots \\ a_2 b_N \\ \vdots \\ a_M b_1 \\ a_M b_2 \\ \vdots \\ a_M b_N \end{pmatrix}, \tag{10.240}$$

$$\begin{aligned} \boldsymbol{a}^{\mathrm{T}} \otimes \boldsymbol{b}^{\mathrm{T}} &= (a_1, a_2, \cdots, a_M) \otimes (b_1, b_2, \cdots, b_N) = \left(a_1 \boldsymbol{b}^{\mathrm{T}}, a_2 \boldsymbol{b}^{\mathrm{T}}, \cdots, a_M \boldsymbol{b}^{\mathrm{T}} \right) \\ &= \left(a_1 b_1, a_1 b_2, \cdots, a_1 b_N, a_2 b_1, a_2 b_2, \cdots, a_2 b_N, \cdots, a_M b_1, a_M b_2, \cdots, a_M b_N \right). \end{aligned} \tag{10.241}$$

We introduce the following two-dimensional fundamental vectors:

$$|1\rangle \equiv \begin{pmatrix} 1 \\ 0 \end{pmatrix}, \ |2\rangle \equiv \begin{pmatrix} 0 \\ 1 \end{pmatrix}, \tag{10.242}$$

$$|1\rangle \equiv (1, 0), \ \langle 2| \equiv (0, 1). \tag{10.243}$$

By using the fundamental vectors in two-dimensional space, we define the vertical and horizontal fundamental vectors in four-dimensional space by using the tensor product as follows:

$$\begin{cases} |1,1\rangle \equiv |1\rangle \otimes |1\rangle = \begin{pmatrix} 1 \\ 0 \\ 0 \\ 0 \end{pmatrix}, \ |1,2\rangle \equiv |1\rangle \otimes |2\rangle = \begin{pmatrix} 0 \\ 1 \\ 0 \\ 0 \end{pmatrix}, \\ |2,1\rangle \equiv |2\rangle \otimes |1\rangle = \begin{pmatrix} 0 \\ 0 \\ 1 \\ 0 \end{pmatrix}, \ |2,2\rangle \equiv |2\rangle \otimes |2\rangle = \begin{pmatrix} 0 \\ 0 \\ 0 \\ 1 \end{pmatrix}, \end{cases} \tag{10.244}$$

$$\begin{cases} \langle 1,1| \equiv \langle 1|\otimes\langle 1| = (1,0,0,0), \ \langle 1,2| \equiv \langle 1|\otimes\langle 2| = (0,1,0,0), \\ \langle 2,1| \equiv \langle 2|\otimes\langle 1| = (0,0,1,0), \ \langle 2,2| \equiv \langle 2|\otimes\langle 2| = (0,0,0,1), \end{cases} \tag{10.245}$$

It is easy to confirm the following equality:

$$\langle i,j| \begin{pmatrix} A_{11} & A_{12} \\ A_{21} & A_{22} \end{pmatrix} \otimes \begin{pmatrix} B_{11} & B_{12} \\ B_{21} & B_{22} \end{pmatrix} |i',j'\rangle = A_{i,i'} B_{j,j'}. \tag{10.246}$$

By extending the above example to general-dimensional fundamental vectors, the $(i,j|i',j')$-components of $\boldsymbol{A}\times\boldsymbol{B}$ for any $M\times M$ matrix $\boldsymbol{A}$ and $N\times N$ matrix $\boldsymbol{B}$ are expressed as

$$\langle i,j|\boldsymbol{A}\otimes\boldsymbol{B}|i',j'\rangle = \langle i|\boldsymbol{A}|i'\rangle\langle j|\boldsymbol{B}|j'\rangle = A_{i,i'} B_{j,j'}. \tag{10.247}$$

For $M\times M$ matrices $\boldsymbol{A}$ and $\boldsymbol{C}$ and $N\times N$ matrices $\boldsymbol{B}$ and $\boldsymbol{D}$, we have

$$(\boldsymbol{A}\otimes\boldsymbol{B})(\boldsymbol{C}\otimes\boldsymbol{D}) = (\boldsymbol{A}\boldsymbol{C})\otimes(\boldsymbol{B}\boldsymbol{D}), \tag{10.248}$$

and

$$\mathrm{Tr}[\boldsymbol{A}\otimes\boldsymbol{B}] = (\mathrm{Tr}[\boldsymbol{A}])(\mathrm{Tr}[\boldsymbol{B}]). \tag{10.249}$$

In deriving the equality in Eq. (10.248), the $(i,j|i',j')$-components of the $MN\times MN$ matrix $(\boldsymbol{A}\otimes\boldsymbol{B})(\boldsymbol{C}\otimes\boldsymbol{D})$ are given by

$$\langle i,j|(\boldsymbol{A}\otimes\boldsymbol{B})(\boldsymbol{C}\otimes\boldsymbol{D})|i',j'\rangle = \sum_{i''=1}^{M}\sum_{j''=1}^{N} \langle i,j|(\boldsymbol{A}\otimes\boldsymbol{B})|i'',j''\rangle\langle i'',j''|(\boldsymbol{C}\otimes\boldsymbol{D})|i',j'\rangle$$
$$\big(i\in\{1,2,\cdots,M\},\ i'\in\{1,2,\cdots,M\},\ j\in\{1,2,\cdots,N\},\ j'\in\{1,2,\cdots,N\}\big). \tag{10.250}$$

For the $M\times M$ and $N\times N$ identity matrices $\boldsymbol{I}^{(M)}$ and $\boldsymbol{I}^{(N)}$, it is valid that

$$\left(\boldsymbol{A}\otimes\boldsymbol{I}^{(N)}\right)\left(\boldsymbol{I}^{(M)}\otimes\boldsymbol{B}\right)=\left(\boldsymbol{I}^{(M)}\otimes\boldsymbol{B}\right)\left(\boldsymbol{A}\otimes\boldsymbol{I}^{(N)}\right)=\boldsymbol{A}\otimes\boldsymbol{B}. \tag{10.251}$$

Moreover, by using mathematical induction, we can confirm the following binomial expansion:

$$\left(\boldsymbol{A}\otimes\boldsymbol{I}^{(N)}+\boldsymbol{I}^{(M)}\otimes\boldsymbol{B}\right)^{n}=\sum_{k=0}^{n}\frac{n!}{k!(n-k)!}\left(\boldsymbol{A}\otimes\boldsymbol{I}^{(N)}\right)^{k}\left(\boldsymbol{I}^{(M)}\otimes\boldsymbol{B}\right)^{n-k}. \tag{10.252}$$

By using Eq. (10.252), we can derive the following equality:

$$\begin{aligned}
\exp\left(\boldsymbol{A}\otimes\boldsymbol{I}^{(N)}+\boldsymbol{I}^{(M)}\otimes\boldsymbol{B}\right)&=\sum_{n=0}^{+\infty}\frac{1}{n!}\left(\boldsymbol{A}\otimes\boldsymbol{I}^{(N)}+\boldsymbol{I}^{(M)}\otimes\boldsymbol{B}\right)^{n}\\
&=\sum_{n=0}^{+\infty}\frac{1}{n!}\sum_{k=0}^{n}\frac{n!}{k!(n-k)!}\left(\boldsymbol{A}\otimes\boldsymbol{I}^{(N)}\right)^{k}\left(\boldsymbol{I}^{(M)}\otimes\boldsymbol{B}\right)^{n-k}\\
&=\sum_{k=0}^{+\infty}\sum_{n=k}^{+\infty}\frac{1}{n!}\frac{n!}{k!(n-k)!}\left(\boldsymbol{A}\otimes\boldsymbol{I}^{(N)}\right)^{k}\left(\boldsymbol{I}^{(M)}\otimes\boldsymbol{B}\right)^{n-k}\\
&=\sum_{k=0}^{+\infty}\sum_{n=k}^{+\infty}\frac{1}{k!(n-k)!}\left(\boldsymbol{A}\otimes\boldsymbol{I}^{(N)}\right)^{k}\left(\boldsymbol{I}^{(M)}\otimes\boldsymbol{B}\right)^{n-k}\\
&=\sum_{k=0}^{+\infty}\sum_{l=0}^{+\infty}\frac{1}{k!l!}\left(\boldsymbol{A}\otimes\boldsymbol{I}^{(N)}\right)^{k}\left(\boldsymbol{I}^{(M)}\otimes\boldsymbol{B}\right)^{l}\\
&=\left(\sum_{k=0}^{+\infty}\frac{1}{k!}\left(\boldsymbol{A}\otimes\boldsymbol{I}^{(N)}\right)^{k}\right)\left(\sum_{l=0}^{+\infty}\frac{1}{l!}\left(\boldsymbol{I}^{(M)}\otimes\boldsymbol{B}\right)^{l}\right)\\
&=\left(\sum_{k=0}^{+\infty}\frac{1}{k!}\left(\boldsymbol{A}^{k}\otimes\boldsymbol{I}^{(N)}\right)\right)\left(\sum_{l=0}^{+\infty}\frac{1}{l!}\left(\boldsymbol{I}^{(M)}\otimes\boldsymbol{B}^{l}\right)\right)\\
&=\left(\left(\sum_{k=0}^{+\infty}\frac{1}{k!}\boldsymbol{A}^{k}\right)\otimes\boldsymbol{I}^{(N)}\right)\left(\boldsymbol{I}^{(M)}\otimes\left(\sum_{l=0}^{+\infty}\frac{1}{l!}\boldsymbol{B}^{l}\right)\right)\\
&=\left(\exp(\boldsymbol{A})\otimes\boldsymbol{I}^{(N)}\right)\left(\boldsymbol{I}^{(M)}\otimes\exp(\boldsymbol{B})\right)\\
&=\exp(\boldsymbol{A})\otimes\exp(\boldsymbol{B}).
\end{aligned} \tag{10.253}$$

By taking the logarithm of both sides of Eq. (10.253), we have

$$\ln(\exp(\boldsymbol{A}))\otimes\boldsymbol{I}^{(N)}+\boldsymbol{I}^{(M)}\otimes\ln(\exp(\boldsymbol{B}))=\ln(\exp(\boldsymbol{A})\otimes\exp(\boldsymbol{B})). \tag{10.254}$$

10.4.4 Quantum Probabilistic Graphical Models and Quantum Expectation-Maximization Algorithm

This section explores a type of probabilistic graphical modeling based on Pauli spin matrices from the quantum statistical mechanical point of view. Our review focuses on the transverse Ising model in statistical mechanical informatics [37, 83, 84]. Note that generalization of the framework is possible.

Consider a graph specified by nodes and edges (V, E) where V is the set of all nodes i and E is the set of all edges $\{i, j\}$. We introduce Pauli spin matrices $\boldsymbol{\sigma}^z$ and $\boldsymbol{\sigma}^x$ as well as an identity matrix $\boldsymbol{I}$ defined by

$$\boldsymbol{\sigma}^z = \begin{pmatrix} +1 & 0 \\ 0 & -1 \end{pmatrix}, \ \boldsymbol{\sigma}^x = \begin{pmatrix} 0 & +1 \\ +1 & 0 \end{pmatrix}, \ \boldsymbol{I} = \begin{pmatrix} +1 & 0 \\ 0 & +1 \end{pmatrix}. \tag{10.255}$$

The Pauli spin matrices at each node $i \in V \equiv \{1, 2, \cdots, N\}$ are defined by

$$\begin{cases} \boldsymbol{\sigma}_1^x \equiv \boldsymbol{\sigma}^x \otimes \boldsymbol{I} \otimes \boldsymbol{I} \otimes \cdots \otimes \boldsymbol{I} \otimes \boldsymbol{I}, & \boldsymbol{\sigma}_1^y \equiv \boldsymbol{\sigma}^y \otimes \boldsymbol{I} \otimes \boldsymbol{I} \otimes \cdots \otimes \boldsymbol{I} \otimes \boldsymbol{I}, & \boldsymbol{\sigma}_1^z \equiv \boldsymbol{\sigma}^z \otimes \boldsymbol{I} \otimes \boldsymbol{I} \otimes \cdots \otimes \boldsymbol{I} \otimes \boldsymbol{I}, \\ \boldsymbol{\sigma}_2^x \equiv \boldsymbol{I} \otimes \boldsymbol{\sigma}^x \otimes \boldsymbol{I} \otimes \cdots \otimes \boldsymbol{I} \otimes \boldsymbol{I}, & \boldsymbol{\sigma}_2^y \equiv \boldsymbol{I} \otimes \boldsymbol{\sigma}^y \otimes \boldsymbol{I} \otimes \cdots \otimes \boldsymbol{I} \otimes \boldsymbol{I}, & \boldsymbol{\sigma}_2^z \equiv \boldsymbol{I} \otimes \boldsymbol{\sigma}^z \otimes \boldsymbol{I} \otimes \cdots \otimes \boldsymbol{I} \otimes \boldsymbol{I}, \\ \vdots & \vdots & \vdots \\ \boldsymbol{\sigma}_{|V|}^x \equiv \boldsymbol{I} \otimes \boldsymbol{I} \otimes \boldsymbol{I} \otimes \cdots \otimes \boldsymbol{I} \otimes \boldsymbol{\sigma}^x, & \boldsymbol{\sigma}_{|V|}^y \equiv \boldsymbol{I} \otimes \boldsymbol{I} \otimes \boldsymbol{I} \otimes \cdots \otimes \boldsymbol{I} \otimes \boldsymbol{\sigma}^y, & \boldsymbol{\sigma}_{|V|}^z \equiv \boldsymbol{I} \otimes \boldsymbol{I} \otimes \boldsymbol{I} \otimes \cdots \otimes \boldsymbol{I} \otimes \boldsymbol{\sigma}^z. \end{cases} \tag{10.256}$$

The vertical and horizontal N-dimensional state vectors are defined by

$$|s_1, s_2, \cdots, s_{|V|}\rangle \equiv |s_1\rangle \otimes |s_2\rangle \otimes \cdots \otimes |s_{|V|}\rangle \ (s_1 \in \Omega, s_2 \in \Omega, \cdots, s_{|V|} \in \Omega), \tag{10.257}$$

$$\langle s_1, s_2, \cdots, s_{|V|}| \equiv \langle s_1| \otimes \langle s_2| \otimes \cdots \otimes \langle s_{|V|}| \ (s_1 \in \Omega, s_2 \in \Omega, \cdots, s_{|V|} \in \Omega), \tag{10.258}$$

where

$$\langle +1| \equiv (1, 0), \ \langle -1| \equiv (0, 1), \ |+1\rangle \equiv \begin{pmatrix} 1 \\ 0 \end{pmatrix}, \ |-1\rangle \equiv \begin{pmatrix} 0 \\ 1 \end{pmatrix}. \tag{10.259}$$

By using the state vector representations, $(s_1, s_2, \cdots, s_{|V|}|s'_1, s'_2, \cdots, s'_{|V|})$-elements of $\boldsymbol{\sigma}_i^x$, $\boldsymbol{\sigma}_j^z$ and $\boldsymbol{\sigma}_i^z \boldsymbol{\sigma}_j^z$ are given as

$$\langle s_1, s_2, \cdots, s_{|V|}|\boldsymbol{\sigma}_i^x|s'_1, s'_2, \cdots, s'_{|V|}\rangle = \left(\prod_{k \in V \setminus \{i\}} \delta_{s_k, s'_k} \right) \langle s_i|\boldsymbol{\sigma}^x|s'_i\rangle$$
$$(s_1 \in \Omega, s_2 \in \Omega, \cdots, s_{|V|} \in \Omega; \ s'_1 \in \Omega, s'_2 \in \Omega, \cdots, s'_{|V|} \in \Omega), \tag{10.260}$$

$$\langle s_1, s_2, \cdots, s_{|V|}|\boldsymbol{\sigma}_i^z|s_1', s_2', \cdots, s_{|V|}'\rangle = \left(\prod_{k\in V\backslash\{i\}} \delta_{s_k,s_k'}\right)\langle s_i|\boldsymbol{\sigma}^z|s_i'\rangle$$
$$(s_1\in\Omega, s_2\in\Omega, \cdots, s_{|V|}\in\Omega;\ s_1'\in\Omega, s_2'\in\Omega, \cdots, s_{|V|}'\in\Omega), \quad (10.261)$$

$$\langle s_1, s_2, \cdots, s_{|V|}|\boldsymbol{\sigma}_i^z\boldsymbol{\sigma}_j^z|s_1', s_2', \cdots, s_{|V|}'\rangle = \left(\prod_{k\in V\backslash\{i,j\}} \delta_{s_k,s_k'}\right)\langle s_i, s_j|(\boldsymbol{\sigma}^z\otimes\boldsymbol{I})(\boldsymbol{I}\otimes\boldsymbol{\sigma}^z)|s_i', s_j'\rangle$$
$$(s_1\in\Omega, s_2\in\Omega, \cdots, s_{|V|}\in\Omega;\ s_1'\in\Omega, s_2'\in\Omega, \cdots, s_{|V|}'\in\Omega). \quad (10.262)$$

The prior density matrix $\boldsymbol{P}(\alpha, \gamma)$ and the data generative density matrix $\boldsymbol{P}(\boldsymbol{d}|\beta)$ for a given data vector $\boldsymbol{d}$ are assumed to be

$$\boldsymbol{P}(\alpha, \gamma) = \frac{\exp\Big(-\frac{1}{2}\alpha\sum_{\{i,j\}\in E}\Big(\boldsymbol{\sigma}_i^z - \boldsymbol{\sigma}_j^z\Big)^2 + \gamma\sum_{i\in V}\boldsymbol{\sigma}_i^x\Big)}{\mathrm{Tr}\Big[\exp\Big(-\alpha\sum_{\{i,j\}\in E}\Big(\boldsymbol{\sigma}_i^z - \boldsymbol{\sigma}_j^z\Big)^2 + \gamma\sum_{i\in V}\boldsymbol{\sigma}_i^x\Big)\Big]}, \quad (10.263)$$

$$\boldsymbol{P}(\boldsymbol{d}|\beta) = \left(\sqrt{\frac{\beta}{2\pi}}\right)^{|V|}\exp\left(-\frac{1}{2}\beta\sum_{i\in V}\Big(d_i\boldsymbol{I}^{(2^{|V|})} - \boldsymbol{\sigma}_i^z\Big)^2\right), \quad (10.264)$$

where α, β, and γ are hyperparameters. The data generative density matrix $\boldsymbol{P}(\boldsymbol{d}|\beta)$ is expressed as a $|\Omega|^{|V|}\times|\Omega|^{|V|}$ diagonal matrix in which all the off-diagonal elements are zero. Each diagonal element $\langle s_1, s_2, \cdots, s_{|V|}|\boldsymbol{P}(\boldsymbol{d}|\beta)|s_1, s_2, \cdots, s_{|V|}\rangle$ $((s_1, s_2, \cdots, s_{|V|})^{\mathrm{T}}\in\Omega^{|V|})$ corresponds to the probability of the data vector $\boldsymbol{d}$ according to additive white Gaussian noise when the state vector $(s_1, s_2, \cdots, s_{|V|})$ is given, and β corresponds to the inverse of variance in the additive white Gaussian noise. By considering a quantum statistical mechanical extension of the Bayes formula, a posterior density matrix $\boldsymbol{P}(\boldsymbol{d}, \alpha, \beta, \gamma)$ and a joint density matrix $\boldsymbol{P}(\boldsymbol{d}|\alpha, \beta, \gamma)$ can be expressed as follows:

$$\boldsymbol{P}(\boldsymbol{d}, \alpha, \beta, \gamma) \equiv \frac{\exp\Big(\ln\Big(\boldsymbol{P}(\boldsymbol{d}|\beta)\Big) + \ln\Big(\boldsymbol{P}(\alpha, \gamma)\Big)\Big)}{\mathrm{Tr}\Big[\exp\Big(\ln\Big(\boldsymbol{P}(\boldsymbol{d}|\beta)\Big) + \ln\Big(\boldsymbol{P}(\alpha, \gamma)\Big)\Big)\Big]}$$
$$= \frac{\exp\Big(-\frac{1}{2}\alpha\sum_{\{i,j\}\in E}\Big(\boldsymbol{\sigma}_i^z - \boldsymbol{\sigma}_j^z\Big)^2 - \frac{1}{2}\beta\sum_{i\in V}\Big(d_i\boldsymbol{I}^{(2^{|V|})} - \boldsymbol{\sigma}_i^z\Big)^2 + \gamma\sum_{i\in V}\boldsymbol{\sigma}_i^x\Big)}{\mathrm{Tr}\Big[\exp\Big(-\frac{1}{2}\alpha\sum_{\{i,j\}\in E}\Big(\boldsymbol{\sigma}_i^z - \boldsymbol{\sigma}_j^z\Big)^2 - \frac{1}{2}\beta\sum_{i\in V}\Big(d_i\boldsymbol{I}^{(2^{|V|})} - \boldsymbol{\sigma}_i^z\Big)^2 + \gamma\sum_{i\in V}\boldsymbol{\sigma}_i^x\Big)\Big]}, \quad (10.265)$$

$$
\boldsymbol{P}\big(\boldsymbol{d}\big|\alpha,\beta,\gamma\big)\equiv\exp\Big(\ln\Big(\boldsymbol{P}(\boldsymbol{d}|\beta)\Big)+\ln\Big(\boldsymbol{P}(\alpha,\gamma)\Big)\Big)
$$

$$
=\frac{\exp\Big(-\frac{1}{2}\alpha\sum_{\{i,j\}\in E}\Big(\sigma_i^z-\sigma_j^z\Big)^2+\frac{1}{2}\beta\sum_{i\in V}(d_i\boldsymbol{I}^{(2^{|V|})}-\sigma_i^z)^2+\gamma\sum_{i\in V}\sigma_i^x\Big)}{\Big(\sqrt{\frac{2\pi}{\beta}}\Big)^{|V|}\mathrm{Tr}\Big[\exp\Big(-\frac{1}{2}\alpha\sum_{\{i,j\}\in E}\Big(\sigma_i^z-\sigma_j^z\Big)^2+\gamma\sum_{i\in V}\sigma_i^x\Big)\Big]}.
\tag{10.266}
$$

The estimates of the states of the hyperparameters $\big(\widehat{\alpha}(\boldsymbol{d}),\widehat{\beta}(\boldsymbol{d}),\widehat{\gamma}(\boldsymbol{d})\big)$ are found that maximize the marginal likelihood $\mathrm{Tr}\Big[\boldsymbol{P}\big(\boldsymbol{d}\big|\alpha,\beta,\gamma\big)\Big]$ as follows:

$$
\big(\widehat{\alpha}(\boldsymbol{d}),\widehat{\beta}(\boldsymbol{d}),\widehat{\gamma}(\boldsymbol{d})\big)\equiv\arg\max_{(\alpha,\beta,\gamma)}\mathrm{Tr}\Big[\boldsymbol{P}\big(\boldsymbol{d}\big|\alpha,\beta,\gamma\big)\Big].
\tag{10.267}
$$

To achieve the estimation criteria for hyperparameters α, β, and γ in Eqs. (10.267), we extend the $\mathcal{Q}$-function in Eq. (10.8) to the following expression from a quantum statistical mechanical point of view:

$$
\mathcal{Q}\Big(\alpha,\beta,\gamma\Big|\alpha',\beta',\gamma',\boldsymbol{d}\Big)\equiv\mathrm{Tr}\Big[\boldsymbol{P}\big(\boldsymbol{d},\alpha',\beta',\gamma'\big)\ln\Big(\boldsymbol{P}\big(\boldsymbol{d}\big|\alpha,\beta,\gamma\big)\Big)\Big]
\tag{10.268}
$$

The quantum EM algorithm can be summarized as a procedure consisting of the following **E-** and **M-step** which are repeated for $t=0,1,2,\cdots$ until $\widehat{\alpha}$ and $\widehat{\beta}$ converge:

E-step: Compute $\mathcal{Q}\big(\alpha,\beta\big|\alpha(t),\beta(t),\boldsymbol{d}\big)$ for various values of α and β.
M-step: Determine $\big(\alpha(t+1),\beta(t+1)\big)$ so as to satisfy the extremum of conditions of $\mathcal{Q}\big(\alpha,\beta\big|\alpha(t),\beta(t),\boldsymbol{d}\big)$ with respect to α and β. Update $\widehat{\alpha}\leftarrow\alpha(t+1)$ and $\widehat{\beta}\leftarrow\beta(t+1)$.

The quantum EM algorithm can obtain the solution of the extremum condition in the marginal likelihood $\mathrm{Tr}\Big[\boldsymbol{P}\big(\boldsymbol{d}\big|\alpha,\beta,\gamma\big)\Big]$, because we have the following equalities:

$$
\begin{cases}
\Big[\frac{\partial}{\partial\alpha}\mathcal{Q}\Big(\alpha,\beta,\gamma\Big|\widehat{\alpha},\widehat{\beta},\widehat{\gamma},\boldsymbol{d}\Big)\Big]_{(\alpha,\beta,\gamma)=(\widehat{\alpha},\widehat{\beta},\widehat{\gamma})}=\Big[\frac{\partial}{\partial\alpha}\ln\Big(\mathrm{Tr}\Big[\boldsymbol{P}\big(\boldsymbol{d}\big|\alpha,\beta,\gamma\big)\Big]\Big)\Big]_{(\alpha,\beta,\gamma)=(\widehat{\alpha},\widehat{\beta},\widehat{\gamma})},\\
\Big[\frac{\partial}{\partial\beta}\mathcal{Q}\Big(\alpha,\beta,\gamma\Big|\widehat{\alpha},\widehat{\beta},\widehat{\gamma},\boldsymbol{d}\Big)\Big]_{(\alpha,\beta,\gamma)=(\widehat{\alpha},\widehat{\beta},\widehat{\gamma})}=\Big[\frac{\partial}{\partial\beta}\ln\Big(\mathrm{Tr}\Big[\boldsymbol{P}\big(\boldsymbol{d}\big|\alpha,\beta,\gamma\big)\Big]\Big)\Big]_{(\alpha,\beta,\gamma)=(\widehat{\alpha},\widehat{\beta},\widehat{\gamma})},\\
\Big[\frac{\partial}{\partial\gamma}\mathcal{Q}\Big(\alpha,\beta,\gamma\Big|\widehat{\gamma},\widehat{\beta},\widehat{\gamma},\boldsymbol{d}\Big)\Big]_{(\alpha,\beta,\gamma)=(\widehat{\alpha},\widehat{\beta},\widehat{\gamma})}=\Big[\frac{\partial}{\partial\alpha}\ln\Big(\mathrm{Tr}\Big[\boldsymbol{P}\big(\boldsymbol{d}\big|\alpha,\beta,\gamma\big)\Big]\Big)\Big]_{(\alpha,\beta,\gamma)=(\widehat{\alpha},\widehat{\beta},\widehat{\gamma})}.
\end{cases}
\tag{10.269}
$$

By substituting Eq. (10.265) into Eq. (10.268), the $\mathcal{Q}$-function can be rewritten as follows:

$$
\mathcal{Q}\big(\alpha,\beta,\gamma\big|\alpha',\beta',\gamma',\boldsymbol{d}\big)=-\frac{1}{2}\alpha\sum_{\{i,j\}\in E}\mathrm{Tr}\big(\boldsymbol{\sigma}^z\otimes\boldsymbol{I}-\boldsymbol{I}\otimes\boldsymbol{\sigma}^z\big)^2\boldsymbol{P}_{ij}\big(\boldsymbol{d},\alpha',\beta',\gamma'\big)
$$

$$-\frac{1}{2}\beta\sum_{i\in V}\mathrm{Tr}\big[d_i\boldsymbol{I}-\boldsymbol{\sigma}^z)^2\boldsymbol{P}_i(\boldsymbol{d},\alpha',\beta',\gamma')\big]$$
$$+\gamma\sum_{i\in V}\mathrm{Tr}\big[\boldsymbol{\sigma}_i^x\boldsymbol{P}_i(\boldsymbol{d},\alpha',\beta',\gamma')\big]$$
$$+|V|\ln\left(\sqrt{\frac{2\pi}{\beta}}\right)$$
$$+\ln\Big(\mathrm{Tr}\Big[\exp\Big(-\frac{1}{2}\alpha\sum_{\{i,j\}\in E}(\boldsymbol{\sigma}^z\otimes\boldsymbol{I}-\boldsymbol{I}\otimes\boldsymbol{\sigma}^z)^2+\gamma\sum_{i\in V}\boldsymbol{\sigma}_i^x\Big)\Big]\Big). \tag{10.270}$$

The extremum conditions of $\mathcal{Q}\Big(\alpha,\beta,\gamma\Big|\alpha(t),\beta(t),\gamma(t),\boldsymbol{d}\Big)$ with respect to α, β and γ, such that,

$$\begin{cases}\frac{\partial}{\partial\alpha}\mathcal{Q}\Big(\alpha,\beta,\gamma\Big|\alpha(t),\beta(t),\gamma(t),\boldsymbol{d}\Big)=0,\\ \frac{\partial}{\partial\beta}\mathcal{Q}\Big(\alpha,\beta,\gamma\Big|\alpha(t),\beta(t),\gamma(t),\boldsymbol{d}\Big)=0,\\ \frac{\partial}{\partial\gamma}\mathcal{Q}\Big(\alpha,\beta,\gamma\Big|\alpha(t),\beta(t),\gamma(t),\boldsymbol{d}\Big)=0\end{cases} \tag{10.271}$$

can be reduced to the following simutaneous update rules in the quantum EM algorithm:

$$\sum_{\{i,j\}\in E}\mathrm{Tr}\Big[(\boldsymbol{\sigma}^z\otimes\boldsymbol{I}-\boldsymbol{I}\otimes\boldsymbol{\sigma}^z)^2\boldsymbol{P}_{ij}(\alpha(t+1),\gamma(t+1))\Big]$$
$$=\sum_{\{i,j\}\in E}\mathrm{Tr}\Big[(\boldsymbol{\sigma}^z\otimes\boldsymbol{I}-\boldsymbol{I}\otimes\boldsymbol{\sigma}^z)^2\boldsymbol{P}_{ij}(\boldsymbol{d},\alpha(t),\beta(t),\gamma(t))\Big], \tag{10.272}$$

$$\frac{1}{\beta(t+1)}=\sum_{i\in V}\mathrm{Tr}\big[(d_i\boldsymbol{I}-\boldsymbol{\sigma}^z)^2\boldsymbol{P}_i(\boldsymbol{d},\alpha(t),\beta(t),\gamma(t))\big], \tag{10.273}$$

$$\sum_{i\in V}\mathrm{Tr}\big[\boldsymbol{\sigma}^x\boldsymbol{P}_i(\alpha(t+1),\gamma(t+1))\big]=\sum_{i\in V}\mathrm{Tr}\big[\boldsymbol{\sigma}^x\boldsymbol{P}_i(\boldsymbol{d},\alpha(t),\beta(t),\gamma(t))\big], \tag{10.274}$$

where

$$\begin{aligned}\langle s_i|\boldsymbol{P}_i(\boldsymbol{d},\alpha,\beta,\gamma)|s_i'\rangle &= \langle s_i|\mathrm{Tr}_{\backslash i}\boldsymbol{P}(\boldsymbol{d},\alpha,\beta,\gamma)|s_i'\rangle\\ &\equiv \sum_{\tau_1\in\Omega}\sum_{\tau_2\in\Omega}\cdots\sum_{\tau_{|V|}\in\Omega}\sum_{\tau_1'\in\Omega}\sum_{\tau_2'\in\Omega}\cdots\sum_{\tau_{|V|}'\in\Omega}\delta_{s_i,\tau_i}\delta_{s_i',\tau_i'}\\ &\quad\times\left(\prod_{j\in V\backslash\{i\}}\delta_{\tau_j,\tau_j'}\right)\langle\tau_1,\tau_2,\cdots,\tau_{|V|}|\boldsymbol{P}(\boldsymbol{d},\alpha,\beta,\gamma)|\tau_1',\tau_2',\cdots,\tau_{|V|}'\rangle\\ &\quad(s_i\in\Omega,\ s_i'\in\Omega.\ i\in V),\end{aligned} \tag{10.275}$$

$$\begin{aligned}\langle s_i, s_j | \boldsymbol{P}_{ij}(\boldsymbol{d}, \alpha, \beta, \gamma) | s_i', s_j' \rangle &= \langle s_i, s_j | \boldsymbol{P}_{ji}(\boldsymbol{d}, \alpha, \beta, \gamma) | s_i', s_j' \rangle \\ &= \langle s_i, s_j | \mathrm{Tr}_{\backslash\{i,j\}} \boldsymbol{P}(\boldsymbol{d}, \alpha, \beta, \gamma) | s_i', s_j' \rangle \\ &\equiv \sum_{\tau_1\in\Omega}\sum_{\tau_2\in\Omega}\cdots\sum_{\tau_{|V|}\in\Omega}\sum_{\tau_1'\in\Omega}\sum_{\tau_2'\in\Omega}\cdots\sum_{\tau_{|V|}'\in\Omega} \delta_{s_i,\tau_i}\delta_{s_j,\tau_j}\delta_{s_i',\tau_i'}\delta_{s_j',\tau_j'} \\ &\times\left(\prod_{k\in V\backslash\{i,j\}}\delta_{\tau_k,\tau_k'}\right)\langle \tau_1, \tau_2, \cdots, \tau_{|V|} | \boldsymbol{P}(\boldsymbol{d}, \alpha, \beta, \gamma) | \tau_1', \tau_2', \cdots, \tau_{|V|}' \rangle \\ &(s_i\in\Omega\ s_j\in\Omega,\ s_i'\in\Omega,\ s_j'\in\Omega,\ i\in V,\ j\in V,\ i<j), \end{aligned} \tag{10.276}$$

$$\begin{aligned}\langle s_i, s_j | \boldsymbol{P}_{ij}(\alpha, \gamma) | s_i', s_j' \rangle &= \langle s_i, s_j | \boldsymbol{P}_{ji}(\alpha, \gamma) | s_i', s_j' \rangle \\ &= \langle s_i, s_j | \mathrm{Tr}_{\backslash\{i,j\}} \boldsymbol{P}(\alpha, \gamma) | s_i', s_j' \rangle \\ &\equiv \sum_{\tau_1\in\Omega}\sum_{\tau_2\in\Omega}\cdots\sum_{\tau_{|V|}\in\Omega}\sum_{\tau_1'\in\Omega}\sum_{\tau_2'\in\Omega}\cdots\sum_{\tau_{|V|}'\in\Omega} \delta_{s_i,\tau_i}\delta_{s_j,\tau_j}\delta_{s_i',\tau_i'}\delta_{s_j',\tau_j'} \\ &\times\left(\prod_{k\in V\backslash\{i,j\}}\delta_{\tau_k,\tau_k'}\right)\langle \tau_1, \tau_2, \cdots, \tau_{|V|} | \boldsymbol{P}(\alpha, \gamma) | \tau_1', \tau_2', \cdots, \tau_{|V|}' \rangle \\ &(s_i\in\Omega\ s_j\in\Omega,\ s_i'\in\Omega,\ s_j'\in\Omega,\ i\in V,\ j\in V,\ i<j). \end{aligned} \tag{10.277}$$

Finally, we explain how the state at each node is estimated from the reduced posterior density matrix $\boldsymbol{P}_i(\boldsymbol{d}, \alpha, \beta, \gamma)$ in Eq. (10.276) for each node $i(\in V)$. The reduced posterior density matrix $\boldsymbol{P}_i(\boldsymbol{d}, \alpha, \beta, \gamma)$ is a real symmetric matrix and can be diagonalized as

$$\begin{aligned}\boldsymbol{P}_i(\boldsymbol{d}, \alpha, \beta, \gamma) &= \begin{pmatrix} \psi_i^{(1)}(+1|\boldsymbol{d}, \alpha, \beta, \gamma) & \psi_i^{(2)}(+1|\boldsymbol{d}, \alpha, \beta, \gamma) \\ \psi_i^{(1)}(-1|\boldsymbol{d}, \alpha, \beta, \gamma) & \psi_i^{(2)}(-1|\boldsymbol{d}, \alpha, \beta, \gamma) \end{pmatrix} \\ &\times\begin{pmatrix} P_i^{(1)}(\boldsymbol{d}, \alpha, \beta, \gamma) & 0 \\ 0 & P_i^{(2)}(\boldsymbol{d}, \alpha, \beta, \gamma) \end{pmatrix} \\ &\times\begin{pmatrix} \psi_i^{(1)}(+1|\boldsymbol{d}, \alpha, \beta, \gamma) & \psi_i^{(2)}(+1|\boldsymbol{d}, \alpha, \beta, \gamma) \\ \psi_i^{(1)}(-1|\boldsymbol{d}, \alpha, \beta, \gamma) & \psi_i^{(2)}(-1|\boldsymbol{d}, \alpha, \beta, \gamma) \end{pmatrix}^{\mathrm{T}}, \end{aligned} \tag{10.278}$$

where the eigenvalues, $P_i^{(1)}(\boldsymbol{d}, \alpha, \beta, \gamma)$ and $P_i^{(2)}(\boldsymbol{d}, \alpha, \beta, \gamma)$, are always real numbers. The vectors $\begin{pmatrix} \psi_i^{(1)}(+1|\boldsymbol{d}, \alpha, \beta, \gamma) \\ \psi_i^{(1)}(-1|\boldsymbol{d}, \alpha, \beta, \gamma) \end{pmatrix}$ and $\begin{pmatrix} \psi_i^{(2)}(+1|\boldsymbol{d}, \alpha, \beta, \gamma) \\ \psi_i^{(2)}(-1|\boldsymbol{d}, \alpha, \beta, \gamma) \end{pmatrix}$ correspond to the eigenvectors for the eigenvalues $P_i^{(1)}(\boldsymbol{d}, \alpha, \beta, \gamma)$ and $P_i^{(2)}(\boldsymbol{d}, \alpha, \beta, \gamma)$, such that

$$P_i(d,\alpha,\beta,\gamma)\begin{pmatrix}\psi_i^{(n)}(+1|d,\alpha,\beta,\gamma)\\ \psi_i^{(n)}(-1|d,\alpha,\beta,\gamma)\end{pmatrix} = P_i(n|d,\alpha,\beta,\gamma)\begin{pmatrix}\psi_i^{(n)}(+1|d,\alpha,\beta,\gamma)\\ \psi_i^{(n)}(-1|d,\alpha,\beta,\gamma)\end{pmatrix}$$
$$(i\in V,\ n\in\{1,2\}). \qquad (10.279)$$

This means that the eigenvectors correspond to all possible states and probabilities of the states $\begin{pmatrix}\psi_i^{(1)}(+1|d,\alpha,\beta,\gamma)\\ \psi_i^{(1)}(-1|d,\alpha,\beta,\gamma)\end{pmatrix}$ and $\begin{pmatrix}\psi_i^{(2)}(+1|d,\alpha,\beta,\gamma)\\ \psi_i^{(2)}(-1|d,\alpha,\beta,\gamma)\end{pmatrix}$ are $P_i^{(2)}(d,\alpha,\beta,\gamma)$ and $P_i^{(2)}(d,\alpha,\beta,\gamma)$, respectively, in the reduced density matrix $P_i(d,\alpha,\beta,\gamma)$. The estimates for the state at each node $i(\in V)$, $\begin{pmatrix}\widehat{\psi}_i\big(+1\big|d,\widehat{\alpha},\widehat{\beta},\widehat{\gamma}\big)\\ \widehat{\psi}_i\big(-1\big|d,\widehat{\alpha},\widehat{\beta},\widehat{\gamma}\big)\end{pmatrix}$, are given by

$$\begin{pmatrix}\widehat{\psi}_i\big(+1\big|d,\widehat{\alpha},\widehat{\beta},\widehat{\gamma}\big)\\ \widehat{\psi}_i\big(-1\big|d,\widehat{\alpha},\widehat{\beta},\widehat{\gamma}\big)\end{pmatrix} \equiv \mathrm{argmax}\, P_i\big(d,\widehat{\alpha},\widehat{\beta},\widehat{\gamma}\big)\ (i\in V). \qquad (10.280)$$

These estimation criteria in Eqs. (10.267) and (10.280) correspond to quantum statistical mechanical extensions of the maximizations of marginal likelihood and posterior marginal.

10.4.5 Quantum Expectation-Maximization (EM) Algorithm for Probabilistic Image Segmentation

This section applies the framework of Sect. 10.4.5 to the EM algorithm for probabilistic image segmentations in Sect. 10.2.3. In our present framework, **Hubbard Operators** [85] are used instead of Pauli spin matrices.

First, we introduce Hubbard operators $X_i^{\tau,\tau'}$ at each node $i(\in V)$ as follows:

$$\begin{cases} X_1^{(\tau,\tau')} \equiv X^{(\tau,\tau')}\otimes I\otimes I\otimes\cdots\otimes I\otimes I,\\ X_2^{(\tau,\tau')} \equiv I\otimes X^{(\tau,\tau')}\otimes I\otimes\cdots\otimes I\otimes I,\\ \quad\vdots\\ X_{|V|}^{(\tau,\tau')} \equiv I\otimes I\otimes I\otimes\cdots\otimes I\otimes X_{|V|}^{(\tau,\tau')}, \end{cases} \quad (\tau\in\Omega,\ \tau'\in\Omega), \qquad (10.281)$$

where

$$X^{(+1,+1)} \equiv \begin{pmatrix}1&0\\0&0\end{pmatrix},\ X^{(+1,-1)} \equiv \begin{pmatrix}0&0\\1&0\end{pmatrix},\ X^{(-1,+1)} \equiv \begin{pmatrix}0&1\\0&0\end{pmatrix},\ X^{(-1,-1)} \equiv \begin{pmatrix}0&0\\0&1\end{pmatrix}. \qquad (10.282)$$

In probabilistic segmentation and clustering, $\rho(D|s, a(+1), a(-1), C(+1), C(-1))$ in Eq. (10.29) and $P(s|\alpha)$ in Eq. (10.30) correspond to the data generative and prior models, respectively. By using the Hubbard operators and extending Eq. (10.29) and Eq. (10.30) from the standpoint of quantum statistical mechanical informatics, the density matrices of the data generative model and the prior model in quantum machine learning systems for probabilistic image processing can be expressed as follows:

$$
\begin{aligned}
&\boldsymbol{R}(\boldsymbol{D}|\boldsymbol{a}(+1),\boldsymbol{a}(-1),\boldsymbol{C}(+1),\boldsymbol{C}(-1))\\
&=\prod_{i\in V}\sum_{s_i\in\Omega}\boldsymbol{X}_i^{(s_i,s_i)}\sqrt{\frac{1}{\det(2\pi\boldsymbol{C}(s_i))}}\exp\left(-\frac{1}{2}(\boldsymbol{d}_i-\boldsymbol{a}(s_i))\boldsymbol{C}^{-1}(s_i)(\boldsymbol{d}_i-\boldsymbol{a}(s_i))^{\mathrm{T}}\right)\\
&=\exp\left(-\frac{1}{2}\sum_{i\in V}\sum_{s_i\in\Omega}\Big((\boldsymbol{d}_i-\boldsymbol{a}(s_i))\boldsymbol{C}^{-1}(s_i)(\boldsymbol{d}_i-\boldsymbol{a}(s_i))^{\mathrm{T}}+\ln(\det(2\pi\boldsymbol{C}(s_i)))\Big)\boldsymbol{X}_i^{(s_i,s_i)}\right),
\end{aligned}
\tag{10.283}
$$

$$
\boldsymbol{R}(\alpha,\gamma)=\frac{\exp\left(-2\alpha\sum_{\{i,j\}\in E}(\boldsymbol{I}^{(2^{|V|})}-\boldsymbol{X}_i^{(+1,+1)}\boldsymbol{X}_j^{(+1,+1)}-\boldsymbol{X}_i^{(-1,-1)}\boldsymbol{X}_j^{(-1,-1)})+\gamma\sum_{i\in V}(\boldsymbol{X}_i^{(+1,-1)}+\boldsymbol{X}_i^{(-1,+1)})\right)}{\mathrm{Tr}\left[\exp\left(-2\alpha\sum_{\{i,j\}\in E}(\boldsymbol{I}^{(2^{|V|})}-\boldsymbol{X}_i^{(+1,+1)}\boldsymbol{X}_j^{(+1,+1)}-\boldsymbol{X}_i^{(-1,-1)}\boldsymbol{X}_j^{(-1,-1)})+\gamma\sum_{i\in V}(\boldsymbol{X}_i^{(+1,-1)}+\boldsymbol{X}_i^{(-1,+1)})\right)\right]},
\tag{10.284}
$$

where

$$
\boldsymbol{a}(+1)=\begin{pmatrix}a_{\mathrm{R}}(+1)\\a_{\mathrm{G}}(+1)\\a_{\mathrm{B}}(+1)\end{pmatrix},\ \boldsymbol{a}(-1)=\begin{pmatrix}a_{\mathrm{R}}(-1)\\a_{\mathrm{G}}(-1)\\a_{\mathrm{B}}(-1)\end{pmatrix},
\tag{10.285}
$$

$$
\boldsymbol{C}(+1)=\begin{pmatrix}C_{\mathrm{RR}}(+1)&C_{\mathrm{RG}}(+1)&C_{\mathrm{RB}}(+1)\\C_{\mathrm{GR}}(+1)&C_{\mathrm{GG}}(+1)&C_{\mathrm{GB}}(+1)\\C_{\mathrm{BR}}(+1)&C_{\mathrm{BG}}(+1)&C_{\mathrm{BB}}(+1)\end{pmatrix},\ \boldsymbol{C}(-1)=\begin{pmatrix}C_{\mathrm{RR}}(-1)&C_{\mathrm{RG}}(-1)&C_{\mathrm{RB}}(-1)\\C_{\mathrm{GR}}(-1)&C_{\mathrm{GG}}(-1)&C_{\mathrm{GB}}(-1)\\C_{\mathrm{BR}}(-1)&C_{\mathrm{BG}}(-1)&C_{\mathrm{BB}}(-1)\end{pmatrix}.
\tag{10.286}
$$

The joint density matrix of $\boldsymbol{s}$ and $\boldsymbol{D}$ is expressed in terms of the data generative and prior density matrix as follows:

$$
\begin{aligned}
&\boldsymbol{P}(\boldsymbol{D}|\alpha,\boldsymbol{a}(+1),\boldsymbol{a}(-1),\boldsymbol{C}(+1),\boldsymbol{C}(-1))\\
&\equiv\exp(\ln(\boldsymbol{P}(\boldsymbol{D}|\boldsymbol{a}(+1),\boldsymbol{a}(-1),\boldsymbol{C}(+1),\boldsymbol{C}(-1)))+\ln(\boldsymbol{P}(\alpha,\gamma))).
\end{aligned}
\tag{10.287}
$$

By using the joint density matrix $\boldsymbol{P}(\boldsymbol{D},\alpha,\gamma,\boldsymbol{a}(+1),\boldsymbol{a}(-1),\boldsymbol{C}(+1),\boldsymbol{C}(-1))$, the posterior density matrix $\boldsymbol{P}(\boldsymbol{D},\alpha,\gamma,\boldsymbol{a}(+1),\boldsymbol{a}(-1),\boldsymbol{C}(+1),\boldsymbol{C}(-1))$ is defined by using Bayes formulas as follows:

$$
\boldsymbol{P}(\boldsymbol{D},\alpha,\gamma,\boldsymbol{a}(+1),\boldsymbol{a}(-1),\boldsymbol{C}(+1),\boldsymbol{C}(-1))\equiv\frac{\boldsymbol{P}(\boldsymbol{D}|\alpha,\gamma,\boldsymbol{a}(+1),\boldsymbol{a}(-1),\boldsymbol{C}(+1),\boldsymbol{C}(-1))}{\boldsymbol{P}(\boldsymbol{D}|\alpha,\gamma,\boldsymbol{a}(+1),\boldsymbol{a}(-1),\boldsymbol{C}(+1),\boldsymbol{C}(-1))},
\tag{10.288}
$$

Estimates of the hyperparameters and parameter vector, $\widehat{\alpha}(\boldsymbol{D})$, $\widehat{\gamma}(\boldsymbol{D})$, $\widehat{\boldsymbol{a}}(+1|\boldsymbol{D})$, $\widehat{\boldsymbol{a}}(-1|\boldsymbol{D})$, $\widehat{\boldsymbol{C}}(+1|\boldsymbol{D})$, $\widehat{\boldsymbol{C}}(-1|\boldsymbol{D})$, are given by

$$\Big(\widehat{\alpha}(\boldsymbol{D}), \widehat{\gamma}(\boldsymbol{D}), \widehat{\boldsymbol{a}}(+1|\boldsymbol{D}), \widehat{\boldsymbol{a}}(-1|\boldsymbol{D}), \widehat{\boldsymbol{C}}(+1|\boldsymbol{D}), \widehat{\boldsymbol{C}}(-1|\boldsymbol{D})\Big)$$
$$= \arg\max_{(\alpha,\gamma,\boldsymbol{\mu}(+1),\boldsymbol{\mu}(-1),\boldsymbol{C}(+1),\boldsymbol{C}(-1))} \mathrm{Tr}\big[\boldsymbol{P}(\boldsymbol{D}|\alpha, \gamma, \boldsymbol{a}(+1), \boldsymbol{a}(-1), \boldsymbol{C}(+1), \boldsymbol{C}(-1))\big], \tag{10.289}$$

The parameter vector $\widehat{\boldsymbol{s}}(\boldsymbol{D}) = \big(\widehat{s}_1(\boldsymbol{D}), \widehat{s}_2(\boldsymbol{D}), \cdots, \widehat{s}_{|V|}(\boldsymbol{D})\big)$ can be estimated from the reduced posterior marginal density matrix at each node i of $\boldsymbol{P}(\boldsymbol{D}, \alpha, \boldsymbol{a}(+1), \boldsymbol{a}(-1), \boldsymbol{C}(+1), \boldsymbol{C}(-1))$ by similar arguments to those for Eqs. (10.278), (10.279), and (10.280).

The $\mathcal{Q}$-function for the EM algorithm in the present framework is defined by

$$\mathcal{Q}\big(\alpha', \gamma', \boldsymbol{a}(+1), \boldsymbol{a}(-1), \boldsymbol{C}(+1), \boldsymbol{C}(-1)|\alpha', \gamma', \boldsymbol{a}'(+1), \boldsymbol{a}'(-1), \boldsymbol{C}'(+1), \boldsymbol{C}'(-1), \boldsymbol{D}\big)$$
$$\equiv \mathrm{Tr}\Big[\boldsymbol{P}\big(\boldsymbol{D}, \alpha, \gamma, \boldsymbol{a}'(+1), \boldsymbol{a}'(-1), \boldsymbol{C}'(+1), \boldsymbol{C}'(-1)\big)$$
$$\times \ln(\boldsymbol{P}(\boldsymbol{D}|\alpha, \gamma, \boldsymbol{a}(+1), \boldsymbol{a}(-1), \boldsymbol{C}(+1), \boldsymbol{C}(-1)))\Big]. \tag{10.290}$$

The EM algorithm is a procedure that performs the following **E-** and **M-step** repeatedly for $t = 0, 1, 2, \cdots$ until $\widehat{\alpha}(\boldsymbol{D})$, $\widehat{\boldsymbol{a}}(+1, \boldsymbol{D})$, $\widehat{\boldsymbol{a}}(-1, \boldsymbol{D})$, $\widehat{\boldsymbol{C}}(+1, \boldsymbol{D})$, $\widehat{\boldsymbol{C}}(-1, \boldsymbol{D})$ converge:

E-step: Compute $\mathcal{Q}\big(\alpha, \boldsymbol{a}(+1), \boldsymbol{a}(-1), \boldsymbol{C}(+1), \boldsymbol{C}(-1)\big|\alpha(t), \boldsymbol{a}(+1, t), \boldsymbol{a}(-1, t), \boldsymbol{C}(+1, t), \boldsymbol{C}(-1, t)\big)$ for various values of $\boldsymbol{a}(+1)$, $\boldsymbol{a}(-1)$, $\boldsymbol{C}(+1)$ and $\boldsymbol{C}(-1)$.

M-step: Determine $\alpha(t+1)$, $\boldsymbol{a}(+1, t+1)$, $\boldsymbol{a}(-1, t+1)$, $\boldsymbol{C}(+1, t+1)$ and $\boldsymbol{C}(-1, t+1)$
so as to satisfy the extremum conditions of $\mathcal{Q}$-function with respect to $\boldsymbol{a}(+1)$, $\boldsymbol{a}(-1)$, $\boldsymbol{C}(+1)$ and $\boldsymbol{C}(-1)$ as follows:

$$(\alpha(t+1), \boldsymbol{a}(+1, t+1), \boldsymbol{a}(-1, t+1), \boldsymbol{C}(+1, t+1), \boldsymbol{C}(-1, t+1))$$
$$\leftarrow \underset{\alpha,\boldsymbol{a}(+1),\boldsymbol{a}(-1),\boldsymbol{C}(+1),\boldsymbol{C}(-1)}{\mathrm{extremum}}$$
$$\mathcal{Q}\big(\alpha, \boldsymbol{a}(+1), \boldsymbol{a}(-1), \boldsymbol{C}(+1), \boldsymbol{C}(-1)\big|\alpha(t), \boldsymbol{a}(+1, t), \boldsymbol{a}(-1, t), \boldsymbol{C}(+1, t), \boldsymbol{C}(-1, t), \boldsymbol{D}\big). \tag{10.291}$$

Update $\widehat{\alpha}(\boldsymbol{D}) \leftarrow \alpha(t+1)$, $\widehat{\boldsymbol{a}}(+1, \boldsymbol{D}) \leftarrow \boldsymbol{a}(+1, t+1)$, $\widehat{\boldsymbol{a}}(-1, \boldsymbol{D}) \leftarrow \boldsymbol{a}(-1, t+1)$, $\widehat{\boldsymbol{C}}(+1, \boldsymbol{D}) \leftarrow \boldsymbol{C}(+1, t+1)$ and $\widehat{\boldsymbol{C}}(-1, \boldsymbol{D}) \leftarrow \boldsymbol{C}(-1, t+1)$.

By using some equalities in Eqs. (10.283), (10.284), (10.287), and (10.288), the EM algorithm using the $\mathcal{Q}$-function can be reduced to the following expression:

$$\frac{1}{|E|}\sum_{\{i,j\}\in E}\mathrm{Tr}\Big[\big(\boldsymbol{I}\otimes\boldsymbol{I}-\boldsymbol{X}^{(+1,+1)}\otimes\boldsymbol{X}^{(+1,+1)}-\boldsymbol{X}^{(+1,+1)}\otimes\boldsymbol{X}^{(+1,+1)}\big)\boldsymbol{P}_{ij}(\alpha(t+1),\gamma(t+1))\Big]$$
$$=\frac{1}{|E|}\sum_{\{i,j\}\in E}\mathrm{Tr}\Big[\Big(\boldsymbol{I}\otimes\boldsymbol{I}-\boldsymbol{X}^{(+1,+1)}\otimes\boldsymbol{X}^{(+1,+1)}-\boldsymbol{X}^{(+1,+1)}\otimes\boldsymbol{X}^{(+1,+1)}\Big)$$
$$\times\boldsymbol{P}_{ij}(\boldsymbol{D},\alpha(t),\gamma(t),\boldsymbol{a}(+1,t),\boldsymbol{a}(-1,t),\boldsymbol{C}(+1,t),\boldsymbol{C}(-1,t))\Big],\qquad(10.292)$$

$$\frac{1}{|V|}\sum_{i\in V}\mathrm{Tr}\Big[\Big(\boldsymbol{X}^{(+1,-1)}+\boldsymbol{X}^{(-1,+1)}\Big)\boldsymbol{P}_{i}(\alpha(t+1),\gamma(t+1))\Big]$$
$$=\frac{1}{|V|}\sum_{i\in V}\mathrm{Tr}\Big[\Big(\boldsymbol{X}^{(+1,-1)}+\boldsymbol{X}^{(-1,+1)}\Big)$$
$$\times\boldsymbol{P}_{i}(\boldsymbol{D},\alpha(t),\gamma(t),\boldsymbol{a}(+1,t),\boldsymbol{a}(-1,t),\boldsymbol{C}(+1,t),\boldsymbol{C}(-1,t))\Big],\qquad(10.293)$$

$$\boldsymbol{\mu}(\xi,t+1)=\frac{\sum_{i\in V}\boldsymbol{d}_i\mathrm{Tr}\Big[\boldsymbol{X}^{(\xi,\xi)}\boldsymbol{P}_{i}(\boldsymbol{D},\alpha(t),\gamma(t),\boldsymbol{a}(+1,t),\boldsymbol{a}(-1,t),\boldsymbol{C}(+1,t),\boldsymbol{C}(-1,t))\Big]}{\sum_{i\in V}\mathrm{Tr}\Big[\boldsymbol{X}^{(\xi,\xi)}\boldsymbol{P}_{i}(\boldsymbol{D},\alpha(t),\gamma(t),\boldsymbol{a}(+1,t),\boldsymbol{a}(-1,t),\boldsymbol{C}(+1,t),\boldsymbol{C}(-1,t))\Big]}\ (\xi\in\Omega),\qquad(10.294)$$

$$\boldsymbol{C}(\xi;t+1)$$
$$=\frac{\sum_{i\in V}(\boldsymbol{d}_i-\boldsymbol{a}(\xi;t))^{\mathrm{T}}(\boldsymbol{d}_i-\boldsymbol{a}(\xi;t))\mathrm{Tr}\Big[\boldsymbol{X}^{(\xi,\xi')}\boldsymbol{P}_{i}(\boldsymbol{D},\alpha(t),\gamma(t),\boldsymbol{a}(+1,t),\boldsymbol{a}(-1,t),\boldsymbol{C}(+1,t),\boldsymbol{C}(-1,t))\Big]}{\sum_{i\in V}\mathrm{Tr}\Big[\boldsymbol{X}^{(\xi,\xi')}\boldsymbol{P}_{i}(\boldsymbol{D},\alpha(t),\gamma(t),\boldsymbol{a}(+1,t),\boldsymbol{a}(-1,t),\boldsymbol{C}(+1,t),\boldsymbol{C}(-1,t))\Big]}\ (\xi\in\Omega),\qquad(10.295)$$

where

$$\langle s_i|\boldsymbol{P}_i(\boldsymbol{D},\alpha,\gamma,\boldsymbol{a}(+1),\boldsymbol{a}(-1),\boldsymbol{C}(+1),\boldsymbol{C}(-1))|s_i'\rangle$$
$$=\langle s_i|\mathrm{Tr}_{\setminus i}\boldsymbol{P}(\boldsymbol{D},\alpha,\gamma,\boldsymbol{a}(+1),\boldsymbol{a}(-1),\boldsymbol{C}(+1),\boldsymbol{C}(-1))|s_i'\rangle$$
$$\equiv\sum_{\tau_1\in\Omega}\sum_{\tau_2\in\Omega}\cdots\sum_{\tau_{|V|}\in\Omega}\sum_{\tau_1'\in\Omega}\sum_{\tau_2'\in\Omega}\cdots\sum_{\tau_{|V|}'\in\Omega}\delta_{s_i,\tau_i}\delta_{s_i',\tau_i'}$$
$$\times\Bigg(\prod_{j\in V\setminus\{i\}}\delta_{\tau_j,\tau_j'}\Bigg)\langle\tau_1,\tau_2,\cdots,\tau_{|V|}|\boldsymbol{P}(\boldsymbol{D},\alpha,\gamma,\boldsymbol{a}(+1),\boldsymbol{a}(-1),\boldsymbol{C}(+1),\boldsymbol{C}(-1)))|\tau_1',\tau_2',\cdots,\tau_{|V|}'\rangle$$
$$(s_i\in\Omega,\ s_i'\in\Omega.\ i\in V),\qquad(10.296)$$

$$\langle s_i,s_j|\boldsymbol{P}_{ij}(\boldsymbol{D},\alpha,\gamma,\boldsymbol{a}(+1),\boldsymbol{a}(-1),\boldsymbol{C}(+1),\boldsymbol{C}(-1)))|s_i',s_j'\rangle$$
$$=\langle s_i,s_j|\boldsymbol{P}_{ji}(\boldsymbol{D},\alpha,\gamma,\boldsymbol{a}(+1),\boldsymbol{a}(-1),\boldsymbol{C}(+1),\boldsymbol{C}(-1)))|s_i',s_j'\rangle$$

$$
\begin{aligned}
&= \langle s_i, s_j|\mathrm{Tr}_{\backslash\{i,j\}}\boldsymbol{P}(\boldsymbol{D},\alpha,\beta,\gamma,\boldsymbol{a}(+1),\boldsymbol{a}(-1),\boldsymbol{C}(+1),\boldsymbol{C}(-1)))|s_i', s_j'\rangle \\
&\equiv \sum_{\tau_1\in\Omega}\sum_{\tau_2\in\Omega}\cdots\sum_{\tau_{|V|}\in\Omega}\sum_{\tau_1'\in\Omega}\sum_{\tau_2'\in\Omega}\cdots\sum_{\tau_{|V|}'\in\Omega}\delta_{s_i,\tau_i}\delta_{s_j,\tau_j}\delta_{s_i',\tau_i'}\delta_{s_j',\tau_j'} \\
&\times\left(\prod_{k\in V\backslash\{i,j\}}\delta_{\tau_k,\tau_k'}\right)\langle\tau_1,\tau_2,\cdots,\tau_{|V|}|\boldsymbol{P}(\boldsymbol{D},\alpha,\gamma,\boldsymbol{a}(+1),\boldsymbol{a}(-1),\boldsymbol{C}(+1),\boldsymbol{C}(-1)))|\tau_1',\tau_2',\cdots,\tau_{|V|}'\rangle \\
&(s_i\in\Omega\ s_j\in\Omega,\ s_i'\in\Omega,\ s_j'\in\Omega,\ i\in V,\ j\in V,\ i<j),
\end{aligned}
\tag{10.297}
$$

$$
\begin{aligned}
\langle s_i|\boldsymbol{P_i}(\alpha,\gamma)|s_i'\rangle &= \langle s_i|\mathrm{Tr}_{\backslash\{i\}}\boldsymbol{P}(\alpha,\gamma)|s_i'\rangle \\
&\equiv \sum_{\tau_1\in\Omega}\sum_{\tau_2\in\Omega}\cdots\sum_{\tau_{|V|}\in\Omega}\sum_{\tau_1'\in\Omega}\sum_{\tau_2'\in\Omega}\cdots\sum_{\tau_{|V|}'\in\Omega}\delta_{s_i,\tau_i}\delta_{s_i',\tau_i'} \\
&\times\left(\prod_{k\in V\backslash\{i\}}\delta_{\tau_k,\tau_k'}\right)\langle\tau_1,\tau_2,\cdots,\tau_{|V|}|\boldsymbol{P}(\alpha,\gamma)|\tau_1',\tau_2',\cdots,\tau_{|V|}'\rangle \\
&(s_i\in\Omega\ s_j\in\Omega,\ s_i'\in\Omega,\ s_j'\in\Omega,\ i\in V),
\end{aligned}
\tag{10.298}
$$

$$
\begin{aligned}
\langle s_i, s_j|\boldsymbol{P_{ij}}(\alpha,\gamma)|s_i', s_j'\rangle &= \langle s_i, s_j|\boldsymbol{P_{ji}}(\alpha,\gamma)|s_i', s_j'\rangle \\
&= \langle s_i, s_j|\mathrm{Tr}_{\backslash\{i,j\}}\boldsymbol{P}(\alpha,\gamma)|s_i', s_j'\rangle \\
&\equiv \sum_{\tau_1\in\Omega}\sum_{\tau_2\in\Omega}\cdots\sum_{\tau_{|V|}\in\Omega}\sum_{\tau_1'\in\Omega}\sum_{\tau_2'\in\Omega}\cdots\sum_{\tau_{|V|}'\in\Omega}\delta_{s_i,\tau_i}\delta_{s_j,\tau_j}\delta_{s_i',\tau_i'}\delta_{s_j',\tau_j'} \\
&\times\left(\prod_{k\in V\backslash\{i,j\}}\delta_{\tau_k,\tau_k'}\right)\langle\tau_1,\tau_2,\cdots,\tau_{|V|}|\boldsymbol{P}(\alpha,\gamma)|\tau_1',\tau_2',\cdots,\tau_{|V|}'\rangle \\
&(s_i\in\Omega\ s_j\in\Omega,\ s_i'\in\Omega,\ s_j'\in\Omega,\ i\in V,\ j\in V,\ i<j).
\end{aligned}
\tag{10.299}
$$

10.5 Quantum Statistical Mechanical Informatics

This section explains some quantum graphical modeling using some quantum mechanical extensions of statistical mechanical informatics, such as quantum statistical mechanical informatics, and particularly, advanced quantum mean-field methods. Fundamental frameworks and recent developments have been explored in some textbooks in statistical mechanics [37, 86]. In some applications of quantum annealing to massive optimization problems, a transverse Ising model is an important quantum probabilistic graphical model [83, 84] and it is known that the density matrices, for example, in Eqs. (10.263), (10.265), and (10.266), in some familiar quantum statistical machine learning systems can be reduced to transverse Ising models.

In quantum statistical mechanical informatics, one of most important schemes is Suzuki-Trotter decompositions [87, 88]. This was used to realize the quantum Monte Carlo methods by mapping d-dimensional density matrices to corresponding $(d+1)$-dimensional probability distributions [89]. Recently, some quantum annealing schemes have been realized as actual quantum computers, for example, the d-wave machine.

In the first part of this section, we explain some basic frameworks in advanced quantum mean-field methods for realizing familiar quantum statistical machine learning systems for the transverse Ising models, including conventional frameworks of quantum belief propagations. In the second part, we propose a quantum adaptive Thouless-Anderson-Palmar (TAP) method and a new approach using the momentum space renormalization group method to realize coarse graining for the transverse Ising model not only for regular graphs but also for random graphs. In the third part, we introduce Suzuki-Trotter decompositions [87, 88], and show the basic scheme for mapping a d-dimensional transverse Ising model to a $(d+1)$-dimensional Ising model and apply the scheme to the message passing rules of the conventional quantum belief propagation.

10.5.1 Advanced Mean-Field Methods for the Transverse Ising Model

This section explores the detailed derivation of the deterministic equations in both the quantum mean-field method and the quantum loopy belief propagation method for the transverse Ising model [83, 84]. Note that the present framework of the quantum mean-field method and the quantum loopy belief propagation method are constructed in real space, while other familiar frameworks in quantum statistical mechanics such as spin wave theory are constructed in momentum space.

For a graph (V, E) with a set of nodes V and set of edges E, we consider a density matrix $\boldsymbol{P}$ as

$$\boldsymbol{P} = \frac{\exp\left(-\frac{1}{k_{\mathrm{B}}T}\left(\frac{1}{2}J\sum_{\{i,j\}\in E}\left(\boldsymbol{\sigma}_i^z-\boldsymbol{\sigma}_j^z\right)^2+\frac{1}{2}h\sum_{i\in V}\left(\boldsymbol{\sigma}_i^z-d_i\boldsymbol{I}^{(2^{|V|})}\right)^2-\gamma\sum_{i\in V}\boldsymbol{\sigma}_i^x\right)\right)}{\mathrm{Tr}\left[\exp\left(-\frac{1}{k_{\mathrm{B}}T}\left(\frac{1}{2}J\sum_{\{i,j\}\in E}\left(\boldsymbol{\sigma}_i^z-\boldsymbol{\sigma}_j^z\right)^2+\frac{1}{2}h\sum_{i\in V}\left(\boldsymbol{\sigma}_i^z-d_i\boldsymbol{I}^{(2^{|V|})}\right)^2-\Gamma\sum_{i\in V}\boldsymbol{\sigma}_i^x\right)\right)\right]}. \tag{10.300}$$

Because $\boldsymbol{\sigma}_i^z\boldsymbol{\sigma}_i^z=\boldsymbol{I}^{(2^{|V|})}$, the density matrix in Eq. (10.300) can be reduced to Eqs. (10.226) and (10.227) with

$$\boldsymbol{H} = -J\sum_{\{i,j\}\in E}\boldsymbol{\sigma}_i^z\boldsymbol{\sigma}_j^z - h\sum_{i\in V}d_i\boldsymbol{\sigma}_i^z - \Gamma\sum_{i\in V}\boldsymbol{\sigma}_i^x. \tag{10.301}$$

Here, all the nodes j connected with the node i by an edge $\{i, j\}$ are referred to as neighboring nodes of the node i, and the set of all neighboring nodes of the node i is denoted by the notation ∂i. The quantum probabilistic graphical model in Eqs. (10.300) and (10.301) is referred to as the **Transverse Ising Model** [83, 84].

First, we explain the conventional quantum mean-field method for the transverse Ising model. We introduce a $2^N \times 2^N$ trial density matrix $\boldsymbol{R}$ and its 2×2 trial reduced density matrix $\boldsymbol{R}_i$ for each node $i(\in V))$ defined by

$$\boldsymbol{R}_i = \mathrm{Tr}_{\backslash i}\boldsymbol{R} = \begin{pmatrix} \langle +1|\boldsymbol{R}_i|+1\rangle & \langle +1|\boldsymbol{R}_i|-1\rangle \\ \langle -1|\boldsymbol{R}_i|+1\rangle & \langle -1|\boldsymbol{R}_i|-1\rangle \end{pmatrix}, \tag{10.302}$$

where

$$\begin{aligned}\langle s_i|\boldsymbol{R}_i|s_i'\rangle &= \langle s_i|\mathrm{Tr}_{\backslash i}\boldsymbol{R}|s_i'\rangle \\ &\equiv \sum_{\tau_1\in\Omega}\sum_{\tau_2\in\Omega}\cdots\sum_{\tau_{|V|}\in\Omega}\sum_{\tau_1'\in\Omega}\sum_{\tau_2'\in\Omega}\cdots\sum_{\tau_{|V|}'\in\Omega}\delta_{s_i,\tau_i}\delta_{s_i',\tau_i'}\left(\prod_{j\in V\backslash\{i\}}\delta_{\tau_j,\tau_j'}\right)\langle\tau_1,\tau_2,\cdots,\tau_{|V|}|\boldsymbol{R}|\tau_1',\tau_2',\cdots,\tau_{|V|}'\rangle \\ &\qquad (s_i\in\Omega,\ s_i'\in\Omega.\ i\in V).\end{aligned} \tag{10.303}$$

By using Eq. (10.303), the average $\mathrm{Tr}(\boldsymbol{\sigma}_i^x\boldsymbol{R})$ can be expressed in terms of the reduced density matrix $\boldsymbol{R}_i$ as follows:

$$\begin{aligned}\mathrm{Tr}(\boldsymbol{\sigma}_i^x\boldsymbol{R}) &= \sum_{s_1\in\Omega}\sum_{s_2\in\Omega}\cdots\sum_{s_{|V|}\in\Omega}\sum_{s_1'\in\Omega}\sum_{s_2'\in\Omega}\cdots\sum_{s_{|V|}'\in\Omega}\langle s_1,s_2,\cdots,s_{|V|}|\boldsymbol{\sigma}_i^x|s_1',s_2',\cdots,s_{|V|}'\rangle \\ &\qquad\times\langle s_1',s_2',\cdots,s_{|V|}'|\boldsymbol{R}|s_1,s_2,\cdots,s_{|V|}\rangle \\ &= \sum_{s_1\in\Omega}\sum_{s_2\in\Omega}\cdots\sum_{s_{|V|}\in\Omega}\sum_{s_1'\in\Omega}\sum_{s_2'\in\Omega}\cdots\sum_{s_{|V|}'\in\Omega}\left(\prod_{k\in V\backslash\{i\}}\delta_{s_k,s_k'}\right) \\ &\qquad\times\langle s_i|\boldsymbol{\sigma}^x|s_i'\rangle\langle s_1',s_2',\cdots,s_{|V|}'|\boldsymbol{R}|s_1,s_2,,\cdots,s_{|V|}\rangle \\ &= \sum_{s_i\in\Omega}\sum_{s_i'\in\Omega}\langle s_i|\boldsymbol{\sigma}^x|s_i'\rangle\sum_{\tau_1\in\Omega}\sum_{\tau_2\in\Omega}\cdots\sum_{\tau_{|V|}\in\Omega}\sum_{\tau_1'\in\Omega}\sum_{\tau_2'\in\Omega}\cdots\sum_{\tau_{|V|}'\in\Omega}\delta_{s_i,\tau_i}\delta_{s_i',\tau_i'} \\ &\qquad\times\left(\prod_{k\in V\backslash\{i\}}\delta_{\tau_k,\tau_k'}\right)\langle\tau_1',\tau_2',\cdots,\tau_{|V|}'|\boldsymbol{R}|\tau_1,\tau_2,,\cdots,\tau_{|V|}\rangle \\ &= \sum_{s_i\in\Omega}\sum_{s_i'\in\Omega}\langle s_i|\boldsymbol{\sigma}^x|s_i'\rangle\langle s_i'|\boldsymbol{R}_i|s_i\rangle \\ &= \mathrm{Tr}(\boldsymbol{\sigma}^x\boldsymbol{R}_i).\end{aligned} \tag{10.304}$$

By similar arguments to those for Eq. (10.304), we derive

$$\mathrm{Tr}\big(\boldsymbol{\sigma}_i^z\boldsymbol{R}\big) = \mathrm{Tr}(\boldsymbol{\sigma}^z\boldsymbol{R}_i). \tag{10.305}$$

Now, we assume that the trial density matrix $\boldsymbol{R}$ is expressed as

$$\boldsymbol{R} = \boldsymbol{R_1}\otimes\boldsymbol{R_2}\otimes\cdots\otimes\boldsymbol{R}_{|V|}. \tag{10.306}$$

In this case, the average $\mathrm{Tr}(\boldsymbol{\sigma}_i^z\boldsymbol{\sigma}_j^z\boldsymbol{R})$ and the entropy $-k_{\mathrm{B}}\mathrm{Tr}\boldsymbol{R}\ln\boldsymbol{R}$ can be expressed as

$$\begin{aligned}
\mathrm{Tr}(\boldsymbol{\sigma}_i^z\boldsymbol{\sigma}_j^z\boldsymbol{R}) &= \mathrm{Tr}\Big(\boldsymbol{\sigma}_i^z\boldsymbol{\sigma}_j^z\big(\boldsymbol{R_1}\otimes\boldsymbol{R_2}\otimes\cdots\otimes\boldsymbol{R}_{|V|}\big)\Big)\\
&= \sum_{s_1\in\Omega}\sum_{s_2\in\Omega}\cdots\sum_{s_{|V|}\in\Omega}\sum_{s'_1\in\Omega}\sum_{s'_2\in\Omega}\cdots\sum_{s'_{|V|}\in\Omega}\sum_{s''_1\in\Omega}\sum_{s''_2\in\Omega}\cdots\sum_{s''_{|V|}\in\Omega}\left(\prod_{k\in V\backslash\{i\}}\delta_{s_k,s'_k}\right)\langle s_i|\boldsymbol{\sigma}^z|s'_i\rangle\\
&\quad\times\left(\prod_{l\in V\backslash\{j\}}\delta_{s'_l,s''_l}\right)\langle s'_j|\boldsymbol{\sigma}^z|s''_j\rangle\langle s''_1|\boldsymbol{R_1}|s_1\rangle\langle s''_2|\boldsymbol{R_2}|s_2\rangle\times\cdots\times\langle s''_{|V|}|\boldsymbol{R}_{|V|}|s_{|V|}\rangle\\
&= \left(\sum_{s_i\in\Omega}\sum_{s'_i\in\Omega}\langle s_i|\boldsymbol{\sigma}^z|s'_i\rangle\langle s'_i|\boldsymbol{R_i}|s_i\rangle\right)\\
&\quad\times\left(\sum_{s_j\in\Omega}\sum_{s''_j\in\Omega}\langle s_j|\boldsymbol{\sigma}^z|s''_j\rangle\langle s''_j|\boldsymbol{R_j}|s_j\rangle\right)\left(\prod_{k\in V\backslash\{i,j\}}\left(\sum_{s'_k\in\Omega}\sum_{s''_k\in\Omega}\delta_{s_k,s'_k}\delta_{s'_k,s''_k}\right)\langle s''_k|\boldsymbol{R_k}|s_k\rangle\right)\\
&= \big(\mathrm{Tr}(\boldsymbol{\sigma}^z\boldsymbol{R_i})\big)\big(\mathrm{Tr}(\boldsymbol{\sigma}^z\boldsymbol{R_j})\big)\left(\prod_{k\in V\backslash\{i,j\}}\big(\mathrm{Tr}(\boldsymbol{R_k})\big)\right)\\
&= \big(\mathrm{Tr}(\boldsymbol{\sigma}^z\boldsymbol{R_i})\big)\big(\mathrm{Tr}(\boldsymbol{\sigma}^z\boldsymbol{R_j})\big),
\end{aligned}\tag{10.307}$$

$$\begin{aligned}
-k_{\mathrm{B}}\mathrm{Tr}(\boldsymbol{R}\ln(\boldsymbol{R})) &= -\mathrm{Tr}\big((\boldsymbol{R_1}\otimes\boldsymbol{R_2}\otimes\cdots\otimes\boldsymbol{R}_{|V|})\ln(\boldsymbol{R_1}\otimes\boldsymbol{R_2}\otimes\cdots\otimes\boldsymbol{R}_{|V|})\big)\\
&= -k_{\mathrm{B}}\sum_{i=1}^{N}\mathrm{Tr}\Big(\big(\boldsymbol{R_1}\otimes\boldsymbol{R_2}\otimes\cdots\otimes\boldsymbol{R}_{|V|}\big)\big(\boldsymbol{I}^{(i-1)}\otimes\ln(\boldsymbol{R_i})\otimes\boldsymbol{I}^{(N-i)}\big)\Big)\\
&= -k_{\mathrm{B}}\sum_{i=1}^{N}\sum_{s_1\in\Omega}\sum_{s_2\in\Omega}\cdots\sum_{s_{|V|}\in\Omega}\sum_{s'_1\in\Omega}\sum_{s'_2\in\Omega}\cdots\sum_{s'_{|V|}\in\Omega}\langle s_1|\boldsymbol{R_1}|s'_1\rangle\langle s_2|\boldsymbol{R_2}|s'_2\rangle\times\cdots\times\langle s_{|V|}|\boldsymbol{R}_{|V|}|s'_{|V|}\rangle\\
&\quad\times\left(\prod_{k\in V\backslash\{i\}}\delta_{s_k,s'_k}\right)\langle s'_i|\ln(\boldsymbol{R_i})|s_i\rangle\\
&= -k_{\mathrm{B}}\sum_{i=1}^{N}\left(\sum_{s_i\in\Omega}\sum_{s'_i\in\Omega}\langle s_i|\boldsymbol{R_i}|s'_i\rangle\langle s'_i|\ln(\boldsymbol{R_i})|s_i\rangle\right)\left(\prod_{k\in V\backslash\{i\}}\left(\sum_{s_k\in\Omega}\sum_{s'_k\in\Omega}\delta_{s_k,s'_k}\langle s_k|\boldsymbol{R_k}|s'_1\rangle\right)\right)\\
&= -k_{\mathrm{B}}\sum_{i=1}^{N}\big(\mathrm{Tr}(\boldsymbol{R_i}\ln(\boldsymbol{R_i}))\big)\left(\prod_{k\in V\backslash\{i\}}\mathrm{Tr}(\boldsymbol{R_k})\right)\\
&= -k_{\mathrm{B}}\sum_{i=1}^{N}\mathrm{Tr}\big(\boldsymbol{R_i}\ln(\boldsymbol{R_i})\big).
\end{aligned}\tag{10.308}$$

The free energy functional can be reduced to

$$\mathcal{F}[\boldsymbol{R}] = \mathcal{F}_{\mathrm{MF}}[\boldsymbol{R}_1, \boldsymbol{R}_2, \cdots, \boldsymbol{R}_{|V|}] \equiv -J \sum_{\{i,j\}\in E} \big(\mathrm{Tr}(\boldsymbol{\sigma}^z \boldsymbol{R}_i)\big)\big(\mathrm{Tr}(\boldsymbol{\sigma}^z \boldsymbol{R}_j)\big) - h \sum_{i\in V} \mathrm{Tr}(\boldsymbol{\sigma}^z \boldsymbol{R}_i)$$
$$-\Gamma \sum_{i\in V} \mathrm{Tr}(\boldsymbol{\sigma}^x \boldsymbol{R}_i) + k_{\mathrm{B}} T \sum_{i\in V} \mathrm{Tr}(\boldsymbol{R}_i \ln(\boldsymbol{R}_i)). \quad (10.309)$$

We define the optimal reduced density matrix $\widehat{\boldsymbol{R}}_i$ for each node $i(\in V)$ by

$$\widehat{\boldsymbol{R}}_i = \arg\underset{\boldsymbol{R}_i}{\mathrm{extremum}} \Big\{ \mathcal{F}_{\mathrm{MF}}\Big[\widehat{\boldsymbol{R}}_1, \widehat{\boldsymbol{R}}_1, \cdots, \widehat{\boldsymbol{R}}_{i-1}, \boldsymbol{R}_i, \widehat{\boldsymbol{R}}_{i+1}, \widehat{\boldsymbol{R}}_{i+2}, \cdots, \widehat{\boldsymbol{R}}_{|V|}\Big] \Big| \mathrm{Tr}\boldsymbol{R}_i = 1 \Big\} \ (i\in V). \quad (10.310)$$

The simultaneous self-consistent equations for reduced density matrices are expressed as

$$\widehat{\boldsymbol{R}}_i = \frac{1}{Z_i} \exp\left(\frac{1}{k_{\mathrm{B}}T} \left(\left(J \sum_{j\in\partial i} \big(\mathrm{Tr}(\boldsymbol{\sigma}^z \widehat{\boldsymbol{R}}_j)\big) + h d_i \right) \boldsymbol{\sigma}^z + \Gamma \boldsymbol{\sigma}^x \right) \right), \quad (10.311)$$

$$Z_i \equiv \mathrm{Tr}\left[\exp\left(\frac{1}{k_{\mathrm{B}}T} \left(\left(J \sum_{j\in\partial i} \big(\mathrm{Tr}(\boldsymbol{\sigma}^z \widehat{\boldsymbol{R}}_j)\big) + h d_i \right) \boldsymbol{\sigma}^z + \Gamma \boldsymbol{\sigma}^x \right) \right) \right]. \quad (10.312)$$

From Eq. (10.311), we can derive the following simultaneous self-consistent equations for the magnetizations $\widehat{m}_i^z \equiv \mathrm{Tr}(\boldsymbol{\sigma}^z \widehat{\boldsymbol{R}}_j)$ $(i\in V)$ and $\widehat{m}_i^x \equiv \mathrm{Tr}(\boldsymbol{\sigma}^x \widehat{\boldsymbol{R}}_j)$ $(i\in V)$:

$$\widehat{m}_i^z = \frac{\dfrac{J}{k_{\mathrm{B}}T} \displaystyle\sum_{j\in\partial i} \widehat{m}_i^z + \dfrac{h}{k_{\mathrm{B}}T} d_i}{\sqrt{\left(\dfrac{J}{k_{\mathrm{B}}T} \displaystyle\sum_{j\in\partial i} \widehat{m}_j^z + \dfrac{h}{k_{\mathrm{B}}T} d_i \right)^2 + \left(\dfrac{\Gamma}{k_{\mathrm{B}}T} \right)^2}}$$
$$\times \tanh\left(\sqrt{\left(\frac{J}{k_{\mathrm{B}}T} \sum_{j\in\partial i} \widehat{m}_j^z + \frac{h}{k_{\mathrm{B}}T} d_i \right)^2 + \left(\frac{\Gamma}{k_{\mathrm{B}}T} \right)^2} \right), \quad (10.313)$$

$$\widehat{m}_i^x = \frac{\dfrac{\Gamma}{k_B T}}{\sqrt{\left(\dfrac{J}{k_B T}\displaystyle\sum_{j\in\partial i}\widehat{m}_j^z + \dfrac{h}{k_B T}d_i\right)^2 + \left(\dfrac{\Gamma}{k_B T}\right)^2}} \times \tanh\left(\sqrt{\left(\frac{J}{k_B T}\sum_{j\in\partial i}\widehat{m}_j^z + \frac{h}{k_B T}d_i\right)^2 + \left(\frac{\Gamma}{k_B T}\right)^2}\right). \tag{10.314}$$

The mean-field free energy $\mathcal{F}_{\mathrm{MF}}\left[\widehat{\boldsymbol{R}}_1, \widehat{\boldsymbol{R}}_2, \cdots, \widehat{\boldsymbol{R}}_{|V|}\right]$ of the present system is expressed as

$$\begin{aligned}\mathcal{F}_{\mathrm{MF}}\left[\widehat{\boldsymbol{R}}_1, \widehat{\boldsymbol{R}}_2, \cdots, \widehat{\boldsymbol{R}}_{|V|}\right] &= \sum_{i\in V}(-k_B T\ln(Z_i)) \\ &= -k_B T\sum_{i\in V}\ln\left(\mathrm{Tr}\left[\exp\left(\frac{1}{k_B T}\left(\left(J\left(\sum_{j\in\partial i}(\mathrm{Tr}(\boldsymbol{\sigma}^z\widehat{\boldsymbol{R}}_j))\right)\boldsymbol{\sigma}^z + \Gamma\boldsymbol{\sigma}^x\right)\right)\right)\right]\right) \\ &= -k_B T\sum_{i\in V}\ln\left(2\cosh\left(\sqrt{\left(\frac{J}{k_B T}\sum_{j\in\partial i}\widehat{\boldsymbol{m}}_j^z\right)^2 + \Gamma^2}\right)\right).\end{aligned} \tag{10.315}$$

Next, we extend the above framework for the mean-field method for the transverse Ising model to the quantum loopy belief propagation method based on the quantum cluster variation method in Ref. [90]. We introduce a $2^N \times 2^N$ trial density matrix $\boldsymbol{R}$ and its 2×2 trial reduced density matrix $\boldsymbol{R}_i$ for each node $i\,(\in V))$ defined by

$$\begin{aligned}\boldsymbol{R}_{ij} &= \boldsymbol{R}_{ji} = \mathrm{Tr}_{\backslash\{i,j\}}\boldsymbol{R} \\ &= \begin{pmatrix} \langle +1,+1|\boldsymbol{R}_{ij}|+1,+1\rangle & \langle +1,+1|\boldsymbol{R}_{ij}|-1,+1\rangle & \langle +1,+1|\boldsymbol{R}_{ij}|+1,-1\rangle & \langle +1,+1|\boldsymbol{R}_{ij}|-1,-1\rangle \\ \langle +1,-1|\boldsymbol{R}_{ij}|+1,+1\rangle & \langle +1,-1|\boldsymbol{R}_{ij}|-1,+1\rangle & \langle +1,-1|\boldsymbol{R}_{ij}|+1,-1\rangle & \langle +1,-1|\boldsymbol{R}_{ij}|-1,-1\rangle \\ \langle -1,+1|\boldsymbol{R}_{ij}|+1,+1\rangle & \langle -1,+1|\boldsymbol{R}_{ij}|-1,+1\rangle & \langle -1,+1|\boldsymbol{R}_{ij}|+1,-1\rangle & \langle -1,+1|\boldsymbol{R}_{ij}|-1,-1\rangle \\ \langle -1,-1|\boldsymbol{R}_{ij}|+1,+1\rangle & \langle -1,-1|\boldsymbol{R}_{ij}|-1,+1\rangle & \langle -1,-1|\boldsymbol{R}_{ij}|+1,-1\rangle & \langle -1,-1|\boldsymbol{R}_{ij}|-1,-1\rangle \end{pmatrix} \\ &(i\in V,\ j\in V,\ i<j),\end{aligned} \tag{10.316}$$

where

$$\begin{aligned}\langle s_i, s_j|\boldsymbol{R}_{ij}|s_i', s_j'\rangle &= \langle s_i, s_j|\boldsymbol{R}_{ji}|s_i', s_j'\rangle \\ &= \langle s_i, s_j|\mathrm{Tr}_{\backslash\{i,j\}}\boldsymbol{R}|s_i', s_j'\rangle \\ &\equiv \sum_{\tau_1\in\Omega}\sum_{\tau_2\in\Omega}\cdots\sum_{\tau_{|V|}\in\Omega}\sum_{\tau_1'\in\Omega}\sum_{\tau_2'\in\Omega}\cdots\sum_{\tau_{|V|}'\in\Omega} \\ &\quad\times\delta_{s_i,\tau_i}\delta_{s_j,\tau_j}\delta_{s_i',\tau_i'}\delta_{s_j',\tau_j'}\left(\prod_{k\in V\backslash\{i,j\}}\delta_{\tau_k,\tau_k'}\right)\langle\tau_1,\tau_2,\cdots,\tau_{|V|}|\boldsymbol{R}|\tau_1',\tau_2',\cdots,\tau_{|V|}'\rangle \\ &\quad(s_i\in\Omega\ s_j\in\Omega,\ s_i'\in\Omega,\ s_j'\in\Omega,\ i\in V,\ j\in V,\ i<j).\end{aligned} \tag{10.317}$$

By similar arguments to those for Eq. (10.304), we derive

$$\mathrm{Tr}\Big(\boldsymbol{\sigma}_i^z\boldsymbol{\sigma}_j^z\boldsymbol{R}\Big) = \mathrm{Tr}\big((\boldsymbol{\sigma}^z\otimes\boldsymbol{I})(\boldsymbol{I}\otimes\boldsymbol{\sigma}^z)\boldsymbol{R}_{ij}\big). \tag{10.318}$$

We now assume that the free energy functional can be expressed as

$$\begin{aligned}
\mathcal{F}[\boldsymbol{R}] &= \mathcal{F}_{\mathrm{Bethe}}\big[\big\{\boldsymbol{R}_i\big|i\in V\big\},\big\{\boldsymbol{R}_{\{i,j\}}\big|\{i,j\}\in E\big\}\big] \\
&\equiv -J\sum_{\{i,j\}\in E}\mathrm{Tr}\big((\boldsymbol{\sigma}^z\otimes\boldsymbol{I})(\boldsymbol{I}\otimes\boldsymbol{\sigma}^z)\boldsymbol{R}_{\{i,j\}}\big) \\
&\quad -h\sum_{i\in V}d_i\mathrm{Tr}(\boldsymbol{\sigma}^z\boldsymbol{R}_i) - \Gamma\sum_{i\in V}\mathrm{Tr}(\boldsymbol{\sigma}^x\boldsymbol{R}_i) \\
&\quad +k_{\mathrm{B}}T\sum_{i\in V}\mathrm{Tr}(\boldsymbol{R}_i\ln(\boldsymbol{R}_i)) \\
&\quad +k_{\mathrm{B}}T\sum_{\{i,j\}\in E}\Big(\mathrm{Tr}\big(\boldsymbol{R}_{\{i,j\}}\ln(\boldsymbol{R}_{\{i,j\}})\big) - \mathrm{Tr}(\boldsymbol{R}_i\ln(\boldsymbol{R}_i)) - \mathrm{Tr}\big(\boldsymbol{R}_j\ln(\boldsymbol{R}_j)\big)\Big) \\
&= -J\sum_{\{i,j\}\in E}\mathrm{Tr}\big((\boldsymbol{\sigma}^z\otimes\boldsymbol{I})(\boldsymbol{I}\otimes\boldsymbol{\sigma}^z)\boldsymbol{R}_{\{i,j\}}\big) \\
&\quad -h\sum_{i\in V}d_i\mathrm{Tr}(\boldsymbol{\sigma}^z\boldsymbol{R}_i) - \Gamma\sum_{i\in V}\mathrm{Tr}(\boldsymbol{\sigma}^x\boldsymbol{R}_i) \\
&\quad +k_{\mathrm{B}}T\sum_{\{i,j\}\in E}\mathrm{Tr}\big(\boldsymbol{R}_{\{i,j\}}\ln(\boldsymbol{R}_{\{i,j\}})\big) + k_{\mathrm{B}}T\sum_{i\in V}(1-|\partial i|)\mathrm{Tr}(\boldsymbol{R}_i\ln(\boldsymbol{R}_i)).
\end{aligned} \tag{10.319}$$

We define the reduced density matrix $\widehat{\boldsymbol{R}}_i$ for each node $i(\in V)$ by

$$\widehat{\boldsymbol{R}}_k = \underset{\boldsymbol{R}_k}{\arg\operatorname{extremum}}\Big\{\mathcal{F}_{\mathrm{Bethe}}\Big[\boldsymbol{R}_k,\Big\{\widehat{\boldsymbol{R}}_i\big|i\in V\backslash\{k\}\Big\},\Big\{\widehat{\boldsymbol{R}}_{\{i,j\}}\big|\{i,j\}\in E\Big\}\Big]\Big|\mathrm{Tr}\boldsymbol{R}_k = 1,\ \boldsymbol{R}_k = \mathrm{Tr}_{\backslash k}\widehat{\boldsymbol{R}}_{\{k,j\}}\ (j\in\partial k)\Big\} \quad (k\in V). \tag{10.320}$$

$$\begin{aligned}
\widehat{\boldsymbol{R}}_{\{k,l\}} = \underset{\boldsymbol{R}_{\{k,l\}}}{\arg\operatorname{extremum}}\Big\{&\mathcal{F}_{\mathrm{Bethe}}\Big[\boldsymbol{R}_{\{k,l\}},\Big\{\widehat{\boldsymbol{R}}_i\big|i\in V\Big\},\Big\{\widehat{\boldsymbol{R}}_{\{i,j\}}\big|\{i,j\}\in E\backslash\{k,l\}\Big\}\Big]\Big| \\
&\mathrm{Tr}\boldsymbol{R}_{\{k,l\}} = 1,\ \widehat{\boldsymbol{R}}_k = \mathrm{Tr}_{\backslash\{k,l\}}\boldsymbol{R}_{\{k,l\}},\ \widehat{\boldsymbol{R}}_l = \mathrm{Tr}_{\backslash\{k,l\}}\boldsymbol{R}_{\{k,l\}}\Big\}\ (\{k,l\}\in E).
\end{aligned} \tag{10.321}$$

To ensure the constraint conditions, we introduce the Lagrange multipliers as follows:

$$\mathcal{L}\big[\big\{\boldsymbol{R}_i\big|i\in V\big\},\big\{\boldsymbol{R}_{ij}\big|\{i,j\}\in E\big\}\big] = -J\sum_{\{i,j\}\in E}\mathrm{Tr}\big((\boldsymbol{\sigma}^z\otimes\boldsymbol{I})(\boldsymbol{I}\otimes\boldsymbol{\sigma}^z)\boldsymbol{R}_{ij}\big)$$

$$
\begin{aligned}
&-h\sum_{i\in V}d_i\mathrm{Tr}(\boldsymbol{\sigma}^z\boldsymbol{R}_i)-\Gamma\sum_{i\in V}\mathrm{Tr}(\boldsymbol{\sigma}^x\boldsymbol{R}_i)\\
&+k_{\mathrm{B}}T\sum_{\{i,j\}\in E}\mathrm{Tr}\big(\boldsymbol{R}_{ij}\ln(\boldsymbol{R}_{ij})\big)+k_{\mathrm{B}}T\sum_{i\in V}(1-|\partial i|)\mathrm{Tr}(\boldsymbol{R}_i\ln(\boldsymbol{R}_i)).\\
&-\sum_{i\in V}\lambda_i(\mathrm{Tr}\boldsymbol{R}_i-1)-\sum_{\{i,j\}\in E}\lambda_{\{i,j\}}\big(\mathrm{Tr}\boldsymbol{R}_{ij}-1\big)\\
&-\sum_{\{i,j\}\in E}\mathrm{Tr}\boldsymbol{\lambda}_{i,ij}\big(\boldsymbol{R}_i-\mathrm{Tr}_{\backslash i}\boldsymbol{R}_{ij}\big)-\sum_{\{i,j\}\in E}\mathrm{Tr}\boldsymbol{\lambda}_{j,ij}\big(\boldsymbol{R}_j-\mathrm{Tr}_{\backslash j}\boldsymbol{R}_{ij}\big)\\
=&\sum_{\{i,j\}\in E}\mathrm{Tr}\Big(\boldsymbol{R}_{ij}\Big(-J(\boldsymbol{\sigma}^z\otimes\boldsymbol{I})(\boldsymbol{I}\otimes\boldsymbol{\sigma}^z)+k_{\mathrm{B}}\ln(\boldsymbol{R}_{ij})+\boldsymbol{\lambda}_{i,ij}\otimes\boldsymbol{I}+\boldsymbol{I}\otimes\boldsymbol{\lambda}_{j,ij}-\lambda_{ij}(\boldsymbol{I}\otimes\boldsymbol{I})\Big)\Big)\\
&+\sum_{i\in V}\mathrm{Tr}\Big(\boldsymbol{R}_i\Big(-hd_i\boldsymbol{\sigma}^z-\Gamma\boldsymbol{\sigma}^x+k_{\mathrm{B}}T\big(1-|\partial i|\big)\ln(\boldsymbol{R}_i)-\sum_{j\in\partial i}\boldsymbol{\lambda}_{i,ij}-\lambda_i\boldsymbol{I}\Big)\Big)\\
&+\sum_{i\in V}\lambda_i+\sum_{\{i,j\}\in E}\lambda_{\{i,j\}}.
\end{aligned}
\tag{10.322}
$$

Here we remark that $\boldsymbol{\lambda}_{i,ij}=\boldsymbol{\lambda}_{i,ji}$ and $\boldsymbol{\lambda}_{j,ij}=\boldsymbol{\lambda}_{j,ji}$ $(\{i,j\}\in E, i<j)$.

We define the reduced density matrix $\widehat{\boldsymbol{R}}_i$ for each node $i\,(\in V)$ and $\boldsymbol{R}_{ij}=\boldsymbol{R}_{ji}$ for each edge $\{i,j\}\in E$ by

$$
\widehat{\boldsymbol{R}}_i=\arg\underset{\boldsymbol{R}_i}{\mathrm{extremum}}\Big\{\boldsymbol{R}_i\Big(-hd_i\boldsymbol{\sigma}^z-\Gamma\boldsymbol{\sigma}^x-\sum_{j\in\partial i}\boldsymbol{\lambda}_{i,ij}+k_{\mathrm{B}}T(1-|\partial i|)\ln(\boldsymbol{R}_i)-\lambda_i\boldsymbol{I}\Big)\Big\}\quad(i\in V),
\tag{10.323}
$$

$$
\widehat{\boldsymbol{R}}_{ij}=\arg\underset{\boldsymbol{R}_{ij}}{\mathrm{extremum}}\Big\{\boldsymbol{R}_{ij}\Big(-J(\boldsymbol{\sigma}^z\otimes\boldsymbol{I})(\boldsymbol{I}\otimes\boldsymbol{\sigma}^z)+\boldsymbol{\lambda}_{i,ij}\otimes\boldsymbol{I}+\boldsymbol{I}\otimes\boldsymbol{\lambda}_{j,ij}+k_{\mathrm{B}}T\ln(\boldsymbol{R}_{ij})-\lambda_{\{i,j\}}(\boldsymbol{I}\otimes\boldsymbol{I})\Big)\Big\}\quad(\{i,j\}\in E).
\tag{10.324}
$$

The simultaneous self-consistent equations for reduced density matrices are expressed as

$$
\widehat{\boldsymbol{R}}_i=\exp\Big(-1+\frac{\lambda_i}{k_{\mathrm{B}}T}\Big)\exp\Bigg(\frac{1}{k_{\mathrm{B}}T}\Big(\frac{1}{|\partial i|-1}\Big)\Big(-hd_i\boldsymbol{\sigma}^z-\Gamma\boldsymbol{\sigma}^x-\sum_{j\in\partial i}\boldsymbol{\lambda}_{i,ij}\Big)\Bigg),
\tag{10.325}
$$

$$
\widehat{\boldsymbol{R}}_{ij}=\exp\Big(-1+\frac{\lambda_{\{i,j\}}}{k_{\mathrm{B}}T}\Big)\exp\Big(\frac{1}{k_{\mathrm{B}}T}\big(J(\boldsymbol{\sigma}^z\otimes\boldsymbol{I})(\boldsymbol{I}\otimes\boldsymbol{\sigma}^z)-\boldsymbol{\lambda}_{i,ij}\otimes\boldsymbol{I}-\boldsymbol{I}\otimes\boldsymbol{\lambda}_{j,ij}\big)\Big),
\tag{10.326}
$$

$$\exp\left(1-\frac{\lambda_i}{k_{\rm B}T}\right)=\mathrm{Tr}\left[\exp\left(\frac{1}{k_{\rm B}T}\left(\frac{1}{|\partial i|-1}\right)\left(-hd_i\boldsymbol{\sigma}^z-\Gamma\boldsymbol{\sigma}^x-\sum_{j\in\partial i}\boldsymbol{\lambda}_{k,kj}\right)\right)\right],\tag{10.327}$$

$$\exp\left(1-\frac{\lambda_{\{i,j\}}}{k_{\rm B}T}\right)=\mathrm{Tr}\left[\exp\left(\frac{1}{k_{\rm B}T}\left(J(\boldsymbol{\sigma}^z\otimes\boldsymbol{I})(\boldsymbol{I}\otimes\boldsymbol{\sigma}^z)-\boldsymbol{\lambda}_{i,ij}\otimes\boldsymbol{I}-\boldsymbol{I}\otimes\boldsymbol{\lambda}_{j,ij}\right)\right)\right].\tag{10.328}$$

By introducing the linear transformations

$$\boldsymbol{\lambda}_{i,ij}=\boldsymbol{\lambda}_{i,ji}=-hd_i\boldsymbol{\sigma}^z-\Gamma\boldsymbol{\sigma}^x-\sum_{k\in\partial i\backslash\{j\}}\boldsymbol{\lambda}_{k\to i},\tag{10.329}$$

Equations (10.325) and (10.326) can be rewritten as

$$\widehat{\boldsymbol{R}}_i=\frac{1}{Z_i}\exp\left(\frac{1}{k_{\rm B}T}\left(hd_i\boldsymbol{\sigma}^z+\Gamma\boldsymbol{\sigma}^x+\sum_{k\in\partial i}\boldsymbol{\lambda}_{k\to i}\right)\right),\tag{10.330}$$

$$\widehat{\boldsymbol{R}}_{ij}=\frac{1}{Z_{\{i,j\}}}\exp\Bigg(\frac{1}{k_{\rm B}T}\Big(J(\boldsymbol{\sigma}^z\otimes\boldsymbol{I})(\boldsymbol{I}\otimes\boldsymbol{\sigma}^z)+h\big(d_i(\boldsymbol{\sigma}^z\otimes\boldsymbol{I})+d_j(\boldsymbol{I}\otimes\boldsymbol{\sigma}^z)\big)+\Gamma\big(\boldsymbol{\sigma}^x\otimes\boldsymbol{I}+\boldsymbol{I}\otimes\boldsymbol{\sigma}^x\big)$$
$$+\sum_{k\in\partial i\backslash\{j\}}\boldsymbol{\lambda}_{k\to i}\otimes\boldsymbol{I}+\sum_{l\in\partial j\backslash\{i\}}\boldsymbol{I}\otimes\boldsymbol{\lambda}_{l\to j}\Big)\Bigg),\tag{10.331}$$

$$Z_i=\mathrm{Tr}\left[\exp\left(\frac{1}{k_{\rm B}T}\left(hd_i\boldsymbol{\sigma}^z+\Gamma\boldsymbol{\sigma}^x+\sum_{k\in\partial i}\boldsymbol{\lambda}_{k\to i}\right)\right)\right],\tag{10.332}$$

$$Z_{\{i,j\}}=\mathrm{Tr}\Bigg[\exp\Bigg(\frac{1}{k_{\rm B}T}\Big(J(\boldsymbol{\sigma}^z\otimes\boldsymbol{I})(\boldsymbol{I}\otimes\boldsymbol{\sigma}^z)+h\big(d_i(\boldsymbol{\sigma}^z\otimes\boldsymbol{I})+d_j(\boldsymbol{I}\otimes\boldsymbol{\sigma}^z)\big)+\Gamma\big(\boldsymbol{\sigma}^x\otimes\boldsymbol{I}+\boldsymbol{I}\otimes\boldsymbol{\sigma}^x\big)$$
$$+\sum_{k\in\partial i\backslash\{j\}}\boldsymbol{\lambda}_{k\to i}\otimes\boldsymbol{I}+\sum_{l\in\partial j\backslash\{i\}}\boldsymbol{I}\otimes\boldsymbol{\lambda}_{l\to j}\Big)\Bigg)\Bigg].\tag{10.333}$$

Then, by substituting Eq. (10.330) and Eq. (10.331) into

$$\boldsymbol{R}_i=\mathrm{Tr}_{\backslash i}\boldsymbol{R}_{ij},\tag{10.334}$$

we derive the following simultaneous self-consistent equations for the effective fields:

$$\exp\left(\frac{1}{k_BT}\boldsymbol{\lambda}_{j\to i}+\frac{1}{k_BT}\left(hd_i\boldsymbol{\sigma}^z+\Gamma\boldsymbol{\sigma}^x+\sum_{k\in\partial i\setminus\{j\}}\boldsymbol{\lambda}_{k\to i}\right)\right)$$
$$=\frac{Z_i}{Z_{\{i,j\}}}\mathrm{Tr}_{\setminus i}\Bigg[\exp\Bigg(\frac{1}{k_BT}\Big(J(\boldsymbol{\sigma}^z\otimes\boldsymbol{I})(\boldsymbol{I}\otimes\boldsymbol{\sigma}^z)+\boldsymbol{I}\otimes\Big(hd_j\boldsymbol{\sigma}^z+\Gamma\boldsymbol{\sigma}^x+\sum_{l\in\partial j\setminus\{i\}}\boldsymbol{\lambda}_{l\to j}\Big)\Big)$$
$$+\frac{1}{k_BT}\Big(hd_i\boldsymbol{\sigma}^z+\Gamma\boldsymbol{\sigma}^x+\sum_{k\in\partial i\setminus\{j\}}\boldsymbol{\lambda}_{k\to i}\Big)\otimes\boldsymbol{I}\Bigg)\Bigg],\tag{10.335}$$

such that

$$\frac{1}{k_BT}\boldsymbol{\lambda}_{j\to i}=-\frac{1}{k_BT}\left(hd_i\boldsymbol{\sigma}^z+\Gamma\boldsymbol{\sigma}^x+\sum_{k\in\partial i\setminus\{j\}}\boldsymbol{\lambda}_{k\to i}\right)$$
$$+\ln\Bigg(\frac{Z_i}{Z_{\{i,j\}}}\mathrm{Tr}_{\setminus i}\Bigg[\exp\Bigg(\frac{1}{k_BT}\Big(J(\boldsymbol{\sigma}^z\otimes\boldsymbol{I})(\boldsymbol{I}\otimes\boldsymbol{\sigma}^z)+\boldsymbol{I}\otimes\Big(hd_j\boldsymbol{\sigma}^z+\Gamma\boldsymbol{\sigma}^x+\sum_{l\in\partial j\setminus\{i\}}\boldsymbol{\lambda}_{l\to j}\Big)\Big)$$
$$+\frac{1}{k_BT}\Big(hd_i\boldsymbol{\sigma}^z+\Gamma\boldsymbol{\sigma}^x+\sum_{k\in\partial i\setminus\{j\}}\boldsymbol{\lambda}_{k\to i}\Big)\otimes\boldsymbol{I}\Bigg)\Bigg]\Bigg).\tag{10.336}$$

Note that Eqs. (10.335) and (10.336) can be regarded as conventional message passing rule quantum loopy belief propagation. The Bethe free energy $\mathcal{F}_{\mathrm{Bethe}}\left[\left\{\widehat{\boldsymbol{R}}_i\middle|i\in V\right\},\left\{\widehat{\boldsymbol{R}}_{ij}\middle|\{i,j\}\in E\right\}\right]$ of the present system is given by

$$\mathcal{F}_{\mathrm{Bethe}}\left[\left\{\widehat{\boldsymbol{R}}_i\middle|i\in V\right\},\left\{\widehat{\boldsymbol{R}}_{ij}\middle|\{i,j\}\in E\right\}\right]=\sum_{i\in V}\left(-k_BT\ln(Z_i)\right)$$
$$+\sum_{\{i,j\}\in E}\left(-k_BT\ln\left(Z_{i,j}\right)+k_BT\ln(Z_i)+k_BT\ln(Z_j)\right).\tag{10.337}$$

The conventional quantum message passing rules in Eqs. (10.335) and (10.336) reduce to Eqs. (10.95) and (10.96) for the case of $\Gamma=0$.

Because we have the orthonormal relationships

$$\begin{cases}\mathrm{Tr}[\boldsymbol{\sigma}^z\boldsymbol{\sigma}^z]=\mathrm{Tr}[\boldsymbol{\sigma}^x\boldsymbol{\sigma}^x]=2,\\ \mathrm{Tr}[\boldsymbol{\sigma}^z\boldsymbol{I}]=\mathrm{Tr}[\boldsymbol{I}\boldsymbol{\sigma}^z]=\mathrm{Tr}[\boldsymbol{\sigma}^x\boldsymbol{I}]=\mathrm{Tr}[\boldsymbol{I}\boldsymbol{\sigma}^x]=0,\\ \mathrm{Tr}[\boldsymbol{\sigma}^z\boldsymbol{\sigma}^x]=\mathrm{Tr}[\boldsymbol{\sigma}^x\boldsymbol{\sigma}^z]=0,\end{cases}\tag{10.338}$$

$$\begin{cases}\mathrm{Tr}[(\boldsymbol{\sigma}^z\otimes\boldsymbol{I})(\boldsymbol{\sigma}^z\otimes\boldsymbol{I})]=\mathrm{Tr}\big[(\boldsymbol{\sigma}^x\otimes\boldsymbol{I})(\boldsymbol{\sigma}^x\otimes\boldsymbol{I})\big]=\mathrm{Tr}[(\boldsymbol{I}\otimes\boldsymbol{\sigma}^z)(\boldsymbol{I}\otimes\boldsymbol{\sigma}^z)]=\mathrm{Tr}\big[(\boldsymbol{I}\otimes\boldsymbol{\sigma}^x)(\boldsymbol{I}\otimes\boldsymbol{\sigma}^x)\big]=4,\\ \mathrm{Tr}\big[(\boldsymbol{\sigma}^z\otimes\boldsymbol{I})(\boldsymbol{\sigma}^x\otimes\boldsymbol{I})\big]=\mathrm{Tr}\big[(\boldsymbol{\sigma}^x\otimes\boldsymbol{I})(\boldsymbol{\sigma}^z\otimes\boldsymbol{I})\big]=\mathrm{Tr}\big[(\boldsymbol{I}\otimes\boldsymbol{\sigma}^x)(\boldsymbol{I}\otimes\boldsymbol{\sigma}^z)\big]=\mathrm{Tr}\big[(\boldsymbol{I}\otimes\boldsymbol{\sigma}^z)(\boldsymbol{I}\otimes\boldsymbol{\sigma}^x)\big]=0,\\ \mathrm{Tr}[(\boldsymbol{\sigma}^z\otimes\boldsymbol{I})(\boldsymbol{I}\otimes\boldsymbol{\sigma}^z)]=\mathrm{Tr}\big[(\boldsymbol{\sigma}^x\otimes\boldsymbol{I})(\boldsymbol{I}\otimes\boldsymbol{\sigma}^x)\big]=\mathrm{Tr}\big[(\boldsymbol{\sigma}^z\otimes\boldsymbol{I})(\boldsymbol{I}\otimes\boldsymbol{\sigma}^x)\big]=\mathrm{Tr}\big[(\boldsymbol{\sigma}^x\otimes\boldsymbol{I})(\boldsymbol{I}\otimes\boldsymbol{\sigma}^z)\big]=0,\end{cases}\tag{10.339}$$

the reduced density matrices $\boldsymbol{R}_i$ and $\boldsymbol{R}_{ij} = \boldsymbol{R}_{ji}$ expand to the following orthonormal expansions:

$$\boldsymbol{R}_i = \frac{1}{2}\big(\boldsymbol{I} + m_i^x \boldsymbol{\sigma}^x + m_i^z \boldsymbol{\sigma}^z\big), \tag{10.340}$$

$$\begin{aligned}\boldsymbol{R}_{ij} &= \boldsymbol{R}_{ji} \\ &= \frac{1}{4}\Big((\boldsymbol{I}\otimes\boldsymbol{I}) + m_i^x\big(\boldsymbol{\sigma}^x\otimes\boldsymbol{I}\big) + m_i^z(\boldsymbol{\sigma}^z\otimes\boldsymbol{I}) + m_j^x\big(\boldsymbol{I}\otimes\boldsymbol{\sigma}^x\big) + m_j^z(\boldsymbol{I}\otimes\boldsymbol{\sigma}^z) \\ &\quad + c_{\{i,j\}}^{zz}(\boldsymbol{\sigma}^z\otimes\boldsymbol{I})(\boldsymbol{I}\otimes\boldsymbol{\sigma}^z) + c_{\{i,j\}}^{xz}\big(\boldsymbol{\sigma}^x\otimes\boldsymbol{I}\big)(\boldsymbol{I}\otimes\boldsymbol{\sigma}^z) \\ &\quad + c_{\{i,j\}}^{zx}(\boldsymbol{\sigma}^z\otimes\boldsymbol{I})\big(\boldsymbol{I}\otimes\boldsymbol{\sigma}^x\big) + c_{\{i,j\}}^{zx}\big(\boldsymbol{\sigma}^x\otimes\boldsymbol{I}\big)\big(\boldsymbol{I}\otimes\boldsymbol{\sigma}^x\big)\Big),\end{aligned} \tag{10.341}$$

where

$$\begin{cases} m_i^{\nu} = \mathrm{Tr}[\boldsymbol{\sigma}^{\nu}\boldsymbol{R}_i] = \mathrm{Tr}\big[\big(\boldsymbol{\sigma}^{\nu}\otimes\boldsymbol{I}\big)\boldsymbol{R}_{ij}\big], \\ m_j^{\nu'} = \mathrm{Tr}\big[\boldsymbol{\sigma}^{\nu'}\boldsymbol{R}_j\big] = \mathrm{Tr}\big[\big(\boldsymbol{I}\otimes\boldsymbol{\sigma}^{\nu'}\big)\boldsymbol{R}_{ij}\big], \\ c_{\{i,j\}}^{\nu,\nu'} = \mathrm{Tr}\big[\big(\boldsymbol{\sigma}^{\nu}\otimes\boldsymbol{I}\big)\big(\boldsymbol{I}\otimes\boldsymbol{\sigma}^{\nu'}\big)\boldsymbol{R}_{ij}\big], \end{cases} \big(\{i,j\}\in E,\ i<j,\ \nu\in\{x,z\}, \nu'\in\{x,z\}\big). \tag{10.342}$$

By using these orthonormal expansions of the reduced density matrices, the Bethe free energy functional in Eq. (10.319) can be rewritten as

$$\begin{aligned}\mathcal{F}[\boldsymbol{R}] &= \mathcal{F}_{\mathrm{Bethe}}\Big[\Big\{m_i^{\nu}\Big|i\in V, \nu\in\{x,z\}\Big\}, \Big\{c_{\{i,j\}}^{\nu,\nu'}\Big|\{i,j\}\in E, \nu\{x,z\}, \nu'\in\{x,z\}\Big\}\Big] \\ &\equiv -J\sum_{\{i,j\}\in E} c_{\{i,j\}}^{z,z} - h\sum_{i\in V} d_i m_i^z - \Gamma\sum_{i\in V} m_i^x \\ &\quad + k_{\mathrm{B}}T\sum_{i\in V}(1-|\partial i|)\mathrm{Tr}(\boldsymbol{R}_i\ln(\boldsymbol{R}_i)) \\ &\quad + k_{\mathrm{B}}T\sum_{\{i,j\}\in E}\mathrm{Tr}\big(\boldsymbol{R}_{\{i,j\}}\ln(\boldsymbol{R}_{\{i,j\}})\big).\end{aligned} \tag{10.343}$$

The extremum conditions

$$\begin{aligned}&\frac{\partial}{\partial m_k^{\nu}}\mathcal{F}_{\mathrm{Bethe}}\Big[\Big\{m_i^{\nu}\Big|i\in V, \nu\in\{x,z\}\Big\}, \Big\{c_{\{i,j\}}^{\nu\nu'}\Big|\{i,j\}\in E, \nu\{x,z\}, \nu'\in\{x,z\}\Big\}\Big] \\ &= 0\ (k\in V,\ \nu\in\{x,z\}),\end{aligned} \tag{10.344}$$

$$\frac{\partial}{\partial c_{\{k,l\}}^{\nu\nu'}}\mathcal{F}_{\mathrm{Bethe}}\Big[\Big\{m_i^{\nu}\Big|i\in V, \nu\in\{x,z\}\Big\}, \Big\{c_{\{i,j\}}^{\nu\nu'}\Big|\{i,j\}\in E, \nu\{x;z\}, \nu'\in\{x,z\}\Big\}\Big]$$

$$= 0 \ (\{k,l\}\in E,\ \nu\in\{x,z\},,\ \nu'\in\{x,z\}), \tag{10.345}$$

can be reduced to the following simultaneous equations:

$$\begin{cases} \dfrac{h}{k_{\mathrm{B}}T}d_i = \dfrac{1}{2}(1-|\partial i|)\mathrm{Tr}\Big[\sigma^z \ln\Big(\widehat{\boldsymbol{R}}_i\Big)\Big] + \dfrac{1}{4}\displaystyle\sum_{\{j\in\partial i, j>i\}} \mathrm{Tr}\Big[(\sigma^z\otimes\boldsymbol{I})\ln\big(\widehat{\boldsymbol{R}}_{ij}\big)\Big] + \dfrac{1}{4}\displaystyle\sum_{\{k\in\partial i, k<i\}} \mathrm{Tr}\Big[(\boldsymbol{I}\otimes\sigma^z)\ln\big(\widehat{\boldsymbol{R}}_{ki}\big)\Big], \\ \dfrac{\Gamma}{k_{\mathrm{B}}T} = \dfrac{1}{2}(1-|\partial i|)\mathrm{Tr}\Big[\sigma^x \ln\Big(\widehat{\boldsymbol{R}}_i\Big)\Big] + \dfrac{1}{4}\displaystyle\sum_{\{j\in\partial i, j>i\}} \mathrm{Tr}\Big[(\sigma^x\otimes\boldsymbol{I})\ln\big(\widehat{\boldsymbol{R}}_{ij}\big)\Big] + \dfrac{1}{4}\displaystyle\sum_{\{k\in\partial i, k<i\}} \mathrm{Tr}\Big[(\boldsymbol{I}\otimes\sigma^x)\ln\big(\widehat{\boldsymbol{R}}_{ki}\big)\Big], \end{cases} (i\in V), \tag{10.346}$$

$$\begin{cases} \dfrac{J}{k_{\mathrm{B}}T} = \dfrac{1}{4}\mathrm{Tr}\Big[\big(\boldsymbol{\sigma}^z\otimes\boldsymbol{I}\big)\big(\boldsymbol{I}\otimes\boldsymbol{\sigma}^z\big)\ln\big(\widehat{\boldsymbol{R}}_{ij}\big)\Big], \\ 0 = \dfrac{1}{4}\mathrm{Tr}\Big[\big(\boldsymbol{\sigma}^z\otimes\boldsymbol{I}\big)\big(\boldsymbol{I}\otimes\boldsymbol{\sigma}^x\big)\ln\big(\widehat{\boldsymbol{R}}_{ij}\big)\Big] = \dfrac{1}{4}\mathrm{Tr}\Big[\big(\boldsymbol{\sigma}^x\otimes\boldsymbol{I}\big)\big(\boldsymbol{I}\otimes\boldsymbol{\sigma}^z\big)\ln\big(\widehat{\boldsymbol{R}}_{ij}\big)\Big], \\ 0 = \dfrac{1}{4}\mathrm{Tr}\Big[\big(\boldsymbol{\sigma}^x\otimes\boldsymbol{I}\big)\big(\boldsymbol{I}\otimes\boldsymbol{\sigma}^x\big)\ln\big(\widehat{\boldsymbol{R}}_{ij}\big)\Big], \end{cases} (\{i,j\}\in E), \tag{10.347}$$

where

$$\widehat{\boldsymbol{R}}_i = \frac{1}{2}\big(\boldsymbol{I} + \widehat{m}_i^x\boldsymbol{\sigma}^x + \widehat{m}_i^z\boldsymbol{\sigma}^z\big)\ (i\in V), \tag{10.348}$$

$$\begin{aligned} \widehat{\boldsymbol{R}}_{ij} &= \widehat{\boldsymbol{R}}_{ji} \\ &= \frac{1}{4}\Big((\boldsymbol{I}\otimes\boldsymbol{I}) + \widehat{m}_i^x\big(\boldsymbol{\sigma}^x\otimes\boldsymbol{I}\big) + \widehat{m}_i^z(\boldsymbol{\sigma}^z\otimes\boldsymbol{I}) + \widehat{m}_j^x\big(\boldsymbol{I}\otimes\boldsymbol{\sigma}^x\big) + \widehat{m}_j^z(\boldsymbol{I}\otimes\boldsymbol{\sigma}^z) \\ &\quad + \widehat{c}_{\{i,j\}}^{zz}(\boldsymbol{\sigma}^z\otimes\boldsymbol{I})(\boldsymbol{I}\otimes\boldsymbol{\sigma}^z) + \widehat{c}_{\{i,j\}}^{xz}\big(\boldsymbol{\sigma}^x\otimes\boldsymbol{I}\big)(\boldsymbol{I}\otimes\boldsymbol{\sigma}^z) \\ &\quad + \widehat{c}_{\{i,j\}}^{zx}(\boldsymbol{\sigma}^z\otimes\boldsymbol{I})\big(\boldsymbol{I}\otimes\boldsymbol{\sigma}^x\big) + \widehat{c}_{\{i,j\}}^{xx}\big(\boldsymbol{\sigma}^x\otimes\boldsymbol{I}\big)\big(\boldsymbol{I}\otimes\boldsymbol{\sigma}^x\big)\Big)\ (\{i,j\}\in E,\ i<j). \end{aligned} \tag{10.349}$$

For $\Gamma = 0$, Eq. (10.347) with Eqs. (10.348) and (10.349) reduces to Eqs. (10.107) and (10.108) with Eqs. (10.72) and (10.102).

Before finishing the present subsection, we briefly review another framework of the quantum advanced mean-field method. As we mentioned above, advanced quantum mean-field methods have also been formulated in the momentum space. One familiar formulation is spin wave theory [91]. A general formulation of the quantum cluster variation method from the viewpoint of spin wave theory was proposed in Refs. [92, 93].

10.5.2 Real-Space Renormalization Group Method for the Transverse Ising Model

We now present sublinear modeling in statistical machine learning procedures by using the real-space renormalization group method for the transverse Ising model in Eq. (10.301) on the ring graph (V, E) of Eq. (10.176) for the case of $|V| = 2^L$ and $h = 0$. The present scheme follows the one in Refs. [37, 94]. Some extensions of the present frameworks for the ring graph in Eq. (10.176) to higher-dimensional graphs such as the torus graph may be available according to the frameworks of Ref. [94].

The important part of the transverse Ising model in Eq. (10.301), $-J(\boldsymbol{\sigma}^z \otimes \boldsymbol{I})(\boldsymbol{I} \otimes \boldsymbol{\sigma}^z) - \Gamma(\boldsymbol{\sigma}^x \otimes \boldsymbol{I})$ can be diagonalized as

$$
-J(\boldsymbol{\sigma}^z \otimes \boldsymbol{I})(\boldsymbol{I} \otimes \boldsymbol{\sigma}^z) - \Gamma(\boldsymbol{\sigma}^x \otimes \boldsymbol{I}) = \begin{pmatrix} -J & 0 & -\Gamma & 0 \\ 0 & J & 0 & -\Gamma \\ -\Gamma & 0 & J & 0 \\ 0 & -\Gamma & 0 & -J \end{pmatrix}
$$
$$
= \begin{pmatrix} \sqrt{\frac{1}{2}\left(1+\frac{J}{\sqrt{J^2+\Gamma^2}}\right)} & 0 & 0 & \sqrt{\frac{1}{2}\left(1-\frac{J}{\sqrt{J^2+\Gamma^2}}\right)} \\ 0 & \sqrt{\frac{1}{2}\left(1-\frac{J}{\sqrt{J^2+\Gamma^2}}\right)} & -\sqrt{\frac{1}{2}\left(1+\frac{J}{\sqrt{J^2+\Gamma^2}}\right)} & 0 \\ \sqrt{\frac{1}{2}\left(1-\frac{J}{\sqrt{J^2+\Gamma^2}}\right)} & 0 & 0 & -\sqrt{\frac{1}{2}\left(1+\frac{J}{\sqrt{J^2+\Gamma^2}}\right)} \\ 0 & \sqrt{\frac{1}{2}\left(1+\frac{J}{\sqrt{J^2+\Gamma^2}}\right)} & \sqrt{\frac{1}{2}\left(1-\frac{J}{\sqrt{J^2+\Gamma^2}}\right)} & 0 \end{pmatrix}
$$
$$
\times \begin{pmatrix} -\sqrt{J^2+\Gamma^2} & 0 & 0 & 0 \\ 0 & -\sqrt{J^2+\Gamma^2} & 0 & 0 \\ 0 & 0 & \sqrt{J^2+\Gamma^2} & 0 \\ 0 & 0 & 0 & \sqrt{J^2+\Gamma^2} \end{pmatrix}
$$
$$
\times \begin{pmatrix} \sqrt{\frac{1}{2}\left(1+\frac{J}{\sqrt{J^2+\Gamma^2}}\right)} & 0 & 0 & \sqrt{\frac{1}{2}\left(1-\frac{J}{\sqrt{J^2+\Gamma^2}}\right)} \\ 0 & \sqrt{\frac{1}{2}\left(1-\frac{J}{\sqrt{J^2+\Gamma^2}}\right)} & -\sqrt{\frac{1}{2}\left(1+\frac{J}{\sqrt{J^2+\Gamma^2}}\right)} & 0 \\ \sqrt{\frac{1}{2}\left(1-\frac{J}{\sqrt{J^2+\Gamma^2}}\right)} & 0 & 0 & -\sqrt{\frac{1}{2}\left(1+\frac{J}{\sqrt{J^2+\Gamma^2}}\right)} \\ 0 & \sqrt{\frac{1}{2}\left(1+\frac{J}{\sqrt{J^2+\Gamma^2}}\right)} & \sqrt{\frac{1}{2}\left(1-\frac{J}{\sqrt{J^2+\Gamma^2}}\right)} & 0 \end{pmatrix}^{\mathrm{T}}. \tag{10.350}
$$

The eigenvalues $\varepsilon_1 = \varepsilon_2 = -\sqrt{J^2+\Gamma^2}$, $\varepsilon_3 = \varepsilon_4 = +\sqrt{J^2+\Gamma^2}$ have the relationship $\varepsilon_1 = \varepsilon_2 < \varepsilon_3 = \varepsilon_4$ and their corresponding eigenvectors are given by

$$\begin{cases} |1\rangle = \begin{pmatrix} \sqrt{\frac{1}{2}\left(1+\frac{J}{\sqrt{J^2+\Gamma^2}}\right)} \\ 0 \\ \sqrt{\frac{1}{2}\left(1-\frac{J}{\sqrt{J^2+\Gamma^2}}\right)} \\ 0 \end{pmatrix}, & |2\rangle = \begin{pmatrix} 0 \\ +\sqrt{\frac{1}{2}\left(1-\frac{J}{\sqrt{J^2+\Gamma^2}}\right)} \\ 0 \\ +\sqrt{\frac{1}{2}\left(1+\frac{J}{\sqrt{J^2+\Gamma^2}}\right)} \end{pmatrix}, \\ |3\rangle = \begin{pmatrix} 0 \\ -\sqrt{\frac{1}{2}\left(1+\frac{J}{\sqrt{J^2+\Gamma^2}}\right)} \\ 0 \\ +\sqrt{\frac{1}{2}\left(1-\frac{J}{\sqrt{J^2+\Gamma^2}}\right)} \end{pmatrix}, & |4\rangle = \begin{pmatrix} \sqrt{\frac{1}{2}\left(1-\frac{J}{\sqrt{J^2+\Gamma^2}}\right)} \\ 0 \\ -\sqrt{\frac{1}{2}\left(1+\frac{J}{\sqrt{J^2+\Gamma^2}}\right)} \\ 0 \end{pmatrix}. \end{cases} \tag{10.351}$$

To realize the coarse graining of the present transverse Ising model for the case of zero temperature $T = 0$ for the density matrix $\boldsymbol{P}$ in Eq. (10.300), we introduce the following projection operator:

$$\mathbb{P}_i^{(2^L)} = \underbrace{\mathbb{P}\otimes\mathbb{P}\otimes\cdots\otimes\mathbb{P}}_{2^L\ \mathbb{P}'s}, \tag{10.352}$$

where

$$\begin{aligned}\mathbb{P} &\equiv \begin{pmatrix} \langle 1| \\ \langle 2| \end{pmatrix}(|1\rangle\langle 1| + |2\rangle\langle 2|) = \begin{pmatrix} \langle 1| \\ \langle 2| \end{pmatrix} \\ &= \begin{pmatrix} \sqrt{\frac{1}{2}\left(1+\frac{J}{\sqrt{J^2+\Gamma^2}}\right)} & 0 & \sqrt{\frac{1}{2}\left(1-\frac{J}{\sqrt{J^2+\Gamma^2}}\right)} & 0 \\ 0 & +\sqrt{\frac{1}{2}\left(1-\frac{J}{\sqrt{J^2+\Gamma^2}}\right)} & 0 & \sqrt{\frac{1}{2}\left(1+\frac{J}{\sqrt{J^2+\Gamma^2}}\right)} \end{pmatrix}.\end{aligned} \tag{10.353}$$

Because it is valid that

$$\mathbb{P}\begin{pmatrix} -J & 0 & -\Gamma & 0 \\ 0 & J & 0 & -\Gamma \\ -\Gamma & 0 & J & 0 \\ 0 & -\Gamma & 0 & -J \end{pmatrix}\mathbb{P}^{\mathrm{T}} = -\sqrt{J^2+\Gamma^2}\begin{pmatrix} \langle 1|1\rangle & \langle 1|2\rangle \\ \langle 2|1\rangle & \langle 2|2\rangle \end{pmatrix} = -\sqrt{J^2+\Gamma^2}\boldsymbol{I}, \tag{10.354}$$

we can derive the following equalities

$$\begin{aligned}&\mathbb{P}_i^{(2^L)}\left(-J\sigma_{2i-1}^z\sigma_{2i}^z - \Gamma\sigma_{2i-1}^x\right)\mathbb{P}_i^{(2^L)\mathrm{T}} \\ &= \mathbb{P}_i^{(2^L)}\Big(\overbrace{(\boldsymbol{I}\otimes\boldsymbol{I})\otimes(\boldsymbol{I}\otimes\boldsymbol{I})\otimes\cdots\otimes(\boldsymbol{I}\otimes\boldsymbol{I})}^{\text{Tensor Products of } (i-1) \text{ Matrices } (\boldsymbol{I}\otimes\boldsymbol{I})}\otimes\left(-J(\sigma^z\otimes\boldsymbol{I})(\boldsymbol{I}\otimes\sigma^z) - \Gamma(\sigma^x\otimes\boldsymbol{I})\right) \\ &\quad\otimes\underbrace{(\boldsymbol{I}\otimes\boldsymbol{I})\otimes(\boldsymbol{I}\otimes\boldsymbol{I})\otimes\cdots\otimes(\boldsymbol{I}\otimes\boldsymbol{I})}_{\text{Tensor Products of } (2^{L-1}-i) \text{ Matrices } (\boldsymbol{I}\otimes\boldsymbol{I})}\Big)\mathbb{P}_i^{(2^L)\mathrm{T}}\end{aligned}$$

$$= \Big(\overbrace{\big(\mathbb{P}(\boldsymbol{I}\otimes\boldsymbol{I})\mathbb{P}^{\mathrm{T}}\big)\otimes\big(\mathbb{P}(\boldsymbol{I}\otimes\boldsymbol{I})\mathbb{P}^{\mathrm{T}}\big)\otimes\cdots\otimes\big(\mathbb{P}(\boldsymbol{I}\otimes\boldsymbol{I})\mathbb{P}^{\mathrm{T}}\big)}^{\text{Tensor Products of } (i-1) \text{ Matrices } (\mathbb{P}(\boldsymbol{I}\otimes\boldsymbol{I})\mathbb{P}^{\mathrm{T}})}\Big)\otimes\Big(\mathbb{P}\big(-J(\boldsymbol{\sigma}^z\otimes\boldsymbol{I})(\boldsymbol{I}\otimes\boldsymbol{\sigma}^z)-\Gamma(\boldsymbol{\sigma}^x\otimes\boldsymbol{I})\big)\mathbb{P}^{\mathrm{T}}\Big)$$
$$\otimes\Big(\underbrace{\big(\mathbb{P}(\boldsymbol{I}\otimes\boldsymbol{I})\mathbb{P}^{\mathrm{T}}\big)\otimes\big(\mathbb{P}(\boldsymbol{I}\otimes\boldsymbol{I})\mathbb{P}^{\mathrm{T}}\big)\otimes\cdots\otimes\big(\mathbb{P}(\boldsymbol{I}\otimes\boldsymbol{I})\mathbb{P}^{\mathrm{T}}\big)}_{\text{Tensor Products of } (2^{L-1}-i) \text{ Matrices } (\mathbb{P}(\boldsymbol{I}\otimes\boldsymbol{I})\mathbb{P}^{\mathrm{T}})}\Big)$$
$$= \Big(\overbrace{\big(\mathbb{P}(\boldsymbol{I}\otimes\boldsymbol{I})\mathbb{P}^{\mathrm{T}}\big)\otimes\big(\mathbb{P}(\boldsymbol{I}\otimes\boldsymbol{I})\mathbb{P}^{\mathrm{T}}\big)\otimes\cdots\otimes\big(\mathbb{P}(\boldsymbol{I}\otimes\boldsymbol{I})\mathbb{P}^{\mathrm{T}}\big)}^{\text{Tensor Products of } (i-1) \text{ Matrices } (\mathbb{P}(\boldsymbol{I}\otimes\boldsymbol{I})\mathbb{P}^{\mathrm{T}})}\Big)\otimes\Big(\mathbb{P}\big(-J(\boldsymbol{\sigma}^z\otimes\boldsymbol{I})(\boldsymbol{I}\otimes\boldsymbol{\sigma}^z)-\Gamma(\boldsymbol{\sigma}^x\otimes\boldsymbol{I})\big)\mathbb{P}^{\mathrm{T}}\Big)$$
$$\otimes\Big(\underbrace{\big(\mathbb{P}(\boldsymbol{I}\otimes\boldsymbol{I})\mathbb{P}^{\mathrm{T}}\big)\otimes\big(\mathbb{P}(\boldsymbol{I}\otimes\boldsymbol{I})\mathbb{P}^{\mathrm{T}}\big)\otimes\cdots\otimes\big(\mathbb{P}(\boldsymbol{I}\otimes\boldsymbol{I})\mathbb{P}^{\mathrm{T}}\big)}_{\text{Tensor Products of } (2^{L-1}-i) \text{ Matrices } (\mathbb{P}(\boldsymbol{I}\otimes\boldsymbol{I})\mathbb{P}^{\mathrm{T}})}\Big)$$
$$= \Big(\overbrace{\boldsymbol{I}\otimes\boldsymbol{I}\otimes\cdots\otimes\boldsymbol{I}}^{(i-1)\ \boldsymbol{I}'\text{s}}\Big)\otimes\Big(-\sqrt{J^2+\Gamma^2}\boldsymbol{I}\Big)\otimes\Big(\underbrace{\boldsymbol{I}\otimes\boldsymbol{I}\otimes\cdots\otimes\boldsymbol{I}}_{(2^{L-1}-i)\ \boldsymbol{I}'\text{s}}\Big), \tag{10.355}$$

$$\mathbb{P}_i^{(2^L)}\Big(-J\boldsymbol{\sigma}_{2i}^z\boldsymbol{\sigma}_{2i+1}^z-\Gamma\boldsymbol{\sigma}_{2i}^x\Big)\mathbb{P}_i^{(2^L)\mathrm{T}}$$
$$= \mathbb{P}_i^{(2^L)}\Big(\overbrace{(\boldsymbol{I}\otimes\boldsymbol{I})\otimes(\boldsymbol{I}\otimes\boldsymbol{I})\otimes\cdots\otimes(\boldsymbol{I}\otimes\boldsymbol{I})}^{\text{Tensor Products of } (i-1) \text{ Matrices } (\boldsymbol{I}\otimes\boldsymbol{I})}$$
$$\otimes\big(-J(\boldsymbol{I}\otimes\boldsymbol{\sigma}^z\otimes\boldsymbol{I}\otimes\boldsymbol{I})(\boldsymbol{I}\otimes\boldsymbol{I}\otimes\boldsymbol{\sigma}^z\otimes\boldsymbol{I})-\Gamma(\boldsymbol{I}\otimes\boldsymbol{\sigma}^x\otimes\boldsymbol{I}\otimes\boldsymbol{I})\big)$$
$$\otimes\ \underbrace{(\boldsymbol{I}\otimes\boldsymbol{I})\otimes(\boldsymbol{I}\otimes\boldsymbol{I})\otimes\cdots\otimes(\boldsymbol{I}\otimes\boldsymbol{I})}_{\text{Tensor Products of } (2^{L-1}-i-1) \text{ Matrices } (\boldsymbol{I}\otimes\boldsymbol{I})}\Big)\mathbb{P}_i^{(2^L)\mathrm{T}}$$
$$= \Big(\overbrace{\big(\mathbb{P}(\boldsymbol{I}\otimes\boldsymbol{I})\mathbb{P}^{\mathrm{T}}\big)\otimes\big(\mathbb{P}(\boldsymbol{I}\otimes\boldsymbol{I})\mathbb{P}^{\mathrm{T}}\big)\otimes\cdots\otimes\big(\mathbb{P}(\boldsymbol{I}\otimes\boldsymbol{I})\mathbb{P}^{\mathrm{T}}\big)}^{\text{Tensor Products of } (i-1) \text{ Matrices } (\mathbb{P}(\boldsymbol{I}\otimes\boldsymbol{I})\mathbb{P}^{\mathrm{T}})}\Big)$$
$$\otimes\Big(\big(\mathbb{P}\otimes\mathbb{P}^{\mathrm{T}}\big)\Big(-J(\boldsymbol{I}\otimes\boldsymbol{\sigma}^z\otimes\boldsymbol{I}\otimes\boldsymbol{I})(\boldsymbol{I}\otimes\boldsymbol{I}\otimes\boldsymbol{\sigma}^z\otimes\boldsymbol{I})-\Gamma(\boldsymbol{I}\otimes\boldsymbol{\sigma}^x\otimes\boldsymbol{I}\otimes\boldsymbol{I})\Big)\big(\mathbb{P}\otimes\mathbb{P}^{\mathrm{T}}\big)\Big)$$
$$\otimes\Big(\underbrace{\big(\mathbb{P}(\boldsymbol{I}\otimes\boldsymbol{I})\mathbb{P}^{\mathrm{T}}\big)\otimes\big(\mathbb{P}(\boldsymbol{I}\otimes\boldsymbol{I})\mathbb{P}^{\mathrm{T}}\big)\otimes\cdots\otimes\big(\mathbb{P}(\boldsymbol{I}\otimes\boldsymbol{I})\mathbb{P}^{\mathrm{T}}\big)}_{\text{Tensor Products of } (2^{L-1}-i-1) \text{ Matrices } (\mathbb{P}(\boldsymbol{I}\otimes\boldsymbol{I})\mathbb{P}^{\mathrm{T}})}\Big)$$
$$= \Big(\overbrace{\big(\mathbb{P}(\boldsymbol{I}\otimes\boldsymbol{I})\mathbb{P}^{\mathrm{T}}\big)\otimes\big(\mathbb{P}(\boldsymbol{I}\otimes\boldsymbol{I})\mathbb{P}^{\mathrm{T}}\big)\otimes\cdots\otimes\big(\mathbb{P}(\boldsymbol{I}\otimes\boldsymbol{I})\mathbb{P}^{\mathrm{T}}\big)}^{\text{Tensor Products of } (i-1) \text{ Matrices } (\mathbb{P}(\boldsymbol{I}\otimes\boldsymbol{I})\mathbb{P}^{\mathrm{T}})}\Big)$$
$$\otimes\Big(-J\big(\big(\mathbb{P}(\boldsymbol{I}\otimes\boldsymbol{\sigma}^z)\mathbb{P}^{\mathrm{T}}\big)\otimes\big(\mathbb{P}(\boldsymbol{I}\otimes\boldsymbol{I})\mathbb{P}^{\mathrm{T}}\big)\big)\big(\big(\mathbb{P}(\boldsymbol{I}\otimes\boldsymbol{I})\mathbb{P}^{\mathrm{T}}\big)\otimes\big(\mathbb{P}(\boldsymbol{\sigma}^z\otimes\boldsymbol{I})\mathbb{P}^{\mathrm{T}}\big)\big)-\Gamma\big(\mathbb{P}(\boldsymbol{I}\otimes\boldsymbol{\sigma}^x)\mathbb{P}^{\mathrm{T}}\otimes\mathbb{P}(\boldsymbol{I}\otimes\boldsymbol{I})\mathbb{P}^{\mathrm{T}}\big)\Big)$$
$$\otimes\Big(\underbrace{\big(\mathbb{P}(\boldsymbol{I}\otimes\boldsymbol{I})\mathbb{P}^{\mathrm{T}}\big)\otimes\big(\mathbb{P}(\boldsymbol{I}\otimes\boldsymbol{I})\mathbb{P}^{\mathrm{T}}\big)\otimes\cdots\otimes\big(\mathbb{P}(\boldsymbol{I}\otimes\boldsymbol{I})\mathbb{P}^{\mathrm{T}}\big)}_{\text{Tensor Products of } (2^{L-1}-i-1) \text{ Matrices } (\mathbb{P}(\boldsymbol{I}\otimes\boldsymbol{I})\mathbb{P}^{\mathrm{T}})}\Big)$$
$$= \Big(\overbrace{\boldsymbol{I}\otimes\boldsymbol{I}\otimes\cdots\otimes\boldsymbol{I}}^{(i-1)\ \boldsymbol{I}'\text{s}}\Big)\otimes\Big(-\frac{J^2}{\sqrt{J^2+\Gamma^2}}(\boldsymbol{\sigma}^z\otimes\boldsymbol{I})(\boldsymbol{I}\otimes\boldsymbol{\sigma}^z)-\frac{\Gamma^2}{\sqrt{J^2+\Gamma^2}}(\boldsymbol{\sigma}^x\otimes\boldsymbol{I})\Big)\otimes\Big(\underbrace{\boldsymbol{I}\otimes\boldsymbol{I}\otimes\cdots\otimes\boldsymbol{I}}_{(2^{L-1}-i-1)\ \boldsymbol{I}'\text{s}}\Big), \tag{10.356}$$

$$\mathbb{P}_i^{(2^L)}\Big(-J\boldsymbol{\sigma}_1^z\boldsymbol{\sigma}_{2^L}^z-\Gamma\boldsymbol{\sigma}_{2^L}^x\Big)\mathbb{P}_i^{(2^L)\mathrm{T}}$$
$$= \mathbb{P}_i^{(2^L)}\Bigg(-J\Big((\boldsymbol{\sigma}^z\otimes\boldsymbol{I})\otimes\ \overbrace{(\boldsymbol{I}\otimes\boldsymbol{I})\otimes(\boldsymbol{I}\otimes\boldsymbol{I})\otimes\cdots\otimes(\boldsymbol{I}\otimes\boldsymbol{I})}^{\text{Tensor Products of } (2^{L-1}-2) \text{ Matrices } (\boldsymbol{I}\otimes\boldsymbol{I})}\ \otimes(\boldsymbol{I}\otimes\boldsymbol{I})\Big)$$

$$\times\Bigg((\boldsymbol{I}\otimes\boldsymbol{I})\otimes\overbrace{(\boldsymbol{I}\otimes\boldsymbol{I})\otimes(\boldsymbol{I}\otimes\boldsymbol{I})\otimes\cdots\otimes(\boldsymbol{I}\otimes\boldsymbol{I})}^{\text{Tensor Products of } (2^{L-1}-2) \text{ Matrices } (\boldsymbol{I}\otimes\boldsymbol{I})}\otimes(\boldsymbol{I}\otimes\boldsymbol{\sigma}^{z})\Big)$$

$$-\Gamma(\boldsymbol{I}\otimes\boldsymbol{I})\otimes\overbrace{(\boldsymbol{I}\otimes\boldsymbol{I})\otimes(\boldsymbol{I}\otimes\boldsymbol{I})\otimes\cdots\otimes(\boldsymbol{I}\otimes\boldsymbol{I})}^{\text{Tensor Products of } (2^{L-1}-2) \text{ Matrices } (\boldsymbol{I}\otimes\boldsymbol{I})}\otimes(\boldsymbol{I}\otimes\boldsymbol{\sigma}^{x})\Big)\Bigg)\mathbb{P}_i^{(2^L)^{\mathrm{T}}}$$

$$= -\frac{J^2}{\sqrt{J^2+\Gamma^2}}\Big(\boldsymbol{\sigma}^z\otimes\Big(\overbrace{\boldsymbol{I}\otimes\boldsymbol{I}\otimes\cdots\otimes\boldsymbol{I}}^{(2^{L-1}-2)\ \boldsymbol{I}'\text{s}}\Big)\otimes\boldsymbol{I}\Big)\Big(\boldsymbol{I}\otimes\Big(\overbrace{\boldsymbol{I}\otimes\boldsymbol{I}\otimes\cdots\otimes\boldsymbol{I}}^{(2^{L-1}-2)\ \boldsymbol{I}'\text{s}}\Big)\otimes\boldsymbol{\sigma}^z\Big)$$
$$-\frac{\Gamma^2}{\sqrt{J^2+\Gamma^2}}\Big(\boldsymbol{I}\otimes\Big(\overbrace{\boldsymbol{I}\otimes\boldsymbol{I}\otimes\cdots\otimes\boldsymbol{I}}^{(2^{L-1}-2)\ \boldsymbol{I}'\text{s}}\Big)\otimes\boldsymbol{\sigma}^x\Big). \tag{10.357}$$

By using these equalities, the first step of the renormalized energy matrix $\boldsymbol{H}^{(2^{L-1})}\equiv\mathbb{P}_i^{(2^L)}\boldsymbol{H}\mathbb{P}_i^{(2^L)^{\mathrm{T}}}$ can be reduced as follows:

$$\begin{aligned}\boldsymbol{H}^{(2^{L-1})} &\equiv \mathbb{P}_i^{(2^L)}\boldsymbol{H}\mathbb{P}_i^{(2^L)^{\mathrm{T}}}\\ &= -2^{L-1}\sqrt{J^2+\Gamma^2}\Big(\overbrace{\boldsymbol{I}\otimes\boldsymbol{I}\otimes\cdots\otimes\boldsymbol{I}}^{(2^{L-1})\ \boldsymbol{I}'\text{s}}\Big)\\ &\quad-\sum_{i=1}^{2^{L-1}}\Big(\overbrace{\boldsymbol{I}\otimes\boldsymbol{I}\otimes\cdots\otimes\boldsymbol{I}}^{(i-1)\ \boldsymbol{I}'\text{s}}\Big)\otimes\Big(\frac{J^2}{\sqrt{J^2+\Gamma^2}}(\boldsymbol{\sigma}^z\otimes\boldsymbol{I})(\boldsymbol{I}\otimes\boldsymbol{\sigma}^z)+\frac{\Gamma^2}{\sqrt{J^2+\Gamma^2}}(\boldsymbol{\sigma}^x\otimes\boldsymbol{I})\Big)\otimes\Big(\underbrace{\boldsymbol{I}\otimes\boldsymbol{I}\otimes\cdots\otimes\boldsymbol{I}}_{(2^{L-1}-i-1)\ \boldsymbol{I}'\text{s}}\Big)\\ &\quad-\frac{J^2}{\sqrt{J^2+\Gamma^2}}\Big(\boldsymbol{\sigma}^z\otimes\Big(\overbrace{\boldsymbol{I}\otimes\boldsymbol{I}\otimes\cdots\otimes\boldsymbol{I}}^{(2^{L-1}-2)\ \boldsymbol{I}'\text{s}}\Big)\otimes\boldsymbol{I}\Big)\Big(\boldsymbol{I}\otimes\Big(\overbrace{\boldsymbol{I}\otimes\boldsymbol{I}\otimes\cdots\otimes\boldsymbol{I}}^{(2^{L-1}-2)\ \boldsymbol{I}'\text{s}}\Big)\otimes\boldsymbol{\sigma}^z\Big)\\ &\quad-\frac{\Gamma^2}{\sqrt{J^2+\Gamma^2}}\Big(\boldsymbol{I}\otimes\Big(\overbrace{\boldsymbol{I}\otimes\boldsymbol{I}\otimes\cdots\otimes\boldsymbol{I}}^{(2^{L-1}-2)\ \boldsymbol{I}'\text{s}}\Big)\otimes\boldsymbol{\sigma}^x\Big).\end{aligned} \tag{10.358}$$

By similar arguments to those for the above procedure, the r-th step of the renormalized energy matrix $\boldsymbol{H}^{(2^{L-r})}\equiv\Big(\mathbb{P}_i^{(2^{L-r})}\mathbb{P}_i^{(2^{L-r+1})}\cdots\mathbb{P}_i^{(2^L)}\Big)\boldsymbol{H}\Big(\mathbb{P}_i^{(2^L)^{\mathrm{T}}}\cdots\mathbb{P}_i^{(2^{L-r+1})^{\mathrm{T}}}\mathbb{P}_i^{(2^{L-r})^{\mathrm{T}}}\Big)$ can be reduced to the following recursion formulas:

$$\begin{aligned}\boldsymbol{H}^{(2^{L-r})} &\equiv \mathbb{P}_i^{(2^{L-r+1})}\boldsymbol{H}^{(2^{L-r+1})}\mathbb{P}_i^{(2^{L-r+1})^{\mathrm{T}}}\\ &= 2^{L-r}\varepsilon_1^{(r)}\Big(\overbrace{\boldsymbol{I}\otimes\boldsymbol{I}\otimes\cdots\otimes\boldsymbol{I}}^{(2^{L-r})\ \boldsymbol{I}'\text{s}}\Big)\\ &\quad-\sum_{i=1}^{2^{L-1}}\Big(\overbrace{\boldsymbol{I}\otimes\boldsymbol{I}\otimes\cdots\otimes\boldsymbol{I}}^{(i-1)\ \boldsymbol{I}'\text{s}}\Big)\otimes\Big(J^{(r)}(\boldsymbol{\sigma}^z\otimes\boldsymbol{I})(\boldsymbol{I}\otimes\boldsymbol{\sigma}^z)+\Gamma^{(r)}(\boldsymbol{\sigma}^x\otimes\boldsymbol{I})\Big)\otimes\Big(\underbrace{\boldsymbol{I}\otimes\boldsymbol{I}\otimes\cdots\otimes\boldsymbol{I}}_{(2^{L-r}-i-1)\ \boldsymbol{I}'\text{s}}\Big)\\ &\quad-J^{(r)}\Big(\boldsymbol{\sigma}^z\otimes\Big(\overbrace{\boldsymbol{I}\otimes\boldsymbol{I}\otimes\cdots\otimes\boldsymbol{I}}^{(2^{L-r}-2)\ \boldsymbol{I}'\text{s}}\Big)\otimes\boldsymbol{I}\Big)\Big(\boldsymbol{I}\otimes\Big(\overbrace{\boldsymbol{I}\otimes\boldsymbol{I}\otimes\cdots\otimes\boldsymbol{I}}^{(2^{L-r}-2)\ \boldsymbol{I}'\text{s}}\Big)\otimes\boldsymbol{\sigma}^z\Big)\end{aligned}$$

$$- \Gamma^{(r)} \Big(\boldsymbol{I} \otimes \Big(\overbrace{\boldsymbol{I} \otimes \boldsymbol{I} \otimes \cdots \otimes \boldsymbol{I}}^{(2^{L-r}-2)\ \boldsymbol{I}'\text{s}} \Big) \otimes \boldsymbol{\sigma}^{x} \Big), \tag{10.359}$$

where

$$\begin{cases} J^{(r)} = \dfrac{(J^{(r-1)})^2}{\sqrt{(J^{(r-1)})^2 + (\Gamma^{(r-1)})^2}}, \\ \Gamma^{(r)} = \dfrac{(\Gamma^{(r-1)})^2}{\sqrt{(J^{(r-1)})^2 + (\Gamma^{(r-1)})^2}}, \end{cases} \tag{10.360}$$

$$\varepsilon_1^{(r)} = -\sqrt{(J^{(r-1)})^2 + (\Gamma^{(r-1)})^2}, \tag{10.361}$$

$$\begin{cases} \boldsymbol{H}^{(2^L)} \equiv \boldsymbol{H}, \\ J^{(0)} \equiv J, \\ \Gamma^{(0)} \equiv \Gamma. \end{cases} \tag{10.362}$$

The inverse of the real-space renormalization group is given by

$$\begin{cases} J^{(r-1)} = \sqrt{J^{(r)}\big(J^{(r)} + \Gamma^{(r)}\big)}, \\ \Gamma^{(r-1)} = \sqrt{\Gamma^{(r)}\big(J^{(r)} + \Gamma^{(r)}\big)}, \end{cases} \tag{10.363}$$

If the hyperparameters $J^{(r)}$ and $\Gamma^{(r)}$ in the r-th renormalized density matrix $\boldsymbol{H}^{(2^{L-r})}$ have been estimated from given data vectors by using the QEM algorithm for a renormalized density matrix on ring graphs $\big(V^{(r)}, E^{(r)}\big)$, we can estimate the hyperparameters $J^{(0)} = J$ and $\Gamma^{(0)} = \Gamma$ of the transverse Ising model (10.301) on the ring graph E of Eq. (10.176) for the case of $|V| = 2^L$ and $h = 0$ by using the inverse transformation rule of the real-space renormalization group procedure (10.363).

10.5.3 Sublinear Modeling Using a Quantum Adaptive TAP Approach and Momentum Space Renormalization Group in the Transverse Ising Model

This section proposes a novel scheme for the momentum space renormalization group approaches in **Adaptive Thouless-Anderson-Palmar(TAP) Approaches** for the transverse Ising model on random graphs. The adaptive TAP approach is a familiar advanced mean-field method for the probabilistic graphical model and many extensions have been proposed [95–98]. Furthermore, sublinear modeling for the

EM procedure in probabilistic graphical models has been realized by introducing **Momentum Space Renormalization Group Approaches** [99, 100]. The method proposed in this section is formulated by combining the adaptive TAP approaches with the momentum space renormalization group approaches. Moreover, our method is applicable not only to regular graphs but also to random graphs.

The density matrix $\boldsymbol{P}$ in Eq. (10.300) can be rewritten as

$$\boldsymbol{P} = \frac{\exp\left(-\frac{J}{2k_{\mathrm{B}}T}\sum_{\{i,j\}\in E}\left(\sigma_i^z - \sigma_j^z\right)^2 - \frac{h}{2k_{\mathrm{B}}T}\sum_{i\in V}\left(\sigma_i^z - d_i \boldsymbol{I}^{(2^{|V|})}\right)^2 - \frac{1}{2k_{\mathrm{B}}T}\sum_{i\in V}\left(\sigma_i^x - \gamma \boldsymbol{I}^{2^{|V|}}\right)^2\right)}{\mathrm{Tr}\left[\exp\left(-\frac{J}{2k_{\mathrm{B}}T}\sum_{\{i,j\}\in E}\left(\sigma_i^z - \sigma_j^z\right)^2 - \frac{h}{2k_{\mathrm{B}}T}\sum_{i\in V}\left(\sigma_i^z - d_i \boldsymbol{I}^{(2^{|V|})}\right)^2 - \frac{1}{2k_{\mathrm{B}}T}\sum_{i\in V}\left(\sigma_i^x - \Gamma \boldsymbol{I}^{2^{|V|}}\right)^2\right)\right]}. \tag{10.364}$$

The density matrix $\boldsymbol{P}$ satisfies the following minimization of the free energy functional:

$$\boldsymbol{P} = \underset{\boldsymbol{R}}{\mathrm{argmin}}\left\{\mathcal{F}[\boldsymbol{R}]\middle|\mathrm{Tr}\boldsymbol{R} = 1\right\}, \tag{10.365}$$

$$\begin{aligned}\mathcal{F}[\boldsymbol{R}] \equiv& \frac{1}{2}J\sum_{\{i,j\}\in E}\mathrm{Tr}\left[\left(\boldsymbol{\sigma}_i^z - \boldsymbol{\sigma}_j^z\right)^2\boldsymbol{R}\right] + \frac{1}{2}h\sum_{i\in V}\mathrm{Tr}\left[\left(\boldsymbol{\sigma}_i^z - d_i\boldsymbol{I}^{(2^{|V|})}\right)^2\boldsymbol{R}\right]\\ &+\frac{1}{2}\sum_{i\in V}\mathrm{Tr}\left[\left(\boldsymbol{\sigma}_i^x - \Gamma\boldsymbol{I}^{(2^{|V|})}\right)^2\boldsymbol{R}\right] + k_{\mathrm{B}}T\mathrm{Tr}[\boldsymbol{R}\ln(\boldsymbol{R})].\end{aligned} \tag{10.366}$$

Because all the off-diagonal elements of $\left(\boldsymbol{\sigma}_i^z - \boldsymbol{\sigma}_j^z\right)^2$ are zero, we have

$$\begin{aligned}\mathcal{F}[\boldsymbol{R}] =& \frac{1}{2}J\sum_{\{i,j\}\in E}\sum_{s_1\in\Omega}\sum_{s_2\in\Omega}\cdots\sum_{s_{|V|}\in\Omega}\langle s_1, s_2, \cdots, s_{|V|}|\left(\boldsymbol{\sigma}_i^z - \boldsymbol{\sigma}_j^z\right)^2|s_1, s_2, \cdots, s_{|V|}\rangle\\ &\times\langle s_1, s_2, \cdots, s_{|V|}|\boldsymbol{R}|s_1, s_2, \cdots, s_{|V|}\rangle\\ &+\frac{1}{2}h\sum_{i\in V}\sum_{s_1\in\Omega}\sum_{s_2\in\Omega}\cdots\sum_{s_{|V|}\in\Omega}\langle s_1, s_2, \cdots, s_{|V|}|\left(\boldsymbol{\sigma}_i^z - d_i\boldsymbol{I}^{(2^{|V|})}\right)^2|s_1, s_2, \cdots, s_{|V|}\rangle\\ &\times\langle s_1, s_2, \cdots, s_{|V|}|\boldsymbol{R}|s_1, s_2, \cdots, s_{|V|}\rangle\\ &+\frac{1}{2}\sum_{i\in V}\mathrm{Tr}\left[\left(\boldsymbol{\sigma}_i^x - \Gamma\boldsymbol{I}^{(2^{|V|})}\right)^2\boldsymbol{R}\right] + k_{\mathrm{B}}T\mathrm{Tr}[\boldsymbol{R}\ln(\boldsymbol{R})]\\ =& \frac{1}{2}J\sum_{\{i,j\}\in E}\sum_{s_1\in\Omega}\sum_{s_2\in\Omega}\cdots\sum_{s_{|V|}\in\Omega}\left(s_i - s_j\right)^2\langle s_1, s_2, \cdots, s_{|V|}|\boldsymbol{R}|s_1, s_2, \cdots, s_{|V|}\rangle\\ &+\frac{1}{2}h\sum_{i\in V}\sum_{s_1\in\Omega}\sum_{s_2\in\Omega}\cdots\sum_{s_{|V|}\in\Omega}(s_i - d_i)^2\langle s_1, s_2, \cdots, s_{|V|}|\boldsymbol{R}|s_1, s_2, \cdots, s_{|V|}\rangle\end{aligned}$$

$$+\frac{1}{2}\sum_{i\in V}\mathrm{Tr}\Big[\big(\boldsymbol{\sigma}_i^x - \Gamma \boldsymbol{I}^{(2^{|V|})}\big)^2 \boldsymbol{R}\Big] + k_{\mathrm{B}}T\mathrm{Tr}[\boldsymbol{R}\ln(\boldsymbol{R})]. \tag{10.367}$$

By introducing the reduced density matrix $\boldsymbol{R}_i$ in Eq. (10.275) and

$$\rho\big(s_1, s_2, \cdots, s_{|V|}\big) \equiv \langle s_1, s_2, \cdots, s_{|V|}|\boldsymbol{R}|s_1, s_2, \cdots, s_{|V|}\rangle,\ \big((s_1, s_2, \cdots . s_{|V|})\in\Omega^{|V|}\big), \tag{10.368}$$

and by extending $\rho\big(s_1, s_2, \cdots, s_{|V|}\big)$ to

$$\rho(\boldsymbol{\phi}) = \rho\big(\phi_1, \phi_2, \cdots, \phi_{|V|}\big)\ \Big(\boldsymbol{\phi} = (\phi_1, \phi_2, \cdots . \phi_{|V|})\in(-\infty, +\infty)^{|V|}\Big), \tag{10.369}$$

the free energy functional can be expressed as

$$\begin{aligned}\mathcal{F}[\boldsymbol{R}] = &\frac{1}{2}J\sum_{\{i,j\}\in E}\int_{-\infty}^{+\infty}\int_{-\infty}^{+\infty}\cdots\int_{-\infty}^{+\infty}\Big(\prod_{k\in V}(\delta(\phi_k - 1) + \delta(\phi_k + 1))\Big)(\phi_i - \phi_j)^2\rho(\boldsymbol{\phi})d\phi_1 d\phi_2\cdots d\phi_{|V|}\\ &+\frac{1}{2}h\sum_{i\in V}\int_{-\infty}^{+\infty}\int_{-\infty}^{+\infty}\cdots\int_{-\infty}^{+\infty}\Big(\prod_{k\in V}(\delta(\phi_k - 1) + \delta(\phi_k + 1))\Big)(\phi_i - d_i)^2\rho(\boldsymbol{\phi})d\phi_1 d\phi_2\cdots d\phi_{|V|}\\ &+\frac{1}{2}\sum_{i\in V}\mathrm{Tr}\Big[\big(\boldsymbol{\sigma}_i^x - \Gamma \boldsymbol{I}^{(2^{|V|})}\big)^2 \boldsymbol{R}_i\Big] + k_{\mathrm{B}}T\mathrm{Tr}[\boldsymbol{R}\ln(\boldsymbol{R})].\end{aligned} \tag{10.370}$$

Now we consider the following approximate free energy:

$$\begin{aligned}\mathcal{F}_{\text{Adaptive TAP}}\big[\rho, \{\boldsymbol{R}_i, \rho_i|i\in V\}\big] \equiv &\frac{1}{2}J\sum_{\{i,j\}\in E}\int_{-\infty}^{+\infty}\int_{-\infty}^{+\infty}\cdots\int_{-\infty}^{+\infty}(\phi_i - \phi_j)^2\rho(\boldsymbol{\phi})d\phi_1 d\phi_2\cdots d\phi_{|V|}\\ &+\frac{1}{2}h\sum_{i\in V}\int_{-\infty}^{+\infty}\int_{-\infty}^{+\infty}\cdots\int_{-\infty}^{+\infty}(\phi_i - d_i)^2\rho(\boldsymbol{\phi})d\phi_1 d\phi_2\cdots d\phi_{|V|}\\ &+\frac{1}{2}\sum_{i\in V}\mathrm{Tr}\Big[\big(\boldsymbol{\sigma}_i^x - \Gamma \boldsymbol{I}^{(2^{|V|})}\big)^2 \boldsymbol{R}_i\Big]\\ &+k_{\mathrm{B}}T\int_{-\infty}^{+\infty}\int_{-\infty}^{+\infty}\cdots\int_{-\infty}^{+\infty}\rho(\boldsymbol{\phi})\ln\big(\rho(\boldsymbol{\phi})\big)d\phi_1 d\phi_2\cdots d\phi_{|V|}\\ &+k_{\mathrm{B}}T\sum_{i\in V}\Big(\mathrm{Tr}\boldsymbol{R}_i\ln\boldsymbol{R}_i - \int_{-\infty}^{+\infty}\rho_i(\phi_i)\ln\big(\rho_i(\phi_i)\big)d\phi_i\Big),\end{aligned} \tag{10.371}$$

where

$$\rho_i(\phi_i) \equiv \int_{-\infty}^{+\infty}\int_{-\infty}^{+\infty}\cdots\int_{-\infty}^{+\infty}\delta(\phi_i - \phi_i')\rho\big(\phi_1', \phi_2', \cdots, \phi_{|V|}'\big)d\phi_1' d\phi_2'\cdots d\phi_{|V|}' \quad (i\in V, \phi_i\in(-\infty, +\infty)). \tag{10.372}$$

The reduced density matrix $\boldsymbol{R}_i$ and the marginal probability density functions $\rho_i(\phi_i)$ and $\rho(\boldsymbol{\phi})$ need to satisfy the consistencies

$$\begin{cases} \int_{-\infty}^{+\infty}\int_{-\infty}^{+\infty}\cdots\int_{-\infty}^{+\infty}\phi_i\rho(\boldsymbol{\phi})d\phi_1 d\phi_2\cdots d\phi_{|V|} = \int_{-\infty}^{+\infty}\phi_i\rho_i(\phi_i)d\phi_i = \mathrm{Tr}\boldsymbol{\sigma}^z\boldsymbol{R}_i \ (i\in V), \\ \sum_{i\in V}\int_{-\infty}^{+\infty}\int_{-\infty}^{+\infty}\cdots\int_{-\infty}^{+\infty}{\phi_i}^2\rho(\boldsymbol{\phi})d\phi_1 d\phi_2\cdots d\phi_{|V|} = \sum_{i\in V}\int_{-\infty}^{+\infty}{\phi_i}^2\rho_i(\phi_i)d\phi_i = 1, \end{cases} \tag{10.373}$$

and the normalizations

$$\begin{cases} \int_{-\infty}^{+\infty}\int_{-\infty}^{+\infty}\cdots\int_{-\infty}^{+\infty}\rho(\boldsymbol{\phi})d\phi_1 d\phi_2\cdots d\phi_{|V|} = 1, \\ \int_{-\infty}^{+\infty}\rho_i(\phi_i)d\phi_i = 1 \ (i\in V). \\ \mathrm{Tr}\boldsymbol{R}_i = 1. \end{cases} \tag{10.374}$$

$\boldsymbol{R}_i$, $\rho_i(\phi_i)$ and $\rho(\boldsymbol{\phi})$ are determined so as to minimize the above approximate free energy $\mathcal{F}\big[\rho, \{\boldsymbol{R}_i, \rho_i|i\in V\}\big]$ under the constraint conditions in Eqs. (10.373) and (10.374). We introduce Lagrange multipliers $\boldsymbol{f} = \begin{pmatrix} f_1 \\ f_2 \\ \vdots \\ f_{|V|} \end{pmatrix}$ and $\boldsymbol{g} = \begin{pmatrix} g_1 \\ g_2 \\ \vdots \\ g_{|V|} \end{pmatrix}$, D, L, λ, and λ_i to ensure the constraint conditions in Eqs. (10.373) and (10.374) as follows:

$$\begin{aligned} &\mathcal{L}_{\text{Adaptive TAP}}\big[\rho, \{R_i, \rho_i|i\in V\}\big] \\ &\equiv \mathcal{F}_{\text{Adaptive TAP}}\big[\rho, \{R_i, \rho_i|i\in V\}\big] \\ &-\sum_{i\in V} g_i\left(\int_{-\infty}^{+\infty}\int_{-\infty}^{+\infty}\cdots\int_{-\infty}^{+\infty}\phi_i\rho(\boldsymbol{\phi})d\phi_1 d\phi_2\cdots d\phi_{|V|} - \int_{-\infty}^{+\infty}\phi_i\rho_i(\phi_i)d\phi_i\right) \\ &-\sum_{i\in V} f_i\left(\int_{-\infty}^{+\infty}\int_{-\infty}^{+\infty}\cdots\int_{-\infty}^{+\infty}\phi_i\rho(\boldsymbol{\phi})d\phi_1 d\phi_2\cdots d\phi_{|V|} - \mathrm{Tr}\boldsymbol{\sigma}^z\boldsymbol{R}_i\right) \\ &-D\left(\sum_{i\in V}\int_{-\infty}^{+\infty}\int_{-\infty}^{+\infty}\cdots\int_{-\infty}^{+\infty}{\phi_i}^2\rho(\boldsymbol{\phi})d\phi_1 d\phi_2\cdots d\phi_{|V|} - 1\right) \\ &-L\left(\sum_{i\in V}\int_{-\infty}^{+\infty}{\phi_i}^2\rho_i(\phi_i)d\phi_i - 1\right) \\ &-\lambda\left(\int_{-\infty}^{+\infty}\int_{-\infty}^{+\infty}\cdots\int_{-\infty}^{+\infty}\rho(\boldsymbol{\phi})d\boldsymbol{\phi} - 1\right) \\ &-\sum_{i\in V}\lambda_i\left(\int_{-\infty}^{+\infty}\rho_i(\phi_i)d\phi_i - 1\right). \end{aligned} \tag{10.375}$$

By taking the first variation of the approximate free energy $\mathcal{L}_{\text{Adaptive TAP}}\big[\widehat{\rho}, \{\boldsymbol{R}_i, \rho_i|i\in V\}\big]$ with respect to the marginals, we can derive the approximate expressions of $\widehat{\boldsymbol{R}}_i$, $\widehat{\rho}_i(\phi_i)$, and $\widehat{\rho}(\boldsymbol{\phi})$ as follows:

$$\widehat{\boldsymbol{R}}_i = \frac{\exp\left(\frac{1}{k_{\mathrm{B}}T}\left(f_i\boldsymbol{\sigma}^z + \Gamma\boldsymbol{\sigma}^x\right)\right)}{\mathrm{Tr}\exp\left(\frac{1}{k_{\mathrm{B}}T}\left(h_i\boldsymbol{\sigma}^z + \Gamma\boldsymbol{\sigma}^x\right)\right)} \quad (i\in V), \tag{10.376}$$

$$\widehat{\rho}(\boldsymbol{\phi}) = \frac{\exp\left(\frac{1}{k_{\mathrm{B}}T}\left(-\frac{1}{2}D\sum_{i\in V}\phi_i^2+\sum_{i\in V}(f_i+g_i)\phi_i-\frac{1}{2}h\sum_{i\in V}(\phi_i-d_i)^2-\frac{1}{2}J\sum_{\{i,j\}\in E}(\phi_i-\phi_j)^2\right)\right)}{\int_{-\infty}^{+\infty}\int_{-\infty}^{+\infty}\cdots\int_{-\infty}^{+\infty}\exp\left(\frac{1}{k_{\mathrm{B}}T}\left(-\frac{1}{2}D\sum_{i\in V}\phi_i^2+\sum_{i\in V}(f_i+g_i)\phi_i-\frac{1}{2}h\sum_{i\in V}(\phi_i-d_i)^2-\frac{1}{2}J\sum_{\{i,j\}\in E}(\phi_i-\phi_j)^2\right)\right)d\phi_1 d\phi_2\cdots d\phi_{|V|}}. \tag{10.377}$$

$$\widehat{\rho}_i(\phi_i) = \frac{\exp\left(\frac{1}{k_{\mathrm{B}}T}\left(-\frac{1}{2}L\phi_i^2+g_i\phi_i-\frac{1}{2}h(\phi_i-d_i)^2\right)\right)}{\int_{-\infty}^{+\infty}\exp\left(\frac{1}{k_{\mathrm{B}}T}\left(-\frac{1}{2}L\phi_i^2+g_i\phi_i-\frac{1}{2}h(\phi_i-d_i)^2\right)\right)d\phi_i} \tag{10.378}$$

where $\boldsymbol{C}$ is the $|V|\times|V|$ matrix in which the (i,j)-elements are defined by

$$C_{ij} \equiv \begin{cases} |\partial i| & (i=j), \\ -1 & (\{i,j\}\in E), \\ 0 & (\text{otherwise}), \end{cases} \tag{10.379}$$

for any nodes $i(\in V)$ and $j(\in V)$. Equations (10.376), (10.377), and (10.378) can be rewritten as

$$\widehat{\boldsymbol{R}}_i = \frac{1}{2\cosh\left(\frac{1}{k_{\mathrm{B}}T}\sqrt{f_i^2+\Gamma^2}\right)}\frac{f_i+\sqrt{f_i^2+\Gamma^2}}{2\sqrt{f_i^2+\Gamma^2}}\begin{pmatrix} 1 & -\frac{\Gamma}{f_i+\sqrt{f_i^2+\Gamma^2}} \\ +\frac{\Gamma}{f_i+\sqrt{f_i^2+\Gamma^2}} & 1 \end{pmatrix}$$
$$\times\begin{pmatrix} \exp\left(+\frac{1}{k_{\mathrm{B}}T}\sqrt{f_i^2+\Gamma^2}\right) & 0 \\ 0 & \exp\left(-\frac{1}{k_{\mathrm{B}}T}\sqrt{f_i^2+\Gamma^2}\right) \end{pmatrix}\begin{pmatrix} 1 & +\frac{\Gamma}{f_i+\sqrt{f_i^2+\Gamma^2}} \\ -\frac{\Gamma}{f_i+\sqrt{f_i^2+\Gamma^2}} & 1 \end{pmatrix}. \tag{10.380}$$

$$\widehat{\rho}(\boldsymbol{\phi}) = \sqrt{\frac{\det\left((h+D)\boldsymbol{I}^{|V|}+J\boldsymbol{C}\right)}{(2\pi)^{|V|}}}$$
$$\times\exp\left(-\frac{1}{2k_{\mathrm{B}}T}\left(\boldsymbol{\phi}-\left((h+D)\boldsymbol{I}^{|V|}+J\boldsymbol{C}\right)^{-1}(\boldsymbol{f}+\boldsymbol{g}+h\boldsymbol{d})\right)^{\mathrm{T}}\left((h+D)\boldsymbol{I}^{|V|}+J\boldsymbol{C}\right)\right.$$
$$\left.\times\left(\boldsymbol{\phi}-\left((h+D)\boldsymbol{I}^{|V|}+J\boldsymbol{C}\right)^{-1}(\boldsymbol{f}+\boldsymbol{g}+h\boldsymbol{d})\right)\right), \tag{10.381}$$

$$\widehat{\rho}_i(\phi_i) = \sqrt{\frac{h+L}{2\pi}}\exp\left(-\frac{1}{2k_{\mathrm{B}}T}(h+L)\left(x-\frac{g_i+hd_i}{h+L}\right)^2\right)\ (i\in V), \tag{10.382}$$

The Lagrange multipliers $\boldsymbol{f}$, $\boldsymbol{g}$, L, and D are often referred to as the **effective fields** and are determined so as to satisfy the consistencies in Eq. (10.373), which reduce to the following simultaneous equations:

$$\boldsymbol{g} + h\boldsymbol{d} = (h + L)\Big((D - L)\boldsymbol{I}^{(2|V|)} + J\boldsymbol{C}\Big)^{-1}\boldsymbol{f}, \tag{10.383}$$

$$\boldsymbol{f} + \boldsymbol{g} + h\boldsymbol{d} = \Big((D - L)\boldsymbol{I}^{(|V|)} + J\boldsymbol{C}\Big)^{-1}\begin{pmatrix} \frac{f_1}{\sqrt{{f_1}^2+\Gamma^2}}\tanh\Big(\frac{1}{k_{\mathrm{B}}T}\sqrt{{f_1}^2+\Gamma^2}\Big) \\ \frac{f_2}{\sqrt{{f_2}^2+\Gamma^2}}\tanh\Big(\frac{1}{k_{\mathrm{B}}T}\sqrt{{f_2}^2+\Gamma^2}\Big) \\ \vdots \\ \frac{f_{|V|}}{\sqrt{{f_{|V|}}^2+\Gamma^2}}\tanh\Big(\frac{1}{k_{\mathrm{B}}T}\sqrt{{f_{|V|}}^2+\Gamma^2}\Big) \end{pmatrix}, \tag{10.384}$$

$$L = -h + \frac{1}{2} + \sqrt{\frac{1}{4} + \frac{1}{|V|}(\boldsymbol{f} + \boldsymbol{g} + h\boldsymbol{d})^{\mathrm{T}}(\boldsymbol{f} + \boldsymbol{g} + h\boldsymbol{d})}, \tag{10.385}$$

$$\frac{1}{\frac{1}{2} + \sqrt{\frac{1}{4} + \frac{1}{|V|}(\boldsymbol{f} + \boldsymbol{g} + h\boldsymbol{d})^{\mathrm{T}}(\boldsymbol{f} + \boldsymbol{g} + h\boldsymbol{d})}} = \frac{1}{|V|}\mathrm{Tr}\Big(\big((h + D)\boldsymbol{I}^{|V|} + J\boldsymbol{C}\big)^{-1}\Big). \tag{10.386}$$

The real symmetric matrix $\boldsymbol{C}$ is diagonalized as

$$\boldsymbol{C} = \boldsymbol{U}\boldsymbol{\Lambda}\boldsymbol{U}^{-1}, \tag{10.387}$$

$$\boldsymbol{\Lambda} \equiv \begin{pmatrix} \lambda_1 & 0 & 0 & \cdots & 0 \\ 0 & \lambda_2 & 0 & \cdots & 0 \\ 0 & 0 & \lambda_3 & \cdots & 0 \\ \vdots & \vdots & \vdots & \ddots & \vdots \\ 0 & 0 & 0 & \cdots & \lambda_{|V|} \end{pmatrix}, \tag{10.388}$$

where $\lambda_1 \geq \lambda_2 \geq \lambda_3 \geq \cdots \geq \lambda_{|V|}$. All the eigenvalues $\lambda_1, \lambda_2, \cdots, \lambda_{|V|}$ are always real numbers. For the eigenvector $\boldsymbol{u}_i = \begin{pmatrix} U_{1i} \\ U_{2i} \\ \vdots \\ U_{|V|i} \end{pmatrix}$ corresponding to the eigenvalue λ_i such that $\boldsymbol{A}\boldsymbol{u}_i = \lambda_i\boldsymbol{u}_i$, for every $i\in\{1, 2, 3, \cdots, M\}$, the matrix $\boldsymbol{U}$ is defined by

$$U \equiv (\boldsymbol{u}_1, \boldsymbol{u}_2, \boldsymbol{u}_3, \cdots, \boldsymbol{u}_M) = \begin{pmatrix} U_{11} & U_{12} & U_{13} & \cdots & U_{1|V|} \\ U_{21} & U_{22} & U_{23} & \cdots & U_{2|V|} \\ U_{31} & U_{32} & U_{33} & \cdots & U_{3|V|} \\ \vdots & \vdots & \vdots & \ddots & \vdots \\ U_{|V|1} & U_{|V|2} & U_{|V|3} & \cdots & U_{|V||V|} \end{pmatrix}. \quad (10.389)$$

It is known that $\boldsymbol{U}$ is a unitary matrix that satisfies $\boldsymbol{U}^{-1} = \boldsymbol{U}^{\mathrm{T}}$ for the real symmetric matrix $\boldsymbol{C}$. By using the diagonal matrix $\boldsymbol{\Lambda}$ and unitary matrix $\boldsymbol{U}$, the density matrix $\boldsymbol{R}$ in Eq. (10.390) can be represented as follows:

$$\boldsymbol{R} = \frac{\exp\Big(-\frac{1}{2k_{\mathrm{B}}T}\boldsymbol{\zeta}^{\mathrm{T}}\big((h\boldsymbol{I}^{(2^{|V|})} + J\boldsymbol{\Lambda})\otimes\boldsymbol{I}^{(2^{|V|})}\big)\boldsymbol{\zeta} - \frac{1}{2k_{\mathrm{B}}T}\boldsymbol{\xi}^{\mathrm{T}}\boldsymbol{\xi}\Big)}{\mathrm{Tr}\Big[\exp\Big(-\frac{1}{2k_{\mathrm{B}}T}\boldsymbol{\zeta}^{\mathrm{T}}\big((h\boldsymbol{I}^{(2^{|V|})} + J\boldsymbol{\Lambda})\otimes\boldsymbol{I}^{(2^{|V|})}\big)\boldsymbol{\zeta} - \frac{1}{2k_{\mathrm{B}}T}\boldsymbol{\xi}^{\mathrm{T}}\boldsymbol{\xi}\Big)\Big]}, \quad (10.390)$$

where

$$\boldsymbol{\zeta} = \begin{pmatrix} \zeta_1 \\ \zeta_2 \\ \vdots \\ \zeta_{|V|} \end{pmatrix} \equiv \big(\boldsymbol{U}^{\mathrm{T}}\otimes\boldsymbol{I}^{(2^{|V|})}\big)\begin{pmatrix} \boldsymbol{\sigma}_1^z \\ \boldsymbol{\sigma}_2^z \\ \vdots \\ \boldsymbol{\sigma}_{|V|}^z \end{pmatrix} - \left(\big(h\boldsymbol{I}^{(|V|)} + J\boldsymbol{\Lambda}\big)^{-1}\boldsymbol{U}^{\mathrm{T}}\begin{pmatrix} d_1 \\ d_2 \\ \vdots \\ d_{|V|} \end{pmatrix}\right)\otimes\boldsymbol{I}^{(2^{|V|})}, \quad (10.391)$$

$$\boldsymbol{\xi} = \begin{pmatrix} \xi_1 \\ \xi_2 \\ \vdots \\ \xi_{|V|} \end{pmatrix} \equiv \big(\boldsymbol{U}^{\mathrm{T}}\otimes\boldsymbol{I}^{(2^{|V|})}\big)\begin{pmatrix} \boldsymbol{\sigma}_1^x \\ \boldsymbol{\sigma}_2^x \\ \vdots \\ \boldsymbol{\sigma}_{|V|}^x \end{pmatrix} - \gamma\begin{pmatrix} \boldsymbol{I}^{(2^{|V|}|V|)} \\ \boldsymbol{I}^{(2^{|V|}|V|)} \\ \vdots \\ \boldsymbol{I}^{(2^{|V|}|V|)} \end{pmatrix}. \quad (10.392)$$

By using the Gram-Schmidt orthonormalization in the framework of Fig. 10.17, we introduce a new unitary matrix

$$\widetilde{\boldsymbol{U}} = \begin{pmatrix} \widetilde{U}_{11} & \widetilde{U}_{12} & \widetilde{U}_{13} & \cdots & \widetilde{U}_{1|\widetilde{V}|} \\ \widetilde{U}_{21} & \widetilde{U}_{22} & \widetilde{U}_{23} & \cdots & \widetilde{U}_{2|\widetilde{V}|} \\ \widetilde{U}_{31} & \widetilde{U}_{32} & \widetilde{U}_{33} & \cdots & \widetilde{U}_{3|\widetilde{V}|} \\ \vdots & \vdots & \vdots & \ddots & \vdots \\ \widetilde{U}_{|\widetilde{V}|1} & \widetilde{U}_{|\widetilde{V}|2} & \widetilde{U}_{|\widetilde{V}|3} & \cdots & \widetilde{U}_{|\widetilde{V}||\widetilde{V}|} \end{pmatrix} \equiv \big(\widetilde{\boldsymbol{u}}_1, \widetilde{\boldsymbol{u}}_2, \widetilde{\boldsymbol{u}}_3, \cdots, \widetilde{\boldsymbol{u}}_{|\widetilde{V}|}\big), \quad (10.393)$$

where

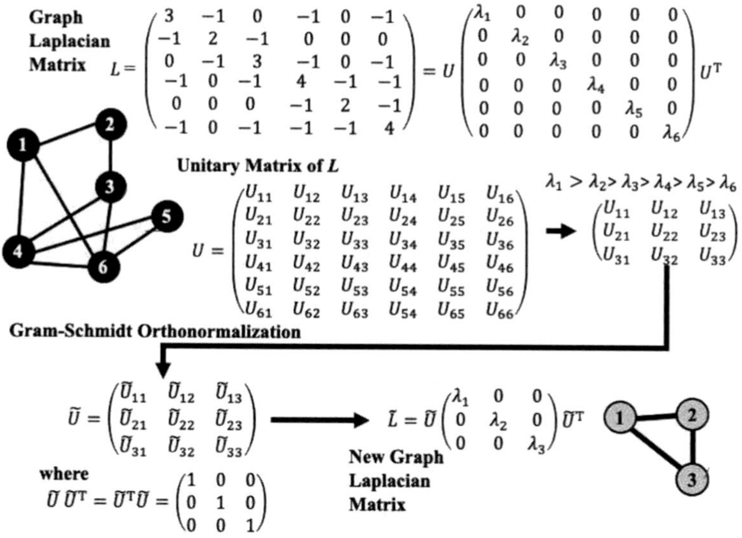

Fig. 10.17 Momentum space renormalization group for graphical models on random graphs

$$\boldsymbol{v}_1 = \begin{pmatrix} U_{11} \\ U_{21} \\ \vdots \\ U_{|\widetilde{V}|1} \end{pmatrix}, \boldsymbol{v}_2 = \begin{pmatrix} U_{12} \\ U_{22} \\ \vdots \\ U_{|\widetilde{V}|2} \end{pmatrix}, \cdots, \boldsymbol{v}_{|\widetilde{V}|} = \begin{pmatrix} U_{1|\widetilde{V}|} \\ U_{2|\widetilde{V}|} \\ \vdots \\ U_{|\widetilde{V}||\widetilde{V}|} \end{pmatrix}, \tag{10.394}$$

$$\begin{cases} \boldsymbol{u}'_1 = \boldsymbol{v}_1, & \widetilde{\boldsymbol{u}}_1 = \dfrac{\boldsymbol{u}'_1}{\sqrt{\boldsymbol{u}'^{\mathrm{T}}_1 \boldsymbol{u}'_1}}, \\ \boldsymbol{u}'_2 = \boldsymbol{v}_2 - \dfrac{\boldsymbol{u}'^{\mathrm{T}}_1 \boldsymbol{v}_2}{\boldsymbol{u}'^{\mathrm{T}}_1 \boldsymbol{u}'_1} \boldsymbol{u}'_1, & \widetilde{\boldsymbol{u}}_2 = \dfrac{\boldsymbol{u}'_2}{\sqrt{\boldsymbol{u}'^{\mathrm{T}}_2 \boldsymbol{u}'_2}}, \\ \boldsymbol{u}'_3 = \boldsymbol{v}_3 - \dfrac{\boldsymbol{u}'^{\mathrm{T}}_1 \boldsymbol{v}_3}{\boldsymbol{u}'^{\mathrm{T}}_1 \boldsymbol{u}'_1} \boldsymbol{u}'_1 - \dfrac{\boldsymbol{u}'^{\mathrm{T}}_2 \boldsymbol{v}_3}{\boldsymbol{u}'^{\mathrm{T}}_2 \boldsymbol{u}'_2} \boldsymbol{u}'_2, & \widetilde{\boldsymbol{u}}_3 = \dfrac{\boldsymbol{u}'_3}{\sqrt{\boldsymbol{u}'^{\mathrm{T}}_3 \boldsymbol{u}'_3}}, \\ \vdots & \\ \boldsymbol{u}'_{|\widetilde{V}|} = \boldsymbol{v}_{|\widetilde{V}|} - \dfrac{\boldsymbol{u}'^{\mathrm{T}}_1 \boldsymbol{v}_{|\widetilde{V}|}}{\boldsymbol{u}'^{\mathrm{T}}_1 \boldsymbol{u}'_1} \boldsymbol{u}'_1 - \dfrac{\boldsymbol{u}'^{\mathrm{T}}_2 \boldsymbol{v}_{|\widetilde{V}|}}{\boldsymbol{u}'^{\mathrm{T}}_2 \boldsymbol{u}'_2} \boldsymbol{u}'_2 + \cdots + \dfrac{\boldsymbol{u}'^{\mathrm{T}}_{|\widetilde{V}|-1} \boldsymbol{v}_{|\widetilde{V}|}}{\boldsymbol{u}'^{\mathrm{T}}_{|\widetilde{V}|-1} \boldsymbol{u}'_{|\widetilde{V}|-1}} \boldsymbol{u}'_{|\widetilde{V}|}, & \widetilde{\boldsymbol{u}}_{|\widetilde{V}|} = \dfrac{\boldsymbol{u}'_{|\widetilde{V}|}}{\sqrt{\boldsymbol{u}'^{\mathrm{T}}_{|\widetilde{V}|} \boldsymbol{u}'_{|\widetilde{V}|}}}. \end{cases} \tag{10.395}$$

By using the new unitary matrix $\widetilde{U}$ and a diagonal matrix $\boldsymbol{\Lambda}$

$$\widetilde{\boldsymbol{\Lambda}} \equiv \begin{pmatrix} \lambda_1 & 0 & 0 & \cdots & 0 \\ 0 & \lambda_2 & 0 & \cdots & 0 \\ 0 & 0 & \lambda_3 & \cdots & 0 \\ \vdots & \vdots & \vdots & \ddots & \vdots \\ 0 & 0 & 0 & \cdots & \lambda_{|\widetilde{V}|} \end{pmatrix}, \tag{10.396}$$

we introduce a renormalized density matrix $\widetilde{\boldsymbol{R}}$ from the standpoint of the momentum space renormalization group for general graphs as

$$\widetilde{\boldsymbol{P}} \equiv \frac{\exp\Big(-\frac{1}{2k_{\mathrm{B}}T}\widetilde{\zeta}^{\mathrm{T}}\Big((h\boldsymbol{I}^{(2^{|\widetilde{V}|})} + J\widetilde{\boldsymbol{\Lambda}})\otimes\boldsymbol{I}^{(2^{|\widetilde{V}|})}\Big)\widetilde{\zeta} - \frac{1}{2k_{\mathrm{B}}T}\widetilde{\xi}^{\mathrm{T}}\widetilde{\xi}\Big)}{\mathrm{Tr}\Big[\exp\Big(-\frac{1}{2k_{\mathrm{B}}T}\widetilde{\zeta}^{\mathrm{T}}\Big((h\boldsymbol{I}^{(2^{|\widetilde{V}|})} + J\widetilde{\boldsymbol{\Lambda}})\otimes\boldsymbol{I}^{(2^{|\widetilde{V}|})}\Big)\widetilde{\zeta} - \frac{1}{2k_{\mathrm{B}}T}\widetilde{\xi}^{\mathrm{T}}\widetilde{\xi}\Big)\Big]}, \tag{10.397}$$

where

$$\widetilde{\zeta} = \begin{pmatrix} \widetilde{\zeta}_1 \\ \widetilde{\zeta}_2 \\ \vdots \\ \widetilde{\zeta}_{|\widetilde{V}|} \end{pmatrix} \equiv \Big(\widetilde{\boldsymbol{U}}^{\mathrm{T}}\otimes\boldsymbol{I}^{(2^{|\widetilde{V}|})}\Big)\begin{pmatrix} \sigma_1^z \\ \sigma_2^z \\ \vdots \\ \sigma_{|\widetilde{V}|}^z \end{pmatrix} - \left((h\boldsymbol{I}^{(|\widetilde{V}|)} + J\widetilde{\boldsymbol{\Lambda}})^{-1}\widetilde{\boldsymbol{U}}^{\mathrm{T}}\begin{pmatrix} \widetilde{d}_1 \\ \widetilde{d}_2 \\ \vdots \\ \widetilde{d}_{|\widetilde{V}|} \end{pmatrix}\right)\otimes\boldsymbol{I}^{(2^{|\widetilde{V}|})}, \tag{10.398}$$

$$\widetilde{\xi} = \begin{pmatrix} \widetilde{\xi}_1 \\ \widetilde{\xi}_2 \\ \vdots \\ \widetilde{\xi}_{|\widetilde{V}|} \end{pmatrix} \equiv \Big(\boldsymbol{U}^{\mathrm{T}}\otimes\boldsymbol{I}^{(2^{|\widetilde{V}|})}\Big)\begin{pmatrix} \sigma_1^x \\ \sigma_2^x \\ \vdots \\ \sigma_{|\widetilde{V}|}^x \end{pmatrix} - \gamma\begin{pmatrix} \boldsymbol{I}^{(2^{|\widetilde{V}|}|\widetilde{V}|)} \\ \boldsymbol{I}^{(2^{|\widetilde{V}|}|\widetilde{V}|)} \\ \vdots \\ \boldsymbol{I}^{(2^{|\widetilde{V}|}|\widetilde{V}|)} \end{pmatrix}, \tag{10.399}$$

$$\begin{pmatrix} \widetilde{d}_1 \\ \widetilde{d}_2 \\ \vdots \\ \widetilde{d}_{|\widetilde{V}|} \end{pmatrix} = \begin{pmatrix} \widetilde{U}_{11} & \widetilde{U}_{12} & \widetilde{U}_{13} & \cdots & \widetilde{U}_{1|\widetilde{V}|} \\ \widetilde{U}_{21} & \widetilde{U}_{22} & \widetilde{U}_{23} & \cdots & \widetilde{U}_{2|\widetilde{V}|} \\ \widetilde{U}_{31} & \widetilde{U}_{32} & \widetilde{U}_{33} & \cdots & \widetilde{U}_{3|\widetilde{V}|} \\ \vdots & \vdots & \vdots & \ddots & \vdots \\ \widetilde{U}_{|\widetilde{V}|1} & \widetilde{U}_{|\widetilde{V}|2} & \widetilde{U}_{|\widetilde{V}|3} & \cdots & \widetilde{U}_{|\widetilde{V}||\widetilde{V}|} \end{pmatrix}\begin{pmatrix} U_{11} & U_{21} & U_{31} & \cdots & U_{|V|1} \\ U_{12} & U_{22} & U_{32} & \cdots & U_{|V|2} \\ U_{13} & U_{23} & U_{33} & \cdots & U_{|V|3} \\ \vdots & \vdots & \vdots & \ddots & \vdots \\ U_{1|\widetilde{V}|} & U_{2|\widetilde{V}|} & U_{3|\widetilde{V}|} & \cdots & U_{|V||\widetilde{V}|} \end{pmatrix}\begin{pmatrix} d_1 \\ d_2 \\ d_3 \\ \vdots \\ d_{|V|} \end{pmatrix}. \tag{10.400}$$

For this density matrix $\widetilde{\boldsymbol{P}}$ in Eq. (10.397), we can formulate the approximate reduced density matrix $\widehat{\widetilde{\boldsymbol{R}}}_i$ and the approximate Gaussian marginal probability density function $\widehat{\widetilde{\rho}}(\widetilde{\boldsymbol{\phi}}) = \widehat{\widetilde{\rho}}(\phi_1, \phi_2, \cdots, \phi_{|\widetilde{V}|})$ and $\widehat{\widetilde{\rho}}(\phi_i)$ for the corresponding quantum adaptive TAP approximation as follows:

$$\widehat{\widehat{\boldsymbol{R}}}_i = \frac{1}{2\cosh\left(\frac{1}{k_{\mathrm{B}}T}\sqrt{\widetilde{f}_i^2+\Gamma^2}\right)}\frac{\widetilde{f}_i+\sqrt{\widetilde{f}_i^2+\Gamma^2}}{2\sqrt{\widetilde{f}_i^2+\Gamma^2}}\begin{pmatrix} 1 & -\frac{\Gamma}{\widetilde{f}_i+\sqrt{\widetilde{f}_i^2+\Gamma^2}} \\ +\frac{\Gamma}{\widetilde{f}_i+\sqrt{\widetilde{f}_i^2+\Gamma^2}} & 1 \end{pmatrix}$$
$$\times\begin{pmatrix} \exp\left(+\frac{1}{k_{\mathrm{B}}T}\sqrt{\widetilde{f}_i^2+\Gamma^2}\right) & 0 \\ 0 & \exp\left(-\frac{1}{k_{\mathrm{B}}T}\sqrt{\widetilde{f}_i^2+\Gamma^2}\right)\end{pmatrix}\begin{pmatrix} 1 & +\frac{\Gamma}{\widetilde{f}_i+\sqrt{\widetilde{f}_i^2+\Gamma^2}} \\ -\frac{\Gamma}{\widetilde{f}_i+\sqrt{\widetilde{f}_i^2+\Gamma^2}} & 1 \end{pmatrix}. \tag{10.401}$$

$$\widehat{\widehat{\rho}}(\phi_1,\phi_2,\cdots,\phi_{|\widetilde{V}|}) = \sqrt{\frac{\det\left((h+\widetilde{D})\boldsymbol{I}^{(|\widetilde{V}|)}+J\widetilde{\boldsymbol{\Lambda}}\right)}{(2\pi k_{\mathrm{B}}T)^{|\widetilde{V}|}}}$$
$$\times\exp\Bigg(-\frac{1}{2k_{\mathrm{B}}T}\left(\widetilde{\boldsymbol{\phi}}-\widetilde{\boldsymbol{U}}\left((h+\widetilde{D})\boldsymbol{I}^{(|\widetilde{V}|)}+J\widetilde{\boldsymbol{\Lambda}}\right)^{-1}\widetilde{\boldsymbol{U}}^{\mathbf{T}}\left(\widetilde{\boldsymbol{f}}+\widetilde{\boldsymbol{g}}+h\widetilde{\boldsymbol{d}}\right)\right)^{\mathrm{T}}$$
$$\times\widetilde{\boldsymbol{U}}\left((h+\widetilde{D})\boldsymbol{I}^{(|\widetilde{V}|)}+J\widetilde{\boldsymbol{\Lambda}}\right)\widetilde{\boldsymbol{U}}^{\mathbf{T}}$$
$$\times\left(\widetilde{\boldsymbol{\phi}}-\widetilde{\boldsymbol{U}}\left((h+\widetilde{D})\boldsymbol{I}^{(|\widetilde{V}|)}+J\widetilde{\boldsymbol{\Lambda}}\right)^{-1}\widetilde{\boldsymbol{U}}^{\mathbf{T}}\left(\widetilde{\boldsymbol{f}}+\widetilde{\boldsymbol{g}}+h\widetilde{\boldsymbol{d}}\right)\right)\Bigg). \tag{10.402}$$

$$\widehat{\widehat{\rho}}_i(\phi_i) = \sqrt{\frac{h+\widetilde{L}}{2\pi k_{\mathrm{B}}T}}\exp\left(-\frac{1}{2k_{\mathrm{B}}T}(h+\widetilde{L})\left(\phi_i-\frac{\widetilde{g}_i+h\widetilde{d}_i}{h+\widetilde{L}}\right)^2\right)\ (i\in\widetilde{V}). \tag{10.403}$$

The reduced density matrix $\widehat{\widehat{\boldsymbol{R}}}_i$ and the marginal probability density functions $\widehat{\widehat{\rho}}_i(\phi_i)$ and $\widehat{\widehat{\rho}}\left(\phi_1,\phi_2,\cdots,\phi_{|\widetilde{V}|}\right)$ need to satisfy the consistencies

$$\begin{cases} \int_{-\infty}^{+\infty}\int_{-\infty}^{+\infty}\cdots\int_{-\infty}^{+\infty}\phi_i\widehat{\widehat{\rho}}\left(\phi_1,\phi_2,\cdots,\phi_{|\widetilde{V}|}\right)d\phi_1 d\phi_2\cdots d\phi_{|\widetilde{V}|} = \int_{-\infty}^{+\infty}\phi_i\widehat{\widehat{\rho}}_i(\phi_i)d\phi_i = \mathrm{Tr}\boldsymbol{\sigma}^{\mathbf{z}}\widehat{\widehat{\boldsymbol{R}}}_i\ (i\in\widetilde{V}), \\ \sum_{i\in\widetilde{V}}\int_{-\infty}^{+\infty}\int_{-\infty}^{+\infty}\cdots\int_{-\infty}^{+\infty}{\phi_i}^2\widehat{\widehat{\rho}}\left(\phi_1,\phi_2,\cdots,\phi_{|\widetilde{V}|}\right)d\phi_1 d\phi_2\cdots d\phi_{|\widetilde{V}|} = \sum_{i\in\widetilde{V}}\int_{-\infty}^{+\infty}{\phi_i}^2\widehat{\widehat{\rho}}_i(\phi_i)d\phi_i = 1. \end{cases} \tag{10.404}$$

The Lagrange multipliers $\widetilde{\boldsymbol{f}}$, $\widetilde{\boldsymbol{g}}$, $\widetilde{L}$, and $\widetilde{D}$ are determined so as to satisfy the consistencies in Eq. (10.404), which reduce to the following simultaneous equations:

$$\widetilde{\boldsymbol{g}}+h\widetilde{\boldsymbol{d}} = (h+\widetilde{L})\widetilde{\boldsymbol{U}}\left((\widetilde{D}-\widetilde{L})\boldsymbol{I}^{(|\widetilde{V}|)}+J\widetilde{\boldsymbol{\Lambda}}\right)^{-1}\widetilde{\boldsymbol{U}}^{\mathbf{T}}\widetilde{\boldsymbol{f}}, \tag{10.405}$$

$$\widetilde{\boldsymbol{f}} + \widetilde{\boldsymbol{g}} + h\boldsymbol{d} = \widetilde{\boldsymbol{U}}\Big((\widetilde{D} - \widetilde{L})\boldsymbol{I}^{(|\widetilde{V}|)} + J\widetilde{\boldsymbol{\Lambda}}\Big)^{-1}\widetilde{\boldsymbol{U}}^{\mathrm{T}} \begin{pmatrix} \frac{\widetilde{f}_1}{\sqrt{\widetilde{f}_1^2+\Gamma^2}}\tanh\left(\frac{1}{k_{\mathrm{B}}T}\sqrt{\widetilde{f}_1^2+\Gamma^2}\right) \\ \frac{\widetilde{f}_2}{\sqrt{\widetilde{f}_2^2+\Gamma^2}}\tanh\left(\frac{1}{k_{\mathrm{B}}T}\sqrt{\widetilde{f}_2^2+\Gamma^2}\right) \\ \vdots \\ \frac{\widetilde{f}_{|\widetilde{V}|}}{\sqrt{\widetilde{f}_{|\widetilde{V}|}^2+\Gamma^2}}\tanh\left(\frac{1}{k_{\mathrm{B}}T}\sqrt{\widetilde{f}_{|\widetilde{V}|}^2+\Gamma^2}\right) \end{pmatrix}, \tag{10.406}$$

$$\widetilde{L} = -h + \frac{1}{2} + \sqrt{\frac{1}{4} + \frac{1}{|\widetilde{V}|}\Big(\widetilde{\boldsymbol{f}} + \widetilde{\boldsymbol{g}} + h\widetilde{\boldsymbol{d}}\Big)^{\mathrm{T}}\Big(\widetilde{\boldsymbol{f}} + \widetilde{\boldsymbol{g}} + h\widetilde{\boldsymbol{d}}\Big)}, \tag{10.407}$$

$$\frac{1}{\frac{1}{2} + \sqrt{\frac{1}{4} + \frac{1}{|\widetilde{V}|}\Big(\widetilde{\boldsymbol{f}} + \widetilde{\boldsymbol{g}} + h\boldsymbol{d}\Big)^{\mathrm{T}}\Big(\widetilde{\boldsymbol{f}} + \widetilde{\boldsymbol{g}} + h\widetilde{\boldsymbol{d}}\Big)}} = \frac{1}{|\widetilde{V}|}\mathrm{Tr}\Big[\Big((\widetilde{D} - \widetilde{L})\boldsymbol{I}^{(|\widetilde{V}|)} + J\widetilde{\boldsymbol{\Lambda}}\Big)^{-1}\Big]. \tag{10.408}$$

10.5.4 Suzuki-Trotter Decomposition in the Transverse Ising Model

In this section, we review the Suzuki-Trotter formulas and extensions from conventional quantum loopy belief propagation using them. In quantum probabilistic graphical models, the state space is defined by all the eigenvectors of the density matrix $\boldsymbol{R}$ and the probability of each eigenvector is given by the eigenvalue as mentioned in Sect. 10.4.2. To compute some statistical quantities by using the Monte Carlo method, it is necessary to diagonalize the energy matrix $\boldsymbol{H}$, which is a massive computation. Instead of such a scheme, quantum Monte Carlo methods based on the Suzuki-Trotter formulas were proposed [89]. One important part of the quantum Monte Carlo method is the mapping from a quantum probabilistic graphical model to a conventional (classical) probabilistic graphical model by introducing the techniques of Suzuki-Trotter decompositions. It is known that some statistical quantities for conventional (classical) probabilistic graphical models can be computed by MCMC methods. This is a basic idea behind quantum Monte Carlo methods. Let us first review the Suzuki-Trotter formulas and explicitly give a detailed scheme of Suzuki-Trotter decompositions for the transverse Ising model in Eqs. (10.226) and (10.227) with Eq. (10.301).

From the definition of the exponential function for square matrices, we have

$$\exp(x(\boldsymbol{A}+\boldsymbol{B})) = \boldsymbol{I} + x(\boldsymbol{A}+\boldsymbol{B}) + \frac{1}{2}x^2(\boldsymbol{A}+\boldsymbol{B})^2 + \mathcal{O}(x^3)\ (x \to 0), \tag{10.409}$$

$$\exp(x\boldsymbol{A}) = \boldsymbol{I} + x\boldsymbol{A} + \frac{1}{2}x^2\boldsymbol{A}^2 + \mathcal{O}(x^3)\ (x \to +0), \tag{10.410}$$

$$\exp(x\boldsymbol{B}) = \boldsymbol{I} + x\boldsymbol{B} + \frac{1}{2}x^2\boldsymbol{B}^2 + \mathcal{O}(x^3)\ (x \to +0). \tag{10.411}$$

From these equalities, the following formula can be confirmed:

$$\exp(x(\boldsymbol{A}+\boldsymbol{B})) = \exp(x\boldsymbol{A})\exp(x\boldsymbol{B}) + \mathcal{O}(x^2)\ (x \to +0). \tag{10.412}$$

Moreover, we have

$$\exp(x\boldsymbol{A}) = \Big[\exp\Big(\frac{x}{M}\boldsymbol{A}\Big)\Big]^M + \mathcal{O}\Big(\frac{x^2}{M}\Big)\ (x^2 \ll M), \tag{10.413}$$

$$\exp(x(\boldsymbol{A}+\boldsymbol{B})) = \Big[\exp\Big(\frac{x}{M}\boldsymbol{A}\Big)\exp\Big(\frac{x}{M}\boldsymbol{B}\Big)\Big]^M + \mathcal{O}\Big(\frac{x^2}{M}\Big)\ (x^2 \ll M). \tag{10.414}$$

Generally, for a graph (V, E) with the set of nodes $V = \{1, 2, \cdots, N\}$ and the set of edges $E = \big\{\{i, j\}\big\}$, we have

$$\exp\Bigg(x \sum_{\{i,j\}\in E} \boldsymbol{A}_{\{i,j\}}\Bigg) = \Bigg[\prod_{\{i,j\}\in E} \exp\Big(\frac{x}{M}\boldsymbol{A}_{\{i,j\}}\Big)\Bigg]^M + \mathcal{O}\Big(\frac{x^2}{M}\Big)\ (x^2 \ll M), \tag{10.415}$$

$$\begin{aligned}&\exp\Bigg(x \sum_{\{i,j\}\in E} \boldsymbol{A}_{\{i,j\}} + x \sum_{\{i,j\}\in E} \boldsymbol{B}_{\{i,j\}}\Bigg) \\ &= \Bigg[\Bigg(\prod_{\{i,j\}\in E} \exp\Big(\frac{x}{M}\boldsymbol{A}_{\{i,j\}}\Big)\Bigg)\Bigg(\prod_{\{i,j\}\in E} \exp\Big(\frac{x}{M}\boldsymbol{B}_{\{i,j\}}\Big)\Bigg)\Bigg]^M + \mathcal{O}\Big(\frac{x^2}{M}\Big)\ (x^2 \ll M).\end{aligned} \tag{10.416}$$

These are referred to as a **Suzuki-Trotter Decomposition** [87, 88].

For the case of $N = 2$, we consider an energy matrix $\boldsymbol{H}$ defined by

$$\boldsymbol{H} = -J\boldsymbol{\sigma}_1^z\boldsymbol{\sigma}_2^z - h_1\boldsymbol{\sigma}_1^z - h_2\boldsymbol{\sigma}_2^z - \Gamma\boldsymbol{\sigma}_1^x - \Gamma\boldsymbol{\sigma}_2^x. \tag{10.417}$$

It is referred to as a quantum transverse Ising model on a chain ($V = \{1, 2\}$, $E = \{\{1, 2\}\}$) with three nodes and two edges. By using the above Suzuki-Trotter formula, we have

$$\begin{aligned}
&\langle s_{1,1}, s_{2,1}|\exp\Big(-\frac{1}{k_{\mathrm{B}}T}\boldsymbol{H}\Big)|s'_{1,1}, s'_{2,2}\rangle \\
&= \lim_{M\to+\infty}\Big[\exp\Big(\frac{1}{k_{\mathrm{B}}TM}(J\boldsymbol{\sigma}_{\mathbf{1}}^{z}\boldsymbol{\sigma}_{\mathbf{2}}^{z}+h_1\boldsymbol{\sigma}_{\mathbf{1}}^{z}+h_2\boldsymbol{\sigma}_{\mathbf{2}}^{z})\Big)\exp\Big(\frac{1}{k_{\mathrm{B}}TM}(\Gamma\boldsymbol{\sigma}_{\mathbf{1}}^{x}+\Gamma\boldsymbol{\sigma}_{\mathbf{2}}^{x})\Big)\Big]^{M} \\
&= \lim_{M\to+\infty}\sum_{\tau_{1,1}\in\Omega}\sum_{\tau_{2,1}\in\Omega}\sum_{s_{1,2}\in\Omega}\sum_{s_{2,2}\in\Omega}\sum_{\tau_{1,2}\in\Omega}\sum_{\tau_{2,2}\in\Omega}\cdots\sum_{s_{1,M}\in\Omega}\sum_{s_{2,M}\in\Omega}\delta_{s_{1,M+1},s'_{1,1}}\delta_{s_{2,M+1},s'_{2,1}} \\
&\quad\times\prod_{m=1}^{M}\Big(\langle s_{1,m}, s_{2,m}|\exp\Big(\frac{1}{k_{\mathrm{B}}TM}(J\boldsymbol{\sigma}_{\mathbf{1}}^{z}\boldsymbol{\sigma}_{\mathbf{2}}^{z}+h_1\boldsymbol{\sigma}_{\mathbf{1}}^{z}+h_2\boldsymbol{\sigma}_{\mathbf{2}}^{z})\Big)|\tau_{1,m}, \tau_{2,m}\rangle \\
&\qquad\times\langle\tau_{1,m}, \tau_{2,m}|\exp\Big(\frac{1}{k_{\mathrm{B}}TM}(\Gamma\boldsymbol{\sigma}_{\mathbf{1}}^{x}+\Gamma\boldsymbol{\sigma}_{\mathbf{2}}^{x})\Big)|s_{1,m+1}, s_{2,m+1}\rangle\Big).
\end{aligned} \tag{10.418}$$

Note that

$$\Gamma\boldsymbol{\sigma}_{\mathbf{1}}^{x}+\Gamma\boldsymbol{\sigma}_{\mathbf{2}}^{x} = \Gamma\boldsymbol{\sigma}^{x}\otimes\boldsymbol{I}+\Gamma\boldsymbol{I}\otimes\boldsymbol{\sigma}^{x}. \tag{10.419}$$

By using Eq. (10.253), Eq. (10.418) can be rewritten as

$$\begin{aligned}
&\langle s_{1,1}, s_{2,1}|\exp\Big(-\frac{1}{k_{\mathrm{B}}T}\boldsymbol{H}\Big)|s'_{1,1}, s'_{2,1}\rangle \\
&= \lim_{M\to+\infty}\sum_{s_{1,2}\in\Omega}\sum_{s_{2,2}\in\Omega}\cdots\sum_{s_{1,M}\in\Omega}\sum_{s_{2,M}\in\Omega}\delta_{s_{1,M+1},s'_{1,1}}\delta_{s_{2,M+1},s'_{2,1}} \\
&\quad\times\prod_{m=1}^{M}\Big(\exp\Big(\frac{1}{k_{\mathrm{B}}TM}(Js_{1,m}s_{2,m}+h_1s_{1,m}+h_2s_{2,m})\Big) \\
&\qquad\times\langle s_{1,m}, s_{2,m}|\Big(\exp\Big(\frac{1}{k_{\mathrm{B}}TM}\Gamma\boldsymbol{\sigma}^{x}\Big)\otimes\boldsymbol{I}\Big)\Big(\boldsymbol{I}\otimes\exp\Big(\frac{1}{k_{\mathrm{B}}TM}\Gamma\boldsymbol{\sigma}^{x}\Big)\Big)|s_{1,m+1}, s_{2,m+1}\rangle\Big).
\end{aligned} \tag{10.420}$$

Moreover, by the definition of the tensor product for $\boldsymbol{A}\otimes\boldsymbol{I}$ and $\boldsymbol{I}\otimes\boldsymbol{A}$ for any matrix $\boldsymbol{A}$ in terms of Eq. (10.238), we have

$$\begin{aligned}
&\langle s_{1,m}, s_{2,m}|\Big(\exp\Big(\frac{1}{k_{\mathrm{B}}TM}\Gamma\boldsymbol{\sigma}^{x}\Big)\otimes\boldsymbol{I}\Big)\Big(\boldsymbol{I}\otimes\exp\Big(\frac{1}{k_{\mathrm{B}}TM}\Gamma\boldsymbol{\sigma}^{x}\Big)\Big)|s_{1,m+1}, s_{2,m+1}\rangle \\
&= \langle s_{1,m}|\exp\Big(\frac{1}{k_{\mathrm{B}}TM}\Gamma\boldsymbol{\sigma}^{x}\Big)|s_{1,m+1}\rangle\langle s_{2,m}|\exp\Big(\frac{1}{k_{\mathrm{B}}TM}\Gamma\boldsymbol{\sigma}^{x}\Big)|s_{2,m+1}\rangle \\
&= \langle s_{1,m}|\begin{pmatrix}\cosh\Big(\frac{1}{k_{\mathrm{B}}TM}\Gamma\Big) & \sinh\Big(\frac{1}{k_{\mathrm{B}}TM}\Gamma\Big)\\ \sinh\Big(\frac{1}{k_{\mathrm{B}}TM}\Gamma\Big) & \cosh\Big(\frac{1}{k_{\mathrm{B}}TM}\Gamma\Big)\end{pmatrix}|s_{1,m+1}\rangle \\
&\quad\times\langle s_{2,m}|\begin{pmatrix}\cosh\Big(\frac{1}{k_{\mathrm{B}}TM}\Gamma\Big) & \sinh\Big(\frac{1}{k_{\mathrm{B}}TM}\Gamma\Big)\\ \sinh\Big(\frac{1}{k_{\mathrm{B}}TM}\Gamma\Big) & \cosh\Big(\frac{1}{k_{\mathrm{B}}TM}\Gamma\Big)\end{pmatrix}|s_{2,m+1}\rangle.
\end{aligned} \tag{10.421}$$

Equation (10.420) can be rewritten in terms of the two-dimensional representation as

$$\begin{aligned}
&\langle s_{1,1}, s_{2,1}|\exp\Big(-\frac{1}{k_{\mathrm{B}}T}\boldsymbol{H}\Big)|s'_{1,1}, s'_{2,1}\rangle \\
&= \lim_{M\to+\infty}\sum_{s_{1,2}\in\Omega}\sum_{s_{2,2}\in\Omega}\cdots\sum_{s_{1,M}\in\Omega}\sum_{s_{2,M}\in\Omega}\delta_{s_{1,M+1},s'_{1,1}}\delta_{s_{2,M+1},s'_{2,1}} \\
&\quad\times\prod_{m=1}^{M}\Bigg(\exp\Big(\frac{1}{k_{\mathrm{B}}TM}(Js_{1,m}s_{2,m}+h_1s_{1,m}+h_2s_{2,m})\Big) \\
&\quad\times\langle s_{1,m}|\begin{pmatrix}\cosh\big(\frac{1}{k_{\mathrm{B}}TM}\Gamma\big) & \sinh\big(\frac{1}{k_{\mathrm{B}}TM}\Gamma\big)\\ \sinh\big(\frac{1}{k_{\mathrm{B}}TM}\Gamma\big) & \cosh\big(\frac{1}{k_{\mathrm{B}}TM}\Gamma\big)\end{pmatrix}|s_{1,m+1}\rangle \\
&\quad\times\langle s_{2,m}|\begin{pmatrix}\cosh\big(\frac{1}{k_{\mathrm{B}}TM}\Gamma\big) & \sinh\big(\frac{1}{k_{\mathrm{B}}TM}\Gamma\big)\\ \sinh\big(\frac{1}{k_{\mathrm{B}}TM}\Gamma\big) & \cosh\big(\frac{1}{k_{\mathrm{B}}TM}\Gamma\big)\end{pmatrix}|s_{2,m+1}\rangle\Bigg).
\end{aligned}\tag{10.422}$$

Eventually, the density matrix $\boldsymbol{P}$ of the transverse Ising model for two nodes in Eq. (10.417), such that

$$\boldsymbol{P}\equiv\frac{\exp\Big(-\frac{1}{k_{\mathrm{B}}T}\boldsymbol{H}\Big)}{\mathrm{Tr}\Big[\exp\Big(-\frac{1}{k_{\mathrm{B}}T}\boldsymbol{H}\Big)\Big]},\tag{10.423}$$

can be reduced to the probability distribution $P^{(M)}(\boldsymbol{s}_1,\boldsymbol{s}_2,\boldsymbol{s}_3,\cdots,\boldsymbol{s}_M,\boldsymbol{s}_{M+1})$ for $\boldsymbol{s}_m=\begin{pmatrix}s_{1,m}\\ s_{2,m}\end{pmatrix}$ $(m=1,2,\cdots,M+1)$ on the $2\times(M+1)$ ladder graph as follows:

$$\begin{aligned}
&\langle s_{1,1}, s_{2,1}|\boldsymbol{P}|s'_{1,1}, s'_{2,1}\rangle \\
&= \lim_{M\to+\infty}\sum_{\boldsymbol{s}_1\in\Omega^2}\sum_{\boldsymbol{s}_2\in\Omega^2}\cdots\sum_{\boldsymbol{s}_M\in\Omega^2}\sum_{\boldsymbol{s}_{M+1}\in\Omega^2}\delta_{s_{1,M+1},s'_{1,1}}\delta_{s_{2,M+1},s'_{1,2}}P^{(M)}(\boldsymbol{s}_1,\boldsymbol{s}_2,\boldsymbol{s}_3,\cdots,\boldsymbol{s}_M,\boldsymbol{s}_{M+1}),
\end{aligned}\tag{10.424}$$

where

$$\begin{aligned}
&P^{(M)}(\boldsymbol{s}_1,\boldsymbol{s}_2,\boldsymbol{s}_3,\cdots,\boldsymbol{s}_M,\boldsymbol{s}_{M+1}) \\
&\equiv\frac{1}{Z(M)}\prod_{m=1}^{M}\Bigg(\exp\Big(\frac{1}{k_{\mathrm{B}}TM}(Js_{1,m}s_{2,m}+h_1s_{1,m}+h_2s_{2,m})\Big) \\
&\quad\times\exp\Big(\frac{1}{k_{\mathrm{B}}TM}\big(K(MT,\Gamma)s_{1,m}s_{1,m+1}+K(MT,\Gamma)s_{2,m}s_{2,m+1}\big)\Big)\Bigg),
\end{aligned}\tag{10.425}$$

$$Z^{(M)} \equiv \sum_{s_{1,2}\in\Omega}\sum_{s_{2,2}\in\Omega}\cdots\sum_{s_{1,M}\in\Omega}\sum_{s_{2,M}\in\Omega}\delta_{s_{1,M+1},s_{1,1}}\delta_{s_{2,M+1},s_{2,1}}$$
$$\times\prod_{m=1}^{M}\left(\exp\left(\frac{1}{k_{\mathrm{B}}TM}(Js_{1,m}s_{2,m}+h_1s_{1,m}+h_2s_{2,m})\right)\right.$$
$$\left.\times\exp\left(\frac{1}{k_{\mathrm{B}}TM}(K(MT,\Gamma)s_{1,m}s_{1,m+1}+K(MT,\Gamma)s_{2,m}s_{2,m+1})\right)\right), \tag{10.426}$$

$$K(T,\Gamma)\equiv k_{\mathrm{B}}T\ln\left(\sqrt{\frac{\cosh\left(\frac{1}{k_{\mathrm{B}}T}\Gamma\right)}{\sinh\left(\frac{1}{k_{\mathrm{B}}T}\Gamma\right)}}\right). \tag{10.427}$$

The density matrix $\boldsymbol{P}$ in Eq. (10.423) of the transverse Ising model for $|V|$ nodes $V=\{1,2,\cdots,|V|\}$, which is given by Eqs. (10.226) and (10.227) with Eq. (10.301), can be reduced to the matrix representation for s probability distribution $P^{(M)}(\boldsymbol{s_1},\boldsymbol{s_2},\boldsymbol{s_3},\cdots,\boldsymbol{s_M},\boldsymbol{s_{M+1}})$ for $\boldsymbol{s_m}=\begin{pmatrix}s_{1,m}\\ s_{2,m}\\ \vdots\\ s_{N,m}\end{pmatrix}$ $(m=1,2,\cdots,M+1)$ on the $|V|\times(M+1)$ ladder graph as follows:

$$\langle s_{1,1},s_{2,1},\cdots,s_{|V|,1}|\boldsymbol{P}|s'_{1,1},s'_{2,1},\cdots,s'_{|V|,1}\rangle$$
$$=\lim_{M\to+\infty}\sum_{\boldsymbol{s_1}\in\Omega^{|V|}}\sum_{\boldsymbol{s_2}\in\Omega^{|V|}}\cdots\sum_{\boldsymbol{s_M}\in\Omega^{|V|}}\sum_{\boldsymbol{s_{M+1}}\in\Omega^{|V|}}\left(\prod_{i\in V}\delta_{s_{i,M+1},s'_{i,1}}\right)P^{(M)}(\boldsymbol{s_1},\boldsymbol{s_2},\boldsymbol{s_3},\cdots,\boldsymbol{s_M},\boldsymbol{s_{M+1}}), \tag{10.428}$$

where

$$P^{(M)}(\boldsymbol{s_1},\boldsymbol{s_2},\boldsymbol{s_3},\cdots,\boldsymbol{s_M},\boldsymbol{s_{M+1}})$$
$$\equiv\frac{1}{Z^{(M)}}\prod_{m=1}^{M}\left(\prod_{\{i,j\}\in E}\exp\left(\frac{1}{k_{\mathrm{B}}TM}Js_{i,m}s_{j,m}\right)\right)$$
$$\times\left(\prod_{i\in V}\exp\left(\frac{1}{k_{\mathrm{B}}TM}K(MT,\Gamma)s_{i,m}s_{i,m+1}\right)\right)\left(\prod_{i\in V}\exp\left(\frac{1}{k_{\mathrm{B}}TM}h_is_{i,m}\right)\right), \tag{10.429}$$

$$
\begin{aligned}
Z^{(M)} \equiv & \sum_{s_1\in\Omega^{|V|}}\sum_{s_2\in\Omega^{|V|}}\cdots\sum_{s_M\in\Omega^{|V|}}\left(\prod_{i\in V}\delta_{s_{i,M+1},s_{i,1}}\right) \\
& \times\prod_{m=1}^{M}\left(\prod_{\{i,j\}\in E}\exp\left(\frac{1}{k_{\mathrm{B}}TM}Js_{i,m}s_{j,m}\right)\right) \\
& \times\left(\prod_{i\in V}\exp\left(\frac{1}{k_{\mathrm{B}}TM}K(MT,\Gamma)s_{i,m}s_{i,m+1}\right)\right)\left(\prod_{i\in V}\exp\left(\frac{1}{k_{\mathrm{B}}TM}h_i s_{i,m}\right)\right).
\end{aligned}
\quad (10.430)
$$

The dynamics of quantum Monte Carlo methods based on Suzuki-Trotter decompositions have been analyzed by using Glauber dynamics [101, 102] and Langevin dynamics [103, 104]. Recently, these analyses are applied to some statistical machine learning systems with quantum annealing [105, 106]. Some statistical analysis of quantum Monte Carlo methods for statistical inferences based on Suzuki-Trotter decompositions [87, 88] are shown in Chaps. 12 and 13 of Part III of this book.

We now try to construct a modification of the conventional quantum message passing rule in Eq. (10.335) for the transverse Ising model in Eqs. (10.226) and (10.227) with Eq. (10.301) by imposing the assumption that all off-diagonal elements of $\boldsymbol{\lambda}_{j\to i}$ and $\boldsymbol{\lambda}_{i\to j}$ for any edge $\{i,j\}(\in E)$ are zero. By using the Suzuki-Trotter formulas in Eqs. (10.415)–(10.416), Eq. (10.335) can be represented as follows:

$$
\begin{aligned}
& \lim_{M\to+\infty}\left[\exp\left(\frac{1}{k_{\mathrm{B}}TM}\Gamma\boldsymbol{\sigma}^{x}\right)\exp\left(\frac{1}{k_{\mathrm{B}}TM}hd_i\boldsymbol{\sigma}^{z}\right)\exp\left(\frac{1}{k_{\mathrm{B}}TM}\boldsymbol{\lambda}_{j\to i}\right)\exp\left(\frac{1}{k_{\mathrm{B}}TM}\sum_{k\in\partial i\backslash\{j\}}\boldsymbol{\lambda}_{k\to i}\right)\right]^{M} \\
& = \frac{Z_i}{Z_{\{i,j\}}}\lim_{M\to+\infty}\mathrm{Tr}_{\backslash i}\left[\exp\left(\frac{1}{k_{\mathrm{B}}TM}\Gamma\boldsymbol{\sigma}^{x}\otimes\boldsymbol{I}\right)\exp\left(\frac{1}{k_{\mathrm{B}}TM}hd_i(\boldsymbol{\sigma}^{z}\otimes\boldsymbol{I})\right)\right. \\
& \times\exp\left(\frac{1}{k_{\mathrm{B}}TM}J(\boldsymbol{\sigma}^{z}\otimes\boldsymbol{I})(\boldsymbol{I}\otimes\boldsymbol{\sigma}^{z})\right)\exp\left(\frac{1}{k_{\mathrm{B}}TM}hd_j(\boldsymbol{I}\otimes\boldsymbol{\sigma}^{z})\right)\exp\left(\frac{1}{k_{\mathrm{B}}TM}\Gamma\boldsymbol{I}\otimes\boldsymbol{\sigma}^{x}\right) \\
& \left.\times\exp\left(\frac{1}{k_{\mathrm{B}}TM}\boldsymbol{I}\otimes\left(\sum_{l\in\partial j\backslash\{i\}}\boldsymbol{\lambda}_{l\to j}\right)\right)\exp\left(\frac{1}{k_{\mathrm{B}}TM}\left(\sum_{k\in\partial i\backslash\{j\}}\boldsymbol{\lambda}_{k\to i}\right)\otimes\boldsymbol{I}\right)\right]^{M},
\end{aligned}
\quad (10.431)
$$

such that,

$$
\begin{aligned}
& \lim_{M\to+\infty}\sum_{s_{i,2}\in\Omega}\cdots\sum_{s_{i,M}\in\Omega}\left(\prod_{m=1}^{M}\langle s_{i,m}|\exp\left(\frac{1}{k_{\mathrm{B}}TM}\sum_{k\in\partial i\backslash\{j\}}\boldsymbol{\lambda}_{k\to i}\right)|s_{i,m}\rangle\exp\left(\frac{1}{k_{\mathrm{B}}TM}hd_i s_{i,m}\right)\right) \\
& \times\delta_{s'_{i,1},s_{i,M+1}}\prod_{m=1}^{M}\left(\langle s_{i,m}|\exp\left(\frac{1}{k_{\mathrm{B}}TM}\boldsymbol{\lambda}_{j\to i}\right)|s_{i,m}\rangle\langle s_{i,m}|\exp\left(\frac{1}{k_{\mathrm{B}}TM}\Gamma\boldsymbol{\sigma}^{x}\right)|s_{i,m+1}\rangle\right) \\
& = \lim_{M\to+\infty}\sum_{s_{i,2}\in\Omega}\cdots\sum_{s_{i,M}\in\Omega}\left(\prod_{m=1}^{M}\langle s_{i,m}|\exp\left(\frac{1}{k_{\mathrm{B}}TM}\sum_{k\in\partial i\backslash\{j\}}\boldsymbol{\lambda}_{k\to i}\right)|s_{i,m}\rangle\exp\left(\frac{1}{k_{\mathrm{B}}TM}hd_i s_{i,m}\right)\right) \\
& \times\left(\delta_{s'_{i,1},s_{i,M+1}}\frac{Z_i}{Z_{\{i,j\}}}\sum_{s_{j,1}\in\Omega}\sum_{s'_{j,1}\in\Omega}\delta_{s_{j,1},s'_{j,1}}\right.
\end{aligned}
$$

$$\times \sum_{s_{j,2}\in\Omega}\cdots\sum_{s_{j,M}\in\Omega}\delta_{s'_{j,1},s_{j,M+1}}\prod_{m=1}^{M}\Bigg(\exp\Big(\frac{1}{k_{\mathrm{B}}TM}(Js_{i,m}s_{j,m})\Big)\exp\Big(\frac{1}{k_{\mathrm{B}}TM}hd_js_{j,m}\Big)$$

$$\times\langle s_{j,m}|\exp\Bigg(\frac{1}{k_{\mathrm{B}}TM}\sum_{l\in\partial j\setminus\{i\}}\boldsymbol{\lambda}_{l\to j}\Bigg)|s_{j,m}\rangle$$

$$\times\langle s_{i,m}|\exp\Big(\frac{1}{k_{\mathrm{B}}TM}\Gamma\boldsymbol{\sigma}^{x}\Big)|s_{i,m+1}\rangle\langle s_{j,m}|\exp\Big(\frac{1}{k_{\mathrm{B}}TM}\Gamma\boldsymbol{\sigma}^{x}\Big)|s_{j,m+1}\rangle\Bigg)\Bigg). \tag{10.432}$$

The sufficient conditions for Eq. (10.432) are given by

$$\delta_{s'_{i,1},s_{i,M+1}}\prod_{m=1}^{M}\Bigg(\langle s_{i,m}|\exp\Big(\frac{1}{k_{\mathrm{B}}TM}\boldsymbol{\lambda}_{j\to i}\Big)|s_{i,m}\rangle\langle s_{i,m}|\exp\Big(\frac{1}{k_{\mathrm{B}}TM}\Gamma\boldsymbol{\sigma}^{x}\Big)|s_{i,m+1}\rangle\Bigg)$$
$$=\delta_{s'_{i,1},s_{i,M+1}}\frac{Z_i}{Z_{\{i,j\}}}\sum_{s_{j,1}\in\Omega}\sum_{s'_{j,1}\in\Omega}\delta_{s_{j,1},s'_{j,1}}$$
$$\times\sum_{s_{j,2}\in\Omega}\cdots\sum_{s_{j,M}\in\Omega}\delta_{s'_{j,1},s_{j,M+1}}\prod_{m=1}^{M}\Bigg(\exp\Big(\frac{1}{k_{\mathrm{B}}TM}Js_{i,m}s_{j,m}\Big)\exp\Big(\frac{1}{k_{\mathrm{B}}TM}hd_js_{j,m}\Big)$$
$$\times\langle s_{j,m}|\exp\Bigg(\frac{1}{k_{\mathrm{B}}TM}\sum_{l\in\partial j\setminus\{i\}}\boldsymbol{\lambda}_{l\to j}\Bigg)|s_{j,m}\rangle$$
$$\times\langle s_{i,m}|\exp\Big(\frac{1}{k_{\mathrm{B}}TM}\Gamma\boldsymbol{\sigma}^{x}\Big)|s_{i,m+1}\rangle\langle s_{j,m}|\exp\Big(\frac{1}{k_{\mathrm{B}}TM}\Gamma\boldsymbol{\sigma}^{x}\Big)|s_{j,m+1}\rangle\Bigg). \tag{10.433}$$

By taking the summations $\sum_{s_{i,2}\in\Omega}\cdots\sum_{s_{i,M}\in\Omega}$ and the limit $M\to+\infty$ on both sides of Eq. (10.433), modified message passing rules can be derived as follows:

$$\exp\Big(\frac{1}{k_{\mathrm{B}}T}\boldsymbol{\lambda}_{j\to i}+\frac{1}{k_{\mathrm{B}}T}\Gamma\boldsymbol{\sigma}^{x}\Big)$$
$$=\frac{Z_i}{Z_{\{i,j\}}}\mathrm{Tr}_{\setminus i}\Bigg[\exp\Bigg(\frac{1}{k_{\mathrm{B}}T}\Big(J(\boldsymbol{\sigma}^{z}\otimes\boldsymbol{I})(\boldsymbol{I}\otimes\boldsymbol{\sigma}^{z})+\Gamma(\boldsymbol{\sigma}^{x}\otimes\boldsymbol{I})\Big)$$
$$+\frac{1}{k_{\mathrm{B}}T}\boldsymbol{I}\otimes\Big(hd_j\boldsymbol{\sigma}^{z}+\Gamma\boldsymbol{\sigma}^{x}+\sum_{l\in\partial j\setminus\{i\}}\boldsymbol{\lambda}_{l\to j}\Big)\Bigg)\Bigg]. \tag{10.434}$$

We remark that the modified message passing rules of Eq. (10.434) can be derived by considering the Bethe free energy functional in the cluster variation method with a ladder-type basic cluster for the probabilistic graphical model [107] in Eqs. (10.429)–(10.430). While the conventional framework of quantum belief propagations was given as a quantum cluster variation method in Ref. [90], some extensions of loopy belief propagations have been proposed in Refs. [108–111] from a quantum statistical mechanical standpoint.

10.6 Concluding Remarks

This chapter explored sublinear modeling based on statistical mechanical informatics for statistical machine learning. In statistical machine learning, we need to compute some statistical quantities in massive probabilistic graphical models. Statistical mechanical informatics can provide us with many statistical approximate computational techniques. One is the advanced mean-field framework, which includes mean-field methods and loopy belief propagation methods such as the Bethe approximation. The advanced mean-field framework can provide good accuracy for statistical quantities, including averages and covariances. Some statistical quantities in probabilistic graphical models sometimes have phase transitions when computing the advanced mean-field method. As we have already shown in Sect. 10.3.3, we have two familiar phase transitions, namely, the first- and second-order phase transitions. Each step of the EM algorithm is often affected by the first-order phase transition because the internal energy in the prior probabilistic model has a discontinuity. This difficulty appears in the convergence procedure of the EM algorithm, in which the trajectory of a hyperparameter passes through not only the equilibrium state but also metastable and unstable states in the loopy belief propagation of probabilistic segmentations in Sect. 10.3.5. We show that some algorithms based on loopy belief propagation in probabilistic segmentations can be accelerated by the inverse real-space renormalization group techniques in Sect. 10.3.6.

The second part of this chapter explored quantum statistical machine learning and some statistical approximate algorithms in quantum statistical mechanical informatics for realizing the framework. Quantum mechanical computations for machine learning are rapidly developing in terms of both academic research and industrial implementation. In Sect. 10.4, we explained the modeling framework of density matrices and some fundamental mathematics for it and expanded the modeling framework to the quantum expectation-maximization algorithm. In Sect. 10.5, we showed the fundamental frameworks of quantum loopy belief propagation and quantum statistical mechanical extensions of the adaptive TAP method. Moreover, we reviewed the Suzuki-Trotter expansion, and the real and the momentum space renormalization group for sublinear modeling of density matrices.

Recently, we have the framework of massive fundamental mathematical modeling in the statistical machine learning theory for many practical applications, such that, mainly the sparse modeling [4, 5] and the deep learning [10]. Many academic researchers are interested in interpretations of such modelings in the stand point of probabilistic graphical models in the statistical mathematics [2, 3, 7] and the statistical mechanical informatics [8, 9, 13, 17]. Now we have novel technologies for realizing quantum computing in the stand point of quantum mechanical extensions of the statistical mechanical informatics, such that, for example, **D-wave Quantum Annealer**. Some results in which the D-Wave quantum annealers have achieved high performance computing have appeared in Refs. [112–116]. Some recent developments of the probabilistic graphical modelings and their static and dynamical analysis of the advanced mean-field methods and the Suzuki-Trotter decompositions as well as the replica methods for realizing sublinear modeling are shown in the subsequent Chaps. 12 and 13 of the present part of this book, in the statistical mechanical point of view.

Acknowledgements This work was partly supported by the JST-CREST program (No. JPMJCR1402) of the Japan Science and Technology Agency and a JSPS KAKENHI Grant (No.18H03303) from the Ministry of Education, Culture, Sports, Science, and Technology. The author is thankful for some valuable comments from Profs. Masayuki Ohzeki and Manaka Okuyama of Tohoku University and Prof. Muneki Yasuda of Yamagata University in Japan, Prof. Federico Ricci-Tersenghi of Università di Roma, La Sapenza in Italy, and Prof. Anthony C.C. Coolen of Radboud University in the Netherlands.

References

1. J.C.D. MacKay, *Information Theory, Inference, and Learning Algorithms* (Cambridge University Press, 2003)
2. D. Koller, N. Friedman, *Probabilistic Graphical Models: Principles and Techniques* (MIT Press, 2009)
3. P.K. Murphy, *Machine Learning: A Probabilistic Perspective* (MIT Press, 2012)
4. I. Rish, G.Y. Grabarnik, *Sparse Modelling: Theory, Algorithms, and Applications* (Chapman & Hall/CRC, 2015)
5. T. Hastie, R. Tibshirani, M.J. Wainwright, *Statistical Learning with Sparsity: The Lasso and Generalizations* (Chapman & Hall/CRC, 2015)
6. J. Hertz, A. Krogh, R.G. Palmer, *Introduction to the Theory of Neural Computation* (CRC Press, 1991)
7. W. Jim, D. Kay, *Statistics and Neural Networks: Advances at the Interface*. Royal Statistical Society Lecture Notes Series, vol. 5, ed. by M. Titterington (Oxford University Press, 2000)
8. A. Engel, C. Van den Broeck, *Statistical Mechanics of Learning* (Cambridge University Press, 2001)
9. A.C.C. Coolen, R. Kühn, P. Sollich, *Theory of Neural Information Processing Systems* (Oxford University Press, 2005)
10. I. Goodfellow, Y. Bengio, A. Courville, *Deep Learning*. Adaptive Computation and Machine Learning Series (MIT Press, 2016)
11. M.J. Wainwright, M.I. Jordan, *Graphical Models, Exponential Families, and Variational Inference*. Foundations and Trends®. Mach. Learn. **1**(1–2), 1–305 (2008). https://doi.org/10.1561/2200000001
12. M. Opper, D. Saad (eds.), *Advanced Mean Field Methods—Theory and Practice* (MIT Press, 2001)
13. H. Nishimori, *Statistical Physics of Spin Glasses and Information Processing: Introduction*. International Series of Monographs on Physics (Oxford Science Publications, 2001)
14. K. Tanaka, Statistical-mechanical approach to image processing (Topical Review). J. Phys. A Math. Gen. **35**(37), R81–R150 (2002). https://doi.org/10.1088/0305-4470/35/37/201
15. T. Tanaka, A statistical-mechanics approach to large-system analysis of CDMA multiuser detectors. IEEE Trans. Inf. Theory **48**(11), 2888–2910 (2002). https://doi.org/10.1109/TIT.2002.804053
16. Y. Kabashima, D. Saad, Statistical mechanics of low-density parity-check codes (Topical Review). J. Phys. A Math. Gen. **37**(6), R1–R43 (2004). https://doi.org/10.1088/0305-4470/37/6/R01
17. M. Mézard, A. Montanari, *Information, Physics and Computation* (Oxford University Press, 2009)

18. A.K. Hartmann, H. Rieger, *Optimization Algorithms in Physics* (Wiley-VCH, 2001)
19. K.A. Hartmann, M. Weigt, *Phase Transitions in Combinatorial Optimization Problems* (Wiley-VCH, 2005)
20. T. Kadowaki, H. Nishimori, Quantum annealing in the transverse Ising model. Phys. Rev. E **58**(5), 5, 5355–5263 (1998). https://doi.org/10.1103/PhysRevE.58.5355
21. A. Das, B.K. Chakrabarti (eds.), *Quantum Annealing and Related Optimization Methods*. Lecture Notes in Physics, vol. 679 (Springer, 2004)
22. C.C. McGeoch, in *Adiabatic Quantum Computation and Quantum Annealing: Theory and Practice* (Morgan & Claypool, 2014)
23. T. Albash, D.A. Lidar, Adiabatic quantum computation. Rev. Modern Phys. **90**(1) (2018). Article ID 015002. https://doi.org/10.1103/RevModPhys.90.015002
24. E.K. Grant, T.S. Humble, *Adiabatic Quantum Computing and Quantum Annealing*. Oxford Research Encyclopedias (Oxford University Press and the American Institute of Physics, 2020). https://doi.org/10.1093/acrefore/9780190871994.013.32
25. A.P. Dempster, N.M. Laird, D.B. Rubin, Maximum likelihood from incomplete data via the EM algorithm. J. R. Stat. Soc. Ser. B (Methodological) **39**(1), 1–38 (1977). With discussion
26. K.L. Mengersen, C.P. Robert, D. Michael Titterington, *Mixtures: Estimation and Applications* (Wiley, 2011)
27. J. Marroquin, S. Mitter, T. Poggio, Probabilistic solution of ill-posed problems in computational vision. J. Am. Stat. Assoc. **82**(397), 76–89 (1987). https://doi.org/10.1080/01621459.1987.10478393
28. W. Qian, D. Michael Titterington, Stochastic relaxations and em algorithms for Markov random fields. J. Stat. Comput. Simul. **40**(1–2), 55–69 (1992) https://doi.org/10.1080/00949659208811365
29. C. Andrieu, N. De Freitas, A. Doucet, M.I. Jordan, An introduction to MCMC for machine learning. Mach. Learn. **50**(1–2), 5–43 (2003). https://doi.org/10.1023/A:1020281327116
30. K. Tanaka, D. Michael Titterington, Statistical trajectory of approximate EM algorithm for probabilistic image processing. J. Phys. A Math. Theor. **40**(37), 11285–11300 (2007). https://doi.org/10.1088/1751-8113/40/37/007
31. J. Inoue, K. Tanaka, Dynamics of the maximum marginal likelihood hyperparameter estimation in image restoration: gradient descent versus expectation and maximization algorithm. Phys. Rev. E **65**(1) (2002). Article ID.016125. https://doi.org/10.1103/PhysRevE.65.016125
32. J. Roy, Glauber: time-dependent statistics of the Ising model. J. Math. Phys. **4**(2), 294–307 (1963). https://doi.org/10.1063/1.1703954
33. F.Y. Wu, The Potts model, Rev. Modern Phys. **54**(1), 235–268 (1982). https://doi.org/10.1103/RevModPhys.54.235
34. C. Domb, On the theory of cooperative phenomena in crystals. Adv. Phys. **9**(34), 149–244 (1960). https://doi.org/10.1080/00018736000101189
35. C. Domb, On the theory of cooperative phenomena in crystals. Adv. Phys. **9**(35), 245–361 (1960). https://doi.org/10.1080/00018736000101199
36. G. Parisi, *Statistical Field Theory* (Addison-Wesley, 1988)
37. H. Nishimori, G. Ortiz, *Elements of Phase Transitions and Critical Phenomena* (Oxford University Press, 2011)
38. D. Ruelle, *Statistical Mechanics: Rigorous Results* (Imperial College Press, 1969)
39. T. Morita, Variational principle for the distribution function of the effective field for the random Ising model in the Bethe approximation. Phys. A Stat. Mech. Appl. **98**(3), 566–572 (1979).https://doi.org/10.1016/0378-4371(79)90154-7
40. T. Morita, Variational principle for regular and random Ising models on the cactus tree or on the usual lattice in the "cactus approximation." Phys. A **105**(3), 620–630 (1981). https://doi.org/10.1016/0378-4371(81)90115-1
41. T. Horiguchi, On the Bethe approximation for the random bond Ising model. Phys. A Stat. Mech. Appl. **107**(2), 360–370 (1981). https://doi.org/10.1016/0378-4371(81)90095-9
42. T. Morita, Cluster variation method of cooperative phenomena and its generalization I. J. Phys. Soc. Jpn. **12**(10), 753–755 (1957). https://doi.org/10.1143/JPSJ.12.753

43. T. Morita, General structure of the distribution functions for the Heisenberg model and the Ising model. J. Math. Phys. **13**(1), 115–123 (1972). https://doi.org/10.1063/1.1665840
44. T. Morita, Cluster variation method and Möbius inversion formula. J. Stat. Phys. **59**(3–4), 819–825 (1990). https://doi.org/10.1007/BF01025852
45. T. Morita, Cluster variation method for non-uniform Ising and Heisenberg models and spin-pair correlation function. Progress Theor. Phys. **85**(2), 243–255 (1991). https://doi.org/10.1143/ptp/85.2.243
46. Y. Kabashima, D. Saad, Belief propagation vs. TAP for decoding corrupted messages. Europhys. Lett. **44**(5), 668–674 (1998). https://doi.org/10.1209/epl/i1998-00524-7
47. J.S. Yedidia, W.T. Freeman, Y. Weiss, Constructing free-energy approximations and generalized belief propagation algorithms. IEEE Trans. Inf. Theory **51**(7), 2282–2312 (2005). https://doi.org/10.1109/TIT.2005.850085
48. A. Pelizzola, Cluster variation method in statistical physics and probabilistic graphical models (Topical Review). J. Phys. A Math. Gen. **38**(2005), R309–R339 (2005). https://doi.org/10.1088/0305-4470/38/33/R01
49. D.L. Donoho, A. Maleki, A. Montanari, Message-passing algorithms for compressed sensing, in *Proceedings of the National Academy of Sciences of the United States of America*, vol. 106, no. 45 (2009), pp. 18914–18919. https://doi.org/10.1073/pnas.0909892106
50. T. Rizzo, A. Lage-Castellanos, F. Ricci-Tersenghi, Replica cluster variational method. J. Stat. Phys. **139**(3), 367–374 (2010). https://doi.org/10.1007/s10955-010-9938-3
51. M. Yasuda, S. Kataoka, K. Tanaka, Statistical analysis of loopy belief propagation in random fields. Phys. Rev. E **92**(4) (2015). Article ID. 042120. https://doi.org/10.1103/PhysRevE.92.042120
52. F. Krzakala, F. Ricci-Tersenghi, L. Zdeborova, R. Zecchina, E.W. Tramel, L.F. Cugliandolo, *Statistical Physics, Optimization, Inference and Message-Passing Algorithms*. Lecture Notes of the Les Houches School of Physics. Special Issue (Oxford University Press, 2013)
53. M. Welling, Y.W. Teh, Approximate inference in Boltzmann machines. Artif. Intell. **143**(1), 19–50 (2003). https://doi.org/10.1016/S0004-3702(02)00361-2
54. M. Yasuda, S. Kataoka, K. Tanaka, Inverse problem in pairwise Markov random fields using loopy belief propagation. J. Phys. Soc. Jpn. **81**(4), 1–8 (2012). Article ID 044801. https://doi.org/10.1143/JPSJ.81.044801
55. F. Ricci-Tersenghi, The Bethe approximation for solving the inverse Ising problem: a comparison with other inference methods. J. Stat. Mech. Theory Exp. (2012). Article ID P08015. https://doi.org/10.1088/1742-5468/2012/08/P08015
56. T. Morita, T. Horiguchi, Exactly solvable model of a spin glass. Solid State Commun. **19**(9), 833–835 (1976). https://doi.org/10.1016/0038-1098(76)90665-7
57. D.J. Thouless, P.W. Anderson, R.G. Palmer, Solution of 'Solvable model of a spin glass'. Philos. Mag. J. Theor. Exp. Appl. Phys. **35**(3), 593–601 (1977). https://doi.org/10.1080/14786437708235992
58. T. Morita, T. Horiguchi, Exactly solvable model of a random classical Heisenberg magnet. J. Phys. C Solid State Phys. **10**(11), 1949–1961 (1977). https://doi.org/10.1088/0022-3719/10/11/029
59. M. Yasuda, K. Tanaka, The relationship between Plefka's expansion and the cluster variation method. J. Phys. Soc. Jpn. **75**(8) (2006). Article ID 084006. https://doi.org/10.1143/JPSJ.75.084006
60. M. Yasuda, K. Tanaka, Approximate learning algorithm in Boltzmann machines. Neural Comput. **21**(11), 3130–3178 (2009). https://doi.org/10.1162/neco.2009.08-08-844
61. M. Yasuda, K. Tanaka, TAP equation for non-negative Boltzmann machine. Philos. Mag. **92**(1–3), 192–209 (2012). https://doi.org/10.1080/14786435.2011.634856
62. M. Yasuda, Y. Kabashima, K. Tanaka, Replica Plefka expansion of Ising systems. J. Stat. Mech. Theory Exp. **2012**(4) (2012). Article ID P04002. https://doi.org/10.1088/1742-5468/2012/04/P04002
63. E.W. Tramel, A. Drémeau, F. Krzakala, Approximate message passing with restricted Boltzmann machine priors. J. Stat. Mech. Theory Exp. **2016**(7) (2016). Article ID 073401 https://doi.org/10.1088/1742-5468/2016/07/073401

64. M. Gabrié, Mean-field inference methods for neural networks (Topical Review). J. Phys. A Math. Theor. **53**(23) (2020). Article ID 223002. https://orcid.org/0000-0002-5989-1018
65. K. Tanaka, J. Inoue, D.M. Titterington, Probabilistic image processing by means of Bethe approximation for Q-Ising model. J. Phys. A Math. Gen. **36**(43), 11023–11036 (2003). https://doi.org/10.1088/0305-4470/36/43/025
66. K. Tanaka, H. Shouno, M. Okada, D.M. Titterington, Accuracy of the Bethe approximation for hyperparameter estimation in probabilistic image processing. J. Phys. A Math. Gen. **37**(36), 8675–8696 (2004). https://doi.org/10.1088/0305-4470/37/36/007
67. S. Kataoka, M. Yasuda, K. Tanaka, Statistical performance analysis in probabilistic image processing. J. Phys. Soc. Jpn. **79**(2) (2010). Article ID 025001. https://doi.org/10.1143/JPSJ.79.025001
68. S. Kataoka, M. Yasuda, K. Tanaka, D.M. Titterington, Statistical analysis of the expectation-maximization algorithm with loopy belief propagation in Bayesian image modeling. Philos. Mag. Study Condens Matter **92**(1-3), 50–63 (2012). https://doi.org/10.1080/14786435.2011.624558
69. K. Tanaka, M. Yasuda, D. Michael Titterington, Bayesian image modelling by means of generalized sparse prior and loopy belief propagation. J. Phys. Soc. Jpn. **81**(11) (2012). Article ID 114802. https://doi.org/10.1143/JPSJ.81.114802
70. K. Tanaka, S. Kataoka, M. Yasuda, Y. Waizumi, C.-T. Hsu, Bayesian image segmentations by Potts prior and Loopy belief propagation. J. Phys. Soc. Jpn. **83**(12) (2014). Article ID 124002. https://doi.org/10.7566/JPSJ.83.124002
71. M.B. Hastings, Community detection as an inference problem. Phys. Rev. E **74**(3) (2006). Article ID 035102(R). https://doi.org/10.1103/PhysRevE.74.035102
72. A. Decelle, F. Krzakala, C. Moore, L. Zdeborová, Asymptotic analysis of the stochastic block model for modular networks and its algorithmic applications. Phys. Rev. E **84**(6) (2011). Article ID 066106. https://doi.org/10.1103/PhysRevE.84.066106
73. S. Kataoka, T. Kobayashi, M. Yasuda, K. Tanaka, Community detection algorithm combining stochastic block model and attribute data clustering. J. Phys. Soc. Jpn. **85**(11) (2016). Article ID 114802. https://doi.org/10.7566/JPSJ.85.114802
74. B. McCoy, T.T. Wu, *The Two-Dimensional Ising Model* (Harvard University Press, 1973). ISBN: 9780674180758
75. R.J. Baxter, *Exactly Solved Models in Statistical Mechanics* (Academic Press, 1982). ISBN: 9780486462714
76. T. Horiguchi, Husimi-Temperley model under a random field. J. Math. Phys. **20**(8), 1774–1775 (1979). https://doi.org/10.1063/1.524265
77. M. Mezard, G. Parisi, M.A. Virasoro, *Spin Glass Theory and Beyond* (World Scientific, 1987)
78. K.H. Fisher, J.A. Hertz, *Spin Glasses* (Cambridge University Press, 1993)
79. Michel Talagrand, *Mean Field Models for Spin Glass. Volume I: Basic Examples* (Springer, 2011)
80. M. Talagrand, *Mean Field Models for Spin Glass. Volume II: Advanced Replica-Symmetry and Low Temperature* (Springer, 2011)
81. K. Tanaka, S. Kataoka, M. Yasuda, M. Ohzeki, Inverse renormalization group transformation in Bayesian image segmentations. J. Phys. Soc. Jpn. **84**(4) (2015). Article ID 045001. https://doi.org/10.7566/JPSJ.84.045001
82. D.A. Harville, *Matrix algebra from a statistician's prespective* (Springer, 1997)
83. S. Suzuki, J. Inoue, B.K. Chakrabarti, *Quantum Ising Phases and Transitions in Transverse Ising Models*. Lecture Notes in Physics Book, vol. 862 (Springer, 2013)
84. A. Dutta, G. Aeppli, B.K. Chakrabarti, U. Divakaran, T.F. Rosenbaum, D. Sen, *Quantum Phase Transitions in Transverse Field Spin Models: From Statistical Physics to Quantum Information* (Springer, 2015)
85. S.G. Ovchinnikov, V.V. Val'kov, *Hubbard Operators in the Theory of Strongly Correlated Electrons* (Imperial College Press, 2004). https://doi.org/10.1142/9781860945977_0001
86. H. Tasaki, *Physics and Mathematics of Quantum Many-Body Systems (Graduate Texts in Physics)* (Springer, 2020)

87. M. Suzuki, Relationship between d-dimensional quantal spin systems and $(d+1)$-dimensional Ising systems—equivalence, critical exponents and systematic approximants of the partition function and spin correlations. Prog. Theor. Phys. **56**(5), 1454–1469 (1976). https://doi.org/10.1143/PTP.56.1454
88. M. Suzuki, Decomposition formulas of exponential operators and Lie exponentials with some applications to quantum mechanics and statistical physics. J. Math. Phys. **26**(4), 601–612 (1985). https://doi.org/10.1063/1.526596
89. J. Gubernatis, N. Kawashima, P. Werner, *Quantum Monte Carlo Methods: Algorithms for Lattice Models* (Cambridge University Press, 2016)
90. T. Morita, Cluster variation method of cooperative phenomena and its generalization II. Quantum statistics. J. Phys. Soc. Jpn. **12**(10), 1060–1063 (1957). https://doi.org/10.1143/JPSJ.12.1060
91. R. Kubo, The spin-wave theory as a variational method and Its application to antiferromagnetism. Rev. Modern Phys. **25**(1), 344–351 (1953). https://doi.org/10.1103/RevModPhys.25.344
92. T. Morita, An approximation scheme of the cluster variation method for quantum lattice gases. Prog. Theor. Phys. **92**(6), 1081–1093 (1994). https://doi.org/10.1143/ptp/92.6.1081
93. T. Morita, A Bose lattice gas equivalent to Heisenberg model and its QCVM study. J. Phys. Soc. Jpn. **64**(4), 1211–1216 (1995). https://doi.org/10.1143/JPSJ.64.1211
94. R. Miyazaki, H. Nishimori, G. Ortiz, Real-space renormalization group for the transverse-field Ising model in two and three dimensions. Phys. Rev. E **83**(5) (2011). Article ID 051103. https://doi.org/10.1103/PhysRevE.83.051103
95. M. Opper, O. Winther, Adaptive and self-averaging Thouless-Anderson-Palmer mean-field theory for probabilistic modeling. Phys. Rev. E **64**(5) (2001). Article ID 056131 https://doi.org/10.1103/PhysRevE.64.056131
96. M. Opper, O. Winther, Expectation consistent approximate inference. J. Mach. Learn. Res. **6**(73), 2177–2204 (2005). https://doi.org/10.5555/1046920.1194917
97. M. Yasuda, C. Takahashi, K. Tanaka, Perturbative interpretation of adaptive Thouless-Anderson-Palmer free energy. J. Phys. Soc. Jpn. **85**(7) (2016). Article ID 075001. https://doi.org/10.7566/JPSJ.85.075001
98. C. Takahashi, M. Yasuda, K. Tanaka, Adaptive Thouless-Anderson-Palmer equation for higher-order Markov random fields. J. Phys. Soc. Jpn. **89**(6) (2020). Article ID 064007. https://doi.org/10.7566/JPSJ.89.064007
99. K. Tanaka, M. Nakamura, S. Kataoka, M. Ohzeki, M. Yasuda, Momentum-space renormalization group transformation in Bayesian image modeling by Gaussian graphical model. J. Phys. Soc. Jpn. **87**(8), 1–2 (2018). Article ID 085001. https://doi.org/10.7566/JPSJ.87.085001
100. K. Tanaka, M. Ohzeki, M. Yasuda, Sublinear computational time modeling by momentum-space renormalization group theory in statistical machine learning procedures. Rev. Socionetwork Strat. **13**(2), 281–306 (2019). https://doi.org/10.1007/s12626-019-00053-1
101. J. Inoue, Deterministic flows of order-parameters in stochastic processes of quantum Monte Carlo method. J. Phys. Conf. Ser. **233** (2010). Article ID 012010. https://doi.org/10.1088/1742-6596/233/1/012010
102. J. Inoue, Pattern-recalling processes in quantum Hopfield networks far from saturation. J. Phys. Conf. Ser. **297** (2011). Article ID 012012. https://doi.org/10.1088/1742-6596/297/1/012012
103. M. Ohzeki, S. Okada, M. Terabe, S. Taguchi, Optimization of neural networks via finite-value quantum fluctuations. Sci. Rep. **8** (2018). Article ID 9950. https://doi.org/10.1038/s41598-018-28212-4
104. S. Arai, M. Ohzeki, K. Tanaka, Dynamics of order parameters of nonstoquastic Hamiltonians in the adaptive quantum Monte Carlo method. Phys. Rev. E **99**(3) (2019). Article ID 032120. https://doi.org/10.1103/PhysRevE.99.032120
105. S. Arai, M. Ohzeki, K. Tanaka, Teacher-student learning for a binary perceptron with quantum fluctuations. J. Phys. Soc. Jpn. **90**(7) (2021). Article ID 074002. https://doi.org/10.7566/JPSJ.90.074002

106. S. Arai, M. Ohzeki, K. Tanaka, Mean field analysis of reverse annealing for code-division multiple-access multiuser detection. Phys. Rev. Res. **3**(3) (2021). Article ID 033006. https://doi.org/10.1103/PhysRevResearch.3.03300
107. K. Tanaka, T. Horiguchi, T. Morita, Critical indices for the two-dimensional Ising model with nearest-neighbor and next-nearest-neighbor interactions. II. Strip cluster approximation. Phys. A Stat. Mech. Appl. **192**(4), 647–664 (1993). https://doi.org/10.1016/0378-4371(93)90114-J
108. M.B. Hastings, Quantum belief propagation: an algorithm for thermal quantum systems. Phys. Rev. B **76**(20) (2007). Article ID 201102(R). https://doi.org/10.1103/PhysRevB.76.201102
109. M.S. Leifer, D. Poulin, Quantum graphical models and belief propagation. Ann. Phys. **323**(8), 1899–1946 (2008). https://doi.org/10.1016/j.aop.2007.10.001
110. F. Krzakala, A. Rosso, G. Semerjian, F. Zamponi, Path-integral representation for quantum spin models: application to the quantum cavity method and Monte Carlo simulations. Phys. Rev. B **78**(13) (2008). Article ID 134428. https://doi.org/10.1103/PhysRevB.78.134428
111. M. Ohzeki, Message-passing algorithm of quantum annealing with nonstoquastic Hamiltonian. J. Phys. Soc. Jpn. **88**(6) (2019). Article ID 061005. https://doi.org/10.7566/JPSJ.88.061005
112. N. Nishimura, K. Tanahashi, K. Suganuma, M.J. Miyama, M. Ohzeki, Item listing optimization for E-commerce websites based on diversity. Front. Comput. Sci. **1** (2019). Article ID 2. https://doi.org/10.3389/fcomp.2019.00002
113. S. Okada, M. Ohzeki, M. Terabe, S. Taguchi, Improving solutions by embedding larger subproblems in a D-wave quantum annealer. Sci. Rep. **9** (2019). Article ID 2098
114. M. Ohzeki, Breaking limitation of quantum annealer in solving optimization problems under constraints. Sci. Rep. **10** (2020). Article ID 3126
115. A.S. Koshikawa, M. Ohzeki, T. Kadowaki, K. Tanaka, Benchmark test of black-box optimization using D-wave quantum annealer. J. Phys. Soc. Jpn. **90**(6) (2021). Article ID 064001. https://doi.org/10.7566/JPSJ.90.064001
116. T. Sato, M. Ohzeki, K. Tanaka, Assessment of image generation by quantum annealer. Sci. Rep. **11** (2021). Article ID 13523

Open Access This chapter is licensed under the terms of the Creative Commons Attribution 4.0 International License (http://creativecommons.org/licenses/by/4.0/), which permits use, sharing, adaptation, distribution and reproduction in any medium or format, as long as you give appropriate credit to the original author(s) and the source, provide a link to the Creative Commons license and indicate if changes were made.

The images or other third party material in this chapter are included in the chapter's Creative Commons license, unless indicated otherwise in a credit line to the material. If material is not included in the chapter's Creative Commons license and your intended use is not permitted by statutory regulation or exceeds the permitted use, you will need to obtain permission directly from the copyright holder.

Chapter 11
Empirical Bayes Method for Boltzmann Machines

Muneki Yasuda

Abstract The framework of the empirical Bayes method allows the estimation of the values of the hyperparameters in the Boltzmann machine by maximizing a specific likelihood function referred to as the empirical Bayes likelihood function. However, the maximization is computationally difficult because the empirical Bayes likelihood function involves intractable integrations of the partition function. The method presented in this chapter avoids this computational problem by using the replica method and the Plefka expansion, which is quite simple and fast because it does not require any iterative procedures and gives reasonable estimates under certain conditions.

11.1 Introduction

Boltzmann machine learning (BML) [1] has been actively studied in the fields of machine learning and statistical mechanics. In statistical mechanics, the problem of BML is sometimes referred to as the *inverse Ising problem* because a Boltzmann machine is the same as an Ising model, and it can be treated as an inverse problem for the Ising model. The framework of the *usual* BML is as follows. Given a set of observed data points, the appropriate values of the Boltzmann machine parameters, namely the biases and couplings, are estimated through maximum likelihood (ML) estimation. Because BML involves intractable multiple summations (i.e., evaluation of the partition function), several approximations have been proposed for it from the viewpoint of statistical mechanics [2]. Examples include methods based on mean-field approximations (e.g., the Plefka expansion [3] and the cluster variation method [4]) [5–11] and methods based on other approximations [12–14].

This chapter focuses on another type of learning problem for the Boltzmann machine. Consider the prior distributions of the Boltzmann machine parameters and assume that the prior distributions are governed by some hyperparameters. The introduction of the prior distributions is strongly connected to regularized ML estimation, in which the hyperparameters can be regarded as regularization coefficients. The reg-

M. Yasuda (✉)
Graduate School of Science and Engineering, Yamagata University, Yamagata, Japan
e-mail: muneki@yz.yamagata-u.ac.jp

© The Author(s) 2022

N. Katoh et al. (eds.), *Sublinear Computation Paradigm*,
https://doi.org/10.1007/978-981-16-4095-7_11

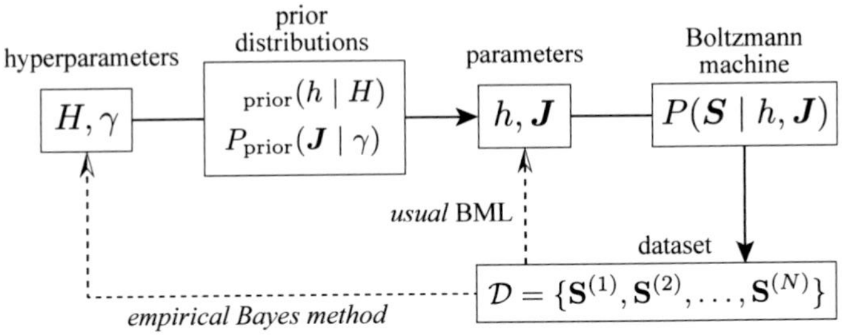

Fig. 11.1 Illustration of scheme of the empirical Bayes method considered in this chapter

ularized ML estimation is important for preventing overfitting to the dataset. As mentioned above, the *usual* BML aims to optimize the values of the Boltzmann machine parameters using a set of observed data points. However, the aim of the problem presented in this chapter is the estimation of the appropriate values of the hyperparameters from the dataset *without* estimating the specific values of the Boltzmann machine parameters. From the Bayesian viewpoint, this can be potentially accomplished by the *empirical Bayes method* (also known as type-II ML estimation or evidence approximation) [15, 16]. The schemes of the *usual* BML and the problem investigated in this chapter are illustrated in Fig. 11.1.

Recently, an effective algorithm was proposed for the empirical Bayes method for the Boltzmann machine [17]. Using this method, the hyperparameter estimates can be obtained without costly operations. This chapter aims to explain this effective method.

The rest of this chapter is organized as follows. The formulations of the Boltzmann machine and its usual and regularized ML estimations are presented in Sect. 11.2. The empirical Bayes method for the Boltzmann machine is presented in Sect. 11.3. Section 11.4 describes a statistical mechanical analysis for the empirical Bayes method and an inference algorithm obtained from the analysis. Experimental results for the presented algorithm are presented in Sect. 11.5. The summary and some discussions are presented in Sect. 11.6. The appendices for this chapter are given in Sect. 11.7.

11.2 Boltzmann Machine with Prior Distributions

Consider a fully connected Boltzmann machine with n (bipole) variables $\boldsymbol{S} := \{S_i \in \{-1, +1\} \mid i = 1, 2, \ldots, n\}$ [1]:

$$P(\boldsymbol{S} \mid h, \boldsymbol{J}) := \frac{1}{Z(h, \boldsymbol{J})} \exp\Big(h \sum_{i=1}^{n} S_i + \sum_{i<j} J_{ij} S_i S_j\Big), \tag{11.1}$$

where $\sum_{i<j}$ is the sum over all distinct pairs of variables, that is, $\sum_{i<j} = \sum_{i=1}^{n}\sum_{j=i+1}^{n}$. $Z(h, \boldsymbol{J})$ is the partition function defined by

$$Z(h, \boldsymbol{J}) := \sum_{\boldsymbol{S}} \exp\Big(h\sum_{i=1}^{n} S_i + \sum_{i<j} J_{ij} S_i S_j\Big),$$

where $\sum_{\boldsymbol{S}}$ is the sum over all possible configurations of $\boldsymbol{S}$, that is,

$$\sum_{\boldsymbol{S}} := \prod_{i=1}^{n} \sum_{S_i=\pm 1}.$$

The parameters $h \in (-\infty, +\infty)$ and $\boldsymbol{J} := \{J_{ij} \in (-\infty, +\infty) \mid i < j\}$ denote the bias and couplings, respectively.

Given N observed data points, $\mathcal{D} := \{\mathbf{S}^{(\mu)} \in \{-1, +1\}^n \mid \mu = 1, 2, \ldots, N\}$, the log-likelihood function is defined as

$$L_{\mathrm{ML}}(h, \boldsymbol{J}) := \frac{1}{nN}\sum_{\mu=1}^{N} \ln P(\mathbf{S}^{(\mu)} \mid h, \boldsymbol{J}). \tag{11.2}$$

The maximization of the log-likelihood function with respect to h and $\boldsymbol{J}$ (i.e., the ML estimation) corresponds to BML (or the inverse Ising problem), that is,

$$\{\hat{h}_{\mathrm{ML}}, \hat{\boldsymbol{J}}_{\mathrm{ML}}\} = \arg\max_{h, \boldsymbol{J}} L_{\mathrm{ML}}(h, \boldsymbol{J}). \tag{11.3}$$

However, the exact ML estimations cannot be obtained because the gradients of the log-likelihood function include intractable sums over $O(2^n)$ terms.

We now introduce the prior distributions of the parameters h and $\boldsymbol{J}$ as $P_{\mathrm{prior}}(h \mid H)$ and

$$P_{\mathrm{prior}}(\boldsymbol{J} \mid \gamma) := \prod_{i<j} P_{\mathrm{prior}}(J_{ij} \mid \gamma), \tag{11.4}$$

where H and γ are the hyperparameters of these prior distributions. One of the most important motivations for introducing the prior distributions is the Bayesian interpretation of the regularized ML estimation [16]. Given the observed dataset $\mathcal{D}$, using the prior distributions, the posterior distribution of h and $\boldsymbol{J}$ is expressed as

$$P_{\mathrm{post}}(h, \boldsymbol{J} \mid \mathcal{D}, H, \gamma) = \frac{P(\mathcal{D} \mid h, \boldsymbol{J}) P_{\mathrm{prior}}(h \mid H) P_{\mathrm{prior}}(\boldsymbol{J} \mid \gamma)}{P(\mathcal{D} \mid H, \gamma)}, \tag{11.5}$$

where

$$P(\mathcal{D} \mid h, \boldsymbol{J}) := \prod_{\mu=1}^{N} P(\mathbf{S}^{(\mu)} \mid h, \boldsymbol{J}).$$

The denominator of Eq. (11.5) is sometimes referred to as *evidence*. Using the posterior distribution, the maximum a posteriori (MAP) estimation of the parameters is obtained as

$$\{\hat{h}_{\text{MAP}}, \hat{\boldsymbol{J}}_{\text{MAP}}\} = \arg\max_{h,\boldsymbol{J}} L_{\text{MAP}}(h, \boldsymbol{J}), \tag{11.6}$$

where

$$\begin{aligned} L_{\text{MAP}}(h, \boldsymbol{J}) &:= \frac{1}{nN} \ln P_{\text{post}}(h, \boldsymbol{J} \mid \mathcal{D}, H, \gamma) \\ &= L_{\text{ML}}(h, \boldsymbol{J}) + \frac{1}{nN} R_0(h) + \frac{1}{nN} R_1(\boldsymbol{J}) + \text{constant}. \end{aligned} \tag{11.7}$$

The MAP estimation of Eq. (11.6) corresponds to the regularized ML estimation, in which $R_0(h) := \ln P_{\text{prior}}(h \mid H)$ and $R_1(\boldsymbol{J}) := \ln P_{\text{prior}}(\boldsymbol{J} \mid \gamma)$ work as penalty terms. For example, (i) when the prior distribution of $\boldsymbol{J}$ is a Gaussian prior,

$$P_{\text{prior}}(J_{ij} \mid \gamma) = \sqrt{\frac{n}{2\pi\gamma}} \exp\Big(-\frac{nJ_{ij}^2}{2\gamma}\Big), \quad \gamma > 0, \tag{11.8}$$

$R_1(\boldsymbol{J})$ corresponds to the L_2 regularization term and γ corresponds to its coefficient; (ii) when the prior distribution of $\boldsymbol{J}$ is a Laplace prior,

$$P_{\text{prior}}(J_{ij} \mid \gamma) = \sqrt{\frac{n}{2\gamma}} \exp\Big(-\sqrt{\frac{2n}{\gamma}}|J_{ij}|\Big), \quad \gamma > 0, \tag{11.9}$$

$R_1(\boldsymbol{J})$ corresponds to the L_1 regularization term and γ again corresponds to its coefficient. The variances of these prior distributions are identical, that is, $\text{Var}[J_{ij}] = \gamma/n$.

The following uses the Gaussian prior for $\boldsymbol{J}$ and the following as a simple test case:

$$P_{\text{prior}}(h \mid H) = \delta(h - H), \tag{11.10}$$

where $\delta(x)$ is the Dirac delta function; that is, in this test case, h does not distribute. It is noteworthy that the resultant algorithm obtained based on the Gaussian prior can be applied to the case of the Laplace prior without modification [17].

11.3 Empirical Bayes Method

Using the empirical Bayes method, the values of the hyperparameters, H and γ, can be inferred from the observed dataset, $\mathcal{D}$. For the empirical Bayes method, a marginal log-likelihood function is defined as

$$L_{\mathrm{EB}}(H, \gamma) := \frac{1}{nN} \ln \big[P(\mathcal{D} \mid h, \boldsymbol{J}) \big]_{h, \boldsymbol{J}}, \tag{11.11}$$

where $[\cdots]_{h,\boldsymbol{J}}$ is the average over the prior distributions, that is,

$$[\cdots]_{h,\boldsymbol{J}} := \int d\boldsymbol{J} \int dh (\cdots) P_{\mathrm{prior}}(h \mid H) P_{\mathrm{prior}}(\boldsymbol{J} \mid \gamma).$$

This marginal log-likelihood function is referred to as the *empirical Bayes likelihood function* in this section. From the perspective of the empirical Bayes method, the optimal values of the hyperparameters, $\hat{H}$ and $\hat{\gamma}$, are obtained by maximizing the empirical Bayes likelihood function, that is,

$$\{\hat{H}, \hat{\gamma}\} = \arg \max_{H,\gamma} L_{\mathrm{EB}}(H, \gamma). \tag{11.12}$$

It is noteworthy that $[P(\mathcal{D} \mid h, \boldsymbol{J})]_{h,\boldsymbol{J}}$ in Eq. (11.11) is identified as the evidence appearing in Eq. (11.5).

The marginal log-likelihood function can be rewritten as

$$L_{\mathrm{EB}}(H, \gamma) = \frac{1}{nN} \ln \Big[\exp \big(nN L_{\mathrm{ML}}(h, \boldsymbol{J}) \big) \Big]_{h, \boldsymbol{J}}. \tag{11.13}$$

Consider the case $N \gg n$. In this case, by using the saddle point evaluation, Eq. (11.13) is reduced to

$$L_{\mathrm{EB}}(H, \gamma) \approx \frac{1}{nN} \ln P_{\mathrm{prior}}(\hat{h}_{\mathrm{ML}} \mid H) + \frac{1}{nN} \ln P_{\mathrm{prior}}(\hat{\boldsymbol{J}}_{\mathrm{ML}} \mid \gamma) + \text{constant}.$$

In this case, the empirical Bayes estimates $\{\hat{H}, \hat{\gamma}\}$ thus converge to the ML estimates of the hyperparameters in the prior distributions in which the ML estimates of the parameters $\{\hat{h}_{\mathrm{ML}}, \hat{\boldsymbol{J}}_{\mathrm{ML}}\}$ (i.e., the solution for BML) are inserted. This indicates that parameter estimations can be conducted independently of hyperparameter estimation. This trivial case is not considered in this section. Remember that the objective is to estimate the hyperparameter values *without* estimating the specific values of the parameters.

11.4 Statistical Mechanical Analysis of Empirical Bayes Likelihood

The empirical Bayes likelihood function in Eq. (11.11) involves intractable multiple integrations. This section presents an evaluation of the empirical Bayes likelihood function using statistical mechanical analysis. The outline of the evaluation is as follows. First, the intractable multiple integrations in Eq. (11.11) are evaluated using the *replica method* [18, 19]. This evaluation leads to a quantity with a certain intractable multiple summation. The quantity is approximately evaluated using the *Plefka expansion* [3]. Thus, from the two approximations, the replica method and Plefka expansion, the evaluation result for the empirical Bayes likelihood function is obtained.

11.4.1 Replica Method

The empirical Bayes likelihood function in Eq. (11.11) can be represented as

$$L_{\mathrm{EB}}(H, \gamma) = \frac{1}{nN} \ln \lim_{x \to -1} \Psi_x(H, \gamma), \tag{11.14}$$

where

$$\Psi_x(H, \gamma) := \Big[Z(h, \boldsymbol{J})^{xN} \exp N\Big(h \sum_{i=1}^{n} d_i + \sum_{i<j} J_{ij} d_{ij} \Big) \Big]_{h, \boldsymbol{J}}, \tag{11.15}$$

and

$$d_i := \frac{1}{N} \sum_{\mu=1}^{N} \mathrm{S}_i^{(\mu)}, \quad d_{ij} := \frac{1}{N} \sum_{\mu=1}^{N} \mathrm{S}_i^{(\mu)} \mathrm{S}_j^{(\mu)}$$

are the sample averages of the observed data points. We now assume that $\tau_x := xN$ is a natural number larger than zero. Accordingly, Eq. (11.15) can be expressed as

$$\begin{aligned} \Psi_x(H, \gamma) = \Big[\sum_{\mathcal{S}_x} \exp \Big\{ h \sum_{i=1}^{n} \Big(\sum_{a=1}^{\tau_x} S_i^{\{a\}} + N d_i \Big) \\ + \sum_{i<j} J_{ij} \Big(\sum_{a=1}^{\tau_x} S_i^{\{a\}} S_j^{\{a\}} + N d_{ij} \Big) \Big\} \Big]_{h, \boldsymbol{J}}, \end{aligned} \tag{11.16}$$

where $a, b \in \{1, 2, \ldots, \tau_x\}$ are the replica indices and $S_i^{\{a\}}$ is the ith variable in the ath replica. $\mathcal{S}_x := \{S_i^{\{a\}} \mid i = 1, 2, \ldots, n;\ a = 1, 2, \ldots, \tau_x\}$ is the set of all vari-

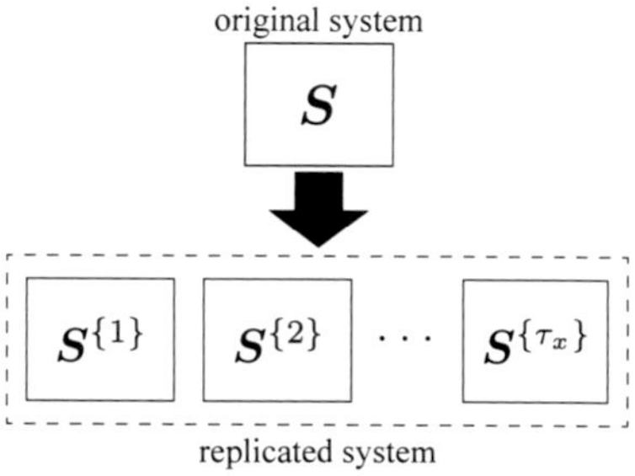

Fig. 11.2 Illustration of the replicated system. The τ_x replicas, $\boldsymbol{S}^{\{1\}}, \boldsymbol{S}^{\{2\}}, \ldots, \boldsymbol{S}^{\{\tau_x\}}$, arise from $Z(h, \boldsymbol{J})^{\tau_x}$ in Eq. (11.15)

ables in the replicated system (see Fig. 11.2) and $\sum_{\mathcal{S}_x}$ is the sum over all possible configurations of $\mathcal{S}_x$, that is,

$$\sum_{\mathcal{S}_x} := \prod_{i=1}^{n} \prod_{a=1}^{\tau_x} \sum_{S_i^{\{a\}}=\pm 1} .$$

We evaluate $\Psi_x(H, \gamma)$ under the assumption that τ_x is a natural number, and then we take the limit of $x \to -1$ from the evaluation result as an analytic continuation,[1] to obtain the empirical Bayes likelihood function (this is the so-called *replica trick*).

By employing the Gaussian prior in Eq. (11.8), Eq. (11.16) becomes

$$\Psi_x^{\mathrm{Gauss}}(H, \gamma) = \exp\Big\{nNHM + \frac{\gamma(n-1)N^2}{4}\Big(C_2 + \frac{x}{N}\Big) - F_x(H, \gamma)\Big\}, \quad (11.17)$$

where

$$M := \frac{1}{n}\sum_{i=1}^{n} d_i, \quad C_k := \frac{2}{n(n-1)}\sum_{i<j} d_{ij}^k, \quad (11.18)$$

and

$$F_x(H, \gamma) := -\ln \sum_{\mathcal{S}_x} \exp\big(-E_x(\mathcal{S}_x; H, \gamma)\big) \quad (11.19)$$

is the replicated (Helmholtz) free energy [20–23], where

[1] The justification for this analytic continuation may not be guaranteed mathematically. Thus, this type of analysis is regarded as "trick."

$$E_x(\mathcal{S}_x; H, \gamma) := -H \sum_{i=1}^{n} \sum_{a=1}^{\tau_x} S_i^{\{a\}} - \frac{\gamma N}{n} \sum_{i<j} d_{ij} \sum_{a=1}^{\tau_x} S_i^{\{a\}} S_j^{\{a\}}$$
$$- \frac{\gamma}{n} \sum_{i<j} \sum_{a<b} S_i^{\{a\}} S_j^{\{a\}} S_i^{\{b\}} S_j^{\{b\}} \tag{11.20}$$

is the Hamiltonian (or energy function) of the replicated system, where $\sum_{a<b}$ is the sum over all distinct pairs of replicas, that is, $\sum_{a<b} = \sum_{a=1}^{\tau_x} \sum_{b=a+1}^{\tau_x}$.

11.4.2 Plefka Expansion

Because the replicated free energy in Eq. (11.19) includes intractable multiple summations, an approximation is required to proceed with the current evaluation. In this section, the replicated free energy in Eq. (11.19) is approximated using the Plefka expansion [3]. In brief, the Plefka expansion is a perturbative expansion in Gibbs free energy that is a dual form of a corresponding Helmholtz free energy.

The Gibbs free energy is obtained as

$$G_x(m, H, \gamma) = -n\tau_x Hm + \operatorname*{extr}_{\lambda} \Big\{ \lambda n \tau_x m - \ln \sum_{\mathcal{S}_x} \exp\big(- E_x(\mathcal{S}_x; \lambda, \gamma)\big) \Big\}. \tag{11.21}$$

The derivation of this Gibbs free energy is described in Sect. 11.7.1. The summation in Eq. (11.21) can be performed when $\gamma = 0$, which gives

$$G_x(m, H, 0) = -n\tau_x Hm + n\tau_x \operatorname*{extr}_{\lambda} \big\{ \lambda m - \ln(2\cosh\lambda) \big\}$$
$$= -n\tau_x Hm + n\tau_x e(m), \tag{11.22}$$

where $e(m)$ is the negative mean-field entropy defined by

$$e(m) := \frac{1+m}{2} \ln \frac{1+m}{2} + \frac{1-m}{2} \ln \frac{1-m}{2}. \tag{11.23}$$

In the context of the Plefka expansion, the Gibbs free energy $G_x(m, H, \gamma)$ is approximated by the perturbation from $G_x(m, H, 0)$. Expanding $G_x(m, H, \gamma)$ around $\gamma = 0$ gives

$$\frac{G_x(m, H, \gamma)}{nN} = -xHm + xe(m) + \phi_x^{(1)}(m)\gamma + \phi_x^{(2)}(m)\gamma^2 + O(\gamma^3), \tag{11.24}$$

where $\phi_x^{(1)}(m)$ and $\phi_x^{(2)}(m)$ are the expansion coefficients defined by

$$\phi_x^{(k)}(m) := \frac{1}{nNk!}\lim_{\gamma\to 0}\frac{\partial^k G_x(m,H,\gamma)}{\partial \gamma^k}.$$

The forms of the two coefficients are presented in Eqs. (11.34) and (11.35) in Sect. 11.7.2.

From Eqs. (11.14), (11.17), (11.24), and (11.33), the approximation of the empirical Bayes likelihood function is obtained as

$$L_{\mathrm{EB}}(H,\gamma) \approx HM - \operatorname*{extr}_m\Big[Hm - e(m) + \Phi(m)\gamma + \phi_{-1}^{(2)}(m)\gamma^2\Big], \tag{11.25}$$

where

$$\Phi(m) := \phi_{-1}^{(1)}(m) - \frac{(n-1)N}{4n}\Big(C_2 - \frac{1}{N}\Big).$$

The forms of $\phi_{-1}^{(1)}(m)$ and $\phi_{-1}^{(2)}(m)$ are presented in Eqs. (11.37) and (11.38) in Sect. 11.7.2.

11.4.3 Algorithm for Hyperparameter Estimation

As mentioned in Sect. 11.3, the empirical Bayes inference is achieved by maximizing $L_{\mathrm{EB}}(H,\gamma)$ with respect to H and γ (cf. Eq. (11.12)). The extremum condition in Eq. (11.25) with respect to H leads to

$$\hat{m} = M, \tag{11.26}$$

where $\hat{m}$ is the value of m that satisfies the extremum condition in Eq. (11.25). By combining the extremum condition of Eq. (11.25) with respect to m with Eq. (11.26),

$$\hat{H} = \operatorname{atanh} M - \Big(\frac{\partial \phi_{-1}^{(1)}(M)}{\partial M}\gamma + \frac{\partial \phi_{-1}^{(2)}(M)}{\partial M}\gamma^2\Big) \tag{11.27}$$

is obtained, where atanh$x$ is the inverse function of $\tanh x$. From Eqs. (11.25) and (11.26), the optimal value of γ is obtained by

$$\hat{\gamma} = \arg\max_{\gamma}\big[-\Phi(M)\gamma - \phi_{-1}^{(2)}(M)\gamma^2\big]. \tag{11.28}$$

Since Eq. (11.28) represents a univariate quadratic optimization, $\hat{\gamma}$ is immediately obtained as follows: (i) when $\phi_{-1}^{(2)}(M) > 0$ and $\Phi(M) \geq 0$ or when $\phi_{-1}^{(2)}(M) = 0$ and $\Phi(M) > 0$, $\hat{\gamma} = 0$, (ii) when $\phi_{-1}^{(2)}(M) > 0$ and $\Phi(M) < 0$, $\hat{\gamma} = -\Phi(M)/(2\phi_{-1}^{(2)}(M))$, and (iii) $\hat{\gamma} \to \infty$, elsewhere. The case of $\phi_{-1}^{(2)}(M) = \Phi(M) = 0$ is ignored because it may be rarely observed in realistic settings. Using Eqs. (11.27) and (11.28), the solution to the empirical Bayes inference can be obtained without any iterative process. The pseudocode of the presented procedure is shown in Algorithm 1. The order of the computational complexity of the presented method is $O(Nn^2)$. Remember that the order of the computational complexity of the exact ML estimation is $O(2^n)$.

Algorithm 1 Proposed Inference Algorithm

1: **Input** Observed dataset: $\mathcal{D} := \{\mathbf{S}^{(\mu)} \in \{-1, +1\}^n \mid \mu = 1, 2, \ldots, N\}$.
2: Compute M, Ω, C_1, and C_2 using the dataset according to Eqs. (11.18) and (11.36).
3: Determine $\hat{\gamma}$ using Eq. (11.28):

$$\hat{\gamma} = \begin{cases} 0 & \text{case (i)} \\ -\Phi(M)/(2\phi_{-1}^{(2)}(M)) & \text{case (ii)} \\ \infty & \text{elsewhere,} \end{cases}$$

where case (i): $\phi_{-1}^{(2)}(M) > 0,\ \Phi(M) \geq 0$ or $\phi_{-1}^{(2)}(M) = 0,\ \Phi(M) > 0$ and case (ii): $\phi_{-1}^{(2)}(M) > 0,\ \Phi(M) < 0$.
4: Using $\hat{\gamma}$, determine $\hat{H}$ using Eq. (11.27).
5: **Output** $\hat{\gamma}$ and $\hat{H}$.

In the presented method, the value of $\hat{H}$ does not affect the determination of $\hat{\gamma}$. Several mean-field-based methods for BML (e.g., listed in Sect. 11.1) have similar procedures, in which $\hat{\boldsymbol{J}}_{\mathrm{ML}}$ is determined separately from $\hat{h}_{\mathrm{ML}}$. This is a common property of the mean-field-based methods for BML, including the current empirical Bayes problem.

Although the presented method is derived based on the Gauss prior presented in Eq. (11.8), the same procedure can be applied to the case of the Laplace prior presented in Eq. (11.9) [17].

11.5 Demonstration

This section discusses the results of numerical experiments. In these experiments, the observed dataset $\mathcal{D}$ was generated by the generative Boltzmann machine (gBM), which has the same form as Eq. (11.1), via Gibbs sampling (with a simulated-annealing-like strategy). The parameters of gBM were drawn from the prior distributions in Eqs. (11.4) and (11.10). This implies that the model-matched case (i.e., the generative and learning models are identical) was considered. In the following, the notation $\alpha := N/n$ and $J := \sqrt{\gamma}$ are used. The standard deviations of the Gaussian prior in Eq. (11.8) and the Laplace prior in Eq. (11.9) can thus be represented as $J/\sqrt{n}$. The hyperparameters of gBM are denoted by H_{true} and J_{true}.

11.5.1 Gaussian Prior Case

We now consider the case in which the prior distribution of $\boldsymbol{J}$ is the Gaussian prior in Eq. (11.8). In this case, the Boltzmann machine corresponds to the Sherrington-Kirkpatrick (SK) model [24], and thus exhibits a spin-glass transition at $J = 1$ when $h = 0$ (i.e., when $H = 0$).

We consider the case $H_{\mathrm{true}} = 0$. The scatter plots for the estimation of $\hat{J}$ for various J_{true} when $H_{\mathrm{true}} = 0$ and $\alpha = 0.4$ are shown in Fig. 11.3. When $J_{\mathrm{true}} < 1$, our estimates of $\hat{J}$ are significantly consistent with J_{true}. This implies that the validity of our perturbative approximation is lost in the spin-glass phase, as is often the case with several mean-field approximations. Figure 11.4 shows the scatter plots for various α. A smaller α causes $\hat{J}$ to be overestimated and a larger α causes it to be underestimated. In our experiments, at least, the optimal value of α seems to be $\alpha_{\mathrm{opt}} \approx 0.4$ when $H_{\mathrm{true}} = 0$. Our method can also estimate $\hat{H}$. The results for the estimation of $\hat{H}$ when $H_{\mathrm{true}} = 0$ and $\alpha = 0.4$ are shown in Fig. 11.5. Figure 11.5a, b shows the average of $|H_{\mathrm{true}} - \hat{H}|$ (i.e., the mean absolute error (MAE)) and the standard deviation of $\hat{H}$ over 300 experiments, respectively. The MAE and standard deviation increase in the region where $J_{\mathrm{true}} > 1$.

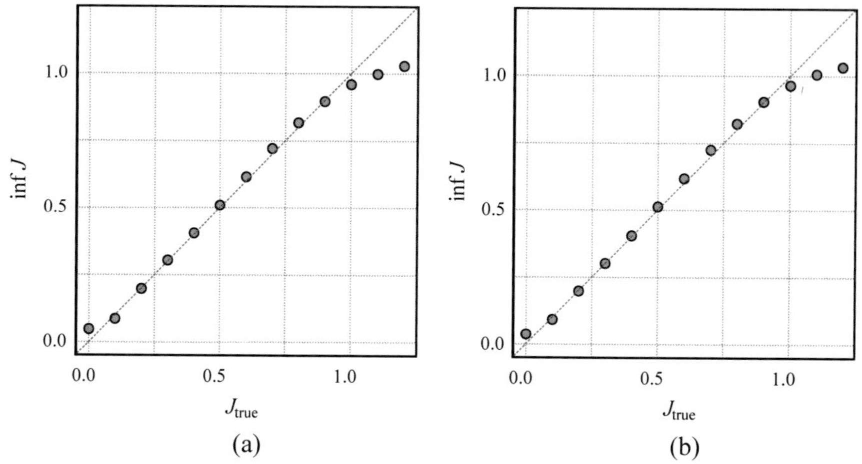

Fig. 11.3 Scatter plots of J_{true} (horizontal axis) versus $\hat{J}$ (vertical axis) when $H_{\mathrm{true}} = 0$ and $\alpha = 0.4$: **a** $n = 300$ and **b** $n = 500$. These plots represent the average values over 300 experiments

11.5.2 Laplace Prior Case

We now consider the case in which the prior distribution of $\boldsymbol{J}$ is the Laplace prior in Eq. (11.9). The scatter plots for the estimation of $\hat{J}$ for various values of J_{true} when $H_{\text{true}} = 0$ are shown in Fig. 11.6. The plots shown in Fig. 11.6 almost completely overlap with those in Fig. 11.4.

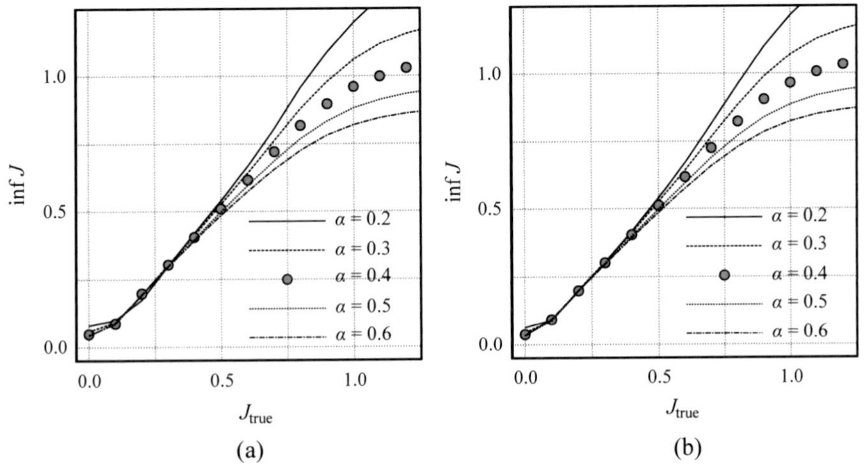

Fig. 11.4 Scatter plots of J_{true} (horizontal axis) versus $\hat{J}$ (vertical axis) for various $\alpha = N/n$ when $H_{\text{true}} = 0$: **a** $n = 300$ and **b** $n = 500$. These plots represent the average values over 300 experiments

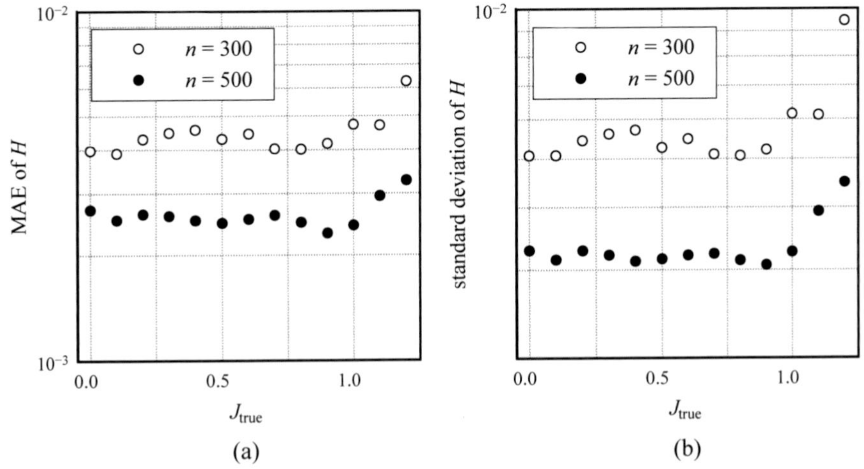

Fig. 11.5 Results of estimation of $\hat{H}$ versus J_{true} when $H_{\text{true}} = 0$ and $\alpha = 0.4$: **a** the MAE and **b** standard deviation. These plots represent the average values over 300 experiments

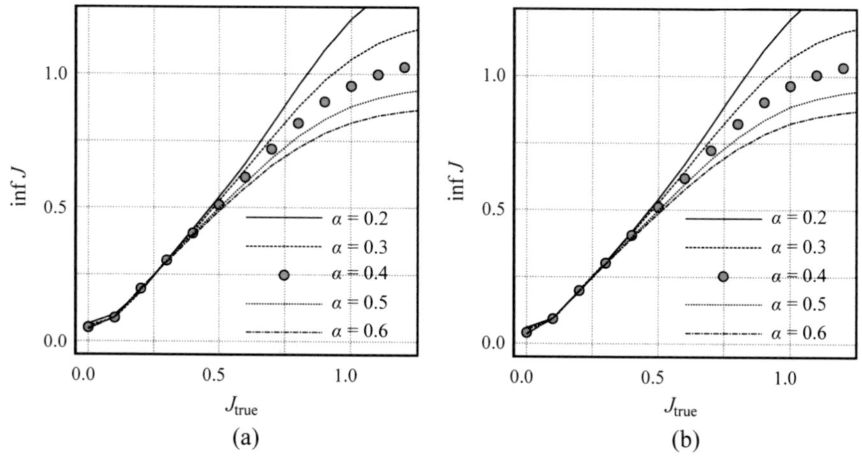

Fig. 11.6 Scatter plots of J_{true} (horizontal axis) versus $\hat{J}$ (vertical axis) for various $\alpha = N/n$, when $H_{\text{true}} = 0$, in the case of the Laplace prior: **a** $n = 300$ and **b** $n = 500$. These plots represent the average values over 300 experiments

11.6 Summary and Discussion

This chapter describes the hyperparameter inference algorithm proposed in [17]. As evident from the numerical experiments, the proposed inference method in both the Gaussian and Laplace prior cases works efficiently except for the spin-glass phase. However, the presented method has the drawback that it is sensitive to the value of $\alpha = N/n$. In the experiments in Sect. 11.5, although $\alpha \approx 0.4$ was appropriate when $H_{\text{true}} = 0$, it is known that the appropriate value decreases as H_{true} increases [17]. Since we cannot know the value of H_{true} in advance, the appropriate setting of α is also unknown. Estimation of α_{opt} is an open problem. It seems to be unnatural that there exists an optimal value of α because larger datasets are better in usual machine learning. Such peculiar behavior can be attributed to the truncating approximation in the Plefka expansion. A more detailed discussion of this issue is presented in [17].

Finally, we review the presented method from the perspective of sublinear computation without considering the aforementioned issues. The Boltzmann machine given in Eq. (11.1) has p parameters, where $p = O(n^2)$. In usual machine learning, $N = O(p)$ is, at least, required to obtain a good ML estimate for the Boltzmann machine. Therefore, a hyperparameter inference "without" the empirical Bayes method (namely, the strategy in which the hyperparameters are inferred through the ML estimate in a similar manner as that discussed in the latter part of Sect. 11.3) requires a dataset of size $O(p)$. However, the presented method requires only $N = O(n) = O(\sqrt{p})$ because $\alpha = O(1)$ with respect to n.

Acknowledgements This work was partially supported by JSPS KAKENHI (Grant Numbers: 15H03699, 18K11459, 18H03303, 25120013, and 17H00764), JST CREST (Grant Number: JPMJCR1402), and the COI Program from the JST (Grant Number JPMJCE1312).

11.7 Appendices

11.7.1 Appendix 1: Gibbs Free Energy

In this appendix, we derive the Gibbs free energy for the replicated (Helmholtz) free energy in Eq. (11.19).

The replicated free energy is obtained by minimizing the variational free energy, defined by

$$f[Q] := \sum_{\mathcal{S}_x} E_x(\mathcal{S}; H, \gamma) Q(\mathcal{S}_x) + \sum_{\mathcal{S}_x} Q(\mathcal{S}_x) \ln Q(\mathcal{S}_x), \tag{11.29}$$

under the normalization constraint, that is, $\sum_{\mathcal{S}_x} Q(\mathcal{S}_x) = 1$, where $Q(\mathcal{S}_x)$ is a test distribution over $\mathcal{S}_x$, and $E_x(\mathcal{S}_x; H, \gamma)$ is the Hamiltonian for the replicated system defined in Eq. (11.20).

The Gibbs free energy is obtained by adding new constraints to the minimization of $f[Q]$. We add the relationship

$$m = \frac{1}{n\tau_x} \sum_{i=1}^{n} \sum_{a=1}^{\tau_x} \sum_{\mathcal{S}_x} S_i^{\{a\}} Q(\mathcal{S}_x) \tag{11.30}$$

as the constraint. Using Lagrange multipliers, the Gibbs free energy is obtained as

$$\begin{aligned} G_x(m, H, \gamma) := \operatorname*{extr}_{Q,\lambda,r} \Big\{ f[Q] - r\Big(\sum_{\mathcal{S}_x} Q(\mathcal{S}_x) - 1\Big) \\ - \lambda\Big(\sum_{i=1}^{n} \sum_{a=1}^{\tau_x} \sum_{\mathcal{S}_x} S_i^{\{a\}} Q(\mathcal{S}_x) - n\tau_x m\Big)\Big\}, \end{aligned} \tag{11.31}$$

where "extr" denotes the extremum with respect to the assigned parameters, and r and λ are the Lagrange multipliers for the normalization constraint of $Q(\mathcal{S}_x)$ and the constraint in Eq. (11.30), respectively. Performing the extremum operation with respect to $Q(\mathcal{S})$ and r in Eq. (11.31) gives

$$G_x(m, H, \gamma) = \operatorname*{extr}_{\lambda} \Big\{ \lambda n\tau_x m - \ln \sum_{\mathcal{S}_x} \exp\big(-E_x(\mathcal{S}_x; H + \lambda, \gamma)\big)\Big\}. \tag{11.32}$$

The replicated free energy in Eq. (11.19) coincides with the extremum of this Gibbs free energy with respect to m, that is,

$$F_x(H, \gamma) = \operatorname*{extr}_{m}\, G_x(m, H, \gamma). \tag{11.33}$$

By performing the shift $H + \lambda \to \lambda$ in Eq. (11.32), Eq. (11.21) is obtained.

11.7.2 Appendix 2: Coefficients of Plefka Expansion

This appendix presents the coefficients of the Plefka expansion in Eq. (11.24). Refer to Ref. [17] for a detailed derivation. The first-order coefficient is given by

$$\phi_x^{(1)}(m) = -\frac{x(n-1)NC_1}{2n}m^2 - \frac{(n-1)K_x}{2nN}m^4, \tag{11.34}$$

where $K_x := \tau_x(\tau_x - 1)/2$. The second-order coefficient is given by

$$\begin{aligned}\phi_x^{(2)}(m) = &-\frac{(n-1)^2\tau_x N\Omega}{2n^2}m^2(1-m^2) - \frac{(n-1)\tau_x NC_2}{4n^2}(1-m^2)^2\\ &-\frac{(n-1)K_xC_1}{n^2}m^2(1-m^2)^2 - \frac{(n-1)K_x}{2n^2N}\big(n+\tau_x-3\big)m^4(1-m^2)^2\\ &-\frac{(n-1)K_x}{4n^2N}(1-m^4)^2,\end{aligned} \tag{11.35}$$

where Ω in the first term of Eq. (11.35) is defined as

$$\Omega := \frac{1}{n}\sum_{i=1}^{n}\omega_i^2, \quad \omega_i := \frac{1}{n-1}\sum_{j\in\partial(i)} d_{ij} - C_1, \tag{11.36}$$

where $\partial(i) := \{1, 2, \ldots, n\} \setminus \{i\}$. When $x = -1$, these coefficients are

$$\phi_{-1}^{(1)}(m) = \frac{(n-1)NC_1}{2n}m^2 - \frac{(n-1)(N+1)}{4n}m^4, \tag{11.37}$$

$$\begin{aligned}\phi_{-1}^{(2)}(m) = &\frac{(n-1)^2N^2\Omega}{2n^2}m^2(1-m^2) + \frac{(n-1)N^2C_2}{4n^2}(1-m^2)^2\\ &-\frac{(n-1)N(N+1)C_1}{2n^2}m^2(1-m^2)^2\\ &-\frac{(n-1)(N+1)}{4n^2}\big(n-N-3\big)m^4(1-m^2)^2 - \frac{(n-1)(N+1)}{8n^2}(1-m^4)^2.\end{aligned} \tag{11.38}$$

References

1. D.H. Ackley, G.E. Hinton, T.J. Sejnowski, A learning algorithm for Boltzmann machines. Cognit. Sci. **9**, 147–169 (1985)
2. Y. Roudi, E. Aurell, J. Hertz, Statistical physics of pairwise probability models. Front. Comput. Neurosci. **3**, 1–22 (2009)
3. T. Plefka, Convergence condition of the TAP equation for the infinite-ranged Ising spin glass model. J. Phys. A Math. Gen. **15**(6), 1971–1978 (1982)
4. A. Pelizzola, Cluster variation method in statistical physics and probabilistic graphical models. J. Phys. A Math. Gen. **38**(33), R309 (2005)
5. H.J. Kappen, F.B. Rodríguez, Efficient learning in Boltzmann machines using linear response theory. Neural Comput. **10**(5), 1137–1156 (1998)
6. T. Tanaka, Mean-field theory of Boltzmann machine learning. Phys. Rev. E **58**, 2302–2310 (1998)
7. M. Yasuda, T. Horiguchi, Triangular approximation for information ising model and its application to Boltzmann machine. Physica A **368**, 83–95 (2006)
8. V. Sessak, R. Monasson, Small-correlation expansions for the inverse Ising problem. J. Phys. A Math. Theoret. **42**(5) (2009)
9. M. Yasuda, K. Tanaka, Approximate learning algorithm in Boltzmann machines. Neural Comput. **21**(11), 3130–3178 (2009)
10. F. Ricci-Tersenghi, The Bethe approximation for solving the inverse Ising problem: a comparison with other inference methods. J. Stat. Mech. Theory Experi. **2012**(08), P08015 (2012)
11. C. Furtlehner, Approximate inverse Ising models close to a Bethe reference point. J. Stat. Mech. Theor. Exp. **2013**(09), P09020 (2013)
12. J. Sohl-Dickstein, P.B. Battaglino, M.R. DeWeese, New method for parameter estimation in probabilistic models: minimum probability flow. Phys. Rev. Lett. **107** (2011)
13. M. Yasuda, Monte Carlo integration using spatial structure of Markov random field. J. Phys. Soc. Jpn. **84**(3) (2015)
14. M. Yasuda, K. Uchizawa, A generalization of spatial monte carlo integration. Neural Comput. **33**(4), 1037–1062 (2021)
15. D.J.C. MacKay, Bayesian interpolation. Neural Comput. **4**(3), 415–447 (1992)
16. C.M. Bishop, *Pattern Recognition and Machine Learning* (Springer, 2006)
17. M. Yasuda, T. Obuchi, Empirical Bayes method for Boltzmann machines. J. Phys. A Math. Theoret. **53**(1), 014004 (2019)
18. M. Mezard, G. Parisi, M. Virasoro, *Spin Glass Theory and Beyond: An Introduction to the Replica Method and Its Applications* (World Scientific, Singapore, 1987)
19. H. Nishimori, *Statistical Physics of Spin Glass and Information Processing—Introduction* (Oxford University Press, 2001)
20. T. Rizzo, A. Lage-Castellanos, R. Mulet, F. Ricci-Tersenghi, Replica cluster variational method. J. Stat. Phys. **139**, 375–416 (2010)
21. M. Yasuda, Y. Kabashima, K. Tanaka, Replica plefka expansion of Ising systems. J. Stat. Mech. Theor. Exp. P04002 (2012)
22. A. Lage-Castellanos, R. Mulet, F. Ricci-Tersenghi, T. Rizzo, Replica cluster variational method: the replica symmetric solution for the 2d random bond ising model. J. Phys. A Math. Theor. **46**(13) (2013)
23. M. Yasuda, S. Kataoka, K. Tanaka, Statistical analysis of loopy belief propagation in random fields. Phys. Rev. E **92**, 042120 (2015)
24. D. Sherrington, S. Kirkpatrick, Solvable model of a spin-glass. Phys. Rev. Lett. **35**, 1792–1796 (1975)

Open Access This chapter is licensed under the terms of the Creative Commons Attribution 4.0 International License (http://creativecommons.org/licenses/by/4.0/), which permits use, sharing, adaptation, distribution and reproduction in any medium or format, as long as you give appropriate credit to the original author(s) and the source, provide a link to the Creative Commons license and indicate if changes were made.

The images or other third party material in this chapter are included in the chapter's Creative Commons license, unless indicated otherwise in a credit line to the material. If material is not included in the chapter's Creative Commons license and your intended use is not permitted by statutory regulation or exceeds the permitted use, you will need to obtain permission directly from the copyright holder.

Chapter 12
Dynamical Analysis of Quantum Annealing

Anthony C. C. Coolen, Theodore Nikoletopoulos, Shunta Arai, and Kazuyuki Tanaka

Abstract Quantum annealing aims to provide a faster method than classical computing for finding the minima of complicated functions, and it has created increasing interest in the relaxation dynamics of quantum spin systems. Moreover, problems in quantum annealing caused by first-order phase transitions can be reduced via appropriate temporal adjustment of control parameters, and in order to do this optimally, it is helpful to predict the evolution of the system at the level of macroscopic observables. Solving the dynamics of quantum ensembles is nontrivial, requiring modeling of both the quantum spin system and its interaction with the environment with which it exchanges energy. An alternative approach to the dynamics of quantum spin systems was proposed about a decade ago. It involves creating stochastic proxy dynamics via the Suzuki-Trotter mapping of the quantum ensemble to a classical one (the quantum Monte Carlo method), and deriving from this new dynamics closed macroscopic equations for macroscopic observables using the dynamical replica method. In this chapter, we give an introduction to this approach, focusing on the ideas and assumptions behind the derivations, and on its potential and limitations.

12.1 Quantum Ensembles and Their Dynamics

We imagine an ensemble of K independent quantum systems $|\psi^\alpha\rangle$, labeled by $\alpha = 1 \ldots K$, all with the same Hamiltonian but distinct initial conditions. Making a measurement of an observable A in this ensemble means randomly picking one of the K systems, with equal probabilities, and measuring A in the selected system. The average of the observable A can then be written as $\langle A\rangle = \mathrm{Tr}(\rho A)$, where ρ, the density matrix, is the Hermitian nonnegative definite operator $\rho = K^{-1}\sum_{\alpha=1}^{K} |\psi^\alpha\rangle\langle\psi^\alpha|$,

A. C. C. Coolen (✉) · T. Nikoletopoulos
Department of Biophysics, Faculty of Science, Radboud University, 6525AJ Nijmegen, The Netherlands
e-mail: a.coolen@science.ru.nl

Saddle Point Science Ltd, York, United Kingdom

S. Arai · K. Tanaka
Graduate School of Information Sciences, Tohoku University, Sendai 980-8579, Japan

© The Author(s) 2022

N. Katoh et al. (eds.), *Sublinear Computation Paradigm*,
https://doi.org/10.1007/978-981-16-4095-7_12

with $\mathrm{Tr}(\rho) = 1$. Since ρ is Hermitian it has a complete basis of eigenstates $\{|k\rangle\}$. Its eigenvalues w_k, which are nonnegative and normalized according to $\sum_k w_k = 1$, can be interpreted as probabilities. We can now write $\langle A\rangle = \sum_n a_n \sum_k w_k |\langle k|n\rangle|^2$. Hence the probability of measuring eigenvalue a_n of observable A in the ensemble is $P_n = \sum_k w_k |\langle k|n\rangle|^2$, where $|\langle k|n\rangle|^2$ is the probability of observing a_n in eigenstate k of the density matrix, and w_k is the probability of finding the ensemble in eigenstate k.

The evolution of the density matrix follows from the evolution of the states $|\psi^\alpha\rangle$, each governed by the Schrödinger equation, giving $\frac{\mathrm{d}}{\mathrm{d}t}\rho = (\mathrm{i}\hbar)^{-1}[H, \rho]$. The solution is $\rho = \mathrm{e}^{-\mathrm{i}Ht/\hbar}\rho_{t=0}\,\mathrm{e}^{\mathrm{i}Ht/\hbar}$. In particular, it follows using the eigenbasis $\{|E\rangle\}$ of H that

$$\langle H\rangle = \sum_E \langle E|\mathrm{e}^{-\mathrm{i}Ht/\hbar}\rho_{t=0}\,\mathrm{e}^{\mathrm{i}Ht/\hbar}H|E\rangle \;=\; \langle H\rangle_{t=0}. \tag{12.1}$$

At equilibrium $[H, \rho] = 0$. The density matrix can therefore be diagonalized simultaneously with H, that is, $\rho = \sum_E f(E)|E\rangle\langle E|$. The values of $f(E)$ define the type of equilibrium ensemble at hand. In the canonical ensemble we have $f(E) = \exp(-\beta E)/\mathcal{Z}(\beta)$, so

$$\rho = \frac{1}{\mathcal{Z}(\beta)}\sum_E \mathrm{e}^{-\beta E}|E\rangle\langle E| \;=\; \frac{1}{\mathcal{Z}(\beta)}\mathrm{e}^{-\beta H}. \tag{12.2}$$

The quantum partition function $\mathcal{Z}(\beta)$ follows from $\mathrm{Tr}(\rho) = 1$: $\mathcal{Z}(\beta) = \mathrm{Tr}(\mathrm{e}^{-\beta H})$. The free energy and the average internal energy are given by $\mathcal{F} = -\beta^{-1}\log\mathcal{Z}(\beta)$ and $\mathcal{E} = -\frac{\partial}{\partial\beta}\log\mathcal{Z}(\beta)$. The expectation values of operators become $\langle A\rangle = \mathcal{Z}(\beta)^{-1}$ $\mathrm{Tr}(\mathrm{e}^{-\beta H}A)$. Note that if the systems of the ensemble evolve strictly according to the Schrödinger equation, there cannot be generic evolution of ρ toward the equilibrium form in Eq. (12.2). For any initial density operator with $\langle H\rangle_{t=0} \neq \mathcal{E}$ this is ruled out by Eq. (12.1). Since the state in Eq. (12.2) describes the result of equilibration of quantum systems in a heat bath with which they can exchange energy, a correct description of the dynamics requires a Hamiltonian that also describes the degrees of freedom of the heat bath.

This is the first obstacle in the analysis of the dynamics of quantum ensembles: it is difficult even to write down the correct microscopic dynamical laws. A similar situation occurs also in the classical setting. Without a heat bath we have a micro-canonical ensemble with conserved energy. Deriving the Gibbs-Boltzmann distribution from the joint dynamics of the system and heat bath requires us to connect deterministic trajectories to invariant measures via ergodic theory and to subsequently derive the form of these measures, which has so far proven possible for only a handful of models.

The approach followed in [1] was to circumvent ensembles altogether and solve the Schrödinger equation for small systems in which a decaying longitudinal field acts as quantum noise (which is indeed what happens in quantum annealing). In classical systems one often *defines* the pain away. One constructs an intuitively reasonable stochastic process that evolves toward the Gibbs-Boltzmann state, usually of the Markov Chain Monte Carlo (MCMC) form. This process is studied as a proxy for the dynamics of the original system. The price paid is that one cannot be sure to what extent the stochastic dynamics are close to those of the original system. The MCMC equations are not even unique, since there are many choices that evolve to the Gibbs-Boltzmann state. The same dynamics strategy can be applied to quantum systems if the latter can be mapped to classical ones. This is achieved by the Suzuki-Trotter formalism [4].

12.2 Quantum Monte Carlo Dynamics

In order to apply quantum annealing to optimization problems formulated in terms of binary variables, one needs spin-$\frac{1}{2}$ particles [1]. These are labeled by $i = 1 \ldots N$, with Pauli matrices $\{\sigma_i^x, \sigma_i^y, \sigma_i^z\}$. In the standard representation of σ^z-eigenstates:

$$\sigma^x = \begin{pmatrix} 0 & 1 \\ 1 & 0 \end{pmatrix}, \quad \sigma^y = \begin{pmatrix} 0 & -\mathrm{i} \\ \mathrm{i} & 0 \end{pmatrix}, \quad \sigma^z = \begin{pmatrix} 1 & 0 \\ 0 & -1 \end{pmatrix}.$$

In quantum annealing one chooses Hamiltonians of the form $H = H_0 + H_1$, in which H_0 is obtained by replacing the classical spins $\sigma_i = \pm 1$ in an Ising Hamiltonian by the matrices σ_i^z and a second part H_1 that acts as a form of quantum noise[1]:

$$H_0 = -\sum_{i<j} J_{ij} \sigma_i^z \sigma_j^z - h \sum_i \sigma_i^z, \qquad H_1 = -\Gamma \sum_i \sigma_i^x. \tag{12.3}$$

H_0 represents the quantity to be minimized in our optimization problem. The classical state achieving this minimum follows from the quantum ground state of the system upon moving the parameters Γ and β^{-1} adiabatically slowly to zero and is hence obtained from the partition function $\mathcal{Z}(\beta) = \mathrm{Tr}(\mathrm{e}^{-\beta H_0 - \beta H_1})$. For excellent reviews of the physics and the applications of the above types of quantum spin systems with transverse fields, we refer to [2, 3].

The Suzuki-Trotter procedure [4] allows us to convert the above quantum problem into a classical one using the operator identity

$$\mathrm{e}^{A+B} = \lim_{M \to \infty} \left(\mathrm{e}^{A/M} \mathrm{e}^{B/M} \right)^M. \tag{12.4}$$

From now on we assume that A and B are Hermitian operators, and we write the basis of eigenstates of A as $\{|n\rangle\}$. We then obtain after some simple manipulations:

---

[1] For simplicity, we choose H_0 here to be quadratic in the spins, and the external field to be uniform, but this is not essential.

$$\mathrm{Tr}(\mathrm{e}^{A+B}) = \lim_{M\to\infty} \sum_{n_1\ldots n_M} \mathrm{e}^{\sum_{k=1}^{M} a_{n_k}/M} \prod_{k,\ \mathrm{mod}(M)} \langle n_k|\mathrm{e}^{B/M}|n_{k+1}\rangle. \tag{12.5}$$

Application to $A = -\beta H_0$ and $B = -\beta H_1$, where the relevant basis is that of the joint eigenstates of all $\{\sigma_i^z\}$, that is, $|s_1,\ldots,s_N\rangle = |s_1\rangle \otimes \ldots \otimes |s_N\rangle$, with $s_i = \pm 1$ and $\sigma_i^z|s_1,\ldots,s_N\rangle = s_i|s_1,\ldots,s_N\rangle$, gives $\mathcal{Z}(\beta) = \lim_{M\to\infty} \mathcal{Z}_M(\beta)$, where

$$\begin{aligned}\mathcal{Z}_M(\beta) &= \sum_{\{s_{ik}=\pm1\}} \mathrm{e}^{(\beta/M)\sum_{k=1}^{M}[\sum_{i<j} J_{ij}s_{ik}s_{jk}+h\sum_i s_{ik}]} \prod_{k,\ \mathrm{mod}(M)} \prod_{i=1}^{N} \langle s_{ik}|\mathrm{e}^{(\beta\Gamma/M)\sigma_i^x}|s_{i,k+1}\rangle \\ &= \mathrm{e}^{\frac{1}{2}NM\log[\frac{1}{2}\sinh(2\beta\Gamma/M)]} \\ &\quad\times \sum_{\{s_{ik}=\pm1\}} \mathrm{e}^{(\beta/M)\sum_{k=1}^{M}[\sum_{i<j} J_{ij}s_{ik}s_{jk}+h\sum_i s_{ik}]+B\sum_{k,\mathrm{mod}(M)}\sum_i s_{ik}s_{i,k+1}}.\end{aligned} \tag{12.6}$$

in which $B = -\frac{1}{2}\log\tanh(\beta\Gamma/M)$. Thus the partition function of the N-spin quantum system is mapped (apart from a constant) onto the limit $M \to \infty$ of that of a classical Ising model with NM spins $\boldsymbol{s} = \{s_{ik}\}$, with Hamiltonian $H(\boldsymbol{s})$ and asymptotic free energy density $f = \lim_{N\to\infty} \lim_{M\to\infty} f_{N,M}$:

$$\begin{aligned}H(\boldsymbol{s}) &= -\frac{1}{M}\sum_{k=1}^{M}\sum_{i<j} J_{ij}s_{ik}s_{jk} - \frac{h}{M}\sum_{k=1}^{M}\sum_{i} s_{ik} \\ &\quad -\frac{B}{\beta}\sum_{k,\mathrm{mod}(M)}\sum_{i} s_{ik}s_{i,k+1},\end{aligned} \tag{12.7}$$

$$\begin{aligned}f_{N,M} &= -\frac{M}{2\beta}\log\left[\frac{1}{2}\sinh(2\beta\Gamma/M)\right] \\ &\quad -\frac{1}{\beta N}\log\sum_{\{s_{ik}=\pm1\}} \mathrm{e}^{\frac{\beta}{M}\sum_{k=1}^{M}[\sum_{i<j} J_{ij}s_{ik}s_{jk}+h\sum_i s_{ik}]+B\sum_{k,\mathrm{mod}(M)}\sum_i s_{ik}s_{i,k+1}}.\end{aligned} \tag{12.8}$$

The new system in Eq. (12.8), for $M\to\infty$ equivalent to the original quantum one, lends itself to constructing a stochastic dynamics. We first write the Suzuki-Trotter Hamiltonian in the standard form of NM interacting Ising spins in an external field:

$$H(\boldsymbol{s}) = -\frac{1}{2}\sum_{ik,j\ell} s_{ik}J_{ik,j\ell}s_{j\ell} - \theta\sum_{ik} s_{ik}, \tag{12.9}$$

$$J_{ik,j\ell} = \frac{1}{M}\delta_{k\ell}J_{ij}(1-\delta_{ij}) + \frac{B}{\beta}\delta_{ij}(\delta_{k,\ell+1}+\delta_{\ell,k+1}), \qquad \theta = h/M. \tag{12.10}$$

The conventional Glauber dynamics by which this classical system evolves toward the equilibrium state with the above Hamiltonian is, after switching to continuous time [5] and denoting by $p_t(\boldsymbol{s})$ the probability of finding the system in state $\boldsymbol{s}$ at time t:

$$\tau \frac{\mathrm{d}}{\mathrm{d}t} p_t(\boldsymbol{s}) = \sum_{i=1}^{N} \sum_{k=1}^{M} \Big\{ p_t(F_{ik}\boldsymbol{s}) w_{ik}(F_{ik}\boldsymbol{s}) - p_t(\boldsymbol{s}) w_{ik}(\boldsymbol{s}) \Big\}, \tag{12.11}$$

$$w_{ik}(\boldsymbol{s}) = \frac{1}{2}[1 - s_{ik} \tanh(\beta h_{ik}(\boldsymbol{s}))], \qquad h_{ik}(\boldsymbol{s}) = \sum_{j\ell} J_{ik,j\ell} s_{j\ell} + \theta. \tag{12.12}$$

This master equation describes a process where at each step a site $i \in \{1, \dots, N\}$ and a Trotter slice $k \in \{1, \dots, M\}$ are picked at random, followed by an attempt to flip the spin s_{ik}. The $w_{ik}(\boldsymbol{s})$ denote transition rates for $s_{ik} \to -s_{ik}$. F_{ik} is an operator that flips spin s_{ik} and leaves all others invariant. The parameter τ defines time units such that the average duration of a single spin update is τ/N. Working out the local fields $h_{ik}(\boldsymbol{s})$ gives

$$h_{ik}(\boldsymbol{s}) = \frac{1}{M} \sum_{j \neq i} J_{ij} s_{jk} + \frac{B}{\beta}(s_{i,k+1} + s_{i,k-1}) + h/M. \tag{12.13}$$

The process in Eqs. (12.11, 12.12) is suitable for numerical simulation and defines the quantum Monte Carlo dynamics for the ensemble with Hamiltonian given by Eq. (12.3) provided we take $M \to \infty$. When applied to quantum annealing models, some authors have called it 'simulated quantum annealing'. The definition in Eqs. (12.11, 12.12), however, is not unique. Many alternative stochastic processes evolve toward the same Gibbs-Boltzmann state (see, e.g., [6]).

12.3 Dynamical Replica Analysis

The remaining challenge is to extract formulae describing the evolution of relevant macroscopic quantities from Eqs. (12.11, 12.12). This was addressed in [7–10] using the so-called dynamical replica method (DRT) [12–14]. In this chapter, we deviate from the definitions in [7–10] and stay closer to the original DRT ideas.

The dynamics (12.11, 12.12) imply that expectation values $\langle G(\boldsymbol{s})\rangle = \sum_{\boldsymbol{s}} p_t(\boldsymbol{s}) G(\boldsymbol{s})$ evolve according to:

$$\tau \frac{\mathrm{d}}{\mathrm{d}t} \langle G(\boldsymbol{s}) \rangle = \sum_{i=1}^{N} \sum_{k=1}^{M} \sum_{\boldsymbol{s}} p_t(\boldsymbol{s}) w_{ik}(\boldsymbol{s}) \Big[G(F_{ik}\boldsymbol{s}) - G(\boldsymbol{s}) \Big]. \tag{12.14}$$

To study the joint dynamics of a set of L observables $\boldsymbol{\Omega}(\boldsymbol{s}) = (\Omega_1(\boldsymbol{s}), \dots, \Omega_L(\boldsymbol{s}))$ we substitute $G(\boldsymbol{s}) = \delta[\boldsymbol{\Omega} - \boldsymbol{\Omega}(\boldsymbol{s})]$. Now $\langle G(\boldsymbol{s}) \rangle = P_t(\boldsymbol{\Omega})$, and

$$\tau \frac{\mathrm{d}}{\mathrm{d}t} P_t(\boldsymbol{\Omega}) = \sum_{i=1}^{N} \sum_{k=1}^{M} \sum_{\boldsymbol{s}} p_t(\boldsymbol{s}) w_{ik}(\boldsymbol{s}) \Big[\delta[\boldsymbol{\Omega} - \boldsymbol{\Omega}(F_{ik}\boldsymbol{s})] - \delta[\boldsymbol{\Omega} - \boldsymbol{\Omega}(\boldsymbol{s})] \Big]. \tag{12.15}$$

If the observables $\Omega_\mu(\boldsymbol{s})$ are $\mathcal{O}(1)$ and macroscopic in nature, their susceptibility to single spin flips $\Delta_{jk\mu}(\boldsymbol{s}) = \Omega_\mu(F_{ik}\boldsymbol{s}) - \Omega_\mu(\boldsymbol{s})$ will be small. We can then define $\boldsymbol{\Delta}_{jk} = (\Delta_{jk1}(\boldsymbol{s}), \ldots, \Delta_{jkL}(\boldsymbol{s})) \in \mathbb{R}^L$, and expand (12.15) in a distributional sense, that is,

$$\tau \frac{\mathrm{d}}{\mathrm{d}t} \int \mathrm{d}\boldsymbol{\Omega}\; P_t(\boldsymbol{\Omega}) G(\boldsymbol{\Omega}) = \int \mathrm{d}\boldsymbol{\Omega}\; G(\boldsymbol{\Omega}) \sum_{\ell \geq 1} \frac{(-1)^\ell}{\ell!} \frac{\partial^\ell}{\partial \Omega_{\mu_1} \ldots \partial \Omega_{\mu_\ell}}$$
$$\times \left\{ \sum_{\mu_1=1}^{L} \cdots \sum_{\mu_\ell=1}^{L} \sum_{i=1}^{N} \sum_{k=1}^{M} \Big\langle w_{ik}(\boldsymbol{s}) \delta[\boldsymbol{\Omega} - \boldsymbol{\Omega}(\boldsymbol{s})] \Delta_{ik\mu_{1'}}(\boldsymbol{s}) \ldots \Delta_{ik\mu_\ell}(\boldsymbol{s}) \Big\rangle \right\}. \quad (12.16)$$

We thereby arrive at the following Kramers-Moyal expansion

$$\tau \frac{\mathrm{d}}{\mathrm{d}t} P_t(\boldsymbol{\Omega}) = \sum_{\ell \geq 1} \frac{(-1)^\ell}{\ell!} \sum_{\mu_1=1}^{L} \cdots \sum_{\mu_\ell=1}^{L} \frac{\partial^\ell}{\partial \Omega_{\mu_1} \ldots \partial \Omega_{\mu_\ell}} \left\{ P_t(\boldsymbol{\Omega}) F^{(\ell)}_{\mu_1 \ldots \mu_\ell}[\boldsymbol{\Omega}; t] \right\}, \quad (12.17)$$

with

$$F^{(\ell)}_{\mu_1 \ldots \mu_\ell}[\boldsymbol{\Omega}; t] = \left\langle \sum_{i=1}^{N} \sum_{k=1}^{M} w_{ik}(\boldsymbol{s}) \Delta_{ik\mu_1}(\boldsymbol{s}) \ldots \Delta_{ik\mu_\ell}(\boldsymbol{s}) \right\rangle_{\boldsymbol{\Omega};t}, \quad (12.18)$$

$$\langle f(\boldsymbol{s}) \rangle_{\boldsymbol{\Omega};t} = \frac{\sum_{\boldsymbol{s}} p_t(\boldsymbol{s}) \delta[\boldsymbol{\Omega} - \boldsymbol{\Omega}(\boldsymbol{s})] f(\boldsymbol{s})}{\sum_{\boldsymbol{s}} p_t(\boldsymbol{s}) \delta[\boldsymbol{\Omega} - \boldsymbol{\Omega}(\boldsymbol{s})]}. \quad (12.19)$$

Asymptotically, that is, for $N, M \to \infty$, only the first term of Eq. (12.17) survives if

$$\lim_{N,M \to \infty} \sum_{\ell \geq 2} \frac{1}{\ell!} \sum_{\mu_1=1}^{L} \cdots \sum_{\mu_\ell=1}^{L} \sum_{i=1}^{N} \sum_{k=1}^{M} \Big\langle |\Delta_{ik\mu_1}(\boldsymbol{s}) \ldots \Delta_{ik\mu_\ell}(\boldsymbol{s})| \Big\rangle_{\boldsymbol{\Omega};t} = 0. \quad (12.20)$$

If all $\Delta_{ik\mu}(\boldsymbol{s})$ scale similarly, that is, $\exists \tilde{\Delta}_{N,M}$ such that $\Delta_{ik\mu}(\boldsymbol{s}) = \mathcal{O}(\tilde{\Delta}_{N,M})$ for $N, M \to \infty$, then Eq. (12.17) retains only its first term if $\lim_{N,M\to\infty} L\tilde{\Delta}_{N,M}\sqrt{NM} = 0$. In that case it reduces to a Liouville equation describing deterministic evolution of $\boldsymbol{\Omega}$:

$$\tau \frac{\mathrm{d}}{\mathrm{d}t} \Omega_\mu = \left\langle \sum_{i=1}^{N} \sum_{k=1}^{M} w_{ik}(\boldsymbol{s}) \Delta_{ik\mu}(\boldsymbol{s}) \right\rangle_{\boldsymbol{\Omega};t}. \quad (12.21)$$

If $\lim_{N,M\to\infty} L\tilde{\Delta}_{N,M}\sqrt{NM} > 0$, we can no longer ignore the fluctuations in our observables $\boldsymbol{\Omega}(\boldsymbol{s})$, which limits our choice of observables.

Equation (12.21) is closed if $\sum_{i=1}^{N} \sum_{k=1}^{M} w_{ik}(\boldsymbol{s}) \Delta_{ik\mu}(\boldsymbol{s})$ is a function of $\boldsymbol{\Omega}(\boldsymbol{s})$ only (which would simply drop out). If this is not the case, we close Eq. (12.21) using a maximum entropy argument: we approximate $p_t(\boldsymbol{s})$ in Eq. (12.21) by a form that assumes that all micro-states with the same value for $\boldsymbol{\Omega}(\boldsymbol{s})$ are equally likely. Now Eq. (12.21) becomes

$$\tau \frac{\mathrm{d}}{\mathrm{d}t}\Omega_\mu = \frac{\sum_{\boldsymbol{s}} \delta[\boldsymbol{\Omega} - \boldsymbol{\Omega}(\boldsymbol{s})] \sum_{i=1}^{N} \sum_{k=1}^{M} w_{ik}(\boldsymbol{s}) \Delta_{ik\mu}(\boldsymbol{s})}{\sum_{\boldsymbol{s}} \delta[\boldsymbol{\Omega} - \boldsymbol{\Omega}(\boldsymbol{s})]}. \tag{12.22}$$

Within the replica formalism [16, 17], this closed equation can also be written as

$$\tau \frac{\mathrm{d}}{\mathrm{d}t}\Omega_\mu = \lim_{n\to 0} \sum_{\boldsymbol{s}^1 \ldots \boldsymbol{s}^n} \left(\prod_{\alpha=1}^{n} \delta[\boldsymbol{\Omega} - \boldsymbol{\Omega}(\boldsymbol{s}^\alpha)] \right) \sum_{i=1}^{N} \sum_{k=1}^{M} w_{ik}(\boldsymbol{s}^1) \Delta_{ik\mu}(\boldsymbol{s}^1). \tag{12.23}$$

The accuracy of Eq. (12.22) depends on our choice for the observables $\Omega_\mu(\boldsymbol{s})$. We want them to be $\mathcal{O}(1)$, obeying $\lim_{N,M\to\infty} L\tilde{\Delta}_{N,M}\sqrt{NM} = 0$, and such that the probability equipartitioning assumption is as harmless as possible. Including $H(\boldsymbol{s})/N$ and $N^{-1} \log p_0(\boldsymbol{s})$ in our set of observables ensures that equipartitioning holds for $t \to 0$ and $t \to \infty$. If we have disorder in the couplings $\{J_{ij}\}$, and for $N \to \infty$ our observables are self-averaging with respect to its realization, we can average over the disorder.[2] This gives

$$\tau \frac{\mathrm{d}}{\mathrm{d}t}\Omega_\mu = \lim_{n\to 0} \sum_{\boldsymbol{s}^1 \ldots \boldsymbol{s}^n} \overline{\left(\prod_{\alpha=1}^{n} \delta[\boldsymbol{\Omega} - \boldsymbol{\Omega}(\boldsymbol{s}^\alpha)] \right) \sum_{i=1}^{N} \sum_{k=1}^{M} w_{ik}(\boldsymbol{s}^1) \Delta_{ik\mu}(\boldsymbol{s}^1)}. \tag{12.24}$$

For the system in Eq. (12.8) and the typical initial conditions in quantum annealing, there are two natural and simple routes for choosing the observables in the DRT method,[3] all involving the normalized distinct energy contributions in Eq. (12.27):

- *Trotter slice-dependent observables*
  We choose, for $k = 1 \ldots M$ (mod M),

$$E_k(\boldsymbol{s}) = -\frac{1}{N}\sum_{i<j} J_{ij} s_{ik} s_{jk}, \quad m_k(\boldsymbol{s}) = \frac{1}{N}\sum_i s_{ik}, \quad \mathcal{E}_k(\boldsymbol{s}) = \frac{1}{N}\sum_i s_{ik} s_{i,k+1}. \tag{12.25}$$

Now $L = 3M$, and the susceptibilities of the observables to single spin flips are, using $\sum_j J_{ij} s_{jk} = \mathcal{O}(1)$ for all k (required for an extensive Hamiltonian):

$$\Delta_{ik} E_q(\boldsymbol{s}) = 2N^{-1} \delta_{qk} s_{ik} \sum_{j\neq i} J_{ij} s_{jk} = \mathcal{O}(N^{-1}), \tag{12.26}$$

$$\Delta_{ik} m_q(\boldsymbol{s}) = -2N^{-1} \delta_{qk} s_{ik} = \mathcal{O}(N^{-1}), \tag{12.27}$$

$$\Delta_{ik} \mathcal{E}_q(\boldsymbol{s}) = -2N^{-1} s_{ik} (\delta_{qk} s_{i,k+1} + \delta_{k,q+1} s_{i,k-1}) = \mathcal{O}(N^{-1}). \tag{12.28}$$

---

[2] Without disorder one does not need the replica formalism yet and can work directly with (12.22).

[3] One can always add further observables, or split the present ones into distinct contributions. This generally improves the accuracy of the theory provided $\lim_{N,M\to\infty} L\tilde{\Delta}_{N,M}\sqrt{NM} = 0$ still holds.

Hence $\tilde{\Delta}_{N,M} = N^{-1}$, so deterministic evolution requires that $M \ll N^{\frac{1}{3}}$ as $M, N \to \infty$. Hence, on choosing Eq. (12.25) we can no longer take $M \to \infty$ before $N \to \infty$, which would have been the correct order, and must rely on these limits commuting.[4]

- *Trotter slice-independent observables*
These are simply averages over all Trotter slices of the previous set in Eq. (12.25), that is,

$$E(\boldsymbol{s}) = \frac{1}{M}\sum_{k=1}^{M} E_k(\boldsymbol{s}), \quad m(\boldsymbol{s}) = \frac{1}{M}\sum_{k=1}^{M} m_k(\boldsymbol{s}), \quad \mathcal{E}(\boldsymbol{s}) = \frac{1}{M}\sum_{k=1}^{M} \mathcal{E}_k(\boldsymbol{s}). \tag{12.29}$$

Hence $L = 3$, and the spin-flip susceptibilities come out as

$$\Delta_{ik} E(\boldsymbol{s}) = 2(NM)^{-1} s_{ik} \sum_{j \neq i} J_{ij} s_{jk} = \mathcal{O}((NM)^{-1}), \tag{12.30}$$

$$\Delta_{ik} m(\boldsymbol{s}) = -2(NM)^{-1} s_{ik} = \mathcal{O}((NM)^{-1}), \tag{12.31}$$

$$\Delta_{ik} \mathcal{E}(\boldsymbol{s}) = -2(NM)^{-1} s_{ik}(s_{i,k+1} + s_{i,k-1}) = \mathcal{O}((NM)^{-1}). \tag{12.32}$$

Now $\tilde{\Delta}_{N,M} = 1/NM$. Deterministic evolution requires $\lim_{N,M\to\infty}(NM)^{-\frac{1}{2}} = 0$, which is always true. We can therefore take our two limits in any desired order without having to worry about fluctuations in our macroscopic observables.

12.4 Simple Examples

We illustrate the previous approach by application to simple models. We investigate the commutation of the limits $N \to \infty$ and $M \to \infty$, and the link between stationary states of the dynamical equations and the equilibrium theory. We start with the simplest case of non-interacting spins in a uniform x field, followed by non-interacting spins in uniform x and z fields and ferromagnetically interacting quantum systems.

12.4.1 Non-interacting Quantum Spins in a Uniform *x* Field

This is the simplest case of Eq. (12.8), where $h = J_{ij} = 0$ for all (i, j). Although this specific model is physically trivial, it is still instructive since it already reveals many general features of the more general dynamical theory. The statics analysis gives

$$\mathcal{Z}_M(\beta) = \left\{ e^{\frac{1}{2}M \log[\frac{1}{2}\sinh(2\beta\Gamma/M)]} \mathrm{Tr}(\boldsymbol{K}^M) \right\}^N, \tag{12.33}$$

with a 2×2 transfer matrix of the one-dimensional Ising chain:

[4] The assumption that the order of the limits $N \to \infty$ and $M \to \infty$ can be changed is also made in equilibrium studies such as [15], where steepest descent integration is used as $N \to \infty$ for fixed M.

$$\boldsymbol{K} = \begin{pmatrix} e^{B} & e^{-B} \\ e^{-B} & e^{B} \end{pmatrix}, \quad \text{eigenvalues: } \lambda_{+} = 2\cosh(B), \;\; \lambda_{-} = 2\sinh(B). \tag{12.34}$$

After some rewriting and insertion of the definition of B we obtain:

$$\begin{aligned} \mathcal{Z}_M(\beta) &= \left\{ e^{\frac{1}{2}M\log[\frac{1}{2}\sinh(2\beta\Gamma/M)]} 2^M [\cosh^M(B) + \sinh^M(B)] \right\}^N \\ &= [2\cosh(\beta\Gamma)]^N. \end{aligned} \tag{12.35}$$

This gives the correct free energy density $f_{N,M} = -\frac{1}{\beta}\log[2\cosh(\beta\Gamma)]$.

Next, we turn to the macroscopic dynamical equations in Eq. (12.21). Since $J_{ij} = 0$, the order parameters $E_k(\boldsymbol{s})$ and $E(\boldsymbol{s})$ are always zero. The two dynamical routes give:

- *Trotter slice-dependent observables*
  The observables are $\{m_k(\boldsymbol{s}), \mathcal{E}_k(\boldsymbol{s})\}$, and we are forced to take $N \to \infty$ before $M \to \infty$. Using identities such as $\tanh[B(s+s')] = \frac{1}{2}(s+s')\tanh(2B)$ we obtain:

$$\tau\frac{\mathrm{d}}{\mathrm{d}t}m_k = -m_k + \frac{1}{2}(m_{k+1}+m_{k-1})\tanh(2B), \tag{12.36}$$

$$\tau\frac{\mathrm{d}}{\mathrm{d}t}\mathcal{E}_k = \tanh(2B)[1+\frac{1}{2}(C_k+C_{k+1})] - 2\mathcal{E}_k, \tag{12.37}$$

  in which, using the equivalence of the N sites i, we have the 2-slice correlators:

$$C_k = \frac{\sum_{\boldsymbol{s}}\left[\prod_q \delta[m_q - m_q(\boldsymbol{s})]\delta[\mathcal{E}_q - \mathcal{E}_q(\boldsymbol{s})]\right] s_{1,k-1}s_{1,k+1}}{\sum_{\boldsymbol{s}}\left[\prod_q \delta[m_q - m_q(\boldsymbol{s})]\delta[\mathcal{E}_q - \mathcal{E}_q(\boldsymbol{s})]\right]}. \tag{12.38}$$

  One can compute these for $N \to \infty$ with fixed M via steepest descent integration:

$$C_k = \frac{\sum_{s_1\ldots s_M} e^{\sum_q (x_q s_q + y_q s_q s_{q+1})} s_{k-1}s_{k+1}}{\sum_{s_1\ldots s_M} e^{\sum_q (x_q s_q + y_q s_q s_{q+1})}}, \tag{12.39}$$

  in which $\boldsymbol{x} = (x_1, \ldots, x_M)$ and $\boldsymbol{y} = (y_1, \ldots, y_M)$ are to be solved from

$$m_k = \frac{\partial \log Z}{\partial x_k}, \quad \mathcal{E}_k = \frac{\partial \log Z}{\partial y_k}, \quad Z(\boldsymbol{x}, \boldsymbol{y}) = \sum_{s_1\ldots s_M} e^{\sum_q (x_q s_q + y_q s_q s_{q+1})}. \tag{12.40}$$

- *Trotter slice-independent observables*
  In this case, we only have $m(\boldsymbol{s})$ and $\mathcal{E}(\boldsymbol{s})$, and working out Eq. (12.21) gives

$$\tau\frac{\mathrm{d}}{\mathrm{d}t}m = -m[1-\tanh(2B)], \qquad \tau\frac{\mathrm{d}}{\mathrm{d}t}\mathcal{E} = (1+C)\tanh(2B) - 2\mathcal{E}, \tag{12.41}$$

with

$$C = \frac{\sum_s \delta[m-m(\mathbf{s})]\delta[\mathcal{E}-\mathcal{E}(\mathbf{s})]s_{1,1}s_{1,3}}{\sum_s \delta[m-m(\mathbf{s})]\delta[\mathcal{E}-\mathcal{E}(\mathbf{s})]}. \tag{12.42}$$

Calculating the 2-slice correlator C using steepest descent results in

$$C = \frac{\sum_{s_1\ldots s_M} \mathrm{e}^{\frac{1}{M}\sum_q (xs_q+ys_qs_{q+1})} s_1 s_3}{\sum_{s_1\ldots s_M} \mathrm{e}^{\frac{1}{M}\sum_q (xs_q+ys_qs_{q+1})}}, \tag{12.43}$$

$$m = \frac{\partial \log Z}{\partial x}, \qquad \mathcal{E} = \frac{\partial \log Z}{\partial y}, \qquad Z(x,y) = \sum_{s_1\ldots s_M} \mathrm{e}^{\frac{1}{M}\sum_q (xs_q+ys_qs_{q+1})}. \tag{12.44}$$

If at time zero the m_k and $\mathcal{E}_k$ in Eqs. (12.36, 12.37) are independent of k, this will remain true at all times[5] and the dynamics in Eqs. (12.36, 12.37) simplifies to Eq. (12.41). Computing C involves solving a one-dimensional Ising model with a constant external field, whereas computing C_k requires solving heterogeneous spin chain models in equilibrium for arbitrary coupling constants and fields. This is the second reason, in addition to the issue with limits, for why it is preferable to work with Trotter slice-independent observables.

For non-interacting spins with $h \neq 0$ the analysis is similar. Here $f = \lim_{M\to\infty} f_{N,M} = -\beta^{-1}\log[2\cosh(\beta\sqrt{\Gamma^2+h^2})]$, with equilibrium magnetisation

$$m = -\partial f/\partial h = \tanh(\beta\sqrt{h^2+\Gamma^2})\frac{h}{\sqrt{h^2+\Gamma^2}}, \tag{12.45}$$

and the Trotter slice-independent observables are predicted to obey

$$\tau\frac{\mathrm{d}}{\mathrm{d}t}m = \frac{1}{2}(1-C)\tanh(\beta h/M) + \frac{1}{2}Q_+(1+C) - m(1-Q_-), \tag{12.46}$$

$$\tau\frac{\mathrm{d}}{\mathrm{d}t}\mathcal{E} = (1+C)Q_- + 2Q_+m - 2\mathcal{E}, \tag{12.47}$$

with $Q_\pm = \frac{1}{2}[\tanh(\beta h/M+2B)\pm\tanh(\beta h/M-2B)]$. Since $\lim_{h\to 0} Q_+ = 0$ and $\lim_{h\to 0} Q_- = \tanh(2B)$, Eqs. (12.46,12.47) indeed revert back to Eq. (12.41) for $h \to 0$. We inspect the fixed-points of Eqs. (12.46, 12.47) after having also added spin interactions in the next section. Clearly, since $\lim_{M\to\infty} Q_+ = \lim_{M\to\infty}(1-Q_-) = 0$ the relaxation time of the system diverges for $M \to \infty$, with closer inspection revealing that $\mathrm{d}m/\mathrm{d}t = \mathcal{O}(M^{-2})$. This makes physical sense: for large M, hence large B, the Trotter slices increasingly prefer identical states, so state changes (in a single slice) become rare as they require the mounting energetic costs of breaking the Trotter symmetry.

[5] In [7, 8, 10] this is called the static approximation.

12.4.2 Ferromagnetic z-interactions and Uniform x and z Fields

We now choose $h \neq 0$, $\Gamma \neq 0$, and $J_{ij} = J_0/N$ for all $i \neq j$, so that the quantum Hamiltonian is $H = -(J_0/N)\sum_{i<j}\sigma_i^z\sigma_j^z - \sum_i(h\sigma_i^z + \Gamma\sigma_i^x)$. This is known as the Husimi-Temperley-Curie-Weiss model in a transverse field [11]. In the statics, after some simple manipulations and using the short-hand $\mathrm{D}z = (2\pi)^{-\frac{1}{2}}\mathrm{e}^{-\frac{1}{2}z^2}\mathrm{d}z$, we find:

$$\mathcal{Z}_M(\beta) = \mathrm{e}^{\frac{1}{2}NM\log[\frac{1}{2}\sinh(2\beta\Gamma/M)]-\frac{1}{2}\beta J_0} \times \int\Big[\prod_{k=1}^{M}\mathrm{D}z_k\Big]\Big\{\mathrm{Tr}\prod_{k=1}^{M}\boldsymbol{K}\Big(z_k\sqrt{\frac{M}{\beta J_0 N}}\Big)\Big\}^N, \tag{12.48}$$

with the non-symmetric transfer matrix

$$\boldsymbol{K}(x) = \begin{pmatrix} \mathrm{e}^{B+\beta h/M+\beta J_0 x/M} & \mathrm{e}^{-B+\beta J_0 x/M} \\ \mathrm{e}^{-B-\beta J_0 x/M} & \mathrm{e}^{B-\beta h/M-\beta J_0 x/M} \end{pmatrix} = \mathrm{e}^{x(\beta J_0/M)\sigma^z}\boldsymbol{K}(0). \tag{12.49}$$

We first turn to the statics of the model. It is not immediately clear whether or not the limits $N, M \to \infty$ in Eq. (12.48) commute. Upon taking the limit $N \to \infty$ first, one obtains via steepest descent integration:

$$\lim_{N\to\infty} f_{N,M} = -\frac{M}{2\beta}\log\Big[\frac{1}{2}\sinh\Big(\frac{2\beta\Gamma}{M}\Big)\Big] -\frac{1}{\beta}\mathrm{extr}_{\boldsymbol{x}}\Big\{\log\mathrm{Tr}\prod_{k=1}^{M}\boldsymbol{K}(x_k) - \frac{\beta J_0}{2M}\boldsymbol{x}^2\Big\}. \tag{12.50}$$

We find the derivatives of the quantity $\Psi(\boldsymbol{x})$ to be extremized, with $\overline{\delta}_{ab} = 1-\delta_{ab}$:

$$\frac{\partial\Psi}{\partial x_q} = \frac{\beta J_0}{M}\Big\{\frac{\mathrm{Tr}\prod_{k=1}^{M}(\overline{\delta}_{kq}\mathbf{I}+\delta_{kq}\sigma^z)\boldsymbol{K}(x_k)}{\mathrm{Tr}\prod_{k=1}^{M}\boldsymbol{K}(x_k)} - x_q\Big\}, \tag{12.51}$$

$$\frac{\partial^2\Psi}{\partial x_q\partial x_r} = \Big(\frac{\beta J_0}{M}\Big)^2\Big\{\frac{\mathrm{Tr}\prod_{k=1}^{M}(\overline{\delta}_{kq}\mathbf{I}+\delta_{kq}\sigma^z)(\overline{\delta}_{kr}\mathbf{I}+\delta_{kr}\sigma^z)\boldsymbol{K}(x_k)}{\mathrm{Tr}\prod_{k=1}^{M}\boldsymbol{K}(x_k)} - \frac{\mathrm{Tr}\prod_{k=1}^{M}(\overline{\delta}_{kq}\mathbf{I}+\delta_{kq}\sigma^z)\boldsymbol{K}(x_k)}{\mathrm{Tr}\prod_{k=1}^{M}\boldsymbol{K}(x_k)}\frac{\mathrm{Tr}\prod_{k=1}^{M}(\overline{\delta}_{kr}\mathbf{I}+\delta_{kr}\sigma^z)\boldsymbol{K}(x_k)}{\mathrm{Tr}\prod_{k=1}^{M}\boldsymbol{K}(x_k)}\Big\} - \frac{\beta J_0}{M}\delta_{qr}. \tag{12.52}$$

In Trotter-symmetric solutions $x_k = m$ for all k, these derivatives simplify to

$$\frac{\partial\Psi}{\partial x_q} = \frac{\beta J_0}{M}\left\{\frac{\text{Tr}[\sigma^z \boldsymbol{K}^M(m)]}{\text{Tr}[\boldsymbol{K}^M(m)]} - m\right\}, \tag{12.53}$$

$$\frac{\partial^2\Psi}{\partial x_q \partial x_r} = \left(\frac{\beta J_0}{M}\right)^2\left\{\frac{\text{Tr}[\sigma^z \boldsymbol{K}^{|q-r|}(m)\sigma^z \boldsymbol{K}^{M-|q-r|}(m)]}{\text{Tr}[\boldsymbol{K}^M(m)]} - \left(\frac{\text{Tr}[\sigma^z \boldsymbol{K}^M(m)]}{\text{Tr}[\boldsymbol{K}^M(m)]}\right)^2\right\} - (\beta J_0/M)\delta_{qr}. \tag{12.54}$$

and m is the solution of

$$m = \frac{\text{Tr}[\sigma^z \boldsymbol{K}^M(m)]}{\text{Tr}[\boldsymbol{K}^M(m)]}. \tag{12.55}$$

Trotter symmetry-breaking bifurcations occur when $\text{Det}[(\beta J_0/M)\boldsymbol{A} - \mathbf{I}] = 0$, where

$$A_{qr} = \frac{\text{Tr}[\sigma^z \boldsymbol{K}^{|q-r|}(m)\sigma^z \boldsymbol{K}^{M-|q-r|}(m)]}{\text{Tr}[\boldsymbol{K}^M(m)]} - m^2. \tag{12.56}$$

We introduce the symmetric matrix $\boldsymbol{Q}(m) = \text{e}^{-\frac{1}{2}m(\beta J_0/M)\sigma^z}\boldsymbol{K}(m)\text{e}^{\frac{1}{2}m(\beta J_0/M)\sigma^z}$, with eigenvalues $\lambda_\pm(x)$ and orthogonal eigenbasis $|\pm\rangle$. Now for any $\ell \in \mathbb{N}$ we have

$$\boldsymbol{K}^\ell(m) = \text{e}^{\frac{1}{2}m(\beta J_0/M)\sigma^z}\Big(\lambda_+^\ell(m)|+\rangle\langle+|+\lambda_-^\ell(m)|-\rangle\langle-|\Big)\text{e}^{-\frac{1}{2}m(\beta J_0/M)\sigma^z}, \tag{12.57}$$

and hence, with the short-hand $\sigma_{ab}^z = \langle a|\sigma^z|b\rangle$ and $\phi = \lambda_-(m)/\lambda_+(m) \in (-1, 1)$:

$$\frac{\text{Tr}[\sigma^z \boldsymbol{K}^M(m)]}{\text{Tr}[\boldsymbol{K}^M(m)]} = \frac{\sigma_{++}^z + \sigma_{--}^z\phi^M}{1+\phi^M}, \tag{12.58}$$

$$A_{qr} = \frac{\sigma_{++}^{z2} + \big[\phi^{|q-r|} + \phi^{M-|q-r|}\big]|\sigma_{+-}^z|^2 + \phi^M\sigma_{--}^{z2}}{1+\phi^M} - m^2. \tag{12.59}$$

Since $\boldsymbol{A}$ has a Toeplitz form, we know its eigenvalues:

$$k = 1\ldots M: \quad a_k = \frac{|\sigma_{+-}^z|^2}{1+\phi^M}\frac{(1-\phi^M)(1-\phi^2)}{1+\phi^2-2\phi\cos(2\pi(k-1)/M)}. \tag{12.60}$$

Finally we need to diagonalize $\boldsymbol{Q}(m)$ for large M. This gives:

$$\boldsymbol{Q}(m) = \begin{pmatrix} e^{B+\beta(h+J_0m)/M} & e^{-B} \\ e^{-B} & e^{B-\beta(h+J_0m)/M} \end{pmatrix} \tag{12.61}$$

$$\lambda_\pm(m) = e^{B\pm\frac{\beta}{M}\sqrt{(h+J_0m)^2+\Gamma^2}+\mathcal{O}(M^{-2})}, \tag{12.62}$$

$$\lim_{M\to\infty} |\pm\rangle = \frac{1}{C_\pm(m)}\Big(\Gamma, -(h+J_0m) \pm \sqrt{(h+J_0m)^2+\Gamma^2}\Big), \tag{12.63}$$

$$C_\pm(m) = \sqrt{2}\Big[(h+J_0m)^2+\Gamma^2 \mp (h+J_0m)\sqrt{(h+J_0m)^2+\Gamma^2}\Big]^{\frac{1}{2}}. \tag{12.64}$$

It follows that

$$\phi = e^{-\frac{2\beta}{M}\sqrt{(h+J_0m)^2+\Gamma^2}+\mathcal{O}(M^{-2})}. \tag{12.65}$$

Hence $\lim_{M\to\infty}\phi=1$, $\lim_{M\to\infty}\phi^M = \exp[-2\beta\sqrt{(h+J_0m)^2+\Gamma^2}]$, $\lim_{M\to\infty}\sigma^z_{++} = -\lim_{M\to\infty}\sigma^z_{--} = (h+J_0m)/\sqrt{(h+J_0m)^2+\Gamma^2}$, and $\lim_{M\to\infty}\sigma^z_{+-} = \Gamma/\sqrt{(h+J_0m)^2+\Gamma^2}$. The equation for the magnetization m and the eigenvalues of $\boldsymbol{A}$ thereby become

$$m = \frac{(h+J_0m)\tanh[\beta\sqrt{(h+J_0m)^2+\Gamma^2}]}{\sqrt{(h+J_0m)^2+\Gamma^2}}, \tag{12.66}$$

$$a_k = \frac{\Gamma^2\tanh[\beta\sqrt{(h+J_0m)^2+\Gamma^2}]}{(h+J_0m)^2+\Gamma^2}\Big[1+2\lim_{M\to\infty}\frac{1-\cos(2\pi(k-1)/M)}{1-\phi^2}\Big]^{-1}. \tag{12.67}$$

Since all a_k are bounded for large M, the condition $\beta J_0 a_k/M = 1$ for bifurcations away from the Trotter-symmetric state are never met, indicating that the state described by Eq. (12.66) is the physical one. The free energy density $f = \lim_{M\to\infty}\lim_{N\to\infty} f_{N,M}$ is

$$\begin{aligned} f &= \frac{1}{2}J_0m^2 - \lim_{M\to\infty}\left\{\frac{M}{2\beta}\log\Big[\frac{1}{2}\sinh\Big(\frac{2\beta\Gamma}{M}\Big)\Big] + \frac{1}{\beta}\log\Big(\lambda_+^M(m)+\lambda_-^M(m)\Big)\right\} \\ &= \frac{1}{2}J_0m^2 - \frac{1}{\beta}\log\Big[2\cosh\Big(\beta\sqrt{(h+J_0m)^2+\Gamma^2}\Big)\Big]. \end{aligned} \tag{12.68}$$

Extremizing the expression in Eq. (12.68) over m reproduces Eq. (12.66).

We return to Eq. (12.48), and now seek to take the Trotter limit $M\to\infty$ first. The complexities are all in the evaluation for large M of the quantity

$$Z_M = \int\Big[\prod_{k=1}^{M} Dz_k\Big]\Big\{\mathrm{Tr}\Big[\prod_{k=1}^{M} e^{z_k\sqrt{\frac{\beta J_0}{MN}}\sigma^z}\begin{pmatrix} e^{B+\beta h/M} & e^{-B} \\ e^{-B} & e^{B-\beta h/M}\end{pmatrix}\Big]\Big\}^N. \tag{12.69}$$

This can be analyzed using random field Ising chain techniques [18]. Alternatively, we can use the fact that in summations of the form $\sum_k z_k$, each z_k effectively scales as $\mathcal{O}(M^{-\frac{1}{2}})$, enabling us to use $e^{-B} = \sqrt{\tanh(\beta\Gamma/M)}$ and a modified version of the Trotter identity, viz. $\prod_{k\leq M}\left(e^{u_k/M}e^{v/M}\right) = e^{M^{-1}\sum_{k\leq M}u_k+v}$, to derive

$$
\begin{aligned}
Z_M &= \mathrm{e}^{NMB} \int \Big[\prod_{k=1}^{M} \mathrm{D}z_k\Big] \Big\{ \mathrm{Tr}\Big[\prod_{k=1}^{M} \mathrm{e}^{z_k\sqrt{\frac{\beta J_0}{MN}}\sigma^z} \Big(\mathbf{1}+\frac{\beta}{M}(h\sigma^z+\Gamma\sigma^x)+\mathcal{O}(\frac{1}{M^2})\Big)\Big]\Big\}^N \\
&= \sqrt{\beta J_0 N}\mathrm{e}^{NMB} \int \frac{\mathrm{d}m}{\sqrt{2\pi}} \mathrm{e}^{-\frac{1}{2}\beta J_0 N m^2} \Big\{\mathrm{Tr}\; \mathrm{e}^{\beta(h+J_0 m)\sigma^z+\beta\Gamma\sigma^x+\mathcal{O}(M^{-1})}\Big\}^N. \qquad (12.70)
\end{aligned}
$$

The free energy density $f = \lim_{N\to\infty} \lim_{M\to\infty} f_{N,M}$ then becomes

$$
f = -\frac{1}{\beta}\mathrm{extr}_m \Big\{ \log\big(\mathrm{e}^{\beta\mu_+(m)} + \mathrm{e}^{\beta\mu_-(m)}\big) - \frac{1}{2}\beta J_0 m^2 \Big\}, \qquad (12.71)
$$

in which $\mu_\pm(m)$ are the eigenvalues of the matrix $\boldsymbol{L}(m) = (h+J_0 m)\sigma^z+\Gamma\sigma^x$:

$$
\boldsymbol{L}(m) = \begin{pmatrix} h+J_0 m & \Gamma \\ \Gamma & -(h+J_0 m) \end{pmatrix}, \quad \mu_\pm(m) = \pm\sqrt{(h+J_0 m)^2+\Gamma^2}. \qquad (12.72)
$$

We now recover Eqs. (12.66, 12.68), so the limits $N\to\infty$ and $M\to\infty$ can be interchanged:

$$
f = \mathrm{extr}_m \Big\{ \frac{1}{2} J_0 m^2 - \frac{1}{\beta}\log\Big[2\cosh\Big(\beta\sqrt{(h+J_0 m)^2+\Gamma^2}\Big)\Big]\Big\}. \qquad (12.73)
$$

We next turn to the DRT dynamics. The energy and the usual initial conditions can once more be expressed in terms of $\{m_k, \mathcal{E}_k\}$ (slice-dependent observables) or $(m, \mathcal{E})$ (slice-independent ones). We define the short-hand $Q_\pm(m) = \frac{1}{2}\tanh(\beta(J_0 m+h)/M+2B) \pm \frac{1}{2}\tanh(\beta(J_0 m+h)/M-2B) \in (-1, 1)$. Upon inserting Eqs. (12.27, 12.28) and Eqs. (12.31, 12.32) into Eq. (12.21), with the fields $h_{ik}(\boldsymbol{s}) = M^{-1}[h+J_0 m_k(\boldsymbol{s})] + (B/\beta)(s_{i,k+1}+s_{i,k-1}) + \mathcal{O}(N^{-1})$, and using expressions such as $\tanh[a+b(s+s')] = \frac{1}{4}(1+s)(1+s')\tanh(a+2b) + \frac{1}{4}(1-s)(1-s')\tanh(a-2b) + \frac{1}{2}(1-ss')\tanh(a)$, one finds the following descriptions:

- *Trotter slice-dependent observables*
  Our observables are $m_q(\boldsymbol{s}) = N^{-1}\sum_i s_{i,q}$ and $\mathcal{E}_q(\boldsymbol{s}) = N^{-1}\sum_i s_{i,q}s_{i,q+1}$, for $q = 1\ldots M$, and we must take the limit $N\to\infty$ before $M\to\infty$. We note that

$$
\begin{aligned}
\tanh(\beta h_{ik}(\boldsymbol{s})) &= \frac{1}{2}(1+s_{i,k+1}s_{i,k-1})Q_+(m_k(\boldsymbol{s})) + \frac{1}{2}(s_{i,k+1}+s_{i,k-1})Q_-(m_k(\boldsymbol{s})) \\
&\quad +\frac{1}{2}(1-s_{i,k+1}s_{i,k-1})\tanh(\beta(h+J_0 m_k(\boldsymbol{s}))/M), \qquad (12.74)
\end{aligned}
$$

so with the correlators C_k in Eq. (12.39) the dynamical laws take the form

$$\tau\frac{\mathrm{d}}{\mathrm{d}t}m_q = \frac{1}{2}(1+C_q)Q_+(m_q) + \frac{1}{2}(m_{q+1}+m_{q-1})Q_-(m_q) - m_q$$
$$+\frac{1}{2}(1-C_q)\tanh\left(\frac{\beta}{M}(h+J_0m_q)\right), \tag{12.75}$$
$$\tau\frac{\mathrm{d}}{\mathrm{d}t}\mathcal{E}_q = \frac{1}{2}(m_{q+1}+m_{q-1})Q_+(m_q) + \frac{1}{2}(1+C_q)Q_-(m_q)$$
$$+\frac{1}{2}(m_q+m_{q+2})Q_+(m_{q+1}) + \frac{1}{2}(1+C_{q+1})Q_-(m_{q+1})$$
$$+\frac{1}{2}(m_{q+1}-m_{q-1})\tanh\left(\frac{\beta}{M}(h+J_0m_q)\right)$$
$$+\frac{1}{2}(m_q-m_{q+2})\tanh\left(\frac{\beta}{M}(h+J_0m_{q+1})\right) - 2\mathcal{E}_q. \tag{12.76}$$

For slice-independent initial conditions, where $m_k = m$ and $\mathcal{E}_k = \mathcal{E}$, this becomes

$$\tau\frac{\mathrm{d}}{\mathrm{d}t}m = \frac{1}{2}(1+C)Q_+(m)+mQ_-(m)-m+\frac{1}{2}(1-C)\tanh\left(\frac{\beta}{M}(h+J_0m)\right), \tag{12.77}$$
$$\tau\frac{\mathrm{d}}{\mathrm{d}t}\mathcal{E} = 2mQ_+(m) + (1+C)Q_-(m) - 2\mathcal{E}, \tag{12.78}$$

with the correlator C in Eq. (12.43).

- *Trotter slice-independent observables*
  For the choice $(m, \mathcal{E})$ there is no constraint on the order of limits, but the quantities $m_k(s)$ appearing inside $\tanh(\beta h_{ik}(s))$ can no longer be replaced by deterministic macroscopic observables, but must now be calculated. Using Trotter slice permutation symmetry wherever possible, one finds

$$\tau\frac{\mathrm{d}}{\mathrm{d}t}m = \frac{1}{2M}\sum_{k=1}^{M}\Big\langle[1+C_k(s)]Q_+(m_k(s)) + [m_{k+1}(s)+m_{k-1}(s)]Q_-(m_k(s))$$
$$+[1-C_k(s)]\tanh(\beta(h+J_0m_k(s))/M)\Big\rangle_{m,\mathcal{E}} - m, \tag{12.79}$$
$$\tau\frac{\mathrm{d}}{\mathrm{d}t}\mathcal{E} = \frac{1}{M}\sum_{k=1}^{M}\Big\langle[m_{k+1}(s)+m_{k-1}(s)]Q_+(m_k(s))\Big\rangle_{m,\mathcal{E}}$$
$$+\frac{1}{M}\sum_{k=1}^{M}\Big\langle[1+C_k(s)]Q_-(m_k(s))\Big\rangle_{m,\mathcal{E}} - 2\mathcal{E}, \tag{12.80}$$

with $C_k(s) = N^{-1}\sum_i s_{i,k+1}s_{i,k-1}$. For large M and N, and in view of the interchangeability of the limits $M \to \infty$ and $N \to \infty$ in the equilibrium calculation, we may anticipate (and can indeed show) that we can neglect the fluctuations in the values of $\{m_k(s)\}$ and simply replace $m_k(s) \to m(s) + o(1)$ in the right-hand sides of the above equations, upon which these simplify to Eqs. (12.77, 12.78).

12.5 Link Between Statics and Dynamics

We now show that for $M \to \infty$, the stationary state of Eqs. (12.77, 12.78) reproduces the equilibrium result in Eq. (12.66) as expected. The fixed-point equations of Eqs. (12.77, 12.78) are

$$m = \frac{1}{2}(1+C)Q_+(m) + mQ_-(m) + \frac{1}{2}(1-C)\tanh\left(\frac{\beta}{M}(h+J_0 m)\right), \tag{12.81}$$

$$\mathcal{E} = mQ_+(m) + \frac{1}{2}(1+C)Q_-(m), \tag{12.82}$$

with the correlator $C = C(m, \mathcal{E}) \in (-1, 1)$ to be solved from

$$C = \frac{\sum_{s_1\ldots s_M} e^{\sum_{k=1}^M (xs_k + ys_k s_{k+1})} s_1 s_3}{\sum_{s_1\ldots s_M} e^{\sum_{k=1}^M (xs_k + ys_k s_{k+1})}}, \tag{12.83}$$

$$m = \frac{1}{M}\frac{\partial \log Z}{\partial x}, \qquad \mathcal{E} = \frac{1}{M}\frac{\partial \log Z}{\partial y}, \qquad Z(x, y) = \sum_{s_1\ldots s_M} e^{\sum_{k=1}^M (xs_k + ys_k s_{k+1})}. \tag{12.84}$$

We compute $Z(x, y)$ via the transfer matrix $\boldsymbol{K}(x, y)$ with elements $K_{ss'} = e^{\frac{1}{2}x(s+s')+yss'}$. This gives $Z(x, y) = \lambda_+^M(x, y) + \lambda_-^M(x, y)$, where $\lambda_\pm(.)$ are the eigenvalues of $\boldsymbol{K}(.)$,

$$\lambda_\pm(x, y) = e^y\Big(\cosh(x) \pm \sqrt{\sinh^2(x) + e^{-4y}}\Big). \tag{12.85}$$

For the equilbrium values of $(m, \mathcal{E})$, Eq. (12.84) are solved by

$$x = \beta(h+J_0 m)/M, \qquad y = B = -\frac{1}{2}\log\tanh\left(\frac{\beta\Gamma}{M}\right), \qquad \text{so } e^{-4y} = \tanh^2\left(\frac{\beta\Gamma}{M}\right). \tag{12.86}$$

This claim is confirmed by substituting these as ansätze into the expressions given in the appendix. The key ingredient $\phi = \lambda_-/\lambda_+$ of our formulae then becomes

$$\log\phi = -\frac{2\beta}{M}\sqrt{(h+J_0 m)^2 + \Gamma^2} + \mathcal{O}(M^{-3}). \tag{12.87}$$

Hence for $M \to \infty$ the formulae for m and $\mathcal{E}$ in Eq. (12.84) become

$$m = \frac{(h+J_0 m)\tanh[\beta\sqrt{(h+J_0 m)^2 + \Gamma^2}]}{\sqrt{(h+J_0 m)^2 + \Gamma^2}}, \qquad \mathcal{E} = 1. \tag{12.88}$$

in which we recognize (12.66). For large M one finds $Q_+(m) = \mathcal{O}(M^{-3})$ and $Q_-(m) = 1 - 2(\beta\Gamma/M)^2 + \mathcal{O}(M^{-3})$, so expansion of the fixed-point equations gives

$$m = M(1-C)\frac{h+J_0m}{4\beta\Gamma^2} + \mathcal{O}(M^{-1}), \tag{12.89}$$

$$\mathcal{E} = \frac{1}{2}(1+C)[1-2(\beta\Gamma/M)^2] + \mathcal{O}(M^{-3}). \tag{12.90}$$

The first equation implies that $C = 1-\tilde{C}/M$ for $M \to \infty$, with $\tilde{C} = \mathcal{O}(1)$. In turn, this gives $\mathcal{E} = 1-\frac{\tilde{C}}{2M}+\mathcal{O}(M^{-2})$. What is left in our proof is to show that m obeys

$$m = \frac{h+J_0m}{4\beta\Gamma^2}\lim_{M\to\infty} M(1-C). \tag{12.91}$$

We hence compute the correlator C to order M^{-1}, using the identities in the appendix:

$$\begin{aligned} C &= \langle+|\sigma^z|+\rangle^2 + \frac{\cosh\left[(\frac{1}{2}M-2)\log\phi\right]}{\cosh\left[\frac{1}{2}M\log\phi\right]}\left(1-\langle+|\sigma^z|+\rangle^2\right) \\ &= \frac{(h+J_0m)^2}{(h+J_0m)^2+\Gamma^2} + \frac{\cosh[\beta(1-4/M)\sqrt{(h+J_0m)^2+\Gamma^2}]}{\cosh[\beta\sqrt{(h+J_0m)^2+\Gamma^2}]} \\ &\times \frac{\Gamma^2}{(h+J_0m)^2+\Gamma^2} + \mathcal{O}\left(\frac{1}{M^2}\right) \\ &= 1-\frac{1}{M}\tanh\left[\beta\sqrt{(h+J_0m)^2+\Gamma^2}\right]\frac{4\beta\Gamma^2}{\sqrt{(h+J_0m)^2+\Gamma^2}} + \mathcal{O}\left(\frac{1}{M^2}\right). \end{aligned} \tag{12.92}$$

We can now read off the value of $\tilde{C}$, and the condition in Eq. (12.91) is found to reduce to Eq. (12.66), so that it is indeed satisfied. This completes the demonstration that for large M, the macroscopic Eqs. (12.77, 12.78) indeed have the equilibrium state as their fixed-point.

12.6 Evolution on Adiabatically Separated Timescales

We return to the dynamical laws in Eqs. (12.77, 12.78). As noted earlier, these exhibit a divergent relaxation time for the magnetization for large M, suggesting that the dynamics have distinct phases. The first phase is studied by choosing $\tau = \mathcal{O}(1)$. Using

$$Q_+(m) = \frac{4\beta^3\Gamma^2(J_0m+h)}{M^3} + \mathcal{O}(M^{-4}), \quad Q_-(m) = 1-\frac{2\beta^2\Gamma^2}{M^2} + \mathcal{O}(M^{-4}), \tag{12.93}$$

we here find that

$$m = m_0 + \mathcal{O}(M^{-1}), \qquad \tau\frac{\mathrm{d}}{\mathrm{d}t}\mathcal{E} = 1+C(m_0,\mathcal{E}) - 2\mathcal{E} + \mathcal{O}(M^{-1}). \tag{12.94}$$

So on these timescales the magnetization does not change, whereas the Trotter energy evolves to the solution of the fixed-point equation $\mathcal{E} = \frac{1}{2} + \frac{1}{2}C(m_0, \mathcal{E})$, in which $C(m_0, \mathcal{E})$ is to be solved from the following equations according to the appendix:

$$m = -\frac{\sinh(x)\tanh[\frac{1}{2}M\log\phi]}{\sqrt{\sinh^2(x)+e^{-4y}}}, \tag{12.95}$$

$$\mathcal{E} = \frac{\sinh^2(x)}{\sinh^2(x)+e^{-4y}} + \frac{\cosh[(\frac{1}{2}M-1)\log\phi]}{\cosh[\frac{1}{2}M\log\phi]}\frac{e^{-4y}}{\sinh^2(x)+e^{-4y}}, \tag{12.96}$$

$$C = \frac{\sinh^2(x)}{\sinh^2(x)+e^{-4y}} + \frac{\cosh[(\frac{1}{2}M-2)\log\phi]}{\cosh[\frac{1}{2}M\log\phi]}\frac{e^{-4y}}{\sinh^2(x)+e^{-4y}}, \tag{12.97}$$

with $\phi = [\cosh(x) - \sqrt{\sinh^2(x)+e^{-4y}}]/[\cosh(x) + \sqrt{\sinh^2(x)+e^{-4y}}]$. Inspection of these equations reveals that the correct scaling with M requires $(x, e^{-2y}) = (u, v)/M$, with $u, v = \mathcal{O}(1)$. Now $\frac{1}{2}M\log\phi = -\sqrt{u^2+v^2} + \mathcal{O}(M^{-2})$, $\mathcal{E} = 1 - \tilde{\mathcal{E}}/M + \mathcal{O}(M^{-2})$, and $C = 1 - 2\tilde{\mathcal{E}}/M + \mathcal{O}(M^{-2})$, in which (u, v) are solved from

$$m_0 = \frac{u\tanh(\sqrt{u^2+v^2})}{\sqrt{u^2+v^2}}, \qquad \tilde{\mathcal{E}} = \frac{2v^2\tanh(\sqrt{u^2+v^2})}{\sqrt{u^2+v^2}}. \tag{12.98}$$

Although the fixed-point equation for $\mathcal{E}$ is now solved to order $\mathcal{O}(M^{-1})$, computation of $\tilde{\mathcal{E}}$ requires higher orders of M^{-1}. Once $\mathcal{E} = 1 - \tilde{\mathcal{E}}/M + \mathcal{O}(N^{-2})$ and $C(m, \mathcal{E}) = 1 - 2\tilde{\mathcal{E}}/M + \mathcal{O}(M^{-2})$, we find $\mathrm{d}m/\mathrm{d}t = \mathcal{O}(M^{-2})$ and $\mathrm{d}\mathcal{E}/\mathrm{d}t = \mathcal{O}(M^{-2})$, so nothing evolves further macroscopically on these finite timescales.

Since we need $\tau = \mathcal{O}(M^{-2})$ to probe the macroscopic evolution of the system on larger timescales, spin flips in the Trotter system are attempted on unit timescales of $\mathcal{O}(M^3N)$.[6] With the choice $\tau = M^{-2}$, and upon defining $M(1-\mathcal{E}) = \tilde{\mathcal{E}}$ and $M(1-C) = \tilde{C}$, the macroscopic laws (12.77, 12.78) become

$$\frac{\mathrm{d}}{\mathrm{d}t}m = \frac{1}{2}\tilde{C}\beta(h+J_0m) - 2m\beta^2\Gamma^2 + \mathcal{O}\left(\frac{1}{M}\right), \tag{12.99}$$

$$\frac{\mathrm{d}}{\mathrm{d}t}\tilde{\mathcal{E}} = 4M\beta^2\Gamma^2 - M^2(2\tilde{\mathcal{E}}-\tilde{C}) - 8\beta^3\Gamma^2 m(J_0m+h) - 2\beta^2\Gamma^2\tilde{C} + \mathcal{O}\left(\frac{1}{M}\right). \tag{12.100}$$

The quantity $\tilde{C} = \tilde{C}(m, \tilde{\mathcal{E}})$ is to be solved together with (x, y) from Eqs. (12.95, 12.96, 12.97). The relevant scaling is still $(x, e^{-2y}) = (u, v)/M$, with $u, v = \mathcal{O}(1)$, but according to Eq. (12.100) we now need more than just the leading order in M^{-1}. Using

$$\log\phi = -\frac{2\sqrt{u^2+v^2}}{M} + \mathcal{O}(M^{-3}), \tag{12.101}$$

[6] This reflects the high energy cost of breaking Trotter symmetry to induce magnetization changes.

the equations for $\mathcal{E}$ and C take the form $\mathcal{E} = \Xi_1(u, v)$ and $C = \Xi_2(u, v)$, where

$$\Xi_\ell(u,v) = \left[\sinh^2\left(\frac{u}{M}\right) + \frac{v^2}{M^2}\right]^{-1}\left[\sinh^2\left(\frac{u}{M}\right) + \frac{v^2}{M^2}\frac{F_\ell(u,v)}{F_0(u,v)}\right], \quad (12.102)$$

$$F_\ell(u,v) = \cosh\left[\left(\frac{1}{2}M - \ell\right)\log\phi\right]. \quad (12.103)$$

Now, after tedious but straightforward expansion in M^{-1} one finds that

$$\frac{F_\ell(u,v)}{F_0(u,v)} = 1 - \frac{2\ell\sqrt{u^2+v^2}}{M}\tanh\left(\sqrt{u^2+v^2}\right) + \frac{2\ell^2(u^2+v^2)}{M^2} + \mathcal{O}(M^{-3}). \quad (12.104)$$

Hence

$$\Xi_\ell(u,v) = 1 - \frac{2\ell v^2}{M}\frac{\tanh(\sqrt{u^2+v^2})}{\sqrt{u^2+v^2}} + \frac{2\ell^2 v^2}{M^2} + \mathcal{O}(M^{-3}). \quad (12.105)$$

It follows that the equations for $\tilde{\mathcal{E}} = M(1-\mathcal{E})$ and $\tilde{C} = M(1-C)$ take the form

$$\tilde{\mathcal{E}} = 2v^2\frac{\tanh(\sqrt{u^2+v^2})}{\sqrt{u^2+v^2}} - \frac{2v^2}{M} + \mathcal{O}(M^{-2}), \quad \tilde{C} = 2\tilde{\mathcal{E}} - \frac{4v^2}{M} + \mathcal{O}(M^{-2}). \quad (12.106)$$

The dynamical equations then become

$$\frac{\mathrm{d}}{\mathrm{d}t}m = \tilde{\mathcal{E}}\beta(h + J_0 m) - 2m\beta^2\Gamma^2 + \mathcal{O}\left(\frac{1}{M}\right), \quad (12.107)$$

$$\frac{\mathrm{d}}{\mathrm{d}t}\tilde{\mathcal{E}} = 4M(\beta^2\Gamma^2 - v^2) - 8\beta^3\Gamma^2 m(J_0 m + h) - 4\beta^2\Gamma^2\tilde{\mathcal{E}} + \mathcal{O}\left(\frac{1}{M}\right). \quad (12.108)$$

What remains is to express v in terms of $(m, \tilde{\mathcal{E}})$, in leading two orders, by solving Eq. (12.106) for $\tilde{\mathcal{E}}$ alongside our equation for m. The latter is

$$m = \frac{u\tanh(\sqrt{u^2+v^2})}{\sqrt{u^2+v^2}} + \mathcal{O}(M^{-2}). \quad (12.109)$$

Equation (12.106) shows that $v = 0$ corresponds to $\tilde{\mathcal{E}} = 0$, and that $\tilde{\mathcal{E}}$ increases with v^2. On intermediate timescales $\tau = M^{-1}$, we have

$$\frac{\mathrm{d}}{\mathrm{d}t}m = \mathcal{O}\left(\frac{1}{M}\right), \quad \frac{\mathrm{d}}{\mathrm{d}t}\tilde{\mathcal{E}} = 4(\beta^2\Gamma^2 - v^2) + \mathcal{O}\left(\frac{1}{M}\right), \quad (12.110)$$

where m remains constant and $\tilde{\mathcal{E}}$ evolves toward the value for which $v = \beta\Gamma + \mathcal{O}(M^{-1})$ (which is also the equilibrium value for v). Thus, in the dynamical equations in Eqs. (12.107, 12.108) describing the process on timescales of $\tau = M^{-2}$ we must substitute $v^2 = \beta^2\Gamma^2 + \mathcal{O}(M^{-1})$. Thus, during the slow process where m evolves we always have

$$\tilde{\mathcal{E}} = 2\beta^2\Gamma^2\, m/u. \tag{12.111}$$

Upon insertion into Eq. (12.107), this results in a closed dynamical equation for m only:

$$\frac{\mathrm{d}}{\mathrm{d}t}m = 2\beta^2\Gamma^2\left(\frac{\beta(h+J_0 m)\tanh(\sqrt{u^2+\beta^2\Gamma^2})}{\sqrt{u^2+\beta^2\Gamma^2}} - m\right), \tag{12.112}$$

without requiring additional approximations, and with u to be solved from[7]

$$m = \frac{u\tanh(\sqrt{u^2+\beta^2\Gamma^2})}{\sqrt{u^2+\beta^2\Gamma^2}}. \tag{12.113}$$

In equilibrium we recover from Eqs. (12.112, 12.113) the correct equilibrium state in Eq. (12.88), with $u = \beta(J_0 m+h)$. Comparison with Eq. (10) in [7] reveals, apart from a harmless difference in time units, that the approximation of [7] (used also in [8–10]) implies replacing u *at any time* by $\beta(J_0 m+h)$. While this indeed holds in equilibrium, the approximation may be dangerous far from equilibrium.

In Fig. 12.1 we test the predictions of Eqs. (12.112, 12.113) against numerical simulations of the process in Eqs. (12.11, 12.12). The approximate co-location of the simulation curves for widely varying values of M confirms that $\tau = \mathcal{O}(1/M^2)$ (inferred from the dynamical theory) indeed captures the characteristic timescale of the macroscopic process. Second, while not showing perfect agreement with the simulation data, which is not expected in view of the probability equipartitioning assumption used to close the macroscopic dynamical equations, away from stationarity the full theory in Eqs. (12.112, 12.113) is reasonably accurate and improves upon the approximation proposed in [7].

12.7 Discussion

In this chapter we aimed to explain the basic ideas and assumptions behind the DRT strategy for deriving and closing macroscopic dynamical equations, and its application to the types of spin systems used in quantum annealing with transverse fields.

---

[7] For certain values of m and $\beta\Gamma$, Eq. (12.113) may have more than one solution u. In such cases the physical solution is the one with the largest absolute value.

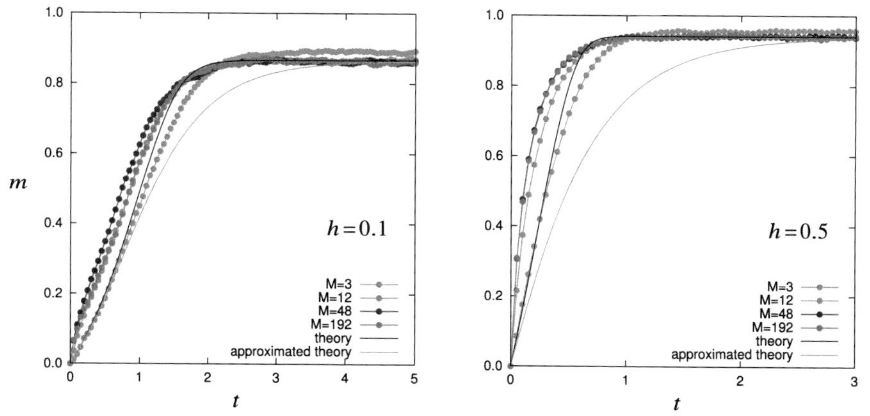

Fig. 12.1 Theory versus computer simulations of the microscopic process in Eqs. (12.11, 12.12) for the Trotter representation of the system with Hamiltonian $H = -(J_0/N)\sum_{i<j}\sigma_i^z\sigma_j^z - \sum_i(h\sigma_i^z + \Gamma\sigma_i^x)$, with $N=10000$ and $M\in\{3, 12, 48, 192\}$. In all cases $J_0=1$, $T=\Gamma=0.5$, and $\tau=1/M^2$ (so time units correspond to NM^3 attempted moves per spin). Left figure: magnetization versus time for $h=0.1$; right figure: the same for $h=0.5$. The simulation data are shown as connected markers. The black curve is the theoretical prediction, that is, the solution of Eqs. (12.112, 12.113). The light blue curve is the approximated theory of [7], obtained by solving Eq. (12.112) with the equilibrium value $u=\beta(J_0m+h)$

We focused on technicalities relating to commutation of the limits $N\to\infty$ and $M\to\infty$, the possible choices of macroscopic observables, the distinct M-dependent timescales in the evolution of the Trotter system, and on how an additional approximation made in earlier studies can be avoided, leading to a more precise dynamical theory. We have tested the theoretical predictions of the theory against numerical MCMC simulations of a ferromagnetic quantum system [11] with transverse external fields in Trotter representation and found good agreement.

Since there was no disorder in the examples used in this text, we could work with the dynamical laws in Eq. (12.22). If, in contrast, there is disorder in the problem, the macroscopic laws need to be averaged over its realization, and the main tool is Eq. (12.24). For models with random interactions, performing this disorder average is, however, relatively painless and does not make the dynamical theory significantly more complicated.

We hope that this introduction to the method may aid the development of further analytical studies of the macroscopic dynamics of quantum annealing, including models with time-dependent control parameters, more realistic quantum systems with disordered spin interactions or with interactions on finitely connected graphs, and more precise analytical descriptions in which the macroscopic dynamical observables are functions [14, 19, 20] instead of scalars.

Acknowledgements The authors are grateful for stimulating discussions with Professor Hidetoshi Nishimori.

Appendix: Mathematical Identities

Here we list some basic properties of relevant transfer matrices and expectation values in the single-site Trotter system. The transfer matrix and its eigenvalues are

$$\boldsymbol{K}=\begin{pmatrix} e^{y+x} & e^{-y} \\ e^{-y} & e^{y-x} \end{pmatrix}, \quad \lambda_{\pm}=e^{y}\Big[\cosh(x)\pm\sqrt{\sinh^2(x)+e^{-4y}}\Big] \tag{12.114}$$

The corresponding normalized eigenvectors are

$$|+\rangle=\frac{1}{L}\Big(e^{-2y},\sqrt{\sinh^2(x)+e^{-4y}}-\sinh(x)\Big), \tag{12.115}$$

$$|-\rangle=\frac{1}{L}\Big(\sqrt{\sinh^2(x)+e^{-4y}}-\sinh(x),\,-e^{-2y}\Big), \tag{12.116}$$

$$L^2=e^{-4y}+\Big(\sqrt{\sinh^2(x)+e^{-4y}}-\sinh(x)\Big)^2. \tag{12.117}$$

From these expressions one can find $\langle\pm|\sigma^z|\pm\rangle=\pm\sinh(x)/\sqrt{\sinh^2(x)+e^{-4y}}$, and compute the following observables (with $\phi=\lambda_-/\lambda_+$):

$$\frac{\sum_{s_1\ldots s_M}s_1\prod_{k=1}^M K_{s_k s_{k+1}}}{\sum_{s_1\ldots s_M}\prod_{k=1}^M K_{s_k s_{k+1}}}=-\frac{\sinh(x)\tanh\left[\frac{1}{2}M\log\phi\right]}{\sqrt{\sinh^2(x)+e^{-4y}}}, \tag{12.118}$$

$$\frac{\sum_{s_1\ldots s_M}s_1 s_2\prod_{k=1}^M K_{s_k s_{k+1}}}{\sum_{s_1\ldots s_M}\prod_{k=1}^M K_{s_k s_{k+1}}}=\frac{\sinh^2(x)}{\sinh^2(x)+e^{-4y}}+\frac{\cosh\left[\left(\frac{1}{2}M-1\right)\log\phi\right]}{\cosh\left[\frac{1}{2}M\log\phi\right]}\frac{e^{-4y}}{\sinh^2(x)+e^{-4y}} \tag{12.119}$$

$$\frac{\sum_{s_1\ldots s_M}s_1 s_3\prod_{k=1}^M K_{s_k s_{k+1}}}{\sum_{s_1\ldots s_M}\prod_{k=1}^M K_{s_k s_{k+1}}}=\frac{\sinh^2(x)}{\sinh^2(x)+e^{-4y}}+\frac{\cosh\left[\left(\frac{1}{2}M-2\right)\log\phi\right]}{\cosh\left[\frac{1}{2}M\log\phi\right]}\frac{e^{-4y}}{\sinh^2(x)+e^{-4y}} \tag{12.120}$$

References

1. T. Kadowaki, H. Nishimori, Quantum annealing in the transverse Ising model. Phys. Rev. E **58**, 5355–5363 (1998)
2. J.I. Inoue, Infinite-range transverse field Ising models and quantum computation. Eur. Phys. J. Special Topics **224**, 149–161 (2015)
3. S. Suzuki, J.I. Inoue, B.K. Chakrabarti, *Quantum Ising Phases and transitions in Transverse Ising Models*. Springer Lecture Notes in Physics 862, 2nd Ed. (2013)

4. M. Suzuki, Relationship between d-dimensional quantal spin systems and $(d + 1)$-dimensional Ising systems. Prog. Theor. Phys. **56**, 1454–1469 (1976)
5. D. Bedeaux, K. Lakatos-Lindenberg, K.E. Shuler, On the relation between Master equations and random walks and their solutions. J. Math. Phys. **12**, 2116–2123 (1971)
6. M. Ohzeki, Quantum Monte Carlo simulation of a particular class of non-stoquastic Hamiltonians in quantum annealing. Sci. Rep. **7**, 41186 (2017)
7. J.I. Inoue, Deterministic flows of order parameters in the stochastic processes of quantum Monte Carlo method. J. Phys. Conf. Ser. **233**, 012020 (2010)
8. J.I. Inoue, Pattern-recalling processes in quantum Hopfield networks far from saturation. J. Phys. Conf. Ser. **297**, 012012 (2011)
9. V. Bapst, G. Semerjian, Thermal, quantum and simulated quantum annealing: analytical comparisons for simple models. J. Phys. Conf. Ser. **473**, 012011 (2013)
10. S. Arai, M. Ohzeki, K. Tanaka, Dynamics of order parameters in nonstoquastic Hamiltonians in the adaptive quantum Monte Carlo method. Phys. Rev. E **99**, 032120 (2019)
11. L. Chayes, N. Crawford, D. Ioffe, A. Levit, The phase diagram of the quantum Curie- Weiss model. J. Stat. Phys. **133**, 131–149 (2008)
12. A.C.C. Coolen, D. Sherrington, Dynamics of fully connected attractor neural networks near saturation. Phys. Rev. Lett. **71**, 3886–3889 (1993)
13. A.C.C. Coolen, D. Sherrington, Order parameter flow in the SK spin-glass I: replica symmetry. J. Phys. A **27**, 7687–7707 (1994)
14. S.N. Laughton, A.C.C. Coolen, D. Sherrington, Order-parameter flow in the SK spin-glass II: inclusion of microscopic memory effects. J. Phys. A **29**, 763–786 (1996)
15. H. Nishimori, Y. Nonomura, Quantum effects in neural networks. J. Phys. Soc. Jpn. **65**, 3780–3796 (1996)
16. M. Mézard, G. Parisi, M.A. Virasoro, *Spin Glass Theory and Beyond* (World Scientific, Singapore, 1987)
17. H. Nishimori, *Statistical Physics of Spin Glasses and Information Processing* (Oxford University Press, 2001)
18. R. Bruinsma, G. Aeppli, One-dimensional Ising model in a random field. Phys. Rev. Lett. **50**, 1494–1497 (1983)
19. A. Mozeika, A.C.C. Coolen, Dynamical replica analysis of processes on finitely connected random graphs: I. Vertex covering. J. Phys. A **41**, 115003 (2008)
20. A. Mozeika, A.C.C. Coolen, Dynamical replica analysis of processes on finitely connected random graphs: II. Dynamics in the Griffiths phase of the diluted Ising ferromagnet. J. Phys. A **42**, 195006 (2009)

Open Access This chapter is licensed under the terms of the Creative Commons Attribution 4.0 International License (http://creativecommons.org/licenses/by/4.0/), which permits use, sharing, adaptation, distribution and reproduction in any medium or format, as long as you give appropriate credit to the original author(s) and the source, provide a link to the Creative Commons license and indicate if changes were made.

The images or other third party material in this chapter are included in the chapter's Creative Commons license, unless indicated otherwise in a credit line to the material. If material is not included in the chapter's Creative Commons license and your intended use is not permitted by statutory regulation or exceeds the permitted use, you will need to obtain permission directly from the copyright holder.

Chapter 13
Mean-Field Analysis of Sourlas Codes with Adiabatic Reverse Annealing

Shunta Arai

Abstract In this chapter, we analyze the typical performance of adiabatic reverse annealing (ARA) for Sourlas codes. Sourlas codes are representative error-correcting codes related to p-body spin-glass models and have a first-order phase transition for $p > 2$, which degrades the estimation performance. In the ARA formulation, we introduce the initial Hamiltonian which incorporates the prior information of the solution into a vanilla quantum annealing (QA) formulation. The ground state of the initial Hamiltonian represents the initial candidate solution. To avoid the first-order phase transition, we apply ARA to Sourlas codes. We evaluate the typical ARA performance for Sourlas codes using the replica method. We show that ARA can avoid the first-order phase transition if we prepare for the proper initial candidate solution.

13.1 Introduction

Problems in information processing have been studied analytically from the viewpoint of statistical mechanics [12]. Associative memory, Sourlas codes, code-division multiple-access (CDMA), and image restoration are very popular examples [5, 6, 21, 24]. Many studies have focused on the degradation of the original signal or information due to noise. The noise can be physically regarded as thermal fluctuations. The original information can be estimated from the degraded data by tuning the strength of thermal fluctuations.

In this chapter, we focus mainly on error-correcting codes such as Sourlas codes, which are described by p-body spin-glass problems [21]. The main idea of error-correcting codes is to add redundancy while sending information to decode the original signal from noisy outputs. In Sourlas codes, the original signal is encoded in the interactions of the spins. To estimate the original signal, we search the ground

S. Arai (✉)
Graduate School of Information Sciences, Tohoku University, 980-8579 Sendai, Japan
e-mail: shunta.arai.d8@tohoku.ac.jp

Sigma-i Co.,Ltd., 108-0075 Minato, Tokyo, Japan

© The Author(s) 2022

N. Katoh et al. (eds.), *Sublinear Computation Paradigm*,
https://doi.org/10.1007/978-981-16-4095-7_13

state of the Hamiltonian or compute the expectation value over the Gibbs–Boltzmann distribution at a finite temperature.

In addition to thermal fluctuations, quantum fluctuations can also be used to infer the original information. Several studies have demonstrated that quantum fluctuations such as the transverse field do not necessarily enhance the performance of decoding for image restoration, Sourlas codes, or CDMA [2, 6, 15, 16]. The optimal estimation performance using quantum fluctuations is inferior to that using thermal fluctuations in Bayes-optimal cases. However, in some non-Bayes optimal cases, the estimation performance using finite quantum fluctuations and thermal fluctuations surpasses that using only thermal fluctuations; for example, when the assigned temperature is lower than the true noise scale. This implies the potential of combining quantum and thermal fluctuations for signal recovery problems.

Signal estimation algorithms using quantum fluctuations are related to optimization algorithms using quantum fluctuations, which is known as quantum annealing (QA) [9] or adiabatic quantum computation (AQC) [3]. The QA algorithm is physically implemented in the quantum annealer [7]. The quantum annealer has been tested in numerous applications, including traffic optimization [11] and in vehicles in factories [14].

In a closed system, the QA procedure is as follows. First, we set the initial state as the trivial ground state of the transverse field term. Next, we gradually decrease the strength of the transverse field. Following the Schrodinger equation, the trivial ground state evolves adiabatically into a nontrivial ground state of the target Hamiltonian, which is consistent with a solution of combinatorial optimization problems. The quantum adiabatic theorem indicates that the total computational time for searching the ground state is characterized by the minimum energy gap between the ground state and first excited state [23]. When the target Hamiltonian has a first-order phase transition, the computational time to find the ground state grows exponentially.

Reverse annealing (RA) is a protocol for restarting quantum dynamics from the final state of the standard QA procedure [17]. The RA algorithm can be used to avoid or mitigate the first-order phase transition and is classified into two methods: *adiabatic reverse annealing* (ARA) [13] and *iterated reverse annealing* (IRA) [26]. ARA and IRA are distinguished by how the final state is utilized. One implements the final state by introducing the initial Hamiltonian, and the other incorporates it as the initial condition.

In a recent study [2], ARA is applied to CDMA multiuser detection. ARA can avoid or mitigate the first-order phase transition in the CDMA model. In this chapter, we apply ARA for Sourlas codes. Sourlas codes have a first-order phase transition for $p > 2$. The existence of the first-order phase transition deteriorates the estimation performance. We evaluate the typical performance of ARA for Sourlas codes using the replica method. We demonstrate that ARA can avoid the first-order phase transition of Sourlas codes if we prepare the proper initial conditions.

13.2 Sourlas Codes Using Quantum Fluctuations

Following a previous study [15], we formulate Sourlas codes using quantum fluctuations. Sourlas codes are set up to send a set of products of p spins $J_{i_1 \dots i_p} = \xi_{i_1} \dots \xi_{i_p}$ through a channel. The symbol $\xi_i = \pm 1 (i = 1 \dots N)$ represents the original signal, which is independently generated from the uniform distribution $P(\xi_i) = 1/2$. We consider the Gauss channel as

$$P(J_{i_1 \dots i_p} | \{\xi\}) = \left(\frac{N^{p-1}}{J^2 \pi p!} \right)^{\frac{1}{2}} \exp \left\{ - \frac{N^{p-1}}{J^2 p!} \left(J_{i_1 \dots i_p} - \frac{J_0 p! \xi_{i_1} \dots \xi_{i_p}}{N^{p-1}} \right)^2 \right\}, \quad (13.1)$$

where J and J_0 are hyperparameters. The ratio J_0/J represents the signal-to-noise ratio. The distribution $P(J_{i_1 \dots i_p} | \{\xi\})$ is the conditional probability of the signal $J_{i_1 \dots i_p}$ for the encoded signal $\xi_{i_1} \dots \xi_{i_p}$. We infer the original signal $\{\xi\}$ from the noisy outputs $\{J_{i_1 \dots i_p}\}$. Using the Bayes formula, we introduce the posterior probability for the estimated signal $\boldsymbol{\sigma} = \{\sigma_1 \dots \sigma_N\} \in \{\pm 1\}^N$ as

$$P(\boldsymbol{\sigma} | \{J_{i_1 \dots i_p}\}) = \frac{P(\{J_{i_1 \dots i_p}\} | \boldsymbol{\sigma}) P(\boldsymbol{\sigma})}{\sum_{\boldsymbol{\sigma}} P(\{J_{i_1 \dots i_p}\} | \boldsymbol{\sigma}) P(\boldsymbol{\sigma})}, \quad (13.2)$$

where $P(\{J_{i_1 \dots i_p}\} | \boldsymbol{\sigma})$ and $P(\boldsymbol{\sigma})$ are the likelihood and prior distribution, respectively. The summation of spin variables $\sum_{\boldsymbol{\sigma}}$ is defined for all possible configurations. The likelihood can be expressed as

$$P(\{J_{i_1 \dots i_p}\} | \boldsymbol{\sigma}) \propto \exp \left(\beta \sum_{i_1 < \dots < i_p} J_{i_1 \dots i_p} \sigma_{i_1} \dots \sigma_{i_p} \right), \quad (13.3)$$

where β is the inverse temperature and the summation $\sum_{i_1 < \dots < i_p}$ runs over all possible combinations of p spins out of N spins. According to Eqs. (13.2) and (13.3), the posterior distribution can be written by using the Gibbs–Boltzmann distribution with the classical Hamiltonian $\mathcal{H}(\boldsymbol{\sigma})$, as follows:

$$P(\boldsymbol{\sigma} | \{J_{i_1 \dots i_p}\}) = \frac{1}{Z} \exp \{ -\beta (\mathcal{H}(\boldsymbol{\sigma}) + \mathcal{H}_{\text{init}}(\boldsymbol{\sigma})) \}, \quad (13.4)$$

$$Z = \sum_{\boldsymbol{\sigma}} \exp \{ -\beta (\mathcal{H}(\boldsymbol{\sigma}) + \mathcal{H}_{\text{init}}(\boldsymbol{\sigma})) \}, \quad (13.5)$$

$$\mathcal{H}(\boldsymbol{\sigma}) = - \sum_{i_1 < \dots < i_p} J_{i_1 \dots i_p} \sigma_{i_1} \dots \sigma_{i_p}, \quad (13.6)$$

where Z is the partition function and $\mathcal{H}_{\text{init}}(\boldsymbol{\sigma})$ is the initial Hamiltonian, which represents the prior information of the estimated signal. We generally assume that the prior of the estimated signal follows a uniform distribution $P(\boldsymbol{\sigma}) = 1/2^N$.

To decode the original signal, one decoding strategy is the maximum a posteriori (MAP) estimation, which corresponds to searching the ground state of the classical Hamiltonian of Sourlas codes in the limit of zero temperature. Another is the marginal posterior mode (MPM) estimation, which corresponds to finding the expectation value over the posterior distribution at a finite temperature. In the limit of zero temperature, the MPM estimation is consistent with the MAP estimation. In this chapter, we mainly consider the MPM estimation. The estimation performance can be evaluated by the overlap between the original and estimated signal as

$$\mathcal{M}(\beta) = \mathrm{Tr}_{\boldsymbol{\xi}} \prod_{i_1<\cdots<i_p} \int dJ_{i_1\ldots i_p} P(\boldsymbol{\xi}) P(\{J_{i_1\ldots i_p}\}|\boldsymbol{\xi}) \xi_i \,\mathrm{sgn}\langle\sigma_i\rangle \tag{13.7}$$

where $\langle\cdot\rangle$ is the expectation over the posterior distribution $P(\boldsymbol{\sigma}|\{J_{i_1\ldots i_p}\})$. This quantity is expected to exhibit a "self-averaging" property in the thermodynamics limit $N \to \infty$. This means that the observables, such as the overlap for a quenched realization of the data $\{J_{i_1\ldots i_p}\}$, and $\boldsymbol{\xi}$, are equivalent to the expectation itself over the data distribution $P(\boldsymbol{\xi})P(\{J_{i_1\ldots i_p}\}|\boldsymbol{\xi})$. In this case, the overlap can be expressed as $\lim_{N\to\infty} M = [\xi_i \mathrm{sgn}\langle\sigma_i\rangle]$, where the bracket $[\cdot]$ indicates the expectation over the data distribution.

Quantum fluctuations can be utilized to decode the original information. The Hamiltonian of Sourlas code using quantum fluctuations is expressed as follows:

$$\hat{\mathcal{H}} = s\hat{\mathcal{H}}_0 + (1-s)\hat{\mathcal{H}}_{\mathrm{TF}}, \tag{13.8}$$

$$\hat{\mathcal{H}}_0 = -\sum_{i_1<\cdots<i_p} J_{i_1\ldots i_p} \hat{\sigma}^z_{i_1} \ldots \hat{\sigma}^z_{i_p}, \tag{13.9}$$

$$\hat{\mathcal{H}}_{\mathrm{TF}} = -\sum_{i=1}^{N} \hat{\sigma}^x_i, \tag{13.10}$$

where $\hat{\sigma}^z_i$ and $\hat{\sigma}^x_i$ are the z and x components of the Pauli matrix at site i. We parameterize the Hamiltonian by the annealing parameter s for the ARA formulation. Note that $\hat{\mathcal{H}}_0$ and $\hat{\mathcal{H}}_{\mathrm{TF}}$ consist of the z and x components of the Pauli matrices, respectively. As in the classical case, we can consider the MPM estimation using quantum fluctuations. The performance of the MPM estimation using quantum fluctuations can be evaluated by the overlap as follows:

$$\begin{aligned} M(\beta, s) &= \mathrm{Tr}_{\{\xi\}} \int \prod_{i_1<\cdots<i_p} dJ_{i_1\ldots i_p} P(\{J_{i_1\ldots i_p}\}|\{\xi\}) P(\{\xi\}) \xi_i \mathrm{sgn}\langle\hat{\sigma}^z_i\rangle_{\mathrm{TF}} \\ &\equiv \left[\xi_i \mathrm{sgn}(\langle\hat{\sigma}^z_i\rangle_{\mathrm{TF}})\right], \end{aligned} \tag{13.11}$$

where $\langle(\cdot)\rangle_{\mathrm{TF}} \equiv \mathrm{Tr}\left((\cdot)\,\hat{\rho}\right)$ denotes the expectation over the density matrix $\hat{\rho} \equiv e^{-\beta\hat{\mathcal{H}}}/\mathrm{Tr}e^{-\beta\hat{\mathcal{H}}}$.

13.3 Replica Analysis for Adiabatic Reverse Annealing

Following Ref. [13], we formulate Sourlas codes using quantum fluctuations in ARA as follows:

$$\hat{\mathcal{H}} = s\hat{\mathcal{H}}_0 + (1-s)(1-\lambda)\hat{\mathcal{H}}_{\text{init}} + (1-s)\lambda\hat{\mathcal{H}}_{\text{TF}}, \tag{13.12}$$

$$\hat{\mathcal{H}}_{\text{init}} = -\sum_{i=1}^{N} \tau_i \hat{\sigma}_i^z, \tag{13.13}$$

where λ $(0 \le \lambda \le 1)$ is the RA parameter. We now introduce the initial candidate solution $\tau_i = \pm 1$ that is expected to be close to the correct ground state ξ_i. We define the probability distribution of the initial candidate solutions as follows:

$$P(\boldsymbol{\tau}) = \prod_{i=1}^{N} P(\tau_i) = \prod_{i=1}^{N} \left(c_1\delta(\tau_i - \xi_i) + c_{-1}\delta(\tau_i + \xi_i)\right), \tag{13.14}$$

where we utilize the symbol $c_1 = c$ and $c_{-1} = 1 - c$. The number c $(0 \le c \le 1)$ denotes the fraction of the original signal $\tau_i = \xi_i$ in the initial candidate solution as

$$c = \frac{1}{N}\sum_{i=1}^{N} \delta_{\tau_i \xi_i}. \tag{13.15}$$

We consider that the ARA formulation is the case when we adopt $P(\boldsymbol{\sigma}^z|\boldsymbol{\tau}) \propto \exp\left(-\beta \hat{H}_{\text{init}}\right)$ as the prior distribution.

The typical behaviors of the order parameters, such as the overlap, can be obtained via the free energy. The free energy density f can be evaluated as $-\beta f = \lim_{N\to\infty}(1/N)[\ln Z]$ in the limit of $N \to \infty$ where $Z = \mathrm{Tr}\exp\left(-\beta\hat{\mathcal{H}}\right)$ is the partition function of Eq. (13.12). In general, the direct computation of the free energy density is hard due to the configuration average of $\ln Z$ and the off-diagonal elements in Eq. (13.12). The configuration average can be found using the replica trick [20]. Even though we can avoid the direct computation of $[\ln Z]$, we cannot apply the standard techniques to evaluate the free energy density due to the non-commutativity of the Hamiltonian.

First, to eliminate the non-commutativity of the Hamiltonian, we apply the Suzuki–Trotter decomposition [22] to the partition function:

$$\begin{aligned} Z &= \lim_{M\to\infty} \mathrm{Tr}\left\{\exp\left(-\frac{\beta}{M}\left(s\hat{\mathcal{H}}_0 + (1-s)(1-\lambda)\hat{\mathcal{H}}_{\text{init}}\right)\right)\exp\left(-\frac{\beta(1-s)\lambda}{M}\hat{\mathcal{H}}_{\text{TF}}\right)\right\}^M \\ &= \lim_{M\to\infty} Z_M, \end{aligned} \tag{13.16}$$

where

$$Z_M = \mathrm{Tr}\exp\left(\frac{\beta s}{M}\sum_{t=1}^{M}\sum_{i_1<\cdots<i_p} J_{i_1\cdots p}\sigma_{i_1}^z(t)\ldots\sigma_{i_p}^z(t) + \frac{\beta(1-s)(1-\lambda)}{M}\sum_{i=1}^{N}\tau_i\sigma_i^z(t)\right.$$
$$\left.+\frac{\beta(1-s)\lambda}{M}\sum_{i=1}^{N}\sigma_i^x(t)\right)\times\prod_{i=1}^{N}\prod_{t=1}^{M}\langle\sigma_i^z(t)|\sigma_i^x(t)\rangle\langle\sigma_i^x(t)|\sigma_i^z(t+1)\rangle, \tag{13.17}$$

where the symbol t is the index of the Trotter slice, M is the Trotter number, and Tr denotes the trace in the z and x basis. We impose the periodic boundary conditions $\sigma_i^z(1) = \sigma_i^z(M+1)$ for all i and introduce the identity operator $\hat{1} = \sum_{\{\sigma^z(t)\}} |\{\sigma^z(t)\}\rangle\langle\{\sigma^z(t)\}|$ and $\hat{1} = \sum_{\{\sigma^x(t)\}} |\{\sigma^x(t)\}\rangle\langle\{\sigma^x(t)\}|$. The detailed calculation is given in Appendix 13.5.

To evaluate $[\ln Z]$, we utilize the replica trick [20]:

$$[\log Z] = \lim_{n\to 0}\frac{[Z^n]-1}{n}, \tag{13.18}$$

where n is the replica number. The replicated partition function can be written as

$$[Z^n] = \lim_{M\to\infty}\sum_{\{\xi_i=\pm 1\}}\sum_{\{\tau_i=\pm\xi_i\}} P(\boldsymbol{\xi})P(\boldsymbol{\tau})\prod_{i_1<\cdots<i_p}\int dJ_{i_1,\ldots,i_p}P(\{J_{i_1,\ldots,i_p}\}|\xi_{i_1}\ldots\xi_{i_p})$$
$$\times\,\mathrm{Tr}\exp\left\{\frac{\beta s}{M}\sum_{t,a}\sum_{i_1<\cdots<i_p} J_{i_1\cdots p}\sigma_{i_1a}^z(t)\ldots\sigma_{i_pa}^z(t) + \frac{\beta(1-s)(1-\lambda)}{M}\sum_{i,t,a}\tau_i\sigma_{ia}^z(t)\right.$$
$$\left.+\frac{\beta(1-s)\lambda}{M}\sum_{i,t,a}\sigma_{ia}^x(t)\right\}\prod_{i,t,a}\langle\sigma_{ia}^z(t)|\sigma_{ia}^x(t)\rangle\langle\sigma_{ia}^x(t)|\sigma_{ia}^z(t+1)\rangle, \tag{13.19}$$

in which a denotes the replica index.

To remove the dependency of the original signal $\{\xi\}$, we apply the gauge transformation $J_{i_1\ldots i_p} \to J_{i_1\ldots i_p}\xi_{i_1}\ldots\xi_{i_p}$ and $\sigma_{ia}^z(t) \to \sigma_{ia}^z(t)\xi_i$ to the partition function $[Z_M^n]$. Performing the Gaussian integration over the distribution in Eq. (13.1), we introduce the following order parameters as

$$m_a(t) = \frac{1}{N}\sum_{i=1}^{N}\sigma_{ia}^z(t), \tag{13.20}$$

$$q_{ab}(t,t') = \frac{1}{N}\sum_{i=1}^{N}\sigma_{ia}^z(t)\sigma_{ib}^z(t'), \tag{13.21}$$

$$R_a(t,t') = \frac{1}{N}\sum_{i=1}^{N}\sigma_{ia}^z(t)\sigma_{ia}^z(t'), \tag{13.22}$$

$$m_a^x(t) = \frac{1}{N}\sum_{i=1}^{N}\sigma_{ia}^x(t). \tag{13.23}$$

The physical meanings of the order parameters are as follows: $m_a(t)$ is the magnetization, $q_{ab}(t, t')$ is the spin-glass order parameter, $R_a(t, t')$ is the correlation between each Trotter slice, and $m_a^x(t)$ is the transverse magnetization. Moreover, we introduce the auxiliary parameters $\tilde{m}_a(t)$, $\tilde{q}_{ab}(t, t')$, $\tilde{R}_a(t, t')$, $\tilde{m}_a^x(t)$ of the order parameters with the delta function and its Fourier integral representation. Under the replica symmetry (RS) ansatz and static approximation, $m_a(t) = m$, $q_{ab}(t, t') = q$, $R_a(t, t') = R$, $m_a^x(t) = m^x$, $\tilde{m}_a(t) = \tilde{m}$, $\tilde{q}_{ab}(t, t') = \tilde{q}$, $\tilde{R}_a(t, t') = \tilde{R}$, $\tilde{m}_a^x(t) = \tilde{m}^x$, we can attain the RS free energy density:

$$-\beta f_{\mathrm{RS}} = \beta s J_0 m^p + \frac{\beta^2 s^2 J^2}{4}(R^p - q^p) + \beta(1-s)\lambda m^x - \beta m\tilde{m} - \beta m^x\tilde{m}^x - \frac{\beta^2}{2}(R\tilde{R} - q\tilde{q}) + \sum_{a=\pm 1} c_a \int Dz \ln 2Y_a, \tag{13.24}$$

$$Y_a \equiv \int Dy \cosh \beta u_a, \tag{13.25}$$

$$u_a \equiv \sqrt{g_a^2 + (\tilde{m}^x)^2}, \tag{13.26}$$

$$g_a \equiv \tilde{m} + a(1-s)(1-\lambda) + \sqrt{\tilde{q}}z + \sqrt{\tilde{R} - \tilde{q}}y, \tag{13.27}$$

where Dz means that the Gaussian measure $Dz := 1/\sqrt{2\pi}dze^{-z^2/2}$, and Dy is the same as Dz. Detailed calculations for deriving the free energy density in Eq. (13.24) are provided in Appendix 13.5. The order parameters and their auxiliary parameters are determined by the saddle-point conditions in the free energy density. The extremization of Eq. (13.24) yields the following saddle-point equations:

$$m = \sum_{a=\pm 1} c_a \int DzY_a^{-1} \int Dy \left(\frac{g_a}{u_a}\right) \sinh \beta u_a, \tag{13.28}$$

$$q = \sum_{a=\pm 1} c_a \int Dz \left\{Y_a^{-1} \int Dy \left(\frac{g_a}{u_a}\right) \sinh \beta u_a\right\}^2, \tag{13.29}$$

$$R = \sum_{a=\pm 1} c_a \int DzY_a^{-1} \int Dy \left\{\left(\frac{(\tilde{m}^x)^2}{\beta u_a^3}\right) \sinh \beta u_a + \left(\frac{g_a}{u_a}\right)^2 \cosh \beta u_a\right\}, \tag{13.30}$$

$$m^x = \sum_{a=\pm 1} c_a \int DzY_a^{-1} \int Dy \left(\frac{\tilde{m}^x}{u_a}\right) \sinh \beta u_a, \tag{13.31}$$

$$\tilde{m} = sJ_0 p m^{p-1}, \tag{13.32}$$

$$\tilde{q} = \frac{s^2 J^2}{2} p q^{p-1}, \tag{13.33}$$

$$\tilde{R} = \frac{s^2 J^2}{2} p R^{p-1}, \tag{13.34}$$

$$\tilde{m}^x = (1-s)\lambda. \tag{13.35}$$

From Eq. (13.11), the overlap function is easily expressed as

$$M(\beta, s, \lambda) = \sum_{a=\pm 1} c_a \int Dz \mathrm{sgn} \left\{ Y_a^{-1} \int Dy \left(\frac{g_a}{u_a} \right) \sinh \beta u_a \right\}. \tag{13.36}$$

In the low-temperature region, the p-body spin-glass model is known to exhibit replica symmetry breaking (RSB) [4]. The stability condition of RS solutions under the static approximation is expressed as

$$\frac{\beta^2 s^2 J^2 p(p-1)}{2} q^{p-2} \left(\sum_{a=\pm 1} c_a A_a \right) < 1, \tag{13.37}$$

$$A_a \equiv \int Dz \left\{ \left(Y_a^{-1} \int Dy \left(\frac{g_a}{u_a} \right) \sinh \beta u_a \right)^2 \right.$$
$$\left. - Y_a^{-1} \left(\int Dy \left(\frac{(\tilde{m}^x)^2}{\beta u_a^3} \right) \sinh \beta u_a + \int Dy \left(\frac{g_a}{u_a} \right)^2 \cosh \beta u_a \right) \right\}^2. \tag{13.38}$$

This condition, called the Almeida–Thouless (AT) condition [1], can be attained by considering perturbations to the RS solutions. This result is consistent with the previous result in Ref. [25] for $p = 2$, $J_0 = 0$, and $\lambda = 1$.

13.4 Numerical Experiments

We numerically solve the saddle-point equations in Eqs. (13.28)–(13.35) with $p = 5$, temperature $T = 0.05$, and signal-to-noise ratio $J_0/J = 1.5$. To evaluate the typical MPM estimation performance, we often utilize the overlap $M(\beta, s, \lambda)$. In this chapter, we focus mainly on the possibility of avoiding the first-order phase transition by ARA. For the sake of simplicity and computational cost, we adopt the magnetization as a measure of the average MPM estimation performance using ARA. Figure 13.1a shows the phase diagram of the Sourlas codes using quantum fluctuations in ARA. We consider three initial conditions: $c = 0.7$, 0.8, and 0.95. Each line represents a point of the first-order phase transition. We call these lines "critical" lines. We can avoid a first-order phase transition by preparing for proper initial conditions. When

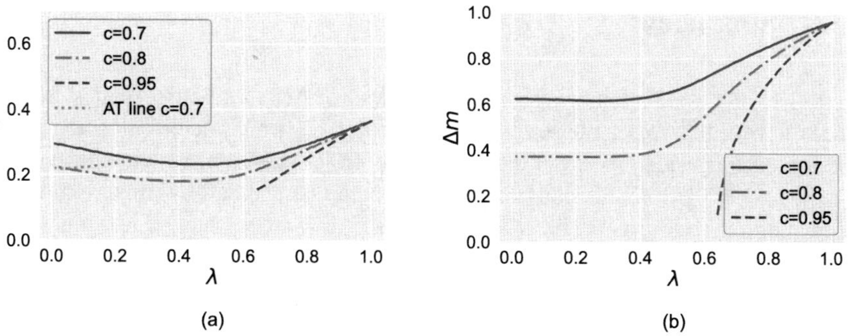

Fig. 13.1 **a** Phase diagram of Sourlas codes in ARA for $c = 0.7$, 0.8, and 0.95. The vertical and horizontal axes represent the annealing parameter and the RA parameter, respectively. Each line represents the point where the first-order phase transition occurs. The AT line indicates where the AT condition is broken above the line. **b** Differences in magnetization between two local minima at the first-order phase transition in Fig. 13.1 (**a**). The vertical axis denotes the differences in the magnetization between two local minima at the first-order phase transition while the horizontal axis represents the RA parameter

we increase the ratio of the ground state in the initial Hamiltonian, the region where we can avoid the first-order phase transition becomes wider.

We also compute the AT condition Eq. (13.37). As shown in Fig. 13.1a, the AT condition is broken between the AT line and the "critical" line for $c = 0.7$. If the fraction of the ground state in the initial candidate solution is not enough, the spin-glass phase emerges and RSB occurs. The emergence of RSB implies the existence of a metastable state. Figure 13.1a shows that we can avoid RSB if we tune the RA parameter λ. For $c = 0.8$, the AT condition is broken in the low λ region. The region where the AT condition is broken is smaller than that for $c = 0.7$. Since we cannot distinguish the AT line from the "critical" line at this scale, we omit the AT line from Fig. 13.1a. For $c = 0.95$, the AT condition holds. Therefore, the local stability of the RS solution is recovered if we can prepare for the proper initial conditions.

To evaluate the extent to which ARA mitigates the difficulty of estimating the original signal, we plot the differences in the magnetization Δm between the two local minima at the first-order phase transition for $c = 0.7$, 0.8, and 0.95. Significant differences in the magnetization result in the separation of the two local minima of the free energy. Figure 13.1b shows that Δm decreases as c increases. The two local minima of free energy are brought closer by ARA. As discussed in Ref. [13], the quantum tunneling rate between two local minima in the free-energy landscape increases if the distance between the two local minima is smaller. Our results demonstrate that ARA for Sourlas codes enhances the quantum tunneling effects if we prepare for an appropriate initial condition. This result is consistent with the CDMA model [2].

13.5 Summary

In this chapter, we explained a mean field analysis of ARA for Sourlas codes. Sourlas codes have a first-order phase transition with $p > 2$, which deteriorates their estimation performance. To avoid the first-order phase transition, we applied ARA to Sourlas codes. The first-order phase transition can be avoided by preparing for the proper initial conditions. The region where the first-order phase transition can be avoided becomes larger as c increases. We investigated the differences in magnetization between the two local minima at the first-order phase transition. When ARA was applied, the two local minima of the free energy came closer if we prepared for the proper initial conditions. ARA improved the probability of escaping the local minimum by quantum tunneling. This study shows that ARA can be useful for error correcting codes.

In the practical case, we need to prepare for the initial candidate solution by using some algorithms. In the previous study [2] for CDMA multiuser detection, we utilized the approximate message passing algorithm [8] to prepare for the initial candidate solution. The performance of ARA in practical case was different from the oracle cases where the initial candidate solution was generated from the original signal. Evaluation of the performance of ARA in the practical case for Sourlas codes is an interesting future direction.

Acknowledgements We are grateful for valuable comments from Kazuyuki Tanaka, Masayuki Ohzeki, Manaka Okuyama, and ACC Coolen. This work was partly supported by JST-CREST (No. JPMJCR1402).

Appendix 1: Derivation of Eq. (13.17)

In this appendix, we derive Eq. (13.15) in detail. We mainly follow the references [10, 18, 19]. We consider the z basis as the computational basis. In this case, Tr is replaced by $\sum_{\{\sigma^z\}}\langle\{\sigma^z\}|(\cdot)|\{\sigma^z\}\rangle$ and $|\{\sigma^z\}\rangle \equiv \otimes_{i=1}^{N}|\sigma_i^z\rangle$. For the z basis, we introduce M copies of the identity operator $\hat{1} = \sum_{\{\sigma^z(t)\}}|\{\sigma^z(t)\}\rangle\langle\{\sigma^z(t)\}|$ into Eq. (13.16),

$$Z_M = \lim_{M\to\infty}\prod_{t=1}^{M}\sum_{\{\sigma^z(t)\}}\exp\left(-\frac{\beta}{M}\sum_{t=1}^{M}(s\mathcal{H}_0 + (1-s)(1-\lambda)\mathcal{H}_{\text{init}})\right)$$
$$\times\prod_{t=1}^{M}\langle\{\sigma^z(t)\}|\exp\left(-\frac{\beta(1-s)\lambda}{M}\hat{\mathcal{H}}_{\text{TF}}\right)|\{\sigma^z(t+1)\}\rangle \tag{13.39}$$

where we introduce the periodic boundary condition $|\{\sigma^z(1)\}\rangle = |\{\sigma^z(M+1)\}\rangle$. To show the dependence of the spin operator on the Trotter index, arguments are added to each Hamiltonian in Eq. (13.39). For x basis, we similarly introduce the M copies of the identity operator $\hat{1} = \sum_{\{\sigma^x(t)\}}|\{\sigma^x(t)\}\rangle\langle\{\sigma^x(t)\}|$ into Eq. (13.39). The last term in Eq. (13.39) can be written as

$$\prod_{t=1}^{M} \sum_{\{\sigma^x(t)\}} \exp\left(-\frac{\beta(1-s)\lambda}{M}\mathcal{H}_{\mathrm{TF}}\right) \prod_{t=1}^{M} \langle\{\sigma^z(t)\}|\{\sigma^x(t)\}\rangle\langle\{\sigma^x(t)\}|\{\sigma^z(t+1)\}\rangle. \tag{13.40}$$

Finally, we can obtain Eq. (13.17) in the main text as

$$\begin{aligned} Z_M = &\prod_{t=1}^{M} \mathrm{Tr} \exp\left(-\frac{\beta}{M}\sum_{t=1}^{M}(s\mathcal{H}_0 + (1-s)(1-\lambda)\mathcal{H}_{\mathrm{init}}) - \frac{\beta(1-s)\lambda}{M}\sum_{t=1}^{M}\mathcal{H}_{\mathrm{TF}}\right) \\ &\times \prod_{i=1}^{N}\prod_{t=1}^{M} \langle\sigma_i^z(t)|\sigma_i^x(t)\rangle\langle\sigma_i^x(t)|\sigma_i^z(t+1)\rangle, \end{aligned} \tag{13.41}$$

where Tr denotes the summation over all the possible spin configurations $\{\sigma_i^z\}$ and $\{\sigma_i^x\}$. Since the first term in Eq. (13.41) consists of the commutable numbers, we can take the configuration average over the data distribution.

Appendix 2: Derivation of the RS Free Energy

We derive the free energy density under the RS ansatz and the static approximation. After the gauge transformation $J_{i_1\ldots i_p} \to J_{i_1\ldots i_p}\xi_{i_1}\ldots\xi_{i_p}$ and $\sigma_{ia}^z(t) \to \sigma_{ia}^z(t)\xi_i$, we integrate over $J_{i_1,\ldots,i_p}$ as

$$\begin{aligned} &\prod_{i_1<\cdots<i_p}\left[\int dJ_{i_1,\ldots,i_p} P(\{J_{i_1,\ldots,i_p}\}|\{\xi\}) \exp\left\{\frac{\beta s}{M}\sum_{a,t} J_{i_1\cdots p}\sigma_{i_1a}^z(t)\ldots\sigma_{i_pa}^z(t)\right\}\right] \\ &= \prod_{i_1<\cdots<i_p} \exp\left\{\frac{N^{p-1}}{J^2 p!}\left(\frac{J_0 p!}{N^{p-1}} + \frac{\beta s J^2 p!}{2MN^{p-1}}\sum_{a,t}\sigma_{i_1a}^z(t)\ldots\sigma_{i_pa}^z(t)\right)^2 - \frac{J_0^2 p!}{J^2 N^{p-1}}\right\} \\ &\simeq \exp\left\{\frac{\beta s J_0 N}{M}\sum_{a,t}\left(\frac{1}{N}\sum_{i=1}^{N}\sigma_{ia}^z(t)\right)^p + \frac{\beta^2 s^2 J^2 N}{4M^2}\sum_{a,b,t,t'}\left(\frac{1}{N}\sum_{i=1}^{N}\sigma_{ia}^z(t)\sigma_{ib}^z(t')\right)^p\right\}, \end{aligned} \tag{13.42}$$

where we use the expression $\sum_{i_1<\cdots<i_p}\sigma_{i_1}^z\cdots\sigma_{i_p}^z = (N^p/p!)\left(\sum_{i=1}^{N}\sigma_i^z/N\right)^p + O(N^{p-1})$. We introduce the delta function and its Fourier integral representation for Eqs. (13.20)–(13.23) as follows:

$$\prod_{a,t}\int dm_a(t)\delta\left(m_a(t) - \frac{1}{N}\sum_{i=1}^{N}\xi_i\sigma_{ia}^z(t)\right)$$

$$= \prod_{a,t} \int \frac{\beta i N dm_a(t) d\tilde{m}_a(t)}{2\pi M} e^{-\frac{\beta \tilde{m}_a(t)}{M}\left(N m_a(t) - \sum_{i=1}^N \xi_i \sigma_{ia}^z(t)\right)}, \quad (13.43)$$

$$\prod_{a,t,t'} \int dR_a(t,t') \delta\left(R_a(t,t') - \frac{1}{N}\sum_{i=1}^N \sigma_{ia}^z(t)\sigma_{ia}^z(t')\right)$$
$$= \prod_{a,t,t'} \int \frac{\beta^2 i N dR_a(t,t') d\tilde{R}_a(t,t')}{4\pi M^2} e^{-\frac{\beta^2 \tilde{R}_a(t,t')}{2M^2}\left(N R_a(t,t') - \sum_{i=1}^N \sigma_{ia}^z(t)\sigma_{ia}^z(t')\right)}, \quad (13.44)$$

$$\prod_{a\neq b,t,t'} \int dq_{ab}(t,t') \delta\left(q_{ab}(t,t') - \frac{1}{N}\sum_{i=1}^N \sigma_{ia}^z(t)\sigma_{ib}^z(t')\right)$$
$$= \prod_{a\neq b,t,t'} \int \frac{\beta^2 i N dq_{ab}(t,t') d\tilde{q}_{ab}(t,t')}{4\pi M^2} e^{-\frac{\beta^2 \tilde{q}_{ab}(t,t')}{2M^2}\left(N q_{ab}(t,t') - \sum_{i=1}^N \sigma_{ia}^z(t)\sigma_{ib}^z(t')\right)}, \quad (13.45)$$

$$\prod_{a,t} \int dm_a^x(t) \delta\left(m_a^x(t) - \frac{1}{N}\sum_{i=1}^N \sigma_{ia}^x(t)\right)$$
$$= \prod_{a,t} \int \frac{\beta i N dm_a^x(t) d\tilde{m}_a^x(t)}{2\pi M} e^{-\frac{\beta \tilde{m}_a^x(t)}{M}\left(N m_a^x(t) - \sum_{i=1}^N \sigma_{ia}^x(t)\right)}. \quad (13.46)$$

The partition function can be written as

$$[Z^n] \simeq \lim_{M\to\infty} \prod_{a,t} \int \frac{\beta i N dm_a(t) d\tilde{m}_a(t)}{2\pi M} \prod_{a,t\neq t'} \int \frac{\beta^2 i N dR_a(t,t') d\tilde{R}_a(t,t')}{4\pi M^2}$$
$$\times \prod_{a\neq b,t,t'} \int \frac{\beta^2 i N dq_{ab}(t,t') d\tilde{q}_{ab}(t,t')}{4\pi M^2} \prod_{a,t} \int \frac{\beta N dm_a^x(t) d\tilde{m}_a^x(t)}{2\pi i M} e^{G1+G2+G3}, \quad (13.47)$$

$$e^{G1} \equiv \exp\left\{\frac{\beta s J_0 N}{M}\sum_{a,t}(m_a(t))^p + \frac{\beta^2 s^2 J^2 N}{4M^2}\left(\sum_{a\neq b,t,t'} q_{ab}^p(t,t') + \sum_{a,t\neq t'} R_a^p(t,t') + nM\right)\right\} \quad (13.48)$$

$$e^{G_2} \equiv \sum_{\{\xi_i=\pm 1\}} \sum_{\{\tau_i=\pm\xi_i\}} P(\boldsymbol{\xi}) P(\boldsymbol{\tau}) \mathrm{Tr} \exp\left\{\frac{\beta}{M}\sum_{a,t}\tilde{m}_a(t)\sum_{i=1}^N \sigma_{ia}^z(t)\right.$$
$$+ \frac{\beta(1-s)(1-\lambda)}{M}\sum_{a,t,i}\tau_i\xi_i\sigma_{ia}^z(t) + \frac{\beta^2}{2M^2}\sum_{a,t\neq t'}\tilde{R}_a(t,t')\sum_{i=1}^N \sigma_{ia}^z(t)\sigma_{ia}^z(t')$$
$$\left. + \frac{\beta^2}{2M^2}\sum_{a\neq b}\sum_{t,t'}\tilde{q}_{ab}(t,t')\sum_{i=1}^N \sigma_{ia}^z(t)\sigma_{ib}^z(t') + \frac{\beta}{M}\sum_{a,t}\tilde{m}_a^x(t)\sum_{i=1}^N \sigma_{ia}^x(t)\right\}$$
$$\times \prod_{a,t,i} \langle\sigma_{ia}^z(t)|\sigma_{ia}^x(t)\rangle\langle\sigma_{ia}^x(t)|\sigma_{ia}^z(t+1)\rangle, \quad (13.49)$$

$$e^{G_3} \equiv \exp\left\{-\frac{\beta N}{M}\sum_{a,t}\tilde{m}_a(t)m_a(t) - \frac{\beta^2 N}{2M^2}\sum_{a,t\neq t'}\tilde{R}_a(t,t')R_a(t,t')\right.$$
$$-\frac{\beta^2 N}{2M^2}\sum_{a<b}\sum_{t,t'}\tilde{q}_{ab}(t,t')q_{ab}(t,t') - \frac{\beta N}{M}\sum_{a,t}\tilde{m}^x_a(t)m^x_a(t)$$
$$\left.+\frac{\beta(1-s)\lambda N}{M}\sum_{a,t}m^x_a(t)\right\}. \tag{13.50}$$

We assume the RS ansatz and the static approximation as

$$m_a(t) = m,\, q_{ab}(t,t') = q\ \ (a \neq b),\, R_a(t,t') = R\ \ (t \neq t'),\, m^x_a(t) = m^x,$$
$$\tilde{m}_a(t) = \tilde{m},\, \tilde{q}_{ab}(t,t') = \tilde{q}\ \ (a \neq b),\, \tilde{R}_a(t,t') = \tilde{R}\ \ (t \neq t'),\, \tilde{m}^x_a(t) = \tilde{m}^x. \tag{13.51}$$

Under the RS ansatz and the static approximation, e^{G_1} is represented as

$$e^{G1} \equiv \exp\left\{\beta n N\left(sJ_0 m^p + \frac{\beta s^2 J^2}{4}\left((n-1)q^p + R^p\right) + \mathcal{O}\left(\frac{1}{M}\right)\right)\right\}. \tag{13.52}$$

We compute e^{G2} under the RS ansatz and the static approximation as follows:

$$e^{G_2} = \sum_{\{\xi_i=\pm 1\}}\sum_{\{\tau_i=\pm\xi_i\}} P(\boldsymbol{\xi})P(\boldsymbol{\tau})\mathrm{Tr}\exp\left\{\frac{\beta\tilde{m}}{M}\sum_{a,t,i}\sigma^z_{ia}(t)\right.$$
$$+\frac{\beta(1-\lambda)(1-s)}{M}\sum_{a,t,i}\tau_i\xi_i\sigma^z_{ia}(t) + \frac{\beta^2\tilde{R}}{2M^2}\sum_{a,t\neq t'}\sum_{i=1}^{N}\sigma^z_{ia}(t)\sigma^z_{ia}(t')$$
$$\left.+\frac{\beta^2\tilde{q}}{2M^2}\sum_{a\neq b}\sum_{t,t'}\sum_{i=1}^{N}\sigma^z_{ia}(t)\sigma^z_{ib}(t') + \frac{\beta\tilde{m}^x}{M}\sum_{a,t}\sum_{i=1}^{N}\sigma^x_{ia}(t)\right\}$$
$$\times\prod_{a,t,i}\langle\sigma^z_{ia}(t)|\sigma^x_{ia}(t)\rangle\langle\sigma^x_{ia}(t)|\sigma^z_{ia}(t+1)\rangle$$
$$= \prod_{i=1}^{N}\sum_{\xi_i=\pm 1}\sum_{\tau_i=\pm\xi_i}\frac{1}{2}P(\tau_i)\int Dz\prod_{a=1}^{n}\int Dy\prod_{t=1}^{M}\mathrm{Tr}\exp\left\{\frac{\beta}{M}\left(\tilde{m}\right.\right.$$
$$\left.\left.+(1-s)(1-\lambda)\tau_i\xi_i + \tilde{q}z + \sqrt{\tilde{R}-\tilde{q}}\,y\right)\sigma^z_{ia}(t) + \frac{\beta\tilde{m}^x}{M}\sigma^x_{ia}(t)\right\}$$
$$\times\prod_{a,t,i}\langle\sigma^z_{ia}(t)|\sigma^x_{ia}(t)\rangle\langle\sigma^x_{ia}(t)|\sigma^z_{ia}(t+1)\rangle$$
$$= \prod_{i=1}^{N}\sum_{\xi_i=\pm 1}\sum_{\tau_i=\pm\xi_i}\frac{1}{2}P(\tau_i)\int Dz\left(\int Dy\, 2\cosh\beta\sqrt{g^2(\tau_i,\xi_i) + (\tilde{m}^x)^2}\right)^n$$

$$\simeq \prod_{i=1}^{N} \sum_{\xi_i=\pm 1} \frac{1}{2} \exp \left\{ n \int Dz \sum_{\tau_i=\pm\xi_i} P(\tau_i) \ln \int Dy 2 \cosh \beta \sqrt{g^2(\tau_i, \xi_i) + (\tilde{m}^x)^2} \right\}$$

$$= \exp \left\{ nN \left(\sum_{a=\pm 1} c_a \int Dz \ln \int Dy 2 \cosh \beta \sqrt{g_a^2 + (\tilde{m}^x)^2} \right) \right\}, \qquad (13.53)$$

where

$$g(\tau_i, \xi_i) = \tilde{m} + (1-s)(1-\lambda)\tau_i \xi_i + \sqrt{\tilde{q}} z + \sqrt{\tilde{R} - \tilde{q}}\, y, \qquad (13.54)$$

$$g_a = \tilde{m} + a(1-s)(1-\lambda) + \sqrt{\tilde{q}} z + \sqrt{\tilde{R} - \tilde{q}}\, y. \qquad (13.55)$$

We apply the Hubbard–Stratonovich transformation,

$$\exp\left(\frac{x^2}{2}\right) = \int Dv_1 \exp(xv_1), \qquad (13.56)$$

to the terms $\left(\beta\sqrt{\tilde{q}}/M \sum_{a,t} \sigma_{ia}^z(t)\right)^2/2$ and $\sum_a \left(\beta\sqrt{\tilde{R} - \tilde{q}}/M \sum_t \sigma_{ia}^z(t)\right)^2/2$. We now perform the inverse operation of the Suzuki–Trotter decomposition and take the trace.

Under the RS ansatz and the static approximation, e^{G_3} is expressed as

$$e^{G_3} = \exp\left\{ \beta n N \left(-m\tilde{m} - m^x \tilde{m}^x - \frac{\beta}{2} R\tilde{R} - \frac{\beta(n-1)}{2} q\tilde{q} + (1-s)\lambda m^x \right) + \mathcal{O}\left(\frac{1}{M}\right) \right\}. \qquad (13.57)$$

In the thermodynamic limit $N \to \infty$, the saddle-point method can be used. The RS free energy density is then expressed as

$$-\beta f_{\mathrm{RS}} = \lim_{n\to 0} \frac{[Z^n] - 1}{nN}$$
$$= \mathop{\mathrm{extr}}_{\substack{m,q,R\\ \tilde{m},\tilde{q},\tilde{R}}} \left[\beta s J_0 m^p + \frac{\beta^2 s^2 J^2}{4}(R^p - q^p) + \beta(1-s)\lambda m^x - \beta m\tilde{m} - \beta m^x \tilde{m}^x \right.$$
$$\left. - \frac{\beta^2}{2}(R\tilde{R} - q\tilde{q}) + \sum_{a=\pm 1} c_a \int Dz \ln \int Dy 2\cosh \beta \sqrt{g_a^2 + (\tilde{m}^x)^2} \right]. \qquad (13.58)$$

The order parameters and their auxiliary parameters can be determined from the saddle-point conditions.

References

1. J.R.L. de Almeida, D.J. Thouless, Stability of the Sherrington-Kirkpatrick solution of a spin glass model. J. Phys. A Math. Gen. **11**(5), 983–990 (1978)
2. S. Arai, M. Ohzeki, K. Tanaka, Mean field analysis of reverse annealing for code-division multiple-access multiuser detection. Phys. Rev. Res. **3** (2021)
3. E. Farhi, J. Goldstone, S. Gutmann, J. Lapan, A. Lundgren, D. Preda, A quantum adiabatic evolution algorithm applied to random instances of an np-complete problem. Science **292**(5516), 472–475 (2001)
4. P. Gillin, H. Nishimori, D. Sherrington, Multispin Ising spin glasses with ferromagnetic interactions. J. Phys. A Math. Gen. **34**(14), 2949–2964 (2001)
5. J.J. Hopfield, Neural networks and physical systems with emergent collective computational abilities. Proce. Nat. Acad. Sci. **79**(8), 2554–2558 (1982)
6. J.I. Inoue, Application of the quantum spin glass theory to image restoration. Phys. Rev. E **63**, 046114 (2001)
7. M.W. Johnson, P. Bunyk, F. Maibaum, E. Tolkacheva, A.J. Berkley, E.M. Chapple, R. Harris, J. Johansson, T. Lanting, I. Perminov, E. Ladizinsky, T. Oh, G. Rose, A scalable control system for a superconducting adiabatic quantum optimization processor. Supercond. Sci. Technol. **23**(6) (2010)
8. Y. Kabashima, A CDMA multiuser detection algorithm on the basis of belief propagation. J. Phys. A: Math. Gen. **36**(43), 11111–11121 (2003)
9. T. Kadowaki, H. Nishimori, Quantum annealing in the transverse ising model. Phys. Rev. E **58**, 5355–5363 (1998)
10. S. Matsuura, H. Nishimori, T. Albash, D.A. Lidar, Mean field analysis of quantum annealing correction. Phys. Rev. Lett. **116** (2016)
11. F. Neukart, G. Compostella, C. Seidel, D. von Dollen, S. Yarkoni, B. Parney, Traffic flow optimization using a quantum annealer. Frontiers in ICT **4**, 29 (2017)
12. H. Nishimori, *Statistical Physics of Spin Glasses and Information Processing: An Introduction* (Oxford University Press, Oxford, 2001)
13. M. Ohkuwa, H. Nishimori, D.A. Lidar, Reverse annealing for the fully connected p-spin model. Phys. Rev. A **98** (2018)
14. M. Ohzeki, A. Miki, M.J. Miyama, M. Terabe, Control of automated guided vehicles without collision by quantum annealer and digital devices. Front. Comput. Sci. **1**, 9 (2019)
15. Y. Otsubo, J.I. Inoue, K. Nagata, K., Okada, M.: Effect of quantum fluctuation in error-correcting codes. Phys. Rev. E **86**, 051138 (2012)
16. Y. Otsubo, J.I. Inoue, K. Nagata, M. Okada, Code-division multiple-access multiuser demodulator by using quantum fluctuations. Phys. Rev. E **90**, 012126 (2014)
17. A. Perdomo-Ortiz, S.E. Venegas-Andraca, A. Aspuru-Guzik, A study of heuristic guesses for adiabatic quantum computation. Quant. Inf. Process. **10**(1), 33–52 (2011)
18. Y. Seki, H. Nishimori, Quantum annealing with antiferromagnetic transverse interactions for the hopfield model. J. Phys. A: Math. Theor. **48**(33) (2015)
19. B. Seoane, H. Nishimori, Many-body transverse interactions in the quantum annealing of thep-spin ferromagnet. J. Phys. A Math. Theor. **45**(43) (2012)
20. D. Sherrington, S. Kirkpatrick, Solvable model of a spin-glass. Phys. Rev. Lett. **35**, 1792–1796 (1975)
21. N. Sourlas, Spin-glass models as error-correcting codes. Nature **339**, 693 EP (1989)
22. M. Suzuki, Generalized trotter's formula and systematic approximants of exponential operators and inner derivations with applications to many-body problems. Commun. Math. Phys. **51**(2), 183–190 (1976)
23. S. Suzuki, M. Okada, Residual energies after slow quantum annealing. J. Phys. Soc. Jpn **74**(6), 1649–1652 (2005)
24. T. Tanaka, Statistical mechanics of CDMA multiuser demodulation. EPL (Europhysics Letters) **54**(4), 540 (2001)

25. D. Thirumalai, Q. Li, T.R. Kirkpatrick, Infinite-range ising spin glass in a transverse field. J. Phys. A Math. Gener. **22**(16), 3339–3349 (1989)
26. Y. Yamashiro, M. Ohkuwa, H. Nishimori, D.A. Lidar, Dynamics of reverse annealing for the fully connected p-spin model. Phys. Rev. A **100**, (2019)

Open Access This chapter is licensed under the terms of the Creative Commons Attribution 4.0 International License (http://creativecommons.org/licenses/by/4.0/), which permits use, sharing, adaptation, distribution and reproduction in any medium or format, as long as you give appropriate credit to the original author(s) and the source, provide a link to the Creative Commons license and indicate if changes were made.

The images or other third party material in this chapter are included in the chapter's Creative Commons license, unless indicated otherwise in a credit line to the material. If material is not included in the chapter's Creative Commons license and your intended use is not permitted by statutory regulation or exceeds the permitted use, you will need to obtain permission directly from the copyright holder.

Part V
Applications

Chapter 14
Structural and Functional Analysis of Proteins Using Rigidity Theory

Adnan Sljoka

Abstract Over the past two decades, we have witnessed an unprecedented explosion in available biological data. In the age of big data, large biological datasets have created an urgent need for the development of bioinformatics methods and innovative fast algorithms. Bioinformatics tools can enable data-driven hypothesis and interpretation of complex biological data that can advance biological and medicinal knowledge discovery. Advances in structural biology and computational modelling have led to the characterization of atomistic structures of many biomolecular components of cells. Proteins in particular are the most fundamental biomolecules and the key constituent elements of all living organisms, as they are necessary for cellular functions. Proteins play crucial roles in immunity, catalysis, metabolism and the majority of biological processes, and hence there is significant interest to understand how these macromolecules carry out their complex functions. The mechanical heterogeneity of protein structures and a delicate mix of rigidity and flexibility, which dictates their dynamic nature, is linked to their highly diverse biological functions. Mathematical rigidity theory and related algorithms have opened up many exciting opportunities to accurately analyse protein dynamics and probe various biological enigmas at a molecular level. Importantly, rigidity theoretical algorithms and methods run in almost linear time complexity, which makes it suitable for high-throughput and big-data style analysis. In this chapter, we discuss the importance of protein flexibility and dynamics and review concepts in mathematical rigidity theory for analysing stability and the dynamics of protein structures. We then review some recent breakthrough studies, where we designed rigidity theory methods to understand complex biological events, such as allosteric communication, large-scale analysis of immune system antibody proteins, the highly complex dynamics of intrinsically disordered proteins and the validation of Nuclear Magnetic Resonance (NMR) solved protein structures.

A. Sljoka (✉)
RIKEN Center for Advanced Intelligence Project, RIKEN, 1-4-1 Nihombashi, Chuo-ku, Tokyo 103-0027, Japan
e-mail: adnan.sljoka@riken.jp

© The Author(s) 2022

N. Katoh et al. (eds.), *Sublinear Computation Paradigm*,
https://doi.org/10.1007/978-981-16-4095-7_14

14.1 Introduction

In the current post-genomics era, advances in experimental and computational techniques have revolutionized biological and biomedical research. High-throughput technologies have paved the way to novel research avenues where we can systematically analyse whole genomes of organisms and individual or collection of proteins, including their structures and interactions with other proteins, which in many cases allow researchers to successfully decipher their biological functions. Proteins are macromolecules that are fundamental to most cellular function [1]. They comprise the highest levels of molecular and cellular structure and organization, and because the majority of physiological and disease processes are manifested within proteins, structural and computational biology research is focused on understanding protein function.

Proteins and other biomolecules are nanomachines. Accurate representation of their three-dimensional structure is a critical first step to understanding how they perform their functions. Advances in molecular biology, instrumentation, and imaging technologies such as X-ray crystallography, nuclear magnetic resonance (NMR), and electron microscopy have led to a revolution in structural biology. These techniques allow us to see beautiful yet complex three-dimensional shapes of protein structures and how they interact with other proteins and ligands. Protein imaging techniques are continuously improving, and for many proteins, we can now characterize their structures at an individual-atom-level resolution. A rapidly growing and revolutionary cryogenic-electron microscopy (cryo-EM) technique has been attracting significant attention, as very recently it has broken various resolution barriers [2] and can now discern individual atoms of very large protein structures (see Fig. 14.1). Cryo-EM complements X-ray crystallography because it reveals atomistic structural details without the need for a crystalline specimen. Protein Data Bank (PDB), a repository of experimentally solved protein structures, together with computationally determined protein structures, make up a rich source of protein structural data. Recent advances in AI and deep learning have provided significant improvements in inferring protein structures from a sequence of amino acids [3]. Deepmind's Alphafold method has demonstrated that deep learning structure predictions can come astonishingly close to experimentally determined structures, and in the near future, we expect this will result in huge growth of macromolecular structural data. The increasing richness of the available protein structural data and the rapidly growing proteomics and bioinformatics big-data repositories open up possibilities to systematically analyse complex biological questions and gain novel biological insights. To facilitate data-driven biological knowledge discovery, many bioinformatics and computational biology tools, software packages, and databases have been developed [4].

Despite tremendous advances in bioinformatics, structural biology and imaging technologies which have generated hundreds of thousands of atomic snapshots of protein structures, many fundamental biological problems such as protein folding, allosteric regulation, receptor signalling, and enzyme catalysis, to name a few, still remain largely unresolved [5–12]. While the static high-quality representation of

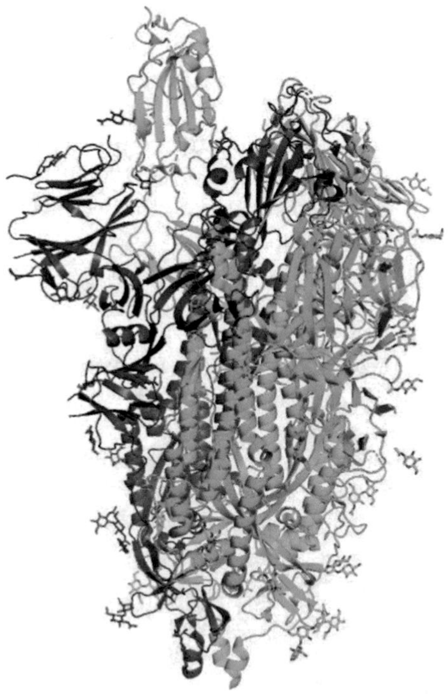

Fig. 14.1 Cryo-EM snapshot structure of viral spike protein of SARS-CoV-2 (a key protein involved in COVID-19), which is a very large protein structure consisting of three chains (distinct colours), each consisting of nearly 1300 amino acids

protein structures can offer clues to structure-function mechanisms, protein function is almost purely controlled by its dynamic character through a delicate mix of rigidity and flexibility. Research must move beyond static snapshot representations of proteins, as the mechanical heterogeneity of protein structures that dictates their dynamic nature is intimately linked to their highly diverse biological functions. Deep understanding of the connection between structures and internal protein flexibility, rigidity, and dynamics is absolutely critical, as it can lead to solutions to protein folding problem, elusive allosteric regulation and other dynamically driven biological secrets of protein regulation.

The primary desire of any protein researcher is to see proteins move in real time at the atomistic level while they carry out their biological functions. Yet, despite many advances in experimental techniques and molecular dynamics simulations, such a goal is still very far from being realized. Analysing and comprehending protein flexibility and dynamics has proven to be extremely difficult. One major challenge is that the main molecular simulation methods, such as classical molecular dynamics simulations, require a prohibitive amount of computational power and are not suitable to reach biologically relevant functional dynamics that occur on longer (millisecond-second) timescales. Furthermore, with rapid growth in the number of experimentally solved biomolecular structures and the increasing size of structural protein databases, including the expanding big-data size sets of computationally predicted protein structures, we are faced with a pressing need to develop fast algorithms and novel mathematical and computational techniques that simplify the classical force fields and can offer experimentally verified accurate predictions of protein flexibility and dynamics.

Techniques inspired from the field of mathematical-structural rigidity theory [13–16] have gained special attention as they are suitable for handling the many challenges with computational analysis of protein flexibility and its dynamics. Biological functions of protein structures are often related to their network (or graph) properties. Mathematical rigidity theory offers considerable promise in deciphering graph theoretical properties of protein networks to better understand protein function [13, 15–18]. In rigidity theory, proteins are modelled as geometric molecular frameworks consisting of atoms and various connecting intermolecular forces. Such frameworks are essentially multigraphs (networks), in which atoms are vertices and edges form various bonding and non-bonding constraints (see Sect. 14.3). The programme FIRST [15] and related methods [19] apply mathematical results that provide combinatorial characterization of rigidity and flexibility on a molecular multigraph, which can rapidly decompose a protein framework (i.e., multigraph) into flexible and rigid regions. Starting with a decomposition of a protein into rigid and flexible regions, fast Monte Carlo geometric simulation methods, such as FRODA and FRODAN [19–22], can sample the highly complex conformational space of proteins and simulate their functionally relevant motions. The main advantage of rigidity theory methods over classical molecular dynamics simulations is that their predictions of rigidity and flexibility are very fast, they are not affected by timescale issues (see Sect. 14.2), and they are suitable for high-throughput and big-data style analyses. Moreover, predictions based on rigidity theory have been widely shown to be consistent with experimental measures of protein flexibility and dynamics [11, 12, 15, 17–19, 22, 24–26].

In this chapter, we first discuss the importance of protein flexibility and dynamics for biological function (Sect. 14.2). We then provide a brief review of fundamental concepts in rigidity theory (Sect. 14.3) that enables us to perform fast predictions of flexibility and dynamics of protein structures. We next discuss how to represent biomolecules as a graph constraint network, the mathematical/algorithmic background for analysing protein networks, and the basic uses of rigidity theory software for analysing protein flexibility and its dynamics. We then review some major advances contributed by the author of this chapter, in which rigidity theory and algorithms were used to elucidate and provide new perspectives on very complex biological phenomena, such as long-range allosteric communication, enzyme catalysis, antibody dynamics, and NMR structural validation (Sect. 14.4). We conclude by reviewing some of these recent developments and some surprising breakthroughs that have led to rich protein function discoveries that were mainly driven by mathematical rigidity theory.

14.2 Protein Structural Flexibility and Dynamics

In this section, we briefly cover for non-biologists the background and the importance of predicting protein flexibility, which is arguably one of the most fundamental research topics in biochemistry, structural biology, and bioinformatics.

14.2.1 Protein Flexibility and Dynamics Is Central to Protein Function

Proteins are polypeptide chains composed of a linear sequence(s) of amino acids [1]. Through a complex protein folding process, forces are exerted on atoms which steer a polypeptide chain(s) into a defined three-dimensional biologically functional native-state structural ensemble. High-resolution X-ray crystallography and other techniques have revealed aesthetic structural complexity of protein structures and have revolutionized our understanding of their function, which have spearheaded the development of novel experimental and computational methods for examining protein function in atomistic detail. It is important to stress that solved protein structures are only snapshots or pictures of proteins at some low-energy state. This can often provide a misleading representation of proteins and potentially misinform about their function, which must include kinetic and thermodynamic descriptions [5] (see Fig. 14.2).

Proteins are composed of rigid and connecting flexible regions that can be highly dynamic, which facilitates sampling a wide variety of conformations spanning a complex multidimensional energy landscape. In this conformational biomolecular dance, proteins undergo dynamical fluctuations even under conditions that are preferentially biased towards a well-defined low-energy 'native' state [5]. Such dynamically driven conformational states and fluctuations are critical to long-range allosteric regulations, ligand recognition, catalytic efficiency, antibody–antigen recognition and the majority of functional mechanisms. Understanding protein flexibility and rigidity and how it is modified by mutations and ligand binding is critical to understanding and modulating protein function [5, 7, 8, 11, 12]. Most globular proteins (excluding intrinsically disordered proteins) function through utilizing a delicate mix of rigidity and flexibility. Achieving appropriate balance between rigidity and flexibility is one of the most important keys for biological function. Protein rigidity is necessary, as it maintains overall structural fold, while flexibility and dynamics enable proteins to perform specific functions. Protein defects can lead to alterations in overall folding, or they can cause proteins to be overly flexible, interfering with protein function, or cause other extreme defects that can result in indestructible rigid protein. These scenarios are related to numerous medical conditions, including neurological disorders, Alzheimer's disease, and Mad Cow disease [22, 27]. Hence, predicting and examining protein flexibility and dynamics is the most important, and probably the

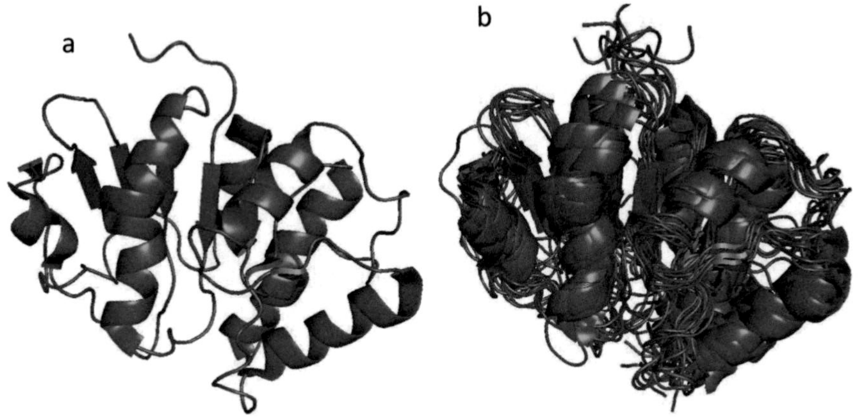

Fig. 14.2 The structure of an enzyme (Protein Data Bank ID 2jz3) showing **a** protein snapshot representation and conformational ensemble depicting its dynamical characteristics **b**

most complex, component of protein research. This is an active area of research in both experimental protein science and computational biology.

Protein structures can have thousands of conformational degrees of freedom. It is therefore easy to imagine that their motions can be extremely complex, and determining flexible and rigid regions and how they move relative to one another can seem like a daunting task. Moreover, many proteins are oligomeric structures consisting of two or more interacting polypeptide chains, and in some cases the structures are very large, consisting of thousands of amino acids (see Fig. 14.1). Protein flexibility and rigidity are often regulated by interactions with small ligands, drugs, hormones, and cations (e.g., calcium and magnesium) and changes in temperature, pressure, and pH [11, 15, 17, 18, 24]. Internal motion and conformational change can be rapid and transient and result in a structural ensemble that can often be spectroscopically indistinguishable from the snapshot ground state determined by X-ray crystallography or other imaging techniques (see Fig. 14.2). Protein dynamics occur across a wide range of timescales, from very rapid short-amplitude motions caused by bond vibrations occurring on a femtosecond range, to side-chain motions on the picosecond to nanosecond timescale, all the way up to very slow larger-amplitude collective domain motions, which are often biologically most significant, occurring in the milliseconds to seconds range [5] (see Fig. 14.3). Dynamics on longer timescales (i.e., millisecond to second timescales) are functionally very important because many biological processes—including allostery, enzyme catalysis, receptor activations, and protein–protein interactions—occur on such timescales [5, 9, 11, 12, 24, 28]. Fluctuations between different low-energy states and the heights of their energy barriers can also be affected by mutations, ligand binding, and changes in temperature or pH. The timescale component of protein dynamics is one critical factor that complicates the computation examination of protein dynamics. Another important characteristic of protein dynamics is the amplitude and directionality of conformational fluctuations

[5]. All these factors combine to contribute to the difficulty in obtaining knowledge about the flexibility and motion of proteins.

Despite this complexity, functional motions will often involve large domain–domain motions (i.e., relative motions dominated by a few rigid bodies) and many degrees of freedom can be neglected or suppressed to study the functionally most important motions. Hence decomposition of a protein into rigid and flexible regions is a highly important aspect of deciphering protein dynamics.

14.2.2 Techniques for Analysing and Predicting Protein Flexibility and Dynamics

In terms of experimental techniques, NMR measurements such as order parameter measurements and chemical shifts are very useful in studying protein dynamics [24, 29]. Mass spectrometry, hydrogen–deuterium exchange, crystallographic B-values, etc. can also provide deep insights into the dynamical nature of protein structures [5, 11, 24, 25]. Fluorescence resonance energy transfer (FRET) [30] measures in particular have high practical value as they can characterize changes in distance for single molecules over time as well as possible corresponding conformational changes. However, the disadvantage of FRET is that only a single distance change is measured. Experimental measurements are useful as they can be used to infer specific information about dynamics across a specific range of timescales (see Fig. 14.3) and are specifically very helpful in supporting and validating computational predictions. The disadvantage of experimental tools is their high cost, susceptibility to uncertainty in measurements, and frequent inability to provide information about very dynamic regions of protein structures. Moreover, protein structures often have to be stabilized to extract structural and dynamical information. Experimental measurements can also take a long time to perform, as they require maintenance of very expensive equipment; yet, such measurements can rarely provide dynamical information about individual atoms.

Computationally, it should be theoretically possible to describe protein dynamics in their entirety. Molecular dynamics (MD) simulation has been the most widely used approach for simulating the motions of proteins and other biopolymers [28]. Molecular dynamics simulations of proteins have been a common tool in biochemistry and biophysics since the 1970s [31]. It has been successfully applied to protein folding problems, the impact of protein motions on enzyme catalysis, and the effects of mutations and ligand binding on protein motions [28]. Its uses have increased in recent years, pointing to the key importance of deciphering the relationships between complex motions and protein function. In molecular dynamics simulations, the trajectories of individual atoms in protein structures can be predicted by repeated numerical solutions of the Newtonian motion equation (i.e., $F = ma$), with forward integration in time, where F represents a force field (energy function). A force field models all potential forces and energies between the molecules and is supposed to be a

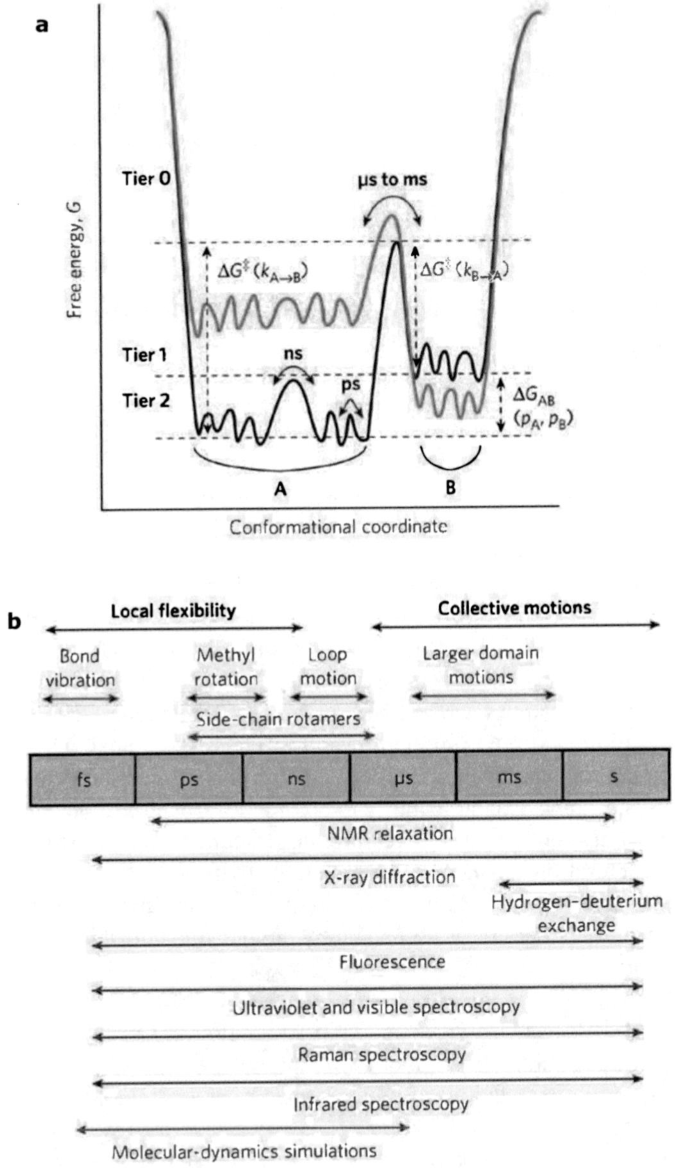

Fig. 14.3 **a** A one-dimensional cross-sectional representation of a high-dimensional protein's energy landscape. Proteins can be defined as multiple collections of low-energy conformational states (defined as minima in the energy surface), with many conformational ensemble substates interconverting between one another on very fast timescales. The time it takes a protein to transition from one low-energy state to another is dependent on the height of the energy barrier between the states. When the barrier is high, this can occur in a relatively long microsecond to second range. **b** Timescales of different dynamic processes in proteins and different experimental methods that can detect fluctuations on each timescale. Longer timescales are largely inaccessible to classical MD simulations. However, rigidity theory methods and simulations are not confined by this timescale issue. Figure adapted from [5]

simple parameterization of the energy surface of the protein. A number of different methods and force field models exist for parametrizing the potential energy surface. Assuming one can use an accurate description of a force field, a difficult and heavily debated concept, molecular dynamics simulation can be extremely useful in tracking the precise position of atoms over time. However, the major downside of molecular dynamics simulations is that they require prohibitively excessive computational power. Indeed, even despite today's computational advances and special-purpose simulation machines [32], in the majority of cases molecular dynamics simulations are largely impractical for investigating biologically relevant protein motions on relatively long microsecond timescales. Stemming from the increase in protein structural data combined with the increasing size of solved structures, advances in emerging Cryo-EM technology and deep learning, it is clear that there is an urgent need to develop alternate efficient and accurate computational methods for molecular flexibility and dynamics simulations.

A large class of computational approaches that simplify classical force fields have been developed. Coarse-grained simulations, normal model analysis, principal component analysis, contact network analysis, and other related methods have become popular alternative approaches to classical MD simulations [33]. In coarse-grained and network approaches, physical units such as individual amino acids or a cluster of amino acids including rigid clusters can be treated as nodes (vertices), where edges indicate possible interactions or contacts. For more precise modelling, individual atoms should be treated as vertices and edges should model pairwise bonded and non-bonded contacts.

Arguably, one of the most powerful ways of analysing the flexibility and rigidity of protein structures, especially using an all atom representation, is based on mathematical rigidity theory [13–16, 19, 34]. Rigorous mathematical results in rigidity theory, whose details are explained below, can be used in combination with fast algorithms to rapidly decompose a protein constraint graph into rigid and flexible regions. Moreover, how rigidity is modified through protein–protein, protein–ligand, or other interactions can be quickly predicted. Such decompositions are very informative as they can be combined with other methods such as MD simulations, normal mode analysis, or Monte Carlo simulations [19, 22] to directly infer information about protein dynamics. This is discussed in more detail below. We now turn the discussion to mathematical formulations and the uses of rigidity theory for the analysis of protein structures.

14.3 Rigidity Theory

In this section, we present a basic introduction and results of rigidity theory that are essential for applications to protein structure and function analysis, with a focus on combinatorial rigidity theory concepts. For a thorough review of rigidity theory see [13, 19, 34].

14.3.1 Combinatorial Rigidity Theory and the Molecular Theorem

In general terms, flexibility is the ability of a material or framework to reversibly change the configuration of its joints, bodies, or building blocks. Rigidity, which is the opposite property of flexibility, describes a state in which no relative motions are allowed between the framework's elements. In a rigid structure, only rigid body motions are possible (i.e., motions arising from congruences of space, rotations, translations, etc.). In biochemistry and biophysics, a notion related to rigidity is the concept of stability and robustness, where internal protein dynamics are not changed in response to small atomic fluctuations and the breaking of a few non-covalent interactions. Although to a non-expert, rigidity and stability may seem like related concepts, care should be taken to understand the potential differences and their implications.

Mathematical *rigidity theory*, sometimes called *structural rigidity* because of its close connections to structural and mechanical engineering, offers the most mathematically sound concepts and algorithms for analysis of rigidity and flexibility of frameworks [13, 14, 34]. Rigidity theory analyses the rigidity and flexibility of frameworks, as specified by geometric constraints such as fixed distances, directions, and volumes defined by a collection of points, lines, planes, or rigid bodies. Frameworks can be natural structures (molecules, crystals, proteins, etc.) or engineered structures (bridges, robots, etc.), and because rigidity is an essential property of most frameworks and materials, rigidity theory naturally has many applications in engineering, robotics, material science, and biology.

Rigidity theory has both geometric and combinatorial characteristics relying on techniques in linear algebra, discrete and algebraic geometry, graph theory, and combinatorics. Rigidity theory has a very long and rich history in mathematics, with early work appearing in the form of Euler's (1766) conjectures on rigidity of polyhedra. Maxwell's (1864) [14, 34] work on counting constraints in a framework for generic rigidity led to the birth of so-called '*combinatorial rigidity*'. Combinatorial characterization of rigidity theory, 140 years later, has turned out to be absolutely crucial for rapid flexibility analysis of materials such as glass networks and protein structures [14].

The classical and simplest frameworks studied in rigidity theory are the bar and joint frameworks (see Fig. 14.4), which are composed of universal (rotating) joints that are connected by bars that fix the distances between pairs of joints. A bar and joint framework is defined as a pair (G, p), where $G = (V, E)$ is an undirected graph and $p : V \to \mathbb{R}^d$, where vertices correspond to joints and edges correspond to bars that connect some pairs of joints; p represents a configuration of joints in $\mathbb{R}^d$. A framework (G, p) in $\mathbb{R}^d$ is rigid if the only edge-length-preserving continuous motions of the vertices are derived from isometries of $\mathbb{R}^d$. If $d \geq 2$, it is NP-hard to determine if a bar and joint framework is rigid [34]. As determining the rigidity of frameworks is very difficult, a common approach is to linearize the problem by differentiating the length/bar constraints of the corresponding pair of connecting

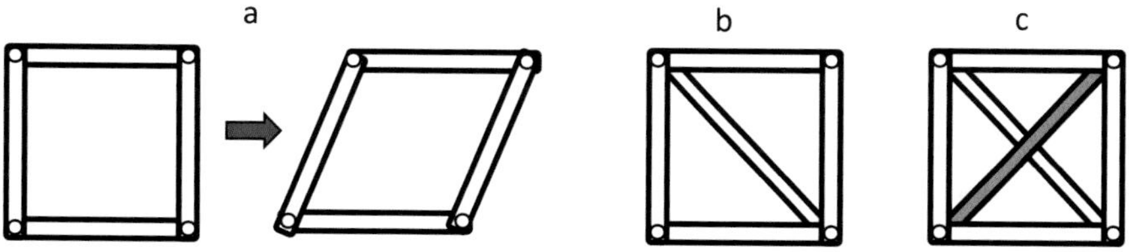

Fig. 14.4 Bar and joint framework examples: **a** is flexible as it can deform its shape (note it is one edge too short in terms of Laman's count, $|E| < 2|V| - 3$); **b** is minimally rigid in 2D (but flexible in 3D as one can rotate two triangles around the diagonal). **c** is redundantly rigid in 2D as it has a redundant (i.e., extra) edge and is minimally rigid in 3D

points/joints, which leads to a system of linear equations (one equation per edge) and a corresponding rigidity matrix. The solution to such a homogenous system can be captured by calculating the rank of the rigidity matrix, which indicates if a framework is infinitesimally rigid [34, 35]. However, in many applications and large frameworks such as proteins, this is not particularly practical owing to numerical errors and uncertainty in rank computations of the rigidity matrix.

A well-known fact within rigidity theory is that if the framework is generic (i.e., it does not have special singular geometry), then rigidity and infinitesimal rigidity coincide [34]. Generic frameworks are very important, as rigidity can be studied by pure graph and combinatorial techniques—a subfield of rigidity theory called combinatorial rigidity theory. A framework is generically rigid if it maintains rigidity even after minor changes to the position of its joints, and almost all frameworks are generic [13, 34, 36]. By assuming that a framework is in a generic position, one can neglect the geometric embedding of joints and actual distances of bars to focus on only the topology of the bar and joint framework and discuss the generic rigidity of (G, p) in terms of graph G.

14.3.1.1 Counting for Rigidity and Flexibility

We now motivate the characterization of rigidity of generic frameworks using combinatorial arguments. For bar and joint frameworks in dimension d, each joint (point, vertex) has d conformational degrees; hence, N joints have a total of dN degrees of freedom. The number of trivial rigid body motions in dimension d or isometries is $d(d+1)/2$. Therefore, in a generic rigid bar and joint framework, the number of bars $\geq dN - d(d+1)/2$. This is known as Maxwell's counting condition. In the plane ($d = 2$), Laman's theorem [34] extends this result by proving that the $2N - 3$ count is both necessary and sufficient for generic rigidity of two-dimensional bar and joint frameworks. More formally, a two-dimensional bar and joint framework is generically *minimally rigidity* if and only if $|E| = 2|N| - 3$ and, for all subsets of edges, $|E'| \leq 2|N'| - 3$. In other words, this remarkable theorem says one can count the vertices and edges in a graph and their distributions over subgraphs to

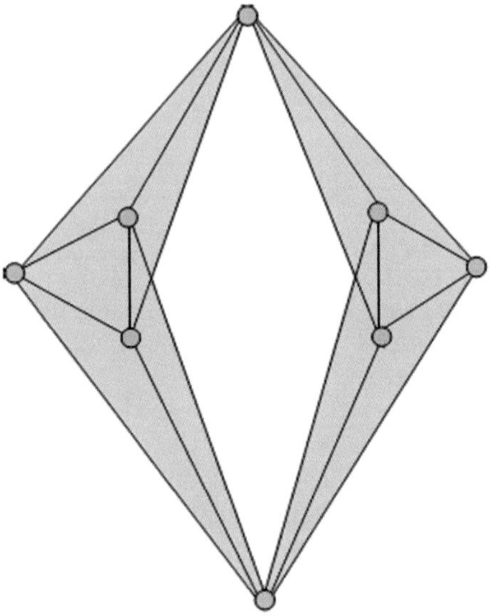

Fig. 14.5 Maxwell's counts in 3D do not guarantee rigidity. A bar and joint framework in 3D (known as the double banana graph) satisfies the $3|N| - 6$ count condition but is flexible (two yellow rigid subgraphs can rotate about an imaginary hinge shown as a red dashed line)

predict generic rigidity of two-dimensional bar and joint frameworks. A framework is minimally rigid if removal of any edge (bar) results in a flexible framework (see Fig. 14.4).

Unfortunately, Maxwell's counting results are not sufficient for minimally rigid bar and joint graphs in dimension 3 and higher. For example, a well-known counterexample is a graph of a double banana, which satisfies Maxwell's $3|N| - 6$ count but is flexible (see Fig. 14.5). Not only is there a lack of a Laman type of a theorem for generic bar and joint frameworks in dimension 3 and higher, there are no known polynomial time algorithms for testing rigidity for general three-dimensional graphs [34]. Extensive research has been conducted on this problem and, to date, only some partial results and approximation algorithms can be found [34, 35]. Fortunately, for different classes of frameworks, called *body-bar* and *body-hinge* frameworks, which includes molecular frameworks, there is a complete and rich combinatorial characterization of rigidity, which is discussed next.

14.3.1.2 Rigidity Model of Molecules and the Molecular Theorem

To build a computational method based on rigidity theory that can provide fast and accurate prediction of protein rigidity and flexibility, three requirements must be met: (i) a realistic physical model of a basic molecular framework; (ii) an accurate model of molecular interactions; and (iii) a fast algorithm for predicting rigidity/flexibility properties of the protein framework model.

Protein structures consist of atoms and various chemical interactions (forces) of different strengths. In rigidity theory, strong interactions between atoms are usually assumed to be fixed rigid constraints in terms of distances and angles. In such a rigidity model of a molecule, bonding interactions are assumed to fix distances between a pair of bonded atoms, and the angles between the bonds of an atom are fixed, allowing only dihedral angle rotations. High frequency motions such as bond vibrations are neglected. This is a sensible modelling assumption as single covalent bond lengths are essentially invariant. For example, the length of a covalent bond between two carbon atoms will vary less than a single percent from its equilibrium value of 1.53 angstroms [14]. Double bonds and peptide bonds lock dihedral angles, and non-covalent interactions such as hydrogen bonds and hydrophobic contacts also impose additional constraints.

A *molecular framework* in rigidity theory is a collection of atoms, which can be modelled as fully rigid bodies with six conformational degrees of freedom of a rigid body and bonds as rotatable hinges, which allow for rotational degrees of freedom between single-bonded atoms. Such frameworks in rigidity theory are a special case of *body-hinge framework*. Hinges (i.e., bonds) remove five degrees of freedom, and for algorithmic and theoretical reasons, it is useful to model hinges as a set of five rigid bars, where each bar (i.e., edge) generically removes a single degree of freedom between bonded atoms. This finally leads to a body-bar framework representation of a molecular body-hinge framework—that is, a collection of rigid bodies connected by linear bars. Special geometric criteria should be considered as bonds are not generic hinges (since bonds intersect at centre of atoms) and the five bars have to pass through the hinge axis to geometrically give the same model as a hinge, but such discussion is beyond the scope of this chapter (details can be found elsewhere; see [13]). Double bonds are modelled as a set of six bars between two atoms. Moreover, non-covalent interactions such as hydrogen bonds and hydrophobic interactions, which are important for overall protein structure folding and rigidity, can also be modelled as a set of one to five bars (where one bar indicates the bond is least restricting and five bars indicate it is most restricting) [25]. This overall model, consisting of rigid bodies for atoms and both covalent bonds and non-covalent interactions, defines the *body-bar framework* model of a protein structure (see Fig. 14.6).

The topological structure of a body-bar (and body-hinge and molecular body-hinge) framework is a multigraph $G = (V, E)$. Vertex set V corresponds to a set of bodies (i.e., atoms) and edge set E to a set of bars (i.e., bond constraints). In accordance with Laman's theorem, an equivalent statement for body-bar frameworks was formulated by Tay [37]. Tay's theorem confirms that the rigidity of generic body-bar frameworks in 3D (which works for all dimensions) can be checked using the $6|V| - 6$ count in a body-bar multigraph. Tay's theorem also extends to generic body-hinge structures [20]. It was proven by Katoh and Tanigawa [38] that the same counting condition stated in Tay's theorem also characterizes the rigidity of generic molecular body-hinge frameworks. This result is known as the molecular theorem, which is here combined with Tay's theorem into one statement.

Theorem 1 (Tay's Theorem/Molecular Theorem) *A generic three-dimensional body-bar framework (body-hinge/molecular framework where bonds (hinges) are*

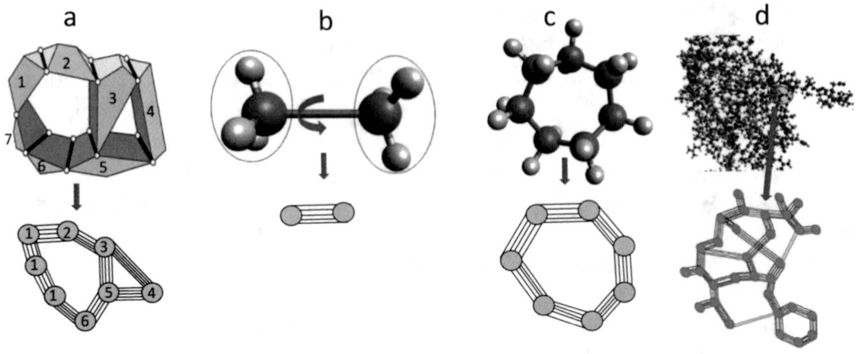

Fig. 14.6 **a** 3D body-hinge framework composed of seven rigid bodies connected by hinges (lines) can be modelled as a body-bar framework (with a corresponding body-bar multigraph shown). **b** A molecule consisting of two carbon atoms and a single bond can be viewed as a body-hinge structure where atoms are rigid bodies (one-valent hydrogen atoms are a part of a carbon atom rigid body, as their angles are fixed and can only spin around their axes) and a hinge is a rotatable bond, with corresponding body-bar multigraph. **c** A ring of seven carbon atoms (ignoring one-valent hydrogens) with a corresponding multigraph. (According to the molecular theorem a ring of seven atoms will have one internal degree of freedom. The total number of edges is $7(5) = 35$, while we need $6|7| - 6 = 36$). **d** Protein structure can be modelled as a molecular body-bar multigraph with black, red, and green lines corresponding to covalent bonds, hydrogen bonds, and hydrophobic contacts, respectively

replaced by five bars) on a multigraph $G = (V, E)$ is minimally rigid if and only if $|E| = 6|V| - 6$, and for all subsets of edges, $|E'| \leq 6|V'| - 6$.

In the stated original form, Tay's theorem leads to an exponential algorithm, as it requires counting the number of edges in every subgraph. However, because these counts of G (same as Laman's counts) define an independent set in a matroid [13, 35], this gives rise to greedy algorithms that can be used to efficiently track these counts. It is well known that all matroidal structures have greedy algorithms. A number of fast polynomial algorithms based on matroid unions, tree decompositions, and extension of bipartite matching algorithms, such as the *pebble game algorithm*, were subsequently developed for tracking these rigidity certifying counts (independence) in graph and subgraphs [16, 39].

14.3.1.3 Pebble Game Algorithm

The pebble game algorithm can very rapidly decompose a body-bar/molecular graph (i.e., protein structure) into rigid and flexible regions and quantify the overall number of degrees of freedom. The main step of the pebble game algorithm is to determine if a constraint (edge) is 'independent' (i.e., removes degrees of freedom) or is 'redundant' as its insertion has no effect on rigidity. The algorithm iteratively builds a maximal independent set of edges. We give a basic procedure of how the main steps of the pebble game algorithm are carried out for Tay's theorem without full details or speedups, which can be found in previous publications [16, 39]. A similar procedure can be derived for Laman's counts or other matroidal independence counting conditions. The implementation of the pebble game algorithm routine given here, which tracks counts in the molecular theorem, is important for the protein flexibility analysis that has been implemented in several software packages. such as FIRST (see below).

The Pebble Game Algorithm $6|V| - 6$:
Input: A multigraph $G = (V, E)$.
Initialize $I(G)$ and $\mathfrak{R}(G)$ to an empty set of edges. Place six pebbles on each vertex of G. (Fig. 14.6a)
Test the edges of E in an arbitrary order.

1. Until every edge in G has been tested, take any untested edge e, and go to step 2. Otherwise go to step 3.
2. Count the number of free pebbles on the endvertices of e, say vertex u and v.
   (a) If the vertices u and v have at least seven free pebbles, then place any pebble from either u or v onto e, directing the edge e from that vertex (Fig. 14.6b). Place e into $I(G)$ (independent edges) and return to step 1.
   (b) Else, search for a free pebble from u and v, by following the directed edges (covered edges) in the partially constructed directed graph $I(G)$ (Fig. 14.6c).
      (i) If the free pebble is found on some vertex w at the end of the directed path P (which starts at u or v), we perform a swap or sequence of swaps (cascade), reversing the entire path P, until a free pebble appears on the initial vertex (u or v) of the path P (i.e., w loses one free pebble, and u or v gains one free pebble) (Fig. 14.6c–e). Return to Step 2.
      (ii) Else, we could not find the seventh free pebble, and the edge is declared redundant (could not be covered by the pebble) (Fig. 14.7). Place e into $\mathfrak{R}(G)$ (redundant edges). Return to step 2.
3. Once all edges have been tested, stop.
   Output: The sets $I(G)$ and $\mathfrak{R}(G) = E - I(G)$.

When the algorithm is finished, $I(G)$ is the maximal independent set of edges (edges that are covered by pebbles). $\mathfrak{R}(G)$ is the set of redundant edges (edges that were not covered by a pebble). Total degrees of freedom (DOF) in a graph = number of remaining free pebbles.

The pebble game algorithm described here tracks the independence of edges in graphs prescribed by the molecular theorem. The initialization of placing six free pebbles on each vertex (corresponds to six trivial rigid body motions) tracks the $6|V|$ part of the count. Pebbles are synonymous with degrees of freedom and removal of a pebble indicates the inserted constraint (edge) is independent. Redundant constraints do not remove degrees of freedom (pebbles) as their insertion (or deletion) from an already rigid region causes no change in rigidity. Every time an edge is pebbled, it grows the set of independent edges. Pebble game algorithms are building a maximal subsets that are independent; at every stage, the edges covered by pebbles will satisfy $|E'| \leq 6|V'| - 6$ on all subsets. The requirement of at least seven free pebbles on the vertices before an edge is pebbled (i.e., declared independent) ensures the critical

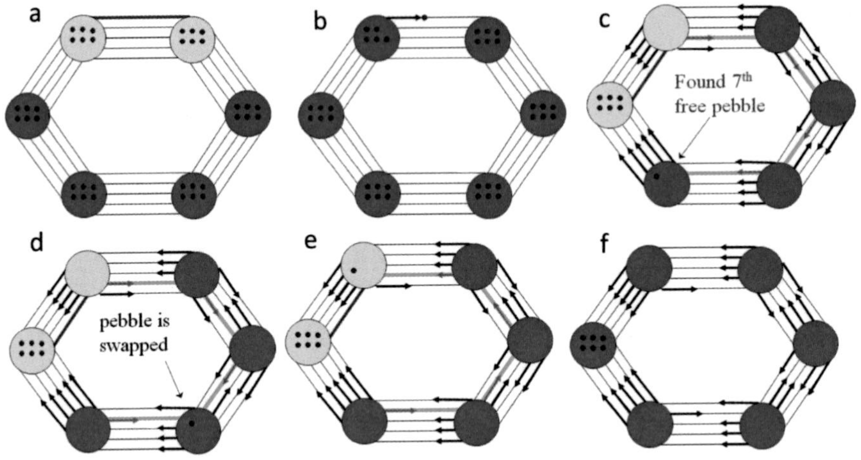

Fig. 14.7 A demonstration of a $6|V| - 6$ pebble game algorithm on a 3D cyclohexane graph. Edges are pebbled one by one (when there is at least seven free pebbles on its end vertices (**a**, **b**). If we cannot locate seven free pebbles we can search for free pebbles along with the partially created directed graph, swapping pebbles back. The graph has six remaining free pebbles and all edges are pebbled, indicating it is minimally rigid

subtraction in $6|V| - 6$ is respected on all subsets of edges. The algorithm is greedy. In other words, regardless of the order the edges are pebbled (i.e., are tested for independence), the algorithm will always give unique answers for total remaining free pebbles, the size of maximal independent $I(G)$ and redundant $\mathfrak{R}(G)$ set of edges. The pebble game algorithm is a very intuitive algorithm, which in the worst case runs in $O(V^2)$ [39], and in practice, it runs in linear time [15] (Fig. 14.8).

There are many extensions one can extract from the pebble game [16]. For example, when we cannot locate the seventh free pebble, the failed search over the directed graph indicates a rigid cluster. By using this procedure, it is possible to find all the maximal rigid clusters and redundantly rigid clusters (Fig. 14.7). Prediction of a highly redundant rigid clusters provides useful importance to a biochemist as these regions will have additional robustness, and will not become unstable (flexible) due to one or few edges breaking. For example, when a hydrogen bond breaks in a significantly redundantly rigid region, it will not alter its rigidity. We can also extract the relative degree of freedom count for any subgraph in G. This is very useful in the prediction of flexibility of particular regions of interest in protein graphs, for example, in antibody protein flexibility studies and in allostery predictions, which is discussed in next section.

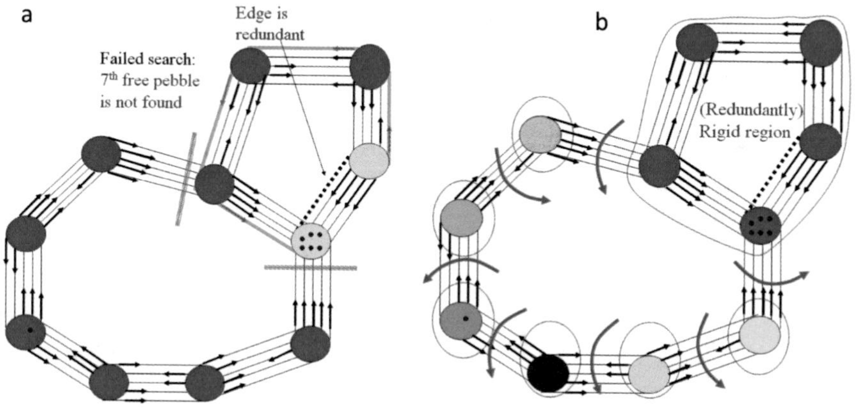

Fig. 14.8 $6|V| - 6$ Pebble game algorithm. **a** When we cannot pebble an edge, it indicates that edge is redundant and the corresponding failed search locates a redundantly rigid subgraph (**b**). Overall, the graph is flexible with one internal degree of freedom, as indicated by the remaining seven free pebbles. Rigid clusters are circled. Each one of the bonds can be moved with one internal rotational degree of freedom

14.4 Protein Flexibility, Dynamics, and Function Analysis with Rigidity Theory

14.4.1 FIRST and Rigid Cluster Decomposition

The pebble game algorithm is the main component of the programme FIRST [15] and other related software for analysing protein rigidity and flexibility. Starting with a protein structure (experimentally or computationally determined structure) in Protein Data Bank File format, the programme FIRST begins by creating a molecular body-bar multigraph. The multigraph consists of all atoms (including hydrogen atoms) represented by vertices, with covalent bonds, hydrogen bonds, hydrophobic contacts, and electrostatic interactions represented by edges. Covalent bonds are modelled as five edges, with six edges for double bonds and peptide bonds (as they do not have bond rotation), while hydrogen bonds and hydrophobic interactions are modelled with between one and five edges [25]. Hydrophobic contacts are defined as a pair of carbon–carbon, carbon–sulfer, or sulfer–sulfer atoms in close contact. Each hydrogen bond is assigned an energy strength in kcal/mol using an energy potential based on hydrogen donor and acceptor geometries. Hydrogen bonds are very important to the overall protein shape and stability. A hydrogen bond cutoff energy value (which mimics temperature) is selected such that all bonds weaker than this cutoff are ignored in the graph. Once the final constraint multigraph is obtained (Fig. 14.6d), FIRST then uses the pebble game algorithm and molecular theorem to decompose the protein into rigid and flexible regions.

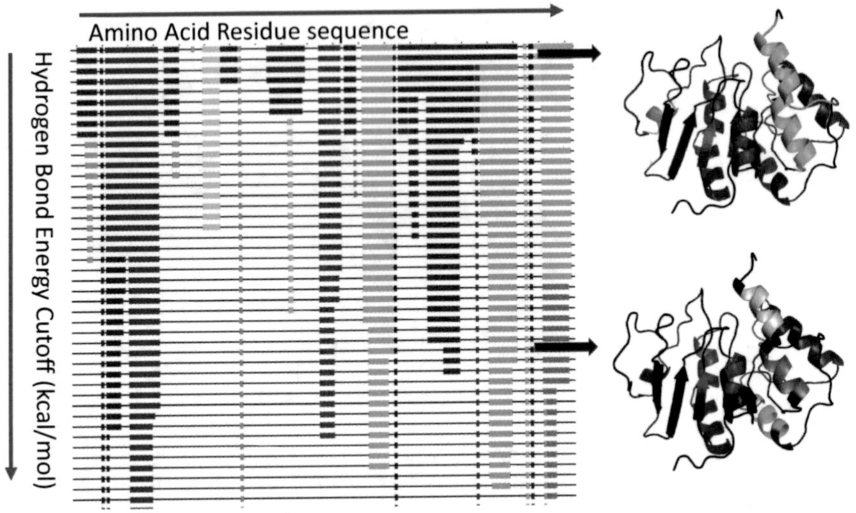

Fig. 14.9 Rigidity and flexibility analysis using FIRST and the pebble game algorithm on protein data from the Protein Data Bank (Protein Data Bank ID, 2jz3). The hydrogen bond dilution plot indicates how the protein breaks down as the hydrogen bond cutoff is increased (i.e., energy is increased), breaking hydrogen bonds one by one. Flexible regions are indicated by thin black lines and rigid regions are indicated by blocks, with separate colours indicating distinct rigid clusters. Flexible regions are coloured black on the protein structure. Initially, with inclusion of all potential hydrogen bonds, the protein is dominated by a few large rigid clusters (indicated by separate colours), and as hydrogen bonds are gradually broken with increasing energy, most of the protein becomes flexible (black) with a few remaining rigid clusters

Figures 14.9 and 14.10 show some examples of rigid cluster decompositions obtained with FIRST and the pebble game algorithm for two proteins. The rigid cluster decomposition on a very large Spike protein complex consisting of nearly 4000 residues was obtained in less than one second of running time (Fig. 14.10) We can monitor gradual changes in the rigid cluster decomposition as hydrogen bonds are removed one by one (i.e., by lowering the hydrogen bond energy threshold) in the order of increasing bond strength. The change in rigidity can be visualized using a hydrogen bond 'dilution plot' (Fig. 14.9). Because the pebble game is a combinatorial integer algorithm (tracking molecular theorem counts) as opposed to a numeric algorithm, FIRST always gives a unique exact answer.

While tremendous computational power and resources are needed to simulate protein flexibility with MD simulations, FIRST can predict rigid clusters and flexible connections in less than one second on a typical PC/laptop. Because of its speed and efficiency, rigidity theory analysis using FIRST and other related programmes have been widely applied to analysing various aspects of protein function and flexibility analysis, such as viral capsids [40] (with enormous structures containing hundreds of copies of protein structures), protein engineering, and prediction and replica-

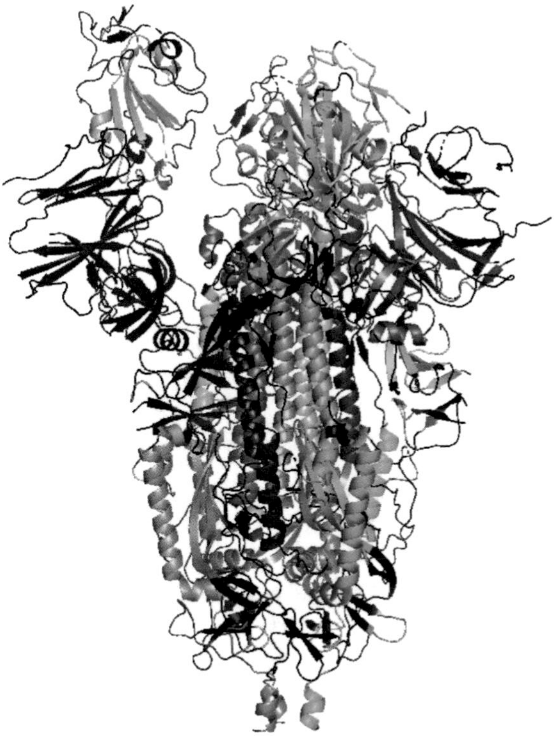

Fig. 14.10 Rigid cluster decomposition obtained with FIRST on a very large SARS-CoV-2 (in COVID-19) spike protein complex (Protein Data Bank ID 6vyb). At -1 kcal/mol energy cutoff, spike protein consists of more than 70 rigid clusters, each containing at least 20 atoms

tion of experimental measures of dynamics such as hydrogen–deuterium exchange, allostery, and enzyme catalysis [11, 12, 15, 17–19, 23, 24, 26].

14.4.2 Large-Scale Rigidity and Flexibility Analysis

As an illustration of the efficiency and wider applicability of rigidity theory for large big-data high-throughput analyses of protein structures, we review a study where the author and colleagues carried out the largest study to date of flexibility predictions of antibody protein structures [41].

Antibodies are proteins produced by B cells that play a main role in the adaptive immune system. They recognize a variety of pathogens and induce further immune response to protect the organism from external disturbance. Molecules that are bound by antibodies are called antigens. The focus of this study was to characterize flexibility of the key hyper-variable binding region on antibody called CDR H3 loop, which is the most important region in binding and recognition of various antigens. More specifically, we analysed whether the conformational flexibility of CDR H3 loop is changed as antibodies undergo affinity maturation. Antibodies can rapidly evolve

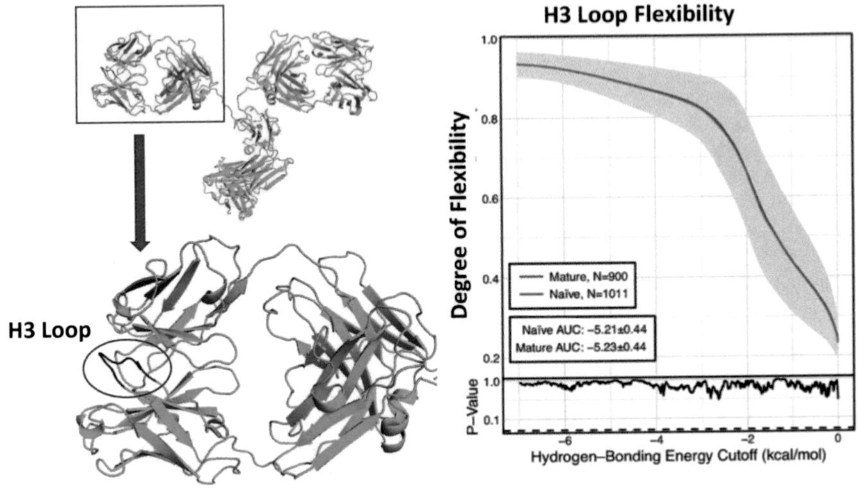

Fig. 14.11 Antibody is a large Y-shaped molecule. CDR H3 loop (shown in red) is located on the surface of each antibody arm, acting as a key region for antigen binding and recognition. In the study, authors applied extensions of the pebble game algorithm to analyse flexibility of the H3 loop using thousands of naïve and mature structures. There was no significant difference in flexibility between the naïve and mature H3 loops (figure on right adapted from [41])

to specific antigens, where affinity maturation drives this evolution through multiple cycles of mutation leading to enhanced antibody specificity and affinity. In this study, we utilized various extensions of the pebble game algorithm, initially developed in [16], which enables quantification of local flexibility of any subgraph, with focus on CDR H3 regions. By analysing thousands of mature and naÃ¯ve antibody crystal structure and homology models, we found no clear statistically significant difference in the flexibility of CDR H3 loops (Fig. 14.11), which was also correlated with experimental measures of flexibility. Such large-scale analysis of the flexibility of protein structures could be carried out because of the speed of the underlying FIRST method and our various pebble game extensions.

14.4.3 Protein Allostery Analysis with Rigidity Theory

We now briefly discuss and review an important application of rigidity theory for analysis of allosteric signalling in protein structures. Allostery is one of the most powerful and fundamental mechanisms regulating protein function [8–12, 42–44]. Allostery refers to the regulation of protein function at a distance, where a perturbation of a protein structure at one part of protein structure (for example, due to a binding or mutational event) can affect conformations and dynamics at another distant site, resulting in regulation of protein function. Allostery is a common event in the cell, and most dynamic protein exhibit some form of allosteric control mechanism. Allostery has been referred to as 'the second secret of life', second only to the genetic code [8]. Monod and Jacob in 1960s [43] first introduced the allostery concept; however, most questions pertaining to allostery are still largely unresolved. Decoding the allosteric mechanism remains one of the key long-standing unsolved problems in the biological sciences.

One of the important areas in allostery research is describing the physical mechanism of distant coupled conformational changes. The utilization and extension of our earlier fundamental work in modelling allostery in frameworks and graphs [16] and a first rigidity-based mechanistic model of allosteric signalling has led to several important breakthroughs in understanding how allostery controls enzyme and receptor function [11, 12, 24, 44]. Our rigidity theory methods predict that if mechanical perturbation of rigidity at one site of the protein can transmit and propagate across a protein structure and, in turn, cause a change in the available conformational degrees of freedom and a change in the conformation and dynamics at a second distant site, resulting in allosteric transmission (Fig. 14.12a). Using various extensions of the pebble game algorithm, we can analyse how long-range conformational coupling occurs in protein structures, map out allosteric pathways (regions in protein that are important for allosteric signalling) and extract various other properties and features of long-range coupling.

A popular hypothesis is that dynamical effects play a central role in enzyme catalysis. Dynamical changes are often manifested in proteins through allosteric effects, where a substrate binding can cause changes in dynamics at remote parts of a protein. In a study published in *Science* [11] concerning bacterial homodimeric fluoroacetate dehalogenase enzyme, experimental NMR chemical shift data suggested that when a substrate binds to one monomer, the second empty monomer undergoes asymmetrically pronounced conformational changes through an increase in flexibility in dynamics, thereby entropically favouring the forward reaction. Our rigidity-based allostery theory was able to verify this and elucidate in great detail the key residues involved in the allosteric pathways responsible for changes in dynamics and how substrate binding enhances allosteric communication between two subunits (Fig. 14.12b). These findings also provided deep insights into the energetic nature of allosteric processes that drive catalysis.

In a follow-up study [24], we showed that when there is a high concentration of substrate, the enzyme undergoes catalysis inhibition through the reduction in dynamics and dampening of interprotomer allosteric effects. Our computational rigidity predictions of allosteric networks and resulting changes in dynamics when additional substrates were bound to the enzyme were validated with NMR and functional experimental studies. These studies represented a major breakthrough in illustrating the role of dynamics and allostery in enzyme function.

Our rigidity-theoretical approaches have been extremely useful for studying allostery in other enzymes and proteins. Indeed, we were able to provide a major advancement and new level of insight regarding key allosteric processes in GPCR activation. GPCRs are situated in the plasma membrane, engage the G-protein and initiate cell signalling [45]. In several studies [12], we have shown how interactions

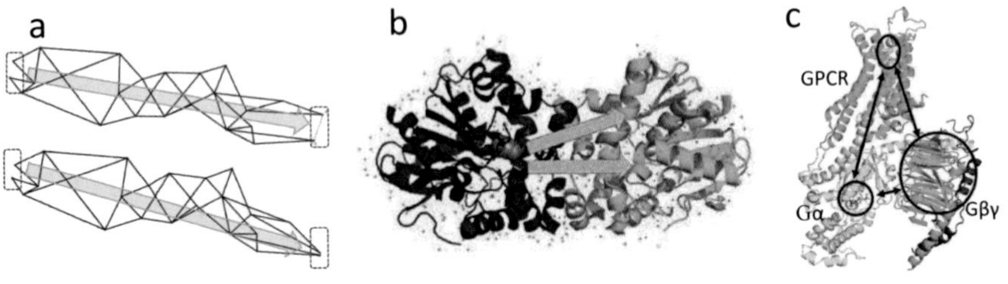

Fig. 14.12 Rigidity theoretical model for allosteric communication. **a** Conformational changes in one region of the framework (or protein structures) can propagate and change conformations and rigidity at distant regions. **b** Rigidity theory allostery analysis showed that homodimeric fluoroacetate dehalogenase enzyme with substrate fluoroacetate molecule (shown as orange spheres) exhibits allosteric communication between the two subunits (shown in distinct colours), which is critical for enzyme catalysis [11, 24]. **c** In a study of human adenosine A2A receptor [12, 18]., a member of superfamily of receptors called G-protein-coupled receptors (GPCRs) a similar approach was used to discover that allosteric communication between receptors and different domains of G-protein is critical for full receptor activation

between GPCR and its natural G-protein binding partner affect activation networks, as is critical for optimal GPCR activation (Fig. 14.12c), or how sodium, calcium, and magnesium can affect this activation process [18]. Our rigidity theory-based approaches offer a new perspective and opportunity to study the various facets of allosteric regulation of protein function, which will allow us to examine complicated signalling events in the cell.

14.4.4 Using Rigidity Theory to Simulate Protein Dynamics

So far, the discussion has focused on infinitesimal flexibility (which is equivalent to finite flexibility, assuming atom positions are in a generic configuration) and not on continuous motions. In other words, FIRST and the pebble game outputs do not simulate protein dynamics and indicate the amplitude of motions. One useful extension is to combine the rigid cluster decomposition with Monte Carlo-based geometric dynamics simulations [20, 21]. Rigid cluster decomposition can remove hundreds of degrees of freedom from the overall protein framework and serve as a natural coarse graining step to speed up protein dynamics simulations [19, 46]. For example, the all-atom geometric simulation method FRODA (Framework Rigidity Optimized Dynamic Algorithm) (which runs about 100,000 times faster than MD simulations) [20] uses rigid clusters as a preprocessing step to explore the conformational space of the protein motions. The rigid clusters, whose size and number depend on the selected energy threshold and the type of protein structure being analysed, can be kept fixed as rigid body geometrical components in the simulation motion (see Fig. 14.13). The atoms belonging to a rigid cluster can only move by utilizing trivial rigid body degrees of freedom. With this in mind, simulations can be focused on sim-

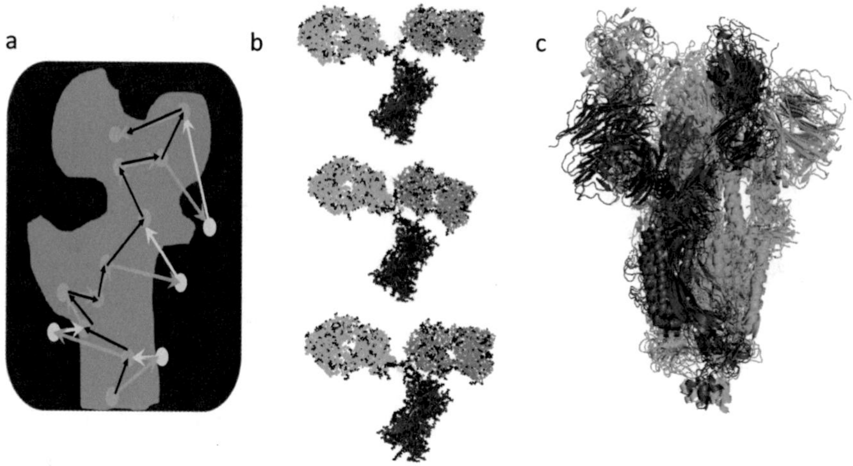

Fig. 14.13 Geometric simulation as used in FRODA/FRODAN (**a**). A part of a 2D slice through the 3N-dimensional conformational space, where red indicates disallowed states and blue indicates allowed states [21]. A random move (green arrows) is accepted if it falls within a blue region (green dots) and rejected if it falls within a red region (yellow dots), followed by enforcement of the constraints (yellow arrows). The black path produces a valid geometric path within the allowed conformational space. Any rigid region (which can be potentially very large) identified with FIRST moves as a single rigid body within FRODA or very small rigid clusters or individual atoms within FRODAN. **b** FRODA was applied to a large antibody protein to explore the large-scale motions of arms (green and orange) of the Y-shaped antibody structure, where three distinct colours represent three separate large rigid bodies. **c** FRODAN dynamics simulation illustrating internal dynamics of a Spike protein [47]

ulating the relevant degrees of freedom belonging to intermediate flexible regions. FRODA rapidly generates geometrically valid conformations that are consistent with bond lengths and angular constraints while maintaining all rigid clusters. In these protein motion simulations, we need to add the van der Waals collisions of atoms as constraints, where only allowed geometries (valid stereochemistry, bonding angles, Ramachandran plots etc.) accessible to protein motions are simulated. Figure 14.13b shows the output of FRODA for an antibody protein, which exemplifies large amplitude motions.

We have applied and extended FRODA, using the related constrained geometric simulation programme FRODAN [21], which, like FRODA, provides very fast motion simulations but is better suited for proteins that are not dominated by large rigid clusters. In a FRODAN simulation, the rigid clusters are typically small, from single atoms up to small rigid cycles (e.g., proline rings and rigid loops). This makes FRODAN useful for simulations of protein motions that include substantial unfolding and refolding and analysing motions of intrinsically disordered proteins. Indeed, we have utilized a similar approach in combination with an experimental measure of dynamics, hydrogen–deuterium exchange, to characterize the highly complex motions and conformational ensemble of a large intrinsically disordered Tau protein [22]. Tau protein is a key protein in a number of pathologies and dementias such as

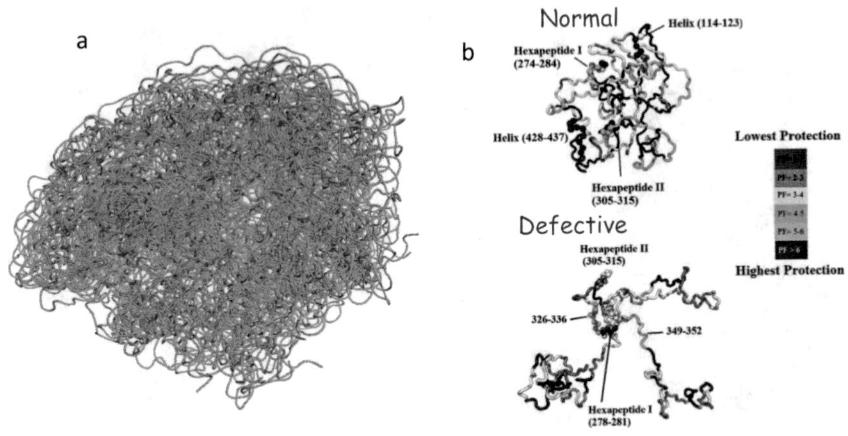

Fig. 14.14 **a** Tau protein is a large intrinsically disordered protein. Because of its high flexibility and disordered structure, it is able to take a wide variety of shapes, which makes it difficult to study with conventional MD simulations. **b** By performing large rigidity theory geometric simulations using FRODAN and its extensions, we were able to characterize the representative structures for the native and defective (i.e., hyperphosphorylated) forms of Tau, which was shown to be in agreement with HDX experimental data (The figure in b is adapted from [22])

Alzheimer's disease, and its primary physiological role is to stabilize microtubules in neuronal axons at all stages of development. One of the main challenges in understanding the Tau structure–function relationship and finding successful therapeutics for Alzheimer's disease is the poor understanding of the atomic structural ensemble and dynamics of the Tau protein. Moreover, Tau protein undergoes modifications to its shape and internal dynamics as mediated by a hyperphosphorylation defect. By performing FRODAN simulations and our various extensions, we were able to show an unprecedented first detailed view of the structural and dynamic characteristics of both the normal and the defective hyperphosphorylated forms of Tau [22]. This study provided a rich understanding of the structural basis of Tau pathology (see Fig. 14.14).

FRODA, FRODAN and our various extensions can be applied to probe the dynamics of very large structures such as Spike proteins [47] or disordered proteins, which provides a significant advantage over traditional MD simulations. Probing motions of intrinsically disordered proteins with MD simulation is extremely challenging, if not essentially impossible, owing to their highly dynamic character. The rigidity theory-inspired methodologies FRODA/N discussed here can be run in either targeted and non-targeted modes, and we have recently combined these techniques with search algorithms in reinforcement learning (under review). The targeted mode employs biasing force during transitioning, while the non-targeted mode explores unbiased random fluctuations, which enables the exploration of a broad conformation space. Additionally, the targeted mode is useful for determining the conformational transition pathways between distinct conformations (i.e., opening and closing motions such as hinge-bending motions, GPCR activation, etc.).

14.5 Protein Structure Validation with Rigidity Theory

We now discuss another application of rigidity theory to structural biology. In a very recent study, we made an important breakthrough in the area of protein structure validation [48, 49].

Experimentally solved protein structures are only useful if they are known to be accurate and realistically represent the protein structures in their native environment. The vast majority of protein structures in the Protein Data Bank [50] have been solved by X-ray crystallography or NMR experiments. Both X-ray crystal structures and NMR structures are only model representations of experimental data, which are prone to uncertainties and errors. It is widely accepted that experimentally solved protein structures must be validated with (i) geometric tests and (ii) how well structures match input experimental data (restraints) [51]. Geometric criteria are easy to check for both X-ray and NMR structures, and measurements like R factor and Rfree values can be used to check how well X-ray structures match input X-ray diffraction data [48]. Unfortunately, no such validation criteria exist for NMR structures [51], and unlike crystal structures, validating the quality of NMR structures has been extremely difficult. In fact, since the first protein was determined by NMR in 1985 until now, there has been no effective method for NMR protein structural validation, which has largely limited the applications and use of NMR structures among protein researchers [51–55]. This has created a problem not only for users of structural information, but also for scientists who use NMR to computationally solve structures and want to know how accurate their solved structure is.

While structures solved by NMR represent less than 10% of all structures in PDB, they are extremely important, as not all proteins can be crystalized and NMR structures also include a high proportion of proteins with under-represented folds (shapes). NMR structures are determined in solution (a protein's natural environment), whereas X-ray structures are determined in a crystalline environment, which arguably makes NMR structures more representative of in vivo structures. Hence, there has been a pressing need to find an acceptable validation measure for NMR structures.

We have developed the method ANSURR (Accuracy of NMR Structures Using Random Coil Index and Rigidity) [48], which addresses this critical long-standing gap for NMR protein structure validation. ANSURR assesses the quality of NMR structures by comparing two measures of local protein rigidity, one derived from the original NMR input data and the other derived from rigidity theory prediction of protein flexibility using structural data. The measure of rigidity using input data is based on the Random Coil Index (RCI), which uses experimental NMR chemical shifts (a readily available data type for each NMR structure) to quantify the extent of disordered structure for each amino acid in solution. The second measure is based on FIRST and our rigidity theory extensions, which involves calculating the dilution plot (see Fig. 14.9) and extracting a flexibility score for each residue. ANSURR then compares these two measures of local rigidity and provides a residue-by-residue test of how well the rigidity of the structure (obtained from rigidity theory) compares

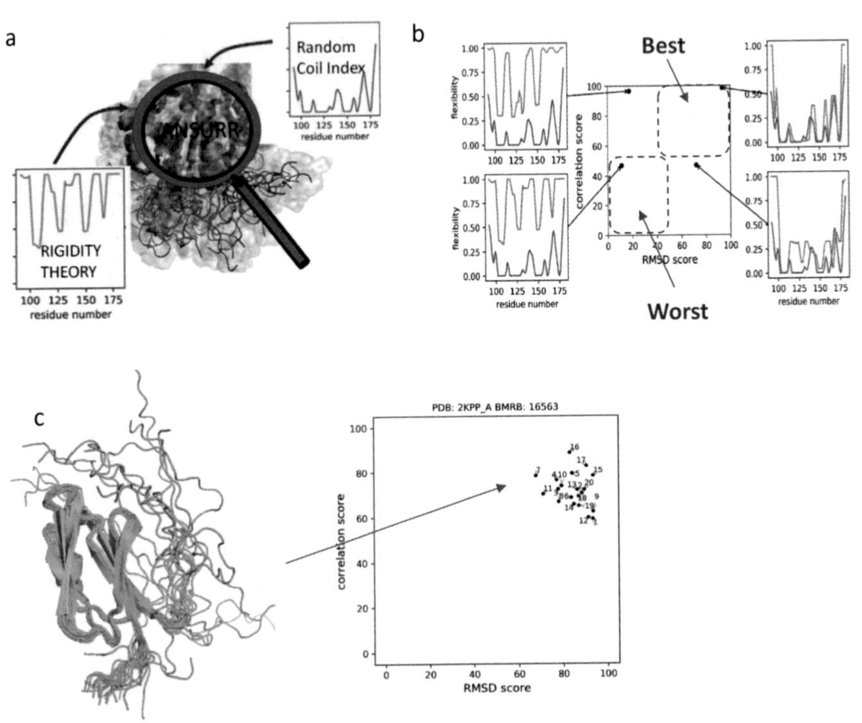

Fig. 14.15 **a** The ANSURR method evaluates the accuracy of nuclear magnetic resonance (NMR) protein structure (which are given as an ensemble of models) by comparing two measures of protein flexibility (orange predicted from structure, using mathematical rigidity theory using extensions of the method FIRST, and blue derived from the random coil index [RCI] using experimental NMR chemical shift data). **b** Analysis of ANSURR using four models from NMR (Protein Data Bank ID, 1e17). ANSURR provides two metrics for accuracy: a correlation score between FIRST (rigidity) and RCI and a root mean square difference (RMSD) score. The structures in the top right portion of the plot (high correlation and high RMSD scores) are high-quality NMR structures, and structures in the bottom left of the plot are considered poor structures (Figure adapted from [48]). **c** ANSURR output for an example NMR structure (Protein Data Bank ID, 2kpp) that has high accuracy for most models in the ensemble

to the experimentally determined (true, RCI chemical shift) rigidity. ANSURR provides two metrics for accuracy measurement. One is a correlation score between FIRST (rigidity) and RCI, which assesses the accuracy of protein folding (secondary structures), and the second is an RMSD score, which measures how well the overall rigidity and flexibility between FIRST and RCI match (Fig. 14.15).

Unlike crystal structures, NMR structures are always represented as an ensemble of (typically around 20) possible structural models. Because it is unclear which models are useful or accurate, this has created substantial and unnecessary confusion for users of NMR structures. A nice feature of ANSURR is its ability to estimate the accuracy of each model.

The performance of ANSURR was tested using several approaches [48]; first, ANSURR was applied to structures refined in an explicit solvent (which was found to be much better than unrefined structures), and then ANSURR was applied to a large set of good and bad structures (using decoy generations). ANSURR was also compared against previously proposed measures of accuracy (mostly restraint-based tests and geometric checks). Several of these indicators, such as restraint violations and restraints per residue, were shown to be poor measures of accuracy. On the other hand, a Ramachandran analysis (a standard check to determine if a protein backbone has a correct geometry) was found to be a useful geometric check of accuracy. A typical comparison of how well a structure compares to another structure is the backbone root mean square deviation, which can show if protein structures resemble each other when superimposed. However, this measure may miss many of the important structural differences found in amino acid side-chain orientations, which are responsible for forming critical hydrogen bonding interactions that have a direct impact on protein stability and functional aspects such as protein dynamics and enzyme catalysis. As rigidity measures are sensitive to side chains, ANSURR can also be used to assess the quality of side-chain atomic positions, which makes it a powerful tool for the assessment and refinement of protein structures.

Recent work [49] applied ANSURR to more than 7000 NMR structures in the PDB, showing that NMR structures span a wide range of accuracy. Most NMR structures have accurate secondary structures, but are too floppy, particularly in their loops. Our studies also indicate that both crystal structures and NMR structures have equally accurate secondary structural elements (helices, sheets), but crystal structures are typically too rigid in disordered regions, whereas NMR structures are too flexible overall.

Development of ANSURR is a major advancement in the long-standing problem of protein structure validation, as it provides the first workable measure of the accuracy of NMR structures and is expected to give researchers more confidence in the use and application of structural NMR. Ultimately, this should lead to a better understanding of how proteins perform their functions, with general implications for structural biology research. This work opens up enormous new research avenues in protein structure determination and the improvement of standards for protein structure refinement.

14.6 Conclusion

Studying the rigidity and flexibility of geometric frameworks has advanced considerably since Maxwell's combinatorial characterization of the rigidity of mechanical frameworks in the 1800s. Mathematical advancements in rigidity theory over the last two decades have been tremendous, opening up many exciting opportunities in applied sciences and engineering. In this chapter, we have reviewed some of the latest advances in rigidity theory and its applications for the analysis of protein function at an atomistic scale. Moreover, we have shown how rigidity theory-based methods and our various algorithms and extensions can rapidly and accurately predict protein flexibility and dynamics, which can be used to decipher various aspects of protein function, including elusive issues of allostery, enzyme catalysis, GPCR signalling, or motions of intrinsically disordered proteins. Our recent development using rigidity theory in protein structure validation has led to a development of a first workable method in validation of NMR protein structures. This advance will provide confidence to users of protein structures and is expected to accelerate and improve the process of protein structure determination and aid computational drug discovery. Rigidity theory is heavily rooted in deep mathematical formulations in the area of discrete applied geometry and combinatorics, which has unfortunately remained largely inaccessible to most researchers in applied science and engineering fields. While there has been some cross-fertilization between the various scientific fields studying different aspects of rigidity and flexibility, stronger interactions and interdisciplinary training are needed between applied and theoretical scientific communities to realize the enormous potential of rigidity theory applications. We advocate that rigidity theory, through both algorithmic and mathematical progress, has significantly advanced such that it could be widely applied in the analysis of structural biological data, which can complement experimental approaches to reveal novel insights on intractable and fundamental biological enigmas of living organism. Rigidity theory exemplifies how mathematics and algorithms can make significant contributions to structural biology, biological big-data analyses, and progress in biological applications.

References

1. K. Roberts, B. Alberts, A. Johnson, P. Walter, T. Hunt, *Molecular Biology of the Cell* (Garland Science, New York, 2002)
2. Yip, K. M., Fischer, N., Paknia, E., Chari, A., and Stark, H. (2020). Atomic-resolution protein structure determination by cryo-EM. Nature, 587(7832), 157–161
3. W. Gao, S.P. Mahajan, J. Sulam, J.J. Gray, Deep learning in protein structural modeling and design. Patterns, 100142
4. M.Y. Galperin, X.M. Fernández-Suárez, D.J. Rigden, The 24th annual Nucleic Acids Research database issue: a look back and upcoming changes. Nucleic acids research **45**(D1), D1–D11 (2017)
5. Henzler-Wildman, K., and Kern, D. (2007). Dynamic personalities of proteins. Nature, 450(7172), 964–972
6. Hartl FU, Hayer-Hartl M (2009) Converging concepts of protein folding in vitro and in vivo. Nat. Struct. Mol. Biol. 16:574–81
7. J.R. Lewandowski, M.E. Halse, M. Blackledge, L. Emsley, Direct observation of hierarchical protein dynamics. Science **348**(6234), 578–581 (2015)
8. A.W. Fenton, Allostery: an illustrated definition for the second secret of life. Trends Biochem. Science **33**, 420–425 (2008)
9. Nussinov R, CJ Tsai (2013) Allostery in disease and drug discovery, Cell, 153(2), 293–305
10. J. Liu, R. Nussinov, Allostery: an overview of its history, concepts, methods, and applications. PLoS Comput. Biol. **12**(6) (2016)
11. Kim TH, Mehrabi P, Ren A, Sljoka A, Ing C, Bezginov A, Ye LB, Pomes R, Prosser RS and Pai EF (2017) The role of dimer asymmetry and protomer dynamics in enzyme catalysis, Science, 355, 262–U287

12. Huang, S., Pandey, A., Tran, D., Villanueva, N., Kitao, A., Sunahara, R., Sljoka, A., and Prosser, R. (2021). Delineating the conformational landscape of the adenosine A2A receptor during G protein coupling. Cell, 184(7), 1884–1894
13. W. Whiteley, Counting out to the fexibility of molecules. Phys. Biol. **2**, S116–S126 (2005)
14. C. F. Mourkazel, P. M. Duxbury in rigidity theory and applications, ed. by M.F. Thorpe, P.M. Duxbury (Kluwer Academic/Plenum Publishers, 1999), p. 69
15. Kuhn LA, Rader DJ, Thorpe MF (2001) Protein flexibility predictions using graph theory, Proteins, 44:150–65
16. A. Sljoka, Algorithms in rigidity theory with applications to protein flexibility and mechanical linkages. Ph.D thesis, York University, Toronto, 2012
17. A.J. Rader, B.M. Hespenheide, L.A. Kuhn, M.F. Thorpe, Protein unfolding: rigidity lost. Proceedings of the National Academy of Sciences **99**(6), 3540–3545 (2002)
18. L. Ye, C. Neale, A. Sljoka, D. Pichugin, N. Tsuchimura, R. Sunahara, S. Prosser, et al, Bidirectional regulation of the A2A adenosine G protein-coupled receptor by physiological cations. Nat. Commun. **1**(9), 1372 (2018)
19. S.M. Hermans, C. Pfleger, C. Nutschel, C.A. Hanke, H. Gohlke, Rigidity theory for biomolecules: concepts, software, and applications. Wiley Interdisciplinary Reviews: Computational Molecular Science **7**(4), (2017)
20. S.A. Wells, S. Menor, B.M. Hespenheide, M.F. Thorpe, Constrained geometric simulation of diffusive motion in proteins. Phys. Biol. **2**, S12736 (2005)
21. D.W. Farrell, K. Speranskiy, M.F. Thorpe, Generating stereochemically acceptable protein pathways. Proteins: Struct. Funct. Bioinf. **78**(14), 2908–2921 (2010)
22. S. Zhu, A. Shala, A. Bezginov, A. Sljoka, G. Audette, D. Wilson, Hyperphosphorylation of intrinsically disordered tau protein induces an amyloidogenic shift in its conformational ensemble. PLoS ONE **10**(3) (2015)
23. S.L. Seyler, A. Kumar, M.F. Thorpe, O. Beckstein, Path similarity analysis: a method for quantifying macromolecular pathways. PLOS Comput. Biol. **11**(10) (2015)
24. P. Mehrabi, C. Di Pietrantonio, T. Kim, A. Sljoka, K. Taverner, C. Ing, N. Kruglyak, R. Pomès, E. Pai, R. Prosser, Substrate-based allosteric regulation of a homodimeric enzyme. Journal of the American Chemical Society **141**(29), 11540–11556 (2019)
25. A. Sljoka, D. Wilson, Probing Protein Ensemble Rigidity and predictions of Hydrogen-Deuterium exchange. Physical Biology **10**, (2013)
26. B. Deng, S. Zhu, A.M. Macklin, J. Xu, C. Lento, A. Sljoka, D. Wilson, Suppressing allostery in epitope mapping experiments using millisecond hydrogen/deuterium exchange mass spectrometry. MAbs **1**, 10 (2017)
27. G. Wieczorek, P. Zielenkiewicz, DeltaF508 mutation increases conformational flexibility of CFTR protein. J Cyst Fibros **7**, 295–300 (2008)
28. F.R. Salsbury Jr., Molecular dynamics simulations of protein dynamics and their relevance to drug discovery. Current opinion in pharmacology **10**(6), 738–744 (2010)
29. I.R. Kleckner, M.P. Foster, An introduction to NMR-based approaches for measuring protein dynamics. Biochimica et Biophysica Acta (BBA). Proteins Proteomics **1814**(8), 942–968
30. E.A. Jares-Erijman, T.M. Jovin, FRET imaging. Nature biotechnology **21**(11), 1387–1395 (2003)
31. McCammon, J. A., Gelin, B. R., and Karplus, M. (1977). Dynamics of folded proteins. Nature, 267(5612), 585–590
32. D.E. Shaw, et al., Anton, a special-purpose machine for molecular dynamics. Commun. ACM (ACM) **51**(7), 9197 (2008)
33. Q. Cui, I. Bahar, *Normal Mode Analysis: Theory and Applications to Biological and Chemical Systems* (CRC press)
34. M. Sitharam, A.S. John, J. Sidman, *Handbook of Geometric Constraint Systems Principles* (CRC Press, 2018)
35. W. Whiteley, Some matroids from discrete applied geometry, in *Matroid Theory*, ed. by J. Bonin, J. Oxley, B. Servatius (Amer. Math. Soc., Providence, 1996), vol. 197 pp. 171–311

36. B. Schulze, A. Sljoka, W. Whiteley, How does symmetry impact the flexibility of proteins? Philos. Trans. Roy. Soc. A **372**, 20120041 (2014)
37. T.S. Tay, Rigidity of multigraphs i: linking rigid bodies in n-space. J. Comb. Theory Ser. B **26**, 95–112 (1984)
38. N. Katoh, S. Tanigawa, A Proof of the Molecular Conjecture. Discrete Comput. Geom. **45**, 647–700 (2011)
39. A. Lee, I. Streinu, Pebble game algorithms and sparse graphs. Discrete Math. **308**(1425), 1437 (2008)
40. B.M. Hespenheide, D.J. Jacobs, M.F. Thorpe, Structural rigidity in the capsid assembly of cowpea chlorotic mottle virus. J. Phys.: Condens. Matter **16**, S5055–S5064 (2004)
41. J.R. Jeliazkov, A. Sljoka, D. Kuroda, N. Tsuchimura, N. Katoh, K. Tsumoto, J.J. Gray, Repertoire analysis of antibody CDR-H3 loops suggests affinity maturation does not typically result in rigidification. Front. Immunol. **9**, 413 (2018)
42. K. Gunasekaran, M. Ma, R. Nussinov, Is allostery an intrinsic property of all dynamic proteins? Proteins: Struct. Funct. Bioinf. **57**, 433443 (2004)
43. J.P. Changeux, F. Jacob, J. Monod, Allosteric proteins and cellular control systems. J Mol Biol **6**, 306–329 (1963)
44. S. Bera, M. Rashid, A. Medvinsky, G.Q. Sun, B.L. Li, C. Acquisti, A. Sljoka, A. Chakraborty, Allosteric regulation of Glutamate dehydrogenase deamination activity. Scientific reports **10**(1), 1–15 (2020)
45. N.R. Latorraca, A.J. Venkatakrishnan, R.O. Dror, GPCR dynamics: structures in motion. Chemical reviews **117**(1), 139–155 (2017)
46. H. Gohlke, M.F. Thorpe, A natural coarse graining for simulating large biomolecular motion. Biophysical Journal **91**(6), 2115–2120 (2006)
47. N. Kumawat, A. Tucs, S. Bera, G. Chuev, M. Fedotova, K. Tsuda, S. Kruchinin, A. Sljoka, A. Chakraborty, Prefusion conformation of SARS-CoV-2 receptor-binding domain favors interactions with human receptor ACE2. bioRxiv (2021)
48. N. Fowler, A. Sljoka, M. Williamson, A method for validating the accuracy of NMR protein structures. Nat. Commun. **11**(1), 6321 (2020)
49. N. Fowler, A. Sljoka, M. Williamson, The accuracy of NMR protein structures in the Protein Data Bank. bioRxiv (2021)
50. H.M. Berman et al., The Protein Data Bank. Nucleic Acids Res. **28**, 235–242 (2000)
51. Gore, S. et al. Validation of structures in the Protein Data Bank. Structure 25, 1916–1927 (2017)
52. A.T. Brunger, Free R-value: A novel statistical quantity for assessing the accuracy of crystal structures. Nature **355**, 472–475 (1992)
53. D.A. Snyder, A. Bhattacharya, Y.P.J. Huang, G.T. Montelione, Assessing precision and accuracy of protein structures derived from NMR data. Proteins: Struct. Funct. Bioinf. **59**, 655-661 (2005)
54. G.W. Vuister, R.H. Fogh, P.M.S. Hendrickx, J.F. Doreleijers, A. Gutmanas, An overview of tools for the validation of protein NMR structures. Journal of Biomolecular NMR **58**, 259–285 (2014)
55. Spronk, C.A.E.M., Nabuurs, S.B., Krieger, E., Vriend, G. and Vuister, G.W. Validation of protein structures derived by NMR spectroscopy. Progr. NMR Spectrosc. 45, 315–337 (2004)

Open Access This chapter is licensed under the terms of the Creative Commons Attribution 4.0 International License (http://creativecommons.org/licenses/by/4.0/), which permits use, sharing, adaptation, distribution and reproduction in any medium or format, as long as you give appropriate credit to the original author(s) and the source, provide a link to the Creative Commons license and indicate if changes were made.

The images or other third party material in this chapter are included in the chapter's Creative Commons license, unless indicated otherwise in a credit line to the material. If material is not included in the chapter's Creative Commons license and your intended use is not permitted by statutory regulation or exceeds the permitted use, you will need to obtain permission directly from the copyright holder.

Chapter 15
Optimization of Evacuation and Walking-Home Routes from Osaka City After a Nankai Megathrust Earthquake Using Road Network Big Data

Atsushi Takizawa and Yutaka Kawagishi

Abstract When a disaster such as a large earthquake occurs, the resulting breakdown in public transportation leaves urban areas with many people who are struggling to return home. With people from various surrounding areas gathered in the city, unusually heavy congestion may occur on the roads when the commuters start to return home all at once on foot. In this chapter, it is assumed that a large earthquake caused by the Nankai Trough occurs at 2 p.m. on a weekday in Osaka City, where there are many commuters. We then assume a scenario in which evacuation from a resulting tsunami is carried out in the flooded area and people return home on foot in the other areas. At this time, evacuation and returning-home routes with the shortest possible travel times are obtained by solving the evacuation planning problem. However, the road network big data for Osaka City make such optimization difficult. Therefore, we propose methods for simplifying the large network while keeping those properties necessary for solving the optimization problem and then recovering the network. The obtained routes are then verified by large-scale pedestrian simulation, and the effect of the optimization is verified.

15.1 Introduction

When a disaster such as a large earthquake occurs, the resulting breakdown in public transportation leaves urban areas with many people who are struggling to return home. With people from various surrounding areas gathered in the city, unusually

A. Takizawa (✉)
Graduate School of Human Life Science, Osaka City University, Sugimoto 3-3-138, Sumiyoshi-ku, Osaka 558-8585, Japan
e-mail: takizawa@osaka-cu.ac.jp

Y. Kawagishi
Graduate School of Engineering, Osaka City University, Sugimoto 3-3-138, Sumiyoshi-ku, Osaka 558-8585, Japan

© The Author(s) 2022

N. Katoh et al. (eds.), *Sublinear Computation Paradigm*,
https://doi.org/10.1007/978-981-16-4095-7_15

heavy congestion may occur on the roads when the commuters start to return home all at once on foot. In Japan, the Great East Japan Earthquake on March 11, 2011 left many people in central Tokyo unable to return home, and roads were flooded with pedestrians attempting to do so. After the Osaka North Earthquake on June 18, 2018, the Shin-Yodogawa Bridge and its surroundings were extremely congested by displaced people crossing the Yodo River from Umeda.

From reflecting on such confusion, many local governments have already decided on countermeasures for people who are struggling to return home [16]. Common among these countermeasures is that people who need to return home from their places of work are urged not to do so immediately after the disaster but rather to remain in place. Meanwhile, although it is known empirically that great confusion arises when difficulties in returning home occur, the associated countermeasures tend to be approximate because it is not known how much congestion occurs and where until after the disaster has occurred. Pedestrian simulation of the whole city would seem useful in such cases, but this has not been attempted until recently because doing so requires large-scale and detailed data and a high-speed calculation environment. However, Hiroi et al. carried out a simulation of mass returning-home behavior on foot after a large earthquake for an area within 40 km from Tokyo Station [3].

In the case of western Japan, such as Osaka City, an earthquake originating from the Nankai Trough is the most dangerous. In Osaka City, the resulting tsunami is predicted to reach the shore in 1 h and 50 minutes and flood about half of the city [14]. One of the major problems with the tsunami is that it will travel up the Yodo River in the northern part of Osaka City and spread to the coastal area. As mentioned above, people returning home after the 2018 Northern Osaka Earthquake became congested around bridges crossing the Yodo River, a phenomena that Kawagishi and Takizawa predicted by means of a large-scale simulation of returning home from Osaka City [7].

However, if the timings of the tsunami flooding and the movement of people overlap, a large-scale secondary disaster may occur. Therefore, in Osaka City, it is necessary to consider risks such as delayed escape from tsunami along with the countermeasures for people who are struggling to return home, but it is difficult to say that the current countermeasures consider such risks. The purpose of the study by Kawagishi and Takizawa [7] was to investigate how a Nankai Trough earthquake would affect the return home of commuters in Osaka City. The results confirmed that bridges over the Yodo River from the center of Osaka City would be congested for a long time with people crossing, and that there would be a danger of delayed escape from tsunami by remaining in the vicinity. However, that study did not consider evacuation behavior from tsunami, and it assumed that people who walk home take the shortest route to do so. Therefore, problems remained, such as excessive concentration of pedestrians on specific roads and bridges.

In the present study, it is assumed that a large earthquake caused by the Nankai Trough occurs at 2 p.m. on a weekday in Osaka City, where there are many commuters. We then assume a scenario in which evacuation from tsunami is carried out in the flooded area and people return home on foot in the other areas. At this time, the evacuation and returning-home routes with the shortest possible travel times are obtained by solving the evacuation planning problem [8, 19]. However, the road network big data for Osaka City make such optimization difficult. Therefore, we propose methods for simplifying the large network while keeping those properties that are necessary for solving the optimization problem and then recovering the network. The obtained routes are then verified by large-scale pedestrian simulation, and the effect of the optimization is verified.

The remainder of this chapter is organized as follows. The next section explains the evacuation planning model. Next, the pedestrian simulation model for a large-scale network model is described. Then, the results are discussed, and conclusions and suggestions for future work are presented.

15.2 Quickest Evacuation Planning Problem

This section describes the quickest evacuation planning problem based on a dynamic network in which the flow rate changes over time. Meanwhile, a network in which the flow rate does not change over time is called a static network.

15.2.1 Dynamic Network

We define a directed graph $D = (V, E)$ for vertex set V and edge set E. In V, the sources (i.e., the starting vertices of the flow) and sinks (i.e., the destinations) are given. A directed edge with a start vertex $u \in V$ and an end vertex $v \in V$ is expressed as $e = (u, v)$, and the start vertex of e is expressed as $tail(e)$ and the end vertex is expressed as $head(e)$. For vertex $v \in V$, $\delta_D^+(v) \subset E$ is defined as a set of edges going out of v and $\delta_D^-(v) \subset E$ is a set of edges going toward v. For each edge $e \in E$, we define a travel time function $\tau : E \to \mathbb{Z}_+$ that denotes the time required to flow on e from $tail(e)$ to $head(e)$. The maximum value of the flow on e is denoted by the capacity function $c : E \to \mathbb{R}_+$. For each vertex $v \in V$, we define a supply function $b : V \to \mathbb{R}_+$ that denotes the amount of supply at that vertex, and the set of vertices with one or more supplies as $S^+ \subseteq V$. Furthermore, the sink set $S^- \subseteq V$ is also defined.

Using the above definitions, a dynamic network $N = (D, c, \tau, b, S^+, S^-)$ is defined, and Fig. 15.1 shows an example of N. Assuming application to evacuation planning, the flow denotes the movement of evacuees, a sink denotes an evacuation site, and the flow reaching a sink denotes the accommodation of evacuees at that evacuation site. An evacuee who arrives at a vertex moves on an edge and is deemed evacuated upon reaching a sink. The total number of evacuees at point $v \in V$ is regarded as the supply at that point $b(v)$.

Next, we define a dynamic flow $f : E \times \mathbb{Z}_+ \to \mathbb{R}_+$ on dynamic network N as the flow rate entering the edge $e \in E$ at discrete time $\theta \in \mathbb{Z}_+$, and it is expressed as

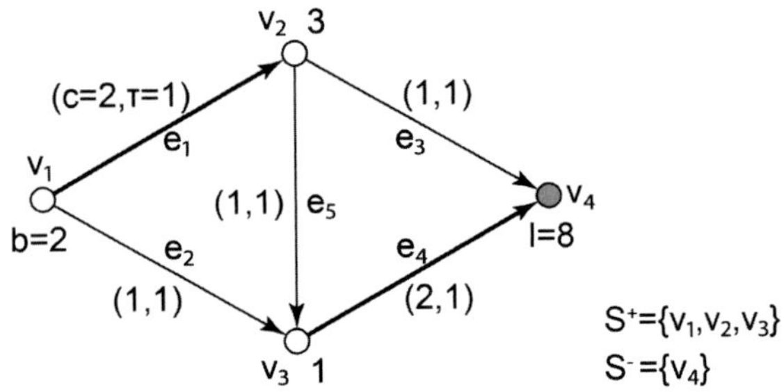

Fig. 15.1 Example of a dynamic network N

$f(e,\theta)$. Note that the flow that enters $tail(e)$ of edge e at time θ arrives at $head(e)$ at time $\theta + \tau(e)$.

On the dynamic flow, the following three constraints are defined. First, the capacity constraint is given by

$$0 \le f(e,\theta) \le c(e) \quad (\forall e \in E, \theta \in \mathbb{Z}_+), \tag{15.1}$$

then the flow conservation law is given by

$$\sum_{e \in \delta_D^+(v)} \sum_{\theta=0}^{\Theta} f(e,\theta) - \sum_{e \in \delta_D^-(v)} \sum_{\theta=0}^{\Theta-\tau(e)} f(e,\theta) \le b(v) \quad (\forall v \in V, \forall \Theta \in \mathbb{Z}_+), \tag{15.2}$$

and the demand constraint is given by

$$\sum_{s \in S^-} \sum_{e \in \delta_D^-(s)} \sum_{\theta=0}^{\Theta-\tau(e)} f(e,\theta) = \sum_{v \in V} b(v) \quad (\exists \Theta \in \mathbb{Z}_+). \tag{15.3}$$

A dynamic flow that satisfies these three constraints is said to be feasible, and the feasible dynamic flow that achieves the minimum time $\Theta*$ is called the quickest flow. The quickest evacuation planning problem is to find the minimum evacuation completion time $\Theta*$.

Considering application to an actual evacuation planning problem, there is an upper limit on the number of evacuees that can be accepted at each sink, which is an evacuation center. As defined by Kamiyama et al. [6], it is assumed that the capacity function $l : S^- \to \mathbb{Z}_+$ pertains to each sink, and the feasible flow f satisfies

$$\sum_{e \in \delta_D^-(s)} \sum_{\theta=0}^{\Theta} f(e,\theta) \le l(s) \quad (\forall s \in S^-, \forall \Theta \in \mathbb{Z}_+). \tag{15.4}$$

15.2.2 Time-Expanded Network

Ford and Fulkerson [1, 2] proposed the time-expanded network to obtain the quickest flow. This is a static network corresponding to dynamic network N with time constraint Θ, and it is designated as $N(\Theta)$. The set of vertices for $N(\Theta)$ is defined by

$$\{v(\theta)|v \in V, \theta \in \{0, \ldots, \Theta\}\}. \tag{15.5}$$

That is, for vertex v of the original network, vertex $v(\theta)$ is provided corresponding to each time $\theta \in \{0, \ldots, \Theta\}$ (see Fig. 15.2).

The edge set of $N(\Theta)$ consists of two parts. First, for each edge $e = (u, v) \in E$ and each time $\theta \in \{0, \ldots, \Theta - \tau(e)\}$, we have edge $e(\theta) = (u(\theta), v(\theta + \tau(e)))$ of capacity $c(e)$. Second, for each vertex $v \in V$ and time $\theta \in \{0, \ldots, \Theta - 1\}$, we add stagnant edges $(v(\theta), v(\theta + 1))$ of capacity $+\infty$ (the horizontal edges in Fig. 15.2). For each vertex $v \in V$, the supply of $v(0)$ is defined as $b(v)$. The supply of $v(\theta)$ for $\theta \in \{1, \ldots, \Theta\}$ is set to zero. Let the sink set of $N(\Theta)$ be $\{s(\theta)|s \in S^-, \theta \in \{0, \ldots, \Theta\}\}$.

15.2.3 Algorithm for Solving Quickest Evacuation Planning Problem

Ford and Fulkerson [1, 2] showed that for the evacuation completion time to be less than Θ in dynamic network $N(\Theta)$, the necessary and sufficient condition is that there exists a flow of size $\sum_{s \in S^+} b(s)$ from source set $\{s(0)|s \in S^+\}$ to the sink set. The existence of such a feasible flow can be examined by obtaining the maximum flow of $N(\Theta)$. To consider the sink capacity for evaluation sites, we add a super sink st

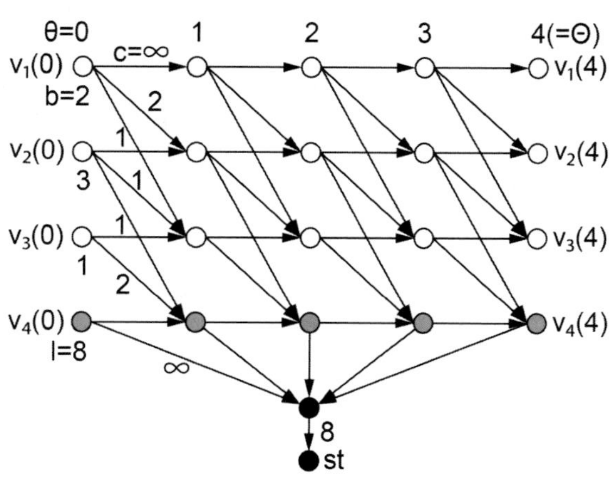

Fig. 15.2 Time-expanded network $N(4)$ of Fig. 15.1 with super sink st

and edges of capacity $l(s)$ from $s(\theta)$ to st for $s \in S^-$ and $\theta \in \Theta$. Then, the necessary and sufficient condition for the evacuation completion time to be less than or equal to Θ in dynamic network N is that the aforementioned feasible flow exists in the time-expanded network $N(\Theta)$.

In this way, it is possible to obtain the quickest flow of evacuation planning in pseudo-polynomial time using the time-expanded network, but as the size of the actual network increases, so does that of the time-expanded one. Moreover, Hoppe and Tardos [4, 5] proposed the quickest transport algorithm without using a time-expanded network. However, although it is a polynomial-time algorithm, it is necessary to minimize the sub-modular function iteratively, and currently this algorithm is inefficient for a large-scale network such as the one in the present study.

Generally, there is more than one quickest flow, of which the one for which the cumulative number of evacuees who have so far been evacuated is the largest at each time before the evacuation completion time Θ is called the universal quickest flow. This is obtained by first finding the evacuation completion time Θ and then finding the flow known as the lexicographic maximum flow [9] on the corresponding time-expanded network. When the sinks are subjected to the capacity constraint, the universal quickest flow does not always exist. However, when this constraint is imposed, the obtained flow is experimentally similar to the universal quickest flow [19].

15.3 Pedestrian Simulation Model

Because both the travel time and time interval of a dynamic network model are approximate, pedestrian simulations are carried out for the obtained route to improve the accuracy, and the travel time and congestion are confirmed. Because the present study deals with a large-scale road network, we use the one-dimensional pedestrian model with high computational efficiency developed by Yamashita et al. [20]. In this model, pedestrians walking in the same direction move in a row on an edge. This row is called a lane, and the number of lanes is determined according to the width of the sidewalk as determined in Sect. 15.4.1. As illustrated in Fig. 15.3, it is assumed that pedestrians move in their specified lane and do not overtake. A discrete-time simulation is performed to determine the speed of each pedestrian in a lane at the next time step from their current speed and the distance between each pedestrian and the one walking immediately in front.

In a lane as illustrated in Fig. 15.3, the leading pedestrian is defined as the one closest to the target node. Let $x_i(t)$ be the distance of the i-th pedestrian from the beginning of the edge from the starting vertex at time t. The velocity $\dot{x}_i(t + \delta t)$ of pedestrian i in the lane at time $t + \delta t$ is considered to depend on the current velocity of the pedestrian and the distance to the pedestrian walking immediately in front, and it is determined by

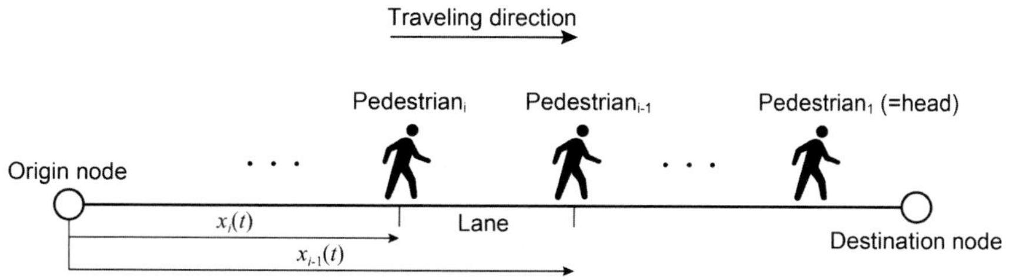

Fig. 15.3 Movement of pedestrians in a lane according to one-dimensional pedestrian model

$$\dot{x}_i(t + \delta t) = \dot{x}_i(t) + \left(a_1(v_0 - \dot{x}_i(t)) - a_2 \exp\left(\frac{r - (x_{i-1}(t) - x_i(t))}{a_3}\right)\right) \delta(t), \tag{15.6}$$

where v_0 is the free walking speed, r is the radius of the pedestrian, and a_1, a_2, and a_3 are parameters. According to a previous study [20], we set $v_0 = 1.023$ [m/s], $r = 0.522$ [m], $a_1 = 0.962$, $a_2 = 0.869$, and $a_3 = 0.214$.

15.4 Data Preparation

The geographic information system (GIS) datasets used in this study are listed in Table 15.1, and Fig. 15.4 shows the city of Osaka covered by this study, the 20-km zone within which people walk home, and the flooded area. In the following, we explain the data preparation.

15.4.1 Road Network

Based on the approach of the Cabinet Office of Japan for people struggling to return home [10], the road network was calculated from the roads in Osaka City except for the expressways, and the range of the buffer was 20 km. Consequently, a large-scale

Table 15.1 GIS datasets used for optimization and simulation

#	Data
1	Sub-regional boundary data [17]
2	Tsunami flooding estimation area [11]
3	Road network [18]
4	Tsunami evacuation buildings [15]
5	Daytime population data [13]

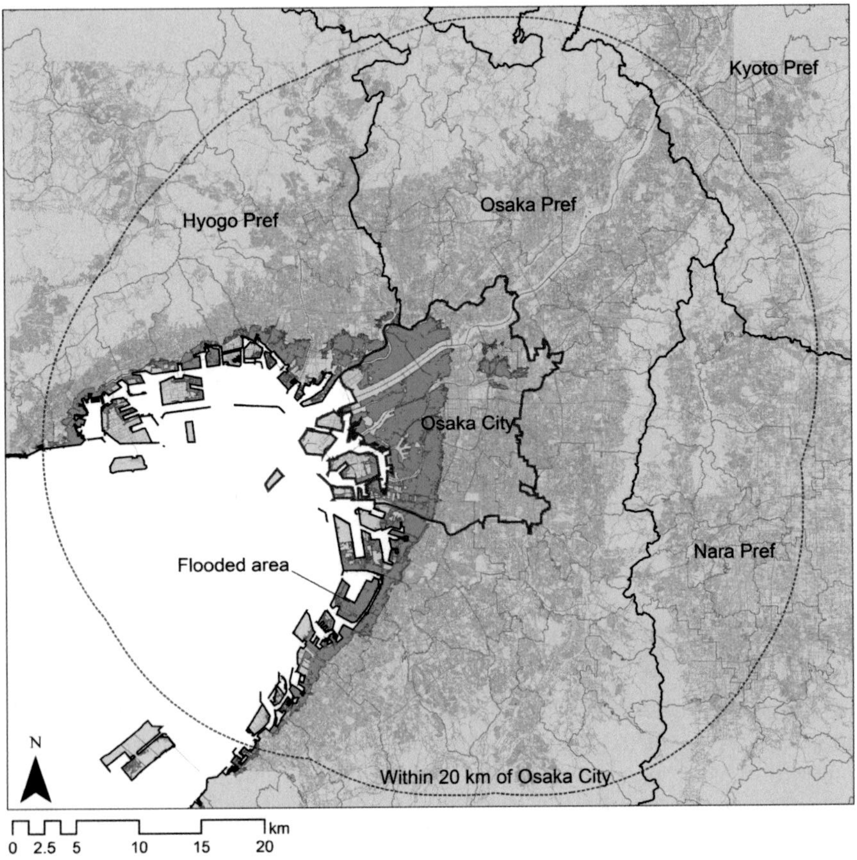

Fig. 15.4 Osaka City and its 20-km surrounding area

road network comprising 815 739 edges and 621 670 nodes was obtained. Simplification of this large-scale road network is described in the next section. In the case of an earthquake due to the Nankai Trough, a seismic intensity of a 6-lower is assumed in Osaka City. There is expected to be little major damage to roads and buildings at this seismic intensity, therefore in this study buildings and roads are assumed to be undamaged.

We assume that pedestrians move on sidewalks, but there are no sidewalk data for this road network. Therefore, referring to the regulations of the Ministry of Land, Infrastructure and Transport [12], we sampled the sidewalk width every 10 blocks using the distance-measuring function of Google Maps for each of six road types obtained from the road network data, and we unified the sidewalk width by each road type.

Next, a sidewalk along which only one person could pass at a time was made to be a lane, and the lane width was made to be uniformly 0.75 m. The number of lanes was set as an even value that did not exceed the determined width of the sidewalk divided by the width of a lane. This was done so that edges opposite to each other had the same number of lanes. For each road type, the maximum and minimum numbers of lanes obtained under these conditions were eight and two, respectively.

15.4.2 Tsunami Evacuation Buildings

As tsunami evacuation buildings, we used 649 buildings designated by Osaka City in 2016. These were inputted as GIS point data, and each point was connected to the nearest road edge by a straight line. The capacity of tsunami evacuees was set for each tsunami evacuation building. In total, 560 816 people could be accommodated in all the tsunami evacuation buildings. Figure 15.5 shows the tsunami evacuation

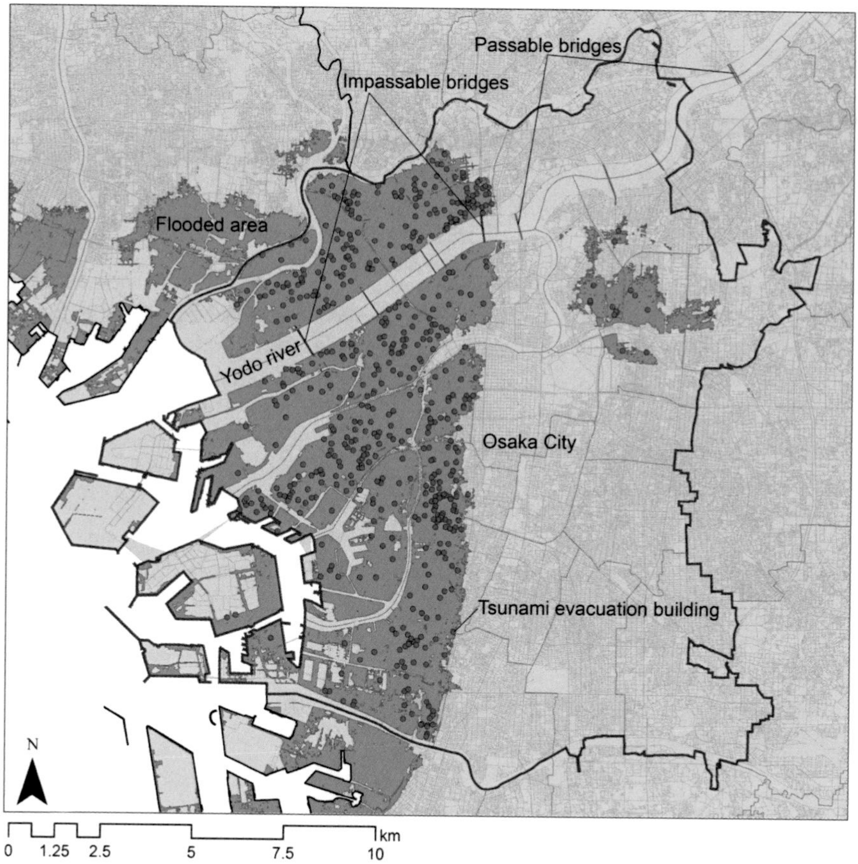

Fig. 15.5 Tsunami evacuation buildings and passable bridges

buildings that were used. As described in Sect. 15.6, when we optimize and simulate the routes including the bridges over the Yodo River, the bridges in the flooded area are set to be impassable.

15.4.3 Daytime Population

The daytime population was calculated from mobile spatial statistics generated from the travel histories of users of mobile phones. As shown in Fig. 15.6, we used 500-m mesh data of the population at 2 p.m. on a weekday in Osaka City in April 2015. There were 2 696 546 residents and commuters in Osaka City during this period, but note that mobile spatial statistics cover only the population between 15 and 79 years of age. We allocated the daytime population equally to nodes of the road network in each mesh, and this became the initial arrangement of evacuees and stranded people. Because the mobile spatial statistics also contain the population of each residential area, we chose the node of the home place for each pedestrian randomly according to this information.

15.4.4 Decisions on Number of People Struggling to Return Home and Number of Evacuees

The polygons of the tsunami-flooded area were superimposed on the road network, and the flooded nodes and edges were determined. For each visitor, the action of evacuate, walk home, or remain in place was chosen according to the flooded condition of the present node, the flooded condition of the home node, and the distance to the home node. Whether or not to return home on foot was determined by the method used by the Cabinet Office to estimate the number of people struggling to return home [10].

Let R denote the set of commuters struggling to return home. In this approach, the probability P_r of resident $r \in R$ deciding to return home on foot is determined by the following equation based on the distance d_r [km] from the current place to the returning place:

$$P_i = \begin{cases} 1 & (d_r < 10), \\ \frac{20-d_r}{10} & (10 \leq d_r < 20), \\ 0 & (20 \leq d_r). \end{cases} \tag{15.7}$$

In this study, the return distance of each visitor is the length of the shortest path from their present node to their home node obtained on the road network before simplification. In the case of resident r whose return distance is $10 \leq d_r < 20$, the action is decided probabilistically according to P_r with uniform distribution. The conditions for each action are summarized in Table 15.2.

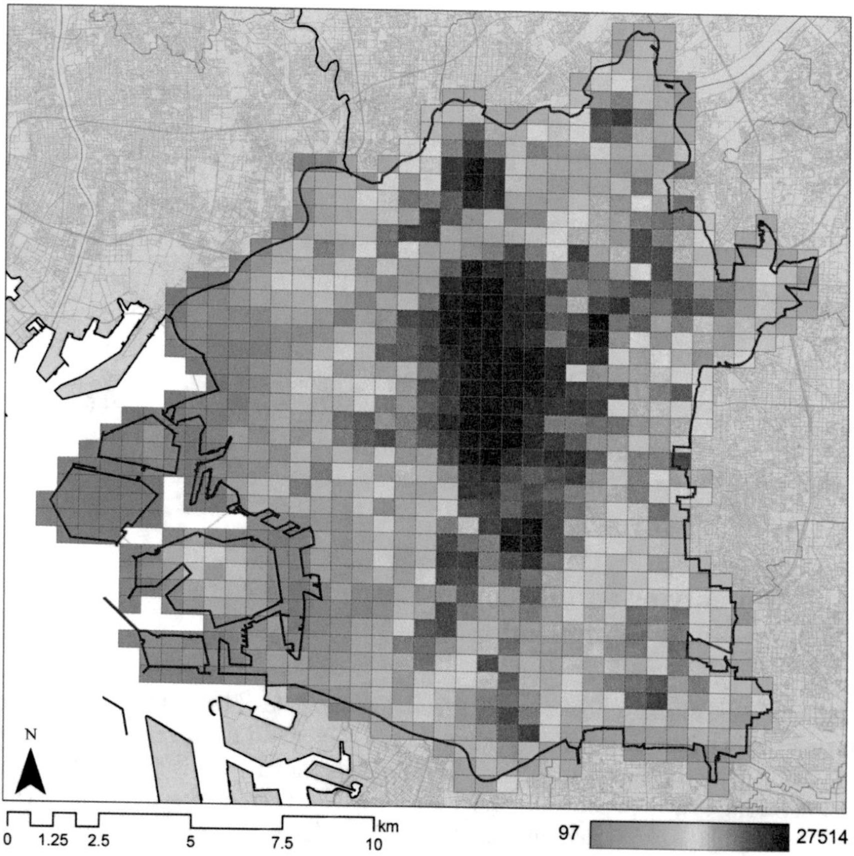

Fig. 15.6 Distribution of commuters in Osaka City at 2 p.m. on a weekday in April 2015

Table 15.2 Decision rules for each action

Action	Conditions		
	Current node	Home node	Return distance
Evacuate	Flooded area	Flooded area	
		Non-flooded area	$10 \leq d_r < 20$ (not returning home) or $20 \leq d_r$
Return home		Non-flooded area	$d_r < 10$ or $10 \leq d_r < 20$ (returning home)
Remain in place	Non-flooded area	Flooded area	
		Non-flooded area	$10 \leq d_r < 20$ (not returning home) or $20 \leq d_r$

Table 15.3 Breakdown of numbers of people involved in each activity

Action	Number of people
Evacuate	701 649
Return home	1 408 990
(via a bridge)	150 994
(others)	1 257 996
Remain in place	585 097
Total	2 696 546

Table 15.3 lists the breakdown of the number of people for each activity classified according to these rules. Of the people who return home on foot, approximately 150 000 cross bridges over the Yodo River, and they become the objects for route optimization. Everyone else returning on foot was deemed to take the shortest route.

15.5 Simplifying and Restoring Large Road Network for Route Optimization

Computing the quickest flow depends greatly on the scale of the network. Although the main part of the quickest-flow algorithm is computing the maximum flow, the effect of parallelization on this algorithm is limited. Therefore, it is difficult to apply this algorithm to a large network, even by using a recent central processing unit with many cores. In this study, we simplify the large-scale road network and optimize the routes for evacuation and returning home using the quickest flow. We also develop a method for restoring the optimized routes to the original road network. The proposed method is outlined below and illustrated in Fig. 15.7.

15.5.1 Simplification of Road Network

The basic idea is to construct a simplified road network by dividing the space by polygons of the sub-regions of the area and connecting their centers of gravity with straight lines between adjacent sub-regions. At this time, the sum of the numbers of lanes of the original edges crossing the line segments shared by two polygons is made to be the number of lanes of a simplified edge. If no original edges crossed between two sub-regions, then the two polygons are not connected by a simplified edge. The length of a simplified edge is the Euclidean distance between centers of gravity, and commuters assigned to nodes in a polygon are aggregated on its center of gravity.

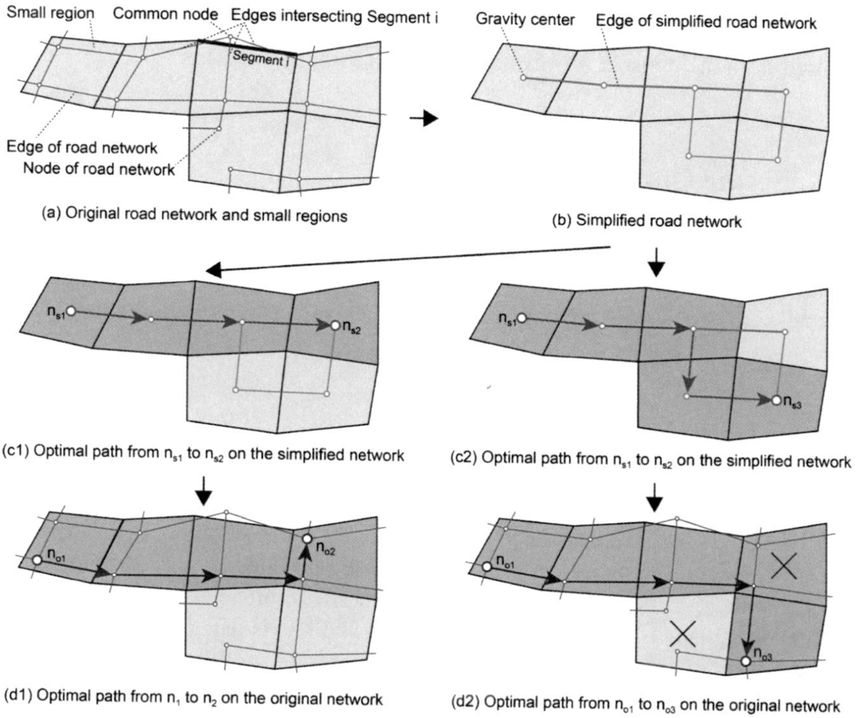

Fig. 15.7 Simplification and restoration of road network

The following procedures were carried out using GIS software to simplify the original road network: recognizing adjacent polygons, decomposing polygons into line segments, generating the centers of gravity of the sub-region polygons, extracting the road edge that crosses the line segment of each pair of adjacent polygons, and generating the simplified road network. Consequently, there were 36 276 edges and 15 853 vertices, these being approximately 4% and 3%, respectively, of those of the original road network.

15.5.2 *Restoring Optimized Routes on Original Road Network*

Let *A* be a set of sub-regions traversed by an origin–destination (OD) path in the set of optimized OD paths on a simplified road network. In this study, we refer to the OD path in the original road network being obtained as the shortest path in the road network in *A* as route restoration. However, with this method, the destination may not be reachable using only the road network in *A* (see Fig. 15.7d2). In that case, the route obtained by the optimization is not used and is replaced by the shortest path in the whole road network. Then, the extent to which the original OD path could be restored from the route in A is evaluated as the reproduction rate.

15.6 Route Optimization Settings

Thus, the routes for evacuation and returning home can be optimized. To prioritize human life, we first secure evacuation routes for tsunami evacuees and then optimize the routes for people walking home. The procedure and settings are described below.

15.6.1 Optimization Steps

First, we explain the concept of optimization for tsunami evacuees. As mentioned in Sect. 15.4, in Osaka City, there are many tsunami evacuation buildings in the expected flooded area, and the plan is to evacuate to those buildings. However, many areas may continue to be flooded for several days even after drainage is carried out, and it is feared that many tsunami evacuation buildings will be isolated by flooding.

In the event of a tsunami disaster in a large city, it is reasonable to suppose that not many evacuees will use the tsunami evacuation buildings, given the limited resources for rescuing evacuees from such buildings. Therefore, it is necessary to clarify which areas contain evacuees who can only evacuate to a tsunami evacuation building. In this study, we optimize the destinations and routes of evacuees in the following three steps.

Step 1
In the simplified road network, the destinations of evacuees are set not as the tsunami evacuation buildings but as the intersections of the boundaries of the flooded-area polygons and the intersecting edges. Then, they are connected to one super sink, the route is optimized by the universal quickest flow, and the evacuation completion time for each evacuee is calculated.

Step 2
For evacuees whose evacuation completion time determined in step 1 exceeds 1 h and 50 minutes, their evacuation routes are optimized again using the universal quickest flow to evacuate to tsunami evacuation buildings. At this time, the optimization is executed by using the residual network of the time-expanded network used in step 1 except for that of evacuees in step 2.

Step 3
The routes of approximately 150 000 commuters walking home across passable four bridges over the Yodo River shown in Fig. 15.5 are optimized using the universal quickest flow. We refer to such pedestrians as “bridge passers.” In this case, sinks are set to nodes on the north side of each bridge and are connected by one super sink. In

addition, the residual network used in the optimization up to step 2 is used. People in areas other than the flooded area return home via the shortest route, this being because there is less congestion than on the bridges, and the optimization problem in this case becomes a general multi-commodity flow problem, which is more difficult than the quickest-flow problem.

15.6.2 Computational Conditions

The time unit of the quickest flow was set to 10 s considering the computational time and available memory. The walking speed of a pedestrian was set to 1 m/s. Meanwhile, the free walking speed in the one-dimensional pedestrian model was set to 1.023 m/s, which is similar to that in the original model [20]. The optimization and simulation code was implemented using Visual C++ 2015, and LEDA 6.4 was also used as a network library to solve the maximum-flow problem. The optimization and simulation were carried out on a personal computer (PC) with Windows 10 Professional 64 bit, an Intel Core i7-6700k, and 32 GB of memory.

15.7 Results of Route Optimization

The optimization results are shown below, where the evacuation completion time is the result of each pedestrian walking along the designated route using the one-dimensional pedestrian model on the original road network.

15.7.1 Computational Times

The computational times for the route optimization for the two types of pedestrian are listed in Table 15.4. Even though the PC that was used was of an older specification dating back several generations, the computation took only a matter of days. In other words, the problem could be computed even with such a low-specification PC. Although there were fewer bridge passers, their optimization took longer, probably because their routes were longer.

Table 15.4 Computational time for each optimization

Pedestrian type	Computational time [h:min]
Evacuee	29:56
Bridge passer	44:46

15.7.2 Reproducibility of Restored Routes

We analyze the reproducibility of the routes optimized by the simplified network after they are restored to the original network. The reproducibility is evaluated by the difference in the length of a route before and after the restoration and the selectivity of the route described above. Table 15.5 lists the mean route lengths before and after network restoration for each type of pedestrian. In the case of evacuees, the mean route length increases after restoration, whereas it decreases for bridge passers. However, the restoration does not cause an extremely large difference in either case.

Table 15.6 lists the selection ratio, which is the percentage of each type of pedestrian using the routes obtained by the universal quickest flow after network restoration. Although the selection ratio for evacuees exceeded 80%, that for bridge passers was only 64%. Because the route became longer for the latter, this is thought to have increased the number of cases in which a route cannot be constructed within the limited range.

15.7.3 Optimization Results

Here, we assess by how much the optimization shortened the travel time compared with that of the shortest route.

First, regarding the movement by evacuation, Fig. 15.8 shows how the cumulative number of evacuees for each type of route varies with time, and Table 15.7 lists the mean evacuation time and evacuation completion time. Although the cumulative numbers of evacuees for both types of route vary similarly, the effect of the optimization is evident because it shortens the evacuation completion time by approximately 1 h compared with that of the shortest route. However, the evacuation completion time

Table 15.5 Mean route lengths for each type of pedestrian before and after network restoration

Pedestrian type	Mean length [m]	
	Before	After
Evacuee	1798	2013
Bridge passer	7712	7593

Table 15.6 Selection ratios for optimized routes

Pedestrian type	Total	Number of optimized-route selectors	Selection ratio
Evacuee	701 649	587 585	0.84
Bridge passer	150994	97 372	0.64

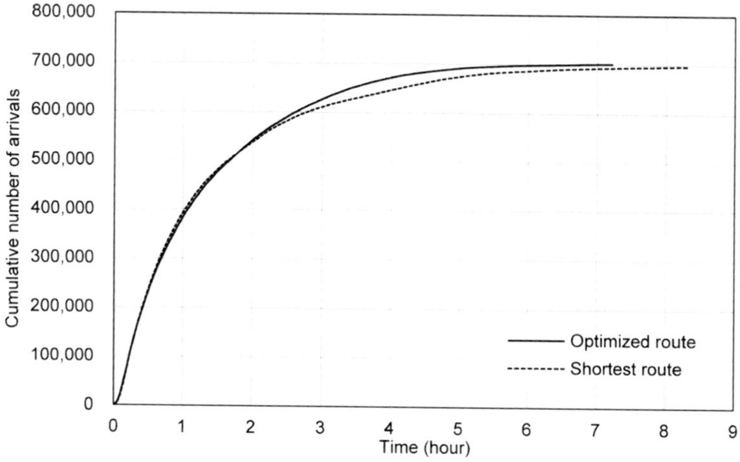

Fig. 15.8 Cumulative number of arriving evacuees for each route type

Table 15.7 Comparison of travel times of evacuees for both route types

Route type	Mean travel time [h:min]	Travel completion time [h:min]
Optimized route	1:18	7:13
Shortest route	1:22	8:18

is over 7 h, which is too long to avoid the impact of the tsunami. This is considered to be a result of interference between the routes of evacuees and people returning home. At the time of optimization, priority was given to evacuees, but this assumption may have collapsed upon restoring the routes. Regardless, it is suggested that evacuees should avoid evacuating outside the flooded area by using the tsunami evacuation buildings as much as possible.

Next, we perform a similar verification for bridge passers. Figure 15.9 shows how the cumulative number of arriving people varies with time, and Table 15.8 compares the mean travel times and travel completion times for both route types. In the case of the shortest route, pedestrian bridge congestion begins early, after which the slope of the straight line of the accumulated number of arriving people is relatively low. As a result, the completion time of returning home was drastically shortened by about 3 h and 20 min by the optimization with consideration of securing routes for tsunami evacuees.

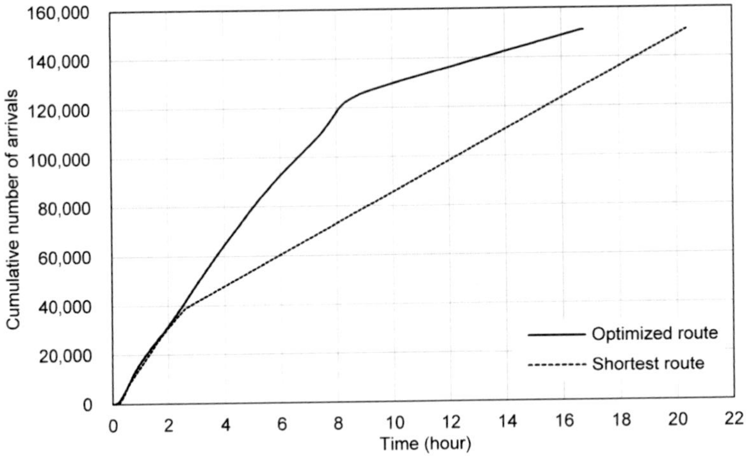

Fig. 15.9 Cumulative number of arriving bridge passers for each route type

Table 15.8 Comparison of travel times of bridge passers for both route types

Route type	Mean travel time [h:min]	Travel completion time [h:min]
Optimized route	5:32	16:47
Shortest route	8:52	20:23

The effect of the optimization was demonstrated, especially for bridge passers. To understand the changes concretely, the total numbers of pedestrians passing along each road for both route types are visualized in Fig. 15.10. In the case of the shortest route, people returning home are concentrated on the Nagara Bridge, but when the route is optimized, two bridges upstream from the Nagara Bridge are used.

People generally use the Shin-Yodogawa Bridge to travel to the north of the Yodo River from Osaka City, but in this case that bridge cannot be used because it is in the tsunami-flooded area. Therefore, with no restrictions, most people returning home would cross the Nagara Bridge, which is the next one upstream of the Shin-Yodogawa Bridge. Bridges further upstream than the Nagara Bridge are not usually used for transportation from Osaka City because they are located more than 3 km away. However, the optimization means that these bridges are also used for returning home, and congestion is reduced.

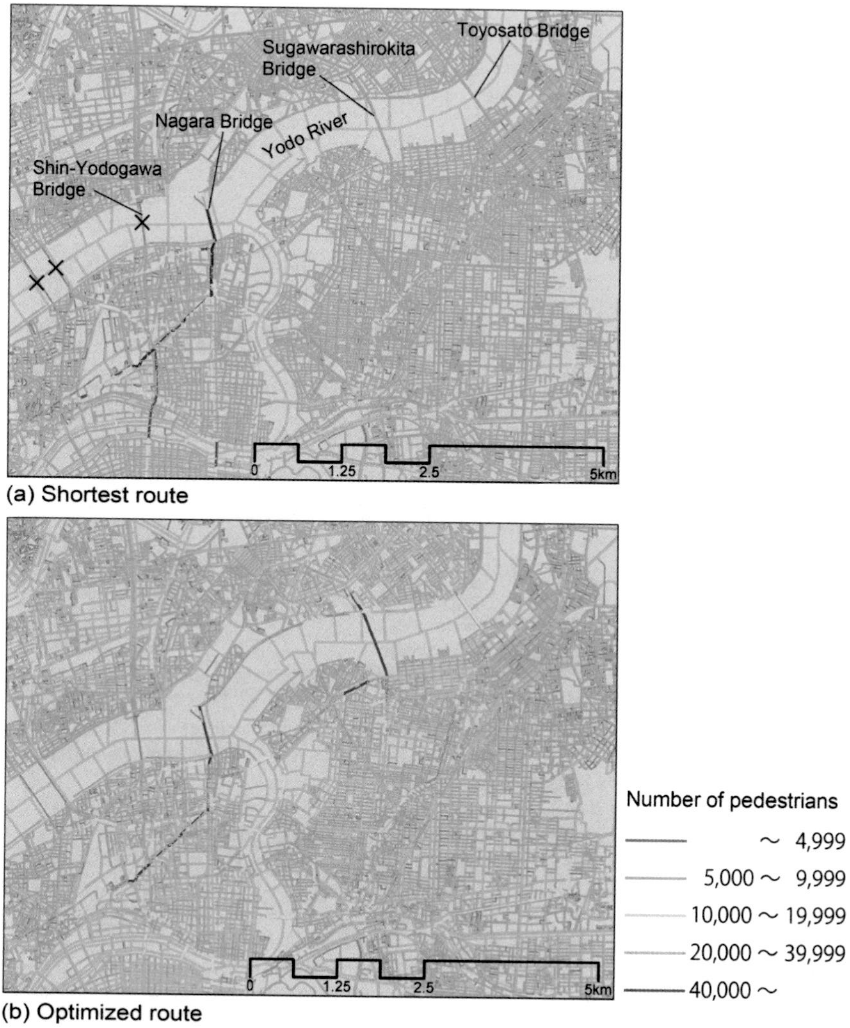

Fig. 15.10 Total number of pedestrians passing at each road edge for each route

15.8 Conclusion

In this study, we proposed a method for network simplification and restoration to optimize the traveling routes of more than 2 million pedestrians with a large-scale and detailed road network in Osaka City and its surrounding area. We then showed that such route optimization worked well.

References

1. L.R. Ford, D.R. Fulkerson, Constructing maximal dynamic flows from static flows. Oper. Res. **6**, 419–433 (1958). https://doi.org/10.1287/opre.6.3.419
2. L.R. Ford, D.R. Fulkerson, *Flows in Networks* (Princeton University Press, 1962)
3. U. Hiroi, T. Oomori, H. Shinkai, Evacuation simulation in metropolitan area and risk maps of heavy traffic and crowd in catastrophic disaster. J. Jpn. Assoc. Earthq. Eng. **16(5)**, 5_111–5_126 (2016). https://doi.org/10.5610/jaee.16.5_111
4. B. Hoppe, É. Tardos, Polynomial time algorithms for some evacuation problems, in *Proceedings of the 5th Annual ACM-SIAM Symposium on Discrete Algorithms (SODA'94)* (1994), pp. 433–441
5. B. Hoppe, É. Tardos, The quickest transshipment problem. Math. Oper. Res. **25**(1), 36–62 (2000). https://doi.org/10.1287/moor.25.1.36.15211
6. N. Kamiyama, A. Takizawa, N. Katoh, Y. Kawabata, Evaluation of capacities of refuges in urban areas by using dynamic network flows, in *The 8th International Symposium on Operations Research and Its Applications*. Lecture Notes in Operations Research, vol. 10 (2009), pp. 453–460
7. Y. Kawagishi, A. Takizawa, Simulation of simultaneous walking home from Osaka city in the case of a major earthquake. Annu. J. Urban Disaster Reduct. Res. **4**, 7–13 (2017). https://doi.org/10.24544/ocu.20181107-012
8. K. Kobayashi, R. Narisawa, Y. Yasui, K. Fujisawa, Experimental analyses of the evacuation planning model using lexicographically quickest flow. Trans. Oper. Res. Soc. Jpn. **59**, 86–105 (2016). https://doi.org/10.15807/torsj.59.86
9. E. Minieka, Maximal, lexicographic, and dynamic network flows. Oper. Res. **21**, 517–527 (1973)
10. Metropolitan Earthquake Countermeasures Council of Cabinet Office, Special Investigation Committee on Tokyo Metropolitan earthquake evacuation measures in Central Disaster Prevention Council (2008), http://www.bousai.go.jp/kaigirep/chuobou/senmon/shutohinan/. Accessed 27 Dec 2020
11. Ministry of Land, Infrastructure, Transport and Tourism of Japan, Tsunami flooding estimation data (2016), https://nlftp.mlit.go.jp/ksj/gml/datalist/KsjTmplt-A40.html. Accessed 27 Dec 2020
12. Ministry of Land, Infrastructure, Transport and Tourism of Japan, Road structure ordinance (1); outline of the road structure ordinance. Explanation of the provisions of the road construction ordinance, https://www.mlit.go.jp/road/sign/pdf/kouzourei_1.pdf. Accessed 27 Dec 2020
13. NTT docomo, Mobile spatial statistics (2015), https://mobaku.jp/. Accessed 27 Dec 2020
14. Osaka City, Announcement of the distribution of seismic intensity, tsunami height, flooded area, and estimated damage due to the Nankai Trough Megathrust earthquake by the Japanese Cabinet Office (2012), https://www.city.osaka.lg.jp/kikikanrishitsu/page/0000182198.html. Accessed 27 Dec 2020
15. Osaka City, List of tsunami and flood evacuation buildings (2016), https://www.city.osaka.lg.jp/kikikanrishitsu/page/0000138173.html. Accessed 27 Dec 2020
16. Osaka City, Measures for people with difficulty returning home in the event of a large-scale disaster (2020), https://www.city.osaka.lg.jp/kikikanrishitsu/page/0000073235.html. Accessed 27 Dec 2020
17. Statistics Bureau of Japan, Population census subregional boundary data (2010), https://www.e-stat.go.jp/gis/statmap-search?page=1&type=2&aggregateUnitForBoundary=A&toukeiCode=00200521&toukeiYear=2010&serveyId=A002005212010. Accessed 27 Dec 2020
18. Sumitomo Electric System Solutions Co., Ltd., Advanced national digital road map database (2015), https://www.seiss.co.jp/ms/gis/map_db.html#ex_map_db. Accessed 27 Dec 2020

19. A. Takizawa, M. Inoue, N. Katoh, An emergency evacuation planning model using the universally quickest flow. Rev. Socionetwork Strat. **6**(1), 15–28 (2012). https://doi.org/10.1007/s12626-012-0024-y
20. T. Yamashita, S. Soeda, M. Onishi, I. Yoda, I. Noda, Development and application of high-speed evacuation simulator with one-dimensional pedestrian model. J. Inf. Process. **53**(7), 1732–1744 (2012)

Open Access This chapter is licensed under the terms of the Creative Commons Attribution 4.0 International License (http://creativecommons.org/licenses/by/4.0/), which permits use, sharing, adaptation, distribution and reproduction in any medium or format, as long as you give appropriate credit to the original author(s) and the source, provide a link to the Creative Commons license and indicate if changes were made.

The images or other third party material in this chapter are included in the chapter's Creative Commons license, unless indicated otherwise in a credit line to the material. If material is not included in the chapter's Creative Commons license and your intended use is not permitted by statutory regulation or exceeds the permitted use, you will need to obtain permission directly from the copyright holder.

Chapter 16
Stream-Based Lossless Data Compression

Shinichi Yamagiwa

Abstract In this chapter, we introduce aspects of applying data-compression techniques. First, we study the background of recent communication data paths. The focus of this chapter is a fast lossless data-compression mechanism that handles data streams completely. A data stream comprises continuous data with no termination of the massive data generated by sources such as movies and sensors. In this chapter, we introduce LCA-SLT and LCA-DLT, which accept the data streams, as well as several implementations of these stream-based compression techniques. We also show optimization techniques for optimal implementation in hardware.

16.1 Introduction to Stream-Based Data Compression

Rapid communication data paths are demanded in computer systems to improve performance, and the fastest data paths have recently reached the order of tens of gigahertz as implemented by optical fiber. One solution to achieving rapid communication data paths is to have parallelized paths in multiple connections, but technological trials have offered no clear solutions because of electrical and physical limitations such as crosstalks and refractions. To overcome the problems associated with high-speed communication, this chapter focuses on data compression on the data path. There are two ways in which this can be implemented. One is software-based compression, which is typically implemented on the lower layer of the communication data path, such as the device-driver level of Ethernet [18]. The other way is hardware-based implementation, which must provide low latency and stream-based compression and decompression.

Well-known algorithms such as Huffman encoding [17] and Lempel-Ziv-Welch (LZW) compression [21, 22] perform data encoding by creating a symbol lookup table (LUT), in which frequent data patterns are replaced by compressed symbols

---

S. Yamagiwa (✉)
Faculty of Engineering, Information and Systems, University of Tsukuba, 1-1-1 Tennodai, Tsukuba, Ibaraki 305-8573, Japan
e-mail: yamagiwa@cs.tsukuba.ac.jp

JST, PRESTO, 4-1-8 Honcho, Kawaguchi, Saitama 332-0012, Japan

© The Author(s) 2022
N. Katoh et al. (eds.), *Sublinear Computation Paradigm*,
https://doi.org/10.1007/978-981-16-4095-7_16

in the table. However, hardware implementation presents the following difficulties: (1) the processing time is unpredictable because the data length is not deterministic, (2) maximal memory must be prepared because the lengths of the data patterns are not deterministic, and (3) blocking decompression is performed. Here, we focus on a stream-based lossless data-compression mechanism that overcomes these problems. The key technology is a histogram mechanism that caches the compressed data. The decompressor must manage the same table contents as the compressor side and reproduce the original data from the table. In this chapter, we introduce challenges to implementing stream-based lossless compression based on hardware. The ultimate goal is to implement compact and fast data-compression hardware without blocking the compression operations upon accepting continuous data streams. We begin by focusing on a technique with a static LUT, called LCA-SLT, and then we show one with a dynamic table, called LCA-DLT. We also describe performance optimizations for LCA-DLT.

16.2 Stream-Based Lossless Data Compression with Static Look-Up Table

16.2.1 Design of LCA-SLT

We begin by focusing on a compression algorithm called online LCA (Lowest Common Ancestor) [12], which converts a symbol pair to an unused symbol with the LUT of symbol pairs managed as shown in Fig. 16.1, which shows an example of compressing the sequence ABCDFFBC to the symbol Z. Online LCA addresses the problems caused by conventional dynamic LUT management and provides a fixed time complexity due to the two-symbol matching. During the decompression, online LCA invokes the opposite mappings by repeating conversions from one symbol to two according to the table starting from the deepest compression step.

Applying the concept of online LCA, we show here the mechanism of LCA-SLT (LCA Static Look-up Table) [20], which prepares statically allocated LUTs that are used for converting symbol pairs. The compressor encodes inputted symbols using the LUTs, and the decompressor does the opposite. The contents of the tables are stored statically and initially before the compression/decompression. The tables are prepared heuristically in the following steps: (1) a test set of the target data is examined by online LCA, (2) the LUTs are created from all the original symbol pairs and their matching symbols, (3) the entries in the LUTs are sorted in ascending order by frequency, and finally (4) the entries in the top ranks are registered as the table contents. These steps implement the best matching patterns in the original data set as determined by the frequency analysis.

As shown in Fig. 16.2, the compressor and decompressor perform online LCA using the tables created from a set of test data patterns. The modules are connected

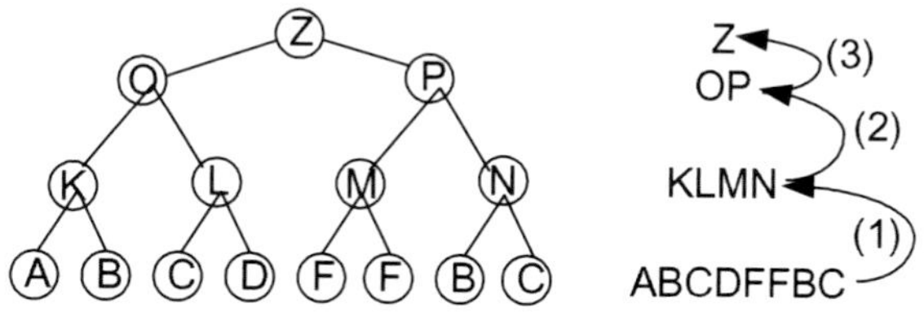

Fig. 16.1 LCA example. If the pairs AB and CD can be converted to K and L, respectively, then the original data become KL. If KL can also be converted to O, then the next pair becomes OP

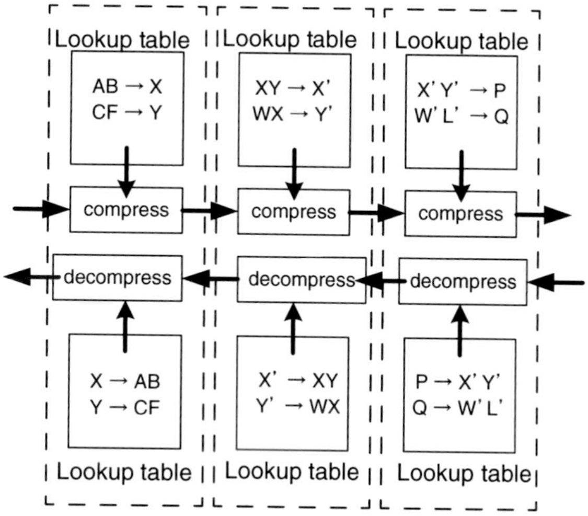

Fig. 16.2 LCA-SLT module comprising a compressor, LUT for compression, decompressor, and LUT for decompression

from the compressed and decompressed data lines one after another and organize a pipeline for recursive compression/decompression operations.

The method with static LUTs has two main advantages. First, the compressed data never include any additional information for table management. Second, the amount of table resources is deterministic. Therefore, LCA-SLT can be implemented on compact hardware and is fast because of its simple compression/decompression operations.

16.2.2 Implementation of LCA-SLT

On hardware, the compressor and decompressor can be implemented using a content-addressable memory (CAM) [8] and a normal memory (MEM), respectively. The CAM is a type of hardware into which a set of data bits is inputted and that outputs a matched address where the data are stored. Figure 16.3 shows the organization of the compression part. As an example, the combination of two symbols becomes 16 bits when the symbol width is 8 bits, and we add another bit per compressed data to mark whether it is compressed, called the *compression mark (CMark) bit*. Figure 16.3 shows a compression pipeline in which four modules are connected. Each module

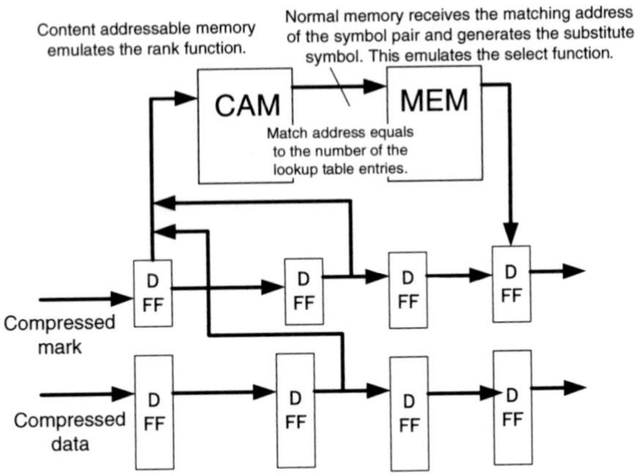

Fig. 16.3 Organization of compression part in LCA-SLT

adds another CMark bit, and the number of bits in the compressed data is extended by one bit per compressed data. Thus, the compression module at the end of the pipeline generates 12-bit compressed data. Decompression involves the same operations as the compression steps but in the opposite direction.

16.2.3 Performance Evaluations

We discuss here the performance of the LCA-SLT. We evaluate the compression ratio and the matching ratio to the symbol pairs in the LUT during the compression. The table is implemented with a fixed number of entries, namely, 32, 64, 128, or 256. For the evaluations, we use Linux source codes of 50 and 200 Mbyte, as well as a DNA sequence of 50 MB downloaded from [2]. Figure 16.4 shows the compression ratio (the data size after compression divided by the original size) and the matching ratio of the symbol pairs during the compression. With increasing number of table entries, the compression ratio improves and the matching ratio of the symbol pairs becomes about 60%.

Next, we show the implementation of the LCA-SLT module with 8-bit symbols and 4-bit CMark on a Xilinx Spartan-6 field-programmable gate array (FPGA; IC code XC6SLX453CSG324). We have two options for implementing the CAM: either shift register LUT (SRL)-based or block RAM (BRAM)-based CAM. We can implement the MEM by applying the BRAM on the FPGA. Table 16.1 shows the compilation reports. The operation timings of both the SRL-based and BRAM-based CAM are precisely the same. However, the number of used slice registers is larger than that of the LUTs in the case of BRAMs because the latches are not packed into the LUTs. The LUTs are used for the combinational logic for the I/O buses around the memory. Besides, the SRL-based case increases the number of LUTs. Therefore, when an application needs many LUTs, such as wide data/address buses

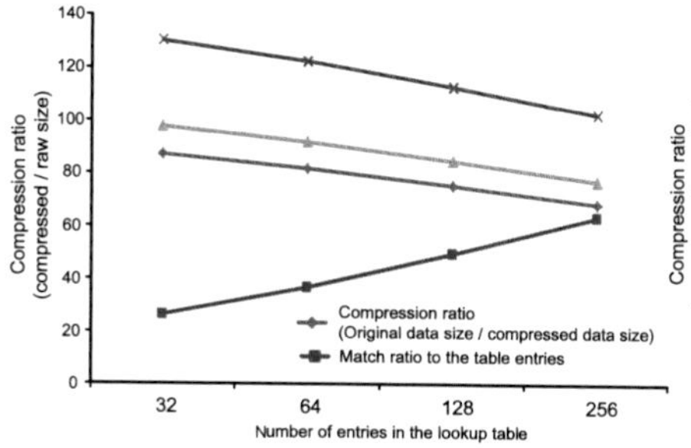

Compression ratio and the matching ratio of the entries in the table, applying the static table of source.50MB to source.50MB.

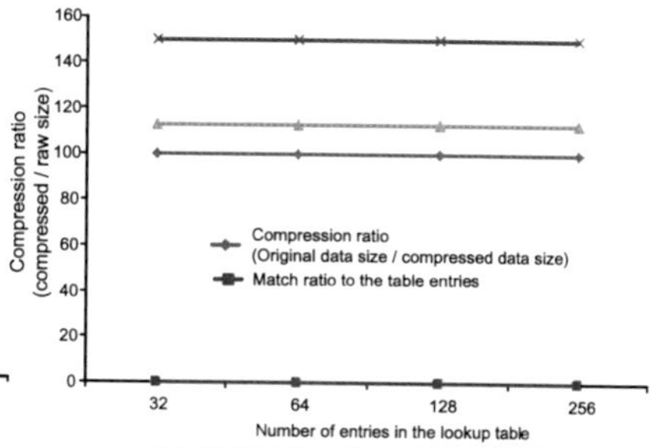

Compression ratio and the matching ratio of the entries in the table, applying the static table of source.50MB to dna.50MB

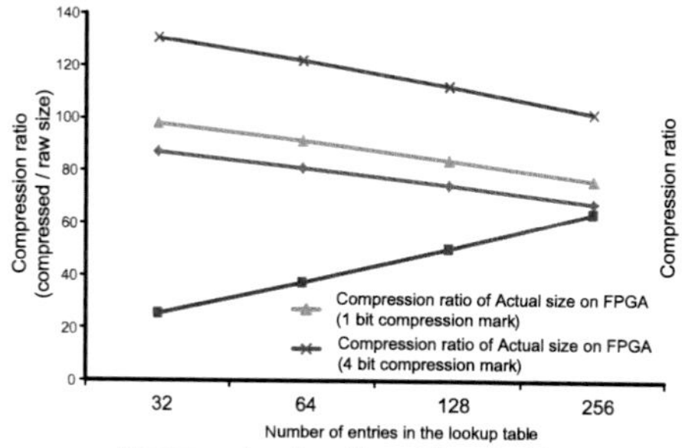

The compression ratio and the matching ratio of the entries in the table, applying the static table of source.50MB to source.200MB.

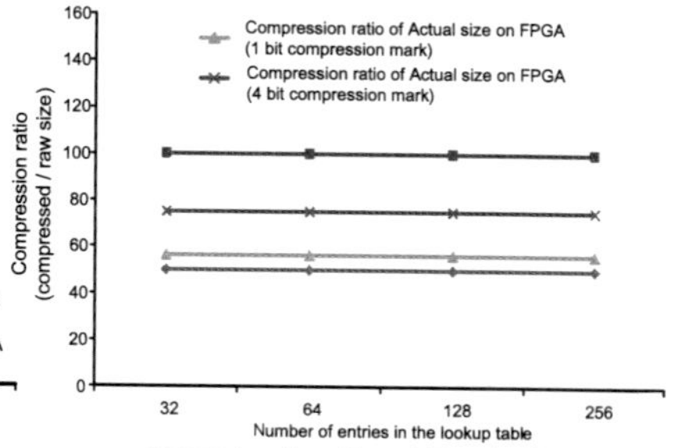

Compression ratio and the matching ratio of the entries in the table, applying the static table of dna.50MB to dna.50MB

Fig. 16.4 Performances of LCA-SLT

for a processor interface, it is effective to implement LCA-SLT. On the other hand, the SRL-based implementation shows that the maximal frequency for the input clock will decrease drastically with increasing number of LUT entries. In the FPGA case, we must consider how the number of table entries affects the performance because the limited number of physical wires in the large-scale integration decreases the routing availability when the matching address bits due to the CAM become wide.

Thus, the LCA-SLT implements a compression mechanism with small overhead for data streams. It is reconfigurable depending on the characteristics of the target data, addressing the desired performance depending on the number of compression/decompression modules or the number of bits in a symbol or the available symbol mapping entries in the LUT.

Table 16.1 Compilation reports regarding hardware implementations of LCA-SLT

128 entries	# of slice registers	# of slice LUTs	# of BRAMs	Max freq.
Using SRL-based CAM	141	2224	1	93 MHz
Using BRAM-based CAM	380	738	21	93 MHz
256 entries	# of slice registers	# of slice LUTs	# of BRAMs	Max freq.
Using SRL-based CAM	144	4135	1	75 MHz
Using BRAM-based CAM	638	1546	41	101 MHz
512 entries	# of slice registers	# of slice LUTs	# of BRAMs	Max freq.
Using SRL-based CAM	152	8128	1	51 MHz
Using BRAM-based CAM	1152	2567	81	81 MHz

16.3 Stream-Based Lossless Data Compression with Dynamic Look-Up Table

16.3.1 Design of LCA-DLT

Next, we focus on another algorithm for stream-based data compression with dynamic table management, called LCA-DLT (LCA Dynamic Look-up Table) [19]. It allocates corresponding symbol LUTs for the compressor and the decompressor, respectively. Each table has any number N of entries and the i-th entry E_i includes a pair of the original symbols $(s0_i, s1_i)$, a compressed symbol S_i, and a frequent counter $count_i$. The compressor side uses the following rules: (1) reading two symbols $(s0, s1)$ from the input data stream and if they match to $s0_i$ and $s1_i$ in a table entry E_i, then after incrementing the $count_i$, it outputs S_i as the compressed data; (2) if the symbols do not match to any entry in the table, it outputs $(s0, s1)$ and register an entry $(s0_k, s1_k, S_k, count_k = 1)$ where S_k is the index number of the entry; (3) if all entries in the table are used, then decrement all $count_i$ $(0 \leq i < N)$ until any count(s) become zero, and then delete the corresponding entries from the table. When compressed data S are transmitted from the compressor, the steps in the decompressor are equivalent to those in the compressor. The symbol matching is performed based on S_k in an entry. If the compressed symbol S_i matches to S_k in a table entry, then $(s0_k, s1_k)$ is outputted. If not, then another symbol S' from the compressed data stream and the pair (S, S') is outputted and then the pair is registered in the table.

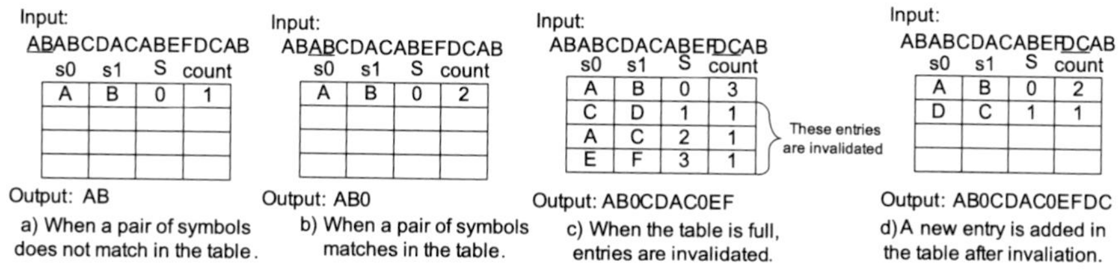

Fig. 16.5 Compression example for the LCA-DLT

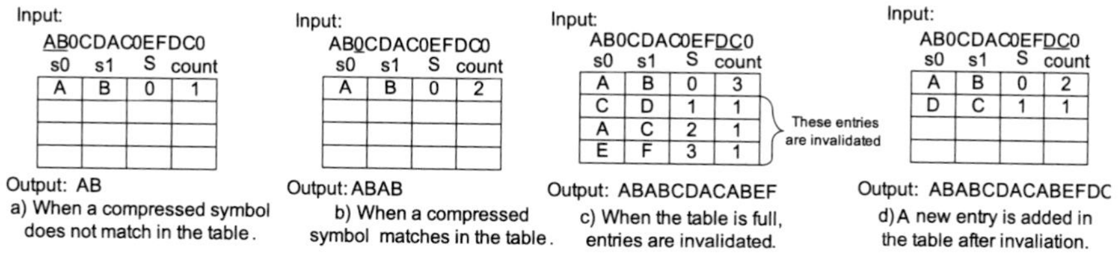

Fig. 16.6 Decompression example for the LCA-DLT

When the table entry is full, the same operations as those of the compressor are performed.

Figures 16.5 and 16.6 show examples of compression and decompression operations, respectively. Here, the input data stream for the compressor is ABABCDACABEFDCAB. First, the compressor reads the first two symbols AB and tries to match that pair in the table (Fig. 16.5a). However, the matching fails, and the compressor registers A and B as the $s0$ and $s1$ in the table. Here, the compressed symbol is assigned in the entry, which is the index 0 of the table. Thus, a rule AB→0 is performed. The *count* is initially set to 1. When the compressor continuously reads a pair of symbols (again AB) and it matches in the table, Fig. 16.5b translates AB to 0. Subsequently the equivalent operations are performed. If the table becomes full (Fig. 16.5c), then the compressor decrements the *count*(s) of all entries until any *count*s become zero. Here, three entries are invalidated from the table in the figure. The compressor will register a new entry to the invalidated entry from the smallest index of the table. Figure 16.5d shows that the compressor added a new entry after the invalidation. Finally, the original input data are compressed to AB0CDAC0EFDC0.

The decompressor reads A first (Fig. 16.6a), but it does not match any compressed symbol in the table (because the table is empty). The decompressor then reads another symbol B and registers AB to a new table entry. The entry saves a rule AB→0. Thus, the output becomes AB. The decompressor reads the next symbol 0 (Fig. 16.6b), which matches to the table entry. The decompressor translates it to AB and outputs it again. After the subsequent decompression operations, when the table becomes full, the decompressor decrements the *count*(s) as well as on the compressor side (Fig. 16.6c). The invalidated entries must be equivalent to those on the compressor side. Therefore, the compressed symbols are consistently associated with the original symbols. Finally, the compressed data inputted to the decompressor are associated and outputted as ABABCDACABEFDCAB, which is the same pattern as the input data on the compressor side.

16.3.2 Implementation of LCA-DLT

Figure 16.7 shows an implementation of the LCA-DLT. The input data are propagated through the latches, and the compressed/decompressed data are processed in a pipeline manner. The LUT in the compressor is organized as shown in Fig. 16.8a. The symbol LUT performs the compressed/decompressed data association. Here, the index becomes the compressed symbol, and the enable signal from the matching part increments the *count*. The full management logic of the LUT activates the invalidate control: it decrements the *count* and resets the valid bits (v in the figure) regarding the invalidated entry. The LUT in the decompressor is organized with a RAM and a CAM as shown in Fig. 16.8b. The management part of *count* also performs equivalently to that of the compressor based on a CAM. Besides, the matching part is implemented simply in a RAM. The compressed data generated from the address are inputted to the RAM, and the original uncompressed data pair is associated.

The invalidate operation looks for the minimal *count*s in the table entries by decrementing those counts. During the operation, the stall signal is outputted to stop the compression/decompression data pipeline. Figure 16.9a shows an implementation based on parallel decrement logic, and Fig. 16.9b shows one based on serial decrement logic. These two implementations have a tradeoff between the amount of logics and the compression speed when the table becomes full.

In the LCA-DLT as in the LCA-SLT, the compressor adds the CMark bit that indicates whether or not the symbol is compressed. Moreover, by combining the compressor and decompressor in a module and cascading the modules as shown in Fig. 16.10, we can compress long symbol patterns corresponding to 2, 4, 8, or 16

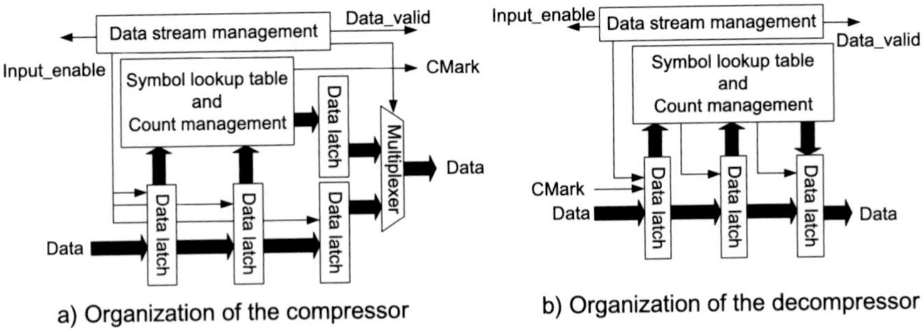

Fig. 16.7 Overall functional block diagrams of the compressor and decompressor in LCA-DLT. The compressor's LUT receives two input symbols from the latches and outputs the selected signal to the multiplexer for the output data. The decompressor's LUT performs the opposite data translation

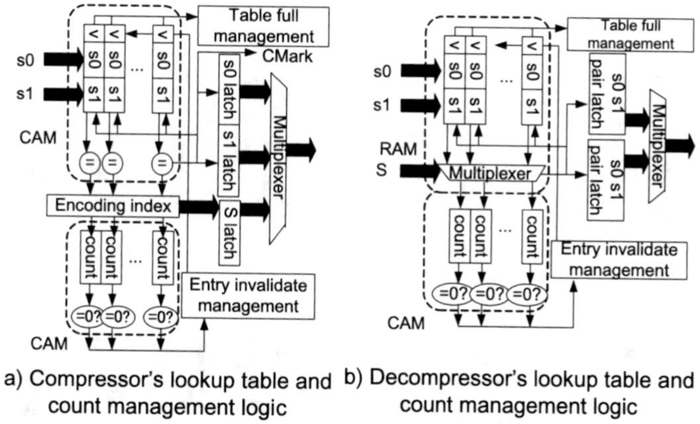

Fig. 16.8 Detailed organization of LUTs in LCA-DLT. The table has 2n entries when a symbol is n bits. The matching part for s0 and s1 must be organized as a content-addressable memory (CAM), which outputs the index (i.e., the address in the CAM) matched to an inputted pair of (s0, s1). The management part for count is also organized by a CAM

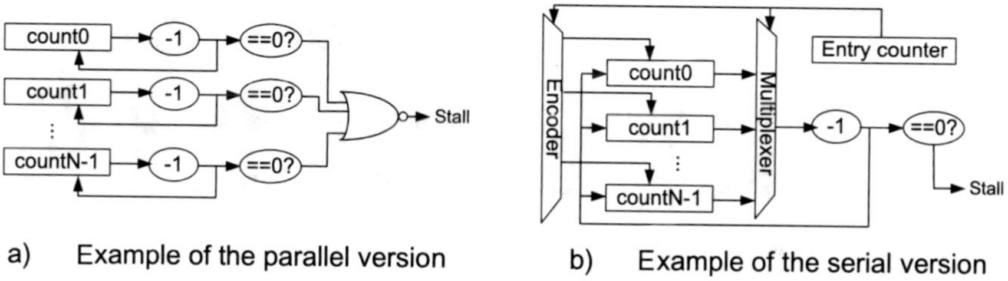

Fig. 16.9 Decrementing logic for entry invalidation in LCA-DLT

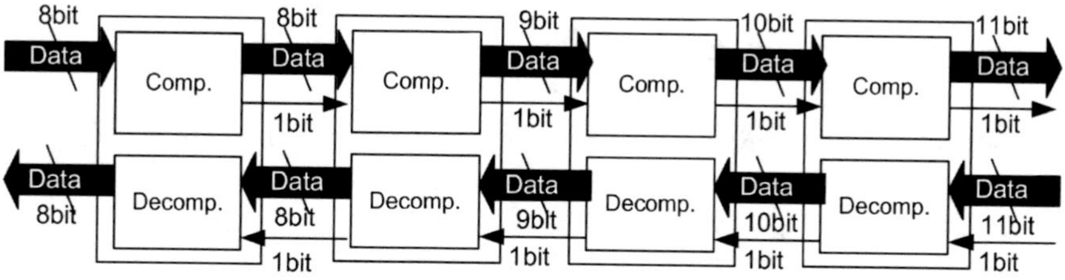

Fig. 16.10 Cascading modules of LCA-DLT. This example compresses long symbol patterns corresponding to 2, 4, 8, and 16 symbols. If the input data at the first compressor are 8 bits long, then the output compressed data become 12 bits because of the CMark bits

symbols when there are four modules. If the input data at the first compressor are 8 bits long, then the output compressed data become 12 bits after four modules because of the CMark bits.

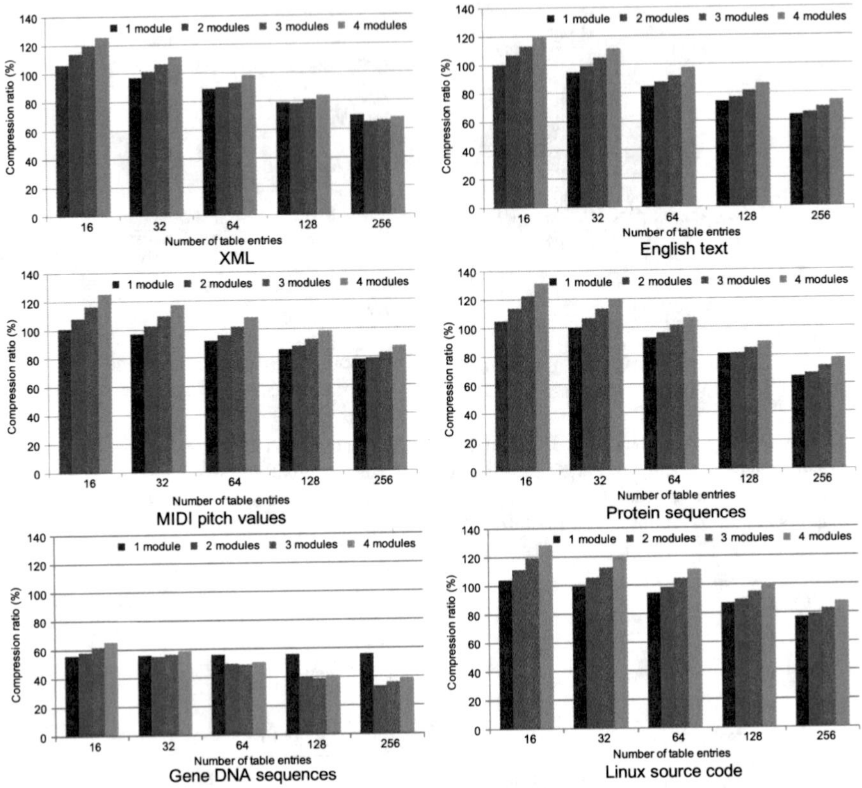

Fig. 16.11 Compression perfomances of LCA-DLT

16.3.3 Performance Evaluations

Figure 16.11 shows the compression ratios $((compressed\_data\_size \div original\_data\_size) \times 100)$. The numbers of table entries are varied from 16 to 256. Focusing on the performance impact of the number of table entries, the compression ratios are improved linearly except for the gene DNA sequence; because the DNA data have a few patterns, all patterns can be saved in 16 entries. Furthermore, focusing on the impact of the number of modules, the compression ratios degrade in the case of more than two modules. This means that a communication data path using too many compression modules becomes disadvantageous because of the CMark bit added after each module.

Figures 16.12 and 16.13 show the hardware performances of the LCA-DLT. It was implemented with only hundreds of slices and a memory block in the FPGA. The LCA-DLT works at 100 MHz with any number of modules, thereby achieving 800 Mbit/s. The LCA-DLT has large impact on resource usage with respect to the logic but not the memory because the recent FPGA does not have any dedicated hardware

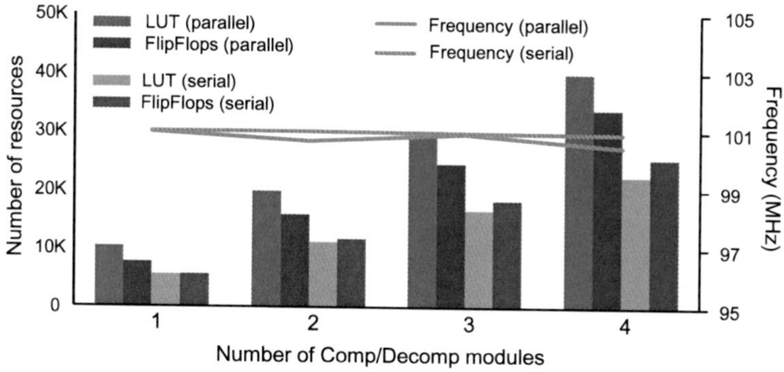

Fig. 16.12 Hardware resources of LCA-DLT. It is compiled with 8-bit data input in the first compressor for the Xilinx Artix7 device (XC7A200T-1FBG676C)

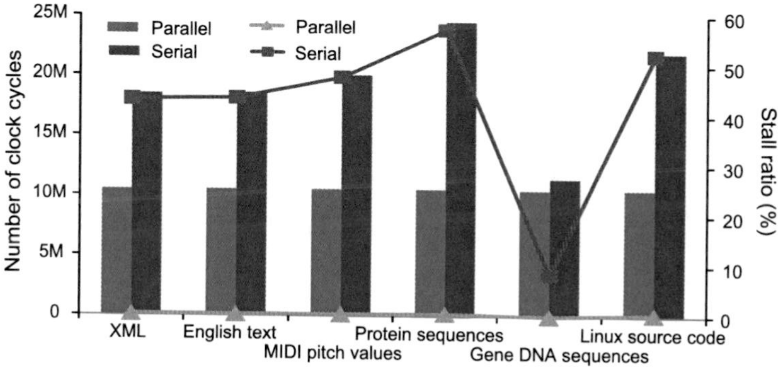

Fig. 16.13 Performance comparison between parallel and serial invalidation mechanisms with two modules

macros for CAMs. It is inevitably implemented by LUT and registers in the FPGA. We also compare the amount of hardware resources among the mechanisms of the parallel and the serial invalidations. The parallel version uses larger hardware resources; regarding the dynamic performance of the LCA-DLT, the parallel version involves very few stalls, but its hardware resources explode. Assuming that the hardware works at 100 MHz, the effective bandwidth in the input of the first compressor is about 800 and 340–730 Mbit/s with the parallel and serial invalidations, respectively. The output bandwidth of the second compressor will be reduced to 35–80% of the original data size. This means that the LCA-DLT realizes a communication data path that can send more data even if the speed of the path is slow, and it also contributes largely to realizing a high-speed communication data path while providing flexible adjustment between the hardware resources and the compression performance.

16.4 Optimization Techniques for LCA-DLT

Here we introduce optimization techniques for implementing the LCA-DLT. We consider two available optimization techniques: lazy management and time-sharing multi-threading.

16.4.1 Lazy Management of Look-Up Tables

First, we consider the techniques of dynamic invalidation on LUTs and lazy compression [11] that eliminate stalls during the LUT invalidations.

16.4.1.1 Dynamic Invalidation for Look-Up Table

With the management technique of dynamic invalidation for the symbol LUT, we prepare a *remove pointer* and an *insertion pointer*. Initially, the remove pointer points to any entry of the symbol LUT. The $count_i$ is decremented when the pointer comes to the table index i, and if the $count_i$ becomes zero after the decrement, then the entry is removed from the table. The pointer is moved to the next table index after any table search operation. By contrast, the insertion pointer initially points also to any empty entry in the symbol LUT; if the entry is used, then the pointer moves to an unused entry. Using these two pointers, we can expect that a moderate number of the entries occupied in the symbol LUT can be removed.

Figure 16.14 shows an example of the dynamic invalidation mechanism for compression. We assume that DCAADCBBDB is inputted to the compressor and that the remove pointer starts on the second entry of the table. First, DC does not match any entry in the table (Fig. 16.14a), and the compressor waits for an empty entry to appear. The remove pointer is moved to the next entry and the count value is decremented. In Fig. 16.14b, the count value of the third entry becomes zero, whereupon the entry is removed. The insertion pointer is moved to point to the empty entry. The new entry for DC is registered to where the insertion pointer is pointing. Now, DC is outputted. During these operations, the input and output of the compressor stall. When the input symbol pair matches an entry, it is compressed as shown in Fig. 16.14c, d, the remove pointer is moved, and the count value is decremented. If the entry that matches the input symbol pair corresponds to the one pointed out by the remove pointer, then the count value does not change, as shown in Fig. 16.14e. Finally, after the initially inserted DC is removed because of the count value, the entry is used as a new one. Because it was not found in the table, DB is outputted. Thus, the compressed data stream becomes DC012DB.

Figure 16.15 shows the steps of the decompression mechanism using the dynamic invalidation. The inputted compressed data stream is the one generated by the compression in Fig. 16.14. The insertion and the remove pointers begin from the same

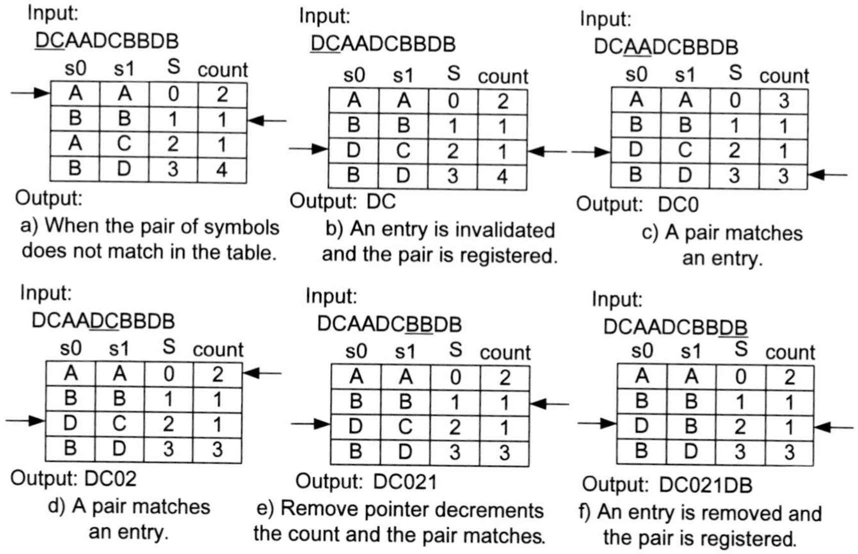

Fig. 16.14 Example of the dynamic invalidation mechanism for compression

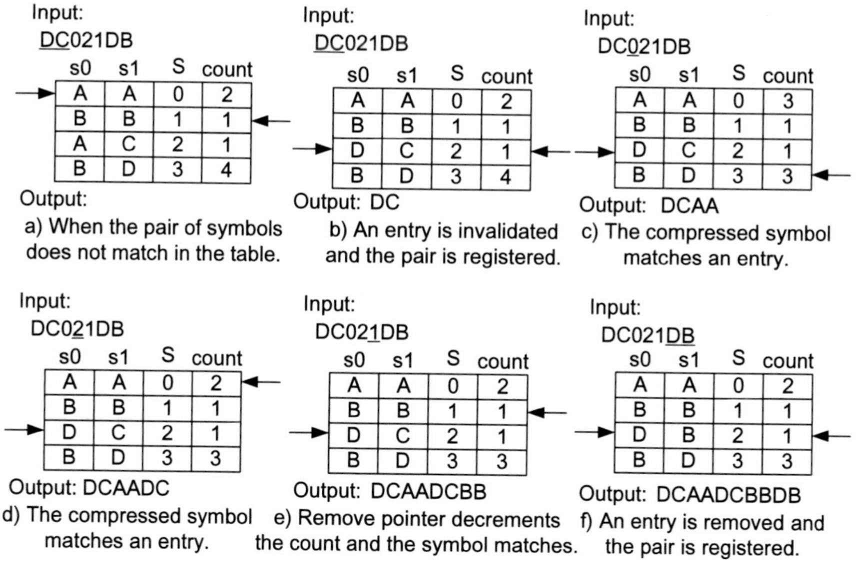

Fig. 16.15 Example of the dynamic invalidation mechanism for decompression

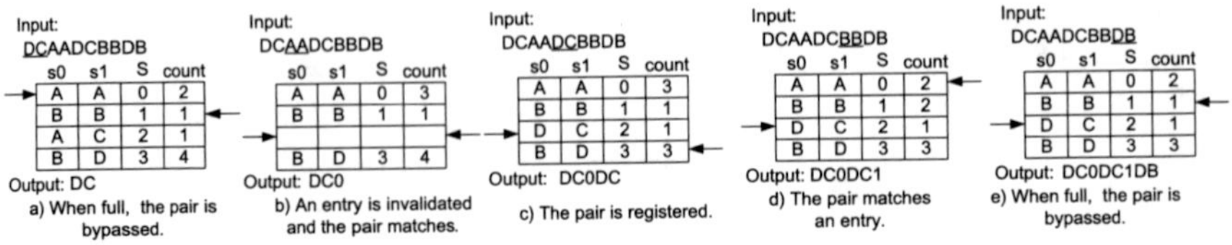

Fig. 16.16 Example of the lazy compression on compressor side

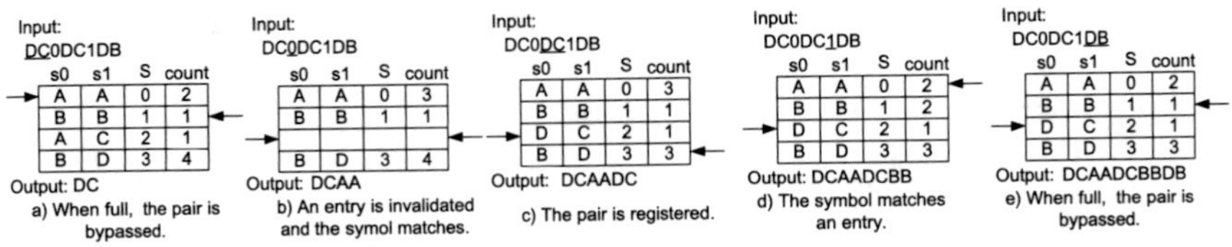

Fig. 16.17 Example of the lazy compression on decompressor side

entries initially defined by the compressor. Although the matching target is the compressed data, the steps are equivalent to the ones performed on the compressor side. In Fig. 16.15a, b, the I/O of the decompressor stall. When matching the compressed symbol in an entry, the decompressor outputs the corresponding symbol pair such as in Fig. 16.15c, d. Again, a stall occurs during the invalidation of an entry as shown in Fig. 16.15e, f. Finally, the original data stream is decoded.

16.4.1.2 Lazy Compression

Another optimization technique is the lazy compression. This technique ignores compression using the symbol lookup table when the symbol lookup table is full. This eliminates stalls and continuously outputs the data to the decompressor side.

Figure 16.16 shows a compression example of lazy compression applied to the LCA-DLT with dynamic invalidation. First, DC does not match any entry in the table. Here, the lazy compression just passes through the symbol pair without registering the pair into the table. Therefore, no stall occurs as in Fig. 16.16a, e. When the symbol pair matches an entry, the pair is compressed to the corresponding symbol as shown in Fig. 16.16b, d. If the table contains empty entry(ies) when the inputted symbol pair does not match any entry, then it is registered to the empty entry and is also passed through to the output as in Fig. 16.16c. The output from the compressor becomes DC0DC1DB, which is larger than DC021DB for the case of eager compression.

Figure 16.17 shows the case for the decompressor. First, D is not included in the table, therefore the input is the original data pair because actually the CMark bit is added to the compressed data. The compressor does not register the pair and passes through DC to the output as shown in Fig. 16.17a, e without any stall. If the compressed data are in the table, then the decompressor translates the original symbol

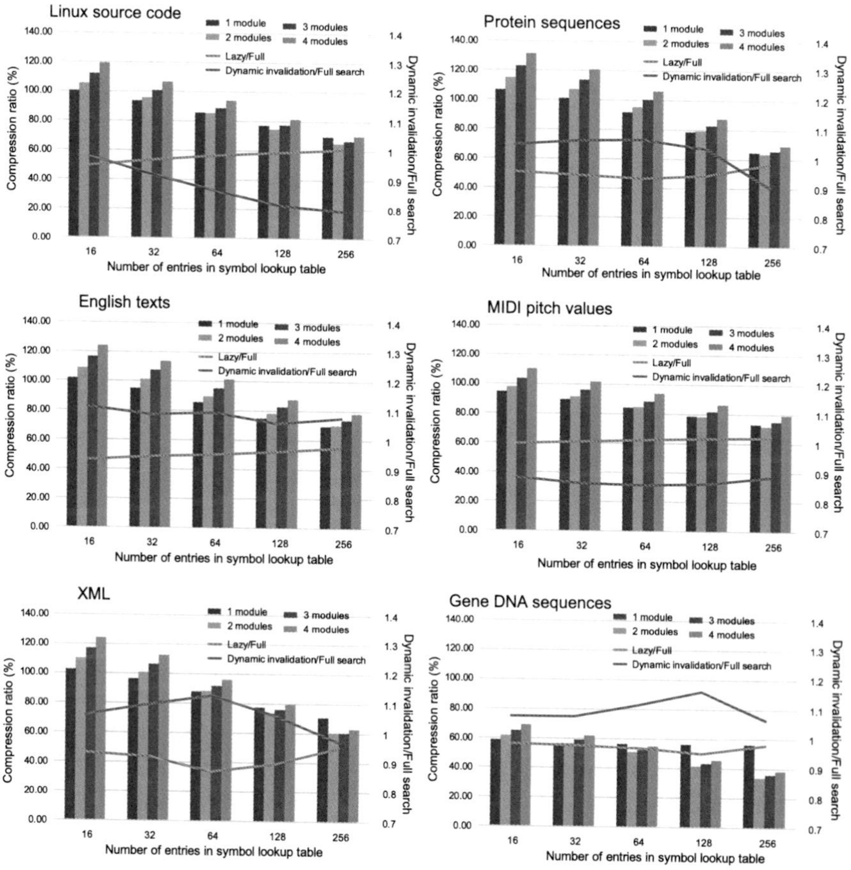

Fig. 16.18 Compression ratios with optimizations. The orange lines show lazy compression against the full search method, and the blue ones show dynamic invalidation against the full search method. The results depicted as lines were from using a compressor with four modules

pair such as in Fig. 16.17b, d. If the symbol is not in the table and there are empty entry(ies), then the inputted symbol pair is registered.

16.4.1.3 Performance Evaluations

Figure 16.18 shows the compression ratios with the above optimizations in the LCA-DLT. The bars show the ratios (i.e., the compressed data size divided by the original data size). We can confirm that the lazy compression effectively eliminates stalls and does not disturb the compression, although it does not compress the inputted data when the data pair does not match entries of the symbol LUT. Overall, both of the proposed mechanisms provide more-effective compression ratios than does the full

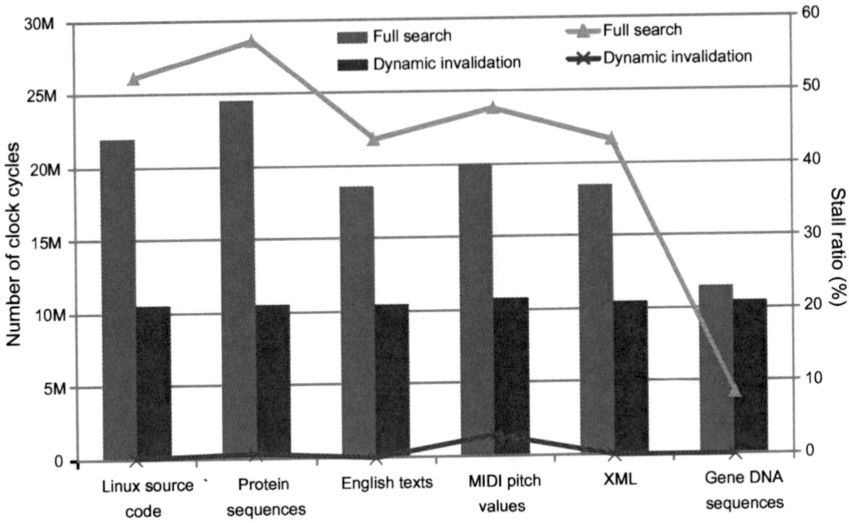

Fig. 16.19 Stall cycles and the stall ratios against the total clock cycles in LCA-DLT with optimizations

search method. These mechanisms work well if the randomness of the data is high (i.e., the data entropy is high).

We measured the stall clock cycles to compare the dynamic performance of hardware implementation with that of the proposed techniques. We used a Xilinx Artix-7 FPGA XC7A200T-1FBG676C. The full search method works at 100 MHz in this device as described in the previous section. By contrast, the implementation with both proposed mechanisms works at 130 MHz because the implementation was simplified by the lazy management of the symbol LUT.

Figure 16.19 shows the stall cycles as the bars and the stall ratios against the total clock cycles as the lines. The total throughput of the data stream becomes much better than that with the full search method. The degradation of the throughput is 30% with the full search but less than 3% with dynamic invalidation. Regarding lazy compression, the compression delay is the number of clock cycles for the input data stream and is also the number of bytes of the input data (i.e., 10M cycles) because lazy compression never causes stalls.

16.4.2 Time-Sharing Multithreading on Compression

16.4.2.1 Design and Implementation of Time-Sharing Multithreading

The time-sharing multi-threading [10] allows the compressor and decompressor to accept multiple different data streams by dividing the dictionary updating operations

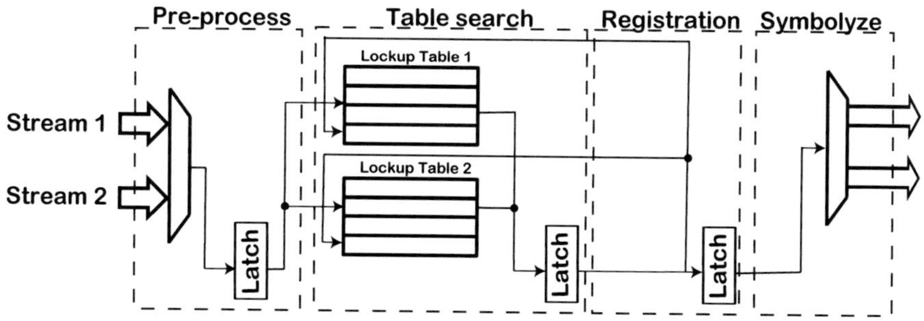

Fig. 16.20 Example structure of time-sharing multi-threading (TSM)

among the various input streams. When N data streams are inputted to the compressor/decompressor, the dictionary updating for each data stream allows NâĹš1 clock cycles to be inserted to solve the updating problem. For example, Fig. 16.20, shows a structure with two compressors that share the pipeline stages for the dictionary updating operations while accepting two different data streams. This mechanism does not cause any stalls during the input data streams, therefore the bandwidth of a data stream of a whole compressor/decompressor module degrades to 1/N. However, the clock frequency is expected to increase.

In implementing the compression mechanism, the following operations are assigned to stages of the encoder pipeline for the compressor hardware. The pre-process operation is performed to prepare the subsequent table matching operation, after which the table search operation is performed. The symbol registration operation to the LUT performs registration of symbols, and finally the symbolizing/lookup operations are performed against the LUT. For decompression, the operations are performed in the opposite way to symbolize the compressed data to an original data pair.

Next we discuss an implementation example of time-sharing multi-threading in the LCA-DLT. Assume that there are two input data streams for the compressor/decompressor, and the pipeline of the compressor is organized as shown in Fig. 16.20. The compression in both data streams takes eight cycles to process a data pair, as does the decompression. The compression pipeline consists of the search stage and the registration stage. The search stage compares the contents of the LUT with the incoming data and then creates a match flag list, and the registration stage updates the corresponding entry in the table according to the match flag list. The decompression pipeline consists of the same stages but is organized in the opposite direction.

16.4.2.2 Performance Evaluations

Here we discuss the performance effect of time-sharing multi-threading. The example structure with two data streams per module explained above is implemented on a

Table 16.2 Performance comparisons of the time-sharing multi-threading (TSM)

Xilinx XCKU025	Frequency (MHz)	Combinational logic	Registers	RAM bits
Compressor with TSM	342	7,347	9,909	5,120
Compressor without TSM	277	9,475	7,503	0
Decompressor with TSM	353	2,145	868	17,408
Decompressor without TSM	328	6,063	2,642	4,096

Xilinx Kintex UltraScale FPGA XCKU025-FFVA1156-1-C, and Table 16.2 shows the comparisons. Compared with the clock frequency without time-sharing multi-threading, that with the optimization increases by a factor of approximately 1.23 for compression and 1.08 for decompression, meaning that the total throughputs of the compressor and decompressor are increased by the same corresponding factors. However, the improvement is shared by the two data streams, so a single data stream achieves approximately 62% of the total throughput without time-sharing multi-threading for compression and 54% for decompression. Regarding the resource usage given in Table 16.2, the optimization reduces the combinational logic by 23–65%, the registers in the compressor module are increased by approximately 32%, and the number of registers is reduced to a third of that for the implementation without the optimization.

16.5 Related Works and Literatures

The most important lossless-compression algorithm is LZW, which is simple and effective and can be found in lossless-compression software such as gz, bzip2, rar, and lzh. However, when attempting to implement a compressor on hardware, the problems discussed in this chapter inevitably arise. To implement compact hardware for LZW, we must prepare memory of the order of kilobytes. For example, Fowers et al. [3] and Kim et al. [5] solved the problem regarding the longest matching by parallelizing the operations. However, it is impossible to increase the size of the sliding dictionary because the number of start indices increases with the length of the symbols. Another important research topic is how to manage the symbol LUT in a limited memory space.

The field of machine learning contains well-known algorithms such as lossy counting [9] and the space saving [13]. However, these algorithms use operations based on pointers and are implemented in software. For a data stream with k different symbols, an attractive algorithm for frequency counting has been proposed in which the top-θk frequent items are counted exactly within $O(1/\theta)$ space [4] for any constant $0 < \theta < 1$. However, this also provides a software solution. Various hardware implementations of lossless data-compression techniques have been investigated in this decade, and a well-known approach is *arithmetic coding* (here in short, AC) [6], which is used widely to compress multimedia data. Arithmetic coding includes heavy computation with floating-point numbers to achieve high compression ratios. To avoid floating-point calculations, arithmetic coding based on binary numbers has been proposed [1, 7, 15]. However, it is not possible to avoid the potential fractal computation, which is why hardware implementations such as those by Pande et al. [16] and Mitchell et al. [14] have been proposed to accelerate the computing speed.

References

1. T.D. Chuang, Y.J. Chen, Y.H. Chen, S.Y. Chien, L.G. Chen, Architecture design of fine grain quality scalable encoder with CABAC for H.264/AVC scalable extension. J. Signal Proces. Syst. **60**(3), 363–375 (2010)
2. Compressed Indexes and their Testbeds: http://pizzachili.dcc.uchile.cl/ (2021)
3. J. Fowers, J.Y. Kim, D. Burger, S. Hauck, *A Scalable High-Bandwidth Architecture for Lossless Compression on FPGAs* (2015)
4. R.M. Karp, S. Shenker, C.H. Papadimitriou, A simple algorithm for finding frequent elements in streams and bags. ACM Trans. Database Syst. **28**(1), 51–55 (2003)
5. J.K. Kim, S. Hauck, D. Burger, A scalable multi-engine xpress9 compressor with asynchronous data transfer, in *IEEE 22nd Annual International Symposium on Field-Programmable Custom Computing Machines (FCCM)* (IEEE, 2014), pp. 161–164
6. G. Langdon, J. Rissanen, Compression of black-white images with arithmetic coding. IEEE Trans. Commun. **29**(6), 858–867 (1981)
7. C.C. Lo, S.T. Tsai, M.D. Shieh, Reconfigurable architecture for entropy decoding and inverse transform in H.264. IEEE Trans. Consum. Electron. **56**(3), 1670–1676 (2010)
8. K. Locke, Parameterizable content-addressable memory. Xilinx XAPP115 (2011)
9. G.S. Manku, R. Motwani, VLDB Endowment, Approximate frequency counts over data streams(2002), pp. 346–357
10. K. Marumo, S. Yamagiwa, *Time-Sharing Multithreading on Stream-Based Lossless Data Compression* (IEEE, 2017), pp. 305–310
11. K. Marumo, S. Yamagiwa, R. Morita, H. Sakamoto, Lazy management for frequency table on hardware-based stream lossless data compression. Information **7**(4), 63 (2016)
12. S. Maruyama, H. Sakamoto, M. Takeda, An online algorithm for lightweight grammar-based compression. Algorithms **5**(2), 214–235 (2012)
13. A. Metwally, D. Agrawal, A.E. Abbadi, An integrated efficient solution for computing frequent and top-k elements in data streams. ACM Trans. Database Syst. **31**(3), 1095–1133 (2006)
14. J.L. Mitchell, W.B. Pennebaker, Optimal hardware and software arithmetic coding procedures for the q-coder. IBM J. Res. Dev. **32**(6), 727–736 (1988)
15. R.R. Osorio, J.D. Bruguera, Arithmetic coding architecture for H.264/AVC CABAC compression system, in *Euromicro Symposium on Digital System Design, 2004. DSD 2004* (2004), pp. 62–69
16. A. Pande, J. Zambreno, P. Mohapatra, Hardware architecture for simultaneous arithmetic coding and encryption (2011)
17. J.S. Vitter, Design and analysis of dynamic Huffman codes. J. ACM **34**(4), 825–845 (1987)
18. S. Yamagiwa, K. Aoki, K. Wada, Performance enhancement of inter-cluster communication with software-based data compression in link layer. Proc. IASTED PDCS **2005**, 325–332 (2005)

19. S. Yamagiwa, K. Marumo, H. Sakamoto, Stream-based lossless data compression hardware using adaptive frequency table management, in *Proceedings of the VERY LARGE DATA BASES/BPOE 2015, LNCS 9495* (Springer, 2015)
20. S. Yamagiwa, H. Sakamoto, in *A Reconfigurable Stream Compression Hardware Based on Static Symbol-Lookup Table*. (IEEE, 2013), pp. 86–93
21. J. Ziv, A. Lempel, A universal algorithm for sequential data compression. IEEE Trans. Inf. Theory **23**(3), 337–343 (1977)
22. J. Ziv, A. Lempel, Compression of individual sequences via variable-rate coding. IEEE Trans. Inf. Theory **24**(5), 530–536 (1978)

Open Access This chapter is licensed under the terms of the Creative Commons Attribution 4.0 International License (http://creativecommons.org/licenses/by/4.0/), which permits use, sharing, adaptation, distribution and reproduction in any medium or format, as long as you give appropriate credit to the original author(s) and the source, provide a link to the Creative Commons license and indicate if changes were made.

The images or other third party material in this chapter are included in the chapter's Creative Commons license, unless indicated otherwise in a credit line to the material. If material is not included in the chapter's Creative Commons license and your intended use is not permitted by statutory regulation or exceeds the permitted use, you will need to obtain permission directly from the copyright holder.